2013

Scottish Bo

3 4144 0088

D0533783

the best campsites

in Britain
& Ireland

alan rogers publishing
expert in camping for 45 years

Compiled by: Alan Rogers Guides Ltd

Designed by: Vine Design Ltd

Additional photography: T Lambelin, www.lambelin.com
Maps created by Customised Mapping (01769 540044)
contain background data provided by GisDATA Ltd

Maps are © Alan Rogers Guides and GisDATA Ltd 2012

© Alan Rogers Guides Ltd 2012

Published by: Alan Rogers Guides Ltd,
Spelmonden Old Oast, Goudhurst, Kent TN17 1HE
www.alanrogers.com Tel: 01580 214000

British Library Cataloguing-in-Publication Data:
A catalogue record for this book is available
from the British Library.

ISBN 978-1-909057-15-9

Printed in Great Britain by Stephens & George Print Group

Contents

Alan Rogers - in search of 'the best'

Alan Rogers Guides were first published over 40 years ago. Since Alan Rogers published the first campsite guide that bore his name, the range has expanded and now covers 27 countries in six separate guides. No fewer than 20 of the campsites selected by Alan for the first guide are still featured in our 2013 editions.

There are well over 5,000 camping and caravanning parks in Britain and Ireland of varying quality: this guide contains impartially written reports on over 600, including many of the very finest, each being individually inspected and selected. We aim to provide you with a selection of the best, rather than information on all – in short, a more selective, qualitative approach. New, improved maps and indexes are also included, designed to help you find the choice of campsite that's right for you.

Finally, for 2013 we have launched the new Alan Rogers Travel Card. Free to readers, it offers exclusive online extras, money saving deals and offers on many campsites. Find out more on page 10.

We hope you enjoy some happy and safe travels – and some pleasurable 'armchair touring' in the meantime!

" ...the campsites included in this book have been chosen entirely on merit, and no payment of any sort is made by them for their inclusion."

Alan Rogers, 1968

How do we find the best?

The criteria we use when inspecting and selecting campsites are numerous, but the most important by far is the question of good quality. People want different things from their choice of site so we try to include a range of campsite 'styles' to cater for a wide variety of preferences: from those seeking a small peaceful park in the heart of the countryside, to visitors looking for an 'all singing, all dancing' park in a popular seaside resort. Those with more specific interests, such as sporting facilities, cultural events or historical attractions, are also catered for.

The size of the park, whether it's part of a chain or privately owned, makes no difference in terms of it being required to meet our exacting standards in respect of its quality and it being 'fit for purpose'. In other words, irrespective of the size of the park, or the number of facilities it offers, we consider and evaluate the welcome, the pitches, the sanitary facilities, the cleanliness, the general maintenance and even the location.

Expert opinions

We rely on our dedicated team of Site Assessors, all of whom are experienced campers, caravanners or motorcaravanners, to visit and recommend campsites. Each year they travel some 100,000 miles around Europe inspecting new campsites for the guide and re-inspecting the existing ones. Our thanks are due to them for their enthusiastic efforts, their diligence and integrity.

We also appreciate the feedback we receive from many of our readers and we always make a point of following up complaints, suggestions or recommendations for possible new campsites. Of course we get a few grumbles too – but it really is a few, and those we do receive usually relate to overcrowding or to poor maintenance during the peak school holiday period. Please bear in mind that, although we are interested to hear about any complaints, we have no contractual relationship with the campsites featured in our guides and are therefore not in a position to intervene in any dispute between a reader and a campsite.

Independent and honest

Whilst the content and scope of the Alan Rogers guides have expanded considerably since the early editions, our selection of campsites still employs exactly the same philosophy and criteria as defined by Alan Rogers in 1968.

'telling it how it is'

Firstly, and most importantly, our selection is based entirely on our own rigorous and independent inspection and selection process. Campsites cannot buy their way into our guides – indeed the extensive Site Report which is written by us, not by the site owner, is provided free of charge so we are free to say what we think and to provide an honest, 'warts and all' description. This is written in plain English and without the use of confusing icons or symbols.

Looking for the best

Highly respected by site owners and readers alike, there is no better guide when it comes to forming an independent view of a campsite's quality. When you need to be confident in your choice of campsite, you need the Alan Rogers Guide.

- Parks only included on merit

- Parks cannot pay to be included

- Independently inspected, rigorously assessed

- Impartial reviews

- Over 40 years of expertise

Written in plain English, our guides are exceptionally easy to use, but a few words of explanation regarding the layout and content may be helpful. For England we have used official tourist board regions and the counties within them. For Wales, Scotland and Ireland (North and South) we use the counties.

Index town
Park name
Postal address (including county) T: telephone number. E: email address
alanrogers.com web address (including Alan Rogers reference number)

A description of the park in which we try to give an idea of its general features – its size, its situation, its strengths and its weaknesses. This section should provide a picture of the park itself with reference to the facilities that are provided and if they impact on its appearance or character. We include details on pitch numbers, electricity (with amperage), hardstandings etc. in this section as pitch design, planning and terracing affect the park's overall appearance. Similarly, we include reference to pitches used for caravan holiday homes, chalets, and the like. Importantly at the end of this column we indicate if there are any restrictions, e.g. no tents, no children, naturist sites.

Facilities
Lists more specific information on the park's facilities and amenities and, where available, the dates when these facilities are open (if not for the whole season). Off site: here we give distances to various local amenities, for example, local shops, the nearest beach, plus our featured activities (bicycle hire, fishing, horse riding, boat launching). Where we have space we list suggestions for activities and local tourist attractions.

Open: Park opening dates.

Directions
Separated from the main text in order that they may be read and assimilated more easily by a navigator en-route. Bear in mind that road improvement schemes can result in road numbers being altered. GPS: references are provided in decimal format. All latitudes are North. Longitudes are East unless preceded by a minus sign e.g. 48.71695 is North, 0.31254 is East and -0.31254 is West.

Charges 2013 (or a general guide)

Maps, campsite listings and indexes

For this 2013 guide we have changed the way in which we list our featured campsites and also the way in which we help you to locate the parks within each region.

We now include a map immediately after our Introduction to that region. These maps show the towns near which one or more of our featured parks are located.

Within each regional section of the guide, we list these towns and the park(s) in that vicinity in alphabetical order.

You will certainly need more detailed maps for navigation, for example the Ordnance Survey road atlas. We provide GPS coordinates for each park to assist you. Our three indexes will also help you to find a park by its reference number and name, by region and park name, or by the town where the park is situated.

Understanding the entries

Facilities

Toilet blocks

We assume that toilet blocks will be equipped with WCs, washbasins with hot and cold water and hot showers with dividers or curtains, and will have all necessary shelves, hooks, plugs and mirrors. We also assume that there will be an identified chemical toilet disposal point, and that the campsite will provide water and waste water drainage points and bin areas. If not the case, we comment. We do mention certain features that some readers find important: washbasins in cubicles, facilities for babies, facilities for those with disabilities and motorcaravan service points. Readers with disabilities are advised to contact the site of their choice to ensure that facilities are appropriate to their needs.

Shop

Basic or fully supplied, and opening dates.

Bars, restaurants, takeaway facilities and entertainment

We try hard to supply opening and closing dates (if other than the campsite opening dates) and to identify if there are discos or other entertainment.

Children's play areas

Fenced and with safety surface (e.g. sand, bark or pea-gravel).

Swimming pools

If particularly special, we cover in detail in our main campsite description but reference is always included under our Facilities listings. We will also indicate the existence of water slides, sunbathing areas and other features. Opening dates, charges and levels of supervision are provided where we have been notified.

Leisure facilities

For example, playing fields, bicycle hire, organised activities and entertainment.

Dogs

If dogs are not accepted or restrictions apply, we state it here. Check the quick reference list at the back of the guide.

Off site

This briefly covers leisure facilities, tourist attractions, restaurants etc. nearby.

Charges

These are the latest provided to us by the parks. In those cases where 2013 prices have not been provided to us by the parks, we try to give a general guide.

Opening dates

These are advised to us during the early autumn of the previous year – parks can, and sometimes do, alter these dates before the start of the following season, often for good reasons. If you intend to visit shortly after a published opening date, or shortly before the closing date, it is wise to check that it will actually be open at the time required. Similarly some parks operate a restricted service during the low season, only opening some of their facilities (e.g. swimming pools) during the main season; where we know about this, and have the relevant dates, we indicate it – again if you are at all doubtful it is wise to check.

Sometimes, campsite amenities may be dependant on there being enough customers on site to justify their opening and, for this reason, actual opening dates may vary from those indicated.

Taking a tent?

In recent years, sales of tents have increased dramatically. With very few exceptions, the campsites listed in this guide have pitches suitable for tents, caravans and motorcaravans. Tents, of course, come in a dazzling range of shapes and sizes. Modern family tents with separate sleeping pods are increasingly popular and these invariably require large pitches with electrical connections. Smaller lightweight tents, ideal for cyclists and hikers, are also visible on many sites and naturally require correspondingly smaller pitches. Many (but not all) sites have special tent areas with prices adjusted accordingly. If in any doubt, we recommend contacting the site of your choice beforehand.

You're on your way!

Whether you're an 'old hand' in terms of camping and caravanning or are contemplating your first trip, a regular reader of our Guides or a new 'convert', we wish you well in your travels and hope we have been able to help in some way.

We are, of course, also out and about ourselves, visiting parks, talking to owners and readers, and generally checking on standards and new developments.

Our Holiday Home section

324

Over recent years, more and more parks in Britain and Ireland have added high quality holiday home accommodation in the form of caravan holiday homes, chalets and lodges. In response to feedback from many of our readers, and to reflect this evolution in campsites, we have decided to introduce a separate section on caravan holiday homes and chalets (see page 324). If a park has decided to contribute to this section, it is indicated above our site report in the main body of the guide with a page reference where the full details are given. We feature parks offering some of the best accommodation available and have included full details of one or two accommodation types at these parks.

Please note however that many other campsites listed in this guide may also have a selection of accommodation for rent.

We wish all our readers thoroughly enjoyable Camping and Caravanning in 2013 – favoured by good weather of course!

The Alan Rogers Team

Scotland
page 263

Northern
Ireland
page 289

Northumbria
page 228

Cumbria
page 217

North West
England
page 209

Yorkshire
page 192

Republic of Ireland
page 296

Heart of England
page 165

Wales
page 236

East of England
page 146

Southern
England
page 103

South West England
page 16

South East
England
page 127

London
page 142

Channel Islands
page 319

FREE

The Alan Rogers
Travel Card

Across the Alan Rogers guides you'll find a network of thousands of quality inspected and selected campsites. We also work with numerous organisations, including ferry operators and tourist attractions, all of whom can bring you benefits and save you money.

Our brand **NEW** Travel Card binds all this together, along with exclusive extra content in our cardholders' area at **alanrogers.com/travelcard**

Advantage all the way

Carry the Alan Rogers Travel Card on your travels and save money all the way.
Enjoy exclusive offers on many partner sites - as well as hotels, apartments and campsite accommodation. We've even teamed up with Camping Cheque, the low season discount scheme, so you can load your card with Cheques before you travel. So register today - hundreds of campsites already have special offers just for you.

Holiday **discounts**, **free** kids' meals, **free** cycle hire, **discounted** meals, **free** sports activities, **free** gifts on arrival, **free** wine with meals, **free** wifi, **free** tennis, **free** spa day, **free** access to local attractions.

Check out all the offers at **alanrogers.com/travelcard** and present your card on arrival.

Benefits that add up

- Offers and benefits on many Alan Rogers campsites across Europe

- Save up to 60% in low season on over 600 campsites

- Savings on rented accommodation and hotels at over 400 locations

- Free cardholders' magazine

- Exclusive cardholders' area on our website – exchange opinions with other members

- Discounted ferries

- Savings on Alan Rogers guides

- Travel insurance deals

Register today - and start saving

Step 1
Register at www.**alanrogers.com/travelcard** (you can now access exclusive content on the website).

Step 2
You'll receive your activated card, along with a Welcome email containing useful links and information.

Step 3
Start using your card to save money or to redeem benefits during your holiday.

Register now at
alanrogers.com/travelcard

The Alan Rogers Awards

The Alan Rogers Campsite Awards were launched in 2004 and have proved a great success.

Our awards have a broad scope and before committing to our winners, we carefully consider more than 2,000 campsites featured in our guides, taking into account comments from our site assessors, our head office team and, of course, our readers.

Our award winners come from the four corners of Europe, from southern Portugal to Croatia, and this year we are making awards to campsites in 10 different countries.

Needless to say, it's an extremely difficult task to choose our eventual winners, but we believe that we have identified a number of campsites with truly outstanding characteristics.

In each case, we have selected an outright winner, along with two highly commended runners-up. Listed below are full details of each of our award categories and our winners for 2012.

Alan Rogers Progress Award 2012

This award reflects the hard work and commitment undertaken by particular site owners to improve and upgrade their site.

Winner	
UK0970	Cofton Country Holidays *England*

Runners-up	
FR86010	Castel Camping Le Petit Trianon *France*
CR6765	Camping Kovacine *Croatia*

Alan Rogers Welcome Award 2012

This award takes account of sites offering a particularly friendly welcome and maintaining a friendly ambience throughout readers' holidays.

Winner	
ES80330	Camping Las Palmeras *Spain*

Runners-up	
FR29180	Camping Les Embruns *France*
IT60280	Camping Vela Blu *Italy*

Our warmest congratulations to all our award winners and our commiserations to all those not having won an award on this occasion.

The Alan Rogers Team

Alan Rogers Active Holiday Award 2012

This award reflects sites in outstanding locations which are ideally suited for active holidays, notably walking or cycling, but which could extend to include such activities as winter sports or watersports.

Winner	
DE3003	Camping Wulfener Hals *Germany*

Runners-up	
IT62030	Caravan Park Sexten *Italy*
AU0065	Camping Seehof *Austria*

Alan Rogers Innovation Award 2012

Our Innovation Award acknowledges campsites with creative and original concepts, possibly with features which are unique, and cannot therefore be found elsewhere. We have identified innovation both in campsite amenities and also in rentable accommodation.

Winner	
NL6470	Camping de Papillon *Netherlands*

Runners-up	
FR85625	Camping Les Moulins *France*
ES92120	Camping Monte Holiday *Spain*

Alan Rogers Small Campsite Award 2012

This award acknowledges excellent small campsites (less than 75 pitches) which offer a friendly welcome and top quality amenities throughout the season to their guests.

Winner	
FR58040	Camping l'Etang de la Fougeraie *France*

Runners-up	
UK0115	Tehidy Holiday Park *England*
CZ4896	Camping Country *Czech Republic*

Alan Rogers Seaside Award 2012

This award is made for sites which we feel are outstandingly suitable for a really excellent seaside holiday.

Winner	
IT60450	Camping Marina di Venezia *Italy*

Runners-up	
FR64060	Camping le Pavillon Royal *France*
PO8202	Turiscampo *Portugal*

Alan Rogers Country Award 2012

This award contrasts with our former award and acknowledges sites which are attractively located in delightful, rural locations.

Winner	
FR74140	Camping Les Dômes de Miage *France*

Runners-up	
UK0710	Hidden Valley Touring Park *England*
NL5823	Camping Waalstrand *Netherlands*

Alan Rogers Family Site Award 2012

Many sites claim to be child friendly but this award acknowledges the sites we feel to be the very best in this respect.

Winner	
IT60200	Camping Union Lido Vacanze *Italy*

Runners-up	
NL6710	Recreatiepark de Achterste Hoef *Netherlands*
ES85400	Camping La Torre del Sol *Spain*

Alan Rogers Readers' Award 2012

We believe our Readers' Award to be the most important. We simply invite our readers (by means of an on-line poll at www.alanrogers.com) to nominate the site they enjoyed most.

The outright winner for 2012 is:

Winner	
FR85150	Camping La Yole *France*

Alan Rogers Special Award 2012

A Special Award is made to campsites which have suffered a very significant setback and have not only returned to their former condition, but can fairly be considered to be even better than before. In 2012 we acknowledge a Spanish campsite which suffered a devastating forest fire and we feel is a worthy recipient of this award.

ES80240	Camping Les Pedres *Spain*

What are you looking for?

Best of British, a group of high quality, family owned touring and holiday parks, provides you with a choice of 50 prestigious parks throughout the UK offering a variety of accommodation. You can take your tent, touring caravan or motorhome or, if you prefer, you can book a caravan holiday home, chalet or lodge for your holiday – the choice is yours! Go to **www.bob.org.uk** for full details of our member parks – some offer online booking facilities – or you can email the parks you are interested in direct from their individual page on **www.bob.org.uk** if you prefer.

A warm welcome wherever you go

Whichever Best of British park you choose, you can be sure that you will receive the warmest of welcomes and a very high standard of customer service.

Visit the Best of British website

Go to **www.bob.org.uk** to register for a **FREE** Best of British loyalty card and see details of the special offers available on the parks, sign up for the e-newsletter, or to request a full colour brochure.

A brochure and/or loyalty card can also be obtained by writing to
PO Box 28249, Edinburgh, EH9 2YZ

the
Best of
British
quality touring and holiday parks

Visit www.bob.org.uk

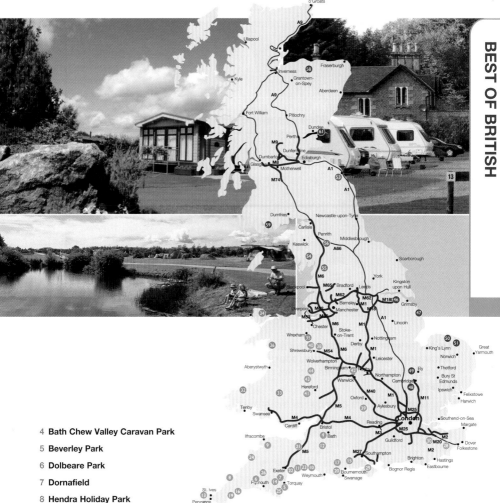

4 Bath Chew Valley Caravan Park

5 Beverley Park

6 Dolbeare Park

7 Dornafield

8 Hendra Holiday Park

9 Hidden Valley Touring & Camping Park

10 Highlands End Holiday Park

11 Oakdown Country Holiday Park

12 The Old Oaks Touring Park

13 Polmanter Touring Park

14 Ross Park

15 Sandy Balls Holiday Centre

16 Seaview International Holiday Park

17 South Lytchett Manor Caravan & Camping Park

19 Trethem Mill Touring Park

20 Wareham Forest Tourist Park

21 Waterrow Touring Park

22 Webbers Park

23 Wood Farm Caravan Park

24 Wooda Farm Holiday Park

25 Woodlands Grove Caravan & Camping Park

26 Woodovis Park

28 Broadhembury Caravan & Camping Park

29 The Orchards Holiday Park

30 Tanner Farm Touring Caravan and Camping Park

32 Cenarth Falls Holiday Park

33 Erwlon Caravan & Camping Park

34 Home Farm Caravan Park

35 Plassey Leisure Park

36 Trawsdir Caravans and Camping Park

38 Beaconsfield Farm

39 Lincoln Farm Park

40 Oxon Hall Touring & Holiday Home Park

41 Poston Mill Park

42 Somers Wood Caravan Park

43 Townsend

44 Westbook Farm Park

46 Brookside Caravan and Camping Park

47 Cherry Tree Touring Park

48 Highfield Farm Touring Park

49 Stroud Hill Park

50 The Old Brick Kilns

51 Two Mills Touring Park

53 Ord House Country Park

54 Park Cliffe Camping and Caravan Estate

55 Riverside Caravan Park

56 Wild Rose Park

58 Aberlour Gardens Caravan Park

59 Brighouse Bay Holiday Park

61 Riverview Caravan Park

The West Country is a region of contrasts, with windswept moorlands and dramatic cliffs towering above beautiful sandy beaches. Its bustling cities are a fascinating mix of history and contemporary culture. Major attractions include medieval Salisbury with its timbered houses and cathedral, and the mysterious ancient monument of Stonehenge.

THE SOUTH WEST COMPRISES: CORNWALL, DEVON, SOMERSET, BATH, BRISTOL, SOUTH GLOUCESTERSHIRE, WILTSHIRE AND WEST DORSET.

With its dramatic cliffs pounded by the Atlantic ocean, and beautiful coastline boasting warm waters, soft sandy beaches and small seaside towns, Cornwall is one of England's most popular holiday destinations. The coast is also a surfers' paradise, while inland the wild and rugged Bodmin Moors dominate the landscape. In Devon, the Dartmoor National Park has sweeping moorland and granite tors, where wild ponies roam freely. Much of the countryside is gentle, rolling, green fields, dotted with pretty thatched cottages. The coastline around Torbay is known as the English Riviera which, due to its temperate climate, allows palm trees to grow. Stretching across East Devon and West Dorset is the fossil-ridden Jurassic Coast, a World Heritage Site. West Dorset is also home to Lyme Regis and Weymouth, which comes alive in summer when regular entertainment, including a carnival and fireworks, is held along the seafront. Famous for its cider and cheese, Somerset is good walking country, with the Exmoor National Park, which also straddles Devon. Wiltshire's natural attractions include the Marlborough Downs, Savernake Forest and the River Avon. It also boasts one of the most famous prehistoric sites in the world, the ancient stone circles of Stonehenge.

Places of interest

Bath: Roman and modern spas; Fashion Museum housing costumes from the 16th century. Bath Abbey with 212 steps to the top of the tower.

Bristol: Brunel's Clifton Suspension bridge; St Nicholas Market and the old city; vibrant harbourside area with bars, restaurants and cultural events.

Cornwall: historic Tintagel Castle, reputed birthplace of King Arthur; Tate Gallery, St Ives; Barbara Hepworth Museum and Sculpture Garden.

Devon: Exeter Cathedral; World Heritage Jurassic Coast; the granite rocks of Dartmoor; pretty harbours at Clovelly and Ilfracombe.

Somerset: Weston-Super-Mare; Wells Cathedral; Glastonbury; Cheddar Gorge and Wookey Hole caves.

West Dorset: Dorchester, home of Thomas Hardy; Isle of Portland; Abbotsbury village, with swannery.

Wiltshire: Longleat stately home and safari park; Stourhead House and gardens; the historic market town of Devizes.

Did you know?

Longleat pioneered the first drive-through safari park outside of Africa in 1966.

Silbury Hill dates back to around 2,400 BC and is the largest Neolithic mound of its kind in Europe.

Cornwall has over 300 beaches, including Fistral Beach, a magnet for surfers and the largest in Cornwall.

Pultney Bridge in Bath is one of only a few bridges in the world with shops built into it.

Avebury houses the largest stone circle in Europe, believed to be 4,500 years old.

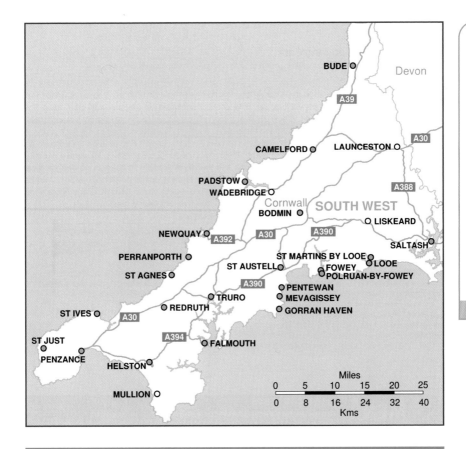

Bodmin

Ruthern Valley Holidays

Ruthernbridge, Bodmin PL30 5LU (Cornwall) T: 01208 831395. E: camping@ruthernvalley.com

alanrogers.com/UK0306

This is a little gem of a site set in eight acres of woodland, tucked away in a peaceful little valley not far from Bodmin. Run by Andrew and Nicola Johnson, the park was landscaped over 30 years ago with an amazing range of trees and shrubs, and there is plenty of animal wildlife. There are 16 touring pitches in a tree-lined field, informally spaced but numbered in the main, six with 10A electricity; a further 13 are in smaller fields and alcove areas in the woods with a small stream meandering through and alive with bluebells when we visited. There are three caravan holiday homes, four wigwams and three camping huts. The bubbling stream is an attraction for children and now there are some chickens and farm animals in an additional field, not to mention some adventure-type play equipment in an area set away from the pitches. A small, basic toilet block and a little shop complete the provision. Ruthern is a special place to unwind and enjoy the simple pleasures of life. Go walking, cycling or birdwatching (38 different species of bird have been recorded).

Facilities

Small, fully equipped toilet block with solar heated water. Washing machines and dryer. Shop with basic provisions shares with reception (reduced hours in low season). Barbecue hire. Play area including five-a-side goal posts. Field with farm animals. Bicycle hire (delivered to site). Free WiFi. Dogs are not accepted. Off site: Fishing 2 miles. Nearest pub 3-4 miles. Riding, pony trekking and golf 4 miles. 10 miles to the coast.

Open: All year.

Directions

Approaching Bodmin from A30/A38 turn right at first mini-roundabout and proceed anti-clockwise on the inner ring road. Go straight over double mini-roundabout, leaving Bodmin on A389/A391 towards St Austell. Ignore first Nanstallon-Ruthernbridge sign, after 1.5 miles, at top of hill, turn right. At Nanstallon village sign (0.75 miles), turn left then filter left. Continue for 1 mile into Ruthernbridge. Turn left immediately before bridge. Site is on left in 300 yds. GPS: 50.46455, -4.8019

Charges guide

Per unit incl. 2 persons and electricity	£ 16.00 - £ 20.00
extra person (over 3 yrs)	£ 3.50 - £ 4.50

FREE Alan Rogers Travel Card
Extra benefits and savings - see page 10

17

Bodmin
Mena Caravan & Camping Park
Lanivet, Bodmin PL30 5HW (Cornwall) T: 01208 831845. E: mena@campsitesincornwall.co.uk
alanrogers.com/UK0270

A family run park, tucked away in the Cornish countryside, yet close to the main routes. It is open all year, and a warm welcome awaits visitors. Set in 15 acres of secluded countryside with rural views, it is spacious and never crowded, offering only 25 level grass pitches on well drained, slightly sloping grass. There are 21 electricity connections (10A) and three hardstandings. Reception has facilities for hot drinks and keeps essentials, which is useful for walkers. The park is on the Land's End to John O'Groats route and gets walkers either at the beginning or end of their walk. There is a small fishing lake and a wooded area. Mena means 'hilltop' in the Cornish language, and the site is actually situated at the geographical centre of Cornwall, overlooked by Helman's Tor, one of the highest points on Bodmin Moor. With its position, visitors can choose between beaches on the north or south coast. Lanivet village has a shop and a pub serving meals. Children will love the chickens and two large Kune pigs.

Facilities

Four toilet and washbasin cabins are in an older wooden building. Two new showers and two toilets are behind the veranda building with laundry facilities. On the opposite side of the site is an en-suite facility for disabled visitors and a large games room with TV, a three-quarter size snooker table and darts. Shop for basics (with gas). Hot drinks machine. Swings, etc. for children in the central grass area. Fishing lake (licence required). Two mobile homes for hire. Caravan storage. WiFi (charged). Dog kennel facilities. Off site: Riding 1.5 miles. Lanivet village with shop and pub 2 miles. Golf 3 miles. Bicycle hire 3 miles. Eden Project 4 miles. Nearest beach 8 miles.

Open: All year.

Directions

From A30 Bodmin bypass, exit at A30/A391 Innis Downs roundabout. Take A389 north (Lanivet, Bodmin). After 0.5 miles take first right (filter lane) and pass under A30. Turn first left (Lostwithiel, Fowey) and in 0.25 miles turn right at top of hill (by Celtic cross). Continue for 0.5 miles and take first right into lane and site in 100 yds. GPS: 50.430267, -4.757167

Charges guide

Per unit incl. 2 persons and electricity	£ 15.00 - £ 19.00
extra person	£ 4.00
child (3-16 yrs)	£ 1.00 - £ 2.50
dog	£ 1.00

Tel 01208 831 845
email mena@campsitesincornwall.co.uk
www.campsitesincornwall.co.uk

Lanivet
Bodmin
Cornwall PL30 5HW

Our park is open all year and is ideally located to visit anywhere in Cornwall. Mena Caravan & Camping Park a secret you will not want to share!

Bodmin
Eden Valley Holiday Park
Lanlivery, Lostwithiel, Bodmin PL30 5BU (Cornwall) T: 01208 872277.
E: enquiries@edenvalleyholidaypark.co.uk **alanrogers.com/UK0280**

A pleasant, peaceful touring park, Eden Valley Holiday Park has plenty of sheltered green space and a natural, uncommercialised atmosphere. This has been enhanced by careful planting of trees and shrubs to form a series of linked paddocks with an unfenced stream running through. With 56 numbered touring pitches in total, each paddock contains 10-15 pitches spread around the perimeter. There are 20 hardstandings and 40 pitches have 10/16A electricity connections. Awning groundsheets must be lifted on alternate days. A separate field contains 35 private caravan holiday homes. A large, well equipped activity play area with adventure type equipment on grass is in one of the hedged paddocks. The park is owned by Darren and Ginny Hopkins and their young family and they welcome families and couples to enjoy their surroundings with colourful trees, grassy paddocks and stream.

Facilities

A smart log cabin toilet block is heated, with en-suite facilities. The more traditional block has individual cubicles. Unit for disabled visitors. Fully equipped laundry room. Motorcaravan service point. Gas supplies. Play area. TV room. Games room. Putting green. Torch useful. Off site: Riding nearby. Freshwater fishing 1.5 miles and sea fishing 3 miles. Golf 1.5 miles. Bicycle hire and beach 4 miles.

Open: Easter/1 April - 31 October.

Directions

Park approach road leads off A390 road 1.5 miles southwest of Lostwithiel. Follow white or brown camping signs. No other approach is advised. GPS: 50.40191, -4.69805

Charges guide

Per unit incl. 2 persons and electricity	£ 13.00 - £ 17.00
extra person	£ 2.00
child (4-15 yrs)	£ 1.50
dog	£1.00 - £ 2.00

No single sex groups (excl. bona fide organisations).

For latest campsite news visit
alanrogers.com

Bodmin
South Penquite Farm

South Penquite, Blisland, Bodmin PL30 4LH (Cornwall) T: 01208 850491. E: thefarm@bodminmoor.co.uk
alanrogers.com/UK0302

South Penquite offers real camping with no frills. It is set on a 200-hectare hill farm, high on Bodmin Moor between the villages of Blisland and St Breward. The farm achieved organic status in 2001 and runs a flock of 300 ewes and a herd of 40 cattle and horses. The camping is small scale and intended to have a low impact on the surrounding environment. Fifty tents or simple motorcaravans (no caravans) can pitch around the edge of three walled fields, roughly cut in the midst of the moor. You can find shelter or a view. Four yurts are available to rent in one field, complete with wood burning stoves.

Facilities

A smart new pine clad toilet block, with a separate provision of four family-sized showers, with solar heated rainwater. Washing machine and dryer. Small fridge and freezer. Home produced meat available. LPG gas. Facilities for field studies and educational groups. Bushcraft days. Fishing (requires an EA rod licence). Dogs are not accepted. Off site: Riding and cycling 1 mile. Pubs 1.5 and 2.5 miles. Sustrans Route 3 passes close by. North and south coasts within easy reach.

Open: 1 May - 1 November.

Directions

On A30 Bodmin Moor pass Jamaica Inn and watch for St Breward sign (right) at end of dual carriageway. Follow narrow road over moor for 2 miles ignoring right turn to St Breward before South Penquite sign. Follow track over bridge through farm gate, then left to camping fields. GPS: 50.5445, -4.671833

Charges guide

Per person	£ 7.00 - £ 8.00
child (5-15 yrs)	£ 3.50 - £ 4.00

No credit cards.

Bude
Wooda Farm Holiday Park

326

Poughill, Bude EX23 9HJ (Cornwall) T: 01288 352069. E: enquiries@wooda.co.uk
alanrogers.com/UK0380

Wooda Farm is spacious and well organised with some nice touches. A quality, family run park, it is part of a working farm set within 40 acres, under two miles from the sandy, surfing beaches of Bude. In peaceful farmland with plenty of open spaces (and some up and down walking), there are marvellous views of sea and countryside. The 220 large touring pitches are spread over four meadows on level or gently sloping grass. There are 142 with 16A electricity connections, and 83 hardstanding, 83 hedged premier pitches (electricity, water, waste water), linked by tarmac roads. A 28 day field with electricity provides extra grass pitches for the peak season. A late arrivals area has electricity. Beside the shop and reception at the entrance are 55 caravan holiday homes for let. A takeaway service is available and an attractive courtyard bar and restaurant with home cooking is popular.

Facilities

Three well maintained and equipped toilet blocks, two heated, include a unit suitable for disabled campers, two baby rooms. En-suite family bathrooms for hire. Laundry rooms. Motorcaravan service point. Self-service shop with off-licence (Easter-mid Sept). Bar/restaurant and takeaway (reduced hours out of season). 9-hole fun golf course (clubs provided). Games room with TV and pool. Tennis. Badminton. Fitness suite. Coarse fishing in 1.5-acre lake (permits from reception, £1.50 per half day, £2.50 per day). Certain breeds of dog not accepted. WiFi. Off site: Local village inn is five minutes walk.

Open: End March - end October.

Directions

Park is north of Bude at Poughill; turn off A39 on north side of Stratton on minor road for Coombe Valley, following camp signs at junctions. GPS: 50.84331, -4.51857

Charges guide

Per unit incl. 2 persons and electricity	£ 16.00 - £ 26.00
extra person	£ 5.00 - £ 6.50

Camping Cheques accepted.

Luxury Holiday Homes - Cottages - Sports Facilities - Fishing - Wi-Fi - Sandy Beaches
In the Countryside - Beside the Sea
Wooda Farm Holiday Park
In the Countryside - Beside the Sea
Bude·Cornwall·EX23 9HJ
Tel: 01288 352069
www.wooda.co.uk

FREE Alan Rogers Travel Card
Extra benefits and savings - see page 10

Bude
Pentire Haven Holiday Park

Stibb Road, Kilkhampton, Bude EX23 9QY (Cornwall) T: 01288 321601. E: holidays@pentirehaven.co.uk
alanrogers.com/UK0385

Pentire Haven is a quiet family site, under new management, located close to the popular resort of Bude. The original part of the site has 220 touring pitches with 16A electrical connections, and some with hardstanding; 54 are terraced super pitches with electricity, water and drainage. The more open area near reception has 100 level, grassy tent pitches in separate fields. The use of natural wood for the swimming pool area and fencing gives it a range style feel. The park has an arrangement with the adjacent residential site (Penstone Manor) to share its amenities, including a bar/restaurant and a pool.

Facilities	Directions
One new toilet block and two older, renovated blocks are both heated and have preset showers and some washbasins in cubicles. Facilities for disabled visitors (shower in 1 block). Washing machine. Shop. Swimming pool (heated 21/7-1/9). Play area. TV room. Free WiFi over site. Entertainment next door at Penstone Manor. Tourist information. Off site: Nearest beach 5 minutes.	Approaching from the south (Bude), head north on the A39. Turn right in direction of Stibb just before entering Kilkhampton and site entrance is almost immediately on right. GPS: 50.869086, -4.494175

Open: 3 April - 31 October.

Charges guide

Per unit incl. 2 persons and electricity	£ 14.00 - £ 23.00
extra person	£ 1.50 - £ 4.00

Bude
Widemouth Bay Caravan Park

Widemouth Bay, Bude EX23 0DF (Cornwall) T: 01288 361208
alanrogers.com/UK0373

Widemouth has a wonderful situation on the edge of Widemouth Bay amidst rural farmland. Covering 50 acres in total, a number of areas have mobile homes carefully fitted into the hillside. There are some 180 touring pitches on undulating meadowland at the top of the hill, with 16A electricity available and some level hardstandings. The views are magnificent. The sandy beach, just a 15 minute walk away, is very popular with bathers and surfers and the indoor heated swimming pool is a bonus. This is a big and lively park in season, very well catered for with a well stocked shop, a bar serving food and nightly entertainment for children and parents.

Facilities	Directions
Two traditional, fully equipped toilet blocks. Facilities for babies and an en-suite unit for visitors with disabilities. Launderette. Microwave. Shop, bar with food, and takeaway (limited hours). Indoor heated pool with lifeguard. Entertainment, quizzes, disco. Kids' club. Amusement arcade. Play area. Internet café/WiFi. Mini Golf. Bus service. Mobile homes to rent.	Using the A39 bypass Bude and after 3 miles watch for right-hand turning for Widemouth Bay. Follow to beach and continue south alongside beach until road bends inland by the Manor Hotel. Lane to site on right. GPS: 50.78033, -4.5613

Open: 5 March - 31 October.

Charges guide

Per unit incl. 2 persons and electricity	£ 14.00 - £ 38.00

Bude
Sandymouth Holiday Park

Sandymouth Bay, Bude EX23 9HW (Cornwall) T: 0844 272 9530. E: enquiries@sandymouthbay.co.uk
alanrogers.com/UK0375

Sandymouth is a popular family park with a good range of amenities. The beautifully maintained site is situated on the side of a valley with wonderful views but also a lot of up and down walking. Serviced pitches, 22 in all, with hardstanding are arranged either side of a tarmac roadway. A number of electric tent pitches are to one side of the large, sloping open tent field where there are ten acres for camping. Pitches here are grassy and enjoy excellent views of Bude and Sandymouth. There is also a good range of fully equipped mobile homes, chalets and lodges available for rent. On-site amenities include an indoor pool (with water slide), sauna and free membership of the Ocean Bar and Club.

Facilities	Directions
Fully equipped toilet block. En-suite facilities for disabled visitors. Shop. Bar. Restaurant/snack bar. Takeaway. Ocean Bar and Club. Indoor swimming pool with small slide. Sauna. Adventure playground. Soft ball area. Minigolf. Activity programme. Children's club. Amusement arcade. Fishing. WiFi (charged). Accommodation for rent. Off site: Summerleaze and Sandymouth beaches. Milky Way Adventure Park 13 miles. Clovelly 13 miles. Fishing.	Approaching on the M5 motorway, leave at exit 27 and take the A361 and A39 towards Bideford and Bude. After passing through Kilkhampton turn right towards Stibb. Follow this road to Stibb and after the village turn left and the park is on the left. GPS: 50.866973, -4.53752

Open: 15 March - 26 November.

Charges guide

Per unit incl. 2 persons and electricity	£ 16.00 - £ 28.00

For latest campsite news visit
alanrogers.com

Camelford

Lakefield Caravan Park

Lower Pendavey Farm, Camelford PL32 9TX (Cornwall) T: 01840 213279.
E: enquiries@lakefieldcaravanpark.co.uk **alanrogers.com/UK0360**

Lakefield is a small, simple touring park on what was a working farm. Now the main focus is on the BHS approved equestrian centre. With only 40 pitches, it is no surprise that the owners, Maureen and Dennis Perring, know all the campers. The well spaced pitches backing onto hedges and with 24 electric hook-ups (16A) are in view of the small, fenced lake watched over by one of Cornwall's first wind farms. The white-washed café/reception, converted from one of the old barns, is open all day between Easter and October offering traditional cream teas. Children will love the goats and 'Wabbit World'.

Facilities	Directions
Simple but adequate toilet block. Washing machine and dryer in the ladies. Toilet for disabled visitors at riding centre. Tea room. Gas supplies (Calor). Torches may be useful. Off site: Golf 2 miles. Fishing: sea 4 miles, coarse 5 miles.	Follow B3266 north from Camelford. Park access is directly from this road on the left just before the turning for Tintagel. GPS: 50.635058, -4.687648

Open: 1 April - 30 September.

Charges guide

Per unit incl. 2 persons and electricity	£ 14.00 - £ 16.50
extra person (5 yrs and over)	£ 1.00

Falmouth

Pennance Mill Farm Chalet & Camping Park

Maenporth, Falmouth TR11 5HJ (Cornwall) T: 01326 317431. E: pennancemill@amserve.com
alanrogers.com/UK0450

Pennance Mill Farm has been in the hands of the Jewell family for three generations and is listed as a typical Cornish farmstead in an Area of Outstanding Natural Beauty; you can enjoy a woodland walk with 200-year-old beech trees. In the high season skittles, country games and barbecue evenings are organised, all in keeping with the relaxed and friendly atmosphere generated by the owners. The camping area is in four sheltered, south-facing and fairly level fields with views over the countryside. It provides 75 pitches, all with 16A electricity and eight with hardstandings. Caravans are accepted but this is not a site for those who like neat, manicured lawns and flower beds.

Facilities	Directions
The two toilet blocks are fully equipped. Original block near the entrance is well kept with hot water. Washing machine and dryer. The newer block in the top meadow is heated. Small farm shop including some basic provisions (open 09.00-10.30 and 17.30-18.30). Gas supplies. Small play meadow with new equipment. Off site: Tennis courts, golf course and pitch and putt within walking distance. Beach, watersports and indoor heated pool 2 miles. Riding 4 miles. Bar/restaurant/takeaway 5 miles. New Maritime Museum. Coastal footpath to the Helford River.	From Truro, follow signs for Falmouth on A39. At first roundabout pass Asda then right at next roundabout 'Industrial Estates' (on Bickland Water Road), next roundabout 'Maenporth'. Follow brown camping signs for 1.5 miles and continue down hill to site on left. GPS: 50.134983, -5.092667

Open: Easter - November.

Charges guide

Per unit incl. 2 persons and electricity	£ 23.00 - £ 26.00
extra person	£ 7.00 - £ 8.00
No credit cards.	

Fowey

Penmarlam Caravan & Camping Park

Bodinnick-by-Fowey, Fowey PL23 1LZ (Cornwall) T: 01726 870088. E: info@penmarlampark.co.uk
alanrogers.com/UK0195

Penmarlam is situated high above the estuary opposite Fowey, close to the village of Bodinnick which is famous for being the home of Daphne du Maurier. The original field is level and sheltered with 29 pitches which are semi-divided by bushes. The newer field with 34 pitches has a slight slope, is divided with wild banks and enjoys good countryside views. Both fields have circular access roads. All pitches have 16A electricity and 14 also have water and drainage. The modern reception, shop and the toilet facilities are well situated between the two fields.

Facilities	Directions
The modern heated toilet block with a baby and toddler room in the ladies' and a separate en-suite unit for disabled visitors, which doubles as a family room with baby changing. Laundry facilities. Well stocked, licensed shop with fresh fruit and vegetables. Coffee machine (reduced hours in low season). Video, DVD and book library. WiFi (charged). Off site: Beach 1 mile.	From main A390 road at East Taphouse take B3359 towards Looe. After 5 miles fork right (Bodinnick and ferry). Site is signed on right 1 mile past village of Lanteglos Highway. GPS: 50.34434, -4.62289

Open: 1 April - 31 October.

Charges guide

Per unit incl. 2 persons and electricity	£ 15.50 - £ 26.50
extra person	£ 4.50 - £ 8.25

FREE Alan Rogers Travel Card
Extra benefits and savings - see page 10

Fowey

Penhale Caravan & Camping Park

Fowey PL23 1JU (Cornwall) T: 01726 833425. E: info@penhale-fowey.co.uk
alanrogers.com/UK0285

Penhale is a traditional campsite on four and half acres of rolling farmland with magnificent views across the countryside to St Austell Bay. The Berryman family run an arable and beef farm alongside the campsite. The atmosphere here is relaxed and there is plenty of room in the touring fields. The fields do slope but a number of pitches have been levelled. In total, there are 56 pitches for all types of units, 41 with 16A electricity hook-ups. Ten holiday caravans occupy a separate field. It is possible to walk to Polkerris beach a mile away and Fowey is just a mile and a half.

Facilities

One fully equipped toilet block at the bottom of the touring fields. Laundry room. Games room. Reception at the farmhouse stocks basic necessities. WiFi. Off site: Garage with shop 600 yds. Sandy beach, pub and watersports centre at Polkerris beach 1 mile. Fishing and shops and restaurants in Fowey 1.5 miles. Bicycle hire 5 miles. Three golf courses within 7 miles.

Open: Easter/1 April - 8 October.

Directions

From the A390 take B3269 for Fowey and 1 mile before town turn right at roundabout by petrol station on the A3082 St Austell road. Site is 600 yds. on left. GPS: 50.34309, -4.66848

Charges guide

Per unit incl. 2 persons and electricity	£ 15.00 - £ 21.00
extra person	£ 4.60 - £ 5.80

Gorran Haven

Sea View International

Boswinger, Gorran Haven, Saint Austell PL26 6LL (Cornwall) T: 01726 843425.
E: holidays@seaviewinternational.com **alanrogers.com/UK0150**

Sea View is an impressive, well cared for park, its quality reflected in the many awards it has won. Located at the gateway to the Roseland Peninsula on the South Coast of Cornwall with views of the sea and nearby Dodman Point, this park offers quality camping pitches, luxury self-catering lodges and caravan holiday homes. With over 200 touring pitches, all with electricity hook-ups and many being 'all service' with a choice of hardstanding or grass, there are pitches to suit all requirements. Available to hire are luxury lodges and a variety of caravan holiday homes, many with sea views.

Facilities

Excellent toilet and shower blocks are well maintained and heated including facilities for disabled visitors and luxury bathroom suites on the family field. Fully equipped campers' kitchens. Laundry. Motorcaravan service point. Well stocked shop and off-licence. Café and takeaway with free WiFi. Heated outdoor swimming pool. Large play area. Tennis and badminton courts, pitch and putt (all free). Extensive dog walk area. Off site: Community bus stops at park. Fishing. Boat launching and riding 2 miles.

Open: 1 April - 31 October.

Directions

From St Austell take the B3273 towards Mevagissey for 3 miles. At top of steep hill, turn right signed Lost Gardens of Heligan and Seaview International. Follow this road and brown signs to park. GPS: 50.2369, -4.820033

Charges guide

Per unit incl. 2 persons and electricity	£ 8.00 - £ 45.00
extra person (over 5 yrs)	£ 3.00 - £ 5.00

Helston

Silver Sands Holiday Park

Gwendreath, Ruan Minor, Helston TR12 7LZ (Cornwall) T: 01326 290631.
E: info@silversandsholidaypark.co.uk **alanrogers.com/UK0070**

Silver Sands is a small, peaceful 'away-from-it-all' park, under new ownership, in a remote part of the Lizard peninsula, the most southerly part of mainland Britain and an Area of Outstanding Natural Beauty. It is tucked away behind two other holiday home parks (possible noise in season). The park itself has 16 caravan holiday homes, along with 36 touring pitches of which 20 have 10A electrical hook-ups. The pitches are large, attractively situated and divided into individual bays by flowering shrubs and bushes. The adjoining tent field has similar pitches (seven with electricity) where the shrubs are growing (some pitches are slightly sloping). A member of the Countryside Discovery group.

Facilities

The fully equipped toilet block includes an en-suite room for disabled visitors, doubling as a family room. Some play equipment. An undeveloped three-acre field for walking, kite flying, etc. Off site: Restaurant nearby, pub within walking distance. Fishing 1 mile. Boat launching 2 or 7 miles. Riding and bicycle hire 5 miles. Golf 6 miles.

Open: Easter - mid October.

Directions

From Helston take A3038 Lizard road. After Culdrose turn left on B3293 passing Goonhilly after 4 miles. At next crossroads turn right (Kennack Sands), continue for 1.5 miles then left to Gwendreath on single track road. Site is 1 mile. GPS: 50.00900, -5.16900

Charges guide

Per unit incl. 2 persons, 2 children and electricity	£ 14.50 - £ 21.00
extra person	£ 3.20 - £ 4.30

For latest campsite news visit
alanrogers.com

Helston

Franchis Holiday Park

Cury Cross Lanes, Mullion, Helston TR12 7AZ (Cornwall) T: 01326 240301. E: enquiries@franchis.co.uk

alanrogers.com/UK0485

A small rural site, Franchis is ideally situated for exploring the Lizard peninsula in an Area of Outstanding Natural Beauty. Mature trees edge the site's two fields (a total of four acres) that slope slightly, with 65 pitches arranged around the perimeters. There are 33 with 10A electricity. Natural woodland areas and a stream will keep children occupied. Continuing past the fields into a wooded area are six small bungalows and six mobile homes, some privately owned and some to rent. There is a small toilet block for each field and a small shop that opens morning and evening. Phil and Kate, the young couple who have owned the site for the last few years, will be pleased to welcome you and advise you in exploring the area. The Lizard is a unique area and well worth exploring with unspoilt coves and the Helford river. Goonhilly Earth station is just up the road and you pass by the extensive Culdrose Naval base on your way to the site. Helston is known for its famous 'floral dance', the origin of which is not certain, but for one day in May each year the inhabitants dress up and dance through the streets to celebrate.

Facilities

Two traditional small toilet blocks with showers on payment (20p/4 mins). Two washing machines and two driers. Freezer for ice blocks. Small shop (2/7-3/9). Tourist information. Small library. Play area. Dog exercise field. Mobile homes and chalets for rent. WiFi (charged). Off site: Riding, golf, beach, fishing and boat launching 2 miles. Sailing 4 miles. Helston 5 miles.

Open: Easter - 31 October.

Directions

From Helston take the A3083 road towards Mullion and the Lizard. After 5 miles and passing the Wheel Inn, watch for site directly on the left. GPS: 50.039, -5.21843

Charges guide

Per unit incl. 2 persons	
and electricity	£ 13.00 - £ 18.00
extra person	£ 1.50 - £ 2.00
dog	free - £ 2.00

Franchis Holiday Park Near Mullion, Helston, Cornwall TR12 7AZ Tel. 01326 240301

Franchis is a small & friendly park perfectly placed for visiting The Lizard and West Cornwall. Special offers run outside of high season; **please phone or visit our website for more details.**

www.franchis.co.uk - enquiries@franchis.co.uk

Helston

Chy Carne Holiday Park

Kuggar, Ruan Minor, Helston TR12 7LX (Cornwall) T: 01326 290200. E: enquiries@camping-cornwall.com

alanrogers.com/UK0075

Situated on the Lizard peninsular, the first impression of Chy Carne is of a traditional site with little stone bungalows and mobile homes at the entrance, but from the touring fields there are spectacular views of the sea and cliffs at Kennack Sands. In season the owners erect large marquees so that the bar and takeaway have their own internal area to eat, drink and relax in. There is plenty of entertainment and music provided. The caravan field is level but the tent field is sloping with some terracing. The 150 pitches are marked by low, white chain fencing, some 100 with 10/16A electricity, and 60 with hardstanding. Some mobile homes and chalets are available to rent. There is a pathway through the fields to Kennack Sands, a blue flag beach with lifeguards in high season. There is also a café and the odd gift shop. The sand is a greyish colour, but it is a very popular beach with an extremely narrow access road. There is a good play area on site. The marquees seem to be the focus of the site and everything happens there.

Facilities

One largish toilet block is near the touring fields, with a small one at the far end. Fully equipped with showers (pink for ladies and blue for men) on payment (50p/5 mins). Double sized shower for use by families and disabled visitors. Laundry/washing up room. Shop, bar and takeaway selling pizzas (July and Aug. when the marquees are put up). Games room with arcade games. Play area. Mobile fire baskets and chimneys available to hire. WiFi. Off site: Beach within walking distance. Fishing 1.5 miles. Riding and golf 5 miles. Bicycle hire 15 miles.

Open: March - November.

Directions

From Helston take A3083 towards the Lizard. Pass sign for Mullion then watch for left turn for Ruan Minor, following signs for Kuggar. Site almost immediately on left on road to Kennack sands. Bear right in Kuggar to site on left. GPS: 50.00404, -5.17625

Charges 2013

Per unit incl. 2 persons	£ 15.00 - £ 17.00
incl. electricity	£ 21,50 - £ 23,50
extra person	£ 4.50 - £ 5.50
child (4-15 yrs)	£ 2.50 - £ 3.50

Helston
Lower Polladras Touring Park
Carleen, Helston TR13 9NX (Cornwall) T: 01736 762220. E: lowerpolladras@btinternet.com
alanrogers.com/UK0475

Lower Polladras is a small, friendly park located north of Helston in beautiful rolling Cornish countryside. There are 44 touring pitches here as well as a number of mobile homes (for rent) and seasonal pitches. The site has a strong conservation interest and is actively working towards carbon neutral status. A two-acre area adjoining the park accommodates play equipment for children and a sports area. The upper level here is reserved for 28-day camping in the peak season. A nature and dog walk has been developed around the perimeter.

Facilities

Two traditional toilet blocks, both clean and light, with preset showers and hairdryer (20p). Baby changing area. Visitors with disabilities should check with site. Shop for basics. Playground. Sports area. Nature and dog walk. Tourist information. Mobile homes for rent. Off site: Helston (shops and restaurants). Golf and boat launching 3 miles. Fishing 4 miles. Riding 6 miles. Walking and cycling. Eden Project. Lizard Peninsula.

Open: 1 April - 2 January.

Directions

Take A394 from Helston towards Penzance. On the edge of Helston, turn right onto B3302, signed Camborne and Hayle. Take second left to Carleen. Once in the village take the second right and follow signs to the park. GPS: 50.130156, -5.337199

Charges guide

Per unit incl. 2 persons and electricity	£ 13.50 - £ 20.50
extra person	£ 2.00 - £ 3.00

Helston
Boscrege Caravan Park
Ashton, Helston TR13 9TG (Cornwall) T: 01736 762231. E: enquiries@caravanparkcornwall.com
alanrogers.com/UK0480

A pretty site covering 12 acres and hidden deep in the countryside in an Area of Outstanding Natural Beauty, Boscrege will suit those who want a quiet base for their Cornish holiday. The main large touring field nestles at the foot of Tregonning Hill with its striking hill top cross, and has neatly cut grass with a gentle slope from the top. The pitches are generously spaced around the edge, backing on to hedging and leaving plenty of room in the centre for ball games. There are two small, attractive paddock areas with 26 caravan holiday homes and a field for touring units, a total of 51 pitches, 40 with 10A electricity.

Facilities

Traditional, fully equipped toilet block is showing its age but has been newly painted. Washing machine, dryer and microwave. Two play areas for smaller children and central ball area. Amusement machines, pool table and TV room. Nature trail and dog-walking area. Plans to include WiFi. Off site: Godolphin House and garden. Whole of the tip of Cornwall easily accessible – the Lizard, Land's End. Fishing 1 mile. Golf, riding and nearest beach (Praa Sands) 2 miles. Bicycle hire and boat launching 5 miles.

Open: Easter/1 April - 31 October.

Directions

From Helston take A394 for Penzance. At top of Sithney Common Hill turn right onto B3302. Pass Sithney General Stores, take next left for Carleen. At Godolphin Cross turn left past Godolphin Arms (Ashton). Proceed up hill bearing left at top until you see camp signs. GPS: 50.12501, -5.36751

Charges guide

Per unit incl. 4 persons and electricity	£ 15.50 - £ 23.45
extra person	£ 2.00

Looe
Trelay Farmpark
Pelynt, Looe PL13 2JX (Cornwall) T: 01503 220900. E: stay@trelay.co.uk
alanrogers.com/UK0400

Situated a little back from the coast, just over three miles from Looe and Polperro in a rural situation, this is a quiet little park. Despite the name, there is no farm. On your right as you drive in, and quite attractively arranged amongst herbaceous shrubs, are caravan holiday homes (15 privately owned, some let by the park). The touring area is behind and slightly above and now also includes holiday homes around the outside edge with some touring pitches in the centre along with the play area. To compensate a new grass area has been developed at the side with views across the countryside, providing a total of 43 touring pitches with 16A electricity with further space for 12 tents.

Facilities

Good, fully equipped toilet block is heated and has large cubicles. Some semi-private washbasins. En-suite unit with ramp for disabled visitors (key from reception); it includes a baby bath. Washing machine and dryer. Gas supplies. Free use of fridge/freezer and ice pack service. Tourist information. Off site: Village with pub, shops and bus service 0.5 miles. Looe and Polperro within 3 miles.

Open: 30 March - end October.

Directions

From A390 Lostwithiel road take B3359 south at Middle or East Taphouse towards Looe and Polperro.The site is signed 0.5 miles past Pelynt on the left. GPS: 50.36225, -4.518883

Charges guide

Per unit incl. 2 persons and electricity	£ 10.50 - £ 16.50
No credit cards.	

For latest campsite news visit
alanrogers.com

Looe
Tencreek Holiday Park

Polperro Road, Looe PL13 2JR (Cornwall) T: 01503 262447. E: tencreek@dolphinholidays.co.uk

alanrogers.com/UK0006

Situated within walking distance of Cornwall's beautiful south coast, Tencreek is a family owned campsite with a friendly welcome which quite rightly justifies its description as a complete holiday park. Of the 350 pitches about 100 are occupied by mobile homes, but the rest are reserved for touring units and tents, with most having hardstanding. The site gently slopes towards the coast and it is claimed that every pitch has a sea view. Although close to many local attractions, there is plenty on offer on site with a well-stocked shop, a fine heated indoor pool, a new, all-weather multisports pitch, a large bar and a cabaret stage for evening entertainment. Over the years the Joce family has continually invested in the park and the result is a well-run site with clean, modern facilities. They are proud to offer a complete holiday package for the whole family and employ a team of professional 'Yellowcoats' who ensure that everyone has a good time! All new arrivals are given a comprehensive welcome pack which gives all necessary information about the park and tips on how to make the most of the surrounding area. Tencreek has direct access to the Coastal Path so it is possible to reach both Looe and Polperro on foot, although this is quite a distance for young children. Buses run to both towns from the end of the lane.

Facilities

Two modern, well kept blocks provide toilets, showers and open style washbasins, plus 12 family washrooms. Facilities for disabled visitors. Full launderette. Shop. Bar with bar meals and takeaway, large screen TV and entertainment. Games room. Indoor pool with lifeguard (all year). Multisport pitch. Play area. Organised entertainment for all ages. WiFi in bar area (free). Caravan holiday homes for rent. Off site: Beach 2 miles. Polperro. Shark fishing in Looe. Porfell Wildlife Park and Sanctuary. Eden Project and Lost Gardens of Heligan.

Open: All year.

Directions

From Plymouth take A38 and after 10 miles at big roundabout turn left towards Looe (clearly signed). Follow signs to Looe on A387 and B3253. In Looe turn right across the bridge for Polperro. After 1.25 miles Tencreek is signed on the left. The lane is narrow but it is only 400 yds and there are passing places. GPS: 50.346191, -4.483177

Charges guide

Per unit incl. 2 persons and electricity	£ 13.75 - £ 30.00
extra person (over 3 yrs)	£ 1.90 - £ 3.00
dog	£ 1.80 - £ 2.00

Mevagissey
Tregarton Park

Gorran, Mevagissey, Saint Austell PL26 6NF (Cornwall) T: 01726 843666. E: reception@tregarton.co.uk

alanrogers.com/UK0155

Run by the welcoming Hicks family, Tregarton Park itself dates back to the 16th century. It is little wonder that the listed buildings have created some problems in providing modern facilities, although the Hicks have done well with their conversions to create a pleasing environment. The 12-acre caravan park is made up of four meadows with wonderful rural views. The 125 pitches, all with 10A electric hook ups, 30 with hardstanding, are generous with most separated by either hedges or fencing. All have been terraced as the park itself is quite hilly. Reception provides a well stocked shop, tourist information and a takeaway service offering freshly cooked food including a daily delivery of Cornish pasties.

Facilities

The fully equipped toilet block has been completely revamped and includes some excellent features. Facilities for disabled visitors. Laundry room. Well stocked shop with groceries and camping supplies (11/5-20/9), takeaway (18/5-20/9). Gas supplies. Heated swimming pool (25/5-6/9). Tourist information. Dog exercise meadow. Adventure playground. All weather tennis. WiFi (charged). Max. 2 dogs. Off site: Bus stop at entrance. Heligan Gardens, Mevagissey and beaches all 2 miles. Bicycle hire 3 miles. Golf 5 miles. Eden Project 9 miles. Fishing trips from Mevagissey and Gorran Haven.

Open: 28 March - 2 November.

Directions

Leave St Austell travelling south on the B3273 and pass through London Apprentice and Pentewen. Follow Tregarton Park's brown tourist signs by turning right at the crossroads at the top of the hill towards Heligan and Gorran Haven. Do not go into Mevagissey. GPS: 50.2588, -4.829417

Charges guide

Per unit incl. 2 persons, electricity and awning	£ 9.00 - £ 25.00
extra person (over 17 yrs)	£ 3.00 - £ 18.00
dog (max. 2)	£ 1.00 - £ 3.00

FREE Alan Rogers Travel Card
Extra benefits and savings - see page 10

Newquay
Newperran Holiday Park

Rejerrah, Newquay TR8 5QJ (Cornwall) T: 01872 572407. E: holidays@newperran.co.uk

alanrogers.com/UK0160

Newperran is a large, level park in rural Cornish countryside. Being on high ground, it is quite open but this also gives excellent views of the coast and surrounding countryside. The owners, Keith and Christine Brewer, have rebuilt the reception, shop and pub to a very high standard. The traditional layout of the park provides a number of flat, well drained meadows divided into over 370 individual pitches with 10/16A electricity. Some fields have larger and reservable spaces with more free space in the centre. There are now 77 fully serviced pitches, some with hardstanding and a TV point. Newperran is only 2.5 miles from Perranporth beach, but there is a free heated swimming pool with sunbathing area and paddling pool on the park. A state-of-the-art entrance barrier is now in place operating on number plate recognition. Newly refurbished heated swimming pool and paddling pool. The pub or 'cottage inn' is a very comfortable area with a log burner for low season warmth and family entertainment such as quiz nights in high season. A new larger restaurant has been added, along with a games room and launderette. This is a well run park with plenty of space and activities for families with a few caravan holiday homes to rent.

Facilities

Toilet facilities comprise four clean blocks, two heated and all refurbished to a very high standard. Facilities include washbasins in cabins, family rooms, baby room, hairdressing room and a unit for disabled visitors. Laundry room. Well stocked self-service licensed shop. Licensed bar (mid May-Oct). Café (all season). New outdoor heated swimming pool with paddling pool (Whitsun-Sept). Adventure playground and separate toddlers' play area. Games room with TV. TV room. Off site: Goonhavern village within walking distance with pubs and post office. Fishing 1 mile. Riding and golf 2 miles. Beach 2.5 miles.

Open: 22 March - 31 October.

Directions

Turn off A3075 to west at camping sign 7 miles south of Newquay and just north of Goonhavern village. GPS: 50.350433, -5.101817

Charges guide

Per pitch incl. 2 persons and electricity	£ 12.00 - £ 23.30
extra person	£ 4.65 - £ 8.50
child (3-15 yrs)	£ 1.50 - £ 5.95

Newquay
Trevella Holiday Park

Crantock, Newquay TR8 5EW (Cornwall) T: 01637 830308. E: holidays@trevella.co.uk

alanrogers.com/UK0170

One of the best known and respected of Cornish parks with its colourful flowerbeds (a regular winner of a Newquay in Bloom award), Trevella is also one of the first to fill up and has a longer season than most. Well organised, the pitches are in a number of adjoining meadows, most of which are on a slight slope. Of the 270 pitches for touring units (any type), some 200 can be reserved and these are marked, individual ones. Over 200 pitches have 10A electricity, with 59 serviced pitches (with hardstanding, electricity and TV hook-ups, water, waste water), some extra large with sewage drain as well. Trevella is essentially a quiet family touring park. Ready erected tents are available to hire. The accent is on orderliness and cleanliness with on-site evening activities limited, although Andy's Kitchen offers good home-cooked food. Access is free to two fishing lakes, (permits from reception); with some fishing instruction and wildlife talks for youngsters in season. There is a pleasant walk around the lakes, which are a haven for wildlife and a protected nature reserve. It is also possible to walk to Crantock beach but check the tides first.

Facilities

Three blocks provide good coverage with individual washbasins in private cabins, hairdressing room, baby rooms and large en-suite family rooms in one block. Laundry. Freezer pack service. Well stocked supermarket (Easter-Oct). Café (including breakfast) and takeaway. Heated outdoor pool. Games room. Separate TV room. Crazy golf. Large adventure playground. Play and sports area. Pets corner. Fishing. Caravan storage. WiFi (charged). Off site: Shuttle bus service to Newquay in high season. Nearest beach 0.5 miles on foot, 1 mile by car. Riding 1 mile. Pubs and restaurants at Crantock 1 mile. Newquay 2 miles. Golf 3 miles.

Open: Easter - 31 October.

Directions

To avoid Newquay leave A30 or A392 at Indian Queens, straight over crossroads with A39 and A3058, left at A3075 junction and first right at camp sign. GPS: 50.3973, -5.096133

Charges guide

Per person	£ 4.65 - £ 8.65
child (3-14 yrs)	£ 1.50 - £ 6.10
pitch incl. electricity	£ 6.35
service pitch	£ 10.90 - £ 15.35

Families and couples only.

For latest campsite news visit
alanrogers.com

Newquay
Treloy Touring Park

Newquay TR8 4JN (Cornwall) T: 01637 872063. E: stay@treloy.co.uk

alanrogers.com/UK0205

Just three miles from the wonderful beaches around Newquay, yet peacefully located away from the crowds, Treloy is a pretty park. Family owned and run, there are 197 large pitches (120-190 sq.m), many level, some slightly sloping, all with 16A electricity (new system) and 30 fully serviced. All are used for touring units and perhaps this contributes towards the relaxed family atmosphere. There are concrete hardstandings for caravans which are attractively interspersed with shrubs and form a pleasant landscape feature. Elsewhere hydrangea edge the roads around the more open pitches and the new trees have grown well. St Mawgan, the RAF air sea rescue base and Newquay's airport are nearby but there is little disturbance. There is an hourly bus service to Newquay from the park entrance which means the coast and beaches can be enjoyed without taking the car. On return to Treloy there is the Park Chef and the Surfrider's Bar for meals and drinks. If you do not fancy the beach there is a pool in the park. This is a real family park providing for all ages.

Facilities

Good overall provision including a smart new block at the top. Baby room with bath. En-suite facilities for disabled visitors (key). Laundry. Gas. Shop with all necessities. Bar (20/5-15/9). Pleasant café with a good reputation and including breakfast (20/5-1/9). Takeaway. Swimming pool (walled and gated). Good fenced play areas and field with goal posts. Nature trail. Family entertainment such as magic shows, bingo, folk and rock music. WiFi (charged). Off site: Golf 0.5 miles. Fishing 1 mile. Riding and boat launching 3 miles. Other beaches such as Watergate Bay, Mawgan Porth and Porth beach are a short car journey.

Open: 29 March - 30 September.

Directions

From A39 St Columb Major take the B3059 for Newquay. Park is signed after 4 miles. GPS: 50.432867, -5.0125

Charges guide

Per unit incl. 2 persons	
and electricity	£ 12.40 - £ 23.45
extra person	£ 4.50 - £ 7.35
child (3-14 yrs)	£ 3.00 - £ 4.35
dog	£ 1.00 - £ 2.50

Newquay
Hendra Holiday Park

Newquay TR8 4NY (Cornwall) T: 01637 875778. E: enquiries@hendra.co.uk

alanrogers.com/UK0210

Hendra, one of Newquay's most popular parks, is now 40 years old, but still at the forefront in providing a wide range of facilities and entertainment, which makes for a memorable holiday experience. It is a large park with 280 caravan holiday homes to rent and 548 touring pitches on well mown, mostly terraced grass fields with country views and mature trees, some pitches are more sheltered than others. With tarmac roads and lighting, 311 pitches have 16A electricity and 28 pitches are fully serviced including water, electricity, light, sewer drainage, satellite TV connections and some innovative awning pads (dogs are not accepted on these pitches). A few camping pods have been added this year. This is an excellent, well maintained site with extremely helpful staff. The main attraction is perhaps the Oasis complex (open to the public) comprising an indoor fun pool with flumes, river rapids and beach. The outdoor heated pool with grass sunbathing area is free to campers. A wide variety of entertainment is on offer: comedians, bands, cabaret, dancing, bingo, discos, as well as the Tavern bar and restaurant, a pizzeria and fish and chip shop. The park is only 1.5 miles from Newquay and its fabulous surfing beaches and a bus to the town passes the gate. Hendra welcomes families and couples. A member of the Best of British group.

Facilities

Three modern fully equipped toilet blocks including facilities for babies and disabled visitors. Large launderette. Motorcaravan services. Gas supplies. Well stocked shop. Various bars, restaurants and takeaway, open all season (limited hours in early season). Pizzeria (main season only). Outdoor swimming pool (25/5-31/8). Indoor pool complex (cost £2.95 per person or, if pre-booked, £14.60 for 7 tickets). Various play areas including one for soft play. Games field. Scooter and skate park. Amusements. Comprehensive evening entertainment. Bicycle hire. WiFi (free). Minigolf. Bowling. Off site: Fishing 1 mile. Beach 1.5 miles. Golf 2 miles.

Open: 30 March - end October.

Directions

Park is on left side of A392 Indian Queens-Newquay road at Newquay side of Quintrell Downs. GPS: 50.402433, -5.04915

Charges guide

Per unit incl. 2 persons	
and electricity	£ 16.55 - £ 24.45
extra person	£ 5.30 - £ 9.60
child (3-14 yrs)	£ 1.60 - £ 6.35
dog	£ 4.30 - £ 5.25

Minimum charges apply at peak times.

FREE Alan Rogers Travel Card
Extra benefits and savings - see page 10

Newquay

Porth Beach Tourist Park

Porth, Newquay TR7 3NH (Cornwall) T: 01637 876531. E: info@porthbeach.co.uk
alanrogers.com/UK0235

The park is just across the road from Porth Beach with its beautiful bay, sandy shoreline and rock pools. Situated in a small, rural valley with a gentle stream to one side you can enjoy the ducks and the wildlife. The 182 good sized grass pitches stretching up the valley in parallel lines accessed by tarmac roadways are level, marked by tram lines and back on to open fencing. Most have 16A electricity, there are also a few with hardstandings. A well equipped toilet block is to be found half way up, heated in cold weather and with air conditioning for warmer times. There is a shop near the entrance, a pub across the road and a restaurant two doors up. Watergate Bay is just around the corner, and Newquay a couple of miles down the road, so if you are a surfer you will be in paradise. For walkers, Porth Headland and the South West Coastal path offer some outstanding views. Porth Beach is said to be the safest beach for swimming in the Newquay area. Altogether a super place for a family holiday.

Facilities

One modern, heated and fully equipped toilet block. Baby bath and facilities for disabled visitors. Launderette. Play area. Mobile homes to rent. Off site: Golf, riding and boat launching 1.5 miles.

Open: 5 March - 31 October.

Directions

From Newquay take the B3276 to Padstow. Site is half a mile on right. GPS: 50.426071, -5.0534

Charges guide

Per unit incl. 2 persons and electricity	£ 13.00 - £ 41.00

Newquay

Trethiggey Touring Park

Quintrell Downs, Newquay TR8 4QR (Cornwall) T: 01637 877672. E: enquiries@trethiggey.co.uk
alanrogers.com/UK0530

Trethiggey is a garden-like park with a ten month season, set some three miles back from the busy Newquay beaches and night life, with an enjoyable, informal style. With natural areas including a small wildlife pond and fishing lakes to enjoy, conservation is high on the agenda. There are 157 pitches, 110 with 16A electricity, some with hardstanding and four with water and waste connection. Some level pitches are formally arranged, with others more informal on gently sloping grass amidst 12 caravan holiday homes. A more open field provides extra pitches and room for tents. Facilities maintain the informal touch with reception alongside the Trethiggey Trading Post which provides basic supplies, an off-licence and a small library. The Mediterranean style bistro and café/bar is a great attraction, with an extensive menu in the main season. A barbecue bar is a nice touch in high season. Goats, chickens and geese are an added attraction for children. The relaxed atmosphere created by the two families who run the site makes this a different, yet popular, site.

Facilities

Two fully equipped, heated shower blocks, one in traditional style. En-suite facilities for families and disabled visitors. Baby bathroom. Motorcaravan service point. Laundry facilities and wetsuit wash. Games room at each toilet block with TV and amusement machines. Shop (all season). Café, bar and takeaway (June-Sept). Adventure play area and recreation field. Coarse fishing. WiFi (charged). Off site: Riding 2 miles. Golf and bicycle hire 3 miles. All the delights of Newquay within 3 miles with nightly minibus service (book in shop). Pub within walking distance.

Open: 2 March - 2 January.

Directions

Site is a few hundred yards south of roundabout where A393 crosses the A3058 at Quintrell Downs (beside the A3058). GPS: 50.396833, -5.0283

Charges guide

Per unit incl. 2 persons and electricity	£ 14.50 - £ 25.40
extra person	£ 4.85 - £ 8.20
child (3-15 yrs)	£ 1.50 - £ 5.65
dog	£ 2.80 - £ 2.95

For latest campsite news visit

alanrogers.com

Newquay
Monkey Tree Holiday Park
Rejerrah, Newquay TR8 5QR (Cornwall) T: 01872 572032. E: enquiries@monkeytreeholidaypark.co.uk
alanrogers.com/UK0165

A busy family park some three miles from the beach, Monkey Tree covers 56 acres and boasts an impressive entrance and smart reception. There are 750 pitches with 500 for touring units, 400 of which have 10/16A electrical connections. There are some hardstanding pitches and 24 extra large ones with water and waste water include the use of private facilities in the toilet block. The park is broken up into a number of hedged fields, the older ones with mature trees and shrubs. Some 50 caravan holiday homes to rent have their own fields as do a number of seasonal caravans. The park has developed an animal enclosure around the fishing lake, with alpacas, pygmy goats and some smaller, cuddly animals.

Facilities

The original block (refurbished) supplements seven new modern timber blocks with heating and facilities for babies and disabled visitors. Private en-suite facilities for super pitches. Laundry. Motorcaravan services. Gas supplies. Shop (mornings only in low season). Club with bar, restaurant and entertainment (main season and B.Hs). Takeaway (high season). Outdoor pool and paddling pool (Whitsun-end Sept). Trampolines (supervised, charged). Bouncy castles. Three adventure play areas. Amusement arcade. Fishing lakes. Off site: Beach 3 miles. Golf 4 miles.

Open: All year.

Directions

Follow A30 ignoring signs for Newquay. At Carland Cross (windmills on right) follow signs for Perranporth. After 1 mile turn right at Boxheater Junction on B3285 (Perranporth and Goonhavern). Follow for 0.5 miles, turn right into Scotland Road for 1 mile to park on left. GPS: 50.352218, -5.091659

Charges guide

Per person	£ 5.00 - £ 8.95
pitch incl. electricity	£ 5.50
incl. services	£ 12.50 - £ 19.75

Newquay
Sun Haven Valley Holiday Park
Mawgan Porth, Newquay TR8 4BQ (Cornwall) T: 01637 860373. E: sunhaven@sunhavenvalley.com
alanrogers.com/UK0215

An attractive, well maintained holiday park, Sun Haven Valley is on the edge of a small valley with views of the opposite hills. Owned and thoughtfully run by the Tavener family, it caters mainly for couples and families with children whose parents are said 'to play with their children'. On a gently sloping hillside, around 30 caravan holiday homes for rent border the top field with a central area of neatly cut grass left free for play. The lower field is edged by a small trout stream (unfenced) and provides over 100 level, grass touring pitches, 86 with 10A electricity and eight with hardstanding, marked by tram lines and accessed by a circular road.

Facilities

A large, centrally situated toilet block is fully equipped with a smaller one in the far corner. Two en-suite family rooms double as facilities for disabled visitors. Laundry. Fridge and freezer. Microwave. Toaster. Basic foodstuffs available in reception. Tourist nformation centre. Play area. TV room. Games room with computers. WiFi in reception (charged). Mobile phone reception poor.

Open: Easter - 31 October.

Directions

From B3276 at Mawgan Porth take narrow unclassified road between surf shop and minigolf (signed Mawgan 2 miles) for 1 mile. Site is on the left. GPS: 50.46203, -5.01385

Charges guide

Per unit incl. 2 adults and electricity	£ 15.00 - £ 31.50
child (5-13 yrs, first one free)	free - £ 3.50

Newquay
Summer Lodge Country Park
Whitecross, Newquay TR8 4LW (Cornwall) T: 01726 860415. E: info@summerlodge.co.uk
alanrogers.com/UK0325

Set some five miles back from Newquay in a rural situation (there is another park nearby), Summer Lodge has facilities for touring units along with some 56 privately owned mobile homes and an additional 35 for rent. Seventy touring pitches (12A electricity) are pleasantly situated in a large, sloping, grassy field with rural views. There is also room for a further 70 tenting places. The mobile homes are situated nearer the entrance in regular rows, close to where the bar and fish and chip café are to be found. Entertainment is offered all season and there is a largish heated swimming pool.

Facilities

Portacabin toilet facilities, somewhat cramped, were clean but with only one shower per sex. Facilities for disabled visitors. Laundry room. Shop, fish and chip café with takeaway. Bar with evening entertainment. Swimming pool with paddling pool (heated May-Oct). Play area. TV in bar. WiFi over site (charged).

Open: March - October.

Directions

From A30 at Indian Queens take A392 Newquay road and site is signed off to left at White Cross. GPS: 50.398322, -4.971258

Charges guide

Contact site for prices.

Newquay
Trevornick Holiday Park

Holywell Bay, Newquay TR8 5PW (Cornwall) T: 01637 830531. E: bookings@trevornick.co.uk

alanrogers.com/UK0220

Trevornick, once a working farm, is a modern, busy and well run family touring park providing a very wide range of amenities close to one of Cornwall's finest beaches. A modern reception with welcoming staff sets the tone for your holiday. The park is well managed with facilities and standards constantly monitored. It has grown to provide caravanners and campers (no holiday caravans but 56 very well equipped Eurotents) with some 550 large grass pitches (350 with 10A electricity and 55 fully serviced with electricity, water, drainage and TV connection with DVD channel) on five level fields and two terraced areas. There are few trees but some good views. Providing 'all singing, all dancing' facilities for fun packed family holidays, the farm buildings now provide the setting for the Farm Club. Recently refurbished, it provides much entertainment, from bingo and quizzes to shows, discos and cabaret. The Stables Grill also opens for breakfast and the Hungry Horse provides takeaway food. The rest of the development provides a pool complex, an 18-hole golf course with a small, quiet club house offering bar meals and lovely views out to sea, and three fishing lakes. Next door is the Holywell Bay Fun Park (reduced rates) and the sandy beach is five minutes by car or a downhill walk from the park.

Facilities

Five modern toilet blocks provide showers, two family bathrooms, baby bath, laundry facilities and provision for disabled visitors. Well stocked supermarket with bread made on site (from late May). Hire shop. Bars (with TV), restaurant, café and takeaway. Entertainment (every night in season). Pool complex with heated outdoor pool, paddling pool, sunbathing decks, solarium, sauna and massage chair. Health and beauty salon. Super Fort Knox style adventure playground, crazy golf, Kiddies Club. Amusement arcade and bowling alley. Teenagers' room. 18-hole pitch and putt with golf pro shop. Bicycle hire. Coarse fishing with three lakes. Dogs are accepted in two fields only. Limited facilities at Easter and from 8 Sept.

Open: 23 May - 14 September.

Directions

From A3075 approach to Newquay-Perranporth road, turn towards Cubert and Holywell Bay. Continue through Cubert to park on the right. GPS: 50.384983, -5.128933

Charges guide

Per unit incl. 2 persons	
and electricity	£ 27.55 - £ 46.45
extra person	£ 5.85 - £ 10.95
child (3-14 yrs)	£ 1.60 - £ 7.95
dog	£ 4.40 - £ 5.60

Families and couples only.
Many special discounts.

Newquay
Carvynick Motorhome Touring Park

Summercourt, Newquay TR8 5AF (Cornwall) T: 01872 510716. E: info@carvynick.co.uk

alanrogers.com/UK0540

Carvynick is unique in having been specially created and developed for American motorhomes. As you approach, you catch a glimpse of large, colourful 'monsters' through the trees. The RVs are parked in fully serviced, landscaped bays which include sewerage connections. In the Paddock area there is also parking for the tow car, whilst in the Copse there is decking and patio areas. A newer area built on a section of the existing golf course has similar facilities and amazing views across to the sea at Newquay. The reception complex is impressive and boasts a heated indoor pool, a badminton court and a small fitness centre with sauna and solarium.

Facilities

Restaurant and bar, separate bar. Indoor heated pool and toddler pool with spectators' lounge. Sauna, solarium and fitness suite. Golf course (5 hole). Badminton court. Games room. Pool table. WiFi. Off site: North and south Cornwall coasts nearby. Eden Valley project 14 miles. St Ives and Tate Gallery within easy reach.

Open: All year.

Directions

From Bodmin on A30 continue past McDonalds and Jet service station on right at Fraddon. Take next exit, A3058, (Summercourt). Continue into village of Summercourt, turn right at lights over A30 and take first turning left for site. GPS: 50.368736, -4.983035

Charges guide

Per motorhome incl. 4 persons,	
electricity, water and sewerage	£ 18.00 - £ 33.00
extra person	£ 3.00

Padstow

Mother Ivey's Bay Holiday Park

Trevose Head, Padstow PL28 8SL (Cornwall) T: 01841 520990. E: info@motheriveysbay.com

alanrogers.com/UK0425

Mother Ivey's Bay has a wonderful clifftop location with amazing sea views and its own sandy beach. It is a well established family park located to the west of Padstow and features low, Cornish walls and colourful displays of plants. The site has been owned by the Langmaid family for over 20 years and is extremely well cared for and maintained. One hundred grassy touring pitches are in two well tended fields with 16A electricity, one slightly sloping, with a further field for 100 in high season. Ten super pitches are also available with electricity, water and drainage. There are some 100 attractively arranged, privately owned mobile homes, with a further 58 available to rent. On-site amenities include a well stocked shop and a children's adventure playground, but the emphasis is on peace and quiet, so there is no bar or restaurant. The amazing beach in its own cliff edge cove, approached via wooden steps, is rather special. It has an almost Mediterranean feel. Padstow needs little introduction and is a delightful fishing village and holiday centre, and more recently has become renowned for its gastronomy. The Obby Oss May Day celebrations are well worth seeing with origins dating back centuries. The South West Coastal Path crosses from Padstow to Rock, using the Black Tor ferry, and offers miles of magnificent coastal walking.

Facilities	Directions
Two clean toilet blocks have all necessary facilities, including preset showers and open washbasins. 6 family shower rooms. Facilities for babies and disabled visitors. Large laundry room. Licensed shops sells fresh bread. Sandy beach. Adventure playground. Tourist information. Mobile homes and chalets for rent. WiFi (charged). Off site: Golf 0.5 miles. Bar and restaurant within 1 mile. Riding 1.5 miles. Shops and restaurants in Padstow 4 miles. Bicycle hire and boat launching 4 miles. Fishing trips. South West Coastal Path.	Follow the A30 dual carriageway to Indian Queens. Follow signs firstly towards Wadebridge (A39), then Padstow (B3274). After 3 miles, turn left towards St Merryn. Follow signs to Trevose Golf Club and then Mother Ivey's Bay. GPS: 50.541334, -5.013923

Charges guide

Per unit incl. 6 persons and electricity	£ 18.00 - £ 54.00
dog	£ 3.00 - £ 5.00

Open: 31 March - 4 November.

Padstow

Padstow Touring Park

Padstow PL28 8LE (Cornwall) T: 01841 532061. E: mail@padstowtouringpark.co.uk

alanrogers.com/UK0430

Padstow Touring Park has wonderful views over the surrounding countryside and is owned and run by the Barnes family. They have worked hard to develop the site, and bushes and shrubs now break up the fields in smaller grass bays or levelled terraces. There are 150 pitches, of which 127 have 'eurobollards' supplying shared water, waste water points and 10A electricity. Some pitches are on hardstanding. The site can accommodate motorcaravans of up to 34 ft. Padstow itself is a mile away, either by public footpath through the fields (20-30 minutes) or by bicycle on the road. A bus service passes (the site is a request stop) and reception holds timetables. Rick Stein's restaurant or bistro may tempt you – and there are many others in Padstow.

Facilities	Directions
Three toilet blocks, including one new with underfloor heating, en-suite shower rooms, facilities for disabled visitors and a family room. Full laundry facilities. Reception/shop for gas, camping equipment and provisions. Play area. WiFi throughout (charged). Off site: Nearest beach is at Padstow, others are within 2 miles. From Padstow there is access to the Camel Trail cycle route. Riding and fishing 2 miles. Golf 5 miles.	Park is situated on the main A389 road into Padstow, on the right 1 mile before the town. If towing or in a motorcaravan avoid A389 between Wadebridge and St Issey; instead take B3274 which can take large units. GPS: 50.52705, -4.949183

Charges guide

Per unit incl. 2 persons and electricity	£ 15.00 - £ 24.50
extra person	£ 3.50 - £ 5.00
child (3-15 yrs)	£ 2.00 - £ 3.50
dog	£ 2.00 - £ 3.00

Open: All year.

For latest campsite news visit

alanrogers.com

Pentewan

Pentewan Sands Holiday Park

Pentewan, Saint Austell PL26 6BT (Cornwall) T: 01726 843485. E: info@pentewan.co.uk

alanrogers.com/UK0250

Pentewan Sands is a popular, well managed family park with an ideal position right beside a wide sandy private beach. A busy, 32 acre holiday park with lots going on, there are 501 touring pitches, 401 with electricity, and 120 caravan holiday homes for hire. The good sized pitches are on level grass with nothing between them. They are marked and numbered by frontage stones, mostly in rows adjoining access roads. A good heated pool with a paddling pool is beside the Beach Club. In 2010 this area was rebuilt providing new indoor pools, a lap pool and a fun pool, a gym, 'kids' zone' and a new bar and restaurant. The bar and restaurant are open all day and serve good value food in season.

Facilities	Directions
Four main toilet blocks receive heavy use in peak season but are clean. Two bathrooms, a baby room and facilities for disabled campers. Laundry room. Motorcaravan service point. Large shop with off-licence, bistro and fast food (Easter-mid Sept). Bar meals (Easter-mid Sept, limited hours low season). Swimming pools (supervised; Whitsun-mid Sept). Entertainment. Playground. Games room. Tennis. Bicycle hire. Dogs are not accepted. WiFi.	From St Austell ring road take B3273 for Mevagissey. Park is 3.5 miles, where the road meets the sea. GPS: 50.288283, -4.78575

Open: 1 April - 31 October.

Charges guide

Per unit incl. 2 persons and electricity	£ 17.45 - £ 35.50
extra person	£ 3.00 - £ 5.50

Seafront pitch plus 10-20%.

Penzance

Wayfarers Camping & Caravan Park

Relubbus Lane, Saint Hilary, Penzance TR20 9EF (Cornwall) T: 01736 763326. E: elaine@wayfarerspark.co.uk

alanrogers.com/UK0065

Wayfarers is a neat and tidy, garden-like park reserved for adults only, in rural Cornwall. Sheltered by perimeter trees and consisting of two finely mown fields interspersed by shrubs and palm-like trees, 30 places are available for caravans (up to 23 ft. single axle), motorcaravans (up to 22 ft) and tents, plus three holiday caravans are available to rent. All have 16A electricity, with hardstanding available on 24. Should you enjoy walking you can follow the River Hayle down to St Erth. There are many more suggestions with maps and a good display of leaflets in the information room, including a star chart.

Facilities	Directions
The modern toilet block is fully equipped. Ladies have a wash cubicle and there are two smart en-suite shower rooms (key system). Fully equipped laundry. Shop stocks basics. No twin-axle caravans. Off site: Two pubs serving food in Goldsithney 1 mile. Fishing and riding 1 mile. Golf 1.5 miles. Beach 2 miles. Bicycle hire, sailing and boat launching 5 miles.	Following the A30 Penzance road take the A394 Helston road after the St Ives turning. Follow for 1 mile then turn left on the B3280 and pass through Goldsithney village and site is 1 mile further on left. Do not use sat nav. GPS: 50.133167, -5.416833

Open: 7 May - 25 September.

Charges guide

Per unit incl. 2 persons and electricity	£ 18.00 - £ 26.00
extra person	£ 6.00

Perranporth

Perran Sands Holiday Park

Perranporth TR6 0AQ (Cornwall) T: 01872 573551. E: nick.cook@bourne-leisure.co.uk

alanrogers.com/UK0135

An amazing site on grassy sand dunes with over 1,100 pitches in total (350 for touring units), so numerous mobile homes are dotted amongst the dunes. It is a village in its own right, with all the facilities that you could need – shops, restaurants, bars, entertainment; a second entertainment area opens in high season. Pitches are on sandy grass, marked by fencing, some level, some sloping, many with rabbit holes, 280 have 10A electricity and a few hardstandings. It is possible to hire tents or even yurts. A magnificent sandy beach is just over the next dune and is popular with surfers.

Facilities	Directions
Three basic toilet blocks (no electrical points) with two family rooms. Facilities for babies and disabled campers. Launderette. Supermarket. Gift shop. Café/bar and grill with terrace. Takeaway food. Sports bar. Heated indoor fun pool with flume and heated outdoor pool (28/5-3/9). Multisports court. Mini 10-pin bowling. Amusements. Pool tables. Surf school (equipment hire). Kids' club. Soft play area. Playland. Road train. Accommodation to hire. WiFi.	From Goonhaven take road for Perranporth. Site entrance on right before going down the hill. GPS: 50.359357, -5.143635

Open: 1 April - 31 October.

Charges guide

Per unit incl. 2 persons and electricity	£ 8.00 - £ 61.00
extra person	free - £ 2.00

FREE Alan Rogers Travel Card
Extra benefits and savings - see page 10

Polruan-by-Fowey

Polruan Holidays Camping & Caravanning

Townsend, Polruan-by-Fowey PL23 1QH (Cornwall) T: 01726 870263. E: polholiday@aol.com
alanrogers.com/UK0190

Polruan is a rural site in an elevated position on the opposite side of the river to Fowey, 200 metres from the Coastal path. With 47 touring pitches and ten holiday caravans to let, this is a very pleasant little site. The holiday homes are arranged in a neat circle, with a central area for some touring units, including seven pitches with gravel hardstanding and electricity, one fully serviced. The remaining touring pitches are in an adjacent field with eight electricity hook-ups, which is part level for motorcaravans and part on a gentle slope for tents. There are marvellous sea views, but it could be a little exposed when the wind blows off the sea. A raised picnic area gives more views across the estuary to Fowey. This is a nice little park in a popular tourist area, within walking distance (downhill all the way, and vice versa!) of the village, where there are various hostelries and a passenger ferry to Fowey. A member of the Countryside Discovery group.

Facilities

The fully equipped, heated, sanitary block has modern, controllable showers, large enough for an adult and child. Laundry room. Motorcaravan service facilities. Range of recycling bins. Reception (with a small terrace) doubles as a shop for everyday needs including fresh fruit and vegetables. Gas. Microwave. Hot drinks machine and freezer for ice packs. Tourist information and bus timetables (for Looe, etc). Sloping field area with swings for children. Max. 2 dogs. WiFi. Off site: Coastal path 200 yds. Fishing 0.5 miles. Riding and bicycle hire 3 miles. Golf 10 miles.

Open: Easter - 1 October.

Directions

From the main A390 at East Taphouse take the B3359 towards Looe. After 5 miles fork right signed Bodinnick and ferry. Watch for signs for Polruan and site to left. Follow these carefully along narrow Cornish lanes to site on right just before village. GPS: 50.32759, -4.62515

Charges guide

Per unit incl. 2 persons and electricity	£ 14.00 - £ 20.00
extra person	£ 4.00 - £ 7.00
child (2-15 yrs)	£ 1.00 - £ 3.00
dog	£ 1.00 - £ 2.00

No credit cards.

Redruth

Lanyon Holiday Park

Loscombe Lane, Four Lanes, Redruth TR16 6LP (Cornwall) T: 01209 313474.
E: info@lanyonholidaypark.co.uk **alanrogers.com/UK0016**

Lanyon's location is a pleasant surprise after the somewhat grey landscape found in parts of the tip of Cornwall. Tucked away down a lane, the holiday caravans are attractively situated with hedged touring fields beyond. A neat tarmac road curves around to reception, the pub and an indoor swimming pool. There are 25 large hedged touring pitches around the edge of two level fields and room for around 40 tents in high season in a separate field. A large play area for children is overlooked by the roof top terrace of the bar. This is a pleasant, relaxed destination for a family holiday with something for everyone and splendid views across the surrounding countryside to the sea. Lanyon is well positioned for travel to the north and south coasts. Stithians Lake is nearby for sailing, fishing and birdwatching. The Great Flat Lode Trail, also nearby, is ideal for walking, cycling and riding. The nearest beach is at Porthreath, although the park itself offers a small heated pool and meals are available in the pub. The holiday homes include 26 that are privately owned and 18 available to rent.

Facilities

One traditional toilet block is attached to reception with heating. Two others are of Portacabin type but well maintained. Baby changing. Showers may be in short supply at peak times. Laundry room. Bar serving meals (22/5-5/9). Heated indoor pool (10x4 m. April-Oct). Games room. Play area and trampoline. Caravan storage. WiFi (charged). Off site: Watersports at Stithians Lake 1 mile. Riding, fishing and bicycle hire 2 miles. Golf and beach 5 miles.

Open: Easter - 31 October.

Directions

From southwest side of Redruth take B3297 Helston road. After 1 mile enter Four Lanes village. Pass two shops then take second right into Loscombe Lane. Follow to park on right. GPS: 50.20292, -5.24554

Charges guide

Per unit incl. 2 persons and electricity	£ 9.00 - £ 23.00
extra person	£ 2.00 - £ 4.00
dog	£ 1.00 - £ 2.00

Minimum stay 5 nights in high season.

For latest campsite news visit
alanrogers.com

Redruth
Globe Vale Holiday Park

Radnor, Redruth TR16 4BH (Cornwall) T: 01209 891183. E: info@globevale.co.uk

alanrogers.com/UK0114

A family run, well maintained, 13-acre site, in countryside where the tin mine chimneys are a stark reminder of the past. The Owen family have worked hard in the past few years to upgrade the site. A number of mobile homes are to be found in the first part of the site amidst a mix of trees and shrubs. A further neatly grassed and sheltered area has serviced pitches on hardstanding. Two large, open fields with wonderful countryside views and Cornish stone walls have some 100 touring pitches around the edges with a central open space. Reception, in the centre of the site, is part of the Owen's home. A very pleasant bar open in peak periods has a popular patio area and serves food and takeaways. For children there is a super play area and large open spaces for running around. Altogether this makes a very good place to stay while visiting the tip of Cornwall. The beaches of Saint Agnes and Portreath are close and Saint Ives, Land's End, Saint Michael's Mount and the Lizard Peninsula are all within close driving distance. The site is on the route of the coast-to-coast cycle route.

Facilities

Smart, well equipped Portacabin toilet facilities. Facilities for disabled campers, ramped access. Laundry room. Bar, restaurant, takeaway. Play area. Caravans to hire. Off site: Bicycle hire 2 miles. Beach 3 miles. 9-hole golf course, riding, boat launching, fishing, sailing all 5 miles.

Open: All year.

Directions

Heading west on A30 take Redruth/Porthtowan exit, then take Porthtowan exit at roundabout and follow site signs. GPS: 50.257212, -5.218644

Charges guide

Per unit incl. 2 persons and electricity	£ 13.00 - £ 24.00
extra person	£ 3.00
dog	£ 2.00

Redruth
Tehidy Holiday Park

Harris Mill, Illogan, Redruth TR16 4JQ (Cornwall) T: 01209 216489. E: holiday@tehidy.co.uk

alanrogers.com/UK0115

Tehidy is a rather special, small park with an emphasis on the environment, so wild flowers abound and a note is kept of all bird sightings. Richard and his family have worked hard to ensure that the facilities on offer are of a high standard. Their newest development, in a secluded area at the top of the park, will provide camping pods, rather like a wooden tent with a hexagonal open cooking shelter. Tehidy also offers 28 level touring pitches all with 10A electricity, some with hardstanding, and 24 mobile homes and six bungalows cottages to let. The pitches are terraced where necessary and some are hedged, with others part fenced and with views across the countryside. The owners live on site and are constantly looking for ways to make improvements and to provide a relaxing environment. The setting on a wooded hillside is peaceful, with a stream at the bottom and direct access to a woodland walk alive with primroses and bluebells in spring. Whilst the grass is neatly cut, the banks are left for nature to develop. The nearest beach is at Portreath, which has a deep rock pool for swimming at low tide. There is a request bus stop outside the entrance for Truro, St Ives and Newquay. This is surfing country but you can also windsurf at St Stithian's reservoir. Tehidy Country Park (250 acres of woodland) is nearby, together with Tehidy Golf Club.

Facilities

Modern fully equipped toilet block. Very smart en-suite family room doubles as a facility for disabled visitors. Laundry facilities. Reception with shop area. Games room and tourist information. Play area with small trampoline. Netball. Picnic tables. Woodland walk. Local takeaway delivery. Pub and restaurant within walking distance. WiFi. Dogs are not accepted. Cottages and mobile homes for rent. Off site: Golf and bicycle hire 1 mile. Beach and riding 2.5 miles. Sailing 4 miles.

Open: 28 March - 1 November.

Directions

Leave A30 at Porthtowan and Portreath exit. Go right on roundabout to Portreath. Left at North Country crossroads. Follow signs to site. GPS: 50.244939, -5.252935

Charges guide

Per unit incl. 2 persons and electricity	£ 15.00 - £ 24.00
extra person	£ 3.00

FREE Alan Rogers Travel Card
Extra benefits and savings - see page 10

Saint Austell

Carlyon Bay Caravan & Camping Park

Cypress Avenue, Carlyon Bay, Saint Austell PL25 3RE (Cornwall) T: 01726 812735.
E: holidays@carlyonbay.net **alanrogers.com/UK0290**

Tranquil open meadows edged by mature woodland, well cared for by the Taylor family who live on site, provide a beautiful holiday setting with the nearest beach five minutes walk from the top gate. The original farm buildings have been converted and added to, providing an attractive covered, central area with a certain individuality of design which is very pleasing. Pitches are in five spacious areas and allow for a family meadow and a dog free meadow (high season only). There are 115 marked pitches with 10/16A electricity, some with hardstanding and eight have full services. All are on flat, terraced or gently sloping grass with flowers and flowering shrubs or edged with trees. The impressively tiled toilet blocks are of good quality and design. In addition to the attractive kidney shaped pool and paddling pool there is now a large rectangular pool (also heated) within a walled and paved area which is excellent for sunbathing. This forms part of the central area at the heart of the site and complete with tables and chairs it is the place to enjoy family entertainment in high season. There is also a pleasant family pub and Kidsworld for children within walking distance.

Facilities

Three individually designed, modern toilet blocks (one heated) provide a full range of comfortable facilities for all your needs. Fully equipped laundry room. Modern reception with little shop. Takeaway (May-mid Sept). Heated swimming and paddling pools (Whitsun-Sept). TV lounge. Crazy golf. Play areas (including adventure type). Eden Project tickets. Off site: Bus service on main road. Coastal footpath nearby. Buses to St Austell and Fowey from park entrance. Pub 1 mile. Sailing 2 miles. Eden Project 2 miles. Golf and riding 3 miles. Bicycle hire 4 miles. Boat launching 5 miles.

Open: Easter/1 April - 28th September.

Directions

From Plymouth direction on A390, pass Lostwithiel and 1 mile after village of St Blazey, turn left at roundabout beside Britannia Inn. After 400 yds. turn right on a concrete road and right again at site sign. GPS: 50.34085, -4.737217

Charges guide

Per unit incl. 2 persons and electricity	£ 16.00 - £ 29.00
incl. services	£ 19.00 - £ 32.00
extra person	£ 5.00 - £ 6.00
child (3-15 yrs)	£ 4.00 - £ 5.00
dog (max. 2)	£ 3.00

Motorcaravan less £1, hiker/tent less £2 per night.
Camping Cheques accepted.

Saint Agnes

Beacon Cottage Farm Holidays

Beacon Drive, Saint Agnes TR5 0NU (Cornwall) T: 01872 552347. E: beaconcottagefarm@lineone.net
alanrogers.com/UK0125

Amazing views greet you as you arrive at Beacon Farm. The stark remains of Wheal Coates tin mine stand out against the cliffs and views over the sea stretch for 25 miles – as far as Saint Ives. A mixed beef and arable farm, Beacon has its own home bred herd of beef cows and calves. The buildings and the impressive stone walls are extremely well maintained. One large, sloping field and a smaller one enjoy sea views but can be less sheltered than the pitches in smaller paddocks which are sheltered by walls and trees. In all there are 70 pitches of varying size, 42 with 10A electricity. This is a truly popular area with walkers and birdwatchers. A ten minute walk takes you to Chapel Porth beach, an unspoilt sandy cove offering excellent swimming and surfing, with caves and rock pools to explore.

Facilities

Good stone built toilet blocks are fully equipped and include a family room. Baby bath and changing mat. Laundry room. Motorcaravan station. Fresh supplies are kept in reception (papers, bread and eggs). Fish and chip van calls once a week. Play area with adventure type equipment. Dog exercise field. Caravan storage. Off site: Fishing and beach 0.5 miles. Riding 1.5 miles. Bicycle hire 2 miles. Golf 3 miles.

Open: Easter/1 April - 30 September.

Directions

From the A30 travelling west take B3277 (signed St Agnes) at Chiverton roundabout. At mini-roundabout approaching St Agnes, turn left for Chapel Porth and follow brown Beacon Cottage Farm signs. GPS: 50.30567, -5.2249

Charges guide

Per unit incl. 2 persons and electricity	£ 19.70 - £ 25.70
extra person	£ 4.70

Min. 7 nights in school holidays.

For latest campsite news visit
alanrogers.com

Saint Austell
Heligan Woods Camping and Caravan Park
Saint Ewe, Saint Austell PL26 6EL (Cornwall) T: 01726 843485. E: heligan@pentewan.co.uk
alanrogers.com/UK0410

A peaceful, attractive park in a mature garden setting, Heligan Woods complements its sister site, Pentewan Sands, with its busy beach life and activities. One can enjoy the mature trees and flowering shrubs here which have been further landscaped to provide an attractive situation for holiday homes (17 to rent). These face out over a part of the 'Lost Valley' of Heligan fame with the touring pitches below on sloping grass, some terraced and others in a more level situation (some with handstanding) amongst trees and shrubs. In all, there are 100 good sized touring pitches, 80 with 16A electricity.

Facilities

Fully equipped and well kept, the modern, heated toilet block includes a unisex room with bath and small size bath. Extra showers in separate block. Fully equipped laundry room. Small shop (Easter-14/09). Adventure playground. Off site: Beach/sailing 1.5 miles. Riding 2 miles. Golf 3.5 miles. Bicycle hire/boat launching. Lost Gardens of Heligan next door.

Open: Mid January - end November.

Directions

From St Austell ring road take B3273 for Mevagissey. After 3.5 miles, pass Pentewan Sands, continue up the hill and turn right following site signs. Park is on left just before reaching Heligan Gardens. GPS: 50.288833, -4.812083

Charges guide

Per unit incl. 2 persons and electricity	£ 11.75 - £ 27.25
extra person	£ 2.50 - £ 4.75

Saint Austell
Meadow Lakes
Hewas Water, Saint Austell PL26 7JG (Cornwall) T: 01726 882540. E: info@meadow-lakes.co.uk
alanrogers.com/UK0415

Meadow Lakes is a well equipped park set in 56 acres of rolling Cornish countryside of woodland and lakes and is a wonderful place for a family holiday. The level grassy or hardstanding touring pitches here are of a good size, most with electrical connections and views of the lakes or surrounding fields. The central farm buildings house all the amenities, including playbarn, games room and shop. Also available are the heated outdoor swimming pool, four coarse fishing lakes (each stocked with a different range of fish), pets corner (small animals and donkeys) and outdoor play area. Lodges, caravans and chalets are available to rent.

Facilities

New sanitary building containing three en-suite units per sex. Launderette. Shop. Heated swimming pool (27/5-4/9). Indoor and outdoor play areas. Tennis. Fishing (free, but rod licence needed). Play areas. Pets corner. WiFi (free). Off site: Golf (18 holes) 3 miles. Riding, bicycle hire and nearest beach 4 miles. Eden Project 8 miles.

Open: 19 March - 31 October.

Directions

Site is 4 miles west of St Austell. Take the A390 and then fork left to join the B3287 and the site is 1 mile further on the left. GPS: 50.30075, -4.85708

Charges guide

Per unit incl. 2 persons and electricity	£ 9.00 - £ 23.00
extra person	£ 5.00

Saint Ives
Ayr Holiday Park
Higher Ayr, Saint Ives TR26 1EJ (Cornwall) T: 01736 795855. E: recept@ayrholidaypark.co.uk
alanrogers.com/UK0030

Ayr Holiday Park has an unparalleled position overlooking Saint Ives Bay and Porthmeor beach and is a popular, well cared for site. On arrival it may seem to be all caravan holiday homes, but behind them is a series of naturally sloping fields with marvellous views providing a total of 90 pitches, of which 40 are for touring caravans and motorcaravans. These pitches are on grass, all with 16A electricity and several fully serviced with hardstanding. An extra field for tents is open in July and August. A state-of-the-art toilet block provides excellent facilities in a colourful and modern design.

Facilities

The excellent toilet block includes two family shower rooms and facilities for baby changing and disabled visitors. Wetsuit showers. Fully equipped laundry room. Motorcaravan point. Games room with TV, hot drinks and snack machines. Adventure play area. Max. 1 dog, contact site first. Bus calls. WiFi (charged). Off site: Tate Gallery and beaches within walking distance. Spar shop and leisure centre with indoor pool nearby. Golf 1 mile. Riding 2 miles. Sea and coarse fishing 2-3 miles.

Open: All year.

Directions

From A30 follow heavy vehicles signs for St Ives (not town centre). After 2 miles join B3311, then B3306 1 mile from St Ives (octagonal building on left). Turn left at mini-roundabout following camping signs through residential areas. Park entrance is 600 yds. at Ayr Terrace. GPS: 50.21261, -5.48928

Charges guide

Per unit incl. 2 persons and electricity	£ 21.25 - £ 44.25
extra person	£ 4.50 - £ 7.25

For latest campsite news visit
alanrogers.com

Saint Ives
Little Trevarrack Holiday Park

Laity Lane, Carbis Bay, Saint Ives TR26 3HW (Cornwall) T: 01736 797580. E: info@littletrevarrack.co.uk

alanrogers.com/UK0035

Little Trevarrack is a traditional Cornish park covering 20 acres, with wonderful views from the top of the site across St Ives bay towards Hayle and the surrounding countryside. It is owned by Neil, son of the owners of Polmanter Park, and Annette Osborne and has a smart, large reception and entrance. There are 234 pitches, in five open fields (the top ones with gentle slopes), 153 with 10A electricity and 15 with water and drain as well. Bushes and hedging have grown to form individual pitches and give a continental appearance to the park. A heated outdoor pool has a paddling pool and sunbathing area.

Facilities

The large, central toilet block is modern and well equipped. Baby room and facilities for disabled visitors in the reception building. Laundry. Heated swimming and paddling pools (27/5-12/9). Games room. Internet access and WiFi (charged). Play area and play field. Wild flower field with paths for dog walking. Max. 2 dogs. No kites allowed. Early and late arrivals area. Off site: Beach and fishing 1 mile (no dogs in high season). Golf 2 miles.

Open: 1 April - 30 September.

Directions

Follow signs for St Ives and take A3074 to Carbis Bay. Site is signed on left opposite junction to Carbis Bay beach. Follow road for 150 yds, cross small crossroads and site is the second turn on the right. GPS: 50.187233, -5.470833

Charges guide

Per unit incl. 2 persons	
and electricity	£ 17.00 - £ 34.00
extra person	£ 4.00 - £ 7.50

Saint Ives
Trevalgan Touring Park

Saint Ives TR26 3BJ (Cornwall) T: 01736 792048. E: recept@trevalgantouringpark.co.uk

alanrogers.com/UK0040

Trevalgan is owned by the same family that owns Ayr Holiday Park. It is a quiet, traditional style of park, located on the cliffs 1.5 miles west of bustling St Ives. It is a truly rural location where you can enjoy spectacular views and an abundance of flora and fauna and plenty of space for children to run. There are 132 clearly marked pitches (88 with 16A electricity and some with water as well) in two level fields edged by Cornish stone walls – it could be a little exposed on a windy day. The park is very popular with walkers with direct access to the coastal path. A member of the Countryside Discovery group.

Facilities

A fully equipped toilet block includes a baby room and facilities for disabled visitors. Seven en-suite rooms. Laundry room. Motorcaravan service point. Small shop (in reception). Mobile shop calls daily. Gas supplies. Games field, adventure play area. Pool. Games room with TV and coffee machine. Off site: Riding and golf within 2 miles. Fishing 3 miles. Bicycle hire 8 miles. Regular bus service to St Ives and back (June-mid Sept).

Open: 1 May - 30 September.

Directions

Approach site down a narrow Cornish lane from the B3306 St Ives-Lands End road, following sign. GPS: 50.20769, -5.51882

Charges guide

Per unit incl. 2 persons	
and electricity	£ 18.40 - £ 29.50
extra person	£ 3.75 - £ 6.00
child (5-16 yrs)	£ 2.00 - £ 3.00

Saint Ives
Polmanter Tourist Park

Halsetown, Saint Ives TR26 3LX (Cornwall) T: 01736 795640. E: reception@polmanter.com

alanrogers.com/UK0050

A popular and attractively developed park, Polmanter is located high up at the back of Saint Ives, with wonderful sea and country views. The Osborne family has worked hard to develop Polmanter as a complete family base. Converted farm buildings provide a cosy bar lounge with conservatory overlooking the heated swimming pool. The 250 touring pitches (no caravan holiday homes) are well spaced in several fields divided by established shrubs and hedges giving large, level, individual pitches with connecting tarmac roads. There are grass and hardstanding multi-serviced pitches with electricity, water, waste water and TV point, serviced pitches with 16A electricity and non-serviced tent pitches.

Facilities

Three modern, fully equipped toilet blocks can be heated and include en-suite family rooms. Facilities for disabled visitors. Baby room. Laundry. Motorcaravan service point. Well stocked shop. Bar with food and family area (all Whitsun-mid Sept). Takeaway. Heated swimming pool (Whitsun-mid Sept). Some entertainment (peak season). Tennis. Putting. Play area. Sports field. Games room. WiFi (charged). Off site: Golf 1 mile.

Open: 1 April - 31 October.

Directions

Take A3074 to St Ives from A30, then first left at mini roundabout taking Holiday Route (B3311) to St Ives. At T-junction, turn right for Halsetown, right again at the Halsetown Inn then first left. GPS: 50.196183, -5.491017

Charges guide

Per unit incl. 2 persons	
and electricity	£ 18.00 - £ 36.00

FREE Alan Rogers Travel Card
Extra benefits and savings - see page 10

Saint Just

Roselands Caravan & Camping Park

Dowran, Saint Just, Penzance TR19 7RS (Cornwall) T: 01736 788571. E: info@roselands.co.uk
alanrogers.com/UK0025

Roselands is a small, family owned park situated on the Cornish moors overlooking the village of St Just and with marvellous views of the sea and countryside around Lands End. In all there are 14 holiday homes to let, 17 level grassy touring pitches (all with 16A electricity) and some provision for tents. The owner's home, providing a bar and conservatory, along with reception and a small shop, sits in the centre of the park. The conservatory acts as a community family room with games, Internet facility and tourist information with a play area outside and a games room nearby. This area is very popular with walkers and birdwatchers. Bicycles are available to hire.

Facilities	Directions
Small traditional toilet block, fully equipped and can be heated. Laundry facilities. Small shop mainly for basics and gas. Bar with bar food served in conservatory (all year). Conservatory with TV and Internet access. Play area. Games room. Bicycle hire. WiFi. Off site: Fishing and golf 1 mile. Riding, beach and surfing at Sennen Cove 2 miles. Boat launching 5 miles. Nearby Lands End and Cape Cornwall. Minack Outdoor Theatre.	Take the A3071 from Penzance for Saint Just. Follow for 5.5 miles then 0.5 miles before Saint Just turn left at sign for site. GPS: 50.11323, -5.658

Open: 1 January - 31 October.

Charges guide

Per unit incl. 2 persons	
and electricity	£ 12.50 - £ 18.50
extra person	£ 4.50
child (under 12 yrs)	£ 3.50
dog	£ 1.00

Saint Martins by Looe

Polborder House Caravan & Camping Park

Bucklawren Road, Saint Martins by Looe PL13 1QS (Cornwall) T: 01503 240265.
E: reception@polborderhouse.co.uk alanrogers.com/UK0320

Polborder House is a lovely site, open all year, which will appeal to those who prefer a quiet, well kept small family site to the larger ones with many on-site activities. With good countryside views, up to 36 touring units can be accommodated on well tended grass. Good sized pitches are marked with some hedging between pairs of pitches to give privacy and most have 16A electrical connections. There are several hardstandings and 17 serviced pitches. Five mobile homes are available to rent. The new owners, Amanda and Dale Byers, live on the park and make everyone very welcome, creating a relaxed and happy atmosphere. The nearest beach is a 20-25 minute walk from a gate in the corner of the park.

Facilities	Directions
Laminated teak with chrome fittings and black surfaces make an unusual but warm, fully equipped, heated sanitary block. Family room planned. Laundry room. En-suite toilet unit for disabled visitors has a ramped approach. Shop (all season) for gas and basics, and some camping accessories. Play area. Hut with tourist information. WiFi (charged). Off site: Restaurant 500 m. Fishing, golf and boat launching within 2 miles. Diving school at Seaton 2 miles. Looe 2.5 miles. Riding 6 miles.	Park is less than half a mile south of the B3253. Turn off 2 miles east of Looe and follow signs to park and Monkey Sanctuary at junctions; care is needed with narrow road. GPS: 50.377217, -4.4185

Open: All year.

Charges guide

Per unit incl. 2 persons	
and electricity	£ 15.00 - £ 24.50
extra person	£ 4.25 - £ 7.00
child (3-15 yrs)	£ 2.25 - £ 4.50
dog	£ 1.00 - £ 2.00

For latest campsite news visit
alanrogers.com

Saltash
Dolbeare Caravan & Camping Park
Saint Ives Road, Landrake, Saltash PL12 5AF (Cornwall) T: 01752 851332. E: reception@dolbeare.co.uk
alanrogers.com/UK0440

Dolbeare Park has a countryside setting (but is very easily accessible from the main A38 road). The site is surrounded by trees and farmland and slopes slightly at the top. Connected by a gravel road, there are 60 hardstanding and gravel pitches, all with 16A electricity connections. A four acre camping paddock can also be used for rallies. For children there is a low level adventure play area and a separate area for games. Giant chess and Connect 4 games will entertain families. Dogs are accepted and a small dog walk is provided at the top of the park. Reception supplies leaflets on local attractions and amenities with a good supply of tourist information and maps. A member of the Best of British group.

Facilities

A modern, bright sanitary block has underfloor heating, family rooms and a room for visitors with disabilities. Small drying room. Laundry next to reception. Fridge and freezer in camping field. Motorcaravan services. Reception doubles as a small licensed shop for basics including takeaway food and gas (limited hours out of main season). Adventure play area. Giant chess and Connect 4. WiFi (charged). Site barrier (£10 deposit). Off site: Fishing 1 mile. Riding 3 miles. Golf 5 miles. Beach 8 miles.

Open: All year.

Directions

After crossing the Tamar Bridge into Cornwall, continue on A38 for a further 4 miles. In Landrake village turn right following signs and site is 0.75 miles on the right. GPS: 50.43064, -4.30551

Charges guide

Per unit incl. 2 persons and electricity	£ 16.50 - £ 23.00
extra person	£ 4.50
child (5-15 yrs)	£ 2.50
dog	£ 1.00 - £ 2.00

Truro
Chacewater Park
Cox Hill, Chacewater, Truro TR4 8LY (Cornwall) T: 01209 820762. E: enquiries@chacewaterpark.co.uk
alanrogers.com/UK0010

For those who want to be away from the hectic coastal resorts and to take advantage of the peace and quiet of an adults only park, this will be an excellent, 'value for money' choice. Chacewater has a pleasant rural situation and the site is run with care and attention by Richard Peterken and his daughters Debbie and Mandy. It provides 100 level touring pitches, all with 10A electricity and 90 with hardstanding, in two large field areas (slight slope) edged with trees or in small bays formed by hedges. There are 29 serviced pitches (electricity, water, and drainage) and an area for dog owners. The modern reception is not at the entrance but through the park to one side in a pleasant courtyard area.

Facilities

The main toilet block provides well equipped showers and two en-suite units. Laundry room. Second fully equipped block near reception providing roomy showers open direct to outside. Gas supplies. Icepack service. Library in reception. Adults only (over 30 yrs). Max. 1 dog, contact site first. Off site: Golf, riding and bicycle hire all within 3 miles. Bus stop 100 yds. Cornish tramways/railway coast to coast trail to walk or cycle nearby.

Open: 1 May - 30 September.

Directions

From A30 take A3047 (Scorrier), continue to roundabout and take left towards St Day. After 500 yds. turn right at crossroads onto B3298 (St Day) and continue for 1 mile. Turn left at the crossroads and continue for 0.75 miles, then left at crossroads (by Truro Tractors). Chacewater is the next right. GPS: 50.250802, -5.172557

Charges guide

Per unit incl. 2 persons and electricity	£ 16.00 - £ 20.00
dog (one only)	£ 1.00

FREE Alan Rogers Travel Card
Extra benefits and savings - see page 10

Truro
Porthtowan Tourist Park

Mile Hill, Porthtowan, Truro TR4 8TY (Cornwall) T: 01209 890256. E: admin@porthtowantouristpark.co.uk
alanrogers.com/UK0014

This delightful and sheltered park is set a mile back from the pretty seaside village of Porthtowan, a haven for surfers but enjoyed by families who can explore the rock pools and coves. The beach has Blue Flag status. In an Area of Outstanding Natural Beauty, tall chimney stacks, stark against the sky, remain a reminder of the tin mining for which this area of Cornwall was once renowned. This is now a peaceful spot with plenty of space on the park and tall trees surrounding the three camping fields. There are 80 pitches around the edges of the fields, on level grass and half with 10A electricity. There are a few hardstandings. The park is attractively laid out with tarmac roads and flowering shrubs. The facilities were spotless when we visited in high season. There is a recycling box for odds and ends left behind by holidaymakers but of potential use to future visitors. A large adventure type play area in the centre of the large top field is popular. There is a waiting list for seasonal pitches and caravan storage. The Coast to Coast Tramway trail passes within half a mile of the site. The Newquay-Saint Ives bus stops in the village.

Facilities

Modern fully equipped toilet block with two en-suite family rooms also suitable for disabled visitors. Shop in reception. Games room with tourist information. Adventure type play area. Fish and chip van calls once a week (variable day). WiFi throughout (charged). Off site: Riding 200 yds. Nearest beach 1 mile. Fishing and golf 8 miles.

Open: 25 March - 30 September.

Directions

From the A30 take exit for Redruth, Porthtowan and Portreath and follow signs for Porthtowan for 2 miles. At T-junction turn right up hill to park on the left just past a restaurant. GPS: 50.27374, -5.23768

Charges guide

Per unit incl. 2 persons
and electricity   £ 13.50 - £ 21.50

Porthtowan Tourist Park
Mile Hill, Porthtowan
Truro, Cornwall TR4 8TY

01209 890256
admin@porthtowantouristpark.co.uk
www.porthtowantouristpark.co.uk

Truro
Killiwerris Camping & Caravan Park

Penstraze, Chacewater, Truro TR4 8PF (Cornwall) T: 01872 561356. E: killiwerris@aol.com
alanrogers.com/UK0012

Tucked down a Cornish lane, Killiwerris is a rare find. It has been developed from a large garden and the field surrounding the house into a small and delightful touring park which provides 20 good sized pitches for caravans and motorcaravans. Of these, 16 are semi-separated either by low fencing or hedging, all with hardstanding in the front field with flowering shrubs sheltered by trees. The birds love it, as do adult humans – the park is adult only so it is very peaceful and now open all year. Three further pitches are found in the back field. Electricity (16A) is available for all the pitches with water points between two. The park is now owned by the Ashurst family and being centrally situated five miles from the city of Truro and four from the coastal village of St Agnes, this is an ideal base to explore the Cornish countryside.

Facilities

Excellent heated toilet block in a log cabin provides en-suite facilities to a very high standard. Separate provision for disabled visitors with ramped access. Separate laundry room. Max. 2 dogs. Off site: Bus stop 8 minutes level walk. Chacewater village (shop, pub, etc) 1 mile. Riding 1.5 miles. Fishing and golf 2 miles. Bicycle hire 2-3 miles. Beach 4.5 miles.

Open: All year.

Directions

Using the A30 towards Penzance, exit at Chiverton Cross roundabout (this is a large roundabout 28 miles west of Bodmin signed for Truro and St Agnes). Take third exit for Blackwater and in 500 yds. turn left into Kea Down Road. Park is 1 mile on right. GPS: 50.2655, -5.155

Charges guide

Per unit incl. 2 persons,	
electricity and awning	£ 16.00 - £ 20.00
extra person	£ 4.00
dog (max. 2)	£ 0.50
No credit cards.	

For latest campsite news visit
alanrogers.com

Truro
Silverbow Park
Goonhavern, Truro TR4 9NX (Cornwall) T: 01872 572347
alanrogers.com/UK0120

Silverbow has been developed by the Taylor family over many years and they are justifiably proud of their efforts. They believe Silverbow is a way of life and staying is an experience – they have certainly created a relaxed and tranquil atmosphere seeking to encourage couples and young families (teenagers are not accepted). Hard work, planting and landscaping has provided a beautiful environment set in 21 acres. There are 90 tourist pitches which are all of good size and include 69 'super' pitches in a newly developed area, with electricity, water and drainage, which are even larger. Many are on a slight slope with some attractive views. There are also 15 park-owned, high quality leisure homes. Much free space is not used for camping, including an excellent sports area with two all-weather tennis courts, as well as wild meadow and wooded areas ideal for walks. A natural area with ponds has been created to encourage wildlife (Silverbow was the first in Cornwall to gain the coveted '5-year Bellamy Gold' award for conservation). The park is 2.5 miles from the long sandy beach at Perranporth (30 minutes walk away from traffic) and six miles from Newquay.

Facilities
Two good toilet blocks include private cabins, four family shower/toilet rooms, two accessible by wheelchair, and a bath on payment. Laundry room. Motorcaravan services. Free freezer service. Shop for basics (mid May-mid Sept). Covered, heated swimming pool and small paddling pool (mid May-mid Sept) gated and sheltered by high surrounding garden walls. Games room. Play field. Tennis. Off site: Gliding, riding and fishing nearby. Concessionary green fees are available at Perranporth golf club. Pub within walking distance.

Open: 4 May - 28 September.

Directions
Entrance is directly off the main A3075 road 0.5 miles south of Goonhavern.
GPS: 50.336567, -5.120633

Charges guide
Per unit incl. 2 persons	£ 15.00 - £ 28.00
extra person	£ 3.00 - £ 6.00
child (2-12 yrs) or adult over 50 yrs.	£ 2.50 - £ 4.50
dog	free - £ 2.00

Children over 12 yrs. with or without parents not accepted. Discounts available.

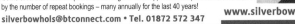

Silverbow Park Goonhavern • TR4 9NX • Truro • Cornwall

Silverbow Park has been developed as a tranquil, family park over the last 40 years. We always aim to be different than many other tourist establishments - a priority of respect for wildlife combined with a warm personal welcome. Dogs can also enjoy a lead free stroll around our Park meadows, but there are also dog-free wildlife areas and ponds, as well as facilities such as heated pool, tennis courts, bowls area etc. These aspects are among the most appreciated aspects of Silverbow, as shown by the number of repeat bookings – many annually for the last 40 years!

silverbowhols@btconnect.com • Tel. 01872 572 347   **www.silverbow.co.uk**

Truro
Trethem Mill Touring Park
Saint Just-in-Roseland, Saint Mawes, Truro TR2 5JF (Cornwall) T: 01872 580504. E: reception@trethem.com
alanrogers.com/UK0090

The Akeroyd family are proud of their park and work hard to keep it really well maintained and have been recognised for their commitment to high standards. They aim to attract couples and families who seek peace and tranquillity, and can manage without a bar and on-site entertainment. Trethem is a 'strictly touring' park with 84 pitches all with electricity, 60 with hardstanding and TV connections and 21 with water and waste water. All pitches are large, most on slightly sloping ground, some terraced, with the lower field more level and sheltered. All are individual or in bays, divided by hedging (some still growing) giving your own area. There is a comfortable and spacious feel as the park covers 11.5 acres, about half of which provides a dog and nature walk and recreation area.

Facilities
The well equipped central toilet block is kept spotlessly clean and is heated in cooler weather. En-suite facilities for disabled visitors which can double as a family room. Baby room (under 4s). Reception/shop, only small but well stocked and licensed. Freezer for ice packs (free). Motorcaravan services. Well equipped adventure playground (closed at 21.00). Large field for ball games. Extra field for dog walking. WiFi throughout park (charged). Off site: Fishing 1.5 miles. Beach, sailing, boat launching and bicycle hire 2 miles. Golf 6 miles. Riding 8 miles.

Open: 29 March - 6 October.

Directions
From Tregony follow A3078 to St Mawes. About 2 miles after passing through Trewithian, watch for caravan and camping sign.
GPS: 50.19003, -5.00096

Charges guide
Per unit incl. 2 persons and electricity	£ 18.00 - £ 30.00
extra person	£ 5.00
child (3-14 yrs)	£ 4.00
dog	£ 1.00

Truro
Carnon Downs Caravan & Camping Park

Carnon Downs, Truro TR3 6JJ (Cornwall) T: 01872 862283. E: info@carnon-downs-caravanpark.co.uk

alanrogers.com/UK0180

Carnon Downs is an excellent all year park run personally and enthusiastically by Simon Vallance, a very forward thinking owner. It has been thoughtfully laid out in a series of fields covering 20 acres so that all pitches back onto attractive hedging or areas of flowering shrubs and arranged to provide some pleasant bays or other, more open grass areas. Gravel roads connect the 150 pitches, most with 10/16A electricity and over 70 with hardstanding. Of these 55 are serviced, with the newer ones being exceptionally large and surrounded by young shrubs. On arrival you will receive a warm welcome, a neatly presented layout plan of the park and a touring information pack. This includes comprehensive details on walks and cycle paths leading from the park.

Facilities

Two excellent modern, light and airy, heated blocks include en-suite units and facilities for disabled visitors. Another well maintained block, also heated, includes some washbasins in cubicles and showers (unisex). Three good family bath/shower rooms, one suitable for use by disabled campers or families. Mother and toddler room, two baby sinks and full sized bath. Two laundries with freezers. Motorcaravan service point (ask at reception). Good adventure-type play area. Football field. Gas, newspapers and caravan accessories. General room with TV. Good dog walks. Caravan storage. Off site: Walks direct from site. Bus outside site for Truro/Falmouth. Pub/restaurant 100 yds. across the road. Golf 1 mile. Riding and bicycle hire 2 miles. Fishing 5 miles.

Open: All year.

Directions

From Truro take A39 Falmouth road. After 3 miles, park entrance is directly off the Carnon Downs roundabout. GPS: 50.22529, -5.08012

Charges guide

Per unit incl. 2 persons	
and electricity	£ 20.00 - £ 29.00
extra person	£ 4.00
child (5-16 yrs)	£ 3.50
all-service hardstanding	£ 2.50

Truro
Cosawes Park

Perranarworthal, Truro TR3 7QS (Cornwall) T: 01872 863724. E: info@cosawes.com

alanrogers.com/UK0185

Cosawes is set in a beautiful wooded valley where there are woodland and river walks and the park offers a quiet and relaxing holiday. The Fraser family have owned the site for many years and the recent upgrading of the facilities is excellent, particularly for a site that is open all year. Cosawes now offers 25 large, serviced pitches on gravel hardstandings, each in its own fenced space. These are particularly popular with motorcaravan owners and very useful for twin-axle vans. This still leaves around 40 grass pitches which are slightly sloping, most with electricity. A separate large residential area is private and away from the touring section. The situation of the park makes it good for visiting both the north and south coasts. Falmouth with its maritime museum is well worth visiting, whilst the north coast is popular for its surfing beaches. Saint Ives, Lands' End and the unique Lizard Peninsula are all within easy reach.

Facilities

Excellent, modern block (with ground source heat pump) beside the new serviced pitches provides two en-suite family rooms also suitable for disabled visitors. Toilets, laundry and dishwashing are downstairs, upstairs are showers and washbasins in cubicles. Fish and chips weekly. Dog walking field. WiFi (charged). Walks from site. Off site: Two pubs within walking distance. Supermarket 3 miles. Sailing and boat launching 3-5 miles. Fishing, golf and bicycle hire 5 miles. Beach at Falmouth 7 miles.

Open: All year.

Directions

Site is midway between Truro and Falmouth. Approaching from Truro via A39, after village of Perranarworthal, the park is clearly signed on right, and is 300 yds. up the lane on left. Use second entrance. GPS: 50.197026, -5.128319

Charges guide

Per unit incl. 2 persons	
and electricity	£ 13.00 - £ 17.00
hardstanding, serviced pitch	£ 17.00 - £ 21.00
extra person	£ 3.00
child (5-16 yrs)	£ 2.00

For latest campsite news visit

alanrogers.com

Truro

Summer Valley Touring Park

Shortlanesend, Truro TR4 9DW (Cornwall) T: 01872 277878. E: res@summervalley.co.uk

alanrogers.com/UK0510

Summer Valley is a quiet and mature, but very pleasant, small rural park suitable for visiting both the north and south coast of Cornwall. South facing, the park consists of a large well kept grass area with reception and facilities to one side. A tarmac road circles this and mature trees edge the whole site providing shelter but still allowing rural views. Caravans go on the central area which slopes gently and is divided down the centre with more mature trees and shrubs. The pitches around the perimeter area are semi-divided by shrubs and used more for tents. There is provision for 60 units of all types, but only 50 are used, 45 with 10/16A electricity connections. A Countryside Discovery site.

Facilities

A good quality toilet block is well maintained. Unisex showers, washbasins in cabins and one shower/toilet en-suite per sex. Laundry facilities. Campers' rest room with library. Reception/licensed shop (basics) with freezer pack service (reduced hours out of main season). Gas supplies. Off site: Shortlanesend with post office and pub within walking distance.

Open: 31 March - 31 October.

Directions

From Truro take B3284 north, signed Perranporth. Follow for 2.5 miles and site is signed on left just through the village of Shortlanesend. GPS: 50.29098, -5.08823

Charges guide

Per unit incl. 2 persons incl. electricity	£ 16.00 - £ 19.00
extra person	£ 3.00

Wadebridge

Saint Mabyn Holiday Park

Longstone Road, Saint Mabyn PL30 3BY (Cornwall) T: 01208 841677. E: info@stmabyn.co.uk

alanrogers.com/UK0230

The beaches of north Cornwall and the wilds of Bodmin Moor are all an easy drive from the site. The park has been extensively improved and is now carefully maintained by the Lloyd family and it provides a spacious and relaxed atmosphere. There are 110 level pitches, 97 with 16A electricity, on well drained and well mown grass with 50 hardstandings. There are caravan holiday homes and lodges to let. A nice, sheltered outdoor pool is an added attraction. However, there is no bar although the local village inn has a good reputation for food. The Camel Trail is only two miles away, providing a means to cycle or walk all the way to Bodmin, Wadebridge or Padstow.

Facilities

The fully equipped modern toilet block includes an en-suite unit per sex. A second, newly renovated block has family rooms and facilites for disabled visitors. Indoor dishwashing area with fridge/freezer and microwave. Laundry. Heated outdoor swimming pool and paddling pool (late May-early Sept). Good, fenced adventure play area. Play area for small children. Games room. WiFi over site. Off site: Riding and golf 3 miles, bicycle hire 5 miles.

Open: Mid March - end October.

Directions

From Bodmin or Wadebridge on A389, take B3266 north (Camelford). At Longstone turn left signed St Mabyn and brown camping sign. Site is 400 yds. on right. GPS: 50.5278, -4.745183

Charges guide

Per unit incl. 2 persons and electricity	£ 16.00 - £ 22.00
extra person	£ 5.00

Wadebridge

Trewince Farm Holiday Park

Saint Issey, Wadebridge PL27 7RL (Cornwall) T: 01208 812830

alanrogers.com/UK0500

A well established and popular park, Trewince Farm is four miles from Padstow and has been developed around a dairy farm with magnificent countryside views. Careful landscaping with flowering shrubs and bushes makes this an attractive setting. There are 35 caravan holiday homes discreetly terraced, some privately owned, some to let. Two touring areas on higher ground provide both hardstanding and level grass pitches with a sheltered tent area. Over half of the 120 touring pitches have 10A electricity and 34 have water and drainage. The park's main feature is an excellent heated swimming pool with paddling pool and paved sunbathing area. Cornish pasty suppers in the barn are organised in the high season.

Facilities

Two fully equipped, well maintained toilet blocks include washbasins in cabins and laundry rooms. Room for children with bath (20p) and facilities for disabled visitors. Well stocked shop by reception. Fish and chip van calls twice weekly. Swimming pool. Play area. Games room. Crazy golf. Fishing lake and woodland walk.

Open: 1 April - 31 October.

Directions

From Wadebridge follow A39 towards St Columb and pick up the A389 for Padstow. Site is signed on left in 2 miles. Follow for short distance to park entrance on right. GPS: 50.506604, -4.911692

Charges guide

Per unit incl. 2 persons and electricity	£ 15.80 - £ 21.80

FREE Alan Rogers Travel Card
Extra benefits and savings - see page 10

Wadebridge
The Laurels Holiday Park

Padstow Road, Whitecross, Wadebridge PL27 7JQ (Cornwall) T: 01209 313474.
E: info@thelaurelsholidaypark.co.uk **alanrogers.com/UK0505**

This is a small park in a garden-like setting of which the managers are very proud. It is very well maintained and provides 32 level pitches with 16A electricity. Some have hardstanding and some are extra large. Neat hedging marks the pitches and the central area with shrubs and plants is kept clear for enjoyment. A good play area for children is well fenced from the A39 which could be the cause of some road noise. The Camel Trail for walking or cycling is close and follows the estuary from Wadebridge to Padstow. A bus stops outside the site.

Facilities

Well kept fully equipped toilet block. Laundry. Facilities for drying wetsuits. Freezer and communal fridge. Play area with trampoline. Off site: Shops 1 mile. Riding, bicycle hire, boat launching 3 miles. Beach 4 miles. Fishing 5 miles. Camel Trail (walking/cycling).

Open: Easter/1 April - 31 October.

Directions

The Park is half a mile from the Royal Cornwall Showground, at the junction between the A39 and A389 Padstow Road, at Whitecross, 2 miles from Wadebridge. GPS: 50.50827, -4.88192

Charges guide

Per unit incl. 2 persons	
and electricity	£ 13.00 - £ 23.00
extra person	£ 2.00 - £ 4.00
dog	£ 1.00 - £ 2.00

Wadebridge
Tristram Camping Park

Polzeath, Wadebridge PL27 6TP (Cornwall) T: 01208 862215. E: info@tristramcampsite.co.uk
alanrogers.com/UK0525

Polzeath has one of the most spectacular surfing beaches in Cornwall and is just round the corner from the popular resorts of Rock and Padstow. The campsite is situated on the cliff just above the bay on sloping grass and a footpath leads to the beach. This is a popular and compact site for families so space can be tight. A few units up to 26 feet can be accommodated but most of the pitches take units of 20 feet. In total there are 107 marked pitches with a smaller area for two-man tents. Two toilet blocks serve the site and 16A electricity is available over most of the site. The coastal path runs along the front of the site. A smart licensed Indian restaurant fronts the reception and toilet block, with a garden overlooking the beach and village. Pubs, various cafés, surf and tourist shops, including a Spar shop, fill the little village, which is teeming with surfers over the summer season.

Facilities

Two solid toilet blocks are fully equipped. 50p token required for showers. Washing machines and dryers. Restaurant. Surf hire (by day/hour). Off site: Shops in village (10 minutes walk). Two golf courses nearby. Foot ferry from Rock for the Camel Trail and Padstow (with Rick Stein's restaurants). Wadebridge 15 miles.

Open: March - October.

Directions

Follow directions to Polzeath from Wadebridge. Go downhill into village then keep left up hill. Site signed on right. Access is just before the public parking barriers. GPS: 50.572947, -4.918816

Charges guide

Per unit incl. 4 persons	
and electricity	£ 31.50 - £ 42.00
Two-man tent	£ 20.00 - £ 25.00
extra person	£ 7.50 - £ 10.00
dog	£ 3.00

For latest campsite news visit
alanrogers.com

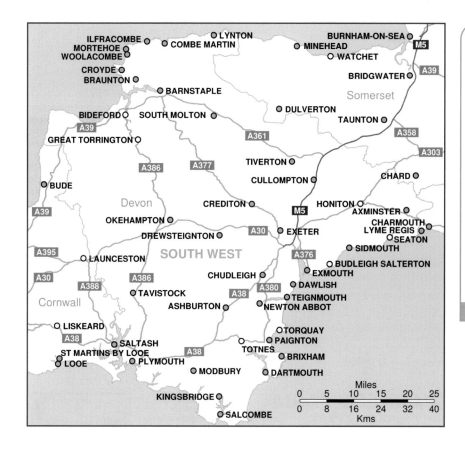

Ashburton
River Dart Country Park
Holne Park, Ashburton TQ13 7NP (Devon) T: 01364 652511. E: info@riverdart.co.uk
alanrogers.com/UK0950

The park is marketed as River Dart Adventures, where campsite and adventure experiences are enjoyed by old and young from all over Europe. It does become busy at weekends and school holidays with supervised activities for seven year olds and upwards, such as climbing and canoeing. The camping and caravanning area is in open parkland overlooking the woods and is mainly on a slight slope with some shade from mature trees. There are 185 individual pitches of very reasonable size, marked by lines on the grass, some slightly sloping, with 105 electrical connections (10/16A) and 12 hardstandings. Once part of a Victorian estate with mature woodland on the edge of Dartmoor in the beautiful Dart valley, the park and its activities are now open to the general public on payment. It features a variety of unusual adventure play equipment (e.g. a giant spider's web) arranged amongst and below the trees, Lilliput Land for toddlers, Jungle Fun, woodland streams and a lake with a 'pirate ship' for swimming, and inflatables, fly fishing and marked nature and forest trails – all free to campers except fishing. There is a Commando assault course, Dare Devil activities (high ropes, water zorbs, mega zip wire) and falconry displays are organised in high season (Thursdays).

Facilities
The woodland amenity block has been refurbished. A new Biomass heating system provides hot water throughout. Washbasins in cubicles, baby facilities, laundry, freezer, en-suite unit for disabled visitors (access by key), family bathroom and drying room. Motorcaravan service point. Shop, restaurant, bar, Sunday carvery and takeaway (all 1/4-25/9). Large TV and games room. Indoor climbing room (some of these open all year for the activities on offer). Tennis. WiFi. Max. two dogs per pitch. Bicycle hire. Off site: Riding 4 miles. Golf 6 miles.

Open: 1 April - 30 September.

Directions
Signed from the A38 at Peartree junction, park is 1 mile west of Ashburton, on the road to Two Bridges. Disregard advisory signs stating 'no caravans' as access to the park is prior to narrow bridge. GPS: 50.51698, -3.78869

Charges guide
Per unit incl. 2 persons
and electricity	£ 21.50 - £ 30.00
extra person (over 3 yrs)	£ 6.65 - £ 7.75
dog (max. 2)	£ 3.25

Camping Cheques accepted.

FREE Alan Rogers Travel Card
Extra benefits and savings - see page 10

Ashburton

Parkers Farm Holiday Park

Higher Mead Farm, Ashburton, Newton Abbot TQ13 7LJ (Devon) T: 01364 654869.
E: parkersfarm@btconnect.com **alanrogers.com/UK0960**

Well situated with fine views towards Dartmoor, Parker's Farm is a modern touring site offering a unique chance to experience Devon country life at first hand, with pigs, sheep, goats, calves and rabbits to feed and touch. The 100 touring pitches are on broad terraces giving groups of flat pitches, all with good views across the valley (over the A38 which may give some road noise). Electricity (12A) is provided throughout and 11 pitches also have large hardstanding with TV and waste water connections. Trees and hedges have matured nicely on the terraces, with many more planted. Caravan holiday homes are available to hire. In addition, the Parker family has added a family bar which provides entertainment during the main season (live singers, family bingo, children's entertainers) and a restaurant using locally sourced ingredients. Farm walks and tractor rides are tremendously popular and take place three evenings a week in high season, on request at other times. Parker's Farm provides a warm welcome – in the words of one camper, 'You come here and feel you belong'.

Facilities

Two modern, fully equipped toilet blocks also provide two family shower rooms. Baby bathroom. En-suite room for disabled visitors. Laundry. Shop (Easter-mid Oct). Restaurant, comfortable bar with family room (Easter, then Whitsun-mid Sept) and entertainment. Games room. Indoor play and TV area. Large outdoor play area. Trampolines. 6 acres of fields for dog walking. Caravan storage. Caravan holiday homes to hire. Rallies welcome. American motorhomes accepted by prior arrangement. Off site: Golf 4 miles. Riding and bicycle hire 5 miles. Coast 12 miles.

Open: Easter - 31 October.

Directions

From Exeter on A38 turn left at Alston Cross signed Woodland Denbury. Site is 400 yds. GPS: 50.527646, -3.723459

Charges guide

Per unit incl. 2 persons	
and electricity	£ 10.00 - £ 25.00
extra person	£ 3.00
child (3-15 yrs)	£ 2.00
dog	£ 1.50

PARKERS FARM
HOLIDAY PARK
01364 654869
Higher Mead Farm, Ashburton
Devon TQ13 7LJ
AA www.parkersfarmholidays.co.uk

- Friendly family run park
- Views to Dartmoor
- Level terraced touring site
- Static caravans to let
- Children's paradise
- 12 miles to the coast
- Dogs very welcome
- Short breaks available
- Bar/restaurant

Axminster

Andrewshayes Holiday Park

Dalwood, Axminster EX13 7DY (Devon) T: 01404 831225. E: info@andrewshayes.co.uk
alanrogers.com/UK1252

The Lawrences have been developing the park for over 50 years so it is well established with visitors returning every year. As the farm has wound down, extra fields have been added providing 230 pitches in total. As the site is on the side of the valley with wonderful views across to the Blackdown Hills, most of the pitches have been terraced with central or circular access roads. One field has mainly seasonal vans, another has 60 privately-owned mobile homes, with a further 20 available to rent and the remainder is for touring. The 130 touring pitches (some with hardstanding) have 10A electricity and a good majority have water and waste water and there are 20 tent pitches.

Facilities

Two fully equipped toilet blocks (one recently built), with family rooms and facilities for disabled visitors. Launderette. Microwave. Bar (weekend evenings only low season). Takeaway (mid July-end Aug). Shop in reception for essentials and Calor gas. Outdoor heated swimming pool (end May-mid Sept). Play area for younger children. Games room with video machines, pool table and soft ball pit area for young ones. Separate TV room. WiFi (charged). Off site: Fishing and bicycle hire 5 miles. Riding 6 miles. Golf 9 miles. Beach 10 miles. Bus service on main road for Lyme, Exeter and Bridport.

Open: Mid March - 31 October.

Directions

From Axminster following the A35 towards Honiton for 3 miles. Watch carefully for site sign at Taunton Cross signed Dalwood and Stockland. Park entrance 150 yds. GPS: 50.782995, -3.069477

Charges guide

Per unit incl. 2 persons	
and electricity	£ 17.00 - £ 25.00
extra person	£ 1.50 - £ 3.00
dog	£ 1.50 - £ 2.50

For latest campsite news visit

alanrogers.com

Axminster

Hawkchurch Country Park

Hawkchurch, Axminster EX13 5UL (Devon) T: 0844 272 9502. E: enquiries@hawkchurchpark.co.uk

alanrogers.com/UK1725

Although just 4 miles from the historic seaside town of Lyme Regis and 2 miles from Axminster itself, Hawkchurch Park enjoys a peaceful, rural situation with wonderful views over the Axe Valley. The park is set on a sloping hillside with a number of camping areas and is edged at the back with tall mature trees. In total there are 299 pitches with around 100 occupied by seasonal units in their own area and another section of 33 privately owned mobile homes. A further nine are available to let. Most of the touring pitches have been levelled and have either concrete or gravel hardstanding, 208 have 16A electricity. Tent pitches are on grass and mostly in their own fields.

Facilities

Two traditional toilet blocks which have been modernised, and one newer block near the tenting area. All are fully equipped and one is heated. Family washroom and baby changing unit. Washing machines. Shop for basics in reception. Bar/restaurant (open weekends and on demand out of main season). Dog walking area. Bicycle hire can be arranged. Off site: Beach at Lyme Regis and Charmouth 4 miles. Golf at Seaton (15 minutes drive).

Open: 15 February - 4 January.

Directions

To avoid narrow roads leave A35 between Charmouth and Axminster at Hunters Lodge pub, travel north on B3165 for 1.5 miles. At Wareham Cross follow sign to left for Hawkchuch and site is almost immediately on left. GPS: 50.7824, -2.930506

Charges guide

Per unit incl. 2 persons and electricity	£ 15.00 - £ 25.00
tent pitch	£ 13.00 - £ 20.00

Barnstaple

Greenacres Touring Caravan Park

Bratton Fleming, Barnstaple EX31 4SG (Devon) T: 01598 763334. E: stephenrj@hotmail.co.uk

alanrogers.com/UK0700

A neat, compact, rural park on the edge of Exmoor, Greenacres is managed and run alongside, but separately from, the farm owned by the family. Drive through the farm access to the park (clearly signed) – you will need to go back and call at the house to book in. No tents are taken. The site has 30 very large, well drained pitches (all with 16A electric hook-ups) with connecting gravel paths to the road – in theory you can get to your unit without stepping on the grass. The top area is level, the lower part next to the beech woods is semi-terraced to provide six hardstandings and some hedged places.

Facilities

The neat, clean toilet block has showers (1 per sex) on payment (20p). Units for disabled visitors (and general use in peak times). Laundry room. Washing lines provided. Gas supplies. Tourist information kiosk. Area for children with football and volleyball nets and swings, separated by a Devon bank from the 2-acre dog exercise field. Off site: Pubs, restaurants and takeaways within 3 mile radius. Fishing 3 miles. Riding 6 miles. Golf 12 miles.

Open: 1 April - 13 October.

Directions

From A361 (M5, exit 27) turn north at South Molton onto A399. Continue for 9 miles, past turning for Exmoor Steam Centre and on to Stowford Cross. Turn left towards Exmoor Zoo and Greenacres Farm is on the left. GPS: 51.147633, -3.917517

Charges guide

Per unit incl. 2 persons and electricity	£ 9.50 - £ 15.00

No credit cards.

Braunton

Lobb Fields Caravan & Camping Park

Saunton Road, Braunton EX33 1HG (Devon) T: 01271 812090. E: info@lobbfields.com

alanrogers.com/UK1140

Lobb Fields has two camping areas providing 180 pitches on sloping grass, with a few hardstandings. Twelve pitches are reserved for seasonal caravans, and 98 have 16A electricity hook-ups. A third field is open for campers for 28 days only in high season. The pitches are marked and grass roads lead to the amenities. As the two toilet blocks are at the very bottom or very top of the fields, some up and down walking is inevitable. Lobbs Fields may be close to many holiday activities, but it is also a peaceful retreat for those wanting a quiet holiday.

Facilities

Two elderly toilet blocks (one in each field) have all the usual facilities. Two family/baby rooms. Laundry. Cleaning and maintenance can be variable. The lower block can be heated and has good facilities for disabled visitors. Hairdryers and irons available from reception (£5 deposit). Takeaway. Play area. Surf shop. WiFi. Off site: Nearest shops less than a mile. Golf, riding and bicycle hire 1 mile.

Open: 29 March - 29 October.

Directions

Take A361 Barnstaple-Braunton road, then B3231 (signed Croyde) to Braunton. Park is 1 mile from Braunton on the right. GPS: 51.11165, -4.181233

Charges guide

Per unit incl. 2 persons	£ 9.00 - £ 22.00
prime pitch	£ 12.00 - £ 27.00
extra person	£ 3.00 - £ 6.00

FREE Alan Rogers Travel Card
Extra benefits and savings - see page 10

Braunton

Hidden Valley Touring & Camping Park

West Down, Ilfracombe EX34 8NU (Devon) T: 01271 813837. E: relax@hiddenvalleypark.com

alanrogers.com/UK0710

The owners, the Legg family, run this aptly named family park to high standards. In a sheltered valley setting between Barnstaple and Ilfracombe, beside a small stream and lake (with ducks), it is most attractive and is also convenient for several resorts, beaches and the surrounding countryside. The original part of the park offers some 67 level pitches (standard, large, super and premium pitch options) on three sheltered terraces. On hardstanding, all have 16A electricity and TV connections (leads for hire), with a water point between each pitch. Kingfisher Meadow, a little way from the main facilities and reached by a tarmac road, provides a further 58 pitches. These are entirely on grass (so suitable for campers with tents) and all have electricity, water, drain and TV hook-up. Two good adventure play areas have wooden equipment and safe bark surfaces (one near a fast flowing stream which is fenced). There is a well stocked shop and a coffee shop serving breakfast and light lunches. Essentially this is a park for those seeking good quality facilities in very attractive, natural surroundings, without too many man-made distractions – apart from some traffic noise during the daytime. It provides a relaxed setting with woodland walks direct from the site. A member of the Best of British group.

Facilities

Two modern heated toilet blocks are tiled and have non-slip floors. Some washbasins in cubicles, some en-suite with toilets in the Kingfisher Meadow block. Bathroom. Baby room. Complete facilities for disabled visitors. Laundry facilities. Motorcaravan service facilities. Gas supplies. Shop. Coffee shop. Play areas. Dogs exercise area. Caravan storage. Off site: Fishing and golf 2 miles. Bicycle hire 4 miles. Beach 4.5 miles. Riding 5 miles.

Open: All year.

Directions

Park is on A361 Barnstaple-Ilfracombe road, 3.5 miles after Braunton. GPS: 51.146533, -4.14555

Charges guide

Per unit incl. 2 persons	£ 16.00 - £ 40.00
extra person	£ 3.00 - £ 5.00
child (2-15 yrs)	free - £ 4.00
dog	£ 1.50

Discounts for over 50s.

Brixham

Hillhead Caravan Club Site

Hillhead, Brixham TQ5 0HH (Devon) T: 01803 853204

alanrogers.com/UK0845

Hillhead is set in 22 acres of beautiful Devon countryside. Originally developed in the 1960s within what is now a coastal protection area two miles from Brixham, the park has benefited from a £3 million redevelopment. It offers a full entertainment programme in peak season. Hillhead comprises 239 pitches, all with 16A electrical hook-ups and many with fine views. Amenities are to a uniformly high standard, notably the main complex based around an attractive courtyard, and housing a shop, bar, games room and Nico's restaurant, serving freshly cooked meals using local produce, and a Sunday carvery. The children's play area is outstanding with a range of imaginative items including a large wooden fort. Hillhead is rightly proud of its strong commitment to sound environmental practice, with a plan to promote species diversity and encourage good practice by site workers and visitors alike.

Facilities

The two sanitary blocks are new and maintained to a high standard. Each block includes three private family bathrooms (key from reception) and facilities for disabled visitors. Laundry facilities. Motorcaravan service point. Shop. Bar and restaurant with takeaway. Swimming pool (heated May-Sept) with paddling pool adjacent. Large play area. Skateboard ramp. Games room. TV. Entertainment in season. Games field. Dog walking area. WiFi (charged). Off site: Bus stop at site entrance. Nearest beach and coastal path 2 miles. Golf (18 holes) and riding 2 miles. Bicycle hire 2.5 miles. Numerous local attractions include South Devon Railway, River Dart boat trips. Paignton Zoo.

Open: 23 March - 2 January.

Directions

Site is well signed from the A379 Paignton-Dartmouth road and is on the B3205 (Slappers Hill Road). Entrance is on the left after 400 yds. GPS: 50.369621, -3.544816

Charges guide

Per person	£ 5.40 - £ 10.00
child (5-16 yrs)	£ 1.85 - £ 4.60
pitch incl. electricity	£ 5.20 - £ 11.55

For latest campsite news visit

alanrogers.com

Pitches from £9

"We left feeling a part of the family"

Hidden Valley
Quality family holidays

Hidden Valley Park, West Down,
Nr. Ilfracombe, North Devon
EX34 8NU

info@hiddenvalleypark.com

01271 813 837

• Luxury 5 star facilities
• Woodland walks & dog exercise areas
• 4 miles from Woolacombe Beach
• Wi-Fi across the park
• Children's play areas
• Coffee shop

www.hiddenvalleypark.com

Brixham
Galmpton Park

Greenway Road, Galmpton, Brixham TQ5 0EP (Devon) T: 01803 842066.
E: galmptontouringpark@hotmail.com **alanrogers.com/UK0850**

Within a few miles of the lively amenities of Torbay, Galmpton Park lies peacefully just outside the village of Galmpton, overlooking the beautiful Dart estuary just upstream of Dartmouth and Kingswear. A family park, now under new ownership, with 120 pitches (60 marked for caravans) which are arranged on a wide sweep of grassy, terraced meadow with some hedging. Each pitch has its own wonderful view of the river. Situated on the hillside, some parts have quite a slope, but there are flatter areas (the owners will advise and assist). There are 90 electrical connections (10A) and 23 pitches have water and drainage. There is a separate tent field. A member of the Countryside Discovery group.

Facilities	Directions
A central, substantial looking toilet block provides clean facilities including three washbasins in cabins, a very attractive under 5's bathroom (key), baby unit and hair care areas. En-suite unit for disabled visitors. Washing machine, dryer, iron and ironing board. Reception/shop sells basics including gas. Bread to order. Adventure play equipment. Max. 2 dogs (not accepted 16/7-30/8). No motorcaravans over 23 ft. Torches useful. Off site: Local pub 5 minutes' walk. Beach 2 miles. Open: May - September.	Take A380 Paignton ring road towards Brixham until junction with the Paignton-Brixham coast road. Turn right towards Brixham, then second right into Manor Vale Road. Continue through the village, past the school to site on right. GPS: 50.391650, -3.568070

Charges guide

Per unit incl. 2 persons and electricity	£ 15.50 - £ 20.50
with water and drainage	£ 18.00 - £ 25.50
extra person	£ 3.50

Chudleigh
Holmans Wood Holiday Park

Harcombe Cross, Chudleigh TQ13 0DZ (Devon) T: 01626 853785. E: enquiries@holmanswood.co.uk
alanrogers.com/UK0940

Close to the main A38 Exeter-Plymouth road, with easy access, this attractive, neat park makes a sheltered base for touring south Devon and Dartmoor. The hedged park is arranged on well kept grass surrounding a shallow depression, the floor of which makes a safe, grassy play area for children. Many attractive trees are growing and the park is decorated with flowers. In two main areas and accessed by tarmac roads, there are 116 level pitches (including a number of seasonal pitches) and 25 smart mobile homes in a private area. There are 100 pitches with 10A electrical hook-ups and 70 with hardstanding, electricity, water and drainage.

Facilities	Directions
The single, good quality toilet block includes facilities for babies and disabled visitors. Laundry room. Play area. Caravan storage. Woodland and meadow walks. Dogs are not accepted. Off site: Bus stop outside gate. Pub/restaurant nearby in Chudleigh village. Spar shop 5 minutes' walk. Sunday market at Exeter Racecourse 2 miles. Haldon Forest for walks 2 miles. Beach 7 miles. Open: Mid March - end October.	From Exeter on A38 Plymouth road, 0.5 miles after racecourse and just after a garage, take Chudleigh exit (signed). Park is immediately on the left. GPS: 50.61985, -3.582833

Charges guide

Per unit incl. 2 persons and electricity	£ 19.00 - £ 25.00
extra person	£ 3.50

Combe Martin
Newberry Valley Park

Woodlands, Combe Martin EX34 0AT (Devon) T: 01271 882334. E: relax@newberryvalleypark.co.uk
alanrogers.com/UK0685

Newberry Valley Park is set in a delightful semi-wooded valley that slopes down towards the rugged North Devon coast, on the edge of Combe Martin. Three wide terraces and several sheltered fields provide 110 good sized touring pitches (most with 16A electricity), with views to the hills. These vary from 18 paved, fully serviced pitches with picnic tables to simple grass areas suitable for tents. Combe Martin Bay has two beaches with rock pools and caves, and is only a five minute walk from the site down a small path. The site provides an atmosphere of peace and tranquillity, except perhaps at high season.

Facilities	Directions
Central modern toilet block with underfloor heating. Facilities for disabled visitors. Family shower room. Laundry with washing machines, dryers and free iron. Motorcaravan service point. Play area. Fishing. Small shop (Apr-Sept) in reception. Off site: Beach 0.25 miles. Shops and restaurants in Combe Martin 0.5 miles. Golf 5 miles. Open: 16 March - 31 October.	From A361 (exit 27 off M5) at South Molton take A399 to Combe Martin and Ilfracombe. The site is 20 miles on this road, through Combe Martin. GPS: 51.204191, -4.042599

Charges guide

Per unit incl. 2 persons and electricity	£ 16.00 - £ 38.00

For latest campsite news visit
alanrogers.com

Crediton
Yeatheridge Farm Caravan Park

East Worlington, Crediton EX17 4TN (Devon) T: 01884 860330. E: yeatheridge@talk21.com
alanrogers.com/UK1060

Yeatheridge is a friendly, family park with riding, fishing lakes, and indoor pools. Based on a 200-acre farm, nine acres have been developed over many years into an attractive touring park. Around the site there are views of the local hills and Dartmoor away to the south, and Exmoor lies to the north. The touring area is very neat and tidy with a spacious feel as units are sited around the perimeter or back onto hedges, leaving open central areas. The 85 numbered pitches are flat, gently sloping or on terraces and are sufficiently large, 80 with electricity. Seasonal units take 25 pitches and there are four caravan holiday homes. You can explore three woodland walks ranging from 1 to 2.5 miles and the banks of the River Dalch. There are two deep coarse fishing lakes (bring your own rod), the top one offering family fishing and the lower one for serious fishing (age 14 or over and free of charge). Horse riding is available on site (best to bring your own hat) with hour-long and park rides available. The ponies and goats are also popular with adults and children alike. The owners, Geoff and Liz, are constantly upgrading the park (they recently opened a new reception and amenity building) and they try very hard to make everyone feel at home.

Facilities

Two toilet blocks provide family rooms, washbasins in cubicles, showers and facilities for babies. En-suite room for disabled visitors. Laundry. Motorcaravan service point. Shop. Bar, restaurant and snack bar (hours vary acc. to season). Unsupervised indoor swimming pools, toddlers' pool and water slide (10.00-20.00). Fenced play area with fort for under 10s (parental supervision). Football field. TV room. Games room. Fishing. Riding. WiFi (charged).

Open: 15 March - 3 October.

Directions

Park is off the B3042 Witheridge-Chawleigh (not in East Worlington). From M5 exit 27 onto A361 to Tiverton. Turn left onto A396 for 0.5 miles then right on B3137 almost to Witheridge, then left on the B3042 for 3 miles to site, well signed down concrete roadway on left. GPS: 50.8887, -3.7501

Charges guide

Per unit incl. 2 persons and electricity	£ 11.00 - £ 20.50
extra person (over 4 yrs)	£ 3.00
dog (first two)	£ 2.00

Yeatheridge Farm Caravan & Camping Park
01884 860330
www.yeatheridge.co.uk
If you are a country lover, there is everything to interest you here.
2 ½ miles of wood & riverside walks. If you wish to explore beautiful Devon, then there could not be a better location.

Croyde
Ruda Holiday Park

Parkdean Holidays, Croyde Bay, Croyde EX33 1NY (Devon) T: 01271 890671.
E: rudatouring@parkdeanholidays.com **alanrogers.com/UK1150**

Ruda Holiday Park is a recent addition to Parkdean Holidays, now comprising 12 parks in Scotland, Wales and southwest England. Ruda is right beside a Blue Flag beach and provides 312 camping and touring pitches in two distinct areas. A large camping area divided into four sections is reserved for tent campers and small motorcaravans (there are some electricity hook-ups around the perimeter and it is served by two clean toilet blocks). Touring caravan and motorcaravan pitches, all with 16A connections, are in a separate field across the road and have direct access to the beach. Here, the toilet facilities are modern with coded entry to stop day visitors using them.

Facilities

Two blocks in the camping fields provide toilets, preset showers and communal washbasins. A third, modern building provides all facilities in the touring field. Laundry. Bar, restaurant, snack bar and takeaway. Amusement arcade. Cascade Tropical pool. Adventure playground. Tennis court. Sports field. Fishing lake. Supermarket, boutique and hire centre. Surfing equipment for hire. Direct access to sheltered beach. Caravan holiday homes and lodges for hire. Dogs are not accepted. WiFi. Off site: Golf 3 miles. Bicycle hire 8 miles. Surfing.

Open: March - November.

Directions

From Barnstaple, take A361 signed Braunton and Ilfracombe. At Braunton, take sharp left (narrow road) towards Croyde (signed) and follow the road all the way to the beach. Entrance to Ruda is on the right. GPS: 51.135183, -4.2352

Charges guide

Per unit incl. 4 persons	£ 13.50 - £ 37.50
pitch with services	£ 17.50 - £ 41.50

Prices are for pitch and up to four persons; maximum of eight persons per pitch.

Cullompton
Forest Glade Holiday Park

Kentisbeare, Cullompton EX15 2DT (Devon) T: 01404 841381. E: enquiries@forest-glade.co.uk

alanrogers.com/UK1000

Forest Glade, owned and run by the Wellard family, is set in eight hectares of the Blackdown Hills (designated an Area of Outstanding Natural Beauty), deep in mid-Devon away from the hectic life on the coast. A sheltered site set amongst woodland with extensive walking opportunities, there are 80 level touring pitches, 62 of which have 10/16A electricity connections, two with full services and 39 with hardstanding. Touring caravans must book in advance, when the easiest route will be advised (phone bookings accepted). Although set in the countryside, the beaches of East Devon are a fairly easy drive away. There is a small, heated, covered pool with a paddling pool, sauna and patio area outside, and a large games room (up a flight of steps, so not suitable for visitors with disabilities). There is also a soft play area for children. The surrounding 300 acres of forest makes this a nature- and dog-lovers' paradise (dogs are accepted). The owners have also developed a nature trail and wildlife pond.

Facilities

One main toilet block, heated in cold weather, has some washbasins in cubicles. Family shower room. Separate suite for disabled visitors. Laundry with washing machines and dryers. Facilities for babies. Extra Portacabin style facilities with toilets, washbasins and showers are at the swimming pool. Well stocked shop includes gas, and a takeaway (evenings except Sun). Microwave in campers' kitchen. Heated swimming pool (free). Sauna (charged). Extensive adventure play area. Games room. All-weather tennis court. WiFi over site (charged). Caravan storage. Off site: Fishing and riding 1.5 miles.

Open: 22 March - 4 November.

Directions

Park is 5.5 miles from M5 exit 28. Take A373 for 3 miles, turning left at camp sign, just past thatched pub on right, towards Sheldon. Park is on left after 2.5 miles. This access is unsuitable for touring caravans owing to a steep hill; phone park for alternative route. GPS: 50.857833, -3.277517

Charges guide

Per unit incl. 2 persons and electricity	£ 15.00 - £ 21.00
extra person	£ 6.50
child (4-18 yrs)	£ 1.80 - £ 3.60

Dartmouth
Little Cotton Caravan Park

Dartmouth TQ6 0LB (Devon) T: 01803 832558. E: enquiries@littlecotton.co.uk

alanrogers.com/UK0835

This lovely, family run park on the outskirts of Dartmouth is ideally situated for exploring this attractive area of South Devon. Well tended and immaculate, the 7.5-acre park is open and grassy. On level and gently sloping ground, it is situated on a hilltop and has views across the other fields. There are 95 pitches, all with 16A electricity and mostly level with some hardstanding available. The park is divided into four areas with one dedicated to rallies. A dog walking area is to one side. Barbecues are allowed off the ground.

Facilities

The modern, heated toilet block is centrally situated. It is very clean, light, airy and warm. Some washbasins are in cubicles. Free showers are preset. Excellent facilities for disabled visitors. Laundry facilities. Unisex baby room. Well stocked shop in reception. Bread and sandwiches to order. Freezer. WiFi (charged). Off site: Dartmouth Castle and the steam railway by ferry. Beach and fishing 2 miles.

Open: 15 March - 31 October.

Directions

Park is on the outskirts of Dartmouth on the A3122 opposite Sainsburys. From Totnes take the A381 (Kingsbridge) and turn left at Halwell on the A3122. Site is on right just before entering Dartmouth. GPS: 50.345106, -3.607606

Charges guide

Per unit incl. 2 persons and electricity	£ 16.00 - £ 22.00

Dartmouth

Woodlands Grove Caravan & Camping Park

Blackawton, Dartmouth, Totnes TQ9 7DQ (Devon) T: 01803 712598. E: holiday@woodlandsgrove.com

alanrogers.com/UK0840

Woodlands is a pleasant surprise – from the road you have no idea of just what is hidden away deep in the Devon countryside. To achieve this, there has been sympathetic development of farm and woodland to provide a leisure park with a falconry centre and zoo park, which is open to the public and offers a range of activities and entertainment appealing to all ages. Taking 350 units, the camping and caravan site overlooks the woodland and the leisure park. The original, main field has been fully terraced to provide groups of four to eight flat, very spacious pitches with hedging, the majority hardstanding (90% have 10A electricity and a shared water tap, drain and rubbish bin). This field is used all season, with other fields brought into use during the busier months. The newest field has 120 pitches (with electricity) designed with a more open feel to provide space for larger groups or rallies. Children (and many energetic parents too!) will thoroughly enjoy a huge variety of imaginative adventure play equipment, amazing water coasters, toboggan runs, the new Sea Dragon Swing Ship, a white knuckle monster, the Avalanche, and much more, hidden amongst the trees. Those more peacefully inclined can follow woodland walks around the attractive ponds. The Empire of the Sea Dragon, an indoor play centre, provides marvellous wet weather facilities comprising five floors of play areas and amazing slides. With a two night stay, campers on the touring park are admitted free of charge to the leisure park. A popular park, early reservation is advisable. A member of the Best of British group.

Facilities

Three modern, heated toilet blocks, with private bathrooms (20p) and 16 family shower cubicles. Facilities for disabled visitors. Two laundry rooms. Motorcaravan service point. Freezer for ice packs. Baby facilities. The leisure park café provides good value meals and takeaways for campers. Café opening hours and camping shop (with gas and basic food supplies) vary. TV/games room. WiFi (charged). Dogs are accepted on the campsite but not in the leisure park (unstaffed day kennels available). Caravan storage. Off site: Dartmouth and the South Hams beaches are nearby. Golf 0.5 miles. Beach 6 miles.

Open: Easter - November.

Directions

From A38 at Buckfastleigh, take A384 to Totnes. Before the town centre turn right on A381 Kingsbridge road. After Halwell turn left at Totnes Cross garage, on A3122 to Dartmouth. Park is on right after 2.5 miles. GPS: 50.357898, -3.675001

Charges guide

Per unit incl. 2 persons and electricity	£ 16.50 - £ 26.00
extra person over 2 yrs	£ 7.75
dog (contact site first)	£ 2.75

Free entry to leisure park for stays 2 nights or more.

FREE Alan Rogers Travel Card
Extra benefits and savings - see page 10

Dawlish
Lady's Mile Holiday Park

Exeter Road, Dawlish EX7 0LX (Devon) T: 01626 863411. E: info@ladysmile.co.uk

alanrogers.com/UK1010

Lady's Mile is a popular, large family touring park that caters well for children. It has extensive grassy fields (with some trees for shade), in addition to the main, landscaped camping area which is arranged in broad terraces. There are 486 good sized pitches, mostly marked by lines but with nothing between them, most with 10A electricity and some with water and hardstanding. To one side of the park there are some caravan holiday homes to let. It is a 20 minute walk to a good sandy beach at Dawlish Warren and 10 minutes to Dawlish beach, but the park also has a good sized, free outdoor swimming pool with a 200 ft. slide, a paddling pool and a paved surround plus a super heated indoor pool (20x10 m) with 100 ft. flume and separate paddling pool (both with lifeguards).

Facilities	Directions
Four toilet blocks are of a good standard and well spaced around the main areas, with an additional shower block. Facilities for disabled visitors. Family bathrooms (50p). Two launderettes. Supermarket with camping accessories. Fish and chip takeaway. Bars and entertainment programme. Restaurant and carvery (half-board option available). Café with pizzeria and snack bar. All Easter-mid Sept. Indoor (Easter-Oct) and outdoor (May-Sept) swimming pools. Adventure play area. WiFi throughout.	Park is 1 mile north of Dawlish with access off A379 (Exeter-Teignmouth) road. GPS: 50.59525, -3.459467

Charges guide

Per unit incl. 2 persons and electricity	£ 16.50 - £ 29.50
extra person over 2 yrs	£ 2.50 - £ 4.75
dog	£ 2.50 - £ 4.75

Low season special offers.
Low season discount for OAPs.

Open: All year.

Dawlish
Golden Sands Holiday Park

Week Lane, Dawlish Warren EX7 0LZ (Devon) T: 01626 863099. E: goldensands@ParkHolidaysUK.com

alanrogers.com/UK1085

Dawlish is a deservedly popular South Devon resort. Golden Sands is one of three Park Holidays sites in this area. There is some up and down walking to access a good range of facilities. There are no touring pitches at Golden Sands. Accommodation is provided in mobile homes and chalets for rent. Dawlish Warren can be accessed on foot and is home to an important nature reserve. The Warren is the main roost for the wildfowl and wading birds of the Exe estuary. By way of contrast, Powderham Castle dates back over 600 years and is the historic home of the Earl of Devon.

Facilities	Directions
Basic toilet block with washbasins and preset showers. Facilities for disabled visitors (but quite hilly ground to access). Laundry facilities. Shop. Playground. Tourist information. Mobile homes and chalets for rent. WiFi throughout (charged). Off site: Beach within walking distance. Golf 1 mile. Riding 4 miles. Dawlish.	Leave M5 at exit 30 and take A379 to Dawlish. Drive through Starcross and continue on A379 for 2 miles. Golden Sands is signed to left 1 mile before Dawlish. GPS: 50.596267, -3.456316

Charges guide

Per unit incl. 2 persons and electricity	£ 16.00 - £ 32.00

Open: 28 March - 31 October.

Dawlish
Peppermint Park

Warren Road, Dawlish Warren, Dawlish EX7 0PQ (Devon) T: 01626 863436. E: info@peppermintpark.co.uk

alanrogers.com/UK1090

Now part of the Park Holidays group, Peppermint Park is a green oasis in a popular holiday area. Extensive, green, sloping fields edged with mature trees have been partly terraced to give level pitches for caravans and some more informal areas that cater for tents. There are 90 holiday homes (many privately owned but some to rent) along with timber lodges to rent close to a small fishing lake. There are 75 touring pitches, 60 with 16A electricity, which are marked and numbered. Tarmac roads thread through the site giving easy access to all areas. Visitors staying at Peppermint Park can use all the facilities at nearby Dawlish Sands and Golden Sands, also part of the Park Holidays Group.

Facilities	Directions
Two fully equipped sanitary blocks can be heated. Two units (WC, washbasin and shower) for disabled visitors. Baby room. Laundry (washing machines, dryers and free irons). Shop with gas. Adventure playground on a hill. Field for ball games. Small coarse fishing lake (£5 for adult day ticket). WiFi throughout.	Leave M5 at exit 30 and take A379 Dawlish road. Pass through Starcross (7 miles), then turn left to Dawlish Warren just before Dawlish. Park is on the left in 1.5 miles. GPS: 50.599367, -3.446967

Charges guide

Per unit incl. 2 persons and electricity	£ 8.00 - £ 27.00

Open: 1 March - 31 October.

For latest campsite news visit
alanrogers.com

Dawlish
Cofton Country Holidays

Starcross, Dawlish EX6 8RP (Devon) T: 01626 890111. E: info@coftonholidays.co.uk

alanrogers.com/UK0970

326

A popular and efficient family run park, Cofton is 1.5 miles from a sandy beach at Dawlish Warren. It has space for 450 touring units on a variety of fields and meadows with beautiful country views. Although not individually marked, there is never a feeling of overcrowding. The smaller, more mature fields, including a pleasant old orchard for tents only, are well terraced. While there are terraces on most of the slopes of the larger, more open fields, there are still some quite steep gradients to climb. There are some 450 electrical connections (10A), 30 hardstandings and 14 'super' pitches. Self-catering accommodation on site includes holiday homes, cottages and apartments. A well designed, central complex overlooking the pool and decorated with flowers and hanging baskets houses reception, a shop and off-licence and a traditional bar, the Cofton Swan. New for 2012 was an extension to this complex with another two bar area suitable for daytime dining and evening entertainment, plus an indoor pool, sauna, steam room and gym, as well as a soft play area for children and a centrally located arcade. The new extension is open all year round except for Christmas and New Year. The outdoor pool with a paddling pool, has lots of grassy space for sunbathing. Coarse fishing is available in five lakes on the park. The adjoining unspoilt woodland of 50 acres provides wonderful views across the Exe Estuary and a woodland trail of two miles to Dawlish Warren.

Facilities

Six amenity blocks are well placed for all areas across the park. Facilities for disabled visitors. Family bathrooms and shower room. Hair dryers. Two launderettes. Gas available. Ice pack hire service. Bar (all year excl. Xmas and New Year). Shop (22/3-1/11). Fish and chip takeaway (22/3-5/10). Free outdoor swimming pool (24/5-14/9). Indoor pool (extra charge) open all year except Xmas and New Year. Arcade. Adventure playground, children's play areas and sports wall. Coarse fishing (from £5 per day). Caravan storage. Off site: Woodland walks and pub 0.5 miles. Beach and boat launching 1.5 miles. Golf 3 miles. Riding 5 miles. Bicycle hire in Dawlish.

Open: All year.

Directions

Access to the park is off the A379 road 3 miles north of Dawlish, just after Cockwood Harbour village. GPS: 50.6126, -3.460467

Charges guide

Per unit incl. 2 persons	
and electricity	£ 12.00 - £ 29.50
hardstanding pitch	£ 15.50 - £ 32.00
serviced pitch	£ 20.00 - £ 36.50
extra person (over 2 yrs)	£ 2.50 - £ 4.00

Small discount for senior citizens outside peak season.

Camping Cheques accepted.

See advertisement on the back cover.

Dawlish

Leadstone Camping

Warren Road, Dawlish Warren, Dawlish EX7 0NG (Devon) T: 01626 864411. E: info@leadstonecamping.co.uk

alanrogers.com/UK1095

Leadstone provides traditional camping at its best in a series of hedged grass fields, sloping in parts, in a natural, secluded bowl. In a designed Area of Outstanding Natural Beauty, the Blue Flag beach and sand dunes of Dawlish Warren are only a half mile walk. The area can get somewhat frenzied in peak holiday times but Leadstone provides a haven of peace and tranquillity. Owned by the same family since 1974, the Leadstone welcome is personal and the site totally relaxed. In all, there are 137 pitches, 102 with 16A electricity. A regular bus service passes the gate every 15 minutes. New for the 2012 season, an impressive timber-clad building houses showers, toilets, a dishwashing room and launderette facilities. It is sympathetically designed in keeping with the site's location on the seaward side of the Warren road where it is subject to Coastal Preservation regulations. The provision is good, if somewhat short on toilets. Extra toilet pods are brought in for peak times. The site is only open for a short season but is popular and well run. Dawlish Warren is renowned for its good weather and average temperatures of over 70 degrees Farenheit are not uncommon.

Facilities

The fully equipped, centrally located new building with showers and toilets is well kept. Unisex showers (20p for 5-6 minutes). Laundry facilities. Basic supplies and gas from reception. Play area with real tractor. Indoor pool. WiFi throughout (charged). Off site: Beach with shops, cafés, etc. at Dawlish Warren 0.5 miles. Golf 0.5 miles. Bicycle hire 2 miles. Riding 5 miles. Boat launching 7 miles.

Open: 7 June - 1 September.

Directions

From Exeter follow the A379 Teignmouth road (M5 exit 30). After Starcross watch for left turn to Dawlish Warren and site is on right after 0.5 miles. GPS: 50.59396, -3.45162

Charges guide

Per unit incl. 2 persons and electricity	£ 18.50 - £ 23.50
extra person	£ 7.50 - £ 10.00
child (3-13 yrs)	£ 3.00 - £ 3.50
dog	£ 2.50 - £ 3.25

Drewsteignton

Woodland Springs Touring Park

Venton, Drewsteignton EX6 6PG (Devon) T: 01647 231695. E: enquiries@woodlandsprings.co.uk

alanrogers.com/UK1250

Hidden away in a corner of the Dartmoor National Park, Woodlands Springs is a haven of peace and tranquillity. Set in a dip, it is sheltered by woodland with some views across the rural countryside. It provides 81 fairly level, grass pitches (45 with hardstanding) and 69 with 16A electricity, with a circular gravel access road and a central toilet block. There is a small shop and off licence; bread is baked daily. A large field provides good dog walking. The resident owners provide a warm welcome on this quiet park that only accepts adults. With 600 miles of public right-of-way on Dartmoor, there is plenty to keep walkers busy. Over 50 species of birds have been seen on the park over the last few years so it would also be a good base for birdwatching.

Facilities

Award winning toilet block including full facilities for disabled campers. Shop (limited hours). Dog kennels for rent. Torches useful. WiFi (charged). Off site: Fishing 3 miles. Riding 5 miles. Bicycle hire 8 miles. Golf 9 miles. Castle Drogo, Spinster's Rock, Finch Foundery and the Stone Lane Gardens nearby.

Open: All year.

Directions

From M5 exit 31 follow the A30 towards Okehampton. After 15 miles at Whiddon Down junction turn on A382 Moretonhampstead road. Stay on A382 for 0.5 miles then left at roundabout. After 1 mile turn left at brown caravan sign, then left and park is 150 yds. down drive. GPS: 50.706417, -3.850667

Charges guide

Per unit incl. 2 persons and electricity	£ 19.00 - £ 22.00
extra person	£ 4.00

For latest campsite news visit

alanrogers.com

Exeter
Crealy Meadows Caravan & Camping Park

Sidmouth Road, Exeter EX5 1DR (Devon) T: 01395 234888. E: stay@crealymeadows.co.uk

alanrogers.com/UK1125

Crealy Meadows is a new park in rural Devon developed by the owners of Crealy Adventure Park and situated adjacent to it. The multi-million pound investment has resulted in a well planned, purpose built park with excellent facilities. At present there are 120 serviced touring pitches (16A electricity, water and drainage) on neatly cut, level grass, and 21 hedged 'super' pitches (120 sq.m) with hardstanding. There are also pre-sited lodge tents in superbly themed safari camp or medieval village settings. These are really rather special and very well equipped with wood-burning stoves and sinks. The Safari tents even boast a sleeping cupboard. Don't be surprised to see a knight of King Arthur's court guarding Camelot village or a lioness and her cubs on watch beside the safari tents. There is direct gated access to the adventure park by means of pass cards which saves the queue at the main entrance. There is no doubt that the adventure park is the main attraction at Crealy Meadows and it certainly provides amenities for all the family including a large animal area with ponies to ride. There is a super indoor adventure zone and for the more adventurous an amazing selection of roller coasters and rides, a number involving water, and a range of eateries. Exmouth with its sandy beaches is about five miles away.

Facilities

Two modern fully tiled toilet blocks with underfloor heating. Roomy showers, family bathrooms and facilities for disabled visitors. Baby changing facilities. Two laundry rooms. Shop. Bar, restaurant and takeaway (2/6-1/9). Family entertainment (high season evenings). Two play areas. WiFi. Dog walk. Only charcoal barbecues permitted. Safari and medieval tents to rent. Access to Adventure Park – pay admission charges once, and receive free entry to the park for the following six days. Unique 'own a pony' experience on Adventure park (booking required). Fishing. Off site: Greendale Farm shop. Woodbury Common and castle. Family pub within 2 miles. Exmouth and beaches 5 miles. Exeter 7 miles.

Open: 1 May - 4 November.

Directions

From M5 exit 30 take A3052 (Sidmouth, Seaton and Crealy). Keep straight on following Crealy signs. Site is on right in under 2 miles. Using the A30/A303 from east, join the M5 at exit 29 and travel south to exit 30, then as above. GPS: 50.703606, -3.414967

Charges guide

Per unit incl. 2 persons and electricity	£ 22.50 - £ 27.50

Exeter
Dartmoor Barley Meadow Camping & Caravanning Club Site

Crockernwell, Exeter EX6 6NR (Devon) T: 01647 281629. E: dartmoor.site@thefriendlyclub.co.uk

alanrogers.com/UK0760

This peaceful little park is located on the northern edge of Dartmoor with easy access from the A30. It is sheltered from the weather by good hedging and, although not always visible from the pitches, there are open views across the moorland to the south. The 60 pitches are mostly on level grass, well spaced, with 25 hardstandings and 38 electric hook-ups (10A). Shrubs divide some of the pitches. This is a Club site, but non-members are welcome. The site would be a suitable base for visiting Exeter, Okehampton and Plymouth, hiking over the moors, or just enjoying the local area.

Facilities

The single heated toilet block is well maintained and provides all facilities including a well equipped room for babies and disabled campers. Laundry. Motorcaravan service point. Small shop for basics. Breakfast menu and newspapers to order. Games room. Playground. Small library. Free WiFi. Only small American RVs (up to 30 ft) accepted. Off site: Fishing 2 miles (river) or 6 miles (lake). Golf 4.5 miles. Riding 8 miles. Castle Drogo, the youngest castle in the U.K. Walks and an inn at Fingle Bridge.

Open: 14 March - 4 November.

Directions

From M5 exit 31, take A30 towards Okehampton. After 10 miles turn left towards Cheriton Bishop. After 0.5 miles pass through village, and continue for 1 mile towards Crockernwell, and site entrance is on left. GPS: 50.717533, -3.78325

Charges guide

Per unit incl. 2 persons and electricity	£ 19.25 - £ 22.65
extra person	£ 7.75 - £ 9.45
child (6-17 yrs)	£ 2.70 - £ 2.95

FREE Alan Rogers Travel Card
Extra benefits and savings - see page 10

Exeter
Webbers Caravan & Camping Park

Castle Lane, Woodbury, Exeter EX5 1EA (Devon) T: 01395 232276. E: reception@webberspark.co.uk
alanrogers.com/UK1100

Set in a lovely location in East Devon, with beautiful views of the Maldon Hills, this large family run park (10 hectares) has developed over 20 years to one that can boast spacious, modern facilities, yet still retain its relaxed, rural atmosphere. The 115 marked, grass pitches are large, with the majority level and a few gently sloping. Some of the higher pitches have marvellous views across the Exe river valley. There are 100 electricity connections (10/16A). The park is surrounded by fields and visitors can watch the wildlife and grazing sheep from a fenced walk around the park perimeter.

Facilities

There are three modern toilet blocks, one is a light and airy building with four family shower rooms, a bathroom (£1) and a unit for disabled visitors (WC, shower and washbasin). Laundry facilities. Motorcaravan service point. Small shop at reception for essentials. Gas supplies. Play area and games field. Off site: Woodbury village within walking distance with excellent pub/restaurant, post office, etc. Fishing and golf (Woodbury Park Golf Club) 1 mile. Riding 4 miles. Bicycle hire and boat launching 5 miles.

Open: 15 March - 29 October.

Directions

From A30, Daisymount exit, take B3180 for 3 miles to Halfway Inn and go straight across at crossroads. Follow B3180 (Budleigh Salterton/Exmouth). After 2 miles turn right (Woodbury). Follow downhill for 1 mile to park on left. GPS: 50.678083, -3.392017

Charges guide

Per unit incl. 2 persons and electricity	£ 13.00 - £ 18.00

Min. booking of 4 nights in high season.

Exmouth
Devon Cliffs Holiday Park

Haven Holidays, Sandy Bay, Exmouth EX8 5BT (Devon) T: 01395 226226
alanrogers.com/UK1260

Haven Holiday's flagship park, Devon Cliffs at Exmouth, is a very large, vibrant holiday resort, complete with its own, almost private, sandy beach. There are over 1,600 caravan holiday homes here (400 for hire). They are arranged in avenues on the attractively landscaped, hilly site around a central complex full of top class amenities. Overlooking this complex is a small, modern touring area providing 43 very neat pitches for caravans and motorcaravans, a good toilet block and its own warden. Fully serviced (electricity, aerial point, water and drain), each pitch has areas of gravel, concrete and grass. Tents are accepted in high season on another area of the park with a second toilet block.

Facilities

Neat, clean toilet facilities with open washbasins, preset showers and hairdryers. Room for disabled visitors. Good family bathroom. Launderette. Shopping arcade. Buffet and grill, two café/bars, fish and chips, Burger King, pizzas, Starbucks. Indoor and outdoor pool complex (outdoor 22/5-31/8). Spa centre. Sports facilities. Amusements hall. Evening entertainment. Children's clubs. Play areas. Beach (lifeguards in high season). Tents accepted 24/7-4/9.

Open: 20 March - 2 November.

Directions

From M5 exit 30, A376 (Exmouth). On outskirts of town (just after garage), turn left at lights following signs for Budleigh Salterton, Littleham, Sandy Bay and the park. GPS: 50.615645, -3.366387

Charges guide

Per unit incl. up to 4 persons and services	£ 17.00 - £ 46.50
extra person	£ 2.00 - £ 3.00

Ilfracombe
Sandaway Beach Holiday Park

Combe Martin Bay, Berrynarbor, Ilfracombe EX34 9ST (Devon) T: 01271 866766
alanrogers.com/UK0695

Sandaway Beach is set in a commanding position on the beautiful North Devon coast and is close to the charming fishing village of Combe Martin. The town is on the western edge of Exmoor National Park and offers all facilities including sea fishing trips. The park has a touring area for 20 caravans or motorcaravans, 12 of which have electricity, water and drainage. There are also two fields for tents at the far end of the park with wonderful coastal views. The remainder of the pitches are for rented caravan holiday home accommodation. Families will enjoy exploring the wild coast with its small coves.

Facilities

The single toilet block is downhill from the touring field and may pose access problems for disabled visitors. There are clean hot showers and two private cubicles. The tent areas have their own toilets. Shop. Bar, restaurant and takeaway. Heated outdoor pool. Enclosed play area. Kids' club. Off site: Bus stop at the gate for Combe Martin and Ilfracombe (4 miles). Boat launching and riding 2 miles.

Open: 15 March - 1 November.

Directions

From A361 turn north at South Molton onto A399 towards Ilfracombe and Combe Martin. Drive through Combe Martin and up steep hill towards Ilfracombe. Park is on right side 1 mile out of town. Entrance is tight, especially from Combe Martin direction. GPS: 51.206393, -4.044642

Charges guide

Per unit incl. 2 persons	£ 24.00 - £ 45.00

For latest campsite news visit
alanrogers.com

Ilfracombe
Stowford Farm Meadows

Berry Down, Combe Martin, Ilfracombe EX34 0PW (Devon) T: 01271 882476. E: enquiries@stowford.co.uk

alanrogers.com/UK0690

Stowford Farm is a friendly, family park set in 500 acres of the rolling North Devon countryside, available for recreation and walking, yet within easy reach of five local beaches. The touring park and its facilities have been developed in the fields and farm buildings surrounding the attractive old farmhouse and provide a village like centre with a comfortable spacious feel. There are 710 pitches on five slightly sloping meadows separated by Devon hedges of beech and ash. The numbered and marked pitches, some with hardstanding, are accessed by hard roads, most have 10/16A electricity and there are well placed water points. Stowford also provides plenty to keep the whole family occupied without leaving the park, including woodland walks and horse riding from the park's own stables.

Facilities

Five identical toilet blocks are fully equipped and provide good facilities, each with laundry facilities. The newest block (field 5) has underfloor heating and facilities for disabled visitors. Extra good facilities for disabled visitors and private family washrooms are beside reception. Well stocked shop (with holiday goods and gas). Good value takeaway with restaurant area. Bars and entertainment in season. Indoor pool (22x10 m; heated Easter-Oct) at a small charge. Riding. 18-hole pitch and putt. Crazy golf. 'Kiddies kar' track (all charged). Games room. Large play area. Games and activities in high season. WiFi. ATM. Woodland walks. Max. 2 dogs. Summer parking. Winter caravan storage. Caravan centre with sales, workshop, accessories and repair centre. Rallies accepted.

Open: All year.

Directions

From Barnstaple take A39 towards Lynton. After 1 mile turn left on B3230. Turn right at garage on A3123 and park is 1.5 miles on the right. GPS: 51.174983, -4.05475

Charges guide

Per unit incl. 2 persons and electricity	£ 8.90 - £ 25.70
extra person	free - £ 4.50
child (5-12 yrs)	free - £ 2.50
dog	£ 1.70 - £ 2.70

Low and mid season discounts for over 50s.

Ilfracombe
Napps Touring Holiday Park

Old Coast Road, Berrynarbor, Ilfracombe EX34 9SW (Devon) T: 01271 882557. E: info@napps.fsnet.co.uk

alanrogers.com/UK1120

Set in an idyllic location in North Devon, this popular, family-run site offers peace and quiet on site, with plenty to see and do off site. A path just outside the gates leads down to a private beach with safe bathing; although it is only 200 yards to the gate, there are 200 steps down to the beach so it is not suitable for wheelchair users. Combe Martin and Ilfracombe beaches are also close by. The 200 touring pitches (100 hardstandings), most with views of Watermouth Bay, are terraced and spacious, 95 are serviced with electricity, water tap and waste point, and another 70 have a 16A hook-up.

Facilities

Two modern toilet blocks include open plan washbasins, showers and family wash cubicles. Laundry. Licensed shop. Gas supplies. Bar with terrace and with light entertainment during high season. Restaurant (mornings and evenings). Takeaway. Heated outdoor pool with paddling pool. Tennis. Games room. Adventure play area. Caravan storage. Off site: Beach 200 yds. Combe Martin, golf and boat launching 1.5 miles. Ilfracombe 3.5 miles. Bicycle hire and riding 5 miles.

Open: 1 March - 31 October.

Directions

Leave M5 at exit 27, take A361 to South Molton and then A399 to Combe Martin. Site is 1.5 miles west of Combe Martin on the A399 (signed). GPS: 51.208517, -4.064083

Charges guide

Per unit incl. 2 persons and electricity	£ 10.00 - £ 27.00
extra person (over 10 yrs)	£ 1.00 - £ 5.00
child (5-10 yrs)	£ 1.00 - £ 4.00
dog	£ 1.00 - £ 2.00

FREE Alan Rogers Travel Card
Extra benefits and savings - see page 10

Ilfracombe
Hele Valley Holiday Park
Hele Bay, Ilfracombe EX34 9RD (Devon) T: 01271 862460. E: holidays@helevalley.co.uk
alanrogers.com/UK1145

Hele Valley is a well-established park which has been in the same family for over 30 years. Located a mile from Ilfracombe in a wooded valley, it is only a few minutes walk from Hele Bay beach. Here, quaint coves and coastal paths reveal a genuine smuggler's cave. Apart from the 80 attractively laid out caravan holiday homes (20 for rent), the park caters for tents, motorcaravans and smaller caravans only, because of the difficult access. Some 50 pitches are set in two lush green fields surrounded by trees and hedges. Being in a valley, some of the pitches are terraced. Eight gravel pitches for motorcaravans have electricity and water, and 50 for tents (12 large ones) have hook-ups.

Facilities

The bright, airy and modern heated toilet block (key access; deposit required) provides a mixture of open and enclosed washbasins, plus long mirrors and free hairdryers. Showers have glass doors. Deluxe baby room. Well fitted unit for disabled visitors. Two good adventure play areas and a play field. Parents note: a steep-sided stream running the length of the park. WiFi (charged).

Open: 1 April - 31 October.

Directions

From Ilfracombe, take A399 east towards Combe Martin. With Ilfracombe pool on left, go down hill for 400 yds. At Hele Valley sign turn sharp right, go down steep road and on to T-junction (right-angled). Turn right to park. GPS: 51.205404, -4.101202

Charges guide

Per unit incl. 2 persons and electricity £ 19.00 - £ 32.00

Ilfracombe
Watermouth Cove Holiday Park
Ilfracombe EX34 9SJ (Devon) T: 01271 862504. E: info@watermouthcoveholidays.co.uk
alanrogers.com/UK1257

This park is set in a lovely position, being at the side of a stream as it flows into the harbour and sea at Watermouth Cove. It has its own private beach from where there are lovely views across the sea to Hangman's Hill. Part of the park is arranged on the fairly level valley floor, whilst the tent area is on the side of the private headland with beautiful views of the coast from the higher ground. Electricity hook-ups (16A) are available. Children will enjoy fishing from the rocks; there is an adventure play area and high season activities are organised for them. A heated outdoor pool is open from May to September.

Facilities

New heated facilities are provided in good quality Portacabin style units. Showers are preset, have non-slip bases and a glass partition. Basic toilets and showers in camping field. Laundry. Drinks machines. Shop. Bar, restaurant and takeaway (weekends only in low season). Heated outdoor pool (26/5-30/9). Play area and activities for children (high season). Beach access. Sea kayaks for hire. Fishing. Entertainment. WiFi (free).

Open: End March - end October.

Directions

From M5 exit 27 follow signs for Barnstaple on the A361. At South Molton roundabout turn right signed A399 and continue for 16 miles following signs to Combe Martin. Go through Combe Martin on the A399. After 2 miles Watermouth Cove is clearly signed on right. GPS: 51.212484, -4.071298

Charges guide

Per unit incl. 2 persons and electricity £ 18.00 - £ 38.50

Kingsbridge
Karrageen Caravan & Camping Park
Bolberry, Malborough, Kingsbridge TQ7 3EN (Devon) T: 01548 561230. E: phil@karrageen.co.uk
alanrogers.com/UK0825

Karrageen is to be found in a wonderful area of Devon, near Kingsbridge and Salcombe, with a mixture of rolling countryside, hidden coves, cliff tops and sandy beaches. You can walk, sail, surf or just relax and enjoy the wonderful scenery. This is a small family park run personally by the Higgin family situated in the hamlet of Bolberry, one mile up the lane from Hope Cove. The main camping field slopes gently with either sea or rural views. It has been terraced with hedging to provide 70 grassy pitches with 54 electricity connections (10A). There are some 20 places specifically designed for touring caravans.

Facilities

Modern toilet block includes two curtained washbasins for privacy. Showers are metered (20p). En-suite provision for disabled visitors doubles as family shower room. Baby room. Laundry room. Separate dishwashing (20p). Freezer for ice packs. Shop with basic camping equipment. Fresh baguettes and croissants daily. Gas. Takeaway (evenings only). Two open areas for ball games. Off site: Fishing, boat launching and beach 1 mile. Golf 3 miles.

Open: Easter - 29 September.

Directions

From Exeter on A38, take the A3121 (Ermington, Modbury). Follow signs to Kingsbridge and Salcombe. At Malborough, turn sharp right through village, following signs for Bolberry for 0.6 miles. Turn right to Bolberry, then after 0.9 miles the park is on the right (narrow lanes). GPS: 50.23929, -3.84004

Charges guide

Per unit incl. 2 adults and 2 children £ 16.00 - £ 31.00
No credit cards.

For latest campsite news visit
alanrogers.com

Digital iPad editions

FREE Alan Rogers bookstore app
- digital editions of all 2013 guides

alanrogers.com/digital

Kingsbridge

Higher Rew Caravan & Camping Park

Malborough, Kingsbridge TQ7 3BW (Devon) T: 01548 842681. E: enquiries@higherrew.co.uk

alanrogers.com/UK0826

The Squire family have developed this rural park over the last 50 years on their farm, which is located about a mile up a single-track lane from South Sands, near Salcombe. There used to be a dairy herd on the farm but the buildings are now used to provide camping facilities which include a covered play area for children under 11 years. For older children there is a play barn with table tennis, skittle alley and a pool table. A large, sloping, open field has been terraced to provide 90 grass pitches, 60 of which have 16A electricity. South Sands is ideal for boating, sailing, windsurfing and safe bathing.

Facilities	Directions
Good quality toilet facilities. Unisex showers are in a separate, light and airy part. Showers are metered (20p for 4 minutes). Freezer for ice packs. Reception with shop for basics (main season). Play area. Tennis court. Skittle alley. Caravan storage. Hog roast on Thursdays at 18.00 (high season). Fish and chip van calls at certain times. Off site: Beach, fishing and sailing 1 mile. Boat launching 3 miles. Golf 4.5 miles. Riding 5 miles.	Park is clearly signed from Malborough. Follow signs to Soar for 1 mile. Turn left at Rew Cross, then first right for Higher Rew. Take care with single track roads, although there are always plenty of passing places. GPS: 50.230174, -3.805647

Open: Easter - October half term.

Charges guide

Per unit incl. 2 persons and electricity (16A)	£ 16.00 - £ 23.00

No credit cards.

Lynton

Channel View Caravan & Camping Park

Manor Farm, Barbrook, Lynton EX35 6LD (Devon) T: 01598 753349. E: relax@channel-view.co.uk

alanrogers.com/UK0680

Channel View is a quiet, family run park situated in a sunny, south-facing position overlooking Lynton and Lynmouth. The gently sloping ground provides fairly level pitches, mostly on hardstandings. The park is divided into two areas, an open area that is sheltered by bushes and trees, and one that is more exposed but enjoys panoramic views over the coast. Of the 75 touring pitches, 60 have 16A electricity and the remainder are fully serviced. The grass is well cared for and there is site lighting, although a torch would be useful. There is a café on the site that also offers takeaways.

Facilities	Directions
The modern, very clean toilet and shower block is partly tiled. Showers are free (three steps to ladies' showers from the toilets). Baby changing/family washroom. Facilities for disabled visitors (Radar key). Laundry with washing machines, dryers and iron. Café. Small shop. Play area. WiFi. Off site: Many walks can be started from the site. Riding and fishing 1 mile. Beach 2 miles.	Take the A399 from Ilfracombe. Turn left on A39 and continue past the turn for Lynton to site on the left after 2 miles. It is not advisable to approach from Lynton and Lynmouth. GPS: 51.21800, -3.82930

Open: 15 March - 15 November.

Charges guide

Per unit incl. 2 persons and electricity	£ 15.00 - £ 20.00
extra person	£ 4.00 - £ 5.00

Modbury

Moor View Touring Park

California Cross, Modbury PL21 0SG (Devon) T: 01548 821485. E: info@moorviewtouringpark.co.uk

alanrogers.com/UK0820

Moor View has a gently sloping position with individual, level, terraced pitches with marvellous views across to the Dartmoor Tors. This is a park in a lovely corner of Devon, run personally by the enthusiastic owners, Edward and Liz Corwood. A member of the Countryside Discovery group and an adults only park, it provides 68 pitches of varying sizes, connected by hardcore roads. All are on hardstanding with 10A electricity, water and drainage. Bushes and shrubs planted between the pitches are growing well giving the park a very attractive appearance. A two-acre field provides space for tents, but there is no electricity. There is a woodland walk at the top of the park.

Facilities	Directions
Traditional style, heated and well maintained toilet facilities have access from a courtyard area, providing all necessary facilities including a laundry room and sink. Shop. Takeaway in season (to order, 18.30-20.30). TV room. WiFi. Off site: A local country pub is within walking distance. The small town of Modbury is 3 miles. Golf and bicycle hire 5 miles. Fishing 6 miles. Nearest beach is 15 minutes away.	On A38 from Exeter, pass exit for A385 (Totnes) and continue for 2 miles. Just past Woodpecker Inn leave A38 at Wrangaton Cross. Turn left, then straight on at crossroads (Kitterford Cross) to California Cross. Leave garage on left and follow towards Modbury. Park is 0.5 miles. GPS: 50.363691, -3.817444

Open: All year.

Charges guide

Per unit incl. 2 persons and electricity	£ 11.75 - £ 21.50

For latest campsite news visit

alanrogers.com

Mortehoe
Warcombe Farm Camping Park

Station Road, Mortehoe EX34 7EJ (Devon) T: 01271 870690. E: info@warcombefarm.co.uk
alanrogers.com/UK0725

This park is set in a quiet position on a hill above Woolacombe. It is a large, fairly open site on gently sloping land. There are 260 level or fairly level pitches, some secluded, others extra large with hardstanding and electricity, and others fully serviced. Shrubs and trees help to divide some of the pitches. Two hardstanding pitches are designed to provide facilities and access for disabled campers. In total, 160 pitches have 16A electricity hook-ups. The site has panoramic views across to the sea and at its centre has a fully fenced, lovely, well kept lake that is a haven for wildlife. Fishing is permitted in the lake with free lessons sometimes available for those who want to learn. An adjoining, newly planted wood of 14 acres is available for walks and dog walking.

Facilities

Two modern toilet blocks are spotlessly clean, with underfloor heating and free preset showers. En-suite for disabled visitors (coded locks). Laundry with washing machines, dryers and iron. Motorcaravan services. Shop. Takeaway (w/ends only in low season). Play area. Fishing. Torches useful. WiFi (charged). Off site: Public footpaths and cycle trails (the Tarka Trail is on the doorstep). Riding and golf 1.5 miles. Woolacombe beach is 1.5 miles.

Open: 15 March - 31 October.

Directions

Approaching from Barnstaple on A361 follow signs for Ilfracombe. At Mullacott Cross (10 miles from Barnstaple) turn left, follow B3343 for Woolacombe. After 1.8 miles turn right for Mortehoe. Park is first on right in 500 yds. GPS: 51.190441, -4.180639

Charges guide

Per unit incl. 2 persons and electricity	£ 15.00 - £ 39.00
extra person	£ 4.00

Newton Abbot
Ross Park

Park Hill Farm, Ipplepen, Newton Abbot TQ12 5TT (Devon) T: 01803 812983.
E: enquiries@rossparkcaravanpark.co.uk **alanrogers.com/UK0910**

Ross Park continues to impress us with the care and attention to detail and the amazing floral displays which are a feature of the park and must be seen to be appreciated. These are complemented by the use of a wide variety of shrubs which form hedging for most of the pitches to provide your own special plot, very much as on the continent. Many pitches have wonderful views over the surrounding countryside and for those who prefer the more open style, one small area has been left unhedged. The park covers 31 acres but 21 acres are managed specifically as conservation areas providing a haven for wildlife which visitors can enjoy. The owners, Mark and Helen Lowe, are rightly proud of their park and strive to provide quality facilities and maintain standards. A member of the Best of British group.

Facilities

Twelve well equipped, heated en-suite units, two with baby facilities, one suitable for disabled campers. Extra en-suite rooms built to a very high standard with underfloor heating. Further separate shower, washbasin and toilet facilities. Laundry room. Utility room with dishwashing and freezer. Dog shower. Motorcaravan services. Recycling bins. Reception with licensed shop. Gas supplies. Bar, bar snacks and restaurant (all Apr-end Oct, plus Christmas and New Year). Games room (table tennis, snooker, pool). Croquet green. Badminton. Volleyball. Large well equipped playground. WiFi (free). Caravan storage. Off site: 18-hole golf course adjacent. Riding 1 mile. Fishing 3 miles. Beach 6 miles.

Open: All year excl. January and February.

Directions

From A381 Newton Abbot-Totnes road, park is signed towards Woodland at Park Hill crossroads and Texaco station. GPS: 50.491940, -3.634240

Charges guide

Per unit incl. 2 persons and electricity	£ 15.00 - £ 28.50
extra person	£ 3.25 - £ 5.50
child (4-16 yrs)	£ 1.50 - £ 3.20

Christmas packages available.
No credit cards.

FREE Alan Rogers Travel Card
Extra benefits and savings - see page 10

Newton Abbot

Dornafield

Two Mile Oak, Newton Abbot TQ12 6DD (Devon) T: 01803 812732. E: enquiries@dornafield.com

alanrogers.com/UK0880

The entrance to Dornafield leads into the charming old courtyard of a 14th-century farmhouse giving a mellow feeling that is complemented by the warm welcome from the Dewhirst family. Having booked in, continue down the lane (with a tree covered bank alive with wild flowers) to the Buttermeadow, a tranquil valley providing 75 individual pitches on flat grass, separated by grassy ridges and in some places, wild rose hedges. You pass the walled orchard, secluded and cosy for tents. Or take the road up the hill to Blackrock Copse with large luxury pitches with all facilities including a chemical disposal point and concealed TV connections. Electricity points are 10A. A member of the Best of British group.

Facilities	Directions
Both modern toilet blocks are excellent and heated, with some washbasins in cubicles and comfortable roomy showers; new 'state of the art' block with underfloor heating and a heat recovery system. Both blocks have facilities for disabled visitors and babies. Laundry rooms. Shop (13/3-2/1). Gas supplies. All-weather tennis court. 7 acres for dog walking. Games room. Play areas. WiFi. Off site: Local inn 0.5 miles. Golf 1 mile.	Park is northwest of A381 Newton Abbot-Totnes road. Leave A381 at Two Mile Oak Inn, opposite garage, and turn left at crossroads after half a mile. Entrance is on the right. GPS: 50.50032, -3.63717

Charges guide

Per unit incl. 2 persons and electricity	£ 15.50 - £ 32.20
extra person	£ 4.00 - £ 8.00

Open: 13 March - 2 January.

Newton Abbot

Woodville Caravan Park

Totnes Road, Ipplepen, Newton Abbot TQ12 5TN (Devon) T: 01803 812240. E: info@woodvillepark.co.uk

alanrogers.com/UK0915

A lovely little site exclusively for adults, Woodville is in a sheltered situation, attractively laid out with a wide variety of shrubs and trees. There are 26 pitches all with hardstanding and 16A electricity. They are accessed by a circular roadway which provides a central lawned area. A caravan storage area is to one side. This is a quiet site with few services, although the park is adjacent to a garden centre which also sells food and drinks. Dainton Park golf course is directly opposite and Ipplepen village is within walking distance and has three pubs. The owners live on the site and take a pride in their park.

Facilities	Directions
A fully equipped toilet block also provides a separate unit for visitors with disabilities. Washing machine and freezer. Vans selling fish and chips and eggs call weekly. Wooden chalet with tourist information doubles as reception (limited opening hours). Off site: Shop and golf course adjacent. Three pubs within walking distance. Bus service nearby. Riding 3 miles. Fishing 5 miles. Beach 7 miles.	From Newton Abbot follow A381 Totnes road for 3 miles. Site is on right just after Fermoys Garden Centre. GPS: 50.49505, -3.62965

Charges guide

Per unit incl. 2 persons and electricity	£ 13.90 - £ 18.50
extra person	£ 4.50 - £ 5.00

Open: 1 March - 2 January.

Newton Abbot

Lemonford Caravan Park

Bickington, Newton Abbot TQ12 6JR (Devon) T: 01626 821242. E: info@lemonford.co.uk

alanrogers.com/UK0980

Lemonford is a well run, neat and tidy site for all ages and families on the southern edge of the national park, some three miles from both Ashburton and Newton Abbot. Personally run by the Ayres family, it is attractively landscaped with a mix of trees and shrubs and covers 7.5 acres. Although close to the main road, it is set in a sheltered, peaceful dip bordered by the pretty River Lemon. There are 87 touring pitches (around 40 used as seasonal pitches) on level grass and grouped in four areas with some new, fully serviced pitches available. Most have 10A electricity (some 16A), 76 have hardstanding. There are several holiday homes in the touring area and at the back of the site, some are available to rent.

Facilities	Directions
Two modern toilet blocks. The newer one can be heated and provides some large private cabins, a ladies' bathroom (£1 payment) and a family bathroom with facilities for disabled visitors. Laundry facilities. Shop. Gas supplies. Freezer service. Play area. No commercial vehicles. Off site: Pub within walking distance. Golf 2 miles. Riding and bicycle hire 3 miles. Fishing 4 miles.	From Exeter, turn off A38 Plymouth road at A382 (Drumbridges) exit. At roundabout take third exit to Bickington. Continue for 3 miles and park is on left at bottom of hill. GPS: 50.5391, -3.704

Charges guide

Per unit incl. 2 persons and electricity	£ 13.50 - £ 22.50
extra person (over 16 yrs)	£ 3.00

Open: All year.

For latest campsite news visit

alanrogers.com

Okehampton
South Breazle Holidays

Bratton Clovelly, Okehampton EX20 4JS (Devon) T: 01837 871752. E: louise@southbreazleholidays.co.uk
alanrogers.com/UK0785

Tucked away down a half mile long Devon lane is a rather special campsite. Purpose built by Steve and Louise, who own and run South Breazle farm, the site is spacious with large pitches around the edge of a well mowed field, accessed by a circular roadway. Pitches are marked with young hedging and all are named, e.g. Badgers's Den or Squirrel's Secret. Yes, you may spot a squirrel in the magnificent tall trees which edge the field but do not block the views across the rolling Devon countryside. In all there are 29 large pitches (180 sq.m), 23 with 16A electricity and water, and some with hardstanding.

Facilities

Comfortable toilet block, with facilities for children and disabled visitors. Washing machine and dryer. Shop for basics and local products. Fun fountain. Recycling. Games field. Walks from site. Free WiFi on every pitch. Barbecues off ground. No dogs allowed (working farm). Seasonal pitches available. Off site: Bicycle hire (can be delivered). Roadford Lake 2 miles for fishing.

Open: 1 March - 31 October.

Directions

Exit A30 at Stowford Cross. Follow signs for Roadford Lake. At top of hill (1 mile) turn right (Bratton Clovelly) then second left (Germansweek). South Breazle Holidays signed 1st right, follow for 0.5 mile to site. GPS: 50.70007, -4.20982

Charges guide

Per unit incl. 2 persons, electricity and water	£ 14.00 - £ 22.00

Paignton
Whitehill Country Park

Stoke Road, Paignton TQ4 7PF (Devon) T: 01803 782338. E: info@whitehill-park.co.uk
alanrogers.com/UK0860

Whitehill Country Park is beautifully situated in rolling Devon countryside, just 2.5 miles from the nearest beaches. Extending over 40 acres, a definite sense of space characterises this park and ten acres of ancient woodland are available for walks and attract a great deal of wildlife. Whitehill is a friendly park with 320 large grassy pitches which are located in separate fields around the site with evocative names, such as Nine Acres, Sweethill and Coombe Meadow. Most pitches have electricity (16A, 15 m. cable). Around 60 pitches are used for caravan holiday homes. A new upmarket development of wooden lodges is now completed in Nine Acres field with views across the rural landscape. These luxurious homes are for private ownership and more may be added. The park was once a stud farm where shire horses were bred for showing and field work. Now the stables and stone farm buildings are used for the wide range of park facilities providing a craft centre for children to try their hand at pottery and painting, even hair braiding. There is also an amusement barn with various video games and amusement machines.

Facilities

Good well equipped sanitary provision includes private, individual washing facilities for ladies and facilities for disabled visitors. Laundry facilities. Gas supplies. Well stocked shop and bar (all season). Café/takeaway (15/6- 13/9 daily, then weekends and holidays). Swimming and paddling pools (heated 21/5-1/9). Three play areas. Electronic games, amusement machines, table tennis, pool tables. Craft centre and nature trail for children. WiFi over site. Dogs accepted in touring area from 28/3-23/5, 3/6-19/7 and 2/9-27/9. Off site: Bus stop at site entrance.

Open: Easter - 29 September.

Directions

Turn left at The Parkers Arms off the A385 Paignton to Totnes road, signed Stoke Gabriel. Site is 1 mile along this road. GPS: 50.417867, -3.609

Charges guide

Per unit incl. 2 persons and electricity	£ 15.60 - £ 30.50
tent pitch incl. 2 persons	£ 13.60 - £ 25.10
extra person	£ 4.30
child (4-14 yrs)	£ 3.30

Camping Cheques accepted.

the great outdoors
touring, camping,
caravans, lodges,
and camping pods

Whitehill Country Park
South Devon

- 10 acres of woodland
- walking & cycling
- conservation awards
- outdoor heated pool
- hayloft bar
- children's play areas
- children's craft room
- shop, café & takeaway

01803 782338 whitehill-park.co.uk countryside holidays by the sea

FREE Alan Rogers Travel Card
Extra benefits and savings - see page 10

Paignton
Beverley Park

Goodrington Road, Paignton TQ4 7JE (Devon) T: 01803 661978. E: info@beverley-holidays.co.uk
alanrogers.com/UK0870

Beverley Park is an amazing holiday centre catering for every need. It has been developed and run by the Jeavons family for over 50 years to very high standards. It is popular, busy and attractively landscaped with marvellous views over Torbay. The pools, a large dance hall, bars and entertainment, are all run in an efficient and orderly manner. The park has 190 caravan holiday homes and 23 lodges, mainly around the central complex. There are 159 touring pitches in the lower areas of the park, all reasonably sheltered, some with views across the bay and some on slightly sloping ground. All pitches can take awnings and 87 have 16A electricity (15 m. cable), 42 have hardstanding and are fully serviced. Tents are accepted and a limited number of tent pitches have electrical connections. The park is open all year and reservations are essential for caravans in high season. Entertainment is organised at Easter and from early May in the Starlight Cabaret bar. There are indoor and outdoor pools, each one heated and supervised. The Oasis fitness centre provides a steam room, jacuzzi and an excellent fitness room. The park is in the heart of residential Torquay, with views across the bay to Brixham and the English Riviera, and sandy beaches less than a mile away. A member of the Best of British group.

Facilities

Good toilet blocks adjacent to pitches, well maintained and heated, include showers, some with washbasins en-suite. Baths (charged). Unit for disabled visitors. Facilities for babies. Laundry. Gas supplies. Motorcaravan service point. Large general shop (25/3-2/11). Restaurant, bars and takeaway (3/5-15/9 and B.Hs). Heated swimming pools (outdoor 3/5-1/9, indoor all year). Fitness centre. Tennis. Crazy golf. Playground. Nature trail. Amusements. Soft play area. WiFi over site. Dogs are not accepted.

Open: All year.

Directions

Park is south of Paignton in Goodrington Road between A379 coast road and B3203 ring road and is well signed on both. GPS: 50.413533, -3.568667

Charges guide

Per unit incl. 2 persons and electricity	£ 16.70 - £ 37.30
Max. 6 persons per reservation.	

Paignton
Widdicombe Farm Tourist Park

The Ring Road, Compton, Paignton TQ3 1ST (Devon) T: 01803 558325. E: info@widdicombefarm.co.uk
alanrogers.com/UK0900

Widdicombe Farm is an adults only park, just three miles from Torquay and with easy access from the A380, well situated for the Torbay area. There are 200 numbered pitches, all with 10A electricity of which most have hardstanding and 48 are fully serviced. Situated on a hillside and surrounded by farmland, the pitches are on terraces with open views across the countryside. Many trees have been planted and there are tarmac access roads and steps linking the terraces. There may be some background traffic noise but it is not too intrusive. Touring areas are separated into sections for couples, tent campers, etc.

Facilities

Three older style toilet blocks are kept very clean (the men's has been refurbished). The original heated block near reception includes facilities for disabled visitors and laundry room. Shop. Restaurant. Bar with entertainment (Easter, then Spring B.H-mid Sept). Certain breeds of dog are not accepted. Caravan storage. Minibus to town can be booked if there are 6 persons. WiFi over site (charged).

Open: 19 March - 29 October.

Directions

From Newton Abbot take A380 south for 5 miles. On outskirts of Torquay turn right at roundabout onto ring road. Site is well signed off this road. GPS: 50.467081, -3.586797

Charges guide

Per unit incl. 2 persons and electricity	£ 12.50 - £ 25.50

For latest campsite news visit
alanrogers.com

Plymouth
Riverside Caravan Park

Leigham Manor Drive, Marsh Mills, Plymouth PL6 8LL (Devon) T: 01752 344122.
E: office@riversidecaravanpark.com **alanrogers.com/UK0810**

As you leave the A38 for Plymouth and negotiate the Marsh Mills roundabout, you can have no idea that there is a lush green touring park tucked away from the modern, out-of-town shopping units in a quiet green valley. Part of the park is being developed to provide a residential area alongside the river Plym which has therefore meant a reduction in the number of touring pitches. However, there are still some 200 spaces available for touring, 80 of which have 10A electricity and many are on hardstanding. There are also a number of grass pitches for tents. Hidden behind a high, evergreen hedge are an attractive swimming pool and children's pool. A play area is nearby and a pleasant restaurant with a bar and games room provide welcome facilities and entertainment in high season. Over 30 years ago this park was a corn field but, with careful development by its owner, it now provides a welcome oasis from which to explore Dartmoor, to enjoy the amazing views from Plymouth Hoe or even to overnight quietly before catching the ferry to France. The wooded valley sides give way to level grass where the trees and shrubs planted all those years ago have matured to give a park-like feel. The River Plym runs down one side of the site but it is carefully fenced.

Facilities

Three modern, fully equipped toilet blocks have cubicles with toilets and washbasins. Laundry room. Motorcaravan service point. Gas supplies. Some basics are kept in reception (more in high season). Bar, restaurant and takeaway (B.Hs and high season) with entertainment for families included. Heated swimming pool and paddling pool (end May-12/9). Games room with TV. Play area. Dogs accepted (max. 2). Off site: Fishing possible in River Plym (licence required). Dry ski slope, supermarket and retail park within walking distance. Bus stop 10 minutes. Bicycle hire, sea fishing and boat launching 3.5 miles. Golf 5 miles. Riding 4 miles. Beach 10 miles.

Open: All year.

Directions

From the A38 Marsh Mills roundabout for Plymouth take the third exit. After a few yards turn left following caravan signs, then right alongside the River Plym to the park. GPS: 50.398167, -4.087333

Charges guide

Per unit incl. 2 persons and electricity	£ 14.00 - £ 28.00
tent pitch without electricity	£ 10.50 - £ 20.00
extra person	£ 5.00
child (0-16 yrs)	free - £ 2.50
dog	£ 2.50

FREE Alan Rogers Travel Card
Extra benefits and savings - see page 10

Salcombe

Bolberry House Farm Caravan & Camping

Bolberry, Malborough, Kingsbridge TQ7 3DY (Devon) T: 01548 561 251. E: enquiries@bolberryparks.co.uk

alanrogers.com/UK0824

Five generations have farmed the land at Bolberry. The present owner's grandfather started the campsite in the field on top of the hill; this main field enjoys marvellous views of the surrounding countryside and out to sea. There are breathtaking sunsets, and even shooting stars – 15 were seen the evening I visited. This is a traditional campsite, which caters for all units in three fields connected by grass paths with some up and down walking – this is a small price to pay for the views! There are around 100 pitches with extra allowed in the peak period, well spaced around the edges of fairly level fields with plenty of central space for children to play. Seventy five have 10A electricity. There are a few static vans to let in a separate area. However, it is not just the situation which makes this site special, but the warm welcome from Fiona and Elaine who run it. There is no reception; the sisters meet all their visitors personally and provide them with comprehensive information and they are real ambassadors for this wonderful area – nothing is too much trouble for them. They believe they live in a magical place and want their visitors to share it, especially families, who can enjoy a bucket-and-spade holiday at Hope Cove, or couples enjoying a walking holiday. The coastal path is close by and many other walks can be enjoyed. The sisters are like walking tourist information centres, with knowledge accumulated by their family over several centuries. Take time to see the model village near the farm house built by their father.

Facilities

Two dated toilet blocks fully equipped. Coin operated showers (20p). Laundry. Play area. Small van open in mornings sells basics. Fish and chip van (Sun). Hog roast (Weds). All main season). Four different takeaways deliver to site. Hope Cove holiday weekend (events, entertainment, music etc) last weekend in August. Off site: Farmhouse teas and pubs within walking distance. Coastal paths half a mile. Hope Cove with sandy beach 1 mile. Fishing 1 mile. Salcombe with creeks and safe sandy beaches 3 miles.

Open: Easter - end September.

Directions

From Totnes follow A381 bypassing Kingsbridge via Chuchstow, following signs for Salcombe. At Malborough turn sharp right through village. Follow signs for Bolberry until you come to park on right (narrow lanes). GPS: 50.238221, -3.831081

Charges guide

Per unit incl. 2 persons	£ 14.00 - £ 24.00
extra person	£ 3.00 - £ 4.00
electricity (10A)	£ 3.00
dog	free - £ 1.00

Bolberry House Farm
NR. SALCOMBE • SOUTH DEVON
Friendly, family run park in a very beautiful and unspoilt coastal area. An ideal base.
Tel: (01548) 561251
Email: enquiries@bolberryparks.co.uk
www.bolberryparks.co.uk

Sidmouth

Oakdown Touring & Holiday Caravan Park

Weston, Sidmouth EX10 0PT (Devon) T: 01297 680387. E: enquiries@oakdown.co.uk

alanrogers.com/UK1020

Oakdown is a very attractive, well planned park which celebrated its 60th birthday in 2011. Run by the Franks family since 1972, the family and their team continue to work hard carrying out developments in keeping with the environment. The park has easy access, beautiful floral displays and a spacious feel. There are 100 level touring pitches arranged in landscaped bays, screened by a wide variety of trees and shrubs and linked by a circular road. All have 10/16A electricity and hardstanding and many have water and drainage. An additional touring area near the golf course, Beech Grove, provides a further 50 large pitches with hedging and 16A electricity. There is a new, fully equipped toilet block here.

Facilities

The original central toilet block has been completely renewed. Well maintained, fully equipped and heated facilities include a private cabin for ladies. Two unisex family bathrooms double as units for disabled visitors. Laundry facilities plus free freezer and microwave. New facilities in Beech Grove include a room for families and disabled visitors, and a laundry room. Motorcaravan service point. Smart new café/shop selling essentials and snacks (mid May-mid Sept). Internet room. Fax service. Centrally heated TV/pool room with book exchange. Two excellent adventure play areas and castle. Lake. Dew pond. Off site: Golf course adjacent. Swimming 1 mile.

Open: 17 March - 7 November.

Directions

Turn south off A3052 (Exeter-Lyme Regis) road between Sidford and Colyford, 2.5 miles east of A375 junction. Park is on left. GPS: 50.7056, -3.18063

Charges guide

Per unit incl. 2 persons and electricity	£ 15.80 - £ 22.90
with water and drainage	£ 21.30 - £ 28.60
extra person (5 yrs and over)	£ 3.10
dog	£ 2.40

For latest campsite news visit
alanrogers.com

Sidmouth
Salcombe Regis Camping & Caravan Park
Salcombe Regis, Sidmouth EX10 0JH (Devon) T: 01395 514303. E: contact@salcombe-regis.co.uk
alanrogers.com/UK1110

On the edge of Salcombe Regis village, 1.5 miles from Sidmouth and less than a mile from the sea. Salcombe Regis Park covers 16 acres of land. It is surrounded by farmland with views of the combe and the sea beyond. The focal point of the main camping area is a large 'village green' where the play area and pitch and putt are located. The reception and pitches are arranged around the green, all connected by a tarmac road. The 110 pitches are level and have their own water supply, with 98 electricity hook-ups (16A). A 25 minute walk across fields takes you to a small, secluded beach, although the walk there is fairly steep – we are told there are 129 steps! There are many footpaths and coastal walks nearby, protected by the National Trust and with views of Sidmouth and Weston Mouth. Sidmouth town, originally a small fishing town but now a seaside resort, is host to the annual International Folk Festival, where for one week in summer the town is filled with folk artists from all over the world.

Facilities

The traditional style toilet block (to one side of the site and a longer walk for some) is kept spotlessly clean by the resident wardens and includes a bathroom for families and disabled visitors. Shop at reception sells basic supplies and local produce. Laundry room with washing machines, dryers and ironing board. Motorcaravan service point. Play area. Pitch and putt. Caravan storage. Torches useful. WiFi (charged). Off site: Fishing, bicycle hire and golf 1.5 miles. Sidmouth and beach 1.5 miles. Riding 3 miles.

Open: Easter - 28 October.

Directions

Park is well signed on the A3052 Exeter-Lyme Regis road. From the east, take first left after Donkey Sanctuary. From the west proceed up the hill out of Sidford. Do not take first road signed Salcombe Regis, but take the next right at top of hill. Follow road round to site on left after golf range. GPS: 50.695717, -3.205367

Charges guide

Per unit incl. 2 persons and electricity	£ 16.50 - £ 22.00
extra person	£ 4.10
child (5-15 yrs)	£ 2.70
dog	£ 1.50

Salcombe Regis CAMPING & CARAVAN PARK Sidmouth, Devon EX10 0JH

Tranquil setting with excellent touring facilities Ideal base for exploring rural East Devon, Superb walking country **Within walking distance of the sea & famous Donkey Sanctuary** Ten Luxuriously equipped Rose Award leisure homes for hire. Situated ½ OFF main A3052 Exeter to Lyme Regis coast road. Spacious level sites with some views. Hardstanding with individual taps/soakaways, available for Tourers/Motor caravans at no extra cost. Heated amenity block.

Tel: (01395) 514303 Fax: (01395) 514313 www.salcombe-regis.co.uk E-mail: contact@salcombe-regis.co.uk FREE colour brochure

South Molton
Riverside Caravan & Camping Park
Marsh Lane, North Molton Road, South Molton EX36 3HQ (Devon) T: 01769 579 269.
E: relax@exmoorriverside.co.uk **alanrogers.com/UK0745**

A very impressive purpose-built campsite beside the River Mole, Riverside is set in 40 acres of meadow and woodland. All the 54 pitches at this park have hardstanding, 16A electricity connection, water, drainage and TV aerial socket. Neat grass, tarmac roads and growing trees and hedges contribute to the attractive, overall impression. The heated toilet block gleams and visitors will appreciate the hairdryers, hand-dryers and shaver points. The owners, Joe and Nicky Penfold, are not resting on their laurels and have developed fishing lakes with specimen carp down by the river and a play area on the opposite bank. A road runs alongside the site, so a little noise can be expected. The ancient market town of South Molton is a mile away and a bus stops outside the site entrance. Exmoor is on hand to explore, as are the North Devon resorts of Woolacombe, Ilfracombe, Combe Martin and Lynton, not to mention the surfing paradise of Croyde Bay.

Facilities

Modern, fully equipped and heated toilet block accessed by code. Facilities for disabled visitors. Laundry room. Shop (limited hours in low season). Play area. Entertainment (B.Hs and high season). Fishing. Caravan storage. Swimming in river. Off site: Market town of South Molton with all facilities 1 mile. Riding 2 miles. Golf 5 miles. Boat launching and beach 12 miles.

Open: All year.

Directions

From M5 exit 27 take the North Devon Link road A361. Near South Molton watch for site sign (direction North Molton). GPS: 51.02918, -3.823467

Charges guide

Per unit incl. 2 persons and electricity	£ 14.00 - £ 25.00
extra person	£ 6.00
child (under 16 yrs)	£ 4.00

FREE Alan Rogers Travel Card
Extra benefits and savings - see page 10

Tavistock
Langstone Manor Holiday Park

Moortown, Tavistock PL19 9JZ (Devon) T: 01822 613371. E: jane@langstonemanor.co.uk

alanrogers.com/UK0802

Situated on the southwest edge of Dartmoor, this holiday park has been developed in the grounds of the old Langstone Manor house. The touring pitches are tucked into various garden areas with mature trees and flowering shrubs, or in the walled garden area with views over the moor. In all there are 42 level grass pitches which vary in size (30 with 10A electricity). A new camping area is popular and has been terraced with open views over farmland and the moor. You pass by a number of holiday caravans on the way to reception and the touring pitches where you will also find some holiday cottages and flats for rent. The pièce de résistance is the unexpected traditional bar and restaurant in the Manor House, complete with a terrace that catches the evening sun. Open in high season and on demand in low season it has an open fire (if needed) and games room. Approaching over a short section of the moor, you realise how well Langstone Manor is situated to explore Dartmoor by foot, by car or on bike (the park has direct access). The market town of Tavistock is 3 miles away and there is a wealth of National Trust houses and gardens to visit nearby.

Facilities

The toilet block is set to one side of the walled garden area, fully equipped and well maintained. Showers on payment (20p tokens from reception and bar). Fully equipped laundry room. Changing mat for babies in the ladies'. Basic supplies kept in reception (order bread the day before). Bar/restaurant with terrace. Games room. Play area. Off site: Golf 1 mile. Leisure centre and pool 2 miles. Fishing 2 miles. Riding 5 miles. Boat launching 10 miles. Sailing 15 miles.

Open: 15 March - end October.

Directions

From Tavistock take B3357 Princetown road. After 2 miles turn right at crossroads (site signed). Pass over cattle grid onto the moor and follow site signs. GPS: 50.5449, -4.084167

Charges guide

Per unit incl. 2 persons and electricity	£ 16.00 - £ 21.00
extra person	£ 4.00
child (3-16 yrs)	£ 2.50 - £ 3.00
dog	free

DIRECT ACCESS ONTO MOOR - DARTMOOR'S BEST KEPT SECRET

Langstone Manor Holiday Park
CAMPING & CARAVANS, PODS

TEL: 01822 613 371
www.langstone-manor.co.uk

Tavistock
Woodovis Park

Woodovis House, Gulworthy, Tavistock PL19 8NY (Devon) T: 01822 832968. E: info@woodovis.com

alanrogers.com/UK0805

Woodovis Park is set in the grounds of Woodovis House, owned in the 19th century by a mine captain in the days when the valley had a thriving copper mining industry. It nestles in a sheltered wooded position covering 14 acres, by the edge of the Tamar Valley on the borders of Devon and Cornwall. John and Dorothy Lewis have been running Woodovis Park since 1999, helped by their very welcoming staff. There are 50 good sized pitches, all with 10A electricity. You have a choice of grass, all weather and 11 super pitches (with 16A, water, waste and TV hook-ups too). Split over two fields and landscaped in between are 35 caravan holiday homes, 24 for hire. A member of the Best of British group.

Facilities

Fully equipped and heated toilet block. Bathroom (coin operated) is useful for disabled visitors or those with babies. Family cubicles. Toilet for disabled visitors at the pool. Fully equipped laundry. Motorcaravan service point. Shop for basics with off-licence doubles with reception. Indoor heated swimming pool (no swimming alone), spa and sauna. Good games room including large size Connect 4! Fenced play area. Pétanque. Archery and 'water-walking' organised weekly during school holidays. WiFi throughout (charged). New play equipment. Bicycle hire. Off site: Pub with restaurant within walking distance. Tamar valley with walking and cycling trails. Fishing 3 miles. Golf, riding and boat launching 7 miles. Canoeing and tree walking 3 miles. Tavistock 4 miles.

Open: 22 March - 3 November.

Directions

From Tavistock follow A390 for Liskeard. After 3 miles turn right at Gulworthy roundabout signed Chipshop, Lamerton and Caravan Park. After 1 mile entrance is signed on left. GPS: 50.548867, -4.21585

Charges guide

Per unit incl. 2 persons and electricity	£ 22.00 - £ 34.00
extra person (over 5 yrs)	£ 5.50
dog	free

For latest campsite news visit
alanrogers.com

Tavistock
Harford Bridge Holiday Park
Peter Tavy, Tavistock PL19 9LS (Devon) T: 01822 810349. E: enquiry@harfordbridge.co.uk
alanrogers.com/UK0790

Harford Bridge has an interesting history – originally the Wheal Union tin mine until 1850, then used as a farm campsite from 1930 and taken over by the Royal Engineers in 1939. It is now a quiet, rural, mature park inside the Dartmoor National Park. It is bounded by the River Tavy on one side and the lane from the main road to the village of Peter Tavy on the other, with Harford Bridge, a classic granite moorland bridge, at the corner. With 16.5 acres, the park provides 120 touring pitches well spaced on a level grassy meadow with some shade from mature trees and others recently planted; 52 pitches have 16A electrical hook-ups and 11 have multi-services, five with hardstanding. Out of season or by booking in advance you may get one of the delightful spots bordering the river (these are without electricity). Some holiday caravans and chalets are neatly landscaped in their own area. At the entrance to the park a central grassy area is left free for games, which is also used by the town band, village fete, etc. While the river (unfenced) will inevitably mesmerise youngsters, a super central play area on a hilly tree knoll will claim them. In early summer there are chicks to watch, horses to make a fuss of and the park ducks are a feature. With its own and the local history, plus its situation, this is a super place to stay.

Facilities

The single toilet block has been modernised and is fully equipped and well kept, with free hot water and showers all year. Facilities for disabled visitors and babies. Good launderette and drying room. Freezer. Motorcaravan service point. Games room with table tennis and separate TV room. Play area. Tennis court (free). Two communal barbecue areas. Fly fishing (by licence, £3 p/day, £10 p/week). WiFi (charged). Off site: Bicycle hire, riding and golf, all within 2.5 miles. West Devon cycle way (Route 27). It is possible to cycle into Tavistock, which has a market twice monthly. Bus stop on main road.

Open: All year.

Directions

Two miles north of Tavistock, off A386 Tavistock-Okehampton road, take the road to Peter Tavy. GPS: 50.5713, -4.114

Charges guide

Per unit incl. 2 persons and electricity	£ 13.60 - £ 18.80
with full services	£ 16.60 - £ 22.55
extra person	£ 5.80
child (3-16 yrs)	£ 2.70

Harford Bridge Park
Dartmoor Holidays by the River Tavy

Peter Tavy, Tavistock, Devon. PL19 9LS
Tel 01822 810 349 - Fax 01822 810028
www.harfordbridge.co.uk
e-mail stay@harfordbridge.co.uk

Beautiful sheltered park set in Dartmoor. Beside the River Tavy offering riverside and other spacious level pitches. Ideally suited for exploring Dartmoor, West Devon and the Tamar Valley Area of Outstanding Natural Beauty. Adjacent to a bus service and Cycle Route 27. Luxury self-catering Holiday Homes & Lodges. Off A386 OkehamptonRoad, two miles from Tavistock, take Peter Tavy turn.
Easy access   Open all Year   All enquiries welcome

Tavistock
The Old Rectory Caravan & Camping Park
Gulworthy, Tavistock PL19 8JA (Devon) T: 01822 832927. E: info@tamarvalleycamping.co.uk
alanrogers.com/UK0795

The Old Rectory is a neat little park where hedging provides bays to give you your own space and shelter. You can share the larger bays with friends or family. The hedging will be taken down a foot or two in the Autumn to allow more enjoyment of the panoramic views across to Dartmoor. There are just eleven touring pitches, eight with 16A electricity, 20 tent pitches, and four timber camping pods are available to rent. A small toilet block is being enlarged to double the facilities. There is no reception office, you simply contact the owners by phone when you arrive.

Facilities

New fully equipped toilet block with free hot showers and facilities for disabled visitors. Washing machine and dryers. Small freezer for ice blocks. Wash bay to clean down bikes or wet suits etc. Eggs, bacon and sausages for sale. Caravan storage. Camping pods to rent. Torches useful. Off site: Nearby activities include canoeing on Tamar river, tree surfing, mountain biking, or walking on Dartmoor. Bicycle hire and golf 2 miles. Fishing 3 miles. Boat launching 4 miles. Riding 5 miles.

Open: All year.

Directions

From Tavistock follow A390 for Liskeard. After 3 miles turn left at Gulworthy roundabout signed Bere Alston. Site on left past school and church hall. GPS: 50.532675, -4.190927

Charges guide

Per unit incl. 2 persons and electricity	£ 15.00 - £ 18.00
extra person (over 5 yrs)	£ 5.00
dog	£ 1.00

Teignmouth

Coast View Holiday Park

Torquay Road, Shaldon, Teignmouth TQ14 0BG (Devon) T: 0844 567 8977. E: info@coastview.co.uk

alanrogers.com/UK1080

On the coast road between Teignmouth and Torquay with magnificent views over Lyme Bay, this family run park has a section of caravan holiday homes and chalets with the touring area higher on the hillside. There are 18 pitches with hardstanding and 16A electricity, and a number with water in a further area. A level area is kept for motorcaravans. Over 100 pitches for tents are on part sloping, part terraced grass on the hillside with adequate protection from the prevailing southwest winds and marvellous views. To the right of the park entrance is an attractive indoor swimming pool and an entertainment area comprising a clubroom with a bar.

Facilities	Directions
The modern toilet block is spacious with free hot showers, open washbasins and a baby room. Laundry facilities. Licensed shop for basic provisions. Indoor pool and paddling pool. Clubroom with bar, restaurant, takeaway, games room and TV room. Full entertainment programme and themed weekends. Adventure playground and indoor soft play area. Crazy golf. WiFi (charged). Open: 15 March - 31 October.	From A380 Exeter-Newton Abbot road, take A381 to Teignmouth. On entering town turn right over Shaldon Bridge on B3199 for Torquay. Park is on right in 1.5 miles. GPS: 50.53455, -3.503167

Charges guide

Per unit incl. up to 5 persons and electricity	£ 20.00 - £ 30.00
fully serviced hardstanding pitch	£ 27.00 - £ 40.00

Tiverton

Minnows Touring Caravan Park

Sampford Peverell, Tiverton EX16 7EN (Devon) T: 01884 821770

alanrogers.com/UK0750

Minnows is an attractive, neat, small park with views across the Devon countryside, and separated by hedging from the Grand Western. Easily accessible from the M5, it is an ideal touring centre for Devon and Somerset, for cycling, walking, fishing or canoeing (own landing stage), or simply for breaking a long journey. Open for eight months of the year, it provides 59 level pitches, all with 16A electricity and hardstandings, 12 with water and waste water (two adapted for continental units and RVs). A further 3.5 acres have been added to the park, providing space for further, and larger pitches, a grass tent area, and a play area.

Facilities	Directions
A fully equipped and well maintained, heated toilet block with pressurised showers. Facilities for babies and disabled visitors. Laundry. Motorcaravan service point. Gas supplies. Shop. Newspaper delivery arranged. Bicycle hire (delivery to site). Play area. American RVs accepted (up to 36 ft, advance booking necessary). All year caravan storage. Site gates closed 20.00-07.30 (with pitch holder access in and out) WiFi over site (charged). Open: 4 March - 4 November.	From M5 exit 27 take A361 (Tiverton). After 600 yds. take first exit (Sampford Peverell). After 100 yds. turn right at roundabout and cross bridge over A361 to second roundabout. Go straight on and park is immediately ahead. GPS: 50.925017, -3.364517

Charges guide

Per unit incl. 2 persons	£ 13.80 - £ 25.90
child	£ 1.30 - £ 2.20
Credit cards accepted for £10 or more.	

Woolacombe

North Morte Farm

Mortehoe, Woolacombe EX34 7EG (Devon) T: 01271 870381. E: info@northmortefarm.co.uk

alanrogers.com/UK0703

North Morte Farm is a family run park adjoining National Trust land and is only 500 yards from Rockham beach. The site has 250 pitches (there are 150 pitches for tents in a separate field) of which 30 are for touring, with hardstanding and their own 16A electricity point. Some have a TV connection and a water point close by. The modern toilet block has free hot showers, a washing up area with free hot water and a fully equipped launderette with ironing facilities. There is a well stocked shop/off licence with gas exchange and a well designed play area for children.

Facilities	Directions
Clean, modern toilet block with free hot water and hairdryers can be heated. Facilities for disabled visitors. Launderette with ironing facilities. Well stocked shop withoff licence with gas exchange. Play area. Public telephone. Off site: Direct access to the southwest coastal path. Shops, post office and restaurants in Mortehoe 5 minutes walk. Fishing 800 yds. Golf and riding 1.6 miles. Open: 1 April - 31 October.	From Barnstable take A361 (Ilfracombe). At Mullacott Cross roundabout take first left (Woolacombe, Mortehoe). After 2 miles turn right (Mortehoe). In Mortehoe turn right opposite car park (lighthouse) and site is 500 yds. GPS: 51.188343, -4.203939

Charges guide

Per unit incl. 2 persons and electricity	£ 15.50 - £ 20.50

For latest campsite news visit

alanrogers.com

Woolacombe
Woolacombe Bay Holiday Village

Sandy Lane, Woolacombe EX34 7AH (Devon) T: 01271 870343. E: goodtimes@woolacombe.com
alanrogers.com/UK1070

Woolacombe Bay Holiday Village, and its sister site Golden Coast Holiday Village nearby, are well known holiday parks providing a range of holiday accommodation, from caravan holiday homes to luxury lodges, apartments and villas, with many on site amenities including pools, restaurants and bars, and providing a wide range of entertainment. A camping section at the Woolacombe Bay park caters for tents and trailer tents only, so touring visitors can enjoy all the activities and entertainment of both parks. Partly terraced out of the hillside and partly on the hilltop with some existing pine trees but with many more trees planted for landscaping, the site has magnificent views out across the bay. Marked and numbered pitches have been provided on grass for 150 tents, 97 with 10/16A electricity. All should be level, having been terraced where necessary and they are connected by gravel roads. Some up and down walking is needed for the toilet block. A bus service (small charge) runs between the two parks, the third and fourth parks in the group (Twitchen Park and Easewell Farm) and the beach during the main season. There is a footpath to the beach from the site. The three larger parks have varied entertainment programmes and children's clubs, and Woolacombe Bay also boasts a health spa and beauty suite.

Facilities

A smart central toilet block has excellent facilities, including en-suite shower and washrooms and separate toilets, baby facilities, and also a sauna and steam room. Laundry rooms. Two units for disabled visitors. Supermarket. Bars, restaurant and entertainment. Indoor (all season and heated) and outdoor pools (21/5-15/9) with flumes and slides. Sauna and gym. Beauty and holistic treatments. Wide range of sporting activities. Tennis. ATM. Dogs are welcome at Woolacombe Bay but not at Golden Coast. WiFi (charged). Off site: Fishing and beach 1 mile. Riding 2 miles. Bicycle hire and golf 3 miles.

Open: 23 March - 5 November.

Directions

Take A361 Barnstaple-Ilfracombe road through Braunton. Turn left at Mullacott Cross roundabout towards Woolacombe then right towards Mortehoe. Now follow the camping signs by turning left and park is on the left. GPS: 51.177117, -4.191317

Charges guide

Per person (tents only)	£ 5.50 - £ 20.95
child (5-15 yrs)	£ 3.25 - £ 10.48
dog (camping only)	£ 1.50

Woolacombe
Golden Coast Holiday Village

Station Road, Woolacombe EX34 7HW (Devon) T: 01271 870343. E: goodtimes@woolacombe.com
alanrogers.com/UK1075

The Golden Coast Holiday Village is part of the Woolacombe Bay Holiday Parks group that includes Woolacombe Bay, Twitchen Park and Easewell Farm. Golden Coast's main interest is a range of brick-built bungalows, lodges and apartments, plus a variety of caravan holiday homes, all of good quality and well equipped. However, two touring areas also provide 101 pitches, all with electricity and about half with all-weather hardstanding. There are indoor and outdoor pools, spa facilities, a cinema and a range of sports facilities for active visitors. Guests at the park can enjoy extensive entertainment and nightly cabaret and a programme of daily activities is arranged for adults and children. A shuttle bus runs between the four parks and to the beach several times a day (it costs £3 per person per holiday). A visit to the Old Mill Inn should not be missed; it serves bar meals, and has an excellent beer garden with adventure play area for the children. The range of amenities and facilities at this large park will suit families looking for a lively holiday filled with activities and entertainment.

Facilities

The toilet block is unisex with recently upgraded facilities and was clean at the time of our visit. Washing machine and dryer. Large, well stocked supermarket, boutique and beauty salon. Indoor and outdoor swimming pools, outdoor flume, sauna and solarium. Bar, club, Old Mill Inn, restaurant and takeaway. Floodlit tennis court. Adventure playgrounds. Snooker. Games room. Soft play area. Ceramics studio. Learn to swim classes. 9-hole golf course. Indoor and outdoor bowls, ten-pin bowling. Nightly entertainment and cabaret. Activities and clubs for children. Fishing. Woodland walks. WiFi (charged). Dogs are not accepted. Off site: Golf, riding and bicycle hire 0.5 miles. Woolacombe beach approx. 2 miles. For walkers there is the coastal path. Amenities at sister parks available to all visitors, with shuttle bus.

Open: 10 February - 26 November.

Directions

From Barnstaple, take A361 (signed Braunton and Ilfracombe). Turn left on B3343 (signed Woolacombe) and follow the road towards the town. The park is on the left near the top of the hill. GPS: 51.1725, -4.172767

Charges guide

Per caravan or motorcaravan	£ 9.20 - £ 65.00
tent - per person	£ 4.60 - £ 21.35
tent - per child (5-15 yrs)	£ 2.30 - £ 10.68

FREE Alan Rogers Travel Card
Extra benefits and savings - see page 10

Woolacombe
Easewell Farm Holiday Village

Mortehoe, Woolacombe EX34 7EH (Devon) T: 01271 870343. E: goodtimes@woolacombe.com
alanrogers.com/UK0720

Near the sandy beaches of Woolacombe, Easewell Farm Holiday Village is part of the Woolacombe Bay Holiday Park group who also own three others, Woolacombe Bay, Golden Coast and Twitchen. A shuttle bus runs between the four holiday villages and to the beach (tickets £3 per person per holiday). This is a traditional style touring park which during the day is a hive of activity, but the nights are quiet and peaceful. The largest of the camping fields is sloping with superb views across the headland to the sea. Two smaller fields are terraced and one area has upgraded hardstandings with new landscaping. Together they provide 330 pitches, 207 with 16A electricity connections and 20 also with TV and water connections. Pea-shingle, all-weather hardstandings have been added. Also available are a lovely four bedroom farmhouse (sleeping ten), a pretty two bedroom cottage (five beds) and a caravan holiday home. The shop is well stocked (gas available), there is a takeaway and restaurant and an attractive bar with patio overlooking a small duck pond. The park has its own, very well maintained, nine-hole golf course which is popular and has reduced fees for campers. One of the huge redundant farm buildings has been put to excellent use: divided into three areas, it provides table tennis and pool, a skittle alley and two lanes of flat green bowling with changing rooms. Walks to the local village and along the coastal path are easy from the site and a bus to Ilfracombe and Barnstaple stops 100 yards from the entrance.

Facilities
The central toilet block has been regularly upgraded and can be heated. Two washbasins in the ladies have hoses for hair washing, controllable showers (no dividers). Small area with baby bath facilities. Laundry. These facilities are arranged around the farmhouse area and include a very well equipped unit for disabled visitors with everything in one large room including a hairdryer. Motorcaravan service point. Shop. Bar. Restaurant and takeaway. Golf. Small heated indoor swimming pool is well used, as are games and TV rooms. Fenced play area with bark base. Indoor skittle alley. Max. 1 dog, not accepted in high season. Off site: Fishing and riding 1 mile. Bicycle hire 3 miles.

Open: End March - end October.

Directions
From Barnstaple, take A361 Ilfracombe road through Braunton. Turn left at Mullacott Cross roundabout on B3343 to Woolacombe, turning right after 2-3 miles to Mortehoe. Park is on right before village.
GPS: 51.1853, -4.198933

Charges guide
Per caravan or motorcaravan	£ 15.00 - £ 55.00
incl. services	£ 19.00 - £ 57.50
tent (per person)	£ 5.00 - £ 18.30
tent - child (5-15 yrs)	£ 2.50 - £ 9.15
dog	£ 1.50

Woolacombe
Twitchen Park Holiday Village

Mortehoe Station Road, Woolacombe EX34 7ES (Devon) T: 01271 870848. E: goodtimes@woolacombe.com
alanrogers.com/UK0730

Set in the grounds of an attractive Edwardian country house, Twitchen Park Holiday Village is owned by Woolacombe Bay Holiday Parks. Its main concern lies in holiday caravans and apartments, although it also provides marked pitches, all for touring units, at the top of the park, with some views over the rolling hills to the sea. With a more recently developed touring field, they include 228 pitches with 16A electricity, many with tarmac hardstanding (not always level), mostly arranged around oval access roads in hedged areas. Further non-electric pitches are behind in two open, unmarked fields which are sloping (blocks are thoughtfully provided, stored in neat wooden boxes next to water points). A smart, modern entertainment complex incorporates a licensed club and family lounge with snacks, a restaurant, teenage disco room, cartoon lounge, outdoor pool and smart indoor pool complex. Twitchen is very popular for families with children. If they become bored, there are always the excellent beaches nearby with a footpath down to the sea. All the facilities of Golden Coast and Woolacombe Bay Holiday Villages and Easewell Farm are free to visitors at Twitchen, with a bus (small charge) running regularly between the four parks and to the beach.

Facilities
There are two toilet blocks, one of which is new and provides family bathrooms and saunas. Laundry facilities at each block plus a good modern launderette at the central complex. Motorcaravan service point. Shop and takeaway. Club, bars, restaurant and entertainment for adults and children, day and evening. Outdoor pool (heated mid May-mid Sept). Attractive indoor pool with sauna, paddling pool, fountain and a viewing area. Putting green. Games rooms. Good adventure play area. ATM. American motorhomes are accepted (up to 30 ft). WiFi (charged). Off site: Beach and golf 1 mile. Fishing, riding and bicycle hire 2 miles.

Open: 23 March - 5 November.

Directions
From Barnstaple take A361 towards Ilfracombe and through Braunton. Turn left at Mullacott Cross roundabout towards Woolacombe and then right towards Mortehoe. Park is on the left before village.
GPS: 51.184683, -4.1977

Charges guide
Per unit incl. 2 persons and electricity	£ 15.75 - £ 57.75
incl. services	£ 20.00 - £ 60.00
dog	£ 1.50

Special offers available.

For latest campsite news visit
alanrogers.com

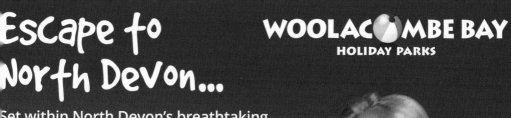

Woolacombe

Woolacombe Sands Holiday Park

Beach Road, Woolacombe EX34 7AF (Devon) T: 01271 870569. E: lifesabeach@woolacombe-sands.co.uk

alanrogers.com/UK0735

With sea views and within walking distance of Woolacombe's lovely sandy beach, this family park has been terraced out of the valley side as you drop down into the village. Apart from its smart entrance, it has been left natural. The pond and stream at the bottom are almost hidden with gated access to the National Trust fields across the valley. The 200 terraced level grass pitches, all with 16A electricity, are accessed by gravel roads with some good up-and-down walking needed to the toilet blocks (may pose a problem for visitors with disabilities). Some 50 mobile homes and 14 bungalows are in the more central area, and tents tend to be placed on the bottom terraces. The park boasts both indoor and outdoor pools (accessed by code) with a full time attendant. Upstairs from the indoor pool is a very pleasant conservatory seating area with great views and an outside seating area adjacent to it. Evenings see Woolly Bear emerge from his shack to entertain children, with adult family entertainment later. A good plus factor is the fact that all facilities open when the site opens. A useful path leads from the site to the beach via the car park and the walk is said to take 15 minutes.

Facilities

Four basic toilet blocks with good hot water are spread amongst the terraces. The newer shower block has separate toilets opposite. Shop. Self-service food bar providing good value meals and breakfast (main season and B.Hs). Two bars and full entertainment programme. Heated indoor and outdoor pools both with paddling pool areas. Fenced play area on bark with plenty of equipment. Ball area with nets. Crazy golf. Kingpin bowling. Off site: Riding next door. Golf, bicycle hire and freshwater fishing 0.5 miles. Beach 15 minutes walk or 0.5 miles.

Open: 1 April - 30 October.

Directions

Follow A361 from Barnstaple through Braunton towards Ilfracombe. At Mullacott Cross roundabout turn left for Woolacombe (B3343). Site clearly signed on left as you go down the hill into the village. GPS: 51.17145, -4.191833

Charges guide

Per person (incl. electricity)	£ 5.00 - £ 15.00
child (4-15 yrs)	£ 2.50 - £ 7.50
dog	£ 5.00

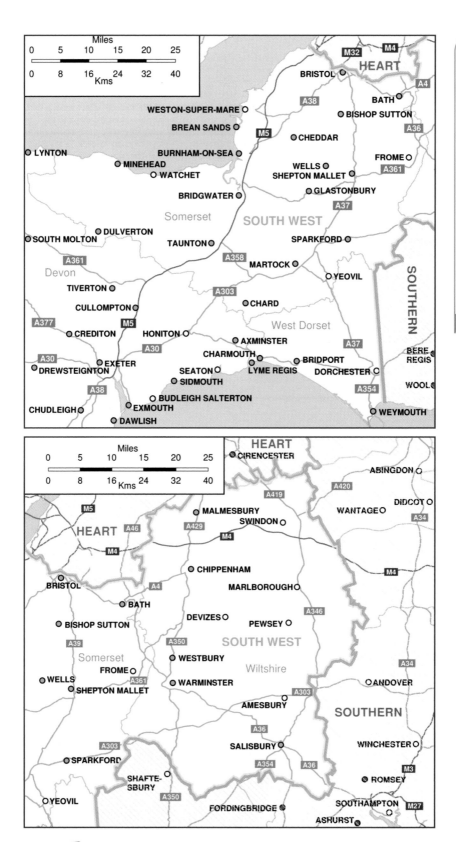

Map 1 (top):

Miles
0 5 10 15 20 25
0 8 16 24 32 40
Kms

HEART

M32 M4

BRISTOL

A4

BATH

A38

BISHOP SUTTON

WESTON-SUPER-MARE

A36

BREAN SANDS

M5

CHEDDAR

FROME

LYNTON

BURNHAM-ON-SEA

WELLS

A361

MINEHEAD

SHEPTON MALLET

WATCHET

BRIDGWATER

GLASTONBURY

A37

Somerset

SOUTH WEST

DULVERTON

SPARKFORD

SOUTH MOLTON

TAUNTON

A361

A358

MARTOCK

Devon

YEOVIL

SOUTHERN

TIVERTON

A303

CULLOMPTON

CHARD

A377

M5

West Dorset

CREDITON

HONITON

A37

A30

AXMINSTER

BERE REGIS

A30

CHARMOUTH

DREWSTEIGNTON

EXETER

SEATON

BRIDPORT

SIDMOUTH

LYME REGIS

DORCHESTER

A38

A354

WOOL

CHUDLEIGH

BUDLEIGH SALTERTON

EXMOUTH

WEYMOUTH

DAWLISH

Map 2 (bottom):

Miles
0 5 10 15 20 25
0 8 16 24 32 40
Kms

HEART

CIRENCESTER

ABINGDON

A420

A419

DIDCOT

M5

MALMESBURY

WANTAGE

HEART

A46

A429

SWINDON

A34

M4

M4

CHIPPENHAM

M4

BRISTOL

A4

MARLBOROUGH

BATH

A346

DEVIZES

BISHOP SUTTON

PEWSEY

A39

A350

SOUTH WEST

Somerset

WESTBURY

Wiltshire

A34

FROME

A361

WELLS

WARMINSTER

ANDOVER

SHEPTON MALLET

A303

AMESBURY

SOUTHERN

A36

A303

SALISBURY

WINCHESTER

SPARKFORD

A354

A36

M3

SHAFTE-SBURY

ROMSEY

A350

YEOVIL

SOUTHAMPTON

M27

FORDINGBRIDGE

ASHURST

Bath

Newton Mill Holiday Park

Newton Road, Bath BA2 9JF (Somerset) T: 0844 272 9503. E: enquiries@newtonmillpark.co.uk

alanrogers.com/UK1460

In a peaceful valley three miles from the centre of the historic city of Bath and with direct access to the local cycle track network, Newton Mill is an excellent base from which to explore the city and the area. There are two meadows for tents and 90 caravan pitches (with 30 long stay) which are located at the other end of the valley. All of these have hardstandings, with 16A electricity and satellite TV hook-ups. This end of the park is closest to the main Bristol to London railway line, not visually obtrusive but occasional rail noise may be noticeable. The site has been created around an old mill, the bar and restaurant now occupying part of the original building, and there is a modern timber chalet-style reception building with a small, well stocked shop. The restaurant (open evenings all year) serves good value, speciality meals. Breakfasts are available (weekends Easter-October, daily in summer). The tent meadow is in an elevated position, or alternatively you may prefer the paddock, a small field alongside the stream, which is a car-free zone with a separate parking area.

Facilities

Two new heated toilet blocks provide excellent modern facilities with some washbasins in cubicles, free hot showers, bathrooms (on payment), baby rooms and a good suite for disabled campers. Launderette. Basic motorcaravan service point. Shop, bar, restaurant with garden seating area. Play area. Boules court. Fishing. Off site: Bus service into Bath runs every ten minutes from Twerton village, a 10 minute walk. Nearby Bristol and Bath Railway Path (a traffic-free cycle way) links to the West Bath Riverside Path, and the Kennet and Avon towpath. Thursday market in Twerton.

Open: All year.

Directions

Site is 2 miles west of Bath city centre. From the north take M4 exit 19, turn onto M32 and almost immediately take A4174 (Avon ring road) for 7.5 miles to A4. Turn left towards Bath and in 5 miles at second roundabout, take second exit (Newton St Looe) and pass The Globe pub. Site entrance is on left in 1 mile. GPS: 51.378133, -2.410817

Charges guide

Per unit incl. 2 persons and electricity	£ 15.00 - £ 25.00

Bishop Sutton

Bath Chew Valley Caravan Park

Ham Lane, Bishop Sutton BS39 5TZ (Somerset) T: 01275 332127. E: enquiries@bathchewvalley.co.uk

alanrogers.com/UK1510

A small and secluded garden site for adults only, Chew Valley has been developed with much tender love and care by the Betton family and is now affiliated to the Caravan Club. Caravans are sited on hardstanding pitches amongst colourful beds of flowers, and cars are tucked away on the nearby car park, providing a tranquil and restful atmosphere. An area of woodland is adjacent with an enclosed dog walking area called Puppies' Parade. The warden will assist you in placing your caravan. There are neat hardstandings for all pitches and 27 spacious, fully serviced pitches, all with 16A electricity connections. This park will particularly appeal to garden and nature lovers. A member of the Best of British group.

Facilities

The heated toilet block (with a 'home from home' feel), provides all the fittings that make life comfortable: separate en-suite units each with WC, basin and shower. One unit has facilities for disabled visitors. Useful utility room with sinks, coin operated washer/driers and ironing facilities, together with a service washes facility for those who do not want to watch their laundry on holiday. Free use of freezer. Motorcaravan service point. Internet access on information room PC and WiFi. Max. 2 dogs. Off site: Village 200 m. with useful general store, post office, newsagent, pub and restaurant. Supermarkets within 15 minutes drive. Fishing 1 mile. Golf 5 miles. Riding 8 miles. Beach 15 miles.

Open: All year.

Directions

From the A37 or A38 take the A368 (which links them) to Bishop Sutton. Ham lane is opposite the Red Lion Public House, and the park is 800 m. along Ham Lane on the left. GPS: 51.336583, -2.597183

Charges guide

Per unit incl. 2 persons and electricity	£ 20.00 - £ 33.00

For latest campsite news visit
alanrogers.com

Brean Sands
Northam Farm Touring Caravan Park

Brean Sands, Burnham-on-Sea TA8 2SE (Somerset) T: 01278 751244. E: stay@northamfarm.co.uk
alanrogers.com/UK1570

Brean has been a popular holiday destination for decades and many large campsites have evolved. Northam Farm, owned by the Scott family, is one of them. It is a large family park with good facilities and an ongoing programme of improvements. There are 350 pitches for seasonal units and these are separated from the four touring fields. Pitches are well established and many have block paved hardstanding. There are two play areas for youngsters, a playing field, bicycle track and football pitch for teenagers, and fishing on the lake for adults. The owners and staff are always available to help visitors enjoy their stay. A monthly newsletter is published giving details of 'what's on' both on and off site. About 500 yards down the road is The Seagull, which is also owned by Northam Farm. Here you will find an excellent restaurant, bar and nightly live entertainment, even during the low season. Just down the road is Brean Leisure Park with its swimming complex, funfair, golf and much more.

Facilities

Three good toilet blocks, well maintained and within reasonable distance of all pitches, provide ample toilets, washbasins and spacious showers (50p). Bathrooms (£1 charge). Baby room. Rooms for visitors with disabilities (radar key access). Laundry. Motorcaravan service point. Dog shower and two exercise areas. Licensed shop well stocked with food, holiday gear and accessories. Snack bar/takeaway. Free entry to live entertainment at The Seagull. Two play areas. Playing field. Fishing lake. Caravan workshop for repairs and servicing. Caravan storage. Dogs are not accepted in some of the fields. A bus stops at the park entrance. Off site: Beach 200 m. across road. Golf, bicycle hire and riding 0.5 miles. Burnham-on-Sea 4 miles. Weston-Super-Mare 8 miles.

Open: March - October.

Directions

From M5 exit 22 follow signs to Burnham-on-Sea, Berrow and then Brean. Continue through Brean and Northam Farm is on the right, 0.5 miles past Brean Leisure Park. GPS: 51.2949, -3.010167

Charges guide

Per unit incl. 2 persons	
and electricity	£ 11.25 - £ 26.25
extra person	£ 2.00 - £ 2.50
child (0-15 yrs)	£ 1.00
dog, awning, fishing	free

One of the most sought after touring parks in Somerset

Northam Farm Holiday Park
Where the sea meets the countryside

Telephone:- 01278 751244 Fax:- 01278 751150
stay@northamfarm.co.uk | www.northamfarm.co.uk

Brean Sands
Warren Farm Holiday Centre

Warren Road, Brean Sands, Burnham-on-Sea TA8 2RP (Somerset) T: 01278 751227.
E: enquiries@warren-farm.co.uk **alanrogers.com/UK1580**

Warren Farm is a popular venue for family campers who want the beach, fun and entertainment. With over 1,000 pitches, the park is divided into several fields, with touring and seasonal pitches kept well apart; Sunnyside, part of Warren Farm, is about 200 yards further down the road and has its own warden. Access roads are wide and all the 565 touring pitches are grassy and level, with 16A electric hook-ups. There are no hardstandings so motorcaravans may have difficulties in extremely wet weather. Play equipment is located in a line through the centre of the camping fields which may be a little noisy. Ranch-style wooden fences break up the fields.

Facilities

Several toilet blocks of varying styles provide WCs, showers (charged) and mostly communal washbasins. Facilities vary depending on which block you are using. The larger blocks have hairdressing stations and laundry facilities. All have facilities for babies. Facilities for disabled visitors in all the fields. A warden looks after each block. Motorcaravan service point. Two shops, snack bar and Chinese takeaway at Sunnyside (opening times vary). Fish bar. Beachcomber Inn. Play equipment for toddlers. Play barn with play centre, bowling alley, bouncy tractor, ball pit, large-screen television, and electronic games. Sports field. Fishing lake. Bicycle hire. No dogs in field six. WiFi.

Open: April - October.

Directions

Leave M5 at exit 22 and follow the B3140 to Burnham-on-Sea, then to Berrow and Brean. Continue through Brean and Warren Farm is on the right 1.5 miles past Brean Leisure Park. GPS: 51.302483, -3.009833

Charges guide

Per unit incl. 2 persons	
and electricity	£ 11.00 - £ 21.00
extra person	£ 2.00
dog	free

FREE Alan Rogers Travel Card
Extra benefits and savings - see page 10

Bridgwater
Mill Farm Caravan & Camping Park
Fiddington, Bridgwater TA5 1JQ (Somerset) T: 01278 732286

alanrogers.com/UK1306

On the edge of the village of Fiddington, in a countryside location at the foot of the Quantock Hills, Mill Farm is just seven miles from Bridgwater and four miles from the sea. This is an extensive and popular family holiday site with three main fields, each taking 50-60 units with a toilet block, a playground and a plentiful supply of water points. Extra fields are opened for the peak season allowing a total capacity of 275 units, all with 10A electricity. The site has a large swimming pool complex with indoor and outdoor pools, free to campers. There is a licensed riding school, rowing boats on the little lake and entertainment during high season and at weekends during mid-season. A well stocked mini-market provides all the usual items. Mill Farm is a good family holiday base, very much children orientated with a wide range of activities to keep them happy.

Facilities

Three toilet blocks include facilities for disabled visitors (Radar key), one washbasin in cubicle for each sex, bathrooms (charged) and baby rooms. Launderette. Shop (all year). Large club room with bar, takeaway (weekends and peak seasons), games room and family entertainment (high season). New sports bar now open. Heated indoor pool with whirlpool and paddling pool (Easter-early Nov) and outdoor pool with giant waterslide (15/5-31/9; no lifeguard, but CCTV monitoring). Pony riding and trekking, canoe hire, and trampolining (charged). Boating lake. WiFi. Off site: Golf 3 miles. Beach and fishing 4 miles.

Open: All year.

Directions

From M5 exit 23 or 24, turn west and pass through Bridgwater and continue on the A39. After 6 miles turn right towards Fiddington. Go along narrow lane with passing places for 1 mile to site entrance. Park where instructed on the long entry driveway and report to reception. GPS: 51.16, -3.120517

Charges guide

Per unit incl. 2 persons and electricity	£ 16.00 - £ 25.00
extra person	£ 3.00 - £ 4.00
child (2-14 yrs)	£ 2.00 - £ 3.00

Mill Farm Caravan and Camping Park
Fiddington, Bridgwater, Somerset

Swimming * Riding * Boating

Activity park with Lots for children, making the ideal family holiday.

ALSO: Hot take-away and shop during high season.

HIRE: Trampolines, Pony rides, Canoes, Pool tables

FREE: Heated Swimming Pool and Large water slide Children's Boating Lake, Swings and Slides, Games room, Hot showers, WIFI

* Club with Entertainment
* Meadow for Rallies
* Holiday Cottage's
* Caravan Storage

01278 732286   www.millfarm.biz

Bridgwater
Secret Valley
Cobbs Cross Farm, Goathurst, Bridgwater TA5 2DN (Somerset) T: 01278 671945.
E: enquiries@secret-valley.co.uk   **alanrogers.com/UK1330**

Hidden in the depths of rural Somerset, Secret Valley is a find. Developed on a 400-acre working farm with four acres of vineyards, it is situated within an Area of Outstanding Natural Beauty and boasts wonderful views across the Quantock Hills – you even get a glimpse of the Bristol Channel. Unusually, accommodation is provided in a peaceful and relaxed setting with wigwams (like wooden pods), yurts, a teepee and even a shepherd's hut on offer, complete with fire pits, barbecues and picnic tables on level grass paddocks. Please note that there are no touring pitches available. Newly converted barns house a communal kitchen and dining area with picnic tables.

Facilities

Fully equipped, clean toilet block. Communal kitchen and dining room with TV and adjacent wet room. Wigwams and yurts (can be heated; kettle, toaster and fridge provided, bring your own linen and crockery). Covered barn for indoor ball games, with toy tractors. Chickens, goats and reindeer. Sandpit. Fly fishing. Guided walks. Wine tasting. Farm tours. Archery and mountain boarding. Other activities (min. 8 persons, charged) pre-booked.

Open: March - November.

Directions

From M5 exit 24, follow A38 south signed South Petherton/Taunton. Turn right at South Petherton signed Goathurst. Follow country lane for 3 miles and pass through Goathurst taking left turn at T-junction after village towards farm and site sign. GPS: 51.10426, -3.078237

Charges guide

Contact site.

For latest campsite news visit

alanrogers.com

Bridport
Freshwater Beach Holiday Park

Burton Bradstock, Bridport DT6 4PT (Dorset) T: 01308 897317. E: office@freshwaterbeach.co.uk

alanrogers.com/UK1780

Family run parks for families with direct access to their own private beach are rare in Britain and this one has the added advantage of being in beautiful coastal countryside in West Dorset. It also has an excellent new leisure centre that includes a gym, ten-pin bowling and an indoor pool. The park is next to the sea and a beach of fine pebbles, sheltered from the wind by pebble banks and has been run by the same family for the last 40 years. Approached by a fairly steep access road, the park itself is on level, open ground. The 500 touring pitches, 400 with 10A electricity, are on an open, undulating grass field connected by tarmac or hardcore roads. Caravan pitches (10x11 m) are marked and evenly spaced in lines. Some tent pitches are in the main field, with others well spaced on a terraced field. In separate areas there are 260 caravan holiday homes, with 60 for hire. This lively holiday park has an extensive range of facilities which include an outdoor pool, a good value licensed restaurant, a main bar and two further small bars with an evening entertainment programme in season. Daytime entertainment caters for all ages. Footpaths lead to the thatched village of Burton Bradstock and West Bay. The overall impression is of a large, busy holiday park with a friendly reception and happy atmosphere.

Facilities

Two fully equipped toilet blocks serve the caravan fields and a third newer block is in the tent field. It is a good provision for a busy beach park. Facilities for disabled visitors (Radar key). Baby care room (key system). Launderette. Bars with wide variety of entertainment and evening shows. Licensed restaurant (weekends only in late season; closed Mondays all season). Main bar and two smaller bars. Supermarket and takeaway. New leisure complex with indoor pool, water play area for young children, gym and 10-pin bowling. Heated, supervised outdoor swimming and paddling pools (24/5-1/9) with lessons. Games room. Activities for children. Two play areas. Internet café and WiFi (charged). Off site: Bus stop on main road. Golf course 0.5 miles.

Open: 15 March - 9 November.

Directions

Park is immediately west of the village of Burton Bradstock, on the Weymouth-Bridport coast road (B3157). GPS: 50.70500, -2.73867

Charges guide

Per unit incl. up to 6 persons, car and awning	£ 16.00 - £ 42.00
car or boat	£ 2.00
electricity	£ 2.00
small tent incl. 2 persons walking or cycling	£ 5.00 - £ 17.00
dog	£ 2.50

Single sex groups not admitted.

Freshwater Beach
HOLIDAY PARK

Great family holidays on Dorset's World Heritage Coast.

Wi Fi

01308 897 317 ● freshwaterbeach.co.uk

FREE Alan Rogers Travel Card
Extra benefits and savings - see page 10

Bridport
Highlands End Holiday Park

West Dorset Leisure Holidays, Eype, Bridport DT6 6AR (Dorset) T: 01308 422139. E: holidays@wdlh.co.uk

alanrogers.com/UK1750

On slightly sloping ground with superb open views, both coastal and inland, Highlands End is quietly situated on the Dorset Heritage Coastline. A path in front of the park runs along the cliff top and then leads down to a shingle beach a little further along. It is a good quality park with 180 caravan holiday homes, mostly privately owned, and 195 touring pitches in two areas nearest to the sea – one has to travel through the holiday homes to reach them. The field for tents has 73 pitches, ten with electricity, and the touring field is all electric with 45 pitches also having water, drainage and hardstanding. A further area is used for tents in high season. A modern, attractive building houses a lounge bar, excellent good value restaurant with takeaway facility, family room and games room with some musical evenings in high season. The park's amenities also include an excellent, air-conditioned indoor heated pool, a tennis court and a nine-hole pitch and putt (all charged). The owners have a long term interest in the fire brigade and an historic fire engine (1936 Leyland Pump Escape) along with memorabilia make an interesting display in the bar. The park is run to high standards and is a member of the Best of British group.

Facilities

Two good quality toilet blocks near the touring sections are well maintained and can be heated. Some washbasins in cubicles with toilets, large, roomy showers. En-suite facilities for disabled visitors. Baby care room. Laundry room. Motorcaravan service point. Well stocked shop (opening times vary), including gas supplies. Bar and restaurant/takeaway (evenings and Sun. lunch). Tennis (charged). Indoor pool (20x9 m), gym, sauna/steam room. Games room. 9-hole pitch and putt. Excellent adventure play area. Large sloping field for games. Facilities open all season. WiFi over site (charged). Off site: Beach 0.5 miles.

Open: 20 March - 8 November.

Directions

Follow Bridport bypass on A35 around town. Park is signed to south (Eype turning), down narrow lane. There is a new exit road. GPS: 50.725333, -2.777

Charges guide

Per unit incl. 2 persons and electricity	£ 15.10 - £ 25.00
all services and hardstanding	£ 17.45 - £ 27.35
extra person	£ 4.20 - £ 5.20
child (4-17 yrs)	£ 3.20
dog (max. 2)	£ 3.20

Highlands End and Golden Cap Holiday Parks
Tel: 01308 422139 Email: holidays@wdlh.co.uk
Eype, Bridport, Dorset DT6 6AR
www.wdlh.co.uk
A World Heritage Coastline on your doorstep
WEST DORSET LEISURE HOLIDAYS

Bridport
Golden Cap Holiday Park

West Dorset Leisure Holidays, Seatown, Chideock, Bridport DT6 6JX (Dorset) T: 01308 422139.
E: holidays@wdlh.co.uk **alanrogers.com/UK1740**

Golden Cap, named after the adjacent high cliff (the highest in southern England) which overlooks Lyme Bay, is only 150 m. from a shingle beach at Seatown and is surrounded by National Trust countryside and the Heritage Coastline. The park is arranged over several fields on the valley floor, sloping gently down towards the sea. It is in two main areas, having once been two parks, each separated into fields with marvellous panoramic views and providing 108 touring pitches. All have electricity and 30 also have hardstanding with drainage and gravel awning area. An extra sloping tent area is used for peak season (torch useful), although it is a five minute walk from here to the toilet blocks and shop. There are 219 caravan holiday homes in their own areas. A small but attractive lake is used for coarse fishing and the heated indoor pool and gym at Highlands End (under the same ownership, 3 miles away) is open for campers at Golden Cap on payment. Beaches are nearby and the coastal path for good walks.

Facilities

The modern toilet block is of good quality with spacious shower cubicles (some with toilet and washbasin). Facilities for disabled visitors. Baby room. Two smaller blocks around the park. Laundry room. Motorcaravan service point. Useful and well stocked shop. Gas supplies. Small play area. Coarse fishing lake (day tickets from shop). American motorhomes are not accepted. WiFi throughout (charged). Off site: Bus stop in village 10 mins. walk. Pub serving food nearby. Beach 150 yds. Golf 2 miles. Bicycle hire, boat launching 3 miles.

Open: 20 March - 8 November.

Directions

Turn off A35 road at Chideock (a bigger village) 3 miles west of Bridport, at sign to Seatown opposite church. Park is less than 1 mile down narrow lane. GPS: 50.715333, -2.821667

Charges guide

Per unit incl. 2 persons and electricity	£ 15.10 - £ 25.00
extra person	£ 4.20 - £ 5.20
child (4-17 yrs)	£ 3.20
all service pitch	£ 17.45 - £ 27.35
pitch with sea view	£ 21.90 - £ 32.50

For latest campsite news visit
alanrogers.com

Bridport

Bingham Grange Touring & Camping Park

Melplash, Bridport DT6 3TT (Dorset) T: 01308 488234. E: enquiries@binghamgrange.co.uk
alanrogers.com/UK1770

Bingham Grange is an attractive, purpose built park for adults only with an excellent restaurant. In a pleasant, rural situation two miles from the market town of Bridport, there are views seaward towards West Bay and inland across Beaminster Downs and Pilsdon Hill. There are over 135 individually landscaped pitches, 118 with 10A electricity, and 83 with hardstanding, 26 serviced. Shrubs and trees are fully developed in the original field and have been planted in the newer field. Pitches here have been levelled and terraced and have super views. Some are non-electric for tents. Paths have been made through the woods to the river and there is access to the public footpaths (Bridport 20 minutes).

Facilities	Directions
Well equipped toilet block, with underfloor heating and a separate, fully equipped room for disabled visitors, with ramped access, and seven luxury en-suite shower rooms. Laundry room with microwave and freezer. Reception with small shop. Popular bar/restaurant with good value menu. Gas available. WiFi (charged). Only adults (over 18 yrs) are accepted and only two per unit at Bank Holidays.	At the roundabouts on the A35 road, on the east side of Bridport, follow signs for Beaminster on the A3066. After 2 miles watch for site entrance on the left. GPS: 50.765076, -2.740911

Open: March - end October.

Charges guide

Per unit incl. 2 persons and electricity (10A)	£ 17.00 - £ 26.00
extra person	£ 7.50

Bristol

Baltic Wharf Caravan Club Site

Cumberland Road, Bristol BS1 6XG (Somerset) T: 01179 268030
alanrogers.com/UK1440

This excellent Caravan Club site in Bristol's redeveloped dockland is well laid out and maintained to a high standard. It is screened from the road by a high wall, with a boatyard on one side and residential apartments on the other, with access via a lockable gate to the Baltic Wharf dockside. The view across the dock towards Clifton village and Bristol is unique and you can even glimpse the suspension bridge. Accessed by a tarmac road, the 55 pitches are on stone chippings and are ideal for all-year-round use (steel pegs are sold at reception). All have electricity (16A) and TV aerial points (reception is poor).

Facilities	Directions
The toilet block provides good clean facilities including controllable showers and washbasins in cubicles (heated in winter). Good facilities for disabled visitors, plus toilets and showers for the walking disabled in the main block. Fully equipped laundry room. Motorcaravan service point. Dogs are welcome but there is no dog walk. Wardens live on the site. Off site: Fishing and boating 400 yds.	From M5, J18, take A4 (Bristol West). Follow signs for Historic Harbour under Suspension Bridge and through Hotwells. Cross dock bridge and site is 500 yds. on left. GPS: 51.446533, -2.61425

Open: All year.

Charges guide

Per person	£ 5.60 - £ 7.60
child (5-16 yrs)	£ 1.55 - £ 3.10
pitch incl. electricity (non-member)	£ 14.00 - £ 17.50

Burnham-on-Sea

Home Farm Holiday Park & Country Club

Edithmead, Burnham-on-Sea TA9 4HD (Somerset) T: 01278 788888. E: SITE@hfhp.co.uk
alanrogers.com/UK1480

Home Farm is neatly and attractively laid out covering 44 acres, and is handy for those using the M5. There are 780 level pitches in total including 180 privately owned holiday homes and a number of seasonal units. These are laid out on level grass, all clearly marked and accessed by tarmac roads. They are divided into various sections, one of which is specifically for those with dogs. The 183 pitches with hardstanding include 20 serviced pitches for RVs and motorcaravans. Electrical connections (10A) are available everywhere. A large, modern outdoor pool with paved surrounds and a paddling section is neatly walled and a recent indoor pool and leisure centre includes access for disabled visitors.

Facilities	Directions
Two refurbished toilet blocks are heated and well situated for touring areas. Bathrooms (£5 key deposit). Baby room. Laundry. Facilities for disabled visitors. Dog shower. Shop (April-end Nov). Club house with TV and entertainment. Restaurants and takeaway (April-Oct). Bar (all season). Outdoor swimming pool (May-Sept). Leisure centre with heated pool, gym (charges apply). Play area. Fishing lake. WiFi zone. Security patrols at night. Barrier card (£2).	Home Farm is 400 yds. from M5 exit 22 and the A38. It is signed from the B3140 into Burnham-on-Sea. GPS: 51.23875, -2.964167

Open: 10 February - 6 January.

Charges guide

Per unit incl. 2 persons, electricity and awning	£ 9.50 - £ 39.95
extra person	£ 3.25 - £ 5.50
child (4-17 yrs)	£ 1.75 - £ 4.75

FREE Alan Rogers Travel Card
Extra benefits and savings - see page 10

Burnham-on-Sea

Holiday Resort Unity

Coast Road, Brean Sands, Burnham-on-Sea TA8 2RB (Somerset) T: 01278 751235. E: admin@hru.co.uk
alanrogers.com/UK1575

Holiday Resort Unity offers everything for everyone, from young children to the 'young at heart'. Apart from the extensive on-site amusements and entertainment programme, campers can also use the swimming pools, funfair and other leisure pursuits at the adjoining Brean Leisure Centre (owned by the same family), some free of charge and others by paying a small fee. Three large touring fields provide pitches that are flat and open, mostly grass but some on concrete hardstandings (for RV's and motorcaravans up to 30 ft, contact site). Most pitches have 16A electricity hook-ups. A separate warden looks after each camping field. New ready-erected euro tents and a substantial number of caravan holiday homes are available for rent. Access to the five-mile stretch of sandy beach is via a footpath opposite the site entrance. Fishing (with a licence) is permitted from Unity Lake in the Yellow Field.

Facilities

Three good toilet blocks provide ample facilities and include en-suite bathrooms. Some toilets and washbasins have been adapted for campers with disabilities (Radar key). Well equipped laundries. Motorcaravan service point. Recycling station. Well stocked shop. Gas exchange. RJ's Club, Sarah's Pantry, Alan's fish and chip bar and Treasure Park Chinese takeaway. Large adventure play area. Buster's Work Out Gym, Sally's sun beds. Mon. market, Sun. car boot sales. All facilities open in high season. Torches advisable. Max. 2 dogs. Bus and land-train services vary according to season. Off site: Beach 100 m. Walking access from park to Brean Leisure Centre. Bus to Weston-Super-Mare and Cheddar Gorge.

Open: 10 February - 20 November.

Directions

From M5 exit 22, follow signs for Burnham-on-Sea (B3140), Berrow and Brean. Holiday Resort Unity is on right along the main street of Brean – it is well signed. Take care as road through Berrow and Brean is rather narrow. GPS: 51.280483, -3.012217

Charges guide

Per unit incl. 4 persons and electricity	£ 10.00 - £ 36.00
extra person	£ 3.50
dog	£ 3.00

Price includes unit, 4 persons, awning, entertainment/swimming and 'Piglet Club'. Credit cards accepted (charge of £2 per transaction).

Chard

Alpine Grove Touring Park

Forton, Chard TA20 4HD (Somerset) T: 01460 63479. E: stay@alpinegrovetouringpark.com
alanrogers.com/UK1415

This peaceful and green site is owned by Richard and Helen Gurd, who go the extra mile to ensure you enjoy your stay here. The pitches vary in size (90-120 sq.m) and are on flat ground served by gravel roads giving easy access. Some informally marked pitches are tucked away in dense foliage and are very private. Electricity (10A) is supplied to 38 of the 40 touring pitches (16 hardstandings). All the standard facilities are near reception, including a free fenced and heated swimming pool (10x5 m). A play area is provided for children under the canopy of mature trees which shade the site. Campers can barbecue on the pitches and use the picnic tables provided or perhaps hire a fire pit for cooking their supper. Torches are essential at night. Nature trails for children are organised within the site.

Facilities

A modest, modern sanitary building provides all usual facilities and is kept clean and smart. Facilities for disabled campers double as a family bathroom. Reception doubles as the shop selling some fresh food, milk, bread and essentials. Heated outdoor swimming pool (20/5-20/9). Play area. Dog sitting service day and evening (extra charge). Washing machine and dryers. Play area with trampoline. Planned walks and some day activities. Two log cabins for hire. Bicycle hire. Barbecues allowed (not electric). WiFi (charged). Off site: Riding alongside site. Public transport in Forton 0.5 miles.

Open: 14 March - 30 September.

Directions

From M5 exit 25 take the A358 signed Chard. From Chard take the Forton road where the site is well signed. From the A35, take A358 via Axminster to Chard, and then Forton. Ignore GPS and approach through Chard. GPS: 50.85779, -2.93597

Charges guide

Per unit incl. 2 persons and electricity	£ 16.00 - £ 20.00
extra person	£ 2.50 - £ 4.00
dog	£ 2.00

For latest campsite news visit
alanrogers.com

Charmouth
Newlands Caravan Park

Charmouth DT6 6RB (Dorset) T: 01297 560259. E: enq@newlandsholidays.co.uk
alanrogers.com/UK1810

Newlands is well situated on the Jurassic Coast, the first natural World Heritage site in England. A family owned park, it is run with care and enthusiasm, occupying a prominent position beside the road into Charmouth village with rural views southwards to the hills across the valley. The terrain is terraced in two fields to provide over 200 well spaced places for touring units, some for seasonal units and over 80 for caravan holiday homes (some for hire). The mainly sloping tent field also has super views towards the sea and Lyme Regis. Electricity (10A) is provided on 160 pitches and 30 have hardstanding, water and drainage. Other accommodation includes around 80 mobile homes, 36 privately owned, smart pine lodges, apartments and motel rooms. All the facilities are located in a modern building to one side of the wide tarmac entrance. The club bar opens each evening and lunch times to suit, and also serves food. Family entertainment includes a children's club during school holidays with Dino Dan, the dinosaur. The indoor pool adjoins the bar area and an adjacent outdoor pool is walled, paved and sheltered.

Facilities

Two modern, heated toilet blocks provide roomy showers. Baby room. Well stocked shop (Mar-Nov). Licensed club bar (limited hours Nov-Mar). Restaurant (18.00-21.00. Mar-Nov plus Xmas/New Year) including takeaway. Outdoor heated pool (supervised in high season; entrance is key coded). Indoor pool and jacuzzi (small charge, closed Dec/Jan). Indoor and outdoor play areas. Family entertainment. Internet access. Off site: Beach 0.5 miles. Fishing 1 mile. Golf 2 miles. Riding 3 miles.

Open: 5 February - 1 December.

Directions

Approaching from Bridport leave the A35 at first sign for Charmouth at start of the bypass and site almost directly on your left. GPS: 50.7385, -2.889833

Charges guide

Per unit incl. up to 6 persons, electricity and awning	£ 17.00 - £ 35.00
fully serviced pitch	£ 20.00 - £ 39.00
dog (max. 2)	£ 1.00 - £ 4.00

Camping Cheques accepted.

Camping & touring pitches located on Dorset's Heritage coastline, a short stroll from the beach and just 3 miles from Lyme Regis. Indoor and outdoor pools, bar & lounge, restaurant, holiday home sales, family dining, kids indoor soft play, nightly and weekly accommodation, luxury pine lodges.

t: 01297 560259 or visit www.newlandsholidays.co.uk e:enq@newlandsholidays.co.uk Charmouth, Dorset DT6 6RB

Charmouth
Monkton Wyld Caravanning & Camping Park

Scotts Lane, Monkton Wyld, Charmouth DT6 6DB (Dorset) T: 01297 631131.
E: holidays@monktonwyld.co.uk **alanrogers.com/UK1730**

Monkton Wyld has pitches for the independent camper and for members of the Camping & Caravanning Club. It prides itself on its conservation efforts and the space and landscaping provided. Every pitch backs against a hedge or flower bed; 150 pitches, of which 92 are hardstanding, have 16A electricity. A further 50 tenting pitches are available in the school holiday period. A number of privately owned holiday homes have a separate area. There is also a range of self-catering accommodation, including a safari tent, cottages, a flat and a large farmhouse. This family run park has matured into an attractive, comfortable, garden-like park with trees and flowering shrubs and is maintained to a high standard.

Facilities

Two well built, heated toilet blocks are fully equipped. Family room with baby changing facilities (wheelchair access). Laundry area. Gas supplies. Shop (Easter-end Sept). Takeaway (May-Aug). Play areas. Caravan storage. Gate locked at 23.00. Caravan holiday homes for private purchase and other self catering accommodation available. Off site: Shops and local pubs within 1 mile.

Open: 9 March - 29 October.

Directions

Park is signed on A35 between Charmouth and Axminster, 2.5 miles west of Charmouth. Turn right at Greenway Head (B3165 Marshwood) and park is on left. Avoid Monkton Wyld hamlet as the road is very steep. GPS: 50.765333, -2.9525

Charges guide

Per unit incl. 2 persons and electricity	£ 19.25 - £ 31.75

FREE Alan Rogers Travel Card
Extra benefits and savings - see page 10

Charmouth
Wood Farm Caravan Park

Axminster Road, Charmouth DT6 6BT (Dorset) T: 01297 560697. E: holidays@woodfarm.co.uk

alanrogers.com/UK1760

Wood Farm is an excellent, family run park, maintained to high standards on sloping, well landscaped ground with rural views across the Marshwood Vale. With an indoor heated pool, tennis court, fishing lakes and a rather good café open all day, it is well worth consideration. All 184 pitches for touring units have hardstanding and 10A electricity (ten for camping), while 57 have water, waste water and TV connections. The ground slopes, so most pitches are terraced with some divided by distinctive, box-like leylandii hedging. Around 80 privately owned caravan holiday homes are in separate areas at the bottom of the site. Three are available to let. Excellent provision is made for disabled visitors, although there is considerable up and down walking due to the terrain. Situated on the western side of Charmouth beside the A35 (some road noise may be expected), the park is only a mile or two from Lyme Regis and its beaches. This area is now part of England's first natural World Heritage site, the Jurassic Coast. Wood Farm is part of the Caravan Club's Affiliated Scheme (non-members are also very welcome). Wood Farm has been in the hands of the same family for over 40 years. A member of the Best of British group.

Facilities

Four modern, well equipped, heated toilet blocks include excellent, new en-suite shower rooms. Good facilities for disabled campers. Baby care unit. Two laundry rooms. Motorcaravan service point. Shop by reception. Super conservatory café with sun terrace and viewing area for the swimming pool serving food all day, including breakfast, and supper on 2/3 nights per week. Fish and chip van calls. Good heated indoor pool and outdoor tennis court (charged). Games room with soft ball area, table tennis and snooker tables. Bridge club. Outdoor draughts. Play field. Two coarse fishing ponds (carp, rudd, roach, tench, perch) adjacent – day and weekly tickets (licence required from park). WiFi over site (charged) Off site: Golf 1 mile. Beaches and shops 1 and 2 miles. Riding 4 miles.

Open: 1 April - 4 November.

Directions

Park is 0.5 miles west of Charmouth village with access near the roundabout at the A35 and A3052 (Lyme Regis) junction. GPS: 50.74216, -2.91588

Charges guide

Per person	£ 5.00 - £ 7.50
child (5-16 yrs)	£ 2.00 - £ 5.50
pitch incl. 10A electricity	£ 6.50 - £ 13.00
'premium' pitch	£ 12.00 - £ 18.50
pup tent, dog, extra car	£ 2.00 - £ 2.50

Weekly offer in low and mid season.

• Breathtaking countryside views
• Superb indoor swimming pool
• Idyllic fishing ponds
• Tennis court
• 'Offshore' Cafe

TEL: (01297) 560697

THE CARAVAN CLUB

WOOD FARM
CHARMOUTH • DORSET

www.woodfarm.co.uk

BEST OF BRITISH   AA

Cheddar
Broadway House Holiday Park

Axbridge Road, Cheddar BS27 3DB (Somerset) T: 0844 272 9501. E: enquiries@broadwayhouse.co.uk

alanrogers.com/UK1410

A well maintained park offering a range of facilities on continental lines, Broadway is now part of the Darwin Group. Occupying a gently sloping area at the foot of the Mendips near Cheddar Gorge, the park has nearly 400 pitches, including 116 for touring units, with 16A electricity, 70 of them on gravel hardstanding have water and drainage and 263 for tents. From the entrance, after an area of neat caravan holiday homes and a separate area of luxury timber lodges, a series of touring areas graduates upwards, culminating in a tent and overflow rally field. The central access avenue is lined by trees with the groups of pitches on either side separated by ranch style fencing or hedging.

Facilities

The large, purpose-built toilet block at the start of the touring area has pushbutton showers and some private cabins. Behind are 10 family shower units, 2 are suitable for disabled visitors. Extra facilities are near reception, with a Portacabin type unit (no showers) in the top tent field. Baby room. Launderette. Motorcaravan service point. Shop. Bar, restaurant and takeaway. Swimming pool. Adventure playground. Crazy golf. BMX track. Games room. Family room and TV. Accommodation to rent.

Open: 1 March - 31 October.

Directions

From M5 exit 22 follow brown tourist signs towards Cheddar. Park entrance is on the A371 between Axbridge and Cheddar. GPS: 51.288214, -2.792303

Charges guide

Per unit	£ 15.00 - £ 30.00

For latest campsite news visit
alanrogers.com

Cheddar
Bucklegrove Holiday Park

Wells Road, Rodney Stoke, Cheddar BS27 3UZ (Somerset) T: 01749 870261. E: info@bucklegrove.co.uk

alanrogers.com/UK1550

Bucklegrove is set right in the heart of Somerset on the southern slopes of the Mendip Hills and close to the tourist attractions of Cheddar Gorge, Wookey Hole and Wells. The 100 individually marked and numbered touring and tenting pitches, most of which have 10A electricity connections, are mainly in the Grove, a level and terraced field, joined by a woodland walk to the lower field. There is also a summer camping meadow just for tents (no electricity here), with plenty of space and great views. The play area (for under 14s) has a safety surface and includes a multiplay unit, slide and spring riders. Campers also have a games room, a heated indoor swimming pool and separate children's pool. Adjoining the pool is a licensed bar with terrace providing simple bar menus and low-key entertainment mainly during high season or depending on the number of campers on site. A new development includes four privately owned lodges.

Facilities

Two toilet blocks house all the usual amenities, including some washbasins in cubicles and some spacious showers. The larger, heated block near reception also provides bathrooms (£1) with baby changing facilities, and a room for visitors with disabilities. Laundry rooms. Freezer for ice packs. Well stocked shop. Indoor swimming pool and paddling pool (22/3-2/11) with terrace bar. Games room. Play area. Dogs are accepted in certain fields (charged). Two luxury log cabins for hire. Off site: Wookey Hole and riding 2 miles. Golf 3 miles. Wells Cathedral 4 miles. Fishing 5 miles. Cheddar 7 miles. Beach at Weston-Super-Mare 12 miles. A bus to Wells and Cheddar stops regularly at the park entrance.

Open: 2 March - 1 December.

Directions

Take A371 Wells to Cheddar road. Park is on right 1 mile past Westbury village. Take care as the road between Wells and Cheddar is rather narrow through some of the villages. GPS: 51.243317, -2.7323

Charges guide

Per unit incl. 2 persons and electricity	£ 15.00 - £ 29.00
extra person	£ 5.00
child (4-17 yrs)	£ 3.00
dog (max. 2)	£ 2.00 - £ 5.00

Cheddar
Cheddar Bridge Touring Park

Draycott Road, Cheddar BS27 3RJ (Somerset) T: 01934 743048. E: enquiries@cheddarbridge.co.uk

alanrogers.com/UK1545

Within easy walking distance of Cheddar village, this is an adult only (over 18 yrs) park. A compact site, there are 50 pitches, mostly on level grass, with 45 electric hook-ups (16A) and 15 gravel hardstandings. A separate area for 20 tents is on the river bank, with its own toilet facilities. Six caravan holiday homes are now also available to rent. Reception keeps basic supplies and gas cylinders. Cream teas are available (which you prepare yourself) and profits go to charity. Note: the site access is over a fairly narrow bridge with low stone walls, passable for twin-axle caravans, but more difficult for very large motorcaravans. Cheddar village has a small supermarket with an ATM, garage, pubs, restaurants and a leisure centre with an indoor pool.

Facilities

Attractive heated sanitary block (close to site entrance, distance from most of the pitches) with washbasins in cubicles, large showers, and family bathroom with shower over the bath. Utility room with sinks, washing machine and dryer. Hot water restricted to 07.00-12.00 and 16.00-21.00. Fishing. Off site: Swimming pool 0.5 miles. Golf and riding 3 miles. Cheddar Gorge and village.

Open: 1 March - end October.

Directions

Site entrance is 100 yds. south of village on the A371, on right hand side, next to Cheddar Football Club. GPS: 51.27315, -2.774583

Charges guide

Per unit incl. 2 persons and electricity	£ 13.00 - £ 20.00
tent incl. 2 persons	£ 10.00 - £ 18.00
extra person	£ 3.00
dog	£ 2.00

Chippenham
Piccadilly Caravan Park

Folly Lane West, Lacock, Chippenham SN15 2LP (Wiltshire) T: 01249 730260. E: piccadillylacock@aol.com
alanrogers.com/UK1660

Piccadilly Caravan Park is set in open countryside close to several attractions, notably Longleat, Bath, Salisbury Plain, Stourhead, and Lacock itself. You will receive a warm welcome from the owner at this small, quiet family owned park that is beautifully kept. Well kept shrubs, plants and trees have been landscaped to give the impression of three separate areas and create a very pleasant ambience. There are 47 well spaced, clearly marked pitches, 12 of which have hardstanding, and two good areas for tents. Electrical connections (10A) are available on 42 pitches. A bus service runs from Lacock village to Chippenham (entry to the Chippenham museum and Heritage centre is free of charge).

Facilities	Directions
There are now two toilet blocks, well maintained and equipped, which can be heated in cool weather. Laundry room with baby changing facilities. Ice pack service. Bark-based playground and a large, grass ball play area. Limited gas supplies. Papers can be ordered. WiFi (free). Off site: Fishing 1 mile. Riding 4 miles. Golf 3 miles.	Park is signed west off A350 Chippenham-Melksham road (turning to Gastard with caravan symbol) by Lacock village. 300 yds. to park. GPS: 51.4138, -2.129683

Open: Easter/1 April - October.

Charges guide

Per unit incl. 2 persons and electricity	£ 19.00

No credit cards.

Chippenham
Plough Lane Caravan Site

Plough Lane, Kington Langley, Chippenham SN15 5PS (Wiltshire) T: 01249 750146.
E: enquiries@ploughlane.co.uk **alanrogers.com/UK1680**

Catering for adults only, this is a good example of a well designed, quality, modern touring site. The 50 pitches (all for touring units) are attractively laid out over four acres, access roads are gravel and the borders are stocked with well established shrubs and trees. The pitches are half grass, half hardstanding and all have 16A electricity, with 25 having full services. The site entrance has a barrier system for security. This site is an ideal base for visiting Bath and the Cotswolds, Avebury and Stonehenge, the Caen Hill locks at Devizes and Bristol.

Facilities	Directions
The sanitary building is heated, spacious, light and airy, and has all the usual facilities including some washbasins in cubicles, with a hairdressing area for ladies. Separate en-suite room for disabled visitors with ramp access. Fully equipped heated laundry. Max. 2 dogs per unit, a gravel dog walking path is provided. This park is for adults only (over 18 yrs). Barrier card deposit. WiFi throughout. Off site: Supermarket, two pubs, and two garages.	From M4 exit 17 turn south on A350 for 2 miles, then left at traffic lights where site is signed. GPS: 51.486367, -2.1257

Open: Easter - October.

Charges guide

Per unit incl. 2 persons and electricity	£ 21.00 - £ 23.00
extra person (max. 2 extra)	£ 5.00

No credit cards.

Glastonbury
The Old Oaks Touring Park

Wick Farm, Wick, Glastonbury BA6 8JS (Somerset) T: 01458 831437. E: info@theoldoaks.co.uk
alanrogers.com/UK1390

The Old Oaks, an adults only park, is tucked below and hidden from the Glastonbury Tor in a lovely secluded setting with views across to the Mendips. The grounds are immaculate with a great deal of attention to cleanliness throughout. In total there are 100 large pitches in a series of paddocks, 97 with 16A electricity, on hardstandings and 30 are fully serviced. Mainly backing on to hedges, they are arranged and interspersed with shrubs and flowers in a circular development, or terraced with fantastic views. There is a quiet orchard area for camping and six camping cabins provide a luxurious alternative to tents, but retain that 'outdoor feel'. A member of the Best of British group.

Facilities	Directions
The heated toilet block is of excellent quality and well equipped. A second block should now be ready. Some washbasins are in cubicles. Two en-suite rooms and a bathroom (£1). Disabled visitors have two rooms. Laundry room. Motorcaravan service facilities. Freezer for ice packs (free). Dog wash. Licensed shop sells local produce, freshly baked cakes and bread (pre-ordered). Pool table. Library room. Bicycle hire. Fishing. Painting holidays. Free Internet in reception. WiFi over site (charged).	Park is north off A361 Shepton Mallet-Glastonbury road, 2 miles from Glastonbury. Take narrow unclassified road signed Wick for 1 mile and park is on the left. GPS: 51.152633, -2.6803

Open: 8 February - 18 November.

Charges guide

Per unit incl. 2 persons and electricity	£ 16.00 - £ 26.50
with full services	£ 18.00 - £ 30.50
extra person	£ 8.00

For latest campsite news visit
alanrogers.com

Dulverton

Exe Valley Caravan Site

Bridgetown, Dulverton TA22 9JR (Somerset) T: 01643 851432. E: info@exevalleycamping.co.uk

alanrogers.com/UK1590

Occupying a prime position in a wooded valley alongside the River Exe, within the National Park, Exe Valley Caravan Site is ideally situated for visiting the Doone Valley, Tarr Steps, Dulverton and many other beautiful venues in the area. This quiet, four-acre adult only campsite is owned and managed by Paul and Christine Matthews. Set beside the River Exe, or the millstream, there are 50 large pitches (mostly grass but with some hardstandings at the top end), of which 41 have 10A electricity and TV hook-ups (cable provided on loan). Reception is now at the entrance. The owner's home is an old mill, complete with water wheel and grindstones that are in working order. Open for visits most Sundays at 10.00, CCTV has been installed so campers may watch the bat colony in the loft from a screen in the mill. A small shop run by the wardens stocks local produce and some camping requirements. Fly fishing along the River Exe is possible from the site or at Wimbleball Reservoir just over four miles away. This part of Somerset is a haven for walking, cycling, pony trekking, or as a place to just sit and relax.

Facilities

The toilet block houses the usual facilities and an en-suite room for disabled visitors (short steep ramp to enter). Excellent laundry with domestic washing and drying machines, plus a microwave and freezer. Motorcaravan service point. Small shop. Bicycle hire. Gas supplies. Free fly fishing. WiFi. This is an adult-only park. Off site: Riding 4 miles. Golf 12 miles. Pub at Bridgetown. Winsford village has a general stores and tea rooms.

Open: 15 March - 21 October.

Directions

Bridgetown is roughly midway between Dunster and Tiverton on the A396. On entering Bridgetown from Tiverton, look for site sign and turn left on minor road. Site is 50 yds. on the right.
GPS: 51.0882, -3.53875

Charges guide

Per unit incl. 2 persons,	
electricity (10A) and TV hook-up	£ 14.00 - £ 20.00
extra person	£ 4.50
awning	£ 1.00
dog	£ 1.00

No credit cards.

EXE VALLEY CARAVAN SITE
Within Exmoor National Park
Tel: 01643 851432   www.exevalleycamping.co.uk

Lyme Regis

Shrubbery Caravan & Camping Park

Rousdon, Lyme Regis DT7 3XW (Dorset) T: 01297 442227. E: info@shrubberypark.co.uk

alanrogers.com/UK1720

Three miles south of historic Lyme Regis, in a good situation to explore the Jurassic Coast, this well cared for park has distant views of the surrounding countryside. There are 120 generous pitches, 20 with hardstanding and more than enough room to pitch for most units. On slightly sloping, neatly cut grass which undulates in places, they are accessed by tarmac roads and all have 10A electricity. The pitches back on to well cut shrubs or the perimeter trees. A modern reception area is welcoming and stocks basic supplies and local provisions. This is a comfortable park where couples and families with young children are welcomed.

Facilities

Excellent heated toilet blocks, the newest (part of the reception building) with en-suite units, bathroom and laundry facilities. Two further blocks nearer the top of the park, fully equipped and well maintained. Facilities for disabled visitors. Simple shop at reception specialising in local produce. General store at adjacent fuel station. Play area. Crazy golf. Off site: Fishing 1 mile. Golf, beach and boat launching 3 miles. Riding 5 miles

Open: 1 April - 31 October.

Directions

From the A35 near Axminster follow A358 towards Seaton. At T-junction turn left on A3052 signed Rousdon and Lyme Regis. Site entrance is on the left a few yards after Rousdon Garage.
GPS: 50.71734, -2.99521

Charges guide

Per unit incl. 2 persons	
and electricity	£ 15.50 - £ 20.50
extra person	£ 3.75
child (4-16 yrs)	£ 3.00
dog	£ 0.75

FREE Alan Rogers Travel Card
Extra benefits and savings - see page 10

Malmesbury
Burton Hill Caravan Park
Arches Lane, Malmesbury SN16 0EH (Wiltshire) T: 01666 826 880. E: audrey@burtonhill.co.uk
alanrogers.com/UK1665

The owners of this park, Audrey and Warren Hateley, tend it with pride. It is a flat, grassy site surrounded by hedges, with open views across farmland on the outskirts of historic Malmesbury. The approach is through a well tended 'village' of park homes. There are 28 numbered touring pitches each with 16A electricity, with eight more for tents. There are limited amenities on-site but you will find a choice of shops, inns and restaurants in the town which is a short walk (10-15 minutes) across the river. Here you can also visit the Abbey House Gardens, Abbey and 15th-century market place.

Facilities

Modern, well equipped and well maintained heated toilet block with free hot water. Separate well equipped facilities for disabled visitors. Washing machine. Motorcaravan service point. Fishing. Max. 2 dogs. Off site: Malmesbury also has a new sports centre and swimming pool. Golf 6 miles.

Open: 1 April/Easter - 31 October.

Directions

From M4 exit 17 follow the A4129 towards Cirencester (5 miles). At approach to Malmesbury at international caravan sign, turn left into Arches Lane, and follow signs. If you miss the turning carry on to roundabout, return and turn right into Arches Lane. GPS: 51.579083, -2.097321

Charges guide

Per unit incl. 2 persons and electricity	£ 18.50
extra person	£ 4.00
child (5-15 yrs)	£ 3.00
dog (max. 2)	free

Martock
Southfork Caravan Park
Parrett Works, Martock TA12 6AE (Somerset) T: 01935 825661. E: southforkcaravans@btconnect.com
alanrogers.com/UK1420

Don't be put off by the address, which is historic – this was once a 17th-century flax mill. Michael and Nancy Broadley now own and run this excellent, modern, well drained site just outside the lovely village of Martock. With 25 touring pitches on grass with a gravel access road (22 with 10A electrical hook-ups and two with water and waste water), it is an orderly, quiet park on two acres of flat, tree lined meadow near the River Parrett. All the expected facilities are close to the entrance and as the owners live on the premises, the park is open all year. Most things are available, including an NCC approved caravan repairs/servicing centre. Despite the rural setting, the A303 trunk road is just five minutes away. This area of south Somerset contains much of interest, including gardens, historic houses and sites, the Fleet Air Arm Museum and Haynes Motor Museum. Information about access to many cycle routes and numerous walks, including the Parrett Trail, is available from reception.

Facilities

The heated, well maintained toilet block is fully equipped and includes some washbasins in cabins and free hot showers. Laundry room with washing machine and dryer. Shop with local produce. Off-licence selling local cider and beer. Play area. Fishing permits from reception. Enclosed dog exercise area. Off site: Fishing (with licences) on the River Parrett a few yards from the park. Pubs with good food in South Petherton and Martock, less than 2 miles in each direction. Golf 5 miles. Bicycle hire 8 miles. Riding 10 miles.

Open: All year.

Directions

From A303 between Ilchester and Ilminster turn north at the roundabout signed for South Petherton. At T-junction in middle of village, turn right towards Martock. Park is at Parrett Works midway between the two villages (about 1.5 miles from South Petherton). GPS: 50.965367, -2.789817

Charges guide

Per unit incl. 2 persons and electricity	£ 17.00 - £ 22.00
extra person	£ 2.50
child (under 5 yrs)	free
dog	£ 1.00

Minehead
Burrowhayes Farm Caravan & Camping Site

West Luccombe, Porlock, Minehead TA24 8HT (Somerset) T: 01643 862463. E: info@burrowhayes.co.uk

alanrogers.com/UK1370

This delightful park with riding stables on site, is on the edge of Exmoor. The stone packhorse bridge over Horner Water beside the farm entrance sets the tone of the park, which the Dascombe family have created over the last forty years having previously farmed the land. The farm buildings have been converted into riding stables with escorted rides available (from Easter). Touring and tent pitches are on a partly sloping field with marvellous views, or a flatter location in a clearing by the river, while 20 caravan holiday homes are in a separate area. Electrical hook-ups are available (16A), although some require long leads (25 m). Six new fully serviced pitches have been added. With walking, birdwatching, plenty of wildlife to observe, pretty Exmoor villages and Lorna Doone country nearby there is much to do. Children can ride, play in the stream or explore the woods at the top of the site. Limited trout fishing is available in Horner Water (NT permit) alongside the park.

Facilities

The heated toilet block provides controllable hot showers, one washbasin cubicle for each sex, hairdressing and shaving areas, laundry room, unit for disabled visitors and babies. A second older block is opened in high season with extra WCs and washbasins. Motorcaravan service point. Well stocked shop doubles with reception (from 1/4). Riding stables. Dogs must be kept on a lead at all times and exercised off site. Off site: Beach and fishing 2 miles. Minehead and bicycle hire 5 miles. Golf 6 miles. Local pub 20 minutes walk.

Open: 15 March - 31 October.

Directions

From A39, 5 miles west of Minehead, take first left past Allerford to Horner and West Luccombe. Site is on right after 400 yds. GPS: 51.203533, -3.5778

Charges guide

Per unit incl. 2 persons and electricity	£ 14.50 - £ 22.00
extra person	£ 5.00 - £ 6.00
child (3-16 yrs)	£ 2.50 - £ 3.00
dog	free

In the heart of Exmoor Country
Burrowhayes Farm
Caravan & Camping Site
Riding Stables
Tel: 01643 862 463
www.burrowhayes.co.uk

Minehead
Halse Farm Touring Caravan & Camping Park

Winsford, Minehead TA24 7JL (Somerset) T: 01643 851259. E: ar@halsefarm.co.uk

alanrogers.com/UK1360

A truly rural park with beautiful, moorland views, you may be lucky enough to glimpse red deer across the valley or see ponies and foals grazing outside the main gate which is adjacent to the moor. Two open, neatly cut fields (level at the top) back onto traditional hedging and slope gently to the middle and bottom where wild flowers predominate. One field provides 10A electricity points and is used for motorcaravans and caravans, the other is for tents. There is no reception – leave your unit by the toilet block and walk down to the farm kitchen to book in. The pretty village of Winsford is one mile (footpath from farm) with a post office, shop, pub and restaurant. Mrs Brown has laminated maps available (at a small cost) detailing six walks of varying distances, starting and finishing at the farm. Also available is a list of the flora and fauna to be found on the site. A member of the Countryside Discovery group.

Facilities

The central toilet block is heated, well equipped and maintained. It includes a toilet, washbasin and shower for visitors with disabilities, washing machine, dryer and iron, and tourist information. Gas is available at the farm. Play equipment. Off site: Winsford village 1 mile. Riding 2 miles. Tarr Steps and Barle Valley 3 miles. Fishing 4 miles. Bicycle hire 15 miles.

Open: 16 March - 31 October.

Directions

Turn off A396 Tiverton-Minehead road for Winsford. In Winsford village turn left in front of Royal Oak (avoiding ford), continue uphill for 1 mile. Cross cattle grid onto moor and turn immediately left to farm. Caravans should avoid Dulverton – keep to the A396 from Bridgetown. GPS: 51.097717, -3.579983

Charges guide

Per unit incl. 2 persons and electricity	£ 15.50 - £ 17.50
extra person	£ 6.25 - £ 7.25
child (5-16 yrs)	£ 2.00
dog	free

Less 10% for 7 days paid in advance
14 days before arrival.

FREE Alan Rogers Travel Card
Extra benefits and savings - see page 10

Minehead
Westermill Farm
Exford, Minehead TA24 7NJ (Somerset) T: 01643 831238. E: info@westermill.com
alanrogers.com/UK1301

This superbly located farm campsite can be found nestling in a valley beside the River Exe. The working farm provides four meadows, all without electricity, and is ideal for 'back to basics' style touring. Uniquely, open fires are permitted in one field with logs being available to purchase. You can marvel at the wildlife, wander around the working farm and sample the farm's own produce in the shop, which also stocks basic provisions. Walking maps can be found at reception which is located in the old dairy.

Facilities

The unheated toilet block houses the usual facilities including showers and washbasins and hot water is provided by solar energy. Laundry facilities. Farm shop (end May - early Sept). Gas supplies. Facility for freezer packs (20p). Fishing in the River Exe. The river is also used for bathing. Off site: Village 2.5 miles. Bicycle hire 6 miles. Riding 15 miles. Beach 15 miles.

Open: All year.

Directions

Leave Exford on Porlock Road with Post Office on right. At Y fork turn left down single track road. Farm is 2 miles on right. Do not use sat nav. GPS: 51.145631, -3.682158

Charges guide

Per person	£ 6.50
car	£ 2.50

No credit cards.

Salisbury
Church Farm Caravan & Camping Park
Sixpenny Handley, Salisbury SP5 5ND (Wiltshire) T: 01725 553005. E: churchfarmcandcpark@yahoo.co.uk
alanrogers.com/UK1655

Sixpenny Handley is a Saxon hilltop village with St Mary's church dating back some 900 years; from the site you can hear the bells and the chimes of its clock. Church Farm, next to the village centre, offers 35 partly sheltered, level, spacious pitches including some hardstandings, all with 10A, arranged around the perimeter of two fields, plus a tent field. It is in an Area of Outstanding Natural Beauty and the views and many walks are an absolute delight. Not forgetting the hundreds of tumuli and prehistoric remains, there are many places for the visitor to discover the delights around this junction of Dorset, Hampshire and Wiltshire. Arrivals to park should be after 2pm.

Facilities

A spacious and modern eco building houses reception, a seasonal café/bar, and up-to-date heated toilet facilities. Dedicated room for disabled visitors. Baby changing. Laundry. Freezer for ice packs. Gas. Motorcaravan service point. Play area with new adventure type equipment. Two holiday caravans for rent. Off site: The village has a bus stop, small shops, a small supermarket and Post Office. The Roebuck Inn offers a varied menu. Golf 4 miles.

Open: All year.

Directions

To avoid the village centre, 1 mile southwest of the Handley Cross roundabout on A354 turn towards Sixpenny Handley, then right by the school and site 300 yds. by church. GPS: 50.955317, -2.006883

Charges guide

Per unit incl. 2 persons and electricity	£ 17.50 - £ 19.50
extra person	£ 7.50 - £ 8.50

Salisbury
Coombe Touring Park
Coombe Nurseries Race Plain, Netherhampton, Salisbury SP2 8PN (Wiltshire) T: 01722 328451.
E: enquiries@coombecaravanpark.co.uk alanrogers.com/UK1650

A touring park with outstanding views over the Chalke Valley, Coombe is adjacent to Salisbury racecourse. There are 100 spacious pitches all on level, well mown grass, 66 with 10A electricity. Tent pitches are generally around the outer perimeter and there are four caravan holiday homes to rent. Many pitches are individual and sheltered by mature hedging. Reception also has a small shop, there are supermarkets in Salisbury (4.5 miles), and pubs in Netherhampton and Coombe Bissett (2 miles) both serving meals.

Facilities

A well built, modern, heated sanitary unit provides an ample supply of WCs, spacious pushbutton showers, washbasins in cubicles for the ladies. A family room (with bath) has facilities for disabled visitors, babies and toddlers. Laundry. Small shop (May-Sept). Gas available. Good tourist information chalet. Open grass play area with slide and new adventure feature. Off site: Golf 400 yds. Riding and tennis in Wilton 2.5 miles. Indoor pool, leisure centre and cinema in Salisbury 4.5 miles.

Open: All year.

Directions

From A36, 2 miles west of Salisbury (east of Wilton roundabout), turn south on A3094 (Netherhampton and Harnham). After 0.5 miles on sharp, left hand bend turn right to Stratford Tony and racecourse. At top of hill and turn left (signed) on narrow lane behind racecourse for 700 yds. to site entrance. GPS: 51.05428, -1.86092

Charges guide

Per unit incl. 2 persons and electricity	£ 15.00 - £ 20.00

No credit cards.

For latest campsite news visit
alanrogers.com

Salisbury
Greenhill Farm Caravan & Camping Park

New Road, Landford, Salisbury SP5 2AZ (Wiltshire) T: 01794 324117. E: info@greenhillholidays.co.uk

alanrogers.com/UK1640

Located on the northern edge of the New Forest National Park, this site occupies 14 out of 50 acres of beautiful forest owned by the family. It is an uncommercialised hideaway and has two distinctive areas: the 'adults only' area, fenced, gated and set around two small lakes, one of which is reserved for coarse fishing; and the 'family' area with a playground, views over the meadow, sightings of deer and a generally open aspect. There are 160 pitches in total, with 50 for tents in a separate hilltop meadow with views over the nearby forest and its own fishing lake. The remainder are for touring units with some seasonal pitches and a number of hardstandings. All pitches are level and with 16A electricity.

Facilities

Two new toilet blocks and two Portacabin style units with excellent facilities include provision for families and disabled visitors. Laundry with washing machine and dryer. Reception/shop. Gas supplies. Takeaway in high season in 'family' area. Room for special events. Bicycle hire. Coarse fishing lakes (£4.00 per rod per day). Torches useful. Off site: Several pubs serving meals are nearby.

Open: All year.

Directions

From M27 exit 2 take A36 north towards Salisbury for 6 miles. Pass through West Wellow and after B.P. garage on left, take next left (New Road), continue to site entrance on left. GPS: 50.96445, -1.62575

Charges guide

Per unit incl. 2 persons and electricity	£ 17.00 - £ 25.00
tent incl. 2 persons	£ 15.00 - £ 25.00

Shepton Mallet
Batcombe Vale Campsite

Batcombe Vale, Shepton Mallet BA4 6BW (Somerset) T: 01749 831207. E: gary.butler1@virgin.net

alanrogers.com/UK1540

Set in a secluded valley with fields gently rising around it, contented cows grazing with watchful buzzards cruising above and views across the distant hills, this is a very special place. Descending slowly down the steep, narrow drive you see the pitches, attractively set and terraced where necessary, in an oval with the lakes below. The grass is left natural around the 32 pitches (20 have 10A electricity) and paths are mown where needed. Batcombe Vale House is an attractive, mellow building covered with wisteria, to one side of the valley overlooking the lakes and the wilder landscape. Trees and shrubs have been skilfully placed to enhance the natural environment providing a range of colours and shapes.

Facilities

The small rustic toilet block covered in honeysuckle meets all needs, including a freezer (ice packs only) and hot water to dishwashing sinks. Launderette. Groundsheet awnings must be lifted daily. Fishing. Rowing boats. Caravan storage. Bed and breakfast available in Batcombe Vale House. Max. 1 dog (unless by prior arrangement; no dangerous breeds). Off site: Bruton and Evercreech 2 miles.

Open: 1 April - end September.

Directions

Bruton is south of Shepton Mallet and Frome and north of Wincanton where A359 intersects B3081. Access to site must be via Evercreech or Bruton (B3081), then follow the brown and white signs. Access drive is steep. GPS: 51.136467, -2.453167

Charges guide

Per unit incl. 2 persons and electricity	£ 21.70
extra person	£ 5.25
Family groups only. No credit cards.	

Shepton Mallet
Greenacres Camping

Barrow Lane, North Wootton, Shepton Mallet BA4 4HL (Somerset) T: 01749 890497. E: stay@greenacres-camping.co.uk **alanrogers.com/UK1490**

Greenacres is a rural site in the Somerset countryside for tents, trailer tents and small motorcaravans only. Hidden away below the Mendips and almost at the start of the Levels, it is a simple green site – a true haven of peace and quiet. The grass is neatly trimmed over the 4.5 acres and hedged with mature trees, though there is a view of Glastonbury Tor in one direction and of Barrow Hill in the other. All of the 40 pitches are around the perimeter of the park, leaving a central area safe for children to play.

Facilities

The central wooden toilet block is simple but clean. Hot showers are accessed directly from outside. Small shop and a van calls in high season with local produce. Play equipment, football, badminton net and play house. The park office (and bicycle hire), is across the lane. New cabin with fridges and freezers for campers' use (free), library and tourist information. WiFi (charged). Dogs are not accepted. No electric barbecues.

Open: April - September.

Directions

From A361 Glastonbury-Shepton Mallet road follow camp signs from Pilton or Steanbow. (Roads are narrow with few passing places). GPS: 51.172367, -2.641883

Charges guide

Per person	£ 8.50
child (2-14 yrs)	£ 3.00

FREE Alan Rogers Travel Card
Extra benefits and savings - see page 10

Sparkford

Long Hazel Park

High Street, Sparkford, Yeovil BA22 7JH (Somerset) T: 01963 440002. E: longhazelpark@hotmail.com

alanrogers.com/UK1500

Pamela and Alan Walton are really enthusiastic about their small, beautifully kept, adults only park in the Somerset village of Sparkford, where they will make you most welcome. This level, landscaped park is surrounded by attractive beech hedging, silver birch and many other ornamental trees and the park has a relaxed, comfortable feel. It provides 50 touring pitches for all types of units (max. 12 m) with 16A electricity hook-ups, 30 pitches with hardstanding, some extra long with grass lawns at the side, and the entrance has been widened for easier access. Part of the park is being developed with holiday lodges for private ownership or rent.

Facilities

The toilet block is clean, well equipped and heated. Well planned en-suite facilities for visitors with disabilities. Washing machine and dryer. Motorcaravan waste water discharge. Shop (all year). Gas supplies. Details of safe cycle routes and walks available at reception. Seasonal pitches available. WiFi over part of site (charged). Off site: Bus service, village inn 100 yds. Spar shop and McDonalds 400 yds. Haynes Motor Museum 1 mile. Golf 5 miles. Riding and fishing 8 miles. Yeovilton Fleet Air Arm Museum.

Open: All year.

Directions

At roundabout on A303 take road into village of Sparkford and park is signed on the left 100 yds. before the inn. GPS: 51.0344, -2.568633

Charges guide

Per unit incl. 2 persons	
and electricity	£ 21.00 - £ 26.00
extra person	£ 5.00
dog	£ 1.00

Taunton

Lowtrow Cross Caravan Site

Upton, Wiveliscombe, Taunton TA4 2DB (Somerset) T: 01398 371199. E: info@lowtrowcross.co.uk

alanrogers.com/UK1355

Lowtrow Cross is a small, adults only park situated just inside Exmoor National Park and is ideal for owners of well behaved dogs. It is quietly located on a hillside giving lovely views north towards the Brendon Hills. There are 18 pitches, three occupied by caravan holiday homes (two for hire) and six seasonal, and all the remaining touring pitches are hardstanding with grass surround, with 16A electricity and TV socket. An adjacent meadow with stunning views over the rolling countryside can be used for tents. Although there is no bar or restaurant on site there is Lowtrow Cross Inn at the gate with local cask beers and excellent food. Lowtrow Cross is well situated for walking, cycling, riding and fishing in the beautiful Exmoor countryside with its wide variety of wildlife. Close by Haddon Moor, with its own herd of ponies and buzzards overhead, overlooks Wimbleball Lake where one can enjoy a variety of water based activities and nature trails. Clatworthy Reservoir is also convenient for walking and fishing, but dogs are not permitted here. Not far away are Dunster Castle, Porlock and the West Somerset Steam railway. The area is well known for its cider and there is a museum of cider-making at Taunton.

Facilities

Traditional heated, well equipped, toilet block but no facilities for disabled visitors. Excellent laundry room. Freezer and microwave. Small shop in reception selling basic foodstuffs; milk, bread, free range eggs, frozen meals, local produce, toiletries and Calor gas. Tourist information. Maps for sale and book exchange. Off site: Lowtrow Cross Inn at gate. Garage 750 m. Excellent fishing and boating 3 miles. Golf and riding 10 miles.

Open: March - October.

Directions

From M5 exit 25 follow signs for Minehead (A358) through Taunton, then 5 miles from Taunton turn west (left) on B3224 signed Raleigh Cross. Shortly after passing Raleigh Cross Inn turn south on the B3190 signed Bampton. Site is on right in 4 miles before Upton village. GPS: 51.053342, -3.419923

Charges guide

Per unit incl. 2 persons	
and electricity	£ 16.00 - £ 20.00
extra adult	£ 5.00
dog	free

Taunton
Cornish Farm Touring Park
Shoreditch, Taunton TA3 7BS (Somerset) T: 01823 327746. E: info@cornishfarm.com

alanrogers.com/UK1340

This neat little park, which opened for its first full season in 2006, is on level ground and conveniently located close to the M5 motorway. There are 49 pitches, all with 10A electricity, of which 25 are on gravel hardstanding. Most pitches are accessed from a gravel road (one-way system) with plenty of fresh water taps, site lighting and some picnic tables. A separate area for tents is close to the toilet block. Light power cables cross the site and there is some background motorway noise. Maximum length for motorcaravans is 30 ft, unless by prior arrangement with the wardens. With its old apple trees this park makes a very pleasant stopover. The centrally situated, modern toilet block is maintained to a high standard and includes underfloor heating. There are no other facilities on the park but a cycle path and a footpath will take you into Taunton town centre, which is worth a visit with its Castle, museum, a variety of livestock and produce markets and an annual flower show. The park is also a good base from which to visit Cheddar Gorge, Wookey Hole, and Clarke's shopping village at Street.

Facilities

One central block has underfloor heating and modern fittings and you can listen to the local radio. Large, dual purpose room providing facilities for disabled visitors and small children. Dusk to dawn low energy lighting. Laundry room. Motorcaravan service point. Camping supplies for sale and plenty of tourist information available. On-site PC repair facility. WiFi. Off site: Village pub and shops are a short walk away. Level cycle/footpath into Taunton (2 miles) which has a castle, museum, and markets. Tesco Express 1 mile. Golf, fishing and bicycle hire 2 miles. Riding 4 miles.

Open: All year.

Directions

From M5 exit 25 follow signs for Taunton. At first set of lights (Creech Castle) turn left (Corfe B3170). Take third left into Ilminster Road (Corfe). Right at roundabout (Blackbrook Way), left at next roundabout and follow to T-junction (B3170). Turn right then next left (Killams Drive). Take second left (Killams Ave) and cross motorway. Site entrance is on left the bridge. GPS: 50.99200, -3.09257

Charges guide

Per unit incl. 2 persons and electricity	£ 14.00 - £ 18.00
extra person	£ 2.10 - £ 3.50

Taunton
Quantock Orchard Caravan Park
Crowcombe, Taunton TA4 4AW (Somerset) T: 01984 618618. E: member@flaxpool.freeserve.co.uk

alanrogers.com/UK1350

Quantock Orchard nestles at the foot of the Quantocks in quiet countryside, close to many of the attractions of the area. Attractively developed, mature apple trees, recently planted trees, shrubs and pretty flower beds with a nice use of heathers, make a pleasant environment. The clock tower on the wooden sanitary block and a dovecote at the entrance add interest. With access from fairly narrow gravel roads, there are 69 touring pitches, part separated by growing shrubs and hedging, of which 40 are for tents. Of various sizes, all touring pitches have 15A electricity, 30 have hardstanding and 8 are fully serviced (two extra large, with patio and barbecue). Levelling blocks are required on some pitches.

Facilities

The central, heated sanitary block is very well maintained. Microwave. Laundry facilities. Facilities for disabled visitors but no shower. Licensed shop. Swimming pool (40x20 ft. and open May-Sept). Leisure suite. Games room, Sky TV. Fenced safe-based play area. Mountain bike hire. Caravan storage (Oct-Mar). Holiday homes for hire. Free WiFi.

Open: All year.

Directions

Park is west off A358 (Taunton-Minehead), 1 mile south of Crowcombe. GPS: 51.1084, -3.22645

Charges guide

Per unit incl. 2 persons and electricity	£ 15.00 - £ 28.50
extra person	£ 6.00

FREE Alan Rogers Travel Card
Extra benefits and savings - see page 10

Taunton
Waterrow Touring Park
Wiveliscombe, Taunton TA4 2AZ (Somerset) T: 01984 623464. E: info@waterrowpark.co.uk

alanrogers.com/UK1520

Beside the River Tone in a pretty part of South Somerset, Tony and Anne Taylor have enthusiastically developed Waterrow into a charming, landscaped touring park for adults only. Nestling in a little sheltered valley, it is very peaceful and possible for an overnight stop (just over 30 minutes from M5) or ideal as a base for exploring nearby Exmoor and the Brendon Hills. There are 48 touring pitches, most of which are on level hardstandings, including five with full services. All have 16A electricity, spring and mains water are available and TV aerial points have been installed (your own lead is required, sometimes quite long). A small area has been set aside for tent campers. A member of the Best of British group.

Facilities

A modern, clean, heated toilet block provides WCs and washbasins, some in curtained cubicles. Heated shower block. Facilities for disabled visitors (key). Laundry facilities. Motorcaravan service point. Limited provisions are available in reception. Regular watercolour painting and drawing courses (May-Oct). Additional fly fishing holidays can be arranged at certain times. WiFi (charged). Caravan storage. Max. 2 dogs. Cottage for hire.

Open: All year.

Directions

From M5 exit 25 take A358 (signed Minehead) round Taunton for 4 miles, then at Staplegrove onto B3227 for 11.5 miles to Wiveliscombe, where straight over at lights to Waterrow (still on B3227). Park is on left shortly after the Rock Inn. Do not use sat nav. GPS: 51.0165, -3.352717

Charges guide

Per unit incl. 2 persons (adults only) and electricity	£ 16.00 - £ 26.00

Warminster
Longleat Caravan Club Site
Warminster BA12 7NL (Wiltshire) T: 01985 844663

alanrogers.com/UK1690

What a magnificent situation in which to find a caravan park, amidst all the wonders of the Longleat Estate including the Elizabethan House, gardens designed by Capability Brown and the Safari Park. Visitors can roam the woodlands (leaflets are available), enjoy the views, watch the wildlife and marvel at the azaleas, bluebells, etc. and listen to the occupants of the Safari Park. The site itself, which sits alongside the National Cycle Network no. 24, is well managed by Caravan Club wardens and is situated in ten acres of lightly wooded, level grassland within walking distance of the house and gardens. There are 165 generous pitches (139 with hardstanding and 26 on grass), all with 16A electricity connections.

Facilities

Two heated toilet blocks provide washbasins in cubicles, controllable showers and a vanity section with mirrors and hairdryers. Baby/toddler room, suite for disabled visitors, laundry room and a family room with a DVD player. Two motorcaravan service points. Play area. Office is manned 09.00-17.30 and stocks basic food items, papers to order and gas is available. Paperback exchange library. Fish and chip van calls some evenings. WiFi. Late arrivals area.

Open: 23 March - 5 November.

Directions

All arrivals must now enter Longleat from A362 (Warminster-Frome). Turn left off A36 Warminster bypass at roundabout onto A362. In 500 yds. at roundabout take 3rd exit (Frome). After some 2 miles turn into Lane End by White Hart Pub, pass Safari Park entrance and Stalls Farm, then left again. Site entrance is in 200 yds. GPS: 51.1907, -2.278517

Charges guide

Per person	£ 5.60 - £ 7.60
pitch incl. electricity (non-member)	£ 13.40 - £ 17.50

For latest campsite news visit
alanrogers.com

Westbury

Brokerswood Country Park

Brokerswood, Westbury BA13 4EH (Wiltshire) T: 01373 822238. E: info@brokerswoodcountrypark.co.uk

alanrogers.com/UK1630

This countryside campsite is located in an 80-acre country park, with ancient broadleaf woodland, plenty of marked walks, a woodland railway which also runs Santa Specials (bookings taken from 1 August). The campsite has 69 pitches arranged around an open meadow area, served by a circular gravel roadway, with low level site lighting. There are 25 hardstanding pitches, and 44 electricity hook-ups (10A). Although fairly recently laid out, the site is maturing well. American RVs and other large units should use the coach entrance and they (and all other arrivals after 18.00) are asked to phone ahead so that arrangements can be made for the barrier.

Facilities

Two well insulated and heated, timber clad buildings are at one end of the site. Some washbasins in cubicles, large, controllable hot showers. Family rooms (on payment). Fully equipped suite for disabled campers with ramped approach and alarm. Laundry and ironing facilities. Motorcaravan services. Gas available. Milk, bread, newspapers to order from reception/shop. Fully licensed café serving meals and refreshments all day. Takeaway food service during peak times. Fishing. Entry barrier (key code). Cycling allowed on site but not in Country Park. Ready erected tents for hire. Off site: Nearest shops are at Dilton Marsh and Westbury.

Open: All year.

Directions

From Trowbridge take A361 south for 2 miles, turning left (east) at Southwick, and follow signs to Country Park. GPS: 51.270283, -2.231417

Charges guide

Per unit incl. 4 persons	
and electricity	£ 12.00 - £ 31.00
extra person (aged 1 or more)	£ 4.95
dog	£ 1.00

Weymouth

Bagwell Farm Touring Park

Chickerell, Weymouth DT3 4EA (Dorset) T: 01305 782575. E: ar@bagwellfarm.co.uk

alanrogers.com/UK1820

A friendly, welcoming, family park, Bagwell Farm is situated between Weymouth and Abbotsbury, close to Chesil Beach. In a valley, yet with an open aspect, there are 320 numbered touring pitches, some taken up by seasonal units. There are 260 electricity connections (10A) and 35 serviced pitches (16A) with hardstanding. Some of the terraced pitches have beautiful views of Chesil Bank and the sea. In addition there is a traditional camping field with a campers' shelter. An attractive bar has been converted from farm buildings where meals are served. Steaks are a speciality – the family farm has a herd of Charolais cattle. The bar is open at weekends in mid-season and daily in high season. A patio overlooks a good pets' corner (also open to the public). There is a large dog walking field, with a wealth of wild flowers in summer. There are clear instructions on how to reach the coastal path and a list of wildlife seen on the park is kept in reception.

Facilities

Modern, heated block with four en-suite family rooms and a unit for disabled visitors (Radar key). Two traditional blocks have two family bathrooms (£1). Launderette. Wet suit wash. Very well stocked shop (open all day). Bar (Easter-Oct). Good fenced play area. Camper's shelter and communal barbecue. WiFi (charged). Bus service on main road. Off site: Situated on the Jurassic Coastline within easy reach of Weymouth (5 miles) and its sandy beach. Many activities available nearby including walking, sailing, diving and exploring the beautiful countryside. Riding 1 mile. Sailing 7 miles.

Open: All year.

Directions

Park is 3 miles west of Weymouth. Follow the B3157 from Weymouth towards Bridport. Park is 1 mile west of Chickerell on the B3157. The entrance is on the brow of a hill – care is needed. GPS: 50.63088, -2.51999

Charges guide

Per unit incl. 2 persons	
and electricity	£ 16.50 - £ 28.00
super-pitch (all services)	£ 20.00 - £ 30.00
extra person	£ 5.00
child (2-15 yrs)	£ 1.00 - £ 1.50
dog	£ 1.00

FREE Alan Rogers Travel Card
Extra benefits and savings - see page 10

Weymouth
East Fleet Farm Touring Park
Fleet Lane, Chickerell, Weymouth DT3 4DW (Dorset) T: 01305 785768. E: enquiries@eastfleet.co.uk

alanrogers.com/UK1800

East Fleet Farm has a marvellous situation on part level, part gently sloping meadows leading to the shores of the Fleet, with views across to the famous Chesil Bank with the sea beyond. This park has been developed by the Whitfield family within the confines of their 300 acre organic arable farm in keeping with its surroundings, yet with modern amenities. It is maturing well as bushes and trees grow. The 400 pitches back onto hedges and are a comfortable size so there is no feeling of crowding. Of these, 350 are level and marked with 10/16A electric hook-ups, over 70 also have hardstanding. The large shop has a very good range of camping equipment and outdoor gear.

Facilities

Two fully equipped toilet blocks include en-suite family rooms. The newest one is very smart in a Norwegian log cabin. En-suite unit for disabled visitors. Laundry room. Motorcaravan service point. Reception plus shop with groceries, bread, papers, gas and camping accessories. Bar serving food with terrace (Easter-Sept). Large play barn with table tennis and gym equipment. Fenced play area. Games field. Nature watch boards. WiFi (charged). Off site: Riding and golf 2 miles. Fishing, boat launching, sailing, bicycle hire and sandy beach 3 miles.

Open: 15 March - 31 October.

Directions

Park is signed at traffic lights on B3157 Weymouth-Bridport road, 3 miles west of Weymouth beside Territorial Army base. Fleet Lane has been widened with plenty of passing places and speed bumps (20 mph). GPS: 50.61927, -2.50040

Charges guide

Per unit incl. 2 persons	£ 14.00 - £ 25.00
incl. electricity	£ 16.00 - £ 28.50
extra person	£ 1.00 - £ 5.00
child (5-12 yrs)	£ 1.00 - £ 2.00

Weymouth
Sea Barn & West Fleet Holiday Farms
Fleet Road, Fleet, Weymouth DT3 4ED (Dorset) T: 01305 782218. E: enquiries@seabarnfarm.co.uk

alanrogers.com/UK1830

Sea Barn and West Fleet are located just half a mile apart in delightful countryside overlooking the Fleet, Chesil Bank and Lyme Bay, all part of the Jurassic coast. Only tents, trailer tents and motorcaravans with tents and awnings are accepted. The parks share some facilities. West Fleet has 250 pitches, 112 with electricity, Sea Barn has the same number of pitches but only 55 electric hook-ups. These are situated in grassy meadows, some sloping, some protected by trees and hedging, many with wonderful views. West Fleet has a newly rebuilt Clubhouse with bar, which serves good local steaks. An outdoor pool and clubhouse are at West Fleet, and a smart new toilet block at Sea Barn. Both have their own reception with well stocked shops. Sea Barn is quieter and popular over a longer period with spectacular views, whereas West Fleet attracts families.

Facilities

A modern block at both sites with en-suite room for disabled visitors and two bathrooms plus a traditional block each for peak season. Laundry facilities at both sites. Heated pool at West Fleet (May-Sept). Bigger shop offering wider range at West Fleet which also has the Club House (evenings), with newly refurbished bar in a stone and brick building (home produced steaks the speciality). Breakfast served. Family entertainment. Adventure play area at West Fleet and smaller area at Sea Barn. Games field. Torches useful. WiFi (charged). Accommodation for rent. Off site: Riding 1 mile. Golf, bicycle hire, boat launching and beach all at Weymouth 5 miles.

Open: West Fleet Easter - September;
Sea Barn 16 March - October.

Directions

From Weymouth take the B3157 coast road for Abbotsbury. Pass Chickerell and turn left at mini-roundabout to Fleet. Pass church on right and continue to top of hill. Sea Barn is to the left, West Fleet to the right. GPS: 50.62539, -2.53865

Charges guide

Per unit incl. 2 persons and electricity	£ 15.00 - £ 26.00
extra person	£ 4.00 - £ 5.00
child (2-15 yrs)	£ 1.00 - £ 3.00
dog (max. 2)	£ 2.00 - £ 3.00

For latest campsite news visit
alanrogers.com

Rich in maritime heritage and historical attractions, the Southern region comprises tranquil English countryside boasting picture-postcard villages, ancient cities and towns, formidable castles and grand stately homes, coupled with a beautiful coastline and lively seaside resorts.

THIS REGION INCLUDES: EAST DORSET, HAMPSHIRE, ISLE OF WIGHT, OXFORDSHIRE, BERKSHIRE AND BUCKINGHAMSHIRE

The south coast is a popular holiday destination for those looking for a beach holiday. Seaside resorts include Swanage, and Bournemouth, with its seven miles of golden sand. Also along this coastal stretch is Durdle Door, a natural arch that has been cut by the sea, and Europe's largest natural harbour at Poole Bay. Nearby, the Isle of Purbeck is not actually an island, but a promontory of low hills and heathland that juts out below Poole Harbour. Across the water is the Isle of Wight, easily reached via a short ferry trip across the Solent. Rural Southern England comprises green, rolling hills and scenic wooded valleys, with numerous walking and bridle paths passing through picturesque villages with quintessential English pubs. The New Forest, well known for its wild roaming ponies, is a distinctive, peaceful retreat. The River Thames weaves its way through the Thames basin and Chilterns area, passing charming riverside villages, castles, stately homes and beautiful countryside, including that around Oxford. This 'city of dreaming spires' has lovely scenic walks, old university buildings to explore, plus a huge selection of restaurants, pubs and shops. Along the river you can go punting, hire a rowing boat, or take one of the many river-boat trips available.

Places of interest

East Dorset: Monkey World near Wareham; village of Cerne Abbas, with Cerne Giant.

Hampshire: Winchester, ancient capital of England; Portsmouth's historic dockyard and Spinnaker Tower; Southampton's West Quay shopping complex and city art gallery.

Isle of Wight: Cowes; Sandown with Dinosaur Isle; Shipwreck Centre in Ryde; Smuggling Museum in Ventnor; Carisbrooke Castle in Newport.

Oxfordshire: Blenheim Palace; Oxford University buildings; Ashmolean Museum, Oxford; River and Rowing Museum, Henley-on-Thames. Bicester Shopping Village.

Berkshire: Windsor, with Legoland, Windsor Castle; Reading.

Buckinghamshire: Bletchley Park and Stowe Landscape Gardens near Milton Keynes; Waddesdon Manor, Aylesbury; Bekonscot Model Village and Railway, Beaconsfield.

Did you know?

The Ashmolean Museum, Oxford was the first museum to be opened to the public in 1683.

There are over 200 scheduled ancient monuments within the New Forest National Park.

The first Cowes regatta was held in 1812, and 'Cowes Week' is now the world's biggest international yachting event.

Quar stone from the Isle of Wight was used in the construction of the Tower of London.

The Spitfire aircraft, used to great effect during the Battle of Britain was devised in Southampton.

The first ever dry dock was constructed in Portsmouth in 1495.

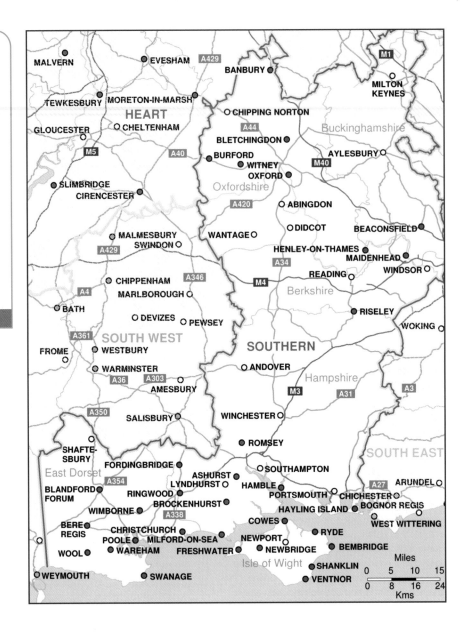

For latest campsite news visit
alanrogers.com

Ashurst
Forest Holidays Ashurst

Forest Holidays, Lyndhurst Road, Ashurst SO4O 7AR (Hampshire) T: 023 8029 2097.
E: info@forestholidays.co.uk **alanrogers.com/UK2300**

Forest Holidays is a partnership between the Forestry Commission and the Camping & Caravanning Club. An attractive site, Ashurst is on the fringe of the New Forest, set in a mixture of oak woodland and grass heathland which is open to the grazing animals of the Forest. Smaller than the Hollands Wood site (23 acres), it provides 280 pitches, some of which have been gravelled to provide semi-hardstanding; otherwise you pitch where you like, applying the 20 ft. rule on ground that can be uneven. There are no electricity connections. Some noise must be expected from the adjacent railway line.

Facilities

The single well kept central toilet block (may be under pressure in main season) provides everything necessary, including hairdryers and a well equipped unit for visitors with disabilities. Good laundry room. Motorcaravan service point. Freezer pack service and charging of batteries (fee). Torches useful. Dogs are not accepted. Off site: Shops and local buses within a five minute walk. Guided forest walks are organised during the main season. Golf 2 miles.

Open: 29 March - 1 October.

Directions

From Southampton, follow A35 west through village of Ashurst, continue over railway bridge and site is 200 yds. on left. GPS: 50.88810, -1.52846

Charges guide

Per unit incl. 2 persons	£ 12.50 - £ 21.15
extra person	£ 4.50 - £ 9.00
child (5-16 yrs)	£ 1.75 - £ 2.60

Discounts for families, backpackers, disabled guests and senior citizens.

Banbury
Barnstones Caravan & Camping Park

Great Bourton, Banbury OX17 1QU (Oxfordshire) T: 01295 750289
alanrogers.com/UK2600

Three miles from Banbury and open all year round, this small, neat park provides an excellent point from which to explore the Cotswolds, Oxford and Stratford-upon-Avon. There are 49 level pitches of which 44 have gravel hardstanding with a grass area for awnings (only breathable groundsheets are allowed) and 10A electricity; 20 of these are fully serviced. Shrubs, flowers and an oval tarmac road convey an attractive, tidy impression throughout. The park provides a pleasant environment for couples and young families, but it is near the main road, so some traffic noise is to be expected.

Facilities

The good toilet block is small, but very clean, heated and well maintained. It is quite adequate for the number of visitors it serves. Good, tiled, adjustable showers. Laundry room and washing up area. Freezer. Gas supplies. Good enclosed play area. Boules. American motorhomes accepted by prior arrangement. Off site: Pub 150 yds. Nearest shop 1 mile. Supermarket, fishing, bicycle hire, golf and riding, all within 3 miles.

Open: All year.

Directions

From M40 take exit 11 for Banbury. Follow signs for Banbury and Southam. At Southam turn right (Great Bourton and Cropredy) and site is just on the right. GPS: 52.104966, -1.338868

Charges guide

Per unit incl. 2 persons and electricity	£ 12.00 - £ 14.00

OAPs less £1 per night. No credit cards.

Banbury
Bo Peep Caravan Park

Aynho Road, Adderbury, Banbury OX17 3NP (Oxfordshire) T: 01295 810605. E: warden@bo-peep.co.uk
alanrogers.com/UK2610

Set amongst 85 acres of farmland and woodland, there is an air of spacious informality about this delightful, friendly park which blends perfectly with the surrounding views. Warm Cotswold stone buildings, dovecotes and extensive planting of trees, shrubs and hedges enhance the natural environment of the park. There are 104 numbered pitches, all with 16A electricity, for caravans and motorcaravans in several areas, each with a different character. A separate four-acre field for tents provides a further 40 pitches, including four electricity points.

Facilities

The two toilet blocks are clean and heated. Large showers and hairdryers. Laundry rooms. Motorcaravan service point. Small shop with off-licence, gas and basic supplies. Information centre with Internet access. Fishing. Caravan storage. Caravan cleaning area. WiFi over site. Off site: Pub and golf 1 mile. Banbury 3 miles. Riding 10 miles. Blenheim Palace 15 miles. Silverstone 16 miles. Day trips to Stratford-upon-Avon and Warwick.

Open: 14 March - 26 October.

Directions

From north on M40 use exit 11, A422 (Banbury) then A4260. At traffic lights in Adderbury turn on B4100 (Aynho). Park is signed 0.5 miles on right. From the south on the M40 use exit 10 onto A43, then B4100 (Aynho and Adderbury). GPS: 52.01585, -1.299433

Charges guide

Per unit incl. 2 persons and electricity	£ 14.00 - £ 20.00

No credit cards.

FREE Alan Rogers Travel Card
Extra benefits and savings - see page 10

Beaconsfield

Highclere Farm Country Touring Park

Newbarn Lane, Seer Green, Beaconsfield HP9 2QZ (Buckinghamshire) T: 01494 874505.
E: highclerepark@aol.com **alanrogers.com/UK2750**

A magnificent sweeping drive provides the entrance to this peaceful park that backs onto fields and woodland. Originally developed around a working farm, the owners continue to keep chickens. There are 115 level pitches all with 10A electricity. Of these, 60 with gravel hardstanding are reserved for caravans and motorcaravans, the remainder being mainly used for tents. The atmosphere is friendly and informal, with reception doubling as a small shop supplying freshly laid eggs. At the top of the park is an open play area and a footpath leading to walks in the surrounding fields.

Facilities

The toilet and shower block is fully equipped and can be heated. Large showers (20p). Unit with toilet and washbasin for disabled visitors. Baby changing. Two new units provide extra large facilities including showers at 50p. Launderette. Fridge and freezer. Shop in reception. Play area. WiFi. Satellite TV connections. Off site: Pub serving food 0.25 miles. Golf 0.5 miles. Riding 2 miles. Bicycle hire 3 miles. Fishing 8 miles.

Open: All year excl. February.

Directions

From M40 exit 2 follow signs for Beaconsfield at first roundabout. Take A355 towards Amersham and after 1 mile turn right (Seer Green and Jordans) following signs to park. GPS: 51.625617, -0.590867

Charges guide

Per unit incl. 2 persons and electricity	£ 20.00 - £ 33.50
extra person	£ 1.00 - £ 2.00

Bembridge

Whitecliff Bay Holiday Park

Hillway, Whitecliff Bay, Bembridge PO35 5PL (Isle of Wight) T: 01983 872671. E: holiday@whitecliff-bay.com
alanrogers.com/UK2510

Whitecliff Bay is a very large complex divided by a road, with a holiday home and chalet park on the right-hand side (230 units), and a touring site on the left-hand side (429 pitches). The large touring site is on a sloping hillside with commanding views over the surrounding countryside. The pitches are spread over three fields, the top and second fields are terraced, but field three is quite level. Most of the pitches have 16A electricity hook-ups, and there are 42 gravel hardstandings, 12 in the top field, the remainder in the lowest field. There are just 18 individual hedged multi-serviced pitches available, so book early if these appeal. On the opposite side of the lane, in the holiday home park, you will find all the main entertainment and leisure facilities. These include The Culver Club with a bar and evening entertainment, several snack bars and takeaways, supervised swimming pools (indoor and outdoor), a sauna, sunbed and soft play zone (under eights). Close to the outdoor pool a very steep path leads down to a sandy beach where there is a small café.

Facilities

Three sanitary units. Showers and a suite (with shower) for disabled campers. A second suite with a hip bath/shower has a similar facility serving as a family room. Motorcaravan service point. Small shop. Playground. At holiday home park: launderette, hairdresser and second larger shop. The Culver Club. Snack bars. Swimming pool (18x18 m, Whitsun-end Aug). Indoor fun pool. Most facilities open Mar-Oct. Free WiFi on main site. Entertainment. Fully equipped tents to rent. Off site: Bus service from park entrance on weekday. Riding 2 miles. Bicycle hire 4 miles.

Open: 22 March - 4 November.

Directions

From A3055 between Ryde and Sandown, turn east at Brading on B3395 for 2 miles passing the Airfield and Propeller Club, fork right (site signed). Follow signs to site, first entry on right is static area, touring entrance is just after. GPS: 50.67498, -1.09606

Charges guide

Per unit incl. up to 6 persons and electricity	£ 6.00 - £ 43.00
dog	£ 1.00

For latest campsite news visit
alanrogers.com

Bere Regis

Rowlands Wait Touring Park

Rye Hill, Bere Regis BH20 7LP (Dorset) T: 01929 472727. E: enquiries@rowlandswait.co.uk

alanrogers.com/UK2050

Rowlands Wait is in a designated Area of Outstanding Natural Beauty and part of the park is officially of Special Scientific Interest. The top of the park, edged by mature woods (full of bluebells in spring) is a haven for tents (and squirrels) with marvellous views and provides 30 areas in three descending fields. The rest of the park is a little more formal, and nearer to the central toilet block. Most pitches back on to hedging or trees and they are generally level. There are 71 pitches in total with 23 seasonal pitches. Many walks are possible from the park with information leaflets available from reception. It is also possible to walk into the village of Bere Regis. The owners Ivor and Stevie Cargill are keen to welcome nature lovers who enjoy bird watching, walking, and cycling. Sightings of various owls and two pairs of buzzards have been reported on the park. The park is a member of the Countryside Discovery group and is open in winter by arrangement. Rallies are welcome.

Facilities	Directions
The refurbished toilet block is fully equipped. New family room and facilities for disabled visitors. Laundry room. Recycling bins. Shop (reduced hours in low season) providing basic essentials and a freezer for ice packs. Play area. Games room. Bicycle hire arranged. Torch useful. Off site: Village (10 minute walk) with shops, two pubs, etc. plus a bus service for Dorchester and Poole. Golf 3 miles. Fishing 5 miles. Riding 9 miles.	Park is 0.5 miles south of Bere Regis on the road to Wool. GPS: 50.743683, -2.22405

Charges guide

Per unit incl. 2 persons	£ 14.50 - £ 18.50
incl. electricity	£ 16.50 - £ 21.50
extra person	£ 3.50 - £ 5.00
child (3-16 yrs)	£ 2.00 - £ 3.25
dog	free - £ 2.50

Open: All year (31 October - 16 March by arrangement).

Blandford Forum

The Inside Park Touring Caravan & Camping Park

Blandford Forum DT11 9AD (Dorset) T: 01258 453719. E: mail@theinsidepark.co.uk

alanrogers.com/UK2070

The Inside Park is set in the grounds of an 18th-century country house that burned down in 1941. Family owned and carefully managed alongside an arable farm, this is a must for those interested in local history or arboriculture and it is a haven for wildlife and birds. The nine acre camping field, a little distant, lies in a sheltered, gently sloping dry valley containing superb tree specimens – notably cedars, with walnuts in one part – and a dog graveyard dating back to the early 1700s under a large Cedar of Lebanon. In total there are 125 spacious pitches, 90 with 10A electricity and some in wooded glades. The six acres adjoining are the old pleasure gardens of the house. The reception/toilet block and games room block are respectively the coach house and stables of the old house. No vehicle access to the park is allowed after 22.30 (there is a separate late arrivals area and car park). Extensive, marked walks are provided through the farmland and a guide is available in the shop.

Facilities	Directions
The toilet block provides some washbasins in cubicles, comfortably sized showers and facilities for disabled visitors and babies. Laundry room. Shop with basics, gas and camping provisions. Spacious games room. Safe based adventure play area. Day kennelling facilities for dogs. Mountain bike course. Winter caravan storage. Free WiFi around reception. Off site: Blandford leisure and swimming centre (temporary membership possible) 2 miles. Riding 2 miles. Golf 3 miles. Beach 25 miles.	Park is 2 miles southwest of Blandford and is signed from the roundabout junction of A354 and A350 roads. GPS: 50.841333, -2.19515

Charges guide

Per unit incl. 2 persons and electricity	£ 19.25 - £ 23.45
extra person	£ 4.25 - £ 4.85
child (3-15 yrs)	£ 1.00 - £ 2.00
dog	£ 1.00 - £ 1.50

Open: Easter - 31 October.

FREE Alan Rogers Travel Card
Extra benefits and savings - see page 10

Bletchingdon
Greenhill Farm Caravan & Camping Park
Greenhill Farm, Station Road, Bletchingdon OX5 3BQ (Oxfordshire) T: 01869 351600.
E: info@greenhill-leisure-park.co.uk **alanrogers.com/UK2590**

On a working farm in a rural setting, this is a newly established site. The approach is a half mile gravel track down into the valley, past recently planted woodlands, fields and the farm. A tarmac path continues round the park giving access to 92 pitches, 80 with 16A electricity and 30 with hardstanding. Growing trees and hedges partition the site and screen the water stands. An adjacent field is available for rallies and there is a second smaller field for tents. There are now two fishing lakes (carp, roach, bream and tench).

Facilities

Three toilet blocks, two of which have ramp access to facilities for disabled visitors and families. Separate laundry room. Shop selling own farm produce (April-Sept). Play area with assault course and football nets. Fishing lakes. Games room which can also be used for meetings. Pets are not accepted 1/10-1/3. Off site: Boat launching and canal walks 1 mile. Golf 2 miles.

Open: All year.

Directions

From M40 exit 9 take A34 to Newbury and Oxford. After 5 miles turn left on B4027 signed Bletchingdon. After 2.5 miles park is on left just past the village. GPS: 51.85754, -1.29142

Charges guide

Per unit incl. 2 persons and electricity	£ 16.00 - £ 18.00
extra person	£ 3.00

Brockenhurst
Forest Holidays Hollands Wood
Forest Holidays, Lyndhurst Road, Brockenhurst SO43 7QH (Hampshire) T: 01590 622967.
E: info@forestholidays.co.uk **alanrogers.com/UK2310**

Forest Holidays is a partnership between the Forestry Commission and The Camping & Caravanning Club. This is a large, spacious 168 acre secluded site in a natural woodland setting (mainly oak). It is set in the heart of the New Forest, with an abundance of wildlife. The site is arranged informally with 600 level unmarked pitches but it is stipulated that there must be at least 20 feet between each unit. There are no electrical connections and traffic noise is possible from the A337 which runs alongside one boundary. Brockenhurst village is only half a mile away, where there are shops for supplies and gas, etc, plus trains and buses. The site is maintained by a hard working team who, with their cheerful attitude, give this place a very friendly ambience. Dogs are also made welcome by the provision of their own shower (hot water).

Facilities

Three refurbished toilet blocks provide all necessary requirements, including for disabled visitors and babies. Good laundry room. All these may be under pressure at peak times. Motorcaravan services. Freezer packs and charging of batteries (fee). Maps and guides. Barbecues allowed (off ground). Milk stocked. Barrier closed 22.30-07.00. Night security. Torches essential. Off site: Bicycle hire and riding 2 miles. Golf 3 miles.

Open: 29 March - 1 October.

Directions

Site entrance is on east side of A337 Lyndhurst-Lymington road, 0.5 miles north of Brockenhurst. GPS: 50.83655, -1.56952

Charges guide

Per unit incl. 2 persons	£ 14.20 - £ 32.65
extra person	£ 4.50 - £ 9.40
child (5-16 yrs)	£ 2.50 - £ 4.70
dog (max. 3)	free
Discounts available.	

Burford
Wysdom Touring Park
The Bungalow, Burford School, Burford OX18 4JG (Oxfordshire) T: 01993 823207
alanrogers.com/UK2620

You'll have to go a long way before you find anything else remotely like this site! The land is owned by Burford School and the site was created to raise money for the school (£50,000 raised in 2009/10). It really is like stepping into their own private garden. This adults only park is screened from the main school grounds by trees and provides 23 pitches (six seasonal), separated by hedges, all with 16A electricity and their own tap. Tents are accepted for short stays by arrangement.

Facilities

The heated sanitary building is clean and well maintained with two unisex showers (payable by token) – there may be a queue at peak times. (Max. 2 dogs per pitch). Tennis courts. WiFi (charged). Tourist information is available in Burford. Off site: Burford is yards away with its famous hill full of antique shops, old coaching inns and quaint shops. Burford Golf Club is next door.

Open: All year (excl. February).

Directions

From roundabout on A40 at Burford, take A361 towards Lechdale on Thames. Park is a few yards on right signed Burford School. Once in drive watch for narrow entrance to site on right in 100 yds. GPS: 51.801983, -1.639367

Charges guide

Per unit incl. 2 persons and electricity	£ 10.00 - £ 15.00

For latest campsite news visit
alanrogers.com

Christchurch
Grove Farm Meadow Holiday Park
Meadowbank Holidays, Stour Way, Christchurch BH23 2PQ (Dorset) T: 01202 483597.
E: enquiries@meadowbank-holidays.co.uk **alanrogers.com/UK2130**

Grove Farm Meadow is a quiet, traditional park with caravan holiday homes and a small provision for touring units. The grass flood bank which separates the River Stour from this park provides an attractive pathway. The river bank has been kept natural and is well populated by a range of water birds. It is popular with bird watchers and there is fishing in the river. There are just under 200 caravan holiday homes (75 for hire), sited in regular rows. For touring units there are 41 level pitches (21 fully serviced and with hardstanding), all clearly numbered with 10A electricity, backing on to fencing or hedging.

Facilities

The new heated toilet block provides a bathroom for each sex (50p). Separate toilets, washbasins and showers. Facilities for disabled visitors with ramped access. Baby room. Laundry facilities. Well stocked shop. Games room with pool table and electronic games. Adventure play area beside the river bank. Fishing (permits from reception). Free WiFi over site. Dogs and tents are not accepted. Off site: Golf 0.5 miles. Large supermarket 1.5 miles. Beach, boat launching and sailing 2 miles.

Open: 1 March - 31 October.

Directions

From A388 Ringwood-Bournemouth road take B3073 for Christchurch. Turn right at the first roundabout and Stour Way is the third road on the right. GPS: 50.750336, -1.807938

Charges guide

Per 'luxury' pitch incl. 2 persons, electricity	£ 16.00 - £ 31.00
standard pitch (no awnings)	£ 10.00 - £ 21.00
extra person (over 5 yrs)	£ 1.00 - £ 2.00

Cowes
Thorness Bay Holiday Park
Thorness Bay, Cowes PO31 8NJ (Isle of Wight) T: 01983 523109. E: holiday.sales@park-resorts.com
alanrogers.com/UK2520

Spread over a large area of rural down and woodland that slopes down to Thorness Bay, this is a large site with around 500 holiday homes. The touring area has 122 pitches, most with 16A electricity including 27 multi-serviced pitches on gravel hardstandings with electricity, water, drain and TV points. These and some grass pitches are on terraces served by tarmac roads. The remainder are on sloping open grassland either divided by ranch style rails or in an open tent area, and all have views of the surrounding countryside. The main activity centre is in the holiday home area, close to the touring site.

Facilities

The toilet block provides showers, WCs and washbasins. Suite for disabled visitors. Baby changing. Laundry facilities. No motorcaravan services. Shop. Indoor pool. Adventure playground. Multisport court. Club for children. Archery. Trampolines. WiFi (charged). Off site: The bay is easily accessed from the main entertainment complex. All the island's attractions are within reach. Golf 4 miles.

Open: Easter - 29 October.

Directions

From East Cowes ferry follow signs to Newport. Follow A3054 (Yarmouth). Continue for 2.5 miles to crossroads, turning right (north) to Thorness Bay. After 2 miles, on sharp right hand bend, turn left, and site is signed. GPS: 50.731133, -1.360467

Charges guide

Per unit incl. up to 6 persons and electricity	£ 12.00 - £ 39.00

Cowes
Waverley Park Holiday Centre
51 Old Road, East Cowes PO32 6AW (Isle of Wight) T: 01983 293452. E: sue@waverley-park.co.uk
alanrogers.com/UK2530

This pleasant, small park (45 pitches) is family owned and set in the grounds of an old country house which was once frequently visited by Dr Arnold, the subject of Tom Brown's Schooldays. The owners have terraced the grass area for touring units and have created 31 large and level, well spaced, fully serviced hardstanding pitches all with impressive views over the Solent. The remaining 14 pitches on a sloping grass area are for caravans and tents (without electricity). To one side there are 75 holiday homes. At the bottom of the park, a gate leads onto the promenade and the pebble beach.

Facilities

A heated toilet block provides the usual facilities, including some spacious cubicles with washbasins en-suite. Suite for disabled visitors with baby changing. Motorcaravan service point. Laundry facilities. Heated outdoor pool and paddling pool with sun terrace. Club with restaurant, bar and outdoor terrace, plus family entertainment in season (Easter-early Sept). Small adventure style playground. Games room. WiFi in some areas (free). Boats accepted by prior arrangement – public slipway nearby.

Open: All year.

Directions

Immediately after leaving Southampton-Cowes car ferry, take first left, then right into Old Road, and park entrance is on left. GPS: 50.76088, -1.28366

Charges guide

Per unit incl. 2 persons and electricity	£ 16.00 - £ 21.00
extra person	£ 6.50 - £ 9.00
During Cowes Week min. pitch fees apply.	

Fordingbridge
Hill Cottage Farm Camping & Caravan Park

Sandleheath Road, Alderholt, Fordingbridge SP6 3EG (Hampshire) T: 01425 650513.
E: hillcottagefarmcaravansite@supanet.com **alanrogers.com/UK2360**

This established, modern site is set in 47 acres of beautiful countryside on the Dorset and Hampshire border. There are 95 pitches, all on hardstandings, 75 with 16A electricity hook-ups, water taps and drainage are arranged around a circular gravel roadway. Secluded and sheltered, they have views across the surrounding countryside. A field, also with electric hook-ups, alongside the camping area is used for tents and rallies, and has space for ball games and a small playground. Also on site there are two small lakes for coarse fishing, and there are many woodland walks in the area. Overall this site is more suitable for adults and younger children – it is not really designed for active teenagers.

Facilities

A large modern barn-style building provides excellent heated facilities. Laundry room. Facilities for disabled visitors and babies. Facilities for tent pitches. First floor games room with full size snooker table, two pool tables and darts board, plus a separate function room. Motorcaravan services. Shop. Playground. WiFi (free). Shepherd's hut for hire. Off site: Village centre with pub, church, Post Office and store is a 20 minute woodland walk. Local attractions include Rockbourne Roman Villa, Cranborne Chase, The Dolls Museum at Fordingbridge, Salisbury, and Ringwood with its Wednesday market.

Open: 1 March - 31 October.

Directions

From Fordingbridge take B3078 westwards for 2 miles to Alderholt. On entering the village, at left hand bend, turn right towards Sandleheath (site signed) and site entrance is 300 yds. on the left. GPS: 50.919017, -1.832783

Charges guide

Per unit incl. 2 persons and electricity	£ 20.00 - £ 27.00
extra person	£ 5.00
child (0-15 yrs)	£ 2.00 - £ 4.00
dog	£ 1.00

Fordingbridge
Sandy Balls Holiday Centre

Godshill, Fordingbridge SP6 2JZ (Hampshire) T: 0845 270 2248. E: post@sandy-balls.co.uk
alanrogers.com/UK2290

Sandy Balls sits high above the sweep of the Avon river near Fordingbridge, amidst woodland which is protected as a nature reserve. It well deserves the entry it has maintained in these guides for over 30 years and continues to improve and develop. Very well run and open all year, the 120-acre park has many private holiday homes as well as 26 caravan holiday homes and 117 lodges for rent. The touring areas have 233 marked, hedged, serviced pitches for caravans and tents on part-hardstanding and part-grass, with 16A electricity and TV connections. In August there is an additional unmarked tent area. In winter only 50 pitches are available. A woodland leisure trail allows wild animals and birds to be observed in their natural surroundings and the attractions of the New Forest are close at hand. The heart of this holiday centre is the architecturally designed, multi-million pound 'village'. Within its traffic-free piazza are the bistro, pub, guest services bureau, gift shop, cycle shop, small supermarket and leisure club, all designed to blend in with the forest surroundings and provide space to relax and meet friends. A member of the Best of British group.

Facilities

Three toilet blocks have underfloor heating and washbasins in cubicles. Portacabin style units with hot water for the tent field. Toilets for disabled visitors and baby facilities. Excellent central launderette. Motorcaravan service point. Entertainment and activity programme (high season). Outdoor pool (25/5-1/9). Indoor pool (66x30 ft). Well equipped gym, jacuzzi, steam room, sauna and hair and beauty suite. Games room. Adventure playground and play areas including indoor soft play area. Tents for rent. River fishing (permit). Riding stables. Bicycle hire. Archery. Dogs only allowed on certain fields. Off site: Golf 6 miles. Beach 20 miles.

Open: All year.

Directions

Park is well signed 1.5 miles east of Fordingbridge on the B3078. GPS: 50.930267, -1.7602

Charges guide

Per unit incl. 2 persons and electricity	£ 10.00 - £ 50.00
extra person	free - £ 5.00
child	free
dog	free - £ 4.00

For latest campsite news visit
alanrogers.com

Freshwater
Heathfield Farm Camping

Heathfield Road, Freshwater PO40 9SH (Isle of Wight) T: 01983 407822. E: web@heathfieldcamping.co.uk
alanrogers.com/UK2500

Heathfield is a pleasant contrast to many of the other sites on the Isle of Wight, in that it is a 'no frills' sort of place, very popular with tent campers, cyclists and small camper vans. Despite its name, it is no longer a working farm. A large, open meadow provides 60 large, level pitches, 50 with 10A electricity. Two small fenced areas provide traffic free zones for backpackers and cyclists' tents. There is no shop as you are only eight minutes walk from the centre of Freshwater. The site overlooks Colwell Bay and across the Solent towards Milford-on-Sea and Hurst Castle. A playing field for ball games also has a picnic table and a communal barbecue. There is a wild flower meadow with the perimeter mown for dog walking. It is ideal for visiting attractions on the western side of the island including Totland and Freshwater Bays, The Needles and Old Battery, Compton Down, and Mottistone Manor Garden. The Military road which runs from Freshwater Bay to St Catherine's Point gives spectacular coastal views.

Facilities

The main toilet unit is housed in a modern, ingeniously customised, Portacabin style unit including a baby changing facility. Showers have two pushbutton controls, one for pre-mixed hot water, the other for cold only. A second similar unit has WCs and washbasins in cubicles, plus facilities for disabled visitors. Laundry facilities. Motorcaravan service point. Gas supplies. Ice pack service. Playing field. Bicycle hire arranged. WiFi (charged). No commercial vehicles are accepted. Gate locked 22.30-07.00. Off site: Bus stop 200 m. Riding, beach and fishing 0.5 miles. Golf 1.25 miles.

Open: 1 May - 30 September.

Directions

From A3054 north of Totland and Colwell turn into Heathfield Road where site is signed. Site entrance is on right after a short distance.
GPS: 50.68940, -1.52704

Charges guide

Per unit incl. 2 persons and electricity	£ 12.50 - £ 19.50
extra person	£ 5.00 - £ 6.50
child (3-15 yrs)	£ 2.00 - £ 4.00
dog	£ 2.00

Min. pitch fee July/Aug £17.

Hamble
Riverside Holidays

Satchell Lane, Hamble, Southampton SO31 4HR (Hampshire) T: 02380 453220.
E: enquiries@riversideholidays.co.uk **alanrogers.com/UK2315**

What makes Riverside so special is its location; close to the River Hamble, Mecca for the international yachtsman. The site is family owned and covers five acres surrounded by trees and hedges; it has 123 pitches of which 77 are level for touring caravans and tents, with 53 electricity hook-ups (16A). The remaining pitches are used for lodges and residential and static caravans on slightly rising ground, but so well spaced and with plenty of grass they are not too obtrusive. A warden-run log cabin reception, with tourist information, including local bus and rail times, is at the entrance. Hamble village, one mile away, with its cobbled streets, pubs and restaurants, is famed the world over for its association with yachting. This is an ideal base for the Southampton Boat Show, Cowes Week and its very own Hamble Week Regatta. At the marina adjacent to the site, a mere two minutes walk, is Oyster Quay with a bar and restaurant overlooking hundreds of yachts worth millions.

Facilities

A brand new lodge contains the sanitary facilities, including family and baby changing rooms. The old Portacabin style unit has been kept for busy periods. Small laundry room alongside. All these facilities could be under pressure in high season. Bicycle hire. Caravan storage. Off site: Fishing, sea fishing, sailing, supermarket, buses and trains in village 1 mile. Riding 3 miles. Golf 4 miles. You can catch a small ferry across to Warsash on the other bank or take a boat up to the Upper Hamble Country Park. The New Forest, Winchester and Portsmouth are nearby.

Open: 1 March - 31 October.

Directions

From M27 exit 8 follow signs for Hamble. Take B3397 with Tesco on left, continue 1.9 miles through lights until Hound roundabout. After 50 yds. turn left into Satchell Lane (signed Mercury Marina) and site is on left in 1 mile. GPS: 50.868835, -1.313586

Charges guide

Per unit incl. 2 persons	
and electricity	£ 15.00 - £ 42.00
extra person	£ 4.00
child (4-16 yrs)	£ 3.00
dog	£ 2.50

Camping Cheques accepted.

Hayling Island
Fishery Creek Caravan & Camping Park

100 Fishery Lane, Hayling Island PO11 9NR (Hampshire) T: 023 924 621654. E: camping@fisherycreek.co.uk
alanrogers.com/UK2221

Fishery Creek is set in a beautiful and quiet location adjoining a tidal creek of Chichester harbour. Of the 150 pitches, 50 are for touring and the remainder are seasonal. All have 16A electricity connections and are individually marked on level grass. From the park you can enjoy a paddle, a spot of fishing, or launch a small boat from the private slipway. Local shops, restaurants and pubs and a coastal path are all within easy access. Unfortunately, access is shared with the local household amenity tip which can cause congestion at weekends.

Facilities

The toilet and shower facilities are housed in separate blocks and have both been recently refurbished. The shower block has underfloor heating. Toilet facility for disabled visitors. Excellent laundry room with TV and a seating area. Motorcaravan service point. Small shop for basics. Play areas. Fishing. Slipway to launch small boats. Off site: Golf and bicycle hire 2 miles. Riding 3 miles.

Open: 1 March - 31 October.

Directions

From A27, follow A3023 onto Hayling Island. At first roundabout turn left then follow brown signs to park. GPS: 50.784205, -0.958565

Charges guide

Per unit incl. 2 persons	
and electricity	£ 19.40 - £ 29.70
extra person	£ 4.00
child (4-14 yrs)	£ 3.30

For latest campsite news visit
alanrogers.com

Henley-on-Thames
Swiss Farm Touring and Camping

Marlow Road, Henley-on-Thames RG9 2HY (Oxfordshire) T: 01491 573419.
E: enquiries@swissfarmcamping.co.uk **alanrogers.com/UK2572**

Nestling at the foot of the Chiltern Hills and just a short stroll from Henley-on-Thames, Swiss Farm is ideally located for those seeking either a relaxing or an active break. The site can offer quiet, communal style pitches or the more family orientated field type. Of the 187 pitches, 156 have 10A electricity, 62 are hardstandings and 31 are fully serviced with 16A electricity and a TV point. This park boasts a heated outdoor, supervised pool, bar and patio barbecue. Reception includes a small shop selling basic provisions. There is an adventure-style wooden children's play area. Just ten minutes walk on a footpath is Henley-on-Thames and there is a bus stop at the site entrance providing services to Wycombe, Marlow, Reading and Henley. Trains from nearby Twyford station take you directly to London's Paddington Station in 40 minutes.

Facilities

Two fully equipped toilet blocks. One private bathroom. Free showers. Facilities for the disabled. Baby changing. Launderette. Basic shop in reception for camping essentials. Bar. Supervised swimming pool. Play area. Patio barbecue. Coarse fishing. WiFi. Dogs welcome in low season only. Off site: Boat launching 0.5 miles. Bicycle hire 1 mile. Golf 2 miles. Toad Hall. Henley-on-Thames. London's Paddington Station 40 minutes.

Open: 1 March - 31 October.

Directions

From M4 exit 8/9 or M40 exit 4A, take A404, A4130 to Henley-on-Thames. Follow Henley-on-Thames signs and site is signed on left just before town. GPS: 51.54594, -0.90504

Charges guide

Per unit incl. 2 persons and electricity	£ 16.00 - £ 27.00
extra person	£ 5.00
child (5-15 yrs)	£ 2.50
dog	£ 2.00

Maidenhead
Hurley Riverside Park

Hurley, Maidenhead SL6 5NE (Berkshire) T: 01628 824493. E: info@hurleyriversidepark.co.uk
alanrogers.com/UK2700

On the banks of the Thames, not far from Henley-on-Thames, you will find the picturesque village of Hurley where some buildings date back to 1086. Just outside the village is Hurley Riverside Park providing facilities for holiday homes, touring units, tents and moorings for boats. The touring area is flat and separated into smaller fields. With the pitches arranged around the outside of each field and the centre left free, the park has a spacious feel. There are 138 touring pitches with 10A electricity including 14 fully serviced and some on long hardstandings. A camping field provides a further 50 pitches including some with electric hook-ups. A very popular park, there is also a large rally field. You can enjoy walks along the banks of the Thames or visit the various pubs and restaurants in the village for a good meal and a pint. A new nature trail has been installed along the length of the touring park and there are large riverside picnic grounds alongside the Thames. Nearby Windsor has its famous castle or for younger members of the family, Windsor is the home of Legoland. At Henley you can watch the regatta. Alternatively, you can just relax in the peaceful settings of the site.

Facilities

Three wooden toilet blocks (raised on legs) include a very good new unisex block with private bathrooms (shower, washbasin, toilet). The other blocks have been renovated and are well equipped. Separate shower and toilet facilities for disabled visitors at reception. Baby area. Launderette. Motorcaravan service point. Well stocked shop at reception. Fishing. WiFi. Temporary moorings. Nature trail, riverside picnic grounds, slipway and fishing in season. Discounted tickets for Legoland Windsor. American RVs accepted. Accommodation to rent. Off site: Golf 5 miles. Riding 10 miles. Legoland at Windsor, Thorpe Park.

Open: 1 March - 31 October.

Directions

From M4 exit 8/9 take A404M towards Wycombe. After 3 miles take A4130 (Henley). Go down steep hill (Hurley village signed on right) – ignore this turning and take next right (site signed from here). GPS: 51.5466, -0.8248

Charges guide

Per unit incl. 2 persons	£ 14.00 - £ 22.00
full services	£ 16.00 - £ 24.00
extra person	£ 3.00
child (5-17 yrs)	£ 1.50
dog	£ 2.00

FREE Alan Rogers Travel Card
Extra benefits and savings - see page 10

Milford-on-Sea
Lytton Lawn Touring Park
Lymore Lane, Milford-on-Sea SO41 0TX (Hampshire) T: 01590 648331. E: holidays@shorefield.co.uk
alanrogers.com/UK2280

Lytton Lawn is the touring arm of Shorefield Country Park, a nearby holiday home park and leisure centre. Set in eight acres, it provides 135 marked pitches with some seasonal available. These include 53 premier pitches (hardstanding, 16A electricity, pitch light, water and waste water outlet) in a grassy, hedged area – this section, with its heated toilet block, is open for a longer season. The rest of the pitches, all with electricity, are in the adjoining, but separate, gently sloping field, edged with mature trees and hedges and with a further toilet block. The larger reception and well stocked shop make this a good, comfortable, self-sufficient site. Visitors to Lytton Lawn are entitled to use the comprehensive leisure facilities at Shorefield itself (2.5 miles away). These include a very attractive indoor pool, solarium, sauna and spa, fitness classes and treatments, all weather tennis courts, outdoor pools, restaurant facilities and entertainment and activity programmes. They are of a very good standard and mostly free (extra charges are made for certain activities including the Reflections day spa).

Facilities

Two modern toilet blocks are well fitted. Washing machine and dryer. Baby changing. Facilities for disabled visitors (Radar key). Motorcaravan service point. Shop (Feb-Dec). Small fenced play area and hedged field with goal posts. Tents for rent. Games room with free WiFi. Off site: Village pub 10 minutes walk. Bicycle hire 1 mile. Sailing, windsurfing and boat launching facilities 1.5 miles. Golf, riding, coarse fishing within 3 miles. The New Forest, Isle of Wight, Bournemouth, Southampton and the beach at Milford-on-Sea are nearby.

Open: All year excl. 3 January - 4 February.

Directions

From M27 follow signs for Lyndhurst and Lymington on A337. Continue towards New Milton and Lytton Lawn is signed at Everton; Shorefield is signed at Downton. GPS: 50.73497, -1.61803

Charges guide

Per unit incl. 6 persons and electricity	£ 12.50 - £ 37.75
premier pitch incl. water, drainage and TV connection	£ 15.25 - £ 41.50
dog	£ 1.50 - £ 3.00

Less 40% Monday-Thursday in certain periods. Min. weekly charge at busy times.

Newbridge
The Orchards Holiday Caravan & Camping Park
Newbridge, Yarmouth PO41 0TS (Isle of Wight) T: 01983 531331. E: info@orchards-holiday-park.co.uk
alanrogers.com/UK2450

In a village situation in the quieter western part of the island, The Orchards Holiday Park, a park for all seasons, has panoramic views of rolling countryside and the Solent. The park's neat 11-acre touring area has 168 marked pitches for tents, caravans and motorcaravans, broken up by apple trees, mature hedges and fences. All pitches have electricity, 62 have hardstandings and 22 are 'all service' pitches, also with hardstanding. A meeting room is suitable for small rallies. A separate area contains 64 caravan holiday homes. The Orchards is a good base from which to explore the island and there are two beaches within five miles. The scenic harbour of Yarmouth is five minutes away, as are the attractions of Fort Victoria and Chessell Pottery, with birdwatching at Newtown Creek.

Facilities

An excellent new facilities centre provides 24 shower and washbasin cubicles, a family bathroom, 2 family shower rooms, fully accessible facilities, spacious laundry and ironing area, walkers' drying room, baby changing room, vegetable preparation and indoor dishwashing area all with underfloor heating. Shop. Gas supplies. Indoor heated pool (Feb-Dec). Outdoor heated pool (May-Sept). Licensed coffee shop. Takeaway (mid Mar-Sept). Play areas. Football pitch. Fitness equipment. TV and amusements rooms. WiFi throughout (charged). Off site: Bus stop at entrance (infrequent). Membership for village social club. Riding 1 mile. Beach 4 miles. Bicycle hire 5 miles. Golf 8 miles.

Open: All year excl. 3 January - mid February.

Directions

Park is in Newbridge village, signed south from B3054 (Yarmouth-Newport) road. GPS: 50.687967, -1.419967

Charges guide

Per unit incl. 2 persons and electricity	£ 17.50 - £ 34.50

No pitch fee for hikers or cyclists. Packages incl. ferry travel – ring park for best deal.

Camping Cheques accepted.

For latest campsite news visit
alanrogers.com

SHOREFIELD

Self-Catering, Camping & Touring

Short breaks & Holidays

Discover   Relax   Explore   Unwind   Enjoy

All six of our holiday parks are set in peaceful, unspoilt parkland in the beautiful South Coast area.

There is a choice of touring pitches or self-catering accommodation depending on which park you choose. There are great leisure facilities and lots of fun entertainment for everyone. Pamper yourself in our Reflections' Elemis Day Spa at Shorefield Country Park, explore the New Forest, or relax on Bournemouth's sandy beaches.

For full details, ask for our brochure or browse online

Telephone **01590 648331**

holidays@shorefield.co.uk

HAMPSHIRE

Shorefield Country Park
Milford-on-Sea, SO41 0LH

Forest Edge Holiday Park
St. Leonards, BH24 2SD

Oakdene Forest Park
St. Leonards, BH24 2RZ

Lytton Lawn Touring Park
Milford-on-Sea, SO41 0TX

DORSET

Swanage Coastal Park
Swanage, BH19 2RS

Merley Court Touring Park
Wimborne, BH21 3AA

www.shorefield.co.uk

Ref: AR

Oxford

Diamond Farm Caravan & Camping Park

Islip Road, Bletchingdon, Oxford OX5 3DR (Oxfordshire) T: 01869 350909. E: warden@diamondpark.co.uk
alanrogers.com/UK2595

Diamond Farm is a spacious, family run site located 5 miles north of Oxford and within easy access of the Cotswolds and Chilterns. The attractive, 300 year old Cotswold stone farmhouse is at the heart of the site, along with a bar and games room. This is a small site with just 37 touring pitches. These are level and all equipped with 16A electricity. A number of hardstandings are also available. A separate field is used for tents (with some electrical connections). On-site amenities include a bar (with TV and full size snooker table), a well equipped children's play area and a heated swimming pool.

Facilities	Directions
Modern toilet block with family room and laundry area. Shop. Bar. Takeaway (weekends). Games room. Swimming pool (May-Sept). Play area. Tourist information. WiFi (free). Off site: Oxford city centre, Blenheim Palace and Bicester Shopping Village all 6 miles. Silverstone 24 miles. Open: All year.	Diamond Farm is on the B4027, 1 mile from the A34 (clearly signed), and 3 miles south of exit 9 of the M40. GPS: 51.84897, -1.25518

Charges guide

Per unit incl. 2 persons and electricity	£ 17.00 - £ 20.00
extra person	£ 3.00 - £ 4.00

Poole

Beacon Hill Touring Park

Blandford Road North, Poole BH16 6AB (Dorset) T: 01202 631631. E: bookings@beaconhilltouringpark.co.uk
alanrogers.com/UK2180

Beacon Hill is located in a marvellous, natural environment of partly wooded heathland, with areas of designated habitation for protected species such as sand lizards and the Dartford Warbler, but there is also easy access to main routes. Wildlife ponds encourage dragonflies and other species, but fishing is also possible. Conservation is obviously important in such a special area but one can ramble at will over the 30 acres, with the hilltop walk a must. Grassy open spaces provide 170 pitches, 151 with 10A electricity, on sandy grass which is sometimes uneven. Of these, 50 are for tents only and a few are seasonal. The undulating nature of the land and trees allows for discrete areas to be allocated for varying needs, for example young families near the play area, families with teenagers close to the bar/games room, those with dogs near the dog walking area, and young people further away. The park provides a wide range of facilities, including an open-air swimming pool and a tennis court. It is well situated for beaches, Poole harbour and ferries for France and the Channel Isles.

Facilities	Directions
Two rather dated, unheated toilet blocks include facilities for disabled guests. Laundry facilities. Well stocked shop at reception. Coffee bar and takeaway (main season). Bar (July/Aug, B.Hs, half-terms). Heated swimming pool (mid May-mid Sept). All weather tennis court (charged). Adventure play areas including a hideaway. Games room with pool tables and amusement machines. TV room. WiFi in some areas (charged). Fishing (charged). Off site: Riding 3 miles. Poole harbour and ferries 3 miles. Golf 4 miles. Beach 6 miles. Brownsea Island, Studland beach with Sandbanks ferry and the Purbecks nearby. Open: 17 March - end September.	Park is 3 miles north of Poole. Take A350 (towards Blandford) at roundabout where A350 joins A35. Park signed to the right (northeast) after 400 yds. GPS: 50.74953, -2.03446

Charges guide

Per unit incl. 2 persons and electricity	£ 14.00 - £ 38.00
extra person	£ 3.75 - £ 7.50
child (3-15 yrs)	£ 2.50 - £ 4.00
dog	£ 1.00 - £ 2.00

Beacon Hill Touring Park

Enjoy individual pitch settings within 30 acres of natural beauty. Relax in the tranquil seclusion of partly wooded heath land hosting an abundance of wildlife.

Gold Award Winners

(O12O2) 631631
www.beaconhilltouringpark.co.uk
bookings@beaconhilltouringpark.co.uk
Blandford Road North • Poole • Dorset • BH16 6AB

Nature & Dog Walks
Coarse Fishing Lakes • Tennis Court
Children Adventure Play Areas • Shop & Take Away
Heated Outdoor Swimming Pool • Bar & Games Room

For latest campsite news visit
alanrogers.com

Poole
Pear Tree Holiday Park

Organford Road, Holton Heath, Poole BH16 6LA (Dorset) T: 0844 272 9504.
E: enquiries@peartreepark.co.uk **alanrogers.com/UK2110**

Pear Tree is a neat, landscaped and well cared for park, set in 7.5 acres with mature trees and views across to Wareham Forest. There are 155 pitches in total, of which 87 are for touring units with hardstanding, 10A electricity, water and drainage. Only breathable groundsheets are permitted for awnings. The tent area is a tranquil, secluded spot with many mature trees. Reception, incorporating tourist information and a small shop supplying milk, bread, gas and other basics, is at the park entrance. The park is well situated for visiting Poole, Corfe Castle, Swanage and the Purbecks.

Facilities

The main heated toilet block (opened by key and recently refurbished) provides some washbasins in cubicles, baby changing unit (two new family rooms with Belfast sink baby bath and a 'wet room' for disabled visitors. Laundry. Separate small portacabin style block near the tent area. All is kept spotlessly clean. Shop (basics only). Play area with range of equipment. All year caravan storage. Off site: The Clay Pipe Inn 500 m. Bicycle hire 0.5 miles.

Open: 1 March - 31 October.

Directions

From the A351 (Wareham-Poole) road, turn west at traffic lights in Holton Heath (signed Organford and Sandford Park). Park is on left after 550 yds. past Sandford Park and The Clay Pipe Inn. GPS: 50.724033, -2.086967

Charges guide

Per unit incl. 2 persons and electricity	£ 18.00 - £ 28.00

Poole
South Lytchett Manor Caravan & Camping Park

Dorset Road, Lytchett Minster, Poole BH16 6JB (Dorset) T: 01202 622577. E: info@southlytchettmanor.co.uk
alanrogers.com/UK2120

Joanne and David are rightly proud of what they have achieved at South Lytchett Manor and, along with their staff, try hard to meet all your needs and make you very welcome. It has an unusual situation on parkland either side of what was once one of the driveways to the manor itself with impressive gates at the entrance. The access to the manor (now a school) is now closed off but there is room for 150 pitches in meadows or bays or beside the roadway. All are level, of a good size, with TV connections and electricity. There are 48 available with hardstanding and some also have water and waste water. They are landscaped with rural views. A member of the Best of British group.

Facilities

Three modern, fully equipped toilet blocks with four en-suite family rooms and facilities for disabled visitors. Motorcaravan service point. Laundry. Well stocked shop with off-licence and gas. Games room. Play area. Playing field. Woodland walk. Dog walk. Tourist information centre. Internet and WiFi. Bicycle hire. Off site: Shops, pubs, ATM 1 mile. Beach and sailing 2 miles. Golf 3 miles.

Open: 1 March - 2 January.

Directions

At the roundabout at the end of the dual carriageway on the A35 to the west of Poole turn north on B3067 to Lytchett Minster. Go through village and site is on the left half a mile past the church, through imposing wrought-iron gates. GPS: 50.73959, -2.05542

Charges guide

Per unit incl. 2 persons and electricity	£ 16.00 - £ 33.00

Ringwood
Forest Edge Holiday Park

229 Ringwood Road, Saint Leonards, Ringwood BH242SD (Hampshire) T: 01590 648331.
E: holidays@shorefield.co.uk **alanrogers.com/UK2285**

This popular family park is part of the Shorefield Group. Offering 120 pitches for tents and touring holidays and 37 caravan holiday homes, it is complemented by the leisure facilities available at Oakdene Forest Park (which is no longer taking any touring units). There is easy access to the level, marked pitches, each with 16A electricity hook-ups. The cheerful, flowery reception and well stocked shop help create a friendly and relaxed atmosphere. Picnic tables are dotted about the park giving it a country feel. A short walk through Hurn Forest leads to Oakdene and its new clubhouse and entertainment centre.

Facilities

The toilet block provides clean but fairly standard facilities. Unit for disabled visitors. Baby area. These facilities may be under pressure in high season. Laundry in a separate room near the adventure play area. Gas supplies. Shop with off-licence. Heated outdoor pool (Whitsun-Sept, weekends only plus school holidays). Football and netball court. Games room. Off site: Riding, fishing and golf 1 mile. Beach 7 miles.

Open: 4 February - 2 January.

Directions

Take the A31 westbound from Ringwood. After 3 miles and two roundabouts, turn left at the second roundabout into Boundary Lane (before reaching Oakdene). Site is signed. GPS: 50.82137, -1.84989

Charges guide

Per unit incl. 6 persons	£ 10.00 - £ 29.50
incl. electricity	£ 12.00 - £ 38.50
dog (max. 2)	£ 1.50 - £ 3.00

FREE Alan Rogers Travel Card
Extra benefits and savings - see page 10

Ringwood
Oakdene Forest Park

Saint Leonards, Ringwood BH24 2RZ (Hampshire) T: 0800 214080. E: holidays@shorefield.co.uk

alanrogers.com/UK2270

This park, part of the Shorefield Group, is a large holiday complex with many caravan holiday homes, but also with a small, basic area set aside for 13 tents, all with 10A electricity (no trailer tents). These pitches are on a rather uneven, grassy field with no shade, but only a short walk from the central facilities. The park provides a wide range of activities and entertainment, both outdoor and indoor, not forgetting the heated, indoor pool with its 34-metre flume and toddlers' beach area. With bars, supermarket, bakery and café, this is ideal for families with children of all ages. Alongside, and with direct access, is Hurn Forest - great for walking and cycling, with the 26 km. Castleman Trailway. Bournemouth and Poole, with their famous beaches and seaside attractions are only eight miles away. In all directions there are nature reserves, country parks and the New Forest with its well known ponies and pretty villages. Further afield are Swanage, Durdle Door and wonderful Weymouth.

Facilities

Portacabin sanitary unit has WCs, showers, washbasins and dishwashing facilities. Launderette. Shop. Restaurant and bars. Takeaway. Indoor pool (all year). Outdoor pools (May-Sept). Gym. Table tennis and pool table. Crazy golf. Compact bowling. Amusement arcade. Play area. Free Squirrel's Kids Club. Bicycle hire. ATM. Free WiFi in main building. Off site: Forest walks. Market, supermarket and restaurant 3 miles. Golf and riding 3 miles. Fishing 5 miles. Beach 9 miles.

Open: April - October.

Directions

From Ringwood take A31 westbound for 4.5 miles (just after Forest Edge) and site is on left. GPS: 50.811936, -1.858323

Charges guide

Per pitch incl. 6 persons and electricity	£ 14.50 - £ 37.00
extra person	£ 4.00

Ringwood
Red Shoot Camping Park

Linwood, Ringwood BH24 3QT (Hampshire) T: 01425 473789. E: enquiries@redshoot-campingpark.com

alanrogers.com/UK2350

Red Shoot is set in the heart of the New Forest, on four acres of level and slightly sloping grass meadows. A simple, rural retreat with panoramic views of the surrounding countryside and forest, it is very popular in high season. A cattle grid at the entrance keeps the New Forest animals outside the park. There are 120 good sized pitches, 45 with 10A electricity, served by a gravel access road. There is no site lighting so a torch would be useful. The adjacent Red Shoot Inn (separate ownership) serves meals and brews its own real ales – Forest Gold and Tom's Tipple. There are ample opportunities for walking, cycling and naturalist pursuits in the area. Local attractions include watersports at the New Forest Water Park near Ringwood, a Doll Museum in Fordingbridge, cider making in Burley, and Breamore House just north of Fordingbridge. Nearby Ringwood has a market on Wednesday.

Facilities

The toilet and shower facilities have been upgraded to a high standard with underfloor heating, including a family shower room/baby bath and changing area. Well equipped laundry room. Good unit for disabled visitors. Very well stocked, licensed shop with fresh bread and croissants. Fenced adventure-style playground. Off site: Fishing 5 miles. Riding 6 miles. Golf 7 miles. Beach 12 miles.

Open: 1 March - 31 October.

Directions

From A338, 1.75 miles north of Ringwood, turn east (signed Linwood and Moyles Court). Follow signs, over a staggered crossroads, and continue straight on for another 1.75 miles to Red Shoot Inn and park. GPS: 50.883917, -1.7347

Charges guide

Per unit incl. 2 persons and electricity	£ 23.00 - £ 33.00
extra person	£ 8.00
child (3-15 yrs)	£ 4.00
dog	£ 1.50

red shoot
camping park

Linwood,
Near Ringwood,
Hampshire,
BH24 3QT

Set in the heart of the New Forest and close to Bournemouth and Ringwood, this is a first class family-run park. Excellent facilities, children's play area and adjacent to Red Shoot Inn.
See our website for full details and saving discounts.

www.redshoot-campingpark.com
01425 473789
Email: enquiries@redshoot-campingpark.com

For latest campsite news visit
alanrogers.com

Ringwood
Shamba Holidays

Ringwood Road, Saint Leonards, Ringwood BH24 2SB (Hampshire) T: 01202 873302.
E: enquiries@shambaholidays.co.uk **alanrogers.com/UK2340**

Shamba is a family run, very modern park, although the aim remains to create a relaxed, pleasant atmosphere. There are 150 pitches, most used for touring units (45 are on a seasonal basis). Surrounded by trees, the camping area is on flat, open grass with 10/16A electricity available on all pitches. A Scandinavian style building forms the focal point and here you will find reception, a bar/restaurant, takeaway and a shop. The indoor swimming pool has walls and a roof which can be opened in good weather. The park's location is excellent for a family holiday on the edge of the New Forest, and for visits to the resorts of Bournemouth and Poole. Within easy reach are the Jurassic Coast, the Sealife Centre and beaches at Weymouth, the Tank Museum at Bovington and Monkey World, as well as the Purbecks and Corfe Castle. Take a trip to Brownsea Island where Baden-Powell started the Scouting movement.

Facilities

Sanitary facilities with underfloor heating include modern showers, washbasins and toilets and family changing rooms. Baby rooms with bath and facilities for disabled visitors. Launderette. Motorcaravan service point. Restaurant (high season and B.Hs). Bar with meals and takeaway (weekends only off season). Indoor swimming pool (12x6 m, heated) and paddling pool. Large play area. Amusements room. Adjacent field for dog walking and football/sports pitch. Off site: Moors Valley Country Park and riding 1 mile. Golf 2 miles. Ringwood, fishing and bicycle hire 2.5 miles. Beach 8 miles.

Open: 1 March - 31 October.

Directions

Take A31 westbound from Ringwood, after 3 miles, at second roundabout, turn back on yourself and after only 20 yds. turn left at park sign.
GPS: 50.825067, -1.853117

Charges guide

Per unit incl. 2 persons and electricity	£ 22.00 - £ 32.00
extra person	£ 5.00
child (6-13 yrs)	£ 4.00
dog	£ 2.50

Camping Cheques accepted.

Ryde
Whitefield Forest Touring Park

Brading Road, Ryde PO33 1QL (Isle of Wight) T: 01983 617069. E: pat&louise@whitefieldforest.co.uk
alanrogers.com/UK2495

This family run park, opened in May 2007, has been sympathetically developed by the owners working closely with the Forestry Commission to maintain the natural beauty of the ancient woodland, Whitefield Forest. There is a mixture of well drained all-weather hardstanding and grass pitches (90 in total) all with 16A electricity hook-up. Varying in size (100-170 sq.m), the pitches are level and sheltered with some on terraces. They are all suitable for tents, caravans and motorcaravans.

Facilities

The excellent well appointed heated toilet block has private cubicles, hairdryers and razor points. Family shower rooms. Baby changing and facilities for disabled visitors. Laundry room. Motorcaravan service point. Paperback book exchange. Adventure type play area with bark surface for children over 5 yrs. WiFi (free). Electric barbecues are not permitted. Suitable for American-style motorhomes and twin-axle caravans. Off site: Network of public footpaths from the site. Supermarket 600 yds.

Open: 22 March - 30 September.

Directions

From Yarmouth follow A3054 to Newport, then to Ryde. Follow the A3055 to Brading and as above.
GPS: 50.70049, -1.14574

Charges guide

Per unit incl. 2 persons and electricity	£ 17.50 - £ 23.50
extra person	£ 7.50 - £ 11.00
child (3-15 yrs)	£ 2.60 - £ 5.25
dog	£ 1.00 - £ 1.50

FREE Alan Rogers Travel Card
Extra benefits and savings - see page 10

Riseley
Wellington Country Park

Riseley, Reading RG7 1SP (Berkshire) T: 01189 326444. E: info@wellington-country-park.co.uk

alanrogers.com/UK2690

This campsite is situated within the very popular 350-acre Wellington Country Park, which is open to the public throughout the year. The park contains a wide range of amenities: a shop, a café, children's play areas, nine-hole crazy golf, animal farm and petting barn, miniature railway (charged), four nature trails, a deer park and a host of play equipment. Entrance to the Park is included in the campsite fees. There are 87 pitches, 30 non-electric for tents, 57 with 6A electricity and 50 hardstandings. A few premium pitches offer slightly more privacy. It is a very pleasant setting and once the park closes at 18.00 all is much quieter. You should aim to arrive before 16.30 (low season) and 17.30 (high season) when the main reception centre closes. Access to the site is through a locked gate (key from reception on check-in). The design of the site with generous individual pitches and some small groups, all within woodland clearings, gives a very rustic and relaxed ambience. The warden lives on the site.

Facilities

The central toilet block provides modern style facilities including washbasins in cubicles and well equipped showers with good dry areas. Ample laundry. Shop stocks basics. Café (during park hours). Calor gas exchange. Country Park with nature walks, deer field, crazy golf, play areas and miniature railway (£1 extra). Family events are held all year round. WiFi over site (charged). Torch useful. Off site: Local shops, bars and entertainment including swimming, cinema, ice-skating, all within a short drive. Wellington Riding School nearby. Bicycle hire and golf 6 miles. Major attractions such as Legoland, Thorpe Park, Windsor etc. all within easy reach.

Open: Early March - 11 November.

Directions

From M4 take exit 11 (A33) south towards Basingstoke. At first roundabout turn left onto the B3339 and park is off next roundabout. From M3 take exit 6 onto A33 towards Reading. Pass Wellington monument on left, turn right at next roundabout (B3339). The park is off the next roundabout. GPS: 51.36001, -0.95513

Charges guide

Per unit incl. 2 persons	£ 17.00 - £ 30.50
extra person	£ 7.50 - £ 8.50
child (3-15 yrs)	£ 6.50 - £ 7.50
dog	£ 3.50

Wellington Country Park
is situated within beautiful woodlands on the Hampshire/ Berkshire border between Reading and Basingstoke. Facilities include toilet/ shower block, shaving points, hair driers and laundry. Campers enjoy 'FREE' access to all Park facilities. Please see website for full details.
www.wellington-country-park.co.uk
Email:- info@wellington-country-park.co.uk
Tel:- 01189 326444

Romsey
Hill Farm Caravan Park

Branches Lane, Sherfield English, Romsey SO51 6FH (Hampshire) T: 01794 340402. E: gjb@hillfarmpark.com

alanrogers.com/UK2380

This 11-acre rural park is ideal for those seeking a quiet base but one that is within easy reach of all the main tourist attractions of Hampshire and Dorset. There are 120 pitches, of which 30 for seasonal units are located in a separate area. The touring area is a large open field surrounded by trees and hedges. All pitches are well marked, numbered and mainly level. All have 6/10A electricity hook-ups, 20 pitches are fully serviced and some are available with hardstanding. Adding to the attractiveness of the site is a pitch and putt golf course, set in a sizeable and well landscaped area. For anyone interested in roses, nearby Mottisfont Abbey (National Trust) has a unique collection of old fashioned varieties. The New Forest with Beaulieu Estate and National Motor Museum is just a short drive away. A trip to the Isle of Wight makes a good excursion – the ferry terminal is within a 30 minute drive.

Facilities

Two very clean, traditionally built toilet blocks include washbasins, both open style and in cubicles, and controllable showers. Facilities for babies and disabled visitors. Motorcaravan service point. Shop in reception for gas supplies and basics. Bread and pasties are cooked on the premises. Tea rooms serving breakfast, lunch and afternoon tea (homemade cakes & desserts). Play area. Pitch and putt golf. Off site: Riding, golf and fishing 3 miles. Bicycle hire 15 miles. Bournemouth and Southampton for shopping, leisure and family entertainment nearby.

Open: 1 March - 31 October.

Directions

From Romsey, drive north on the A27 for 3.5 miles, turning right into Branches Lane and site is a further 0.5 miles on right. GPS: 51.00627, -1.57682

Charges guide

Per unit incl. 2 persons and electricity	£ 17.00 - £ 32.00
extra person	£ 7.00
child (4-16 yrs)	£ 2.50 - £ 6.00

Minimum booking requirement for B.Hs, July and August weekends. No credit cards.

For latest campsite news visit
alanrogers.com

Shanklin
Lower Hyde Holiday Park

Landguard Road, Shanklin PO37 7LL (Isle of Wight) T: 01983 866131. E: holiday.sales@park-resorts.com
alanrogers.com/UK2475

This site is located on the edge of Shanklin, within walking distance of shops and services and only 1.5 miles from the beach. Lower Hyde is a large holiday park complex with around 200 caravan holiday homes for rent and 114 privately owned. The separate touring area has 85 well spaced and numbered pitches, all with 16A electricity and 26 with full services (hardstanding, water, waste water drain, electricity and TV hook-up). There is a further area for tents (no electricity). The touring area is in an elevated position with good views over the surrounding countryside. The pitches are large and flat, easily accessed, with tarmac roads and low-level lighting. There is a permanent warden for the touring pitches.

Facilities

The toilet block has WCs, open washbasins, showers, a family shower room and two bathrooms. Separate baby room. Suite for disabled visitors. Launderette. Shop. Bar. Restaurant and takeaway. Indoor and outdoor pools. Adventure playground. Clubs for children. Entertainment. Multisports court. Soccer. Archery. Fencing. Tennis. ATM. WiFi (charged). Off site: Fishing 1.5 miles. Golf 2.5 miles.

Open: 2 April - 29 October.

Directions

From Newport take A3020 towards Sandown and Shanklin. At Blackwater join A3056 to Sandown. Shortly after supermarket on left, turn right into Whitecross Lane (Landguard Camping). Keep on to site past Landguard. GPS: 50.633317, -1.180983

Charges guide

Per unit incl. up to 6 persons and electricity	£ 12.00 - £ 39.00

Shanklin
Ninham Country Holidays

Ninham, Shanklin PO37 7PL (Isle of Wight) T: 01983 864243. E: office@ninham-holidays.co.uk
alanrogers.com/UK2465

Ninham is an attractive, well maintained park tucked in a wooded valley, but only ten minutes drive to the bustling resort of Shanklin with its long, sandy beaches and good shops and restaurants. Two touring areas, one open all season, have spacious grass and gravel pitches, some open and some separated by hedges, with water and electrical hook-ups. There are two (unfenced) lakes for carp fishing, and numerous cycle paths, which can be used to access local amenities. Children will enjoy the heated outdoor pool, and the games room offers pool, table tennis and other activities.

Facilities

Clean and well maintained toilet facilities are housed in two traditional buildings, and a Portacabin style unit. No facilities for visitors with disabilities. Space for baby changing. Laundry facilities. No shop, but supermarkets nearby. Small outdoor pool with toddler pool and terrace (end May-Sept). Games room. Play areas. Coarse fishing (charged). Bicycle hire. Free WiFi. Accommodation to rent.

Open: 30 April - 4 September.

Directions

From Ryde-Fishbourne (A3055), turn onto A3056 at lake. Entrance is 0.5 miles on left after the Morrison's roundabout. GPS: 50.640607, -1.192424

Charges guide

Per unit incl. 2 persons and electricity	£ 16.50 - £ 23.00
extra person	£ 5.50 - £ 8.00

Swanage
Swanage Coastal Park

Priestway, Swanage BH19 2RS (Dorset) T: 01590 648331. E: holidays@shorefield.co.uk
alanrogers.com/UK2000

Swanage Coastal Park has a stunning location with views over Swanage Bay and the Purbeck Hills. Owned by Shorefield Holidays, it offers a quiet holiday on the hills above the town with its lovely sandy beach. Over 100 caravan holiday homes are on terraces up the hillside, two-thirds being privately owned. Near the entrance are six touring pitches, with a further five by the central toilet block. All have 6A electricity. Larger units may find access roads difficult to negotiate with parked cars and tight bends. It is advisable to telephone in advance for availability. In high season a large field is provided for tents (no electricity). Swanage is at the start of the Jurassic Coast, a World Heritage Site, and there is direct access to the coastal paths and to Durlston Country Park and Castle.

Facilities

Two toilet blocks, one old but clean and the other newer with all the usual facilities. Laundry room. Play area. Membership of Health and Fitness Club at next door park allows use of the indoor pool, gym, sauna, solarium, bar and restaurant as paying customers (all year). It also has a shop (open B.Hs. and high season). Eurostyle tents and holiday homes to rent. Off site: Beach and town 1 mile. Bicycle hire, fishing and boat launching 1 mile.

Open: 14 March - 30 October.

Directions

From A351 Wareham-Swanage road turn right 800 yds. after Welcome to Swanage sign and follow signs to the park. Note: narrow roads with parked cars and sharp bends. GPS: 50.60605, -1.974983

Charges guide

Per pitch (max. 6 persons) incl. electricity	£ 10.00 - £ 19.00
	£ 11.00 - £ 25.50
dog	£ 1.50

FREE Alan Rogers Travel Card
Extra benefits and savings - see page 10

Swanage

Ulwell Cottage Caravan Park

Ulwell, Swanage BH19 3DG (Dorset) T: 01929 422823. E: enq@ulwellcottagepark.co.uk

alanrogers.com/UK2020

Nestling under the Purbeck Hills on the edge of Swanage, in the Dorset and East Devon Coast World Heritage Site, Ulwell Cottage is a family run holiday park with an indoor pool and a wide range of facilities. Pool may have limited supervision in the winter months. A good proportion of the park is taken by caravan holiday homes (140), but an attractive, undulating area accessed by tarmac roads is given over to 77 numbered touring pitches interspersed with trees and shrubs. All have 16A electricity, eight are fully serviced and 16 are available with hardstanding. The colourful entrance area is home to the Village Inn with a courtyard adjoining the heated, supervised indoor pool complex (both open all year and open to the public) and modern reception. The hill above the touring area, Nine Barrow Down, is a Site of Special Scientific Interest for butterflies and overlooks Round Down. It is possible to walk to Corfe Castle this way. With Brownsea Island, Studland Bay, Corfe village and the Swanage Railway close by, Ulwell Cottage makes a marvellous centre for holidays.

Facilities

The modern, cheerful toilet block at the top of the site is heated and includes a unit for disabled visitors. Laundry room and baby sinks. Well stocked shop with gas (Easter-mid Sept). Bar snacks and restaurant meals with family room. Takeaway (July/Aug). Indoor pool with lifeguard (times vary acc. to season). Playing fields and play areas. WiFi throughout (charged). Off site: Beach, fishing and golf 1 mile. Bicycle hire, sailing and riding 2 miles.

Open: 1 March - 7 January.

Directions

From A351 Wareham-Swanage road, turn onto B3351 Studland road just before Corfe Castle. Follow signs to right (southeast) for Swanage and drop down to Ulwell. Park is on right 100 yds. after 40 mph. sign. GPS: 50.626460, -1.969403

Charges guide

Per unit incl. up to 6 persons	£ 25.00 - £ 46.00
full services incl. hardstanding	£ 27.00 - £ 49.00
extra tent, car or boat	£ 4.00

Discounted rates for two persons or three persons only.

For a brochure call:
01929 422823
website: www.ulwellcottagepark.co.uk
e-mail: enq@ulwellcottagepark.co.uk

Find a warm welcome at this family run park in the Isle of Purbeck, an area of outstanding natural beauty and breath taking World Heritage coastline. Nearby sandy beaches, coastal walks and golf.
● **77 Touring Pitches** with hard standings, electric, water and drainage hook-ups and views of the surrounding hills
● **Superb meals at the 'Village Inn'** ● **Heated Indoor Pool** ● **General Shop**

Ventnor

Appuldurcombe Gardens Holiday Park

Wroxall, Ventnor PO38 3EP (Isle of Wight) T: 01983 852597. E: info@appuldurcombegardens.co.uk

alanrogers.com/UK2480

Originally part of the grounds of an historic house, this pretty family holiday park is situated in 14 acres of beautiful countryside in the valley of Stenbury Downs and St Martin's Downs, close to the sandy beaches at Sandown, Shanklin and Ventnor. The camping field is set in a grassy meadow through which a stream meanders, with a tranquil seating area close by. With hard access roads, there are 100 spacious marked pitches for touring units and tents, all with 14A electricity. There are 30 serviced pitches with hardstanding. The old walled orchard contains 40 good quality caravan holiday homes. There is also the access-friendly Orchard Lodge (all accommodation on one level with ramp access to outside), plus two self-contained apartments.

Facilities

Two good toilet blocks are fully tiled with free hot water throughout. Facilities for visitors with disabilities (but not for children). Launderette. Motorcaravan services planned. Shop. Café. Bar and family entertainment room. All amenities open from Spring B.H.-early Sept. Outdoor swimming pool (8x18 m) and toddlers' pool. Play area. Crazy golf. WiFi (charged). Off site: Fishing, golf, riding, bicycle hire, boat launching, beach, sailing, all within 2-3 miles.

Open: March - November.

Directions

From Newport take A3020 towards Shanklin. 2 miles past Godshill turn right at Whiteley Bank roundabout towards Wroxall (B3320). Pass Donkey Sanctuary and turn right into Appuldurcombe Road. Park entrance (narrow road) is second on right. Do not use sat nav. GPS: 50.61891, -1.22657

Charges guide

Per unit incl. 2 persons and electricity	£ 15.25 - £ 26.25
extra person	£ 4.75 - £ 7.00
child (3-15 yrs)	£ 2.85 - £ 5.25
dog	£ 2.00

For latest campsite news visit
alanrogers.com

Wimborne
Merley Court Touring Park

Merley, Wimborne BH21 3AA (Dorset) T: 01590 648331. E: holidays@shorefield.co.uk
alanrogers.com/UK2080

Merley Court is part of the Shorefield Group and all aspects of this well planned, attractively landscaped park are constantly maintained to the highest of standards. Tarmac roads connect 162 touring pitches, all of which have 16A electricity, on neat lawns or one of the many hardstandings. This provision includes 19 serviced pitches with water, waste disposal and satellite TV. The entire park is interspersed with a variety of shrubs, plants and the odd ornamental urn. Some attractive tent pitches are to be found in a small wooded valley. A well furnished club complex provides a lounge bar where meals are available. There is also a snack bar, takeaway, large games room with pool tables and a family room leading onto a spacious sheltered patio. This in turn leads to the paved walled swimming pool area. There are woodland walks (including dog walks) directly from the site connecting to the disused railway line where nature has returned with an abundance of wild flowers, which in turn leads to Delph woods with designated nature trails.

Facilities

Three heated toilet blocks, two with showers, are of good quality. Separate facilities for disabled visitors and babies. Laundry facilities. Motorcaravan service point. Shop with caravan accessories and gas. Café and takeaway. Bar with food (limited hours in low and mid season). Outdoor pool (30x20 ft) with section for children (Whitsun-early Sept). Tennis and short tennis courts. Play area. Games room with pool tables. Tourist information. Barrier card £5 deposit. WiFi throughout (charged). Off site: Fishing, riding and golf all within 2 miles. Bicycle hire and Poole 5 miles. Bournemouth 8 miles. Tower Park leisure and entertainment centre nearby. Kingston Lacy House. Knoll Gardens. Brownsea Island. Moors Valley Country Park.

Open: All year excl. 3 January - 5 February.

Directions

Site clearly signed at the junction of the A31 and A349 roads (roundabout) on the Wimborne bypass. GPS: 50.785733, -1.98525

Charges guide

Per unit incl. 6 persons and electricity	£ 14.50 - £ 38.50
all service pitch	£ 20.00 - £ 42.50
dog	£ 1.50 - £ 3.00

No extra pup tent as well as awning.

Wimborne
Wilksworth Farm Caravan Park

Cranborne Road, Wimborne BH21 4HW (Dorset) T: 01202 885467.
E: rayandwendy@wilksworthfarmcaravanpark.co.uk **alanrogers.com/UK2060**

First opened by the parents of the present owners, the careful and sympathetic development of Wilksworth continues with the aim of providing all the 'mod cons' yet remain in keeping with the environment. It is a spacious, quiet park, well suited for families with a heated outdoor pool which has been totally refurbished in a beautiful Spanish style. The rural situation is lovely, just outside Wimborne and around 12 miles from the beaches between Poole and Bournemouth. The park takes 65 caravans and 25 tents mainly on grass. All pitches have electricity, ten also have water and drainage. There are 77 privately owned caravan holiday homes in a separate area. With a duck pond at the entrance, the park has been well planned on good quality ground with fairly level grass and some views.

Facilities

The central, well equipped toilet block has underfloor heating, washbasins in cubicles, a family bathroom and a shower/bath for children with baby changing. Facilities for disabled visitors. Laundry room. Modern reception and shop (basics only, limited hours, Easter-30 Sept). Gas supplies. Freezer for ice packs. Coffee shop serving simple meals with takeaway service (weekends and B.Hs. only outside the main season). Heated 40x20 ft. swimming pool (May-Sept). Small paddling pool with slide. Adventure play area. BMX track. Golf practice net. Two tennis courts. Games room. Winter caravan storage.

Open: Easter/1 April - 30 October.

Directions

Park is 1 mile north of Wimborne, west off the B3078 road to Cranborne. GPS: 50.8167, -1.9904

Charges guide

Per unit incl. 2 persons and electricity	£ 20.00 - £ 32.00
full services	£ 2.00
extra person	£ 4.00
child (3-15 yrs)	£ 3.00
dog	£ 2.00

No credit cards.

Wareham

Wareham Forest Tourist Park

North Trigon, Wareham BH20 7NZ (Dorset) T: 01929 551393. E: holiday@warehamforest.co.uk

alanrogers.com/UK2030

This peacefully located and spacious park, on the edge of Wareham Forest, has 200 pitches and is continually being upgraded by its enthusiastic owners, Tony and Sarah Birch. The focal point of the park is the modern reception and shop, located by the pools. Four main areas provide a wide choice of touring pitches from grass to hardstanding and luxury, all with 16A electricity. Tent campers have their own choice of open field or pinewood. The site has provided direct access for walkers into the forest or the seven miles of the Sika cycle trail may be used. The lovely market town of Wareham is accessible by bike without having to use the roads. This park has an almost continental feel, with plenty of space. Even when it is busy, it is calm and peaceful in its forest setting. In low season you may be lucky enough to spot the herd of Sika deer which live in the forest. The park is well situated to explore the Dorset coast and Thomas Hardy country. A member of the Best of British group.

Facilities

Two well maintained toilet blocks are of a good standard with some washbasins in cubicles, and several family bathrooms (one with baby bath). Main block was recently refurbished and both blocks are centrally heated. Facilities for disabled visitors. Well equipped laundry rooms. Motorcaravan service point. Small licensed shop with gas. Swimming pool (60x20 ft, heated 20/5-15/9). Large adventure play area. Barrier closed 23.00-07.00. Resident wardens on site. Caravan storage. WiFi. Off site: Cycle trail and walking in the forest. Bicycle hire and golf 3 miles. Fishing 5 miles. Riding 8 miles.

Open: All year.

Directions

From A31 Bere Regis, follow A35 towards Poole for 0.5 miles and turn right where signed to Wareham. Drive for a further 1.5 miles. First park on the left as you enter forest. GPS: 50.721733, -2.156217

Charges guide

Per unit incl. 2 persons and electricity	£ 13.70 - £ 35.20
'superior' pitch fully serviced	£ 19.45 - £ 38.70
extra person	£ 3.10 - £ 5.60
child (5-15 yrs)	£ 2.00 - £ 3.90
dog	free - £ 1.75

Couples and families only.

Wimborne

Woolsbridge Manor Farm Caravan Park

Three Legged Cross, Wimborne BH21 6RA (Dorset) T: 01202 826369. E: woolsbridge@btconnect.com

alanrogers.com/UK2150

Close to the Moors Valley Country Park, this friendly, family run site is within easy reach of the south coast, the resorts of Christchurch, Bournemouth and Poole, and the ancient market town of Wimborne Minster. Entry is restricted to couples and families. The seven-acre camping meadow has 100 large, level pitches (51 seasonal) all with 16A electricity and arranged on either side of a central tarmac road. Reception has a well stocked shop and a good selection of tourist information. The site is part of a working beef cattle farm, so parents should be aware of moving farm machinery and tractors.

Facilities

The neat, refurbished toilet block is well maintained and has ample facilities. Four newly built family rooms each with shower, WC, basin, handrails and ramped access provided for disabled visitors, babies and toddlers. Washing machine, dryer and ironing facilities. Shop. Gas. Playground. Fishing. American RVs accepted, advance booking appreciated. Torches useful. Caravan storage. Off site: Old Barn Farm inn and restaurant 400 yds. Riding, golf and bicycle hire 0.5 miles. Boat launching and sailing 5 miles.

Open: 1 March - 31 October.

Directions

From Ringwood take the A31 southwest to Ashley Heath roundabout (junction of A31 and A338 to Bournemouth). Take left hand slip road to the roundabout, avoiding underpass, and turn right (north) onto unclassified road (Three Legged Cross and Moors Valley Country Park). Follow signs to Country Park, pass entrance on right, continue for 400 yds. to entrance. GPS: 50.842982, -1.859982

Charges guide

Per unit incl. 2 persons and electricity	£ 17.50 - £ 24.50
extra person	£ 6.50 - £ 7.00
child (under 16 yrs)	£ 4.50 - £ 5.00
dog	£ 2.00

For latest campsite news visit

alanrogers.com

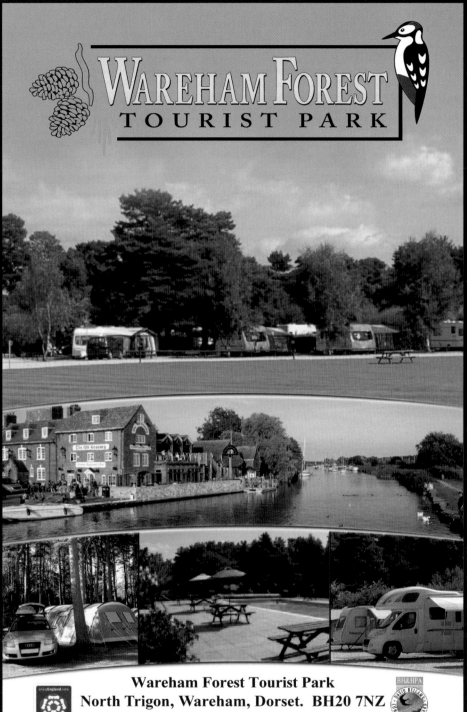

WAREHAM FOREST
TOURIST PARK

Wareham Forest Tourist Park
North Trigon, Wareham, Dorset. BH20 7NZ

 01929 551393

www.warehamforest.co.uk

~ ONLINE BOOKING AVAILABLE ~

Witney

Lincoln Farm Park

High Street, Standlake, Witney OX29 7RH (Oxfordshire) T: 01865 300239. E: info@lincolnfarmpark.co.uk

alanrogers.com/UK2570

From its immaculately tended grounds and quality facilities, to the efficient and friendly staff, this park is a credit to its owner. Situated in a small, quiet village, it is well set back and screened by mature trees, with wide gravel roads, hedged enclosures, brick pathways and good lighting. All the 90 numbered, level touring pitches are generously sized and have 10/16A electricity connections, 75 with gravel hardstanding and grass for awnings, and 22 are fully serviced (fresh and waste water, electricity and satellite TV). Gazebos or extra tents are not permitted on pitches. Although only a relatively small site its leisure facilities are quite outstanding. The indoor leisure centre has two heated pools, a pool for toddlers, spa pools, saunas, steam room and a fitness suite. A member of the Best of British group.

Facilities

Two heated toilet blocks are well maintained and exceptionally clean, with showers and washbasins in cubicles. A well equipped, separate unit for disabled visitors. Two family bathrooms (with baby bath and changing facilities). Laundry facilities, freezers, fridges and microwaves. Motorcaravan service point. Well stocked shop. Information kiosk. Outdoor chess/draughts, putting green and adventure play area. Indoor swimming pools. WiFi. Games room. Off site: Bird hides 250 yds. Fishing (lake and river) 300 yds and 5 miles. Riding centre and water sports nearby. Golf 5 miles. Oxford 14 miles.

Open: 1 February - mid November.

Directions

Take A415 Witney-Abingdon road and turn into Standlake High Street by garage; park is 300 yds. on the right. GPS: 51.7232, -1.428783

Charges guide

Per unit incl. 2 persons and electricity	£ 17.80 - £ 31.40
extra person	£ 4.20
child (5-14 yrs)	£ 2.60
dog	£ 1.30

Low season offers.

Wool

Whitemead Caravan Park

East Burton Road, Wool BH20 6HG (Dorset) T: 01929 462241. E: whitemeadcp@aol.com

alanrogers.com/UK2090

The Church family continue to make improvements to this attractive little park which is within walking distance of the village of Wool, between Dorchester and Wareham. Very natural and with open views over the Frome Valley water meadows, it provides 95 numbered pitches on flat grass sloping gently north and is orchard-like in parts. The 76 touring pitches are well spaced, mostly backing onto hedges or fences and all have 10A electrical connections. All roads are now tarmac. There are no caravan holiday homes but 19 pitches are seasonal. There may be some rail noise but this is not intrusive at night. The park is 4.5 miles from the nearest beach at Lulworth.

Facilities

The toilet block provides showers, private cubicles and a baby room. Washing machine and dryer. Shop (limited hours) with off-licence, gas supplies and information room/library. Games room with pool table and darts. Playground. Caravan storage. WiFi throughout (free). Off site: The Ship Inn 300 yards. Bicycle hire 2 miles. Riding, fishing and golf 3 miles.

Open: 15 March - 31 October.

Directions

Turn off main A352 on eastern edge of Wool, just north of level crossing, onto East Burton road. Site is 350 yds. on right. GPS: 50.68164, -2.22595

Charges guide

Per unit incl. 2 persons	£ 14.50 - £ 22.00
extra person (over 5 yrs)	£ 4.50 - £ 5.00
dog	£ 0.75 - £ 2.00

No credit cards.

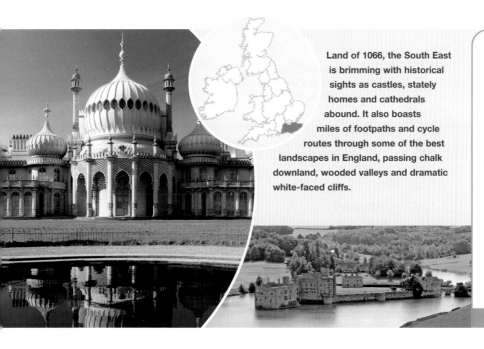

Land of 1066, the South East is brimming with historical sights as castles, stately homes and cathedrals abound. It also boasts miles of footpaths and cycle routes through some of the best landscapes in England, passing chalk downland, wooded valleys and dramatic white-faced cliffs.

THE SOUTH EAST COMPRISES: EAST SUSSEX, WEST SUSSEX, SURREY AND KENT

The chalk countryside of golden downland in Sussex offers many opportunities for an active holiday, from walking and cycling to more adventurous pursuits such as rock climbing or ballooning. Once an ancient forest, much of the Weald is now taken up with farmland, but some areas still remain, including Ashdown Forest, a walkers' paradise with stunning views of the High Weald and South Downs. The many rivers of the county have cut their way through gaps in the chalk landscape, ending spectacularly in white cliffs on the coast. Here you will find the Regency resorts of Bognor Regis and Brighton with its Royal Pavilion, famous pier and quirky shops. Often referred to as the 'Garden of England', Kent is a richly fertile region flourishing with hop gardens, fruit orchards and flowers. It is also home to the world-renowned Canterbury Cathedral, several splendid castles, hidden towns, and quaint villages with oast houses. Surrey too boasts a rich heritage with numerous stately homes and National Trust sites plus large areas of ancient woodland. With a network of rivers, an enjoyable way to explore the beautiful countryside is by boat, stopping off at a riverside pub – or two!

Places of interest

East Sussex: Royal Pavilion, Brighton; the cinque ports towns of Hastings and Rye. Eastbourne with its Victorian pier.

West Sussex: Chichester cathedral; Arundel, with its Norman castle and charming antique shops; Goodwood Racecourse.

Surrey: Guildford castle and cathedral; Mole Valley; Royal Horticultural Society's gardens at Wisley; Chessington World of Adventures; Dorking, a renowned centre for antiques; Runnymede; Thorpe Park in Chertsey.

Kent: Leeds Castle and gardens with maze; Canterbury Cathedral, Roman museum and river tours; Dover, with museum and castle; traditional seaside resort of Broadstairs; Chartwell, family home of Sir Winston Churchill. Turner Art Gallery, Margate.

Did you know?

The Battle of Hastings was actually fought six miles away at Senlac Hill.

Brighton is home to Britain's oldest electric railway, opened by Marcus Volks in 1883.

The modernist De La Warr Pavilion, Bexhill was designed by Serge Chermayeff and Erich Mendelsohn and opened in 1935.

Fishbourne Palace, covering six acres, is the largest Roman site discovered in Britain.

Runnymede takes its name from the meadow where the Magna Carta, the great charter of English liberties, was sealed by King John in 1215.

Oscar Wilde wrote The Importance of Being Earnest in 1895 while living in Worthing.

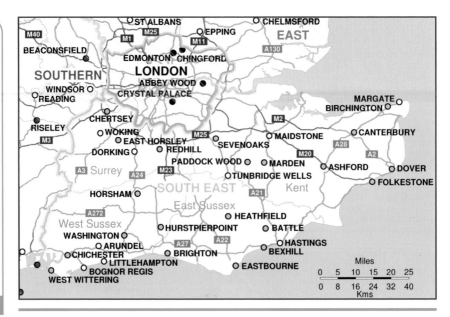

Ashford

Broadhembury Caravan & Camping Park

Steeds Lane, Kingsnorth, Ashford TN26 1NQ (Kent) T: 01233 620859. E: holidaypark@broadhembury.co.uk

alanrogers.com/UK3040

In quiet countryside just outside Ashford and within easy reach of London, Dover, Folkestone and the Kent coast, this sheltered park is attractively landscaped. There are areas for family camping with play areas and amenities designed with children in mind and separate quiet meadows just for adults with new luxury facilities. In total the park takes 101 touring units of any type. The well kept pitches are on level grass and backed by tall, neat hedges, 90 with electricity connections (10/16A). In addition, eight pitches are fully serviced and ten more have double hardstanding plus a grass area for an awning. The welcome is friendly at this popular park and it is often full in the main season.

Facilities

Well equipped toilet block for the family areas and new, block for the couples meadows, both kept very clean. Underfloor heating. Private cabins. High quality facilities for disabled visitors (doubles as family bathroom). Laundry room. Campers' kitchen, with microwaves, fridge and freezer. Motorcaravan service point. Well stocked shop (bread and papers to order). Internet access. Pool room. Games room with video games, table football and table tennis. Two play areas with wood-chip bases. WiFi over site (charged). Dog exercise field – max. 2 per pitch. Large units are accepted if pre-booked. Off site: Fishing 300 m.

Open: All year.

Directions

From M20 exit 10 take A2070. After 2 miles follow sign for Kingsnorth. Turn left at second crossroads in Kingsnorth village. GPS: 51.10647, 0.86809

Charges guide

Per unit incl. 2 persons and electricity	£ 21.50 - £ 25.00
extra person	£ 5.50
child (5-16 yrs)	£ 2.00 - £ 3.50
tent incl. 2 persons	£ 18.00 - £ 22.50

Less 10% for bookings of 7 nights or more.

Battle
Crazy Lane Tourist Caravan Park

Crazy Lane, Sedlescombe, Battle TN33 0QT (East Sussex) T: 01424 870147. E: info@crazylane.co.uk
alanrogers.com/UK2960

This simple, neat, two-acre park has just 36 pitches arranged on grassy terraces, all with 10A electricity and 4 with hardstanding. Many pitches are used by seasonal units so it may be best to phone to make sure space is available before travelling long distances. There is a sloping field towards the top of the site, popular with tent users. With easy access from the A21 (some background road noise), the park is set in the heart of 1066 Country with its historical links. Other local attractions within easy reach include the pretty village of Sedlescombe, a steam railway, an organic vineyard and the seaside at Hastings. This is an ideal park for couples.

Facilities

New solar heated toilet facilities are unisex providing excellent private rooms, each with WC, shower and washbasin. Laundry facilities. Shop at reception. Caravan storage. Off site: Bus stop and pub in village. Golf 0.5 miles. Riding 2 miles. Fishing 3.5 miles. The fascinating towns of Battle and Rye, plus Hastings (6.5 miles) with its beaches, markets and Heritage Shipwreck Centre.

Open: March - October.

Directions

From the A21, 6 miles north of Hastings and 100 yds. south of junction with B2244 (to Sedlescombe), turn right into Crazy Lane. Site is immediately on the right. GPS: 50.92453, 0.53495

Charges guide

Per unit incl. 2 persons and electricity	£ 17.00 - £ 21.00
extra person (over 8 yrs)	£ 1.50
dog	£ 1.00

No credit cards.

Crazy Lane Tourist Park
Whydown Farm, Crazy Lane, Sedlescombe Battle TN33 0QT East Sussex
Tel/Fax: +44 (0)1424 870147 • info@crazylane.co.uk

WELCOME!
Gill and Ron Morgan would like to welcome you to Crazy Lane Tourist Caravan Park. This family-run park is in a quiet, secluded, sun-trapped valley in the heart of '1066' country within easy reach of beach and historical sites.

Battle
Brakes Coppice Park

Forewood Lane, Crowhurst, Battle TN33 9AB (East Sussex) T: 01424 830322. E: brakesco@btinternet.com
alanrogers.com/UK2965

Brakes Coppice Park is a small and secluded site set in woodland just a mile away from historic Battle. Reached by an uneven, winding private track, it is signed to prevent visitors taking a wrong turn to the nearby farm of the same name. Ideal for tents, but welcoming any type of unit, the site has 30 grassy pitches, 21 with 6A electricity and TV aerial points, in a gently sloping field. An adjacent area of 15 small pitches has been set aside for adults only. A further area near a small fishing lake provides a few extra pitches. As well as fishing, visitors can enjoy walking in the surrounding woods.

Facilities

The single toilet block is simple but adequate. Facilities for disabled visitors. Laundry. Shop. Gas supplies. Fishing permits from reception. Off site: Pubs and shops in Crowhurst and Battle. Crowhurst station 10 mins. walk.

Open: 1 March - 31 October.

Directions

From Battle follow the A2100 towards Hastings for 2 miles. Turn right on Telham Lane (signed Crowhurst). Continue into Foreword Lane and turn left on private track shortly after passing sign for Crowhurst village. GPS: 50.89065, 0.507083

Charges guide

Per unit incl. 2 persons	£ 15.00 - £ 19.00
incl. electricity	£ 17.00 - £ 21.00
extra person	£ 4.00
child (5-15 yrs)	£ 2.00
dog	£ 0.50

FREE Alan Rogers Travel Card
Extra benefits and savings - see page 10

Bexhill-on-Sea

Chestnut Meadow Camping & Caravan Park

Ninfield Road, Sidley, Bexhill-on-Sea TN39 5JG (East Sussex) T: 01424 892361.
E: info@chestnutmeadow.co.uk **alanrogers.com/UK2945**

In a peaceful country location near Bexhill, with Hastings and rural East Sussex to explore close by, a family, long used to camping themselves, have developed this into an attractive park. The well drained sheltered meadow is virtually surrounded by trees, with a glimpse of the sea. Flowers and shrubs enhance the entrance and buildings. The 75 large touring pitches (up to 150 sq.m) are marked by posts with numbered buckets which you can use for recycling. Electricity (16A) is available on 74 pitches and 22 have hardstanding beneath the grass, eight with their own water and drainage.

Facilities

Excellent new, heated sanitary building. Shop with local produce at reception. Bar, café (good value, serving breakfast through to evening meal) and takeaway (all high season and weekends). Launderette. Games hall with snooker, pool, table tennis, air hockey, table football. Large, new, fenced play area. WiFi. Off site: Golf and riding 1 mile. International fishing lakes 5 miles. Beach 3 miles. Drusillas Family Park 16 miles.

Open: Mid March - mid January.

Directions

The park is northwest of Bexhill on the A269 Ninfield Road between Sidley and Ninfield, with a 110 yd. entrance drive. GPS: 50.865412, 0.447312

Charges guide

Per unit incl. 2 persons	
and electricity	£ 19.00 - £ 28.00
extra person	£ 4.50
child (5-17 yrs)	£ 2.50

Bexhill-on-Sea

Kloofs Camping & Caravan Park

Sandhurst Lane, Whydown, Bexhill-on-Sea TN39 4RG (East Sussex) T: 01424 842839.
E: camping@kloofs.com **alanrogers.com/UK2955**

This peaceful, rural park is situated in a quiet, country lane with rural views, yet within easy reach of several well known towns on the East Sussex coast. Set in three acres, Kloofs is owned and run by Terry and Helen Griggs who have taken great care in making this a most attractive and well maintained park. There are 50 level, generously sized touring pitches, in two separate areas. Most are on hardstanding, making them suitable for all-weather touring, and have 10/16A electricity, water and drainage. It is evident that considerable investment has been made to ensure visitors have a comfortable stay.

Facilities

One main, centrally heated toilet block is modern and spotlessly clean. Washbasins in cubicles and spacious hot showers. Large shower room for families and en-suite facility for disabled visitors. A second block has additional toilet and shower facilities accessible to disabled visitors. Heated kitchen area. Laundry facilities. Shop in reception for basics and camping gas. Wooden adventure-style play area, fenced. Small library. Off site: Footpath from site to local village for pubs and other eating places 1.4 miles.

Open: All year.

Directions

From the north (Battle), take A269 and turn right into Pear Tree Lane, then right at crossroads. Sandhurst Lane is 300 yds. on left and site is signed a short way down on right. GPS: 50.8560, 0.4271

Charges guide

Per unit incl. 2 persons, electricity and water	£ 25.00
extra person	£ 7.50
child (5-17 yrs)	£ 3.50

Birchington

Quex Caravan Park

Park Road, Birchington CT7 0BL (Kent) T: 01843 841273. E: info@keatfarm.co.uk
alanrogers.com/UK3110

Although there is a large number of privately owned holiday homes at Quex, they do not intrude on the touring area which is in a sheltered glade under tall trees. Here there are 40 shady touring pitches all with 10A electricity hook-ups. This park does not accept tents but will accept trailer tents. This is an attractive and well maintained park, which is well located for the Thanet coast. Local attractions include Quex House and gardens and, of course, the popular seaside resorts of Margate, Ramsgate and Broadstairs. Reception provides a good selection of tourist information and can provide a local map.

Facilities

The central sanitary unit is in a heated chalet style building with all the usual facilities. Laundry room with sink, washing machine and dryer. Well stocked shop. Playground. Café. Takeaway. More than one dog per pitch by prior arrangement only. Off site: Supermarkets close. Fishing, golf and riding 3 miles.

Open: 7 March - 7 November.

Directions

From roundabout at junction of A28 and A299, take A28 east (Birchington and Margate). At Birchington go straight on at roundabout by church, take next right, right again, and left at mini-roundabout. Site is on right in half a mile. GPS: 51.367583, 1.3324

Charges guide

Per unit incl. 2 persons	
and electricity	£ 13.00 - £ 20.00
unit over 7 metres incl. electricity	£ 20.00 - £ 25.00

For latest campsite news visit
alanrogers.com

Brighton

Brighton Caravan Club Site

East Brighton Park, Brighton BN2 5TS (East Sussex) T: 01273 626546

alanrogers.com/UK2930

Brighton is without doubt the South of England's most popular seaside resort, and Brighton Caravan Club's site is a first class base from which to enjoy the many and diverse attractions both in the town and this area of the south coast. A wide tarmac road winds its way through the site from reception, with gravel pitches on either side, leading to terraces with grass pitches on the lower slopes of the valley. The 269 pitches all have 16A electricity, 96 have hardstanding and 12 have water, drainage and TV sockets. Three grass terraces are for tents and these have hard parking nearby.

Facilities

Two heated sanitary blocks include all washbasins in private cabins. In the main season a third timber-clad building provides additional services near the tent area. Well equipped room for wheelchair users, another one for walking disabled, and two baby and toddler wash rooms. Laundry facilities. Motorcaravan service point. Gas available. Milk and bread from reception. Play area with safety base. WiFi. Off site: Brighton 2 miles.

Open: All year.

Directions

From north on M23/A23, join A27 (Lewes). Exit for B2123 (Falmer/Rottingdean). At roundabout turn left on B2123. Continue for 2 miles then turn right at lights by Downs Hotel into Warren Ave. After 1 mile turn left at lights into Wilson Ave, across racecourse. In 1.75 miles at foot of hill (just before lights) turn left and follow lane to site. GPS: 50.820975, -0.097799

Charges guide

Per person	£ 5.40 - £ 7.60
child (5-16 yrs)	£ 1.55 - £ 3.10
pitch incl. electricity (non-member)	£ 13.70 - £ 17.50

Canterbury

Yew Tree Park

Stone Street, Petham, Canterbury CT4 5PL (Kent) T: 01227 700306. E: info@yewtreepark.com

alanrogers.com/UK3060

Yew Tree Park is a small, quiet site located in the Kent countryside overlooking the Chartham Downs. Just five miles south of Canterbury and eight miles north of the M20, it is ideally placed either to explore the delights of the ancient city or the many attractions of eastern and coastal Kent. With some caravan holiday homes, the site also has 45 pitches for touring units and tents. The 27 pitches with 10A electricity are marked on mainly level grass either side of the entrance road, the remainder unmarked on a rather attractive, sloping area, left natural with trees and bushes creating cosy little recesses in which to pitch.

Facilities

Two brick-built sanitary blocks (one for each sex) can be heated. Washbasins (H&C) and four showers (on payment). Extra toilets on the edge of the camping area. Toilet/shower room for families and disabled visitors. Washing machine, dryer and iron. Gas supplies. Outdoor heated swimming pool (53x30 ft; June-Sept). Play area. WiFi throughout (charged). Torches may be useful. Dogs are not accepted. Off site: Pub (serving food) 100 m.

Open: Easter - September.

Directions

From south, take exit 11 from the M20. From Canterbury, ignore signs to Petham and Waltham on B2068 and continue towards Folkestone. From either direction, turn into road beside the Chequers Inn, turn left into park. GPS: 51.2168, 1.058183

Charges guide

Per unit incl. 2 persons and electricity	£ 18.50 - £ 23.50
extra person	£ 4.00 - £ 5.00

Canterbury

Canterbury Camping & Caravanning Club Site

Bekesbourne Lane, Canterbury CT3 4AB (Kent) T: 01227 463216. E: canterbury.site@thefriendlyclub.co.uk

alanrogers.com/UK3070

Situated just off the A257 Sandwich road, about 1.5 miles from the centre of Canterbury, this site is an ideal base for exploring Canterbury and the north Kent coast, as well as being a good stopover to and from the Dover ferries, and the Folkestone Channel Tunnel terminal. There are 200 pitches, 109 with 10/16A electric hook-ups and, except at the very height of the season, you are likely to find a pitch, although not necessarily with electricity. Most of the pitches are on well kept grass with hundreds of saplings planted, but there are also 72 pitches with hardstanding (more are planned).

Facilities

Two modern toilet blocks, the main one with a laundry room. Motorcaravan service point. Reception shop with a small range of essential foods, milk and gas. Excellent tourist information room. Play area with equipment on bark chippings. WiFi throughout (charged). Off site: Golf adjacent. Shop 0.5 miles. Bicycle hire 2 miles.

Open: All year.

Directions

From A2 take Canterbury exit and follow signs for Sandwich (A257). Pass Howe military barracks, turn right into Bekesbourne Lane opposite golf course. Do not use sat nav. GPS: 51.2769, 1.113533

Charges guide

Per person	£ 7.75 - £ 9.45
child (6-18 yrs)	£ 2.70 - £ 2.95
pitch (non-member)	£ 7.10

FREE Alan Rogers Travel Card

Extra benefits and savings - see page 10

Chertsey

Chertsey Camping & Caravanning Club Site

Bridge Road, Chertsey KT16 8JX (Surrey) T: 01932 562405

alanrogers.com/UK2810

This long-established site (1926) is splendidly located on the banks of the River Thames, only a few minutes walk from the shops and amenities of Chertsey. A flagship site for the Club, it was totally redeveloped a few years ago at a cost of over £1 million. There are 200 pitches including 56 new serviced pitches with hardstanding and 16A electricity, and 15 super service pitches which have TV aerial points, water and waste drainage. The work included a new road system, heated toilet blocks with facilities for disabled visitors, recreation hall and much more.

Facilities

The well equipped toilet blocks can be heated and include washbasins in cabins and facilities for disabled visitors. Hairdryers. Laundry. Motorcaravan service point. Well stocked shop for essentials and gas (08.00-11.00 and 16.00-18.00). Fish and chip van calls at weekends. Recreation hall. Play area. Fishing. Dog walk areas. Caravan storage. Torches are necessary. WiFi over site (charged). Off site: Golf and bicycle hire 1 mile. Bus service in Chertsey 1.5 miles. Trains in Weybridge 3 miles.

Open: All year.

Directions

From M25 use exit 11. Turn left at roundabout on A317 towards Shepperton and continue to second set of lights. Turn right, then first left watching for Club camp sign just before Chertsey bridge; narrow opening. GPS: 51.38986, -0.49008

Charges guide

Per person	£ 7.85 - £ 11.30
child (6-18 yrs)	£ 2.85 - £ 6.50
pitch (non-member)	£ 14.95 - £ 18.40

Chichester

Chichester Camping & Caravanning Club Site

345 Main Road, Southbourne PO10 8JH (West Sussex) T: 01243 373202

alanrogers.com/UK2320

This small, neat site is just to the west of Chichester and north of Bosham harbour. Formerly an orchard, it is rectangular in shape with 58 pitches on flat, well mown lawns on either side of gravel roads. All pitches have 16A electricity, 42 with level hardstanding. Although the A27 bypass takes most of the through traffic, the site is by the main A259 road so there may be some traffic noise in some parts (not busy at night). Opposite the park are orchards through which paths lead to the seashore. Arrival must be before 20.00 unless prior arrangements have been made with the site manager.

Facilities

The well designed, brick built toilet block is fully tiled and heated in cool weather, with facilities for campers with disabilities. Washing machines and dryers. Gas supplies. No ball games permitted. Dogs can be walked in the lane by the entrance. WiFi over site (charged). Off site: Shops, restaurants and pubs within easy walking distance in the nearby village and the park is on a main bus route. Excellent caravan shop nearby. Bicycle hire 1 mile.

Open: 2 February - 19 November.

Directions

Park is on A259 at Southbourne, 750 yds. west of Chichester Caravans. Coming from the west, it is 2.8 miles from A27/A259 junction near Havant. GPS: 50.84498, -0.90299

Charges guide

Per person	£ 7.85 - £ 11.70
child (6-18 yrs)	£ 2.85 - £ 6.75
pitch (non-member)	£ 7.10

Chichester

Chichester Lakeside Park

Vinnetrow Road, Chichester PO20 1QH (West Sussex) T: 0845 815 9775. E: lakeside@ParkHolidaysUK.com

alanrogers.com/UK2875

Located just outside the historic city of Chichester, this large site is a member of the Park Holidays group. Set amidst ten fishing lakes, it is within easy access of a sandy beach and the traditional resort of Bognor Regis. The 115 touring pitches with 16A electricity are on three sides of a large, level and grassy field, the fourth side being used for seasonal units and storage. The central, unmarked space is for tents and caravans with no electric hook-ups and a large, fenced area provides space for sports and organised events for the whole park. The larger part of the park is occupied by 400 holiday caravans and the central entertainment area.

Facilities

Two dated toilet blocks are likely to be under pressure at busy times. Facilities for disabled visitors. Shop. Dated bar and snack bar. Entertainment complex. Swimming pool. Fishing. Playing field. Club for children (high season). Tourist information. Mobile homes for rent. WiFi over site (charged). Off site: Riding 2 miles. Golf 2.5 miles. Beach 3 miles. Nearby resort of Bognor Regis. Chichester.

Open: 1 March - 31 October.

Directions

The park is well signed on either side of a roundabout at the junction of the A27 and A259. Turning south on Vinnetrow Road, the park is 200 yards on the right. GPS: 50.823885, -0.75119

Charges guide

Per unit incl. 2 persons and electricity	£ 9.00 - £ 26.00
extra person	£ 2.00 - £ 4.00

For latest campsite news visit

alanrogers.com

Chichester
Warner Farm Touring Park
Warner Lane, Selsey, Chichester PO20 9EL (West Sussex) T: 01243 604499. E: touring@bunnleisure.co.uk
alanrogers.com/UK2885

This site is a member of the Bunn Holiday Villages group, owners of several large holiday home parks which surround the pretty holiday town of Selsey. Warner Farm is a top quality touring park with 174 large grassy pitches and 47 on hardstanding, all with electrical connections. Pitches have a generally open aspect and there is a large area at the back of the site, the 'camping field', which offers an unmarked camping area, as well as providing picnic tables and barbecues. There are 42 serviced pitches with electricity, water and waste water. The site is modern and well maintained, and benefits from free access to the extensive leisure facilities on offer at the neighbouring holiday villages. These include the Oasis Pool and Leisure Complex with two indoor pools, a funfair, bars and restaurants and a lively 'top name' entertainment programme and kids' club. Surprisingly perhaps, the site retains a pleasant rural feel with plenty of space despite its proximity to the sea and the resort of Selsey.

Facilities

Modern toilet block with facilities for disabled visitors. Preset showers in large cubicles. Washing machines and dryers. Small shop. Takeaway. Play area. Multisports area. Communal barbecues, picnic area and dog walking area. Free shuttle bus to neighbouring parks. WiFi throughout (charged). Off site: Nearest beach 900 m. Oasis Pool and Leisure Complex, indoor pools, funfair, bars, restaurants, entertainment and kids' club. Bicycle hire. Tennis.

Open: 1 March - 30 October.

Directions

Head for Chichester on A27. At Whyke roundabout join B2145 and follow signs to Selsey. At Selsey go across mini-roundabout and continue past entrance to Bunn Leisure. After next mini-roundabout take second right into School Lane, right again into Paddock Lane and then first left into Warner Lane. Follow signs to park. GPS: 50.73815, -0.79913

Charges guide

Per unit incl. up to 4 persons	
and electricity	£ 22.50 - £ 39.00
extra person	£ 10.00
extra child (0-18 yrs)	£ 8.00
dog	£ 3.00

Dover
Hawthorn Farm Caravan & Camping Site
Martin Mill, Dover CT15 5LA (Kent) T: 01304 852658. E: info@keatfarm.co.uk
alanrogers.com/UK3100

Hawthorn Farm is a large, relaxed park near Dover. Set in 27 acres, it is an extensive park taking 226 touring units of any type on several large meadows which could accommodate far more, plus 160 privately owned caravan holiday homes in their own areas. Campers not requiring electricity choose their own spot, most staying near the toilet blocks, leaving the farthest fields to those liking solitude. There are 112 pitches with 10/16A electricity, 46 of which are large and separated by hedges, the remainder in glades on either side of tarmac roads. There are 15 new hardstandings available. A well run, relaxed park with plenty of room, mature hedging and trees make an attractive environment. A torch would be useful. Being only four miles from Dover docks, it is a very useful park for those using the ferries and is popular with continental visitors.

Facilities

Two heated toilet blocks are well equipped and of good quality. Facilities for disabled visitors. Baby room. Launderette. Motorcaravan services. Breakfast and other meals are served at the shop (all season). Gates close at 20.00 (22.00 in July/Aug), £10 deposit for card. Caravan storage. Off site: Martin Mill railway station 500 yds. Riding 0.5 miles. Golf 3 miles. Bicycle hire, fishing and boat launching 4 miles.

Open: 1 March - 31 October.

Directions

Park is north of the A258 road (Dover-Deal), with signs to park and Martin Mill where you turn off 4 miles from Dover. GPS: 51.16855, 1.346333

Charges guide

Per unit incl. 2 persons	
and electricity	£ 14.00 - £ 21.00
extra person	£ 3.00 - £ 3.50
child (5-16 yrs)	£ 2.00 - £ 2.25
dog	£ 1.50

Less 10% for 4 nights booked (and paid for on arrival).

FREE Alan Rogers Travel Card
Extra benefits and savings - see page 10

East Horsley

Horsley Camping & Caravanning Club Site

Ockham Road North, East Horsley KT24 6PE (Surrey) T: 01483 283273

alanrogers.com/UK2820

London and all the sights are only 40 minutes away by train, yet Horsley is a delightful, quiet unspoilt site with a good duck and goose population on its part lily covered lake (unfenced). It provides 130 pitches, of which 73 have 10A electrical connections and 51 are on hardstandings. Seventeen pitches are around the bank of the lake, the rest further back in three hedged, grass fields with mostly level ground but with some slope in places. A new area has been developed in woodland. There is a range of mature trees and a woodland dog walk area (may be muddy). The soil is clay based so rain tends to settle – sluice gates remove extra water from the lake area when the rain is heavy. Basic provisions, gas and books are kept in reception and resident managers will make you comfortable.

Facilities

Two purpose built, heated toilet blocks with good design and fittings, with some washbasins in cabins, a Belfast sink and parent and child room with vanity style basin, toilet and wide surface area. Laundry room and new drying areas. Well designed facilities for disabled visitors. Small shop in reception. Play area. Recreation hall with table tennis. Fishing is possible from May (adult £6.10, children £3.10 per day, NRA licence required). WiFi (charged). Off site: Shops and the station are 1 mile. Pubs 1.5-2 miles. Golf 1.5 miles. Riding 2 miles.

Open: 1 April - 31 October.

Directions

From M25 exit 10, towards Guildford, after 0.5 miles take first left B2039 to Ockham and East Horsley, continuing through Ockham towards East Horsley. After 2 miles start to watch for brown site sign (not easy to see) and site is on right in 2.5 miles. GPS: 51.28504, -0.44869

Charges guide

Per person	£ 7.65 - £ 10.15
child (6-18 yrs)	£ 2.65 - £ 2.85
pitch (non-member)	£ 14.75 - £ 17.25

Eastbourne

Bay View Park

327

Old Martello Road, Pevensey Bay BN24 6DX (East Sussex) T: 01323 768688. E: holidays@bay-view.co.uk

alanrogers.com/UK2920

This friendly beachside park is located at the end of a private road right beside the beautiful Sussex coast and its pebble beach and the park's own brand new 9-hole golf course. Two separate areas of grass (some areas are a little uneven) are surrounded by low banks and hedges to give some shelter if it is windy. Careful use of wooden fencing adds to the attractiveness, whilst also keeping the rabbits off the flowers. The 94 touring pitches (80 sq.m, most with 16A electricity and some with hardstanding) are neatly marked and numbered. Several caravan holiday homes for hire are positioned at the back of the park. The golf course clubhouse provides tea, coffee and snacks. Visitors can enjoy all the attractions of Sussex, as well as swimming, fishing and windsurfing. This is an ideal park for a family beach holiday. A cycle path leads to Pevensey Bay and Eastbourne's Sovereign Harbour marina with its shops, restaurants and cinema.

Facilities

Each area has toilet facilities, one a new, fully equipped block with private cubicles (shower, washbasin and WC) and facilities for babies and disabled visitors. Heated when required, both blocks are kept very clean. Fully equipped laundry room. Motorcaravan services. Well stocked shop. Golf (9-holes). Clubhouse for tea, coffee and snacks. Gas. Play area (10 yrs and under). Winter caravan storage. Off site: Sailing club. Sea fishing. Indoor swimming pool 1 mile. Bicycle hire (delivery to site) 1 mile. Riding 5 miles.

Open: 1 March - 31 October.

Directions

From the A27/A259 roundabout at Pevensey take A259 through Pevensey Bay. Park and golf course are signed after 1 mile (private access road) to the left, 2 miles east of Eastbourne. GPS: 50.79998, 0.33797

Charges guide

Per unit incl. 2 persons and electricity	£ 20.00 - £ 24.00
extra person	£ 4.00
child (5-16 yrs)	£ 2.00
dog	£ 1.00

Couples and families only. No commercial vehicles, large vans or pick-ups.

Eastbourne
Fairfields Farm Caravan & Camping Park
Eastbourne Road, Westham, Pevensey BN24 5NG (East Sussex) T: 01323 763165.
E: enquiries@fairfieldsfarm.com **alanrogers.com/UK2915**

Part of a working, family-run farm, this is a simple peaceful park which is ideally located to enjoy the Sussex countryside and coast, just a short distance from Eastbourne. A single, rectangular meadow is split by a line of attractive silver birch trees and provides 66 large pitches, all but four with electricity connections. The farm and its rural landscape stretch towards the sea at Pevensey Bay. Beyond the camping field there is a duck pond with grassy surrounds and picnic benches, pens with numerous small animals and pets and a pleasant walk to a fishing lake. Children are invited to feed the animals (with special food on sale). Within walking distance are the villages of Westham and Pevensey with several pubs and restaurants, as well as Pevensey Castle which has a history spanning 16 centuries. Eastbourne has a promenade, beautiful beaches and a retail complex and cinema at the Sovereign Centre.

Facilities

The single, central toilet block is traditional in style and very clean. An adjacent building houses showers and toilets for disabled visitors. Laundry facilities. Farm shop. Small animals and pets. Fishing lake (licence required). WiFi throughout (free). Off site: Pubs, restaurants and fish and chip shop within walking distance. Beach 1.5 miles. Golf 4 miles. Eastbourne 5 miles.

Open: 22 March - 31 October.

Directions

From the roundabout junction of the A27 and the A259 (petrol station) take exit to Pevensey and the Castle. Go around the castle walls and into Westham village. At end of high street turn left (B2191), over level crossing and park is on left.
GPS: 50.81358, 0.32448

Charges guide

Per unit incl. 2 persons	£ 17.00 - £ 20.00
incl. electricity	£ 21.00 - £ 24.00
extra person	£ 3.00
child (3-13 yrs)	£ 2.50
dog	£ 2.50

FAIRFIELDS FARM
fairfields farm CARAVAN AND CAMPING PARK
This seasonal touring park provides good, clean facilities in peaceful surroundings. On site you will find a duck pond, farm pets, beautiful lakeside walk and free fishing
Eastbourne Road - Westham - Pevensey - East Sussex - BN24 5NG
Tel: 01323 763165 - Email: enquiries@fairfieldsfarm.com - www.fairfieldsfarm.com
Free WiFi

Folkestone
Black Horse Farm Caravan Club Site
385 Canterbury Road, Densole, Folkestone CT18 7BG (Kent) T: 01303 892665
alanrogers.com/UK3090

This neat, tidy and attractive six-acre park, owned by the Caravan Club, is situated amidst farming country in the village of Densole on the Downs just four miles north of Folkestone, eight west of Dover and 11 south of Canterbury. Accessed directly from the A260, the tarmac entrance road leads past reception towards the top field which has gravel hardstanding pitches with a grass area for awnings (possibly some road noise), past hedging to the smaller middle area, then to the large bottom field, which has been redeveloped to provide some larger pitches (including 15 for tents and some to accommodate larger motorcaravans). There are 118 pitches in total, 77 hardstanding, all with 16A electricity.

Facilities

The carefully thought out and well constructed toilet blocks, one below reception and the other at the far end of the site, have washbasins in private cabins with curtains, good sized shower compartments, a baby room and facilities for disabled visitors, laundry and dishwashing facilities, all well heated in cool weather. Motorcaravan service point. Gas supplies. Play area. A fish and chip van calls on Thursdays (April-Sept). Caravan storage. Off site: Riding 1 mile. Golf and fishing 5 miles.

Open: All year.

Directions

Directly by the A260 Folkestone-Canterbury road, 2 miles north of junction with A20. Follow signs for Canterbury. GPS: 51.132617, 1.158483

Charges guide

Per person	£ 4.30 - £ 6.20
child (5-16 yrs)	£ 1.30 - £ 2.20
pitch incl. electricity (non-member)	£ 12.90 - £ 16.00

FREE Alan Rogers Travel Card
Extra benefits and savings - see page 10

Folkestone
Little Satmar Holiday Park

Winehouse Lane, Capel-le-Ferne, Folkestone CT18 7JF (Kent) T: 01303 251188. E: info@keatfarm.co.uk

alanrogers.com/UK3095

Capel-le-Ferne is a relatively little known seaside town midway between Dover and Folkestone. Little Satmar is a quiet site a short walk from the delightful cliff top paths which run between these towns and which offer fine views across the English Channel. The site is a member of the Keat Farm group and is located about a mile from the village. There are 61 touring pitches, 51 of which have 10A electricity. The pitches generally have a sunny, open setting, a few with rather more shade. Privately owned mobile homes occupy 78 pitches between the entrance to the site and reception, but these are quite separate from the touring field.

Facilities

Two toilet blocks (one in a Portacabin style unit) are modern and kept very clean and the main block has now been fitted with heating. Washing and drying machines. Shop (with gas). Play area. For more than 1 dog per unit, contact park. Off site: Bus at end of lane to Dover and Folkestone. Port Lympne Zoo, seafront funpark nearby.

Open: 1 March - 31 October.

Directions

Leave A20 Dover-Folkestone road at Capel-le-Ferne exit and follow signs to the village. Site is clearly signed to right after 0.75 miles.
GPS: 51.101917, 1.222933

Charges guide

Per unit incl. 2 persons and electricity	£ 14.00 - £ 21.00
extra person	£ 3.00 - £ 3.50
child (5-16 yrs)	£ 2.00 - £ 2.25
dog	£ 1.50

For latest campsite news visit
alanrogers.com

Heathfield
Horam Manor Touring Park
Horam, Heathfield TN21 0YD (East Sussex) T: 01435 813662. E: camp@horam-manor.co.uk
alanrogers.com/UK2900

This family-run park is situated on a manor estate, perfect for touring East Sussex. The first field now offers level pitches throughout, all with 16A hook-ups and including 20 hardstandings. In total there are 90 spacious pitches, all with electricity. A brand new toilet block has underfloor heating, large showers, private washing cubicles and carefully designed facilities for disabled visitors. The park is set back form the main road and is a haven of peace and tranquillity, although in high season it becomes busy. For younger visitors there is a play area. On the manor estate, amenities include horse riding, fishing, the Lakeside Café and peaceful walks through the woods. Local buses serve all major towns in the area or you can bring your bike and explore the countryside on the Cuckoo Trail (2 minutes from the park).

Facilities

New heated toilet block, private cubicles, large showers. New room for disabled visitors, family room with shower, washbasin, toilet and baby bath. Tourist information. Gas supplies. New play area. WiFi throughout (charged). Off site: Horam Manor adjacent with café, fishing and riding. Shops and inns within walking distance. Tennis (small fee) 200 yds. Golf within 1 mile. The coastal towns of Brighton, Hastings and Eastbourne are within easy reach, as is the famous Pantiles at Tunbridge Wells.

Open: 1 March - 31 October.

Directions

Horam is on the A267 between Tunbridge Wells and Eastbourne and entry to the park is signed at the recreation ground at southern edge of the village. GPS: 50.931783, 0.240167

Charges guide

Per unit incl. 2 adults, 2 children	
and electricity	£ 22.50 - £ 25.00
extra person	£ 6.50
extra child	£ 2.50

Horsham
Honeybridge Park
Honeybridge Lane, Dial Post, Horsham RH13 8NX (West Sussex) T: 01403 710923.
E: enquiries@honeybridgepark.co.uk **alanrogers.com/UK2940**

This 15 acre park is situated amidst beautiful woodlands and countryside on the edge of the South Downs, within an Area of Outstanding Natural Beauty. Of the 150 pitches, 120 are for touring, some are on hardstandings and all have 16A electricity. The remaining pitches are occupied by holiday homes but these are in a separate area. Some pitches are hedged for privacy, others are on slightly sloping grass, well spaced and generously sized. A large wooden, adventure-style playground is provided for children away from the pitches, and simple family entertainment is organised on special occasions. A large games room provides table tennis, pool, a library and TV with freeview channels.

Facilities

Two modern toilet facilities (one new) are heated in cool weather and include spacious facilities for disabled visitors (Radar key). Laundry facilities. Motorcaravan service point. Licensed shop and café. Play area. Games room with library. Security barrier (card access) is locked 23.00-07.00. Caravan for hire. Off site: Bus 0.5 miles. Pub/restaurant in nearby Dial Post village. Old Barn Nurseries serves meals during the day. Fishing 1 mile. Riding 5 miles. Billingshurst and Horsham are both 8 miles. Golf and beach at Worthing 10 miles.

Open: All year.

Directions

Two miles south of the junction of A24 and A272 at Dial Post, turn east by Old Barn Nurseries. Follow signs to site (about 0.5 miles). GPS: 50.94864, -0.35274

Charges guide

Per unit incl. 2 persons	
and electricity	£ 18.60 - £ 26.00
extra person	£ 3.30 - £ 7.00
child (5-14 yrs)	£ 2.50
dog	£ 1.40

FREE Alan Rogers Travel Card
Extra benefits and savings - see page 10

Hurstpierpoint
Apollo Sun Club

The Weald, Langton Lane, Hurstpierpoint BN6 6AA (West Sussex) T: 07932 812343

alanrogers.com/UK2942

We plan to visit the Apollo Sun Club during 2013. For further information about this naturist club before we do so, please contact the Club.

Apollo Sun Club

Come and enjoy the freedom and relaxation of naturism at our beautiful club in West Sussex.

We are 10miles from Brighton, one of England's most vibrant cities. We have full facilities to help you enjoy your stay, excellent toilets, solar heated pool, sauna & bbq area. Local amenities include supermarket, pubs & restaurants all in local village.

Further info at: www.apollosunclub.co.uk - Bookings to: brianasc@btinternet.com

Marden
Tanner Farm Touring Caravan & Camping Park

Goudhurst Road, Marden TN12 9ND (Kent) T: 01622 832399. E: enquiries@tannerfarmpark.co.uk

alanrogers.com/UK3030

Tanner Farm is a quality park, developed as part of a family working farm in the heart of the Weald of Kent. It is surrounded by orchards, oast houses, lovely countryside and delightful small villages and the owners are much concerned with conserving the natural beauty of the environment. The park extends over 15 acres, most of which is level with part on a gentle slope. The grass meadowland has been semi-landscaped by planting saplings, etc. which units back onto, as the owners do not wish to regiment pitches into rows. There are 100 pitches, all with 16A electricity, 38 with hardstanding, 25 with water tap and 12 with waste water point also. A member of Best of British and Countryside Discovery groups.

Facilities

Two heated, well cared for sanitary units include some washbasins in private cubicles in both units. Purpose built facilities for disabled visitors. Bathroom (£1 token) and baby facilities in the newer block (closed Nov-Easter). Launderette. Motorcaravan service point. Reception, shop and tourist information (hours and stock limited in winter) with meeting/conference facilities. Gas supplies. WiFi in reception area. Off site: Riding and golf within 6 miles. Shopping facilities at Maidstone and Tunbridge Wells.

Open: All year.

Directions

Park is 2.5 miles south of Marden on B2079 towards Goudhurst. GPS: 51.1471, 0.47482

Charges guide

Per person	£ 5.50 - £ 7.10
child (5-16 yrs)	£ 1.60 - £ 2.55
pitch incl. electricity (non-member)	£ 3.75 - £ 9.90
tent pitch	£ 1.75 - £ 6.90

Only one car per pitch permitted.

Paddock Wood
The Hop Farm Touring & Camping Park
Maidstone Road, Paddock Wood TN12 6PY (Kent) T: 01622 870858. E: touring@thehopfarm.co.uk
alanrogers.com/UK3055

Set in 400 acres of the Garden of England, The Hop Farm is a popular family visitor attraction. There are plenty of activities to entertain children including adventure play areas (indoor and outdoor), a driving school, funfair rides, the Magic Factory and the Great Goblin Hunt. This is also the venue for many special events throughout the summer including music festivals, shows and other gatherings. To one side and overlooking all this activity and the attractive cluster of oasts is the touring park which provides over 300 grass and hardstanding pitches on flat, open fields. Electricity (16A) and water are available. There is also plenty more space for tents. The principal toilet block is clean and provides straightforward, simple facilities. It can be supplemented by Portacabin style units when events bring extra campers. Entry to the visitor attraction is half price for caravanners and campers and includes the Shires Restaurant and the Happy Hopper's café. This park would particularly suit those looking to enjoy the visitor attraction or attend one of the events.

Facilities

Brick built toilet block with open washbasins, preset showers (with curtain) and toilets. Further Portacabin style units when the park is full for events. Small shop (in reception) for essentials. Restaurant and café at the visitor attraction (half price entry for campers). Nature walks. Boat launching. Fishing. Dogs accepted but not permitted inside the visitor attraction. Activities and entertainment at the visitor attraction. Off site: Shops, restaurants and golf courses nearby.

Open: 1 March - 31 October.

Directions

The Hop Farm is located on the A228 near Paddock Wood. Follow the brown tourist signs from exit 4 of the M20 or exit 5 of the M25 onto the A21 south. GPS: 51.200725, 0.39333

Charges guide

Per unit incl. 4 persons and electricity	£ 18.45 - £ 26.45
extra person (over 3 yrs)	£ 2.50
dog	£ 1.50

THE HOP FARM TOURING & CAMPING PARK
A great value touring and camping park surrounded by over 400 acres of beautiful countryside and woodland backing on to the River Medway - right in the heart of Kent!
Enquiries & Bookings 01892 838161
touring@thehopfarm.co.uk · www.thehopfarm.co.uk/touring

MAIDSTONE ROAD, BELTRING, NR TONBRIDGE, PADDOCK WOOD, KENT TN12 6PY

Redhill
Alderstead Heath Caravan Club Site
Dean Lane, Merstham, Redhill RH1 3AH (Surrey) T: 01737 644629
alanrogers.com/UK2800

Alderstead Heath is a surprisingly rural site given that it lies just 35 minutes from central London by train. It is also well located for exploring the North Downs and is situated on the Pilgrim's Way. There are 150 touring pitches, all with 16A electrical connections. Most pitches are on well kept grass, but there are also 68 hardstandings. Given the proximity of the M25 and M23 motorways, there is a certain amount of background traffic noise in parts of the site, but this is not obtrusive. An attractive wooded area surrounds the site and concrete tracks there were laid during the war for tanks in preparation for the D-Day landings. Part of the site is used for seasonal pitches.

Facilities

Two well maintained toilet blocks, include a parent and toddler bathroom. The main block houses facilities for disabled visitors. Laundry facilities. Motorcaravan service point. Reception stocks a small range of essential foods, milk and gas. Two small play areas. Football field. Good tourist information room. WiFi throughout. Off site: Golf 2 miles. Fishing 3 miles.

Open: All year.

Directions

Leave M25 at exit 8 and join A217 (signed Reigate). Fork left after 300 yds. (signed Merstham). After a further 2.5 miles turn left at T-junction and join A23. After 500 yds. turn right into Shepherd's Hill and after 1 mile left into Dean Lane. Site is on right after 175 yds. Avoid sat nav route via M23/A23 (J7), where Dean Lane is very narrow. GPS: 51.283284, -0.138702

Charges guide

Per person	£ 4.60 - £ 6.20
child (5-16 yrs)	£ 1.30 - £ 2.20
pitch (non-member)	£ 13.15 - £ 16.00

FREE Alan Rogers Travel Card
Extra benefits and savings - see page 10

Sevenoaks
Thriftwood Camping & Caravan Park

Plaxdale Green Road, Stansted, Sevenoaks TN15 7PB (Kent) T: 01732 822261.
E: info@thriftwoodholidaypark.com **alanrogers.com/UK3038**

Thriftwood Holiday Park is a well located base for exploring Kent, and has good access to a major motorway network. London can be reached in around 50 minutes from Borough Green station (two miles). There is an attractive touring area here with a good number of hardstandings available, and grassy tent pitches around the edge. Some pitches may require the use of levelling blocks. Around 150 pitches have electrical connections. The toilet block has recently been refurbished to a very high standard. Amenities include a swimming pool and a convivial bar/club house where meals may be ordered. There is some entertainment, mainly in high season. The historic town of Sevenoaks is within easy reach, along with its magnificent Elizabethan place, Knole House. Tonbridge and Royal Tunbridge Wells are also close at hand, and, by way of contrast, the large shopping centres at Bluewater and Lakeside are easily accessible, as well as Brands Hatch racing circuit.

Facilities

Recently refurbished toilet block with facilities for disabled visitors. Shop (in reception). Bar/snack bar/club house. Swimming pool (Easter-end Sept). Play area. Games arcade. Nature walks. Tourist information. Mobile homes for rent. Off site: Hotel/restaurant 150 yds. All amenities and railway station in Borough Green 2 miles. Brands Hatch 2 miles. Fishing 3 miles. Golf 5 miles.

Open: All year excl. February.

Directions

Leave M20 motorway at exit 2 and take northbound A20 towards West Kingsdown and Brands Hatch. After passing across 2 roundabouts, turn right into Labour in Vain Road and follow signs to the site. GPS: 51.324233, 0.292382

Charges guide

Per unit incl. 2 persons and electricity	£ 18.00 - £ 40.00
extra person	£ 5.00
child (5-12 yrs)	£ 2.00
dog	£ 2.00

Sevenoaks
Gate House Wood Touring Park

Ford Lane, Wrotham Heath, Sevenoaks TN15 7SD (Kent) T: 01732 843062.
E: contact@gatehousewoodtouringpark.com **alanrogers.com/UK3120**

This sheltered park has been created in a former quarry where all the pitches are on well drained grass. A spacious paved entrance with an attractive reception building and well stocked shop, leads on to the park itself. The 54 pitches are level and open with a few small trees, two brick built barbecue units, and 36 electric hook-ups (10A). A playground has swings, seesaw and a slide, all set on a safety base, and the entire site is enclosed by grassy banks on three sides, with a wild flower walk around the top. Local attractions include Brands Hatch Circuit (four miles), the International Karting Circuit at Buckmore Park (seven miles), and the nearby Country Parks at West Malling and Trosley.

Facilities

Comprehensive toilet facilities are smart and well maintained, including a well equipped room which is designed for disabled visitors. The laundry and dishwashing room is at one end of the modern heated building and has a fridge/freezer. Shop (in reception) has fresh bread daily. Children's play area. WiFi (charged). No dogs or other pets. Caravans/motorcaravans greater than 28 ft. overall are not admitted. Commercial vehicles are not accepted. Off site: Within walking distance are three pubs and a good Cantonese restaurant. Golf 1 mile. Trains to London Victoria from Borough Green (2 miles). Riding 3 miles. Fishing 7 miles.

Open: 1 March - 31 October.

Directions

From M26 exit 2a, take A20 eastwards towards Wrotham Heath and Maidstone. Just past junction with A25, and opposite the Royal Oak pub, turn left into Ford Lane, and park is immediately on left. GPS: 51.300133, 0.345383

Charges guide

Per unit incl. 2 persons and electricity	£ 16.00 - £ 20.00
extra person	£ 4.00
child (5-12 yrs)	£ 2.50
No credit cards.	

For latest campsite news visit
alanrogers.com

Washington
Washington Caravan & Camping Park
Old London Road, Washington RH20 4AJ (West Sussex) T: 01903 892869. E: washcamp@amserve.com
alanrogers.com/UK2950

Washington is a pleasant campsite to the north of Worthing with a bias towards tenting families and groups. It provides only 21 hardstanding pitches for caravans and motorcaravans, and a large gently sloping grassy field with enough space for 80 tents. There are 23 electric hook-ups (16A). There is some road noise from the A24. Local attractions (all with free admission, check opening times) include Highdown Chalk Gardens at Worthing, Nutbourne Vineyard near Pulborough, and Steyning Museum. Parham House is another beautiful privately owned house and garden worthy of a visit. Brighton with its famous Pavilion, plenty of shops and seafront is within easy reach.

Facilities

A heated wooden chalet-style building houses the sanitary facilities including spacious shower rooms (20p) and indoor dishwashing and laundry facilities. No on-site shop but eggs, bread, butter and milk can be bought from the reception office. Drinks machine and freezer. Off site: Bus stop 200 yds in village. Eating out options include the local pub and a nearby restaurant. Beach 9 miles.

Open: All year.

Directions

Site entrance is just east of the junction of A24 and A283 at Washington, 6 miles north of Worthing. GPS: 50.90875, -0.4056

Charges guide

Per unit incl. 2 persons	£ 21.00
extra person	£ 4.00 - £ 5.00
tent	£ 6.00 - £ 12.00
electricity on meter	£ 0.50
car	£ 5.00

Weekly terms acc. to time of year.

West Wittering
Nunnington Farm Campsite
Rookwood Road, West Wittering PO20 8LZ (West Sussex) T: 01243 514013.
E: nunningtonfarm@hotmail.com **alanrogers.com/UK2895**

This no-frills, basic, family run farm site for touring units only can be found on the coast a mere seven miles from Chichester. There are 200 touring pitches, 110 with 15A electricity connections. The pitches are large, level and grassy, providing a comfortable feeling, even when the site is full. The safe, sandy beaches of The Witterings, only a mile away, make this an especially good venue for families in the holidays and a quieter one for off-season visitors. The easily accessible pets corner is an attraction for children of all ages. Visitors with tents are very welcome here and a second field is opened in busy periods, but with no electricity.

Facilities

Three rather dated but clean, central toilet blocks provide all facilities including showers in cubicles, open washbasins, baby bath, washing machines and ramped facilities for disabled visitors (key access). Motorcaravan service point. Gates closed 23.00-07.00. Off site: Local shops 300 yds. Bus service to Chichester every 30 mins. Beach and boat mooring 1 mile. Bicycle hire 2 miles. Golf 3 miles.

Open: Easter - second week October.

Directions

From A27 at Chichester, take A286 signed The Witterings and continue to roundabout. Take second exit on B2179 for West Wittering and site is on left after 2 miles. GPS: 50.78377, -0.88588

Charges guide

Per unit incl. 2 persons and electricity	£ 23.00 - £ 26.00
extra person	£ 5.00
child (under 17 yrs)	£ 1.00
boat	£ 2.00

No credit cards.

FREE Alan Rogers Travel Card
Extra benefits and savings - see page 10

The largest city in Europe, covering over 600 square miles, London is jam packed with hundreds of magnificent museums, impressive art galleries, historic buildings and monuments, beautiful parks, bustling shopping centres and markets; it really has something to offer everyone.

WE HAVE CHOSEN FOUR PARKS WHICH HAVE EASY ACCESS TO CENTRAL LONDON, INCLUDING ONE IN HERTFORDSHIRE

Despite its size, London is relatively easy to explore, largely thanks to the efficient underground service. Buses are also very useful and allow you to see the famous sights as you travel, in particular, the open-top tourist buses which ply the streets offer a good introduction to the city. Among London's many landmarks are the Tower of London, Trafalgar Square, Piccadilly Circus, Buckingham Palace, Big Ben and the Houses of Parliament, to name but a few! Running through the heart of London is the River Thames, dividing north and south; over the years many attractions, restaurants and chic bars have appeared along its banks. Being one of the most multicultural cities in the world, there is a huge choice of restaurants offering a diverse variety of cuisine; food markets are dotted all around the capital. Shopping is another major feature of the city, from the famous Harrods store and Harvey Nichols, to commercial Oxford Street and the street markets of Camden Town and Portobello Road. If all the crowds become too much then head to one of London's beautiful parks such as St. James's Park next to Buckingham Palace, or Hyde Park, where you can take a boat trip along the Serpentine.

Places of interest

London Eye: world's highest observation wheel, reaching 443 feet. With 32 capsules, carrying 25 passengers in each, it offers breathtaking views.

Tower of London: home of the Crown Jewels and the Yeoman Warders.

Tate Modern: contemporary art gallery housed in the converted Bankside Power Station.

Natural History Museum: over 70 million items relating to the life and earth sciences.

Kew Gardens: beautiful botanical gardens, with over 40,000 varieties of plants.

Imperial War Museum: charting the impact of conflict from WWI to the present day.

Hampton Court Palace: one of the best palaces in Britain, with a maze.

British Museum: houses a treasure trove of objects from all over the globe.

Did you know?

One in eight of the UK population live in London and over 300 languages are spoken.

Following expansion in the 1930s and '40s, less than 50% of London's Underground railway is actually below ground.

Founded in 1753, the British Museum is the oldest public museum in the world.

The Great Fire of London destroyed over 13,000 houses and 87 churches.

London's licensed taxi drivers have to pass a test known as the Knowledge, which requires them to learn over 300 routes in the centre of the city.

At over 900 years old, the Tower of London has been a palace, prison, treasury, arsenal and even a zoo.

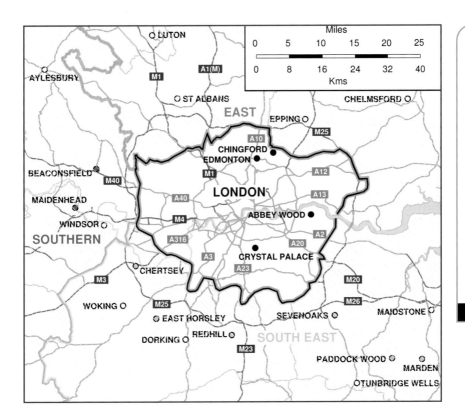

Abbey Wood

Abbey Wood Caravan Club Site

Federation Road, Abbey Wood, London SE2 0LS (London) T: 020 8311 7708

alanrogers.com/UK3260

Situated close to Abbey Wood, it is hard to believe that this park is in London and the wardens have made every effort to create an attractive environment. There are 100 level caravan pitches, all with 16A electricity and TV aerial connections; of these, 73 have hardstandings. A large tent area provides an additional 100 pitches. Many pitches benefit from the shade of mature trees. A secure fence around the perimeter is linked to closed-circuit TV cameras, and just outside is a late arrivals area with electricity and toilets; also protected by cameras. This park attracts many UK and overseas visitors as it offers a very good base from which to visit central London. A train service runs every 15 minutes from Abbey Wood station (five minutes walk) to either Charing Cross or Cannon Street (around 35 minutes).

Facilities

Three modern, fully equipped toilet blocks, two with underfloor heating, one designed to be open all year, include washbasins in cubicles, generous showers, baby/toddler washroom. Good private facilities for disabled visitors. Laundry facilities. Motorcaravan service point. Gas. Bread, milk and cold drinks from reception (high season). Play area. Good travel and information centre. WiFi over site (charged). Off site: Sports centre 1 mile. Golf 4 miles.

Open: All year.

Directions

From east on M2/A2 or from central London: on A2 (third exit) turn off at A221 into Danson Road (Bexleyheath, Welling, Sidcup). Follow Bexleyheath sign to Crook Log (A207 junction); at lights turn right and immediately left into Brampton Road. In 1.5 miles at lights turn left into Bostal Road (A206); in 0.75 miles at traffic lights turn right into Basildon Road (B213). In 300 yds. turn right into McLeod Road, in 0.5 miles at roundabout turn right into Knee Hill, in 100 yds. take second right into Federation Road. Site on left in 50 yds. From M25, north, west or south approach: leave at exit 2 onto A2 (signed London), then as above. GPS: 51.48693, 0.11757

Charges guide

Per person	£ 6.00 - £ 7.75
child (5-16 yrs)	£ 1.85 - £ 3.10
pitch incl. electricity (non-member)	£ 13.70 - £ 15.60

Tent campers apply to site.

FREE Alan Rogers Travel Card
Extra benefits and savings - see page 10

Chingford
Lee Valley Campsite

Sewardstone Road, Chingford, London E4 7RA (London) T: 020 8529 5689. E: scs@leevalleypark.org.uk
alanrogers.com/UK3250

This attractive site provides an excellent base from which to visit London, having both easy access to the M25 and excellent public transport links into the centre of London. Close to Epping Forest in the heart of the Lee Valley, this site is on a hillside overlooking the King George reservoir in a very pleasant and relaxed setting. Like its sister sites, it is understandably very popular with foreign tourers. With capacity for 200 units the site is mostly level, with several bush sheltered avenues and plenty of trees throughout providing shade. There are 20 pitches with tarmac hardstanding and 100 with 10A electricity. American motorhomes are not accepted. Just outside the gate is a bus stop (reception have full details of good value Travelcard schemes). The bus (no. 215) will take you to Walthamstow Central Underground station from where a frequent service runs to central London.

Facilities

Three blocks offer good facilities (one is heated in low season), all recently totally refurbished. Good en-suite room for disabled visitors. Baby changing area. Laundry. Motorcaravan service point. Well stocked shop. Gas available. Playground. Off site: Fishing 500 yards. Shops within 2 miles. Riding 1 mile. 9-hole golf 1 mile, 18-hole golf 3 miles. Waltham Abbey 3 miles. River Lee Country Park and Epping Forest nearby.

Open: 1 April - 4 November.

Directions

From M25 take exit 26 on A112 to Chingford and site is on right in 3 miles. From A10 take A110 (Chingford). After passing between reservoirs, at next traffic lights turn left on A112. Site on left after 2 miles. GPS: 51.653983, -0.006517

Charges guide

Per unit incl. 2 persons	£ 24.90 - £ 38.20
child (under 16 yrs)	£ 2.50 - £ 5.50
electricity	£ 3.80

Min. charge £8.60 per unit/night.

Crystal Palace
Crystal Palace Caravan Club Site

Crystal Palace Parade, London SE19 1UF (London) T: 020 8778 7155
alanrogers.com/UK3270

The Caravan Club's site at Crystal Palace in south London provides easy access to the city centre and its many attractions. The 126 pitches are pleasantly arranged in terraces overlooking the ruins of the old Crystal Palace, its park and National Sports Centre, and are allocated by the site warden. It is surprisingly quiet given its location (with the exception of police sirens and over-flying aircraft). In peak season advance booking is always necessary. Sixty-eight pitches are on gravel hardstandings, useful for out of season stays. There are places for 126 caravans and motorcaravans, all with 16A electricity.

Facilities

The main toilet block can be heated in cool weather and has curtained washbasins for ladies. Another block provides basic unisex showers and toilets. Facilities for disabled visitors. Laundry room. Motorcaravan service facilities. Small shop in reception. Gas available. WiFi over site (charged). Off site: Shops, pubs, etc. 400 yds. Many buses stop outside the site, including services to central London. National Cycle Network.

Open: All year.

Directions

On A205 South Circular travelling east, pass Dulwich College and golf course, turn right at traffic lights. Within 400 yds, at lights, turn right into Sydenham Hill. In 350 yds. at roundabout turn left. Site is 1 mile the opposite mini-roundabouts. Travelling west on A205 South Circular, immediately after passing under Catford railway bridge, keep left onto A212 (Crystal Palace). After 2.75 miles, site is on left. GPS: 51.42587, -0.07379

Charges guide

Per person	£ 6.05 - £ 7.80
child (5-16 yrs)	£ 1.85 - £ 3.25
pitch incl. electricity (non-member)	£ 13.70 - £ 17.50

Tent campers apply to site.

For latest campsite news visit
alanrogers.com

Edmonton
Lee Valley Camping & Caravanning Park

Meridian Way, Edmonton, London N9 0AR (London) T: 020 8803 6900. E: leisurecentre@leevalleypark.org.uk

alanrogers.com/UK3230

Certainly one of the only sites in this guide with a multiplex cinema just outside the gate, you are greeted here by a very attractive entrance with flower displays. The site offers 140 spacious level pitches, with hardstandings and 100 with electricity hook-ups. The pitches are well laid out around a large field and there is a tent area just behind two grassy mounds. The grass and gardens are well trimmed and kept very tidy. The site also offers hook-up points for tents. The adjacent sports complex was rebuilt for use during the 2012 Olympics. The cinema complex incorporates a pizza restaurant, and from here you can hop on a bus to Edmonton Green or Ponders End station from where there is a regular service into central London (journey time around 40 minutes). The site managers have detailed information about the various Travel Card schemes available. Alternatively, historic Waltham Abbey, Epping Forest and the 1,000-acre River Lee Country Park are all within easy access.

Facilities

Two modern, heated toilet blocks include spacious showers and two large en-suite units for disabled visitors. Baby changing area. All facilities are accessed by combination locks. Laundry. Motorcaravan service point. Barbecue area. Kitchen. Shop. Play area. Badminton. Off site: Cinema at entrance. Golf adjacent. Supermarket and fishing 0.5 miles. Riding 4 miles.

Open: All year excl. Christmas, Boxing Day and New Year's Day.

Directions

From M25 take exit 25. Follow signs for the city. At first set of traffic lights turn left (Freezywater). Continue on for 6 miles. Follow signs for Lee Valley Leisure Complex. After roundabout (where the A110 crosses), turn left at second set of traffic lights onto the complex. Follow site signs. GPS: 51.632383, -0.038383

Charges guide

Per unit incl. 2 persons	£ 24.90 - £ 38.20
extra person	£ 6.00 - £ 9.50
child (under 16 yrs)	£ 2.50 - £ 5.50
electricity	£ 3.80

Min. charge £ 9.60

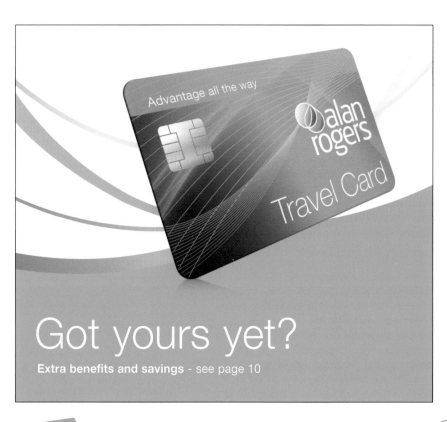

The East of England is a perfect mix of soft and gentle countryside, ancient cities, historical towns, and storybook villages. It is an unspoilt region with endless skies and a maze of inland waterways ideal for birdwatching and boating, while the traditional beach resorts offer old-fashioned seaside fun.

THIS REGION INCLUDES THE COUNTIES OF ESSEX, SUFFOLK, NORFOLK, CAMBRIDGESHIRE, HERTFORDSHIRE AND BEDFORDSHIRE

Bedfordshire and Hertfordshire are the smallest counties in the region, with peaceful canals, undulating countryside with chalk downs, and some of the greatest stately homes in the country. Essex is full of quaint villages with a smattering of old towns and traditional seaside resorts, including Colchester and Southend-on-Sea. The River Cam winds its way through Cambridgeshire; punting along the river in Cambridge is a good way to relax and take in the many famous university buildings that dominate the waterfront along the 'Backs'. Further along the river is the ancient cathedral city of Ely, once an island before the Fen drainage. The flat Fenland has a network of rivers and canals, ideal for narrowboat trips, as are the Norfolk Broads. Norfolk itself is very flat, sparsely populated and tranquil, popular with walkers and cyclists, while the numerous nature reserves attract a variety of wildlife. It also has a beautiful coastline; the seaside towns of Great Yarmouth and Hunstanton are major draws. This unspoilt coastline stretches into Suffolk, 'Constable Country'. Full of space, with picturesque villages set amongst lush green countryside, dotted with timbered cottages and ruined abbeys, the county is home to Newmarket, the horse racing capital of the world.

Places of interest

Essex: Clacton-on-Sea; Walton-on-the-Naze, with nature reserve; Waltham Abbey; Epping; Chelmsford; Colchester.

Suffolk: Ipswich; Lowestoft; market town of Bury St Edmonds with Georgian theatre; Aldburgh with its annual festival.

Norfolk: bustling city of Norwich; seaside resort of Great Yarmouth; waterways of the Norfolk Broads; Sandringham Palace near King's Lynn; Banham Zoo.

Cambridgeshire: museums, historic college buildings and punting in Cambridge; Ely cathedral and stained glass museum; Imperial War Museum in Duxford; St. Ives riverside town with popular Monday market; Wildfowl & Wetland Trust near Wisbech.

Hertfordshire: St Albans and nearby Butterfly World project; historic Knebworth House with gardens and miniature railway.

Bedfordshire: Wrest Park gardens; Woburn with abbey and safari park; Whipsnade Wild Animal Park; Shuttleworth Collection near Biggleswade with birds of prey.

Did you know?

Newmarket has been recognised as the Headquarters of Racing for over 300 years.

The tractor was invented in Biggleswade, Bedfordshire, in 1901 by Daniel Albone.

Danbury Common, Essex, is home to Britain's largest population of adders.

The artist John Constable was born in 1776 in the village of East Bergholt. Nearby Flatford Mill, was portrayed in his most famous scene, 'The Haywain'.

Oliver Cromwell's head is buried in an unmarked grave close to the entrance of Sidney Sussex College chapel, Cambridge.

Epping Forest was the haunt of the renowned highwayman, Dick Turpin.

Aldeburgh

Church Farm Holiday Park

Church Farm Road, Aldeburgh IP15 5DW (Suffolk) T: 01728 453433. E: aldeburgh@amberleisure.com

alanrogers.com/UK3350

This area of the Suffolk coast has always been a popular destination for visitors and Church Farm Holiday Park has an enviable location on the outskirts of Aldeburgh. The park includes a large area designated for caravan holiday homes as well as a separate touring area situated to the front of the park. The touring area provides 68 pitches for caravans and motorcaravans (tents and trailer tents are not accepted). Pitches are separated by attractive hedging that blends in well with the natural environment. Sixty-two pitches have 16A electricity, water, waste water and a night light.

Facilities

The single toilet block has been fully upgraded with heating, free showers, toilets and washbasins (entry card with deposit). Access to the toilets and showers are via two steps, making it unsuitable for wheelchair users. However ambulant toilets are provided. Laundry room. Motorcaravan service point. Gas supplies. Off site: Bus service 0.5-1 mile. Shops, pubs, etc. 15 minutes walk. Beach 5 minutes walk. Fishing and bicycle hire 1 mile. Riding 6 miles.

Open: Easter - 31 October.

Directions

On arrival at Aldeburgh, site is signed at roundabout towards Thorpeness. Where road meets seafront, site is on left. From town centre follow road along seafront to site on left at end of town. GPS: 52.15827, 1.60330

Charges guide

Per pitch incl. all persons	£ 20.00 - £ 24.00
incl. services	£ 28.00 - £ 32.00

Cheques are not accepted.
Credit cards 2.5% surcharge.

FREE Alan Rogers Travel Card
Extra benefits and savings - see page 10

Banham
Applewood Caravan & Camping Park

Banham Zoo, The Grove, Banham NR16 2HE (Norfolk) T: 01953 888370. E: caravanpark@banhamzoo.co.uk
alanrogers.com/UK3385

Applewood is a 13-acre touring park, adjacent to the famous Banham Zoo. One day's entrance fee gives unlimited access whilst on the campsite. Applewood has 200 pitches with 190 on level grass and ten on hardstanding; 120 have 10A electric hook-ups. The large central area has unmarked pitches for those who do not need electricity. Other pitches surrounding this area are in small groups separated by neat laurel hedges. There is a further area with pitches and a large field for rallies. Just four minutes walk from the park is a small supermarket, a pub/restaurant, a fish and chip shop and gift shops.

Facilities

Two toilet blocks, one new and one refurbished provide clean and adequate facilities. Room for disabled visitors. Washing machine and dryer. Play area. Motorcaravan services. Rally field and function room. Gas supplies. Off site: Zoo adjacent. The Appleyard with shops and restaurant. Snetterton race circuit 3 miles. Diss 8 miles. Thetford and Norwich 15 miles.

Open: 10 February - 31 October.

Directions

Leave A11 at Attleborough, take B1077 south. Follow signs to New Buckenham and Banham Zoo. At T-junction with B1113 turn west. Continue through Banham. Park is on the left, entrance through Banham Zoo (not clearly signed). GPS: 52.44636, 1.02514

Charges guide

Per unit incl. electricity	£ 17.50 - £ 19.50

Beccles
Waveney River Centre

Staithe Road, Burgh Saint Peter, Beccles NR34 0BT (Norfolk) T: 01502 677 343.
E: info@waveneyrivercentre.co.uk **alanrogers.com/UK3380**

Set in the Norfolk Broads adjacent to the River Waveney, this site has something for everybody. There are 17 mainly level, grass touring pitches all with 16A electric hook-up, plus 35 large tent pitches, many with electricity. The facilities are of the highest standard and include an indoor swimming pool complex with a café. There is a pub on site which serves meals, and has nightly entertainment. A games arcade for children (in the pub), a wildlife garden and an adventure play area will keep children busy. There is boat hire available and launching facilities for own boats. A foot ferry service across to the marshes opened in 2012, offering miles of rambling and wildlife watching in the wetlands. The local area is an ideal base for visiting the local town of Beccles, as well as Norwich, Great Yarmouth and Lowestoft. Although the site has a great variety of facilities, it has retained a tranquil atmosphere and will suit those looking for peace and quiet as well as families wanting a more active holiday.

Facilities

Two very clean toilet blocks (both key access), one superbly fitted with 9 private rooms (WC, shower sink, hairdryer). Well equipped facilities for disabled visitors. A second smaller block has toilets and washbasins, facilities for children in disabled toilet. Laundry facilities. Fully stocked shop. Pub serving food. Indoor heated swimming pool with sauna, café with pool viewing area and outside decking. Play area. Evening entertainment. Fishing (charged). Boat hire. Free WiFi in bar and café (charged over site). Luxury holiday lodges for rent. Off site: Golf and riding 8 miles. Beach 15 miles.

Open: All year.

Directions

Follow A143 (Beccles-Great Yarmouth) into Haddiscoe. Turn right at village hall into Wiggs Road, signed Waveney River Centre. After 2 miles turn left into Burgh Road. Proceed for 2.5 miles to site (with care along single track road with passing places). GPS: 52.481911, 1.6696

Charges guide

Per unit incl. 2 persons and electricity	£ 14.00 - £ 35.00
dog (max. 2)	£ 3.00

Camping Cheques accepted.

Cambridge

Highfield Farm Touring Park

Long Road, Comberton, Cambridge CB23 7DG (Cambridgeshire) T: 01223 262308.
E: enquiries@highfieldfarmtouringpark.co.uk **alanrogers.com/UK3560**

Situated five miles from Cambridge, this eight-acre park is set in a delightfully quiet touring location yet close to major routes around Cambridge. The welcome is always warm from the friendly family owners. The facilities are of high quality and the grass and hedges are well cared for. Conifer hedges divide the site into five areas. There are also some shady glades for those who wish to retreat even further and one area is reserved for those without children. The pitches are fairly level and on grass with 60 numbered pitches for caravans and motorcaravans, and 60 for tents. All have 10A electricity and 40 are on hardstanding. A good dog walk is provided, which can be extended to a pleasant 1.5 mile walk, with seats, around the farm perimeter. The site is a very good base for visiting the famous University town of Cambridge and a walking tour around the town exploring the colleges is highly recommended. The town can be accessed by car (park and ride recommended), by bus or by bike via a special cycle route. A member of the Best of British group.

Facilities

Three heated toilet blocks provide more than adequate coverage and good facilities, all very clean and well maintained. No dedicated provision for disabled visitors, although one block has extra wide doors and easy access. Laundry room. Small play area. Good shop. Motorcaravan service point. Excellent tourist information room. Gates closed midnight to 07.30.
Off site: Comberton village 0.5 miles. Golf 2 miles. Fishing 3.5 miles. Cambridge 5 miles. Duxford War Museum and National Trust properties.

Open: 29 March - 31 October.

Directions

From M11 exit 12, take A603 towards Sandy. After 0.5 miles turn right, B1046 to Comberton. Turn right just before village signed Madingley (also caravan sign). Site on right just north of village.
GPS: 52.194981, 0.031103

Charges guide

Per unit incl. 2 persons and electricity	£ 19.50 - £ 23.50
extra person	£ 4.00
child (5-16 yrs)	£ 2.50
dog	£ 1.00

No credit cards.

FREE Alan Rogers Travel Card
Extra benefits and savings - see page 10

Bury Saint Edmunds

The Dell Caravan & Camping Park

Beyton Road, Thurston, Bury Saint Edmunds IP31 3RB (Suffolk) T: 01359 270121.
E: thedellcaravanpark@btinternet.com **alanrogers.com/UK3345**

Close to the A14 and surrounded by farmland, this small touring site, four miles east of Bury St Edmunds, provides a convenient base to explore the nearby town and surrounding villages or as a stopover point. The current owners have created 50 spacious pitches within the main touring area, divided into two sections – one of which is reserved for adults only. All pitches have 10A electricity. A separate field with a further ten pitches situated under trees is available for contractors working locally, as well as any visitors who prefer shaded areas. The main touring field has some shade from well maintained hedges and the trees bordering the site.

Facilities	Directions
Excellent and ample toilets and spacious shower facilities (free) are provided within a purpose built sanitary block. Ladies' toilets include a private bathroom and toilet. Family bathroom with bath, shower and baby changing facilities. Separate toilet/shower for disabled visitors. Laundry room. Motorcaravan service point. Off site: Pubs and restaurants in Thurston and neighbouring villages.	From A14 take exit for Thurston and Benton, 4 miles east of Bury St Edmunds. Follow signs to Thurston. Park is on left, shortly after arriving at Thurston and signed from Beyton. GPS: 52.24053, 0.82437

Charges guide

Per unit incl. 2 persons and electricity	£ 15.00 - £ 19.00
extra person	£ 3.00

Open: All year.

Clacton-on-Sea

Homestead Lake Park

Thorpe Road, Weeley, Clacton-on-Sea CO16 9JN (Essex) T: 01255 833492.
E: lakepark@homesteadcaravans.co.uk **alanrogers.com/UK3300**

This well laid out, 25-acre park was opened in 2002. It is hidden from the road at the rear of Homestead Caravans' sales area and workshops in the countryside of the Tendring district, at Weeley near Clacton. It offers 50 fully serviced, hardstanding pitches on gently sloping ground overlooking a fishing lake and recently built holiday lodge accommodation on the other side of the lake. Tents accepted for short stays only on a limited number of pitches. The park makes an ideal spot to stay either for fishing, for a relaxing weekend, or as a base for touring this part of Essex.

Facilities	Directions
The toilet block offers clean and spacious facilities including an en-suite unit for disabled visitors. Baby changing facilities. Coffee shop/café and snack bar. Fishing lake. Woodland walks. Caravan sales, workshops and accessory shop. A large rally field is also available. Off site: Clacton-on-Sea, Frinton, Harwich and Brightlingsea within a 10-mile radius.	From Colchester take A120, then A133 signed Clacton. At roundabout, turn left on B1033 into Weeley and site and showrooms are on left just past council offices. GPS: 51.85989, 1.12021

Charges guide

Per unit incl. 2 persons and electricity	£ 15.50 - £ 22.50
extra person	£ 4.00

Open: 1 March - 31 October.

Colchester

Fen Farm Caravan & Camping Site

Moore Lane, East Mersea, Colchester CO5 8FE (Essex) T: 01206 383275. E: fenfarm@talk21.com
alanrogers.com/UK3290

Tents were first pitched at Fen Farm in 1923 and since then the park has 'grown rather than developed' – something of which owners Ralph and Wenda Lord and their family are proud. The 70 touring pitches are all unmarked, on level grass and within four fields that have a spacious feel to them. An area for 90 holiday homes is separate and screened from the touring area. All pitches have 10A electricity connections and three have hardstanding and are fully serviced. A limited number of seasonal pitches are available on the smaller field, with outstanding views and direct access to the beach. This is an attractive well laid out site with trees and two ponds.

Facilities	Directions
The toilet block in the main touring field includes a family room and shower/toilet for disabled visitors. Laundry room. Gas supplies. Two play areas. Caravan and boat storage. WiFi throughout (charged). Off site: Well stocked shop adjacent sells groceries, bread and milk. 'Pick your own' fruit farm and tea room. Shops, pubs, restaurants and banks in West Mersea. Pub within walking distance. Chinese and Indian takeaways will deliver to site.	From Colchester, take B1025 to Mersea Island. After crossing causeway, take left fork to East Mersea. Follow road for 2.75 miles to Dog and Pheasant pub. Site entrance is next right. NB. Access across the causeway onto Mersea Island is restricted at high tide. GPS: 51.78996, 0.98460

Charges guide

Per unit incl. up to 6 people and electricity	£ 18.00 - £ 25.00

Open: 19 March - 31 October.

For latest campsite news visit
alanrogers.com

Cromer
Woodhill Park

Cromer Road, East Runton, Cromer NR27 9PX (Norfolk) T: 01263 512242. E: info@woodhill-park.com

alanrogers.com/UK3500

Woodhill is a seaside site with good views and a traditional atmosphere. It is situated on the clifftop, in a large, gently sloping, open grassy field, with 300 marked touring pitches. Of these, 210 have 16A electricity, seven are fully serviced and many have wonderful views over the surrounding coastline and countryside. A small number of holiday homes are available with magnificent sea views. Although the site is fenced, there is access to the clifftop path which takes you to the beach. Locally, it is possible to take a boat trip to see the seals off Blakeney Point. Nearby attractions include the Shire Horse Centre at West Runton and the North Norfolk Steam Railway. Green technology plays a major role with solar panels added to one of the block roofs to heat the water. Access to nearby towns and resorts is available using the local bus stop outside the entrance, or by the tourist railway.

Facilities	Directions
Two modern toilet blocks with all necessary facilities including two family rooms with bath, showers, basin and WC, and four rooms with shower, basin and WC. Washing machine and dryer. Well stocked shop (19/3-31/10). Good, large adventure playground and plenty of space for ball games. Crazy golf. Giant chess and golf course adjacent to the site. Bicycle hire. Off site: Beach 0.5 miles. Fishing and shop 1 mile. Golf and riding 2 miles. Bird Reserve at Cley. National Trust properties. North Norfolk Tourist Railway. Boat trips.	Site is beside the A149 coast road between East and West Runton. GPS: 52.93742, 1.26250

Charges guide

Per unit incl. 2 persons	
and electricity	£ 15.65 - £ 18.95
extra person	£ 2.60
child (4-16 yrs)	£ 1.05
dog	£ 2.15 - £ 3.75

Open: 19 March - 31 October.

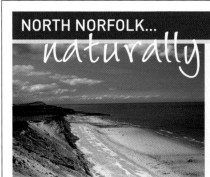

East Harling
The Dower House Touring Park

Thetford Forest, East Harling NR16 2SE (Norfolk) T: 01953 717314. E: info@dowerhouse.co.uk

alanrogers.com/UK3390

Set on 20 acres in the heart of Britain's largest forest on the Suffolk and Norfolk borders, The Dower House provides quiet woodland walks and cycle ways, with an abundance of wildlife. David and Karen Bushell continue to upgrade the facilities without compromising the park's natural features. There are 160 large pitches, 72 with 10A electricity. Most are reasonably level, although given the forest location there are a few tree roots. Six pitches for visitors with mobility problems are linked by a path to the main facilities. Torches are recommended as the site is unlit at night (ideal for stargazing!).

Facilities	Directions
Two toilet blocks, one with a baby room. A separate building houses the showers and a unit for disabled visitors. Washing machine and dryer. Well stocked shop. Information room. Quiet rooms (no games machines). Heated outdoor swimming pool (31/5-1/9, under 15s must be with an adult). Paddling pool. Bicycle hire. Caravan storage. Torches necessary. WiFi throughout (free) Off site: Fishing nearby 1.5 miles. Riding 3 km. Snetterton motor racing circuit and Sunday market 2-3 miles. Many walks and cycle rides in the forest.	From A11 (Thetford-Norwich) road, 7 miles east of Thetford, turn right on B1111 to East Harling. Turn right at church and in just under a mile turn right on unpaved road (site signed). Entrance in 0.8 miles. GPS: 52.42829, 0.89631

Charges guide

Per unit incl. 2 persons	£ 9.75 - £ 23.25
incl. electricity	£ 13.25 - £ 26.95
extra person	£ 5.00
child (4-15 yrs)	£ 2.00

Open: 22 March - 6 October.

Fakenham

The Old Brick Kilns Caravan & Camping Park

Little Barney Lane, Barney, Fakenham NR21 0NL (Norfolk) T: 01328 878305.
E: enquiries@old-brick-kilns.co.uk **alanrogers.com/UK3400**

This is an excellent tranquil, family run park and a friendly, helpful atmosphere prevails. The park's development on the site of old brick kilns has resulted in land on varying levels. This provides areas of level, well drained pitches with many on hardstanding. There are 65 pitches in total, all with 16A electricity and 30 are fully serviced. A wide range of trees and shrubs provide shelter and are home for a variety of wildlife. There are garden areas, including a butterfly garden, and a conservation pond is the central feature. There is a large, comfortable bar area and restaurant open five days a week. Strictly no arrivals before 13.30. A member of the Best of British group.

Facilities

Very good heated toilet blocks provide very clean facilities. Baby room. Facilities for disabled guests (Radar). Laundry room. Motorcaravan service point. Good shop with gas supplies. Bar/restaurant (5 days a week, April-Oct) and takeaway food (July/Aug) with patio area outside. Giant chess. Small library. TV/games room. Fenced play area. Fishing. WiFi (charged). B&B also available. Caravan storage. Off site: Thursford collection 2 miles. Golf 5 and 8 miles. Riding and bicycle hire 6 miles. Beach 7 miles. Boat launching 8 miles. Stately homes. Birdwatching.

Open: All year excl. 2 January - 14 March.

Directions

From Fakenham take A148 Cromer road north east. After 6 miles, at Thursford, fork right on B1354 signed Melton Constable. In 0.4 miles, turn right to Barney, and then first left along a narrow country lane with passing places, for 0.5 miles.
GPS: 52.85804, 0.97583

Charges guide

Per unit incl. 2 persons	
and electricity	£ 16.00 - £ 22.00
'super pitch'	£ 20.00 - £ 26.00
extra person	£ 4.00
child (up to 15 yrs)	£ 1.00 - £ 3.00
dog (max. 2)	£ 1.00

Great Yarmouth

Long Beach Caravan Park

Long Beach, Hemsby, Great Yarmouth NR29 4JD (Norfolk) T: 01493 730023. E: info@long-beach.co.uk
alanrogers.com/UK3492

This is a large caravan park alongside the sandy dunes bordering the sea. There are 270 reasonably level grassy pitches with 150 for touring, 90 with 10/16A electricity. About 30 touring pitches, open all season, are in the Long Beach site dotted amongst the static caravans close to all the main facilities. Most of the touring pitches are in the Hemsby Touring Park, a few hundred yards further inland and only open during school holidays and some Bank Holidays. Here there are two large grassy fields with little shade and many of these pitches are a long way from the toilet block and other facilities. The beach and dunes extend for many miles along the coast offering plenty of opportunity for walking, beach activities and fun in the local amusement arcades. The nearby nature reserve is within walking distance. Not far away is the small seaside resort of Hemsby, the popular Great Yarmouth, the historic cathedral city of Norwich and the famous Norfolk Broads. There is a busy entertainment programme in July and August.

Facilities

Several small old, but clean, toilet blocks in main section plus one modern toilet block in the Hemsby section offering all necessary facilities. Shop, bar, restaurant, games room (open all season) in main section. Beach with miles of sand dunes. Play area. Sea fishing. WiFi (charge). Off site: Hemsby close by. Bicycle hire (800 yds). Great Yarmouth 5 miles, Norwich 18 miles.

Open: 14 March - 4 November.

Directions

Hemsby is 5 miles north of Great Yarmouth. Leave Great Yarmouth on the A149, bypass Caister and at Hemsby turn east towards beach and site.
GPS: 52.7017, 1.7028

Charges guide

Per unit incl. 4 persons	
and electricity	£ 15.50 - £ 26.50
extra person	£ 3.50
dog	£ 3.50
High season minimum stay 7 days (Sat-Sat).	

LONG BEACH ESTATE COMPANY

Estate Office - Long Beach - Hemsby - GREAT YARMOUTH - NR29 4JD
Tel. 01493 - 73 00 23 - info@long-beach.co.uk - www.long-beach.co.uk

For latest campsite news visit
alanrogers.com

Great Yarmouth
The Grange Touring Park

Ormesby St Margaret, Great Yarmouth NR29 3QG (Norfolk) T: 01493 730306. E: info@grangetouring.co.uk

alanrogers.com/UK3490

This family touring site has a pleasant atmosphere and visitors are given a warm and friendly welcome by the resident wardens. There are 70 level pitches with 16A electricity, 14 with hardstanding, and ten pitches for tents, all arranged on well trimmed grass with tarmac access roads. There are some mature trees throughout the site providing shade to many of the pitches. Adjacent to the campsite is The Grange, a free house offering meals, beers and real ale, plus play equipment for children (open all year). The site owner also has a holiday campsite at Hemsby (four miles) with its own wide sandy beach, which guests at The Grange are welcome to use. There is a little road noise from the bypass. The nearest beach is a mile away and local attractions include Caister Castle and Motor Museum and the Norfolk Rare Breed Centre. Great Yarmouth Centre and The Broads are within five miles.

Facilities

A modern, heated toilet building is spacious and well maintained, housing all the usual facilities including free showers. Baby room in the ladies'. Family room. Two fully equipped wet rooms for disabled visitors. Motorcaravan service point. Laundry room with washing machine and dryer. Washing lines are provided at the rear of the building. Gas supplies. Swings for children. Internet and copying facilities in reception, and WiFi over site (£3 per hour or per 24 hours if using own computer). Off site: Bus service 250 yds. Beach, shops and supermarket 1 mile. Riding and bicycle hire 2 miles. Golf 3 miles. Fishing 4 miles. Great Yarmouth 5 minutes drive.

Open: Mid March - early October.

Directions

Site is just north of Great Yarmouth. Entrance is just south of the roundabout at the northern edge of the Caister bypass. GPS: 52.66812, 1.71097

Charges guide

Per unit incl. up to 4 persons and electricity	£ 15.50 - £ 22.50
extra person	£ 3.50
child (under 5 yrs)	free
dog	free - £ 3.50

THE GRANGE TOURING PARK

Yarmouth Road, Ormesby St. Margaret,
Great Yarmouth, Norfolk NR29 3QG
www.grangetouring.co.uk
info@grangetouring.co.uk
Tel: 01493 730306 - 01493 730023
Fax: 01493 730188

This level grassy park will accommodate seventy touring outfits and tents and adjoins the grounds of the Grange Free House. It is very conveniently situated as a touring centre for Great Yarmouth, the Norfolk Broads and the historic Cathedral City of Norwich. We are approximately one mile from the beach.

Great Yarmouth
Clippesby Hall

Clippesby, Great Yarmouth NR29 3BL (Norfolk) T: 01493 367800. E: holidays@clippesby.com

alanrogers.com/UK3485

Set in the heart of the Broads National Park this is a spacious, high quality site where you can be sure of a warm welcome from the Lindsay family, who have lived in the Hall for many years. Clippesby offers the choice of pitching amongst the shady woodland, on the gently sloping lawns of the hall with colourful mature trees and shrubs or in a new area, The Meadow, which offers fully serviced pitches with hardstanding. The 120 pitches are well spaced and clearly numbered (80 have 10A electricity). Children can roam at will in safety, and parents can relax and unwind at this beautiful park.

Facilities

Three timber heated toilet blocks provide very clean, modern facilities. Some cabins with washbasin and WC. En-suite room for disabled visitors. Family room with bath and baby changing. Laundry. Gas. Shop (Easter-end Oct). Café and family bar/restaurant (Easter-end Oct). Pizza takeaway. Small swimming pool and paddling pool (end May-end Sept). Adventure play area. Football. Bicycle hire. Max. 1 dog per pitch. Dog walk. WiFi (free). Off site: Bus service 1.5 miles. Fishing and boat launching 2 miles. Riding 3 miles. Golf, beach and sailing 5 miles. Great Yarmouth 7 miles. Norwich 15 miles. The Broads for cycling, walking and boating.

Open: All year.

Directions

From the A47 Norwich-Great Yarmouth road at Acle roundabout take exit for Filby (A1064). After 1.5 miles fork left on B1152 signed Potter Heigham. Take first left and park is 100 yds. on the right. GPS: 52.67283, 1.58299

Charges guide

Per unit incl. 2 persons and electricity	£ 16.00 - £ 36.25
extra person	£ 5.85
child	£ 2.95
dog (max. 1)	£ 4.00

FREE Alan Rogers Travel Card
Extra benefits and savings - see page 10

Great Yarmouth
Rose Farm Touring Park
Stepshort, Belton, Great Yarmouth NR31 9JS (Norfolk) T: 01493 780896.
E: myhra@rosefarmtouringpark.fsnet.co.uk **alanrogers.com/UK3382**

Rose Farm, open all year, although close to Great Yarmouth is quietly situated offering campers space with peace and tranquillity. There are 145 reasonably level pitches, 20 are on hardstanding and the remainder on grass; 90 have 16A electricity. The park is split into three separate areas. The first is large and open, surrounded by fencing, the second area is long with pitches either side of the road and beyond this is an open area mainly for tents. A new toilet/shower block here offers top quality facilities, both blocks are immaculate with thoughtful decor.

Facilities

The two attractive blocks offer excellent facilities including two family rooms with shower, toilet and basin. Washing machine and dryer, iron and ironing board. Facilities for disabled visitors (pitching can be arranged in advance). Adventure playground. TV/information room. Dog walk. WiFi. Off site: Shops nearby. Bus stop. Sailing 2 miles. Fishing and golf 3 miles. Riding and bicycle hire 4 miles. Beach 5 miles.

Open: All year.

Directions

From Great Yarmouth and Gorleston take the A143 signed Beccles and Diss. At dual carriageway (Bradwell) turn right (signed Holiday Parks) to Burgh Castle. In 0.75 miles, take next right, site on right in 25 yds. GPS: 52.57136, 1.66876

Charges guide

Per unit incl. 2 persons	£ 17.00 - £ 21.00
tent with 2 persons	£ 13.00 - £ 18.50

Special offers available. No credit cards.

Harleston
Little Lakeland Caravan Park
Wortwell, Harleston IP20 0EL (Norfolk) T: 01986 788646. E: information@littlelakeland.co.uk
alanrogers.com/UK3480

This peaceful hideaway with its own fishing lake is tucked behind the houses and gardens that border the village main street. It is a traditional, mature little park with just 58 pitches. There are several caravan holiday homes and long stay units, but there should always be around 22 places with 10A electricity for touring units. The pitches are mostly individual ones separated by mature hedges and trees giving varying amounts of shade. Fishing in the attractive lake is free of charge and solely for the use of campers (bream, tench, roach, perch and carp). A member of the Countryside Discovery group.

Facilities

A modern, heated toilet block provides washbasins all in cubicles for ladies, and one for men. Fully equipped laundry. Separate en-suite room for disabled visitors also has facilities for baby changing. A further unit (also heated) by reception provides a shower, WC and basin per sex. Reception stocks gas, and essentials (newspapers to order). Small play area. Library of paperback books in the summer house. Fishing (max. 4 rods per unit). WiFi (charged). Off site: Pub (with food) 500 yds.

Open: 15 March - 31 October.

Directions

From Diss, leave A143 at roundabout (Wortwell). Continue to village, pass The Bell pub, a garage on right, then turn right at first bungalow (Little Lakeland Lodge) watching carefully for signs. Site is down lane, 250 yds. on right. GPS: 52.41628, 1.35282

Charges guide

Per unit incl. 2 persons and electricity	£ 17.50 - £ 20.50

No credit cards.

Hunstanton
Searles Leisure Resort
South Beach Road, Hunstanton PE36 5BB (Norfolk) T: 01485 534211. E: bookings@searles.co.uk
alanrogers.com/UK3520

This is a high quality 'all-in' family holiday park on the north Norfolk coast offering everything for a great seaside family holiday. There is a beach within walking distance, a covered 'town plaza' including a sports bar, Chinese restaurant and American diner plus fish and chip bar, club house, pools, Country Club, golf course and driving range, fishing lakes and bowling greens; there should be something to entertain everyone. There are 823 pitches with 323 of varying sizes for touring, 129 with 16A electricity. Some are on hardstanding and fully serviced, with others on grass. An open area is reserved for tents.

Facilities

Three large, modern, clean toilet blocks with washbasins and toilets in cubicles. Facilities for disabled visitors. Baby room. Launderette. Food hall. Restaurants, bars and cafés. Hair and beauty salon. Indoor and outdoor heated swimming pools. Gym. Tennis. Soft play area. Golf (9-hole course, driving range and putting course). Fishing lake. Bowling green. Bicycle, pedalo hire. WiFi. Off site: Nearest beach 400 yds. Hunstanton 0.5 miles. Stately homes.

Open: All year, excl. 25 December.

Directions

From King's Lynn take A149 north to Hunstanton. At first roundabout take B1161. After 0.3 miles cross roundabout (supermarket), site immediately on left. GPS: 52.93033, 0.48289

Charges guide

Per pitch	£ 11.00 - £ 39.00
fully serviced pitch	£ 17.00 - £ 54.00
dog	£ 3.25

For latest campsite news visit
alanrogers.com

Huntingdon
Wyton Lakes Holiday Park

Banks End, Wyton, Huntingdon PE28 2AA (Cambridgeshire) T: 01480 412715. E: loupeter@supanet.com

alanrogers.com/UK3555

Wyton Lakes is a family run, adults only park with four well stocked fishing lakes, very close to the River Great Ouse, between Huntingdon and Saint Ives. There are 80 level pitches of medium size with 60 for caravans and motorcaravans and 20 for tents. The tent pitches are on grass and have no electricity. The other pitches are mainly on hardstanding with gravel for awnings and all have 16A electricity and a water tap. Most of the pitches border the lakes making fishing possible from the pitch. Well placed as a centre for touring, the park has easy access for large outfits. The old market towns of Huntingdon and Saint Ives are only three miles away and the delightful village of Houghton with its old mill, pub and riverside walks is just a mile. Just across the road is a large garden centre with a restaurant and coffee shop.

Facilities

Heated toilet block with all necessary facilities including those for campers with disabilities. Laundry with washer and dryer. Coarse lake and river fishing on payment (carp, bream, tench, perch, roach and rudd). Small riverside walk. WiFi (charged). Off site: Garden centre, restaurant and coffee shop opposite entrance. Interesting old village of Houghton, pub, shop, National Trust mill, riverside walks, 1 mile. St Ives, Huntingdon, boat hire and golf 3 miles. Huntingdon Race Course 4 miles. Paxton Pits Nature Reserve. Hinchingbrooke Park.

Open: 1 April - 28 October.

Directions

From the A14 take exit 26 (St Ives). Take A1096 north towards St Ives over four roundabouts. Turn left onto A1123, signed Huntingdon and site entrance is on the left in 2 miles opposite garden centre. GPS: 52.33664, -0.13872

Charges guide

Per unit incl. 2 persons and electricity	£ 17.00
tent pitch incl. 2 adults	£ 14.00 - £ 17.00
extra adult	£ 2.00

Adults only (over 18 yrs). No credit cards.

Wyton Lakes Holiday Park
Banks End, Wyton
Huntingdon Cambs PE28 2AA
Tel: 01480 412 715 or 07785 29 44 19
loupeter@supanet.com
www.wytonlakes.com
Adults only

Ipswich
Low House Touring Caravan Centre

Bucklesham Road, Foxhall, Ipswich IP10 0AU (Suffolk) T: 01473 659437. E: low.house@btinternet.com

alanrogers.com/UK3310

Set in a sheltered 3.5 acres, this site has 30 level, grass pitches and an abundance of shrubs and flowers. The park has been divided into two areas bordered by mature trees and the grounds are well maintained. There are many different varieties of trees with a tree walk leading round two sides of the park. All the pitches have 10/16A electrical connections and they back onto trees that provide plenty of shade and the opportunity to observe a range of wildlife. A good bus service to Ipswich stops nearby. Low House lies between Felixstowe (eight miles) and Ipswich (four miles) and would be a useful stopover for the Felixstowe port or Harwich.

Facilities

The older style, heated sanitary block is spotlessly clean with hot showers (50p). Motorcaravan service point. No on-site provisions but a supermarket is 2 miles (towards Ipswich). Frozen goods can be stored. Small, secure play area. Pet area with rabbit, hens and guinea fowl. Off site: Pub in Bucklesham village (1.5 miles) and other good pubs nearby. Golf 2 miles. Fishing 3 miles.

Open: All year.

Directions

Turn off A14 (was A45) Ipswich ring road (south) via slip road onto A1156 (signed Ipswich East). Follow road over bridge crossing over the A45 and almost immediately turn right (no sign). After 0.5 miles turn right again (signed Bucklesham) and site is on left after 400 yds. GPS: 52.03402, 1.24507

Charges guide

Per unit incl. 2 adults, 2 children and electricity	£ 14.00 - £ 20.00
extra person	£ 3.00
child (5-14 yrs)	£ 2.00
dog	free

No large commercial vehicles. No credit cards.

FREE Alan Rogers Travel Card
Extra benefits and savings - see page 10

Ipswich
Westwood Park Caravan Park

Old Felixstowe Road, Bucklesham, Ipswich IP10 0BW (Suffolk) T: 01473 659637.
E: info@westwoodcaravanpark.co.uk **alanrogers.com/UK3335**

This park opened in Easter 2007 and has been developed on land previously owned by the neighbouring farm. The park is situated between Felixstowe and Ipswich and is within easy reach of the River Deben and Woodbridge. The 90 level grass and hardstanding pitches are of varying size to accommodate both small and large caravans, motorcaravans and tents. All pitches have 10A electricity. When they are available, the seasonal hardstanding super pitches, equipped with 16A electricity, can be used by touring units. Families are welcome and a grass area has been fenced off for football and other games at the far end of the park. A dog walking area has been created, screened by shrubs along two sides of the park, and a nature area to encourage local wildlife is also being developed.

Facilities

A brand new, but traditionally built, toilet block in the centre of the park includes facilities for disabled visitors (£5 deposit for key). Laundry. Purpose built reception provides local information and sells a limited range of provisions e.g. milk. Recycling facilities planned. Grass play area for children. WiFi (charged). Off site: Free range eggs from a farm (short walk). Bus service to Ipswich nearby. Pubs serving meals in nearby Bucklesham and surrounding villages. Fishing 2 miles. Golf 3 miles. Beach 5 miles.

Open: All year excl. 16 January - 28 February.

Directions

Site is near Bucklesham. From the A12 (south) or A14(12) (north) take A14 towards Felixstowe. Continue for 5 miles and turn left signed Kirton. Continue for 5 miles and turn left signed Kirton, Bucklesham and Brightwell. Continue for 1 mile: park is on the right, immediately after Tenth Road on the left. GPS: 52.02316, 1.28389

Charges guide

Per unit incl. 2 persons, 2 children and electricity	£ 18.00 - £ 20.00
extra person	£ 2.50

Camping Cheques accepted.

Westwood Caravan Park

Suffolk's premier family touring caravan & camping site in the heart of the countryside, peaceful & tranquil, just outside the picuresque village of Bucklesham.
Hard standing seasonal pitches available.

Bucklesham - Ipswich IP10 0BW

info@westwoodcaravanpark.co.uk | www.westwoodcaravanpark.co.uk | Tel. 01473 - 659 637

Ipswich
Orwell Meadows Leisure Park

Priory Lane, Ipswich IP10 0JS (Suffolk) T: 01473 726666. E: recept@orwellmeadows.co.uk
alanrogers.com/UK3315

This popular, family park is set on the edge of the Orwell Country Park near Ipswich with its many miles of walks and the famous Orwell Bridge with views of the Suffolk countryside. The park is run by David and Sally Miles and offers an ideal spot for a family holiday with an outdoor swimming pool and a good clubhouse with a bar, restaurant and a shop. Spacious pitches are around the edges of several separate meadows (surrounded on three sides by earth banks), all offering 16A electricity hook-ups. There is much to see and do in the area. Visit towns such as Ipswich and Colchester or unspoilt villages such as Framlingham (with its castle) and Aldeburgh, plus the rest of Constable country.

Facilities

The modern toilet block includes clean and spacious free showers. It is kept to a very high standard. En-suite facilities for disabled visitors. Well stocked shop. Bar and restaurant. Outdoor pool. Play area. TV/family room. Max. two dogs per unit. Off site: Market town of Bury St Edmunds.

Open: March - January.

Directions

From A14 Ipswich bypass take Nacton/Ipswich exit (north of the A14) and follow signs for Orwell Country Park (narrow lane). Cross single-track bridge over the A14 to the site entrance 20 yds. on left. Follow signs past house/reception up hill and park on the left and walk back to reception. GPS: 52.02044, 1.19161

Charges guide

Per unit incl. 2 persons and electricity	£ 15.50 - £ 22.00
extra person	£ 4.00 - £ 6.00
child (3-12 yrs)	£ 3.00 - £ 4.00
dog (max. 2)	£ 2.00

Weekly specials available.

For latest campsite news visit
alanrogers.com

Kings Lynn
The Garden Caravan Site

Barmer Hall, Syderstone, Kings Lynn PE31 8SR (Norfolk) T: 01485 578220. E: nlmason@tiscali.co.uk
alanrogers.com/UK3460

In the quiet Norfolk countryside, this imaginative touring park is a sun trap set in an enclosed walled garden. Sheltered from the winds by the high walls, visitors can relax in peace and tranquillity. Attractive mature trees, shrubs and climbers provide shade at various times of the day. The Mason family run the site in a relaxed way and the atmosphere is superb. There are 30 pitches, all with 16A electricity and TV hook-up, but little shade. Some are slightly sloping and will require blocks. Reception is housed in a small kiosk (not always manned, so pitch yourself and pay later). Barmer Hall is not far from Sandringham, and all the attractions on the Norfolk coast. This area is well known for its seaside resorts of Brancaster and Hunstanton, the latter being the only seaside resort in Norfolk to face west. It is also a haven for birdwatchers as Titchwell and Snettisham are close by.

Facilities

The single toilet block (heated) has all the usual facilities including a toilet and washbasin for campers with disabilities. Spin dryer and iron. No shop, but gas (not Camping Gaz), ices, soft drinks and fresh, free range eggs are available. Off site: Golf 10 miles. Norfolk Lavender, Langham Glass and the Thursford collection of steam engines and mechanical organs.

Open: 1 March - 1 November.

Directions

About 6 miles west of Fakenham leave A148. Take B1454 signed Docking and Hunstanton. After 3 miles turn right Barmer Hall (site signed). Road marked 'unsuitable for motor vehicles' but continue for 0.3 miles. Beyond Hall turn left to site. GPS: 52.86414, 0.69116

Charges guide

Per unit incl. 2 persons	£ 15.00 - £ 20.00

No credit cards.

Lowestoft
Kessingland Beach Holiday Park

Kessingland, Lowestoft NR33 7RN (Suffolk) T: 01502 740636.
E: holidaysales.kessinglandbeach@park-resorts.com **alanrogers.com/UK3370**

Set near the most easterly point in the UK, this park offers all you need for that total family holiday experience – pool tables, an amusement arcade and indoor and outdoor swimming pools. If you so wish you need never leave Kessingland Beach until your holiday ends. There is evening entertainment, as well as a selection of bars and a restaurant. Although mainly a large park for static caravan holiday homes, there is a touring area to the west of the park with quite spacious pitching. Electricity hook-ups are available. The toilet block is older in style but has been refurbished.

Facilities

The toilet block has been refurbished, but access is unsuitable for wheelchairs. Laundry. Shop. Bars, restaurants, fish and chips. Entertainment complex. Indoor and outdoor swimming pools. All-weather sports court. Adventure play areas. Tennis courts. Amusements. WiFi (charged). Off site: Beach and sea fishing 200 yds. Bicycle hire 1 mile. Golf and riding 3 miles. Boat launching 5 miles.

Open: 20 March - 26 October.

Directions

From Lowestoft, north, on A12 ignore first turning to Kessingland village and continue along A12 to next roundabout. Take left turning on roundabout signed Kessingland Beach. From A12 south, turn right at roundabout signed Kessingland Beach. At beach take sharp right continuing along to park entrance (narrow road). GPS: 52.40715, 1.72470

Charges guide

Per unit incl. electricity	£ 6.00 - £ 40.00
tent pitch	£ 5.00 - £ 34.00
dog (max. 2)	£ 1.00 - £ 3.00

Digital iPad editions

)alan rogers

Available on the App Store

FREE Alan Rogers bookstore app - digital editions of all 2013 guides
alanrogers.com/digital

Mundesley-on-Sea

Sandy Gulls Caravan Park

Cromer Road, Mundesley-on-Sea NR11 8DF (Norfolk) T: 01263 720513. E: info@sandygulls.co.uk

alanrogers.com/UK3410

This is an adults only park on the outskirts of Mundesley-on-Sea. One of the only clifftop parks with space for touring units on this coastline, there are panoramic views from most pitches. All 40 pitches (14 on hardstanding) have 10A electricity and TV aerial hook-ups. The unmarked pitches are arranged on an unshaded sloping meadow, so levelling blocks are advised. Primarily a caravan holiday home park, there are mobile homes to rent. The facilities are well maintained but some distance from the pitches. Access to the Blue Flag beach is via a large tarmac ramp. The village of Mundesley is only a mile away with a nine-hole golf course and a variety of shops and pubs. There is much to see and do in this area of Norfolk with a steam railway further along the coast. North Walsham is within easy reach and has a good range of shops and supermarkets.

Facilities

The heated toilet block is modern and spacious offering large shower rooms and open washbasins, all kept very clean. TV aerial hook-ups. WiFi (charged). Off site: Shops and pubs nearby. Mundesley-on-Sea 1 mile. Tennis, boat launching, riding and golf nearby. National Trust. Tourist railway. Norfolk Broads.

Open: March - November.

Directions

Site is 1 mile north of Mundesley (7 miles south of Cromer) on the main coast road.
GPS: 52.88457, 1.42074

Charges guide

Per unit incl. up to 4 persons and electricity	£ 13.00 - £ 24.00
dog	free

Nestling on the Mundesley cliffs, the area's only cliff top touring park, affording panoramic sea views. Norfolk Broads National Park is only a short drive away. The park offers easy access to clean, sandy, Blue Flag beaches. Mundesley has been voted one of the country's best kept seaside villages. Electric & TV hookups. This small, family-operated park has been owned and run for more than twenty five years by the current family.

SANDY GULLS CARAVAN PARK, CROMER ROAD, MUNDESLEY, NORFOLK, NR11 8DF

North Walsham

Two Mills Touring Park

Yarmouth Road, North Walsham NR28 9NA (Norfolk) T: 01692 405829. E: enquiries@twomills.co.uk

alanrogers.com/UK3420

Two Mills is a quiet, adults only site with a long season. Set in the bowl of a former quarry, the park is a real sun trap, both secluded and sheltered, with birdsong to be heard at all times of the day. Neatly maintained with natural areas, varied trees, wild flowers and birds, the owners, Barbara and Ray Barnes, want to add their own touches to this popular park. Following the purchase of an adjacent field, there are now 81 average sized, level pitches for touring units, including 72 serviced pitches (patio, water and waste water drainage), and 48 on hardstanding. All have 10/16A electricity. This is a good centre from which to explore the north Norfolk coast, the Broads or for visiting Norwich. A footpath from the park joins the Weavers Way. A member of the Best of British group.

Facilities

Two neat, clean, central toilet blocks can be heated, and include some washbasins in cabins and en-suite facilities for disabled visitors. Washing machine, dryer and spin dryer. Small shop at reception. TV room/library with tea and coffee facilities. WiFi (charged). Dogs are accepted by arrangement only. Off site: Hotel/pub 100 yds. North Walsham 20 minutes walk. Bicycle hire 1.5 miles. Fishing, golf and coast 5 miles.

Open: 1 March - 31 December.

Directions

From A149 Stalham-North Walsham road, watch for caravan sign 1.5 miles before North Walsham (also signed White Horse Common). The road runs parallel to the A149 and site is on right after 1.25 miles. From North Walsham take Old Yarmouth road past hospital, and park is on left after 1 mile.
GPS: 52.80661, 1.41708

Charges guide

Per unit incl. 2 persons and electricity	£ 16.00 - £ 20.00
full service pitch	£ 18.00 - £ 23.50
extra person	£ 4.00
dog (by arrangement)	£ 1.00
Senior citizen discounts.	

For latest campsite news visit
alanrogers.com

Norwich
Deer's Glade Caravan & Camping Park

White Post Road, Hanworth, Norwich NR11 7HN (Norfolk) T: 01263 768633. E: info@deersglade.co.uk

alanrogers.com/UK3455

In 2003, David and Heather Attew decided that they had an area that would make a superb setting for a caravan park and that they could give up farming. In early 2004 they opened this top quality park, which has since developed into a very popular site. Not far from the Norfolk Broads and close to the East Anglia coast, the park is open all year round. There are 129 level pitches (35 with hardstandings, eight pods). One hundred pitches have 16A electricity and TV aerial points. New hedging between pitches is becoming established. Internet access is possible from all the pitches. Amenities are of a high standard and include two toilet blocks, a play area, small shop and a popular, well stocked fishing lake. As its name suggests, you would not be surprised to wake and see deer wandering on this park and in the surrounding woodland areas. If you do miss them, a short walk will take you to Gunton Park where deer are bred and wander in herds.

Facilities

Two spacious toilet blocks are of a very high standard and include vanity style washbasins for ladies. Room for disabled visitors and families. Laundry. Motorcaravan service point. Shop (all year). Play area. Fishing lake (charged). Bicycle hire. Caravan valet service. Dog kennels. WiFi (charged). Off site: Bus service under 1 mile. Pub 1.5 miles. Woodland walks. Riding 2 miles. Small supermarket 3 miles. Beach and golf 5 miles. Blicking Hall. Felbrigg Hall. Market town of Aylsham. Cromer. Birdwatching. Poppy railway line (Sheringham to Holt).

Open: All year.

Directions

From Norwich take A140 towards Cromer and 5 miles beyond Aylsham turn right towards Suffield Green (White Post Road). Park is 0.5 miles on the right. GPS: 52.85781, 1.28765

Charges guide

Per unit incl. 2 persons
and electricity   £ 12.50 - £ 16.50

Norwich
Little Haven Caravan & Camping Park

The Street, Erpingham, Norwich NR11 7QD (Norfolk) T: 01263 768959. E: patlhaven@tiscali.co.uk

alanrogers.com/UK3450

Within easy reach of the coast and the Broads, this is a very attractive, peaceful little site with good facilities. Only adults are accepted. There are 24 grassy pitches, all with 16A electricity and five with hardstanding. They are arranged around a central lawn, beautiful flower beds and a decorative pergola with seating area; a credit to the owner, who does all the work herself. There is no shop, but two pubs serving food and traditional ales are within walking distance. An ideal base for cycling and walking (the Weavers Way footpath is within half a mile) or just relaxing. Also close by is the magnificent Blickling Hall with its superb state rooms, gardens and park. The famous Norfolk Broads and the fine Norfolk beaches are also close at hand. A short drive takes you to the historic market town of Aylsham or to the seaside resort of Cromer.

Facilities

The well maintained toilet block is heated and includes spacious hot showers and a covered dishwashing and laundry area. Off site: Bus service on the main A140 road. Riding 1 mile. Fishing 3 miles. Bicycle hire 5 miles. Beach 6 miles. Golf 10 miles.

Open: 1 March - 31 October.

Directions

From A140 Norwich-Cromer road, 6 miles north of Aylsham, turn left signed Erpingham 1 mile, plus camping sign (narrow road). Site is 175 yds. on right. GPS: 52.84208, 1.27090

Charges guide

Per unit incl. 2 persons,
electricity and awning   £ 13.00
No credit cards.

Peterborough
Ferry Meadows Caravan Club Site
Ham Lane, Peterborough PE2 5UU (Cambridgeshire) T: 01733 233526. E: enquiries@caravanclub.co.uk
alanrogers.com/UK3580

Three miles from bustling Peterborough and closer still to the East of England Showground, the immaculate Ferry Meadows is an ideal family holiday site occupying 30 acres of the 500-acre Nene Country Park. Open all year the site provides 265 pitches (16A electricity) – 130 grass pitches on one side of the park, informally laid out in small groups and surrounded by a variety of mature trees, and gravel hardstandings just across the road for caravans and motorcaravans. A very small area (no electricity) is reserved for tents. Families with children may prefer the grass area, from where they can keep a watchful eye on the well equipped playground.

Facilities

Two modern, well appointed and heated toilet blocks are of the usual high standard, with en-suite facilities for disabled visitors in one block. Baby/toddler washroom. Laundry room. Motorcaravan service point. The office stocks basic provisions. Good play areas. TV socket and lead. WiFi (charged). Off site: Steam railway 500 yds. Restaurants within 0.5 miles. Shops 1 mile.

Open: All year.

Directions

Leave the A1 on A605, turn east, signed Showground, Peterborough. At fourth roundabout turn left, signed Ferry Meadows. Entrance is on the left just beyond railway. GPS: 52.56053, -0.30593

Charges guide

Per person	£ 5.10 - £ 6.90
child (5-16 yrs)	£ 1.55 - £ 2.55
pitch incl. electricity (non-member)	£ 13.10 - £ 16.60

Pidley
Stroud Hill Park
Fen Road, Pidley PE28 3DE (Cambridgeshire) T: 01487 741333. E: office@stroudhillpark.co.uk
alanrogers.com/UK3575

Open all year round for adults only, Stroud Hill Park is a well designed, high quality park; a credit to its owners, David and Jayne Newman. The park has been landscaped to create a terraced effect and now incorporates a large fishing lake (well stocked with carp, tench, bream, rudd and roach) plus a superb tennis court. There are 60 large, slightly sloping pitches, fully serviced with 16A electricity, fresh water and drainage, 44 with hardstanding. Affiliated to the Caravan Club, non-members are equally welcome. A member of the Best of British group.

Facilities

Toilets and spacious en-suite shower facilities are in the main building. Well equipped room for disabled visitors. All spotlessly clean. Small, licensed shop stocks basic provisions, homemade cakes, local produce, gas and camping accessories. Attractive bar and superb café/restaurant. Fishing (£5 per day). All-weather tennis court. WiFi (charged). Off site: Golf course, 10-pin bowling and paintball adjacent to site. Riding 0.5 miles. Peterborough, Cambridge, Ely, Huntingdon and Saint Ives.

Open: All year.

Directions

Leave A1 near Huntingdon, take A14 east. Leave A14 at A141 (March). In Warboys, at roundabout, turn right on B1040 signed Pidley. In Pidley turn left just beyond church, Fen Road. Site is 1 mile on right. GPS: 52.38926, -0.03966

Charges guide

Per unit incl. 2 persons and full services	£ 24.00 - £ 26.50
extra person	£ 2.50

Polstead
Polstead Camping & Caravanning Club Site
Holt Road, Bower House Tye, Polstead CO6 5BZ (Suffolk) T: 01787 211969. E: polsteadtouring@hotmail.com
alanrogers.com/UK3340

This lovely touring park in the peaceful Suffolk countryside (in the heart of Constable Country) is an ideal base from which to explore many places of interest. These include Flatford Mill, the scene for Constable's famous painting, Sudbury (the birthplace of Gainsborough), Long Melford with its Hall and Colchester, Britain's oldest town. The very neat and well cared for park is attractively presented and offers 60 level pitches, 54 with 10/16A electricity. Well established hedges separate most of the pitches, 35 of which have gravel hardstanding. This is a Club site, but non-members are welcome.

Facilities

The toilet block was completely refurbished in 2010 to an exceedingly high standard. Spacious showers. Facilities for disabled visitors (wet room including a toilet with handrails); this doubles as a baby changing/family room. Laundry. Reception sells a good range of supplies. Fish and chips delivered by arrangement on Saturdays. Rally field. Children's trim trail. Free WiFi over site. Caravan storage. Off site: Riding 600 yds. Beach 15 miles.

Open: All year.

Directions

From A1071 Hadleigh-Sudbury road, just past the Brewers Arms public house, turn left just before a water tower towards Polstead; park is 250 yds. on the right. GPS: 52.02865, 0.89569

Charges guide

Per unit incl. 2 persons	£ 15.50 - £ 18.90
extra person	£ 7.75 - £ 9.45
awning	free

For latest campsite news visit
alanrogers.com

Sheringham
Woodlands Caravan Park

Holt Road, Upper Sheringham NR26 8TU (Norfolk) T: 01263 823802.

E: enquiries@woodlandscaravanpark.co.uk **alanrogers.com/UK3435**

328

This pleasant caravan park is set in parkland in the beautiful surroundings of north Norfolk's protected heathland, next to Sheringham Park (National Trust). There are 225 sloping grass pitches with 216 having 10A electricity. They are in two main areas for caravans and motorcaravans (tents are not accepted). A major feature of this site is the superb new toilet block with electronically controlled showers. There are many lovely local walks including one to the beach (1.5 miles). The park is within easy reach of Holt, Cromer and Sheringham, with the major birdwatching areas of Blakeney, Cley and Salthouse also within 30 minutes drive. There is a good bar on site offering entertainment at weekends and the excellent Pinewood Park Leisure Club with 25 m. pool, spa and children's pools and beauty room is adjacent to the park. The Club has swimming pools, sauna, spa, gym and other fitness facilities at a discounted rate for those staying at Woodlands.

Facilities

One excellent new toilet block provides all the necessary facilities including those for disabled visitors, baby changing and laundry. Well stocked shop. Gas supplies. Lounge bar and family bar with musical entertainment most weekends. Barbecues. Play area (fenced and gated). Pinewood Park Leisure Club with indoor pool, gym, sauna. etc (all year). Off site: Bicycle hire and fishing 1.5 miles. Norfolk coast, golf and riding 2 miles. Sailing 7 miles. Scenic railway. Stately homes.

Open: 20 March - 31 October.

Directions

From Cromer take the A148 towards Holt, pass signs for Sheringham Park and site is on right (camping sign) just before Bodham village.
GPS: 52.92093, 1.17445

Charges guide

Per unit incl. electricity	£ 18.00 - £ 27.00
awning	£ 4.00

Our family run touring caravan site is situated close to the seaside town of Sheringham. We have serviced pitches with great onsite facilities including a 25m indoor pool, gym, sauna and steam rooms, indoor bowls and a club house. Online booking is available on our website: **woodlandscaravanpark.co.uk**

Located in the beautiful countryside of North Norfolk

HOLT ROAD, UPPER SHERINGHAM, NORFOLK NR26 8TU - **01263 823802**

Sheringham
Kelling Heath Holiday Park

Weybourne, Holt, Sheringham NR25 7HW (Norfolk) T: 01263 588181. E: info@kellingheath.co.uk

alanrogers.com/UK3430

Not many parks can boast their own railway station and Kelling Heath's own halt on the North Norfolk Steam Railway gives access to the beach at Sheringham. Set in 250 acres of woodland and heathland, this very spacious holiday park offers freedom and relaxation with 300 large, level, grass touring pitches, all with 16A electricity and six are fully serviced. Together with 384 caravan holiday homes (36 to let, the rest privately owned), they blend easily into the part-wooded, part-open heath. A wide range of facilities provides activities for all ages. 'The Forge' has an entertainment bar and a family room, with comprehensive entertainment all season. The leisure centre provides an indoor pool, spa pool, sauna, steam rooms and gym. An adventure playground with assault course is near. The central reception area is attractively paved to provide a village square with an open air bandstand where one can sit and enjoy the atmosphere. The park's natural environment allows for woodland walks, a nature trail and cycling trails, and a small lake for fishing (permit holders only). Other amenities include two hard tennis courts, a small, outdoor heated fun pool and play areas (some rather hidden from the pitches).

Facilities

Three toilet blocks include facilities for disabled visitors, a baby room and laundry facilities. Well stocked shop. Gas. Bar, restaurant and takeaway (all season). Indoor leisure centre with pool, gym, etc. with trained staff (membership on either daily or weekly basis). Outdoor heated pool (25/5-5/9). Adventure play area. Tennis. Fishing. Bicycle hire. Entertainment programme. Special environmental Acorn activities for the family. WiFi (charged). Torches useful. Off site: The Norfolk coast, Felbrigg Hall, the Walsingham Shrine and Norfolk Broads.

Open: 10 February - 2 January.

Directions

On A148 road from Holt to Cromer, after High Kelling, turn left just before Bodham village (international sign) signed Weybourne. Follow road for 1 mile to park. GPS: 52.92880, 1.14953

Charges guide

Per unit incl. electricity	£ 18.20 - £ 33.00
with full services	£ 23.70 - £ 40.95
dog (max. 2)	£ 3.15 - £ 5.20

Min. 7-day stay in high season.
No single sex groups.

Swaffham
Breckland Meadows Touring Park

Lynn Road, Swaffham PE37 7PT (Norfolk) T: 01760 721246. E: info@brecklandmeadows.co.uk

alanrogers.com/UK3470

Open all year, this compact, adult only park offers peace and tranquillity yet is only ten minutes walk from the historic market town of Swaffham. The site makes a good base to explore East Anglia and the local area with a wide range of diverse attractions. There are 40 average sized pitches, with hardstanding, 16A electricity and TV hook-ups. There are two main roads close to the park but well established hedges and trees help minimise any noise. There is a small shop selling basic supplies, ices and drinks with a good library.

Facilities

The modern, well cared for toilet block provides all the usual facilities, including spacious showers and facilities for disabled visitors. Laundry room. Gas supplies. WiFi throughout (free). Off site: Swaffham with a range of shops, bars, restaurants, museums, Saturday market 0.5 miles. Bicycle hire 1 mile. Golf 2 miles. Riding 4 miles. Fishing 5 miles. Iceni village. Gooderstone Water Gardens.

Open: All year.

Directions

Park is 0.5 miles west of Swaffham on Low Road (old A47). Entrance on right just beyond garage. GPS: 52.65115, 0.67687

Charges guide

Per unit incl. 2 persons	£ 11.95 - £ 13.95
extra person	£ 3.00

No credit cards.

For latest campsite news visit
alanrogers.com

Wisbech
Parklands Caravan & Camping Park
Sutton Road, Four Gotes, Wisbech PE13 5PH (Cambridgeshire) T: 01945 420505.
E: enquiries@parklandsholidays.co.uk **alanrogers.com/UK3585**

A small, quiet, secluded family run site occupying five acres of level grassland on the borders of Cambridgeshire, Lincolnshire and Norfolk. The site is surrounded by tall conifers giving shelter from the wind. There are 58 good sized, level grass pitches, with 56 for touring and 45 have 10A electricity. The pitches are separated by low hedges and a few trees giving little shade but some will get some shade from the high conifer hedging surrounding the site. Access is easy for large outfits. There is a shop, small swimming pool, and a bar serving takeaway food to order. No charcoal barbecues.

Facilities

Small heated toilet block with good sized adjustable showers and facilities for campers with disabilities. Washing machine. Small swimming pool (April-Sept, heated May-Sept), corner spa, sunbathing area. Shop with bread and newspapers to order (all season). Bar/takeaway food/breakfast rolls (weekends only in low season). Games/TV/entertainment room with darts, pool table and table tennis. Play area. Putting green. Evening music (weekends low season). WiFi throughout (charged). Off site: Lake and river fishing nearby. Golf course with restaurant. Market town of Wisbech with shops, bars, restaurants, Peckover House (NT) 5 miles. King's Lynn 15 miles. Sandringham 22 miles. Many walks and cycle rides on local quiet country roads.

Open: 15 March - 15 October.

Directions

Parklands is on A1101 between Wisbech and Long Sutton. From Wisbech go north to Four Gotes. Site is on right 800 yds. after entering village. GPS: 52.732953, 0.14698

Charges guide

Per unit incl. 2 persons	
and electricity	£ 14.60 - £ 18.80
extra person	£ 3.00 - £ 5.00
child	£ 2.00 - £ 3.00

Camping Cheques accepted.

Woodbridge
Run Cottage Touring Park
Alderton Road, Hollesey, Woodbridge IP12 3RQ (Suffolk) T: 01394 411309. E: contact@run-cottage.co.uk
alanrogers.com/UK3322

This small and very attractive site in the heart of unspoilt Suffolk countryside offers an opportunity to explore many of the local attractions on Suffolk's Heritage Coast. Facilities on the site are limited but certainly adequate, and the resident owners, Michele and Andy Stebbens, are always available to ensure that you have an enjoyable stay. The site is open all year round and all pitches have 10A electricity, with six on hardstanding. This is a popular site and advance booking is strongly recommended. Local attractions include Sutton Hoo, Orford Castle and Framlingham Castle. The market town of Woodbridge is only six miles away. Within a short drive are the pretty coastal towns of Southwold, Dunwich, Orford and Aldeburgh.

Facilities

New, well finished sanitary block with free hot water is easily accessed and is well equipped. Reception contains a comprehensive selection of tourist leaflets and details of local attractions. Off site: Excellent pubs and restaurants within 1 mile. Riding and Suffolk Punch Horse Trust 1 mile. Beach, fishing and bicycle hire 1.5 miles. Golf 5 miles.

Open: All year.

Directions

From A12 (Ipswich-Lowestoft) turn right at the roundabout at Melton onto A1152 (Bawdsey, Orford). In 1.5 miles, at roundabout, turn right onto B1083 (Bawdsey, Hollesley). Within 0.75 miles take left fork to Hollesley. At Duck Corner cross road, turn right and continue through village to site on the left, 100 yds. past Red Brick Bridge. Note: Do not follow sat nav directions. GPS: 52.04503, 1.42683

Charges guide

Per unit incl. 2 persons and electricity	£ 18.00
extra person (over 3 yrs)	£ 3.50
dog (max. 2)	free

Run Cottage Touring Park, Alderton Road, Hollesey, Woodbridge, Suffolk. IP12 3RQ Tel: 01394 411 309 Website:http://www.run-cottage.co.uk Email: contact@run-cottage.co.uk

Close to the town of Woodbridge, we are a small family run touring park with 20 pitches. Set in a 2.5 acre parkland. Setting with a large pond and views over open farmland, we offer peace and tranquillity. A place to escape the hustle and bustle of today's busy lifestyle.

FREE Alan Rogers Travel Card
Extra benefits and savings - see page 10

Woodbridge
Moat Barn Touring Caravan Park

Dallinghoo Road, Bredfield, Woodbridge IP13 6BD (Suffolk) T: 01473 737520
alanrogers.com/UK3330

Mike Allen opened this small adults only touring park in April 2000 on the Suffolk Heritage Cycle Route, and also the Hull-Harwich National Cycle Route. The main touring area is bordered by established hedging and incorporates a circular roadway. The park currently provides 34 level grass pitches, all with 10A electricity. The park is popular with both walkers and cyclists and provides a tranquil environment to explore nearby Woodbridge and surrounding areas. The park has limited provision for large units (for example, American motorhomes).

Facilities

The well equipped sanitary block can be heated. Motorcaravan service point. Bicycle hire. Free WiFi. B&B accommodation available. Off site: Nearby pub serving food. Public footpath.

Open: 1 March - 15 January.

Directions

From A12 take turning signed Bredfield (left from south, right from north). At village pump in Bredfield turn right, follow road past public house and church. Continue through S-bends and, after 200 yds, site entrance is on left, just after farm buildings. GPS: 52.13510, 1.31710

Charges guide

Per unit incl. 2 persons and electricity	£ 18.00

Woodbridge
Steadings Park Camping and Caravan Site

Ipswich Road, Newbourne, Woodbridge IP12 4NS (Suffolk) T: 01473 736505.
E: reception@steadingspark.co.uk **alanrogers.com/UK3324**

Steadings Park is a small, rural campsite bordering the Newborne Spring Nature Reserve and the River Deben. This quiet retreat provides the perfect base for walkers and cyclists to explore the pleasant, rolling Suffolk countryside and coast. There are 60 pitches spread across nine acres. The main touring field has spacious, flat pitches, 40 with 5-16A electricity on well-drained ground. A further small sheltered field for tents is conveniently located near the new sanitary block. New caravan holiday homes were installed in 2012 in a secluded garden area, equipped with hot tubs, decking and a barbecue area. Amenities here include a large dog walking field and a designated children's ball games area.

Facilities

New heated sanitary block with open washbasins, free hot showers and wet room for disabled visitors (key access). Washing machine and dryer. Fridge/freezer available. Shop. Play area. Dog walking area. Bicycle hire. WiFi over site (charged). Large RVs and club rallies are welcome. Off site: The Fox Inn pub and restaurant. Restaurants, tea shops and shopping in historic Woodbridge. Golf, boat launching, sailing and beach all 1.5 miles. Dry ski slope 5 miles. Boat trips and crab lines. Orford Castle.

Open: 1 March - 3 January.

Directions

From A14 travelling west take exit 58 signed A12N, Woodbridge. Continue along A12 and at roundabout take third exit towards Newbourne. After 800 yds. turn right, signed Fox Inn and Katie's Garden, then follow signs to park. GPS: 52.04129, 1.30217

Charges guide

Per unit incl. 2 persons and electricity	£ 16.00 - £ 20.00
tent pitch with 2 persons	£ 10.00 - £ 14.00
extra person (any age)	£ 2.50

Woodbridge
The Moon & Sixpence

Newbourne Road, Waldringfield, Woodbridge IP12 4PP (Suffolk) T: 01473 736650.
E: info@moonandsixpence.eu **alanrogers.com/UK3320**

This excellent site offers 60 large touring pitches that are positioned in the centre of an established and very spacious caravan holiday home park. The site is extremely well maintained and all the 60 touring pitches are equipped with 5A electricity, TV point, water tap and a drain. In the centre of the site, and easily accessible to all, is an unsupervised lake with a sandy beach. An area at one end of the lake is set aside for ten pitches for adults only, all with views of the lake.

Facilities

Exceptionally well finished, centrally placed unisex sanitary block consists of 11 fully equipped private rooms with WCs, washbasins, showers, baths and wet rooms. No specific facilities for disabled visitors but access to the block is via a ramp. Laundry facilities. Well stocked shop. Bar and restaurant (main season). TV room. Two adventure play areas. Dog walk trails. Lake with beach. Tennis. Golf. WiFi (free). Off site: Boat launching and fishing 2 miles. Bicycle hire and riding 5 miles.

Open: 1 April - 31 Ocotber.

Directions

From the A12 (Ipswich-Lowestoft) turn right at roundabout, towards Waldringfield and follow signs to site. After one and a half miles, turn left at Waldringfield Golf Club to site, three-quarters of a mile on the left. GPS: 52.06252, 1.29858

Charges guide

Per person (over 2 yrs) incl. unit and services	£ 9.50 - £ 16.50
dog	£ 1.25

For latest campsite news visit
alanrogers.com

Spanning central England, from the ancient borders of Wales in the west across to Lincolnshire on the east coast, the Heart of England is rich in glorious rolling countryside, magnificent castles, fine stately houses and beautiful gardens.

THE REGION COMPRISES LINCOLNSHIRE, RUTLAND, NORTHAMPTONSHIRE, NOTTINGHAMSHIRE, WEST MIDLANDS, DERBYSHIRE, STAFFORDSHIRE, LEICESTERSHIRE, WARWICKSHIRE, HEREFORDSHIRE, WORCESTERSHIRE, GLOUCESTERSHIRE & SHROPSHIRE

The charming and diverse countryside of the Heart of England includes: the Lincolnshire Wolds, with the dramatic open landscape of the Fens; the ragged crags, dales and moorland of the Peak District National Park in Derbyshire and Staffordshire; the heathered hilltops of Shropshire; the famous Sherwood Forest, in the heart of Nottinghamshire; and the miles of lush green countryside of Herefordshire, dotted with black and white timber houses. Rutland Water is a mecca for watersports and the whole region offers superb opportunities for walking, cycling and more daring activities such as rock climbing and caving. The Cotswolds to the west of the region is the largest Area of Outstanding Natural Beauty in England and Wales. Here you will find many traditional English villages, with charming country pubs and cottage gardens. Other significant features of the region are the rivers and canals. Passing pretty towns and villages, a large canal network threads its way through the area, weaving through the Lincolnshire Fens, past the waterside bars and restaurants of Birmingham and along to estuaries of the rivers of Severn and Avon.

Places of interest

Lincolnshire: Skegness and seal sanctuary.

Rutland: market towns of Oakham and Uppingham; Rutland water outdoor centre.

Northamptonshire: Silverstone; Althorp House; Abington Park Museum.

Nottinghamshire: Nottingham Castle and city of caves. Sherwood Forest.

West Midlands: Birmingham; Cadbury World.

Derbyshire: Bakewell; Buxton; Peak District National Park; Chatsworth House.

Staffordshire: Alton Towers; Stoke-on-Trent.

Leicestershire: Snibston Discovery Park; Twycross Zoo. Great Central steam railway.

Warwickshire: Warwick Castle; Kenilworth Castle; Stratford-upon-Avon.

Herefordshire: Hereford Cathedral.

Worcestershire: Severn Valley Railway.

Gloucestershire: Gloucester cathedral and falconry; Cheltenham. Forest of Dean.

Shropshire: Shrewsbury and Whitchurch.

Did you know?

The last battle of the English Civil War was on 3 September 1651 at Worcester.

The World Toe Wrestling Championship, held every June in Wetton, is a registered international sport.

The hollow trunk of the 'Mighty Tree' in Sherwood Forest is reputedly where Robin Hood and his Merry Men hid from the Sheriff of Nottingham.

Quite different from the more familiar tart, the Bakewell pudding was first created in the 1860s.

Rutland is the smallest county in Britain, measuring just 16 miles by 16 miles.

The Emperor Fountain at Chatsworth House, designed in 1844 by Joseph Paxton is the tallest in Britain at just over 260 feet.

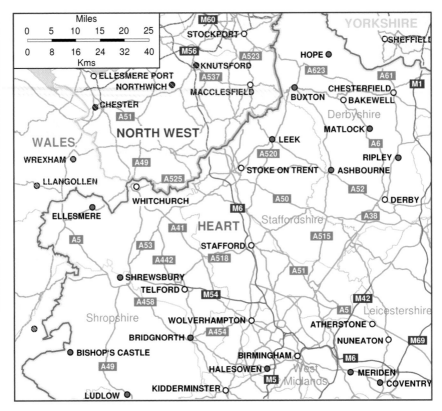

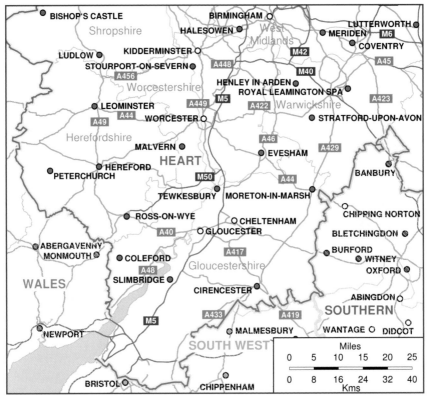

For latest campsite news visit
alanrogers.com

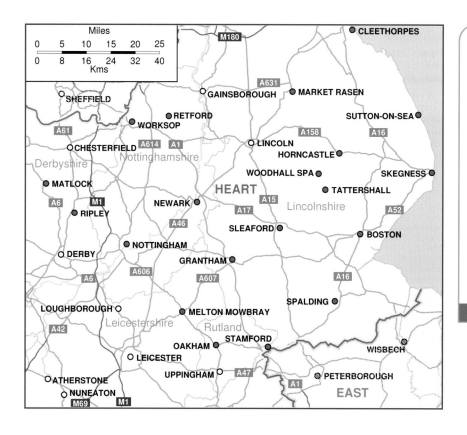

Ashbourne

Callow Top Holiday Park

Buxton Road, Sandybrook, Ashbourne DE6 2AQ (Derbyshire) T: 01335 344020. E: enquiries@callowtop.co.uk

alanrogers.com/UK3855

Situated just north of the market town of Ashbourne, Callow Top nestles within an elevated country setting. The park's location makes it well placed to allow visitors to explore the picturesque villages, bustling market towns and the many attractions of the Peak District. It is ideal for both walking and cycling holidays. Spread over seven separate areas at the top of a hill, there are 200 flat pitches of which 100 are for touring units. Those on hardstanding have 10A electricity, the grass pitches have no power supply. Water points tend to be rather scarce. Some of the pitches are rather small and on these, cars are parked away from the pitch. The focal point of the park is an old farmhouse which has been converted into an 'Olde English' style inn/restaurant serving award-winning real ale brewed in its own micro-brewery and a good selection of pub food (closed Tuesdays). The inn also has a family room and a large beer garden. There are also cottages for rent. Dove Dale, Tissington and High Peak trails and the Manifold Valley are nearby.

Facilities

Three heated toilet blocks (only one open in low season) provide unisex showers (20p). Toilet for disabled visitors. Laundry room. Motorcaravan service point. Calor gas. Shop. Inn/restaurant. Snack bar and takeaway. Heated swimming and paddling pools (May-Sept). Bicycle hire. Games room. Play area. Entertainment (w/ends and high season). Fishing. WiFi (free). Winter caravan storage. Off site: Ashbourne (supermarket etc) 1 mile. Golf 1 mile. Riding 3 miles. Carsington Water (boat launching) 4 miles. Alton Towers 10 miles.

Open: 22 March - 10 November.

Directions

At Sandybrook, 0.5 miles north of Ashbourne, turn west off the A515 (Ashbourne-Buxton) into site road which becomes steep. Site is signed.
GPS: 53.02693, -1.74646

Charges guide

Per unit incl. 2 persons	£ 17.00 - £ 23.50
incl. hardstanding and electricity	£ 20.50 - £ 29.50
extra person	£ 2.50
child (4-16 yrs)	£ 1.50

FREE Alan Rogers Travel Card
Extra benefits and savings - see page 10

Ashbourne
Peak Gateway Leisure Club

Osmaston, Ashbourne DE6 1NA (Derbyshire) T: 01335 344643. E: info@peakgateway.com

alanrogers.com/UK3854

The motto of this park is 'more than just a campsite', and it lives up to that. This is a place that caters for all ages and interests, with children at its heart. A former WWII RAF flying school, the buildings centred around the officers' mess have been sensitively converted to their present functions. The owner and the manager are enthusiastically adding activities, entertainment and attractions to the park and refurbishment of some parts is well underway. There are 30 touring pitches (20 hardstanding), all with 10A electricity and a further 40 well-spaced pitches for tents. There is a new toilet block in the tent field. Privately owned caravan holiday homes occupy a further 42 pitches. The park is busy at weekends.

Facilities

High standard heated toilet blocks with free showers and hairdryers. Laundry room. Rooms for families and disabled visitors. Further toilet block for the tent field, also with dishwashing facilities. Two bars with family room, breakfast café, takeaway and bar meals. Dance hall. Small shop. Games room and TV. Buggy racing (150cc) at weekends. Disco (Sat. in high season; check events programme for dates). Varied entertainment programme all season especially B.Hs, Halloween, etc. (bookings required). WiFi over part of site (charged). Only 1 dog per pitch is permitted. Off site: Leisure centre in town (free Sat. shuttle bus provided). Golf and bicycle hire 1 mile. Riding 2 miles. Fishing 4 miles.

Open: All year.

Directions

The entrance is off the A52 one mile southeast of Ashbourne. From Ashbourne southern bypass turn right 300 yards after roundabout. From Derby on the A52, 1 mile after the turn to Osmaston village, turn left. Site is clearly signed.
GPS: 53.003151, -1.721273

Charges guide

Per unit incl. 2 persons	
and electricity	£ 20.00 - £ 25.00
child (6-17 yrs)	£ 2.00
small dog (max. 1)	£ 3.00

Ashbourne
Rivendale Caravan & Leisure Park

328

Buxton Road, Alsop-en-le-Dale, Ashbourne DE6 1QU (Derbyshire) T: 01335 310311.
E: enquiries@rivendalecaravanpark.co.uk **alanrogers.com/UK3850**

This unusual park has been developed in the bowl of a hill quarry which was last worked over 50 years ago. The steep quarry walls shelter three sides with marvellous views over the Peak District National Park countryside to the south. Near the entrance to the park is a renovated stone building which houses reception, shop, bar and a café/restaurant. Nearby are 136 level and landscaped pitches, mostly of a generous size with 16A electricity and a mix of hardstanding and grass. In two separate fields and a copse there is provision for 50 tents and that area includes a fishing lake. All the touring pitches are within easy reach of the central stone-built toilet block which is in keeping with the environment and provided with underfloor heating.

Facilities

Good toilet facilities include some washbasins in cubicles for ladies, and an excellent en-suite room for disabled visitors. Laundry room. Shop (all essentials). Bar (evenings) and café with home-made and local food (open mornings, lunch and evenings, both with limited opening in low season). Packed lunches from reception. Special events monthly and games in main season. Hot tubs for hire, delivered to your pitch. Fly fishing lake. WiFi in some areas (charged). For rent on the park are B&B rooms, camping pods, lodges and yurts. Off site: Bicycle hire nearby. Riding 5 miles. Sailing and boat launching 8 miles. Golf 10 miles. Alton Towers 35 minutes drive.

Open: 1 February - 5 January.

Directions

Park is 7 miles north of Ashbourne on the A515 to Buxton, on the eastern side of the road. It is well signed between the turnings east to Alsop Moor and Matlock (A5012), but take care as this is a very fast section of the A515. GPS: 53.106383, -1.760567

Charges guide

Per unit incl. 2 persons	
and electricity	£ 18.50 - £ 24.00
extra person	£ 2.50
child (4-15 yrs)	£ 2.00
dog	£ 2.00

Camping Cheques accepted.

Ashbourne
Woodland Caravan Park
Snelston Hall, Ashbourne DE6 2ET (Derbyshire) T: 01335 346 120.
alanrogers.com/UK3860

Set in woodland within the privately owned grounds of Snelston Hall, this site presents a charming, tranquil haven for those seeking a leafy retreat. The 900-acre estate has walks on private and public footpaths. The 52 pitches, constructed from local limestone are level, each with electric hook-up. Expect to see shafts of light falling on irregularly arranged pitches allowing a sense of privacy within the tall trees that give the site its name. These trees help screen out low level traffic noise, which is much reduced at night. Modern, clean, toilet blocks are tastefully coloured to blend with the surroundings.

Facilities

One modern, clean, toilet block (key access) with room for visitors with disabilities. Laundry. Kitchen area with microwave. Motorcaravan services – ask at reception for help with grey waste. Separate, enclosed area for dog walking (breeds restricted). Reception offers advice on waymarked walks and allows access to the large private estate. Off site: Darley Motorcycle Circuit 1 mile. Spa town of Ashbourne 4 miles. Tissington Trail with bicycle hire 5 miles. Peak District National Park 6 miles.

Open: 22 March - 30 September.

Directions

Leave the A50 at Sudbury and take A515 signed Ashbourne. Follow road for 7 miles. Just before Darley Moor Motor Cycle Circuit (on your right) turn left (signed Snelston and Woodland Caravan Park) and turn almost immediately right into Woodland Park. GPS: 52.98102, -1.7531

Charges guide

Per unit incl. 2 persons	
and electricity	£ 15.00 - £ 24.00
extra person	£ 2.00

Bishop's Castle
The Green Caravan Park
Wentnor, Bishop's Castle SY9 5EF (Shropshire) T: 01588 650605. E: karen@greencaravanpark.co.uk
alanrogers.com/UK4440

Remotely situated in a pleasant valley, in a designated Area of Outstanding Natural Beauty, and sandwiched between the Stiperstones and The Long Mynd, The Green would make an ideal base for some serious walking; a footpath to the Stiperstones passes through the site. The 15-acre site is delightful, and is divided into several fields. There are 160 pitches, taking 41 seasonal units, and around 20 holiday homes, with approximately 140 pitches for tourists (41 with 16A electric hook-ups). The main field has some hardstandings. The East Onny is a small, shallow river which runs through the site, much enjoyed by the youngsters, who can spend many hours catching minnows.

Facilities

One main sanitary block, rather austere in appearance, built into the side of a large barn. However, it provides adequate and plentiful facilities with spacious hot showers (coin operated) and laundry facilities, but there is no dedicated unit for disabled campers. Small shop in new reception building. Playground. Off site: Four pubs within 3 miles, one next door. Fishing 3 miles. Riding 4 miles. Bishops Castle with museums. Leisure Centre.

Open: Easter - 31 October.

Directions

From Shrewsbury take A49. Right turn at Marsh Brook. At T-junction turn right onto A489 for 5 miles. Turn right at brown campsite sign. Site is just after The Inn on the Green. GPS: 52.53375, -2.91375

Charges guide

Per unit incl. 2 persons	
and electricity	£ 14.50 - £ 16.00
extra person	£ 3.50

Boston
Long Acres Touring Park
Station Road, Old Leake, Boston PE22 9RF (Lincolnshire) T: 01205 871555.
E: enquiries@longacres-caravanpark.co.uk **alanrogers.com/UK3695**

An attractive, adults only site on the Lincolnshire Fens north of Boston, yet only six miles from the coastline of the Wash, Long Acres is a purpose-built site opened in 2008 and attractively laid out to take maximum advantage of the great variety of trees and shrubs. Ranged on either side of the site's single road, the 40 pitches, all with 10A electric hook-ups, are on hardstandings separated by well tended grass to cater for tents and awnings. The beaches and attractions of Skegness are just 17 miles away.

Facilities

A single well equipped, central toilet block provides preset showers, open-style washbasins with hairdryers, a small freezer for ice packs, and an en-suite unit for disabled visitors. Motorcaravan service point. Reception has tourist information, maps of walking and cycling routes, sample menus from local pubs and a small library. Area available for small rallies. Boules pitch. WiFi over site (charged). Off site: Fishing 1 mile. Golf 7 miles. Bicycle hire 10 miles.

Open: 1 March - 31 October.

Directions

The site is best approached from the A16 Boston -Louth road. At Sibsey turn east on B1184 towards Old Leake. At T-junction turn left and in 1.7 miles turn right along Common Side Road to site on left. GPS: 53.057487, 0.063732

Charges guide

Per unit incl. 2 persons	
and electricity	£ 17.50 - £ 20.00
extra person	£ 4.00

FREE Alan Rogers Travel Card
Extra benefits and savings - see page 10

Bridgnorth

Stanmore Hall Touring Park

Stourbridge Road, Bridgnorth WV15 6DT (Shropshire) T: 01746 761761. E: stanmore@morris-leisure.co.uk

alanrogers.com/UK4400

This attractive park is situated in the former grounds of Stanmore Hall, where the huge lily pond, fine mature trees and beautifully manicured lawns give a mark of quality. There are 135 generously sized pitches, 130 with 16A electricity including 30 hardstanding super pitches with TV connections. Also available are 23 standard pitches, but most are on grass. Some pitches are reserved for adult only use (over 18 years). Access and internal roads are tarmac; site lighting is adequate and reassuring. The park is a member of the Caravan Club's 'managed under contract' scheme but non-members are also very welcome. A size restriction of 30ft exists for motorcaravans.

Facilities

The upgraded, centrally-heated sanitary block is accessed by key. Facilities are excellent and provide washbasins in cubicles and a room for disabled guests and baby care. Full laundry facilities. Motorcaravan service points. A well equipped shop stocks camping and caravan accessories. A TV booster system is available. Play area. Max. 2 dogs per unit. WiFi over site (charged). Off site: Fishing 1.5 miles.

Open: All year.

Directions

Site is 1.5 miles from Bridgnorth on the A458 (signed Stourbridge). If using sat nav approach from Bridgnorth only. GPS: 52.52715, -2.378617

Charges guide

Per unit incl. 2 persons and electricity	£ 22.60 - £ 25.30
extra person	£ 6.60 - £ 7.00

Buxton

Clover Fields Touring Caravan Park

1 Heath View, Harpur Hill, Buxton SK17 9PU (Derbyshire) T: 01298 78731. E: cloverfields@tiscali.co.uk

alanrogers.com/UK3845

The Redferns are more than happy to welcome you to their family owned, adults only park (over 18 yrs). It is located on the outskirts of the spa town of Buxton within easy reach of the Peak District National Park. You will be able to relax here in the 'away from it all' atmosphere. There are just 25 pitches with 20 more planned, serviced by a first rate toilet block. The pitches are divided by low hedges, part hardstanding and part grass, all with 16A electricity, a water tap and a concealed dustbin. There is a little noise from the adjacent road. Recently added is a newly constructed and stocked fishing pond.

Facilities

The toilet and shower block is modern and clean with many complimentary toiletry items. Facilities for disabled visitors. Gas supplies. Laundry room. Motorcaravan service point. Small shop selling essentials, home made jam and chutney and caravan accessories. Newspapers and milk delivered to your pitch. Plant sales. Barbecues provided by reception. Small library. Fishing. Torches recommended. Off site: Supermarket and fish and chip shop in Buxton. Opera House and Pavilion. Golf 3 miles.

Open: All year.

Directions

From Buxton, at Harpur Hill just to southeast, turn right off A515 (Buxton-Ashbourne) onto B5053. Turn immediately right towards Harpur Hill. Site entrance is 0.5 miles on left (easily missed) at start of 40 mph limit. GPS: 53.23066, -1.8878

Charges guide

Per unit incl. 2 persons and electricity	£ 20.00 - £ 23.00
extra adult	£ 5.00

No credit cards.

Buxton

Lime Tree Holiday Park

Dukes Drive, Buxton SK17 9RP (Derbyshire) T: 01298 22988. E: info@limetreeparkbuxton.com

alanrogers.com/UK3840

Lime Tree is in a convenient, edge of town location that makes a very good base for touring the Peak District. The site has three widely spaced main areas, touring pitches on two levels with a toilet block on the upper level, a caravan holiday home area which has the reception shop and games room, and above and a short distance away a large, mainly sloping field for tents. The toilet block for the tents and a play area are above reception. Touring pitches (65) are mainly on hardstandings with 10/16A electricity supply. With good views, the park is situated next to a thickly wooded, limestone gorge.

Facilities

A modern toilet building serves the touring area, including some washbasins in cubicles, controllable showers, baby room and a family room with facilities for disabled visitors. The refitted, original unit serves the tent area. Both can be heated and have top quality fittings. Laundry. Shop. Basic play area. Games/TV room. WiFi. Off site: Pub serving food nearby. Swimming, riding and golf 1 mile. Fishing, bicycle hire, sailing and boat launching 5 miles.

Open: 1 March - 31 October.

Directions

Park is on outskirts of Buxton and signed from the A515 Buxton-Ashbourne road 1 mile south of town. From town, just after hospital bear sharp left into Dukes Drive, go under railway viaduct and site is on right. From south watch for sharp turn right at foot of hill (signed in advance). GPS: 53.250230, -1.896673

Charges guide

Per unit incl. 2 persons and electricity	£ 22.00
extra person	£ 6.00

For latest campsite news visit

alanrogers.com

Cirencester
Hoburne Cotswold

Broadway Lane, South Cerney, Cirencester GL7 5UQ (Gloucestershire) T: 01285 860216.
E: enquiries@hoburne.co.uk **alanrogers.com/UK4100**

Since this park is adjacent to the Cotswold Water Park, those staying here will have easy access to the varied watersports available. On the park itself there is a lake with pedaloes for hire. The wide range of other amenities includes outdoor and indoor heated swimming pools and an impressive, large indoor leisure complex. There are 189 well marked touring pitches for any type of unit, all with hardstanding (only fairly level) and a grass surround for awning or tent. Pitches are of a good size but with nothing between them, and very little shade; all have electricity (10A, some need long leads).

Facilities	Directions
Four small toilet blocks are clean and well maintained with preset showers and background heating. Baby changing facilities. Basic facilities for disabled visitors. The site has heavy weekend trade. Launderette. Supermarket. Indoor leisure complex including a pool with flume. Outdoor pool (mid May-early Sept). Clubhouse with bar, food and entertainment and free WiFi. Events weekends during season. Football pitch. Tennis. Adventure playground. Crazy golf. Fishing lake. Animals are not accepted. Off site: Swindon and Cheltenham. Fishing and walking.	Three miles southeast of Cirencester on A419, turn west towards Cotswold Water Park at new roundabout on bypass onto B4696 signed South Cerney. Continue past Water Park for 1.5 miles. Road leading to campsite is on right. Take second right and follow signs. Bus stop outside campsite entrance. GPS: 51.66018, -1.91910

Open: March - October.

Charges guide	
Per unit incl. max. 6 persons and electricity	£ 15.45 - £ 34.75
serviced 'super' pitch	£ 16.50 - £ 36.85

Cleethorpes
Thorpe Park Holiday Centre

Humberston, Cleethorpes DN35 0PW (Lincolnshire) T: 01472 813395
alanrogers.com/UK3655

Thorpe Park is a Haven Holiday Park at Cleethorpes on the north Lincolnshire coast. The touring site, although part of one of the largest caravan parks in Europe, is neat and compact. There are 81 landscaped Euro pitches with brick-built hardstandings, electricity, water and drainage, and a further 55 in an open area, most with electricity available. A third area has 17 tent pitches (no electricity). There is direct access to the beach, and the park's main entertainment complex is a short walk away. A shuttle train will take you to more distant parts of the park, including a nine-hole golf course.

Facilities	Directions
Three modern toilet blocks. The one in the main area has pushbutton showers in well fitted cubicles, open style washbasins and an excellent room for disabled visitors and families. Motorcaravan services. Supermarket. Fish and chips. Launderette. Entertainment complex. Heated indoor pool and outdoor flumes. Play area. Crazy golf. Climbing wall. Tennis. Multisports court. Fishing lakes. Roller rink. 9-hole and family golf courses. Bicycle hire.	From M180 take A180 to Grimsby, turn south on A16 towards Louth, then east on A1098 to Humberston and follow signs for Pleasure Island and Holiday Parks. Park is to right at roundabout. GPS: 53.5347, 0.00412

Open: Easter - 2 November.

Charges guide	
Per unit incl. up to 4 persons	£ 17.00 - £ 67.00
extra person	£ 3.00

Coleford
Forest Holidays Christchurch

Bracelands Drive, Christchurch, Coleford GL16 7NN (Gloucestershire) T: 01594 837258.
E: fod.site@forestholidays.co.uk **alanrogers.com/UK4160**

Set high above the Wye Valley, a partnership between the Forestry Commission and the Camping and Caravanning Club, Forest Holidays makes a perfect family holiday destination. With 280 unmarked pitches (240 for touring), this 20-acre site occupies an open grassy area in the heart of the Forest of Dean. There are seven hardstandings and 102 pitches with 10A electrical hook-ups. A new reception block includes a shop, café and ranger station. A large viewing gallery overlooks the site and the Forest Rangers will hold events on the life and work of the forest, such as Young Explorers and Forest Survival.

Facilities	Directions
Two sanitary units with spacious, well equipped showers, some vanity style basins with dividers. The central block has a laundry room. Units for disabled visitors and baby changing in both blocks. Adventure playground. No specified dog walk, but trails and footpaths surround the site. Limited television and mobile reception. WiFi. Off site: Fishing and swimming 1 mile. Coleford 1.5 miles.	From Monmouth take A4136 east for 5 miles turning north at crossroads at Pike House Inn and site is on left after 0.5 miles. GPS: 51.813333, -2.62735

Open: All year.

Charges guide	
Per unit incl. 2 persons	£ 12.20 - £ 19.90
incl. electricity	£ 17.00 - £ 29.50

FREE Alan Rogers Travel Card
Extra benefits and savings - see page 10

Coventry

Hollyfast Caravan Park

Wall Hill Road, Allesley, Coventry CV5 9EL (Warwickshire) T: 024 7633 6411.
E: sales@hollyfastcaravanpark.co.uk **alanrogers.com/UK4075**

Hollyfast is situated in beautiful countryside on the outskirts of Coventry, part of the park being set within a lovely woodland area giving peace and tranquillity all year round. Located on the Birmingham side of Coventry, this means a short drive into the centre of Coventry and a fifteen minute drive to Birmingham's National Exhibition Centre. You will receive a friendly welcome and be directed to a very clean and well spaced site with 40 touring pitches of varying sizes with 16A electricity connections. Cars are parked away from pitches. A new toilet block provides very clean facilities, along with a games room. Rallies are welcome and a club house is provided with a stage, a TV and kitchen areas for these groups. Under the same ownership, there is a motorcaravan sales centre with a shop selling parts and accessories.

Facilities

The modern toilet block provides simple, clean facilities with good sized showers (3 per sex) and open washbasins. Toilet and shower for disabled campers. Shop. Club house for rallies. Large outdoor ranch style children's play centre and indoor games room. Deposit for barrier (£25). Torches useful. Off site: The local area has shops, three pubs (hot and cold food), a golf course and a riding centre. Bus stop 1 mile for Coventry. Interesting British Road Transport Museum. Birmingham, Stratford-upon-Avon, Leamington Spa and Warwick are within driving distance.

Open: All year.

Directions

From M1/M45 take A45 towards Birmingham. Turn right on A4114 and follow brown and white caravan signs. After turning by the White Lion pub, site is 0.5 miles on left. From north take M6 north of Birmingham or the M1 north (Nottingham), follow M42 to NEC, A45 towards Coventry and onto the A4114 and as above. GPS: 52.44588, -1.55572

Charges guide

Per unit incl. 2 persons	
and electricity	£ 17.50 - £ 21.00
extra person	£ 3.00
child (5-15 yrs)	£ 2.00
dog	£ 1.50

Ellesmere

Fernwood Caravan Park

Lyneal, Ellesmere SY12 0QF (Shropshire) T: 01948 710221. E: enquiries@fernwoodpark.co.uk
alanrogers.com/UK4380

Fernwood is set in an area known as the Shropshire Lake District – the mere at Ellesmere is the largest of nine meres – and the picturesque Shropshire Union Canal is only a few minutes walk. The landscaped park is tranquil and presented to a very high standard, the natural vegetation blending harmoniously with trees and shrubs. In addition to 163 caravan holiday homes, with two units for hire, there are 30 touring pitches (caravans, motorcaravans and trailer tents only) in several well cut, grassy enclosures (including 30 seasonal long stays). Some are in light woodland, others in more open, but still relatively sheltered situations. All pitches have 10A electricity and six also have water and drainage. One area is set aside for units with adults only. Siting is carried out by the management and there is always generous spacing, even when the site is full.

Facilities

The small toilet block for touring units has background heating for cooler days and includes some washbasins in cabins and facilities for disabled campers. Baby changing facilities planned. Basic motorcaravan services. Dishwashing facilities in laundry room, also additional sanitary facilities for ladies and men. Shop doubles as reception (from 1/4-30/10, hours vary). Coarse fishing lake. Forty acres of woodland for walking. Grassy play area for children. Off site: Shrewsbury, Oswestry and Chester are all within easy travelling distance.

Open: 1 March - 30 November.

Directions

Park is just northeast of Lyneal village, signed southwest off the B5063 Ellesmere-Wem road, 1.5 miles from junction of the B5063 with the A495. GPS: 52.899167, -2.816017

Charges guide

Per unit incl. 2 persons	
and electricity	£ 22.00 - £ 26.00
multi-service pitch	£ 25.50 - £ 29.50

One night free for every 7 booked in advance.

For latest campsite news visit
alanrogers.com

Evesham
Ranch Caravan Park
Honeybourne, Evesham WR11 7PR (Worcestershire) T: 01386 830744. E: enquiries@ranch.co.uk
alanrogers.com/UK4180

This quiet, attractive caravan park set in the Vale of Evesham covers an area of 50 acres of flat, partly undulating, hedged meadows. The park lies between Bidford-on-Avon and Broadway and is only half an hour's drive from Stratford. The park takes 120 touring units – caravans, motorcaravans and trailer tents, but not other tents. The spacious pitches are not marked but the staff help to position units. All have 10A electrical connections and there are 21 hardstandings including eight fully serviced pitches (electricity, TV, water and drainage). There are 193 caravan holiday homes in their own section. The Vale of Evesham is often overshadowed by its next door neighbour, the Cotswolds. It is, however, populated by some of the prettiest villages in the area and it is well worth exploring in its own right. Hidcote Manor Gardens, Broadway Tower, and the Fleece Inn at Bretforton are all within a short drive. The riverside town of Evesham is an attractive market town some six miles to the west, and is well worth a visit.

Facilities

Two very well appointed, modern sanitary blocks with free hot showers and heating, one of which includes facilities for disabled visitors, plus baby changing area. Laundry facilities. Motorcaravan service point. Shop. Clubhouse (weekends only in early and late season) offering wide range of good value meals with entertainment arranged throughout the season. Heated pool (55x30 ft; Spr. B.H.-mid Sept). Gym and sauna (charged). Games room with TV. Playground. WiFi. Off site: Riding and bicycle hire 2 miles. Fishing 4 miles. Golf 6 miles.

Open: 1 March - 30 November.

Directions

From A46 Evesham take B4035 towards Chipping Campden. After Badsey and Bretforton before Weston Subedge pass over old railway bridge, turn left at crossroads to Honeybourne. Park is through village on left before station. GPS: 52.09722, -1.83124

Charges guide

Per unit incl. 2 persons	
and electricity	£ 23.00 - £ 27.00
incl. water and drainage	£ 26.50 - £ 30.50
extra person (over 5 yrs)	free - £ 4.50
dog	free - £ 2.50

One free night for every 7 booked.
Note: tents are not accepted.

RANCH CARAVAN PARK AA

An established family-run holiday park located in Honeybourne, 6 miles from Evesham. Level pitches in a landscaped setting. Well situated for visiting the Cotswolds and Shakespeare Country.

Honeybourne, Evesham, Worcestershire
Tel. 01386 830 744 - www.ranch.co.uk - enquiries@ranch.co.uk

Grantham
Wagtail Country Park
Cliff Lane, Marston, Grantham NG32 2HU (Lincolnshire) T: 07814 481088. E: info@wagtailcountrypark.co.uk
alanrogers.com/UK3775

There has been a small campsite here for many years, but the new owner has transformed the appearance of the original camping area alongside an attractive little fishing lake and is in the process of creating a new, larger lake with additional pitches and facilities. There are currently just 11 pitches, all with electricity, on gravel hardstanding and separated by raised flower beds or timber beams. The new development will offer a further 20 pitches, including a couple on grass and ten fully serviced with water and drainage. There will also be five privately owned wooden chalets. Judging by the quality of the changes that have already been made, there is every indication that this will be an attractive 'country park' which will continue to appeal to fishing enthusiasts and to nature lovers who prefer a simple, unsophisticated site in a peaceful rural setting.

Facilities

Two small heated buildings provide spacious controllable showers and open-style washbasins. A new heated toilet block with full facilities is planned including a unit for disabled visitors and laundry facilities. Motorcaravan service point. Security barriers plus overnight pitch for late arrivals. Calor gas. Secure caravan storage. Fishing (£3 per person). No special provision for children and lake not fenced. Off site: Shopping Outlet and Garden Centre 3 miles. Belton House and golf 5 miles. Grantham 6 miles. Riding 7 miles. Belvoir Castle 12 miles. Newark 14 miles. Sailing at Rutland Water 25 miles. Coast 40 miles.

Open: All year.

Directions

Site is off A1 between Grantham and Newark. Turn east towards Marston at filling station 1.2 miles north of Gonerby Services, Grantham. In 500 yds. turn right into Green Lane towards Barkston, then right again in 0.75 miles into Cliff Lane where park is signed. GPS: 52.961229, -0.667269

Charges guide

Per unit incl. 2 persons	
and electricity	£ 16.00 - £ 20.00
extra person	£ 5.90
child	£ 1.50

No credit cards.

FREE Alan Rogers Travel Card
Extra benefits and savings - see page 10

Grantham
Woodland Waters

Willoughby Road, Ancaster, Grantham NG32 3RT (Lincolnshire) T: 01400 230888.
E: info@woodlandwaters.co.uk **alanrogers.com/UK3765**

This attractive holiday park occupies 70 acres of woodland, gently sloping grassland and lakes, with the caravan park itself occupying about 20 acres. There are 120 pitches although only 60 are regularly used (all with 10A electricity and water taps nearby). There is a rally field of 20 pitches with hook-ups, plus areas for camping and for those not requiring electricity. The land slopes gently down to the 14-acre lake and the pitches nearer the water are more level, although probably not suitable for those with younger children since there is no fencing. Reception is housed in a neat, modern building at the park entrance.

Facilities

A single, modern, heated toilet block is well maintained and kept clean. Open style washbasins and free showers (controllable for ladies). Facilities for disabled visitors. A second block provides extra facilities as required. Small laundry room, but no laundry sinks. Motorcaravan service point. Bar and restaurant with takeaway (all year). Play area. Four fishing lakes. Chalets to rent. WiFi. Off site: Limited bus service from near entrance. Shop and trains in village 1 mile. Go-karting and paintball 1 mile. Golf 3 miles. Riding 6 miles. Skegness 50 miles.

Open: All year.

Directions

Ancaster is 8 miles northeast of Grantham and 19 miles south of Lincoln. The park entrance is off the A153 Grantham-Sleaford road, 600 yds. west of the junction with the B6403 High Dyke road (Ermine Street). GPS: 52.98053, -0.54698

Charges guide

Per unit incl. 4 persons and electricity	£ 17.50 - £ 19.50
extra person	£ 2.00
child	£ 1.00

2.5% surcharge on credit card payments.

Henley-in-Arden
Island Meadow Caravan Park

The Mill House, Aston Cantlow, Henley-in-Arden B95 6JP (Warwickshire) T: 01789 488273.
E: holiday@islandmeadowcaravanpark.co.uk **alanrogers.com/UK4090**

This peaceful, traditional, family run site is in a rural location, surrounded by the River Alne and its mill race. A good base for walking, cycling and birdwatching, it has 80 pitches in total, with 56 holiday homes (four for rent) located around the perimeter. The 24 touring pitches are on the spacious, central grassy area of the site, all have 10A electric hook-ups. Only environmentally friendly groundsheets are permitted. Note: The site is on an island with obvious hazards for small children. There is an excellent playground in the village centre (five minutes walk via footpath across Mill Meadow).

Facilities

Two sanitary units, both heated. The original provides adequate WCs and washbasins for men, and the more modern unit has been provided for women, with separate access shower unit for the men, and a wet room style suite for disabled visitors on one end. Laundry with washing machine, sink and ironing facility. The millpond and its weir offer good coarse fishing. Off site: The village has its own Club (campers welcome) and the local pub serves a good range of meals. Golf 3 miles.

Open: 1 March - 31 October.

Directions

From A46 (Stratford-Alcester) follow signs for Mary Arden's House. At Wilmcote follow signs to Aston Cantlow and site. GPS: 52.23549, -1.80265

Charges guide

Per unit incl. 2 persons and electricity	£ 21.00
extra person	£ 2.00
child (5-12 yrs)	£ 1.00
tent (2 man)	£ 15.00

Gazebos only by prior arrangement. No credit cards.

For latest campsite news visit
alanrogers.com

Hereford

Lucksall Caravan & Camping Park

Mordiford, Hereford HR1 4LP (Herefordshire) T: 01432 870213. E: karen@lucksallpark.co.uk

alanrogers.com/UK4310

Set in 17 acres and bounded on one side by the River Wye, and over 90 acres of woodland on the other, Lucksall has 139 large, well spaced and level touring pitches, all with 16A electricity and 70 with hardstanding. The river is open to the site with lifebelts and safety messages in evidence. Canoes are available for hire or bring your own (launching facilities); fishing permits may be obtained from reception. A large, fenced playground and a large grassy area for games are provided. A well stocked shop selling a variety of goods is in reception (a mini market is within 1.5 miles). Café/takeaway now open.

Facilities

Three centrally heated toilet blocks provide top of the range facilities, two separate units with ramped entrances for disabled campers. Laundry room. Family room. WiFi (free). Only breathable groundsheets are permitted. Off site: Golf 5 miles. Bicycle hire 9 miles. Riding 10 miles. Sustrans cycle route nearby.

Open: 1 March - 30 November.

Directions

Between Mordiford and Fownhope, 5 miles southeast of Hereford on B4224, the park is well signed. GPS: 52.02302, -2.63052

Charges guide

Per unit incl. 2 persons	£ 18.00 - £ 26.00
extra person (over 17 yrs)	£ 3.50
small 3-man tent	£ 15.00 - £ 23.00

Hope

Laneside Caravan Park

Station Road, Hope Valley, Hope S33 6RR (Derbyshire) T: 01433 620215. E: laneside@lineone.net

alanrogers.com/UK3807

Laneside Caravan Park is in a beautiful location facing Win Hill, Lose Hill, and the high gritstone hills of The Dark Peak, while the gentler rolling hills of The White Peak are to the south. The park is on the floor of Hope Valley with the River Noe running alongside. There are 160 marked level pitches, 95 on grass and 30 on hardstanding for touring units, while 35 are seasonal; 110 have 16A electric hook-ups. The two toilet blocks have recently been refurbished. The site welcomes families (although there is no swimming pool on site) and quiet couples, but no single-sex groups or unaccompanied teenagers.

Facilities

Two heated toilet blocks with family/disabled showers. Covered pot washing facility. Laundry room with baby changing station. Motorcaravan service point. Site shop with basics. Gas exchange and basic camping spares. Information room. Dog walk. Payphone. Picnic benches. Large riverside recreation area with picnic benches and boules courts. Security barriers and CCTV protection. WiFi. Off site: Shops, pub and restaurant in Hope. Caverns at Castleton 5 minutes. Golf 2 miles. Bicycle hire 4 miles. Chatsworth 15 minutes.

Open: Mid March to early November.

Directions

From east via A619/A623, at Tideswell crossroads (Anchor pub), turn right onto B6049 (Castleton, Bradwell). Turn left at T-junction (A6187) opposite Travellers' Rest. Follow signs towards Hope. 500 yds. after Travellers' Rest, just before Hope, look for sign (Laneside) on right directing left into park. GPS: 53.345159, -1.735706

Charges guide

Per unit incl. 2 persons and electricity	£ 15.25 - £ 20.75
extra person (over 5 yrs)	£ 2.75

Horncastle

Ashby Park

West Ashby, Horncastle LN9 5PP (Lincolnshire) T: 01507 527966. E: ashbyparklakes@btconnect.com

alanrogers.com/UK3680

Ashby Park is a pleasant, well run site located in 70 acres of former gravel pits that now provide seven attractive fishing lakes. There is a series of clearings occupied by privately owned caravan holiday homes, seasonal caravans and 70 touring pitches. Most are on grass, but some have hardstanding. All have access to 16A electricity and 25 pitches also have hardstanding, water tap and drainage. Lakeside pitches will no doubt appeal to anglers, whereas families with young children will probably prefer to be further away from the lakes, as they are unfenced. One field caters for dog owners.

Facilities

Three toilet blocks are well maintained and equipped, with open style washbasins and controllable showers; all hot water is metered (20p). Good en-suite facilities for disabled visitors. Laundry room with washing machine and dryer. Limited dishwashing (in the new block – a long walk from lakeside pitches). Motorcaravan service point. Gas supplies. Fishing (day ticket £6). WiFi. Off site: Golf 0.5 miles. Pubs and restaurants in Horncastle 2-3 miles.

Open: 1 March - 30 November.

Directions

Horncastle is 20 miles east of Lincoln on A158 to Skegness. Site is 2.6 miles north of the town and is signed to the east from A158 and to the west from A153 Sleaford-Louth road. Follow signs to site. GPS: 53.233293, -0.122426

Charges guide

Per unit incl. 2 persons and electricity	£ 19.00
extra person	£ 4.00
serviced pitch	£ 20.00 - £ 26.50

FREE Alan Rogers Travel Card
Extra benefits and savings - see page 10

Leek
Glencote Caravan Park

Station Road, Cheddleton, Leek ST13 7EE (Staffordshire) T: 01538 360745. E: canistay@glencote.co.uk

alanrogers.com/UK3970

Nestled in the Churnet Valley, three miles south of the market town of Leek, a pleasant stay awaits you at this, well managed, family run park of six acres. Each of the 74 level touring pitches, accessed via tarmac roads, has grass and a paved hardstanding, 16A electrical connections and a dedicated water supply. Pretty flowerbeds, trees and varied wildlife make a very pleasant environment. Alongside a fenced coarse fishing pool is a grass play area and this whole corner is enclosed by banks with an abundance of attractive shrubs and flowers.

Facilities

The clean toilet block is centrally situated and can be heated. Facilities include one private cabin for ladies, a combined shower and toilet for disabled visitors, a small laundry room, two dishwashing sinks and one vegetable preparation sink under cover. Gas supplies. Max. 2 dogs per unit. WiFi over site (charged). Information centre and small library. Off site: Small supermarket and post office in Cheddleton 0.5 miles. Pubs within walking distance.

Open: 1 February - end December.

Directions

Park is signed off A520 Leek-Stone road, 3.5 miles south of Leek on northern edge of Cheddleton Village. GPS: 53.06994, -2.02901

Charges guide

Per unit incl. 2 persons and electricity	£ 24.00
extra person	£ 5.00
child (5-16 yrs)	£ 2.50
dog	£ 1.00

Leominster
Townsend Touring & Caravan Park

Townsend Farm, Pembridge, Leominster HR6 9HB (Herefordshire) T: 01544 388527.

E: info@townsendfarm.co.uk **alanrogers.com/UK4345**

This is a modern, family run campsite hidden in a natural dip next to a working farm, but within a short walk of Pembridge. It has tarmac roads, good site lighting, well spaced pitches and a drive-over motorcaravan service point. There is plenty of open space and a small fishing lake with ducks (completely unfenced). There are 60 pitches in total, 23 with gravel hardstanding, the remainder on grass, and all have access to 16A electricity hook-ups, water and drainage. Reception is at the farm shop by the entrance, stocking a wide variety of fresh fruit, vegetables and eggs; a butchery section has farm produced meats. Three standard and one jumbo sized pods are available for rent.

Facilities

A modern building with blown-air heating, accessed through a foyer with a payphone and tourist information. It is surrounded by wide decking with ramps giving easy access for wheelchairs to all facilities including the dishwashing area and laundry room. Inside are spacious controllable showers, some washbasins in cubicles, a suite for disabled guests, family bathroom and baby changing facilities. Off site: Bicycle hire 0.5 miles.

Open: 1 February - 6 January.

Directions

Site is beside the A44, 7 miles west of Leominster, just inside the 30 mph. speed limit on eastern edge of Pembridge village. GPS: 52.21792, -2.88845

Charges guide

Per unit incl. 2 persons, electricity, water and drainage	£ 19.00 - £ 26.00
extra person	£ 5.00
child (5-15 yrs)	£ 2.00

Ludlow
Ludlow Touring Park

Overton Road, Ludlow SY8 4AP (Shropshire) T: 01584 878788. E: ludlow@morris-leisure.co.uk

alanrogers.com/UK4395

Ludlow Touring Park opened in May 2012 and is part of the Morris Leisure Group. The 135 pitches are all level with 107 on hardstanding and the remainder on grass. They include some spacious, fully serviced pitches (16A electricity, TV connections, water, waste water and a small light). There is a small children's play area and plenty of space for dog walking. Some pitches are reserved for adults (over 16 years). Ludlow, in the shadow of its castle, is two miles to the north and has plenty to offer the visitor, including its Festival (last week in June and first week in July), antique shops and boutiques.

Facilities

The modern, heated toilet block provides washbasins and showers in cubicles plus facilities for children and disabled visitors. Laundry. Motorcaravan service point. Small shop (caravan accessories and basics). No bar or restaurant, but fish and chip van visits Sat. evenings. Children's play area. WiFi over site (charged). Off site: Fishing and riding 2 miles. Golf 3 miles. Acton Scott Victorian Farm 10 miles.

Open: All year.

Directions

From Bridgnorth take A49 (S) around Ludlow and follow signs for Livestock Market. At B4361 junction, follow signs for Livestock Market, turn right heading back toward Ludlow. Park entrance is 1/4 mile on right. GPS: 52.344365, -2.718183

Charges guide

Per unit incl. 2 persons and electricity	£ 23.60 - £ 26.30
extra person	£ 6.90 - £ 7.30

For latest campsite news visit
alanrogers.com

Ludlow
Westbrook Park

Little Hereford, Ludlow SY8 4AU (Shropshire) T: 01584 711280. E: info@bestparks.co.uk

alanrogers.com/UK4390

A beautifully kept, traditional, quiet touring campsite in a working cider apple orchard, Westbrook Park is bordered on one side by the River Teme and is within walking distance of the village and pub. There are 60 level pitches with 16A electric hook-ups, gravel or concrete/gravel all-weather hardstandings with water and waste water drainage. Some pitches have semi-shade, others have none. All the pitches at Westbrook have recently been upgraded. The new spacious, hardstanding pitches, with new and improved electricity supply, TV aerial, water and waste water have been very well received. A member of the Best of British group.

Facilities

A modern, timber-clad, heated toilet block provides spacious hot showers (coin operated), washbasins in curtained cubicles, a basic laundry room. Facilities for disabled visitors (WC and basin). Gas supplies. Playground. Fishing (£4 per day). Riverside walks. No gazebos. No cycling. Only well behaved dogs accepted. Off site: Burford House Gardens.

Open: 1 March - 30 November.

Directions

From A49 between Ludlow and Leominster, turn east at Woofferton on A456 (Tenbury Wells, Kidderminster). After 2 miles turn right just before river bridge and Temeside Inn. Turn left after 150 yds. Park is on left. GPS: 52.307377, -2.665815

Charges guide

Per unit incl. 2 persons and electricity	£ 20.00 - £ 27.00
extra person	£ 4.00

Lutterworth
Stanford Hall Caravan Park

Stanford Road, Swinford, Lutterworth LE17 6DH (Leicestershire) T: 01788 860387.
E: stanfordpark@yahoo.co.uk **alanrogers.com/UK3890**

This picturesque and tranquil site is ideally situated for an overnight stop where you are guaranteed a warm welcome and a pleasant stay. Formerly a Caravan Club site, it is set in the rural grounds of the Stanford Hall Estate, just a mile from the M1. There are 123 pitches (30 of which are seasonal), 80 on grass and 43 on hardstanding, all with 16A electricity. There are no shower or toilet facilities on the park, so your unit must be self contained. The site experiences high levels of repeat bookings so you are advised to contact them in advance of busy weekends to avoid disappointment.

Facilities

There are no toilets or shower facilities on site which means each unit must be totally self-contained. Tents are not accepted. Motorcaravan services. A small shop sells basics. Newspapers can be ordered daily. Picnic tables. Information room. Off site: Supermarkets and banks in Lutterworth. Warwick Castle 25 miles. NEC, Birmingham 30 miles. Stratford Upon Avon 35 miles. Silverstone, Rockingham and Mallory Park race circuits and Althorpe are all within easy reach. Good location for walking.

Open: All year.

Directions

From north on M1 and from M6 leave at exit 19 and at roundabout take first exit (Swinford) and follow signs for Stanford Hall. Site is on left on Stanford Road. From south on M1, leave at exit 18 onto A428, A5 north and then follow signs for Stanford Hall. GPS: 52.406493, -1.149361

Charges guide

Per unit incl. 2 adults, 2 children and electricity	£ 14.00
extra person	£ 1.50

Malvern
Kingsgreen Caravan Park

Kingsgreen, Berrow, Malvern WR13 6AQ (Worcestershire) T: 01531 650272

alanrogers.com/UK4190

An attractive, welcoming and well kept site with views of the Malvern Hills, Kingsgreen is in a lovely rural location. An ideal site for adults who like the quiet life, there are no amusements for children. The surrounding countryside is ideal for walking or cycling, and the small, fenced fishing lakes on the site are well stocked (£4 per day). There are 45 level, grass and gravel pitches, all with 13A electricity, plus an additional area for tents. Some old orchard trees provide a little shade in parts.

Facilities

Modern heated toilet facilities (key on deposit) provide hot showers (25p token from reception) and a separate unit for disabled visitors (WC and washbasin). No baby changing facilities. Laundry room with coin-operated washing machine and dryer. Gas. Fishing. Off site: Nearest shop and pub 1.5 miles. Riding 3 miles. Golf 5 miles.

Open: 1 March - 31 October.

Directions

From M50 exit 2, take A417 towards Gloucester, then first left, where site is signed, also signed the Malverns, back over the motorway. Site is 2 miles from the M50. GPS: 52.00211, -2.33929

Charges guide

Per unit incl. 2 persons and electricity	£ 15.00 - £ 17.50
extra person (over 2 yrs)	£ 1.50
No credit cards.	

FREE Alan Rogers Travel Card
Extra benefits and savings - see page 10

Market Rasen
Walesby Woodlands Caravan Park
Walesby, Market Rasen LN8 3UN (Lincolnshire) T: 01673 843285. E: walesbywoodlands@hotmail.co.uk
alanrogers.com/UK3660

Alongside the Lindsey walking trail and surrounded by mature Forestry Commission woodland, this small, attractive touring park is very peaceful. The new owners, John and Brenda, will make you very welcome. They have upgraded the facilities and have plans for further improvements whilst still maintaining the site's identity as a tranquil retreat. There are 60 well spaced pitches, 52 with 10A electricity, marked out in a single, mainly flat, grassy field divided by a central gravel road with with a double row of trees providing useful visual screening. About a mile away is the town of Market Rasen.

Facilities

The single, heated toilet block is spacious and ample for the site. Pushbutton showers and open style washbasins. Toilet facilities for disabled visitors. Laundry room. Some basic supplies kept in reception. Coffee shop open at busy weekends. Battery charging. Gas supplies. No kite flying (overhead wires). Off site: Golf 1.5 miles. Shops, supermarkets, pubs and restaurants 1-2 miles.

Open: 1 March - 30 November, Christmas and New Year.

Directions

Market Rasen is on A46, 17 miles northeast of Lincoln. Park is just over a mile northeast of town. Take B1203 towards Tealby, then turn left 800 yds. along Walesby Road. Site is on left and well signed. GPS: 53.40135, -0.321

Charges guide

Per unit incl. 2 persons and electricity	£ 19.00
extra person	£ 2.50

Matlock
Lickpenny Touring Park
Lickpenny Lane, Tansley, Matlock DE4 5GF (Derbyshire) T: 01629 583040. E: lickpenny@btinternet.com
alanrogers.com/UK3815

This spacious caravan park on a hill above Matlock has 122 terraced pitches, all on hardstandings and with 16A electricity. Most have good countryside views. There are 100 touring pitches, 27 of which are fully serviced and 22 are seasonal. Tents are not accepted. There are rows of mature trees and pitches are large and separated by shrubs and bushes. The enthusiastic owners have taken full advantage of the fact that this was previously a market garden. High standards have been maintained and some facilities improved. Recreational grassy areas and attractive flower borders are well tended, whilst the top corner of the park has been kept as woodland.

Facilities

Two well equipped, heated toilet blocks have free preset showers and some washbasins in cubicles. Good facilities for disabled visitors. Family room with small bath, toilet and washbasin. Bathroom for children. Laundry room with washing machines, dryers, irons and ironing boards. Motorcaravan service point. Play area. Security barrier. Tents are not accepted. WiFi throughout (charged).

Open: All year.

Directions

Matlock is 18 miles west of M1 exit 28. From motorway, follow signs for Matlock on A38, A61 and A615. After 5 miles on A615 turn north on Lickpenny Lane to site (signed). GPS: 53.134787, -1.491190

Charges guide

Per unit incl. 2 persons and electricity	£ 17.50 - £ 22.00
extra person	£ 5.00

Matlock
Middlehills Farm Caravan and Campsite
Grangemill, Matlock DE4 4HY (Derbyshire) T: 01629 650368. E: middlehillsfarm@yahoo.co.uk
alanrogers.com/UK3825

Middlehills Farm, close to the towns of Bakewell and Matlock, is a well established, family run site to which visitors return year after year to enjoy the relaxed friendly atmosphere. This is simple country camping and caravanning at its best with no frills. It is well placed for visiting many of the local attractions, and the owners, Liz and Nick Lomas, will be pleased to make suggestions. This secluded, 7.5-acre park is located on a family hill farm within the Peak District National Park and comprises three gently sloping fields – one with electricity points. A total of 90 grassy pitches include ten with electricity (10A) and two hardstandings. Water points and drains tend to be rather scarce. There is a small children's farm. The site is not lit at night, so a torch would be useful.

Facilities

One small shower block with washbasins and showers in cubicles (£1 for 5 mins). A second (Portacabin type) unit has toilets and washbasins. One new block on the edge of a barn serves the upper field. All the units have a dishwashing facility. There are no facilities for disabled visitors. Small shop sells basics. No bar or restaurant. Children's adventure play area. Small children's farm.

Open: Easter - 31 October.

Directions

From M1 exit 28, take A38 for Ripley, turn onto A610 to Ambergate then A6 to Cromford. In Cromford turn left at lights and then right onto A5012 for 4 miles. Pass Holly Bush Inn and in 400 yds, turn left over cattle grid. GPS: 53.116541, -1.64391

Charges guide

Per unit incl. 2 persons and electricity	£ 17.00
extra person	£ 7.00

For latest campsite news visit
alanrogers.com

Melton Mowbray
Eye Kettleby Lakes CaravanTouring & Camping Park

Eye Kettleby, Melton Mowbray LE14 2TD (Leicestershire) T: 01664 565900. E: info@eyekettlebylakes.com

alanrogers.com/UK3895

Set in the rolling Leicestershire countryside, this six-acre site with its seven lakes is a fishermen's paradise. The adults only touring area comprises 53 spacious, level, touring pitches set around a small lake. Forty-seven of these are hardstanding super pitches with 16A electricity, water and drainage. The toilet blocks are of an exceptionally high standard with individual en-suite shower rooms, and the facilities for disabled visitors are large and well appointed with underfloor heating. A number of luxury lodges, each with its own hot tub, are available for rent. There is an intimate bar and a restaurant that just serves breakfast. There are numerous walks from the site and in the area. Oakham, a traditional pretty market town is ten miles away. The cities of Leicester and Nottingham are approximately 15 miles from the site, as is Rutland water, which is ideal for sailing and other watersports.

Facilities

Three superbly fitted, heated toilet blocks with free hot water and individual en-suite rooms. Laundry room. Large, well appointed wet room with en-suite facilities and hairdryer for disabled visitors. Dishwashing in heated room. Motorcaravan service point. Shop. Bar with TV and free WiFi (open daily and evenings Thu-Sat). Breakfast (daily 08.00-10.00). Takeaway food delivered. Small games area with pool table. Fishing. Bicycle hire. Off site: Riding and golf 3 miles. Sailing and boat launching 15 miles. Rockingham Castle 22 miles.

Open: All year.

Directions

From Melton Mowbray take A607 towards Leicester. After 1.5 miles turn left towards Great Dalby, site in 1 mile (signed). GPS: 52.74168, -0.90952

Charges guide

Per unit incl. 2 persons, electricity and water	£ 17.00 - £ 20.00
superior pitch	£ 20.00 - £ 25.00
tent pitch (2 persons)	£ 15.00 - £ 18.00
dog (max. 3)	£ 1.00

Meriden
Somers Wood Caravan Park

Somers Road, Meriden CV7 7PL (Warwickshire) T: 01676 522978. E: enquiries@somerswood.co.uk

alanrogers.com/UK4070

Somers Wood is a quiet, peaceful park, attractively situated amongst pine trees. This is a very pleasant park which only accepts adults and does not take tents. It is especially useful for those visiting the various shows at the NEC in Birmingham when it can get very busy. From the reception building at the entrance, an oval gravel road provides access to 48 pitches, all on hardstanding and with 10A electricity hook-ups. Areas of woodland, carpeted with flowers in summer, surround the site and partition it into small intimate areas that create a rural feel. Log buildings blend comfortably into the surroundings providing reception, the owners' home, separate sanitary facilities and tourist information. There are also wooden tables and chairs. The site is beside an 18-hole golf course and a fishing lake, both of which may be used by visitors and next to a bridle path which can be used to exercise dogs. A member of the Best of British group.

Facilities

The central, heated, completely refurbished sanitary block is fully equipped, with facilities for disabled visitors. Shower cubicles are especially large. Laundry service at reception. WiFi on payment. Off site: Local shops and restaurant less than 1 mile and visitors also welcome to use the bar and restaurant at the golf club next door.

Open: All year.

Directions

From M42 exit 6 (NEC) take A45 towards Coventry. Keep in left lane down to roundabout and exit on A452 (signed Leamington/Meriden), then turn left into Hampton Lane at the next roundabout. Site is signed with golf and fishing centres on the left. GPS: 52.43930, -1.66947

Charges guide

Per unit incl. 2 persons and electricity	£ 18.00 - £ 24.00
extra person	£ 4.00
extra dog	£ 1.50
Special offers for some weeks.	

FREE Alan Rogers Travel Card
Extra benefits and savings - see page 10

Moreton-in-Marsh

Moreton-in-Marsh Caravan Club Site

Bourton Road, Moreton-in-Marsh GL56 0BT (Gloucestershire) T: 01608 650519
alanrogers.com/UK4130

This excellent, busy but rural, site is attractively located within mature woodland in the heart of the Cotswolds and offers what one would hope for from a camping holiday. Within easy walking distance (250 yards) of the interesting market town of Moreton-in-Marsh, there is ample choice for food and pubs. The town's main street is part of the Roman Fosse Way. The site has 183 pitches, all with 16A electricity and TV sockets, 171 with hardstanding. A size limit of 8.2 metres for motorcaravans and caravans exists.

Facilities

The two main toilet blocks have been renovated and offer excellent facilities. A separate toilet block exists with disabled toilet and baby room containing a small toilet and bath with seat for children. Large laundry. Play area. Crazy golf. Volleyball. Boules. 5-a-side football. Adventure climbing frame. WiFi (charged). No kite flying (power cables). Off site: Shops, pubs and restaurants 400 yds. Golf 11 miles. Cotswold Falconry Centre, Hidcote Manor Gardens, Snowshill Manor and the Rollright Stones.

Open: All year.

Directions

From Evesham on A44, site on left after Bourton-on-the-Hill village, 150 yds. before town sign. From Moreton-in-Marsh take A44 towards Evesham and site is on right, 150 yds. past the Wellington museum. GPS: 51.988857, -1.710278

Charges guide

Per person	£ 5.40 - £ 7.60
child (5-16 yrs)	£ 1.50 - £ 3.10
pitch incl. electricity (non-member)	£ 13.20 - £ 17.50

Newark

Milestone Caravan Park

Great North Road, Cromwell, Newark NG23 6JE (Nottinghamshire) T: 01636 821244.
E: enquiries@milestonepark.co.uk alanrogers.com/UK3945

Situated just off the A1 north of Newark, Milestone has a good deal more to offer than simply a stopover option. Its 102 good sized, level touring pitches all have 16A electricity and nearby water points. Grass pitches are available, but most are all-weather in a variety of locations. Six are outside the barrier for those in transit (although key access is always available), then comes a pleasantly landscaped area and finally terraces overlooking an attractive fishing lake. An embankment built to muffle traffic noise provides a pleasant grassed walk with views across an adjoining lake and the surrounding countryside. This is a Caravan Club affiliated site.

Facilities

Two heated toilet blocks provide pushbutton showers and open-style washbasins (may be under pressure at busy times). Excellent en-suite facilities for disabled visitors. Laundry facilities. Motorcaravan service points. Tourist information, guides and children's quiz sheets on the site's wildlife. No play area. Fishing (charged). Lakeside cabin with nature and fishing displays). No WiFi. Off site: Large fishing lake adjacent. Village has shop, small brewery and buses to Newark. Riding and boat launching 3 miles.

Open: All year.

Directions

From the south on A1, 3.7 miles after A46 junction, take slip road to Cromwell and site is on the left after the village. From the north on A1, 9 miles after Markham Moor junction, take slip road for Cromwell, turn right over bridge and right again to site. GPS: 53.14985, -0.80693

Charges guide

Per unit incl. 2 persons and electricity	£ 15.90 - £ 22.40
extra person	£ 5.30 - £ 6.90

Newark

Orchard Park

Marnham Road, Tuxford, Newark NG22 0PY (Nottinghamshire) T: 01777 870228.
E: info@orchardcaravanpark.co.uk alanrogers.com/UK3950

This well established, family run touring and caravan park has been created in an old fruit orchard in a quiet location, yet is very convenient for the A1. It has a friendly feel, with just 77 pitches, all with 10A electricity, 34 with hardstanding and about 30 occupied by seasonal units. There is also a spacious camping field with good views. Reception is at the owner's house and a nearby cabin has information on attractions including Sundown Adventureland, Laxton Medieval village and Victorian Times, Rufford Abbey, Clumber Park, Sherwood Forest and the Robin Hood Centre.

Facilities

The heated toilet block has pushbutton showers, open style washbasins and a well equipped room for disabled visitors. Laundry with washing machines, dryer, free spin dryer, iron and a freezer for ice-packs. Small shop with basics and gas. Picnic area. Excellent children's adventure trail and nature walk. Apples, pears and blackberries can be picked in season. WiFi over most of site (charged).

Open: March - October.

Directions

Tuxford is 18 miles west of Lincoln. Park is east of A1. Leave at signs for Tuxford and turn east on A6075 towards Lincoln (A57), continue through village and turn south towards Marnham. Site is on right after railway bridge. GPS: 53.2296, -0.8695

Charges guide

Per unit incl. 2 persons and electricity	£ 17.00 - £ 20.00
extra person	£ 4.00

For latest campsite news visit
alanrogers.com

Newark

Smeaton's Lakes Touring Caravan & Fishing Park

Great North Road, South Muskham, Newark-on-Trent NG23 6ED (Nottinghamshire) T: 01636 605088.
E: lesley@smeatonslakes.co.uk **alanrogers.com/UK3940**

This 82-acre site is really ideal for anglers, with four fishing lakes (coarse, carp and pike) and river fishing on the Trent. There are 130 pitches of which 100 have 16A electricity connections. Non-anglers might choose this park if visiting antique fairs or events at nearby Newark Showground, or Newark town (1 mile) with its castle, air museum and various weekly markets. During your stay, you might visit Southwell Minster, Sherwood Forest, Clumber Park, Lincoln with its castle and cathedral, or Nottingham.

Facilities

Two toilet blocks (with keypad access) are heated and include a good unit for disabled visitors, but no laundry room. Small shop with gas, soft drinks, dairy produce, etc. Newspapers can be ordered. On-site concessions for lake and river fishing. Entry barrier with key access. Security cameras and night-time height barrier (about 6 ft). Off site: Bus stop at the end of the entry lane – buses run into Newark twice hourly until 10 pm. Riding and boat launching 2 miles. Golf 3 miles.

Open: All year.

Directions

Park is 1 mile north of Newark. From south on A1, take A46 west (signed Newark, then Leicester) and turn north on A6065/A616 towards South Muskham. Pass through village and continue on A616 to site on the left. GPS: 53.0936, -0.820667

Charges guide

Per unit incl. 2 persons	
and electricity	£ 16.00 - £ 20.00
extra person	£ 4.00

Nottingham

Thornton's Holt Camping Park

Stragglethorpe, Radcliffe-on-Trent, Nottingham NG12 2JZ (Nottinghamshire) T: 0115 933 2125.
E: camping@thorntons-holt.co.uk **alanrogers.com/UK3935**

Thornton's Holt is an attractively laid out, great family camping park at Stragglethorpe, a scattered rural hamlet 3.5 miles southeast of the city of Nottingham. The 155 spacious pitches are arranged in four separate areas, including one with an orchard setting. With a mixture of grass and gravel hardstanding, most have access to 10A electricity. The owners encourage a friendly farm-type atmosphere with free range chickens, ducks and guinea fowl wandering around the park. You may also encounter Spike and Spartacus, the resident horses, as well as dogs and a cat. Amenities include a heated indoor swimming pool (charged) and a large play area for children.

Facilities

The single, unheated toilet block should now be replaced. Open washbasins, showers on payment (20p). Basic facilities for disabled visitors. Laundry. Shop (1/4-31/10). Heated indoor swimming pool (1/4-31/10). Play area. Bungalow (4 persons) for rent. Caravan storage. Off site: Pub/restaurant adjacent. Supermarket 1 mile. Golf 0.5 miles. Cotgrave Country Park 0.5 miles. National Watersports Centre 2 miles. Vale of Belvoir 4 miles.

Open: All year.

Directions

From A46, join A52 westbound. Pass Radcliffe-on-Trent and after 1.5 miles turn left at traffic lights (white house) into Stragglethorpe Road signed Cotgrave and Cropwell Bishop. Site is on left just after railway bridge. GPS: 52.932024, -1.053404

Charges guide

Per unit incl. 2 persons	
and electricity	£ 16.00 - £ 21.00
extra person (over 5 yrs)	£ 2.50

Oakham

Greendale Farm Caravan & Camping Park

Pickwell Lane, Whissendine, Oakham LE15 7LB (Rutland) T: 01664 474516. E: enq@rutlandgreendale.co.uk
alanrogers.com/UK3904

This is a delightful little adults only park set in rolling countryside, ideal for those seeking peace and tranquillity. It is very eco-friendly and extremely well appointed for such a small site. There are only 13 pitches, all with 10/16A electricity, so it is worth checking availability! Reception, the shop and the toilet facilities are housed in a modern building adjoining the owners' house. The shop is well stocked with essentials and local produce. Cooked breakfasts are available on Sundays. It also has one of the best presented and most comprehensive information displays we have seen on any campsite.

Facilities

Each of the two rooms of the well kept toilet block has a power shower, WCs and two washbasins (cubicles for ladies). Washing machine, tumble dryer and spin dryer. Small open-air, solar-heated swimming pool (6x3 m; June-Sept; £1 charge). Two bicycles for hire. WiFi over site (charged). Off site: Village with bus service 0.5 miles. Supermarket in Oakham and riding 4 miles. Fishing 3 miles. Golf 8 miles. Barnsdale Garden 8 miles.

Open: 15 April - 30 September.

Directions

Whissendine is just off A606 Oakham-Melton Mowbray road. Approach from this road and NOT through village. From Oakham ignore first turning to Whissendine, continue 2 miles and turn right at campsite sign. GPS: 52.711833, -0.788617

Charges guide

Per unit incl. two adults	
and electricity	£ 18.00 - £ 24.00
extra person	£ 5.00

FREE Alan Rogers Travel Card
Extra benefits and savings - see page 10

Oakham

Rutland Caravan & Camping Park

Park Lane, Greetham, Oakham LE15 7FN (Rutland) T: 01572 813520.
E: info@rutlandcaravanandcamping.co.uk **alanrogers.com/UK3903**

First opened in 2002, this family run site is situated in the heart of England's smallest county – Rutland. The family continue to invest in the site which is currently rather open. The 256 pitches have limited shade and are not fenced. There are four separate pitching areas, one reserved for adults and another for families, with two for tents. Hardstanding is provided on 66 pitches, 10A electricity on 156 pitches and full services on 10 pitches. There may be some noise from nearby RAF Cottesmore. The site is beside the village of Greetham with a footpath from the site.

Facilities

Two modern heated toilet blocks. Private bathroom. Baby changing facility. Facilities for disabled visitors. Laundry. Motorcaravan services. Small shop (essentials only). Gas and camping gas. Play area. Picnic tables. Five-a-side football pitch. Security barrier (£10 deposit for card). WiFi (charged). Off site: Fishing, riding and bicycle hire 3 miles. Golf 4 miles. Rutland Water 4 miles. Oakham 5 miles.

Open: All year.

Directions

From A1 turn off on B668 towards Greetham Village. Turn right at crossroads before village and take second left. From Oakham, take B668 through Greetham. Turn left at crossroads at end of village then take second left. GPS: 52.72402, -0.63288

Charges guide

Per unit incl. 2 persons and electricity	£ 15.75 - £ 24.30

Peterchurch

Poston Mill Caravan Park

Golden Valley, Peterchurch HR2 0SF (Herefordshire) T: 01981 550225. E: info@poston-mill.co.uk
alanrogers.com/UK4300

Set in pleasant undulating farmland in the heart of the Golden Valley, Poston Mill Park is a mile from the delightful village of Peterchurch. It is an ideal location for relaxation or exploring. There are currently 43 touring pitches set on level grass or hardstanding with mature trees around the perimeter of the park. All pitches are fully serviced with 16A electricity, water and TV connections (leads for hire). An area is set aside for tents. An attractive walk along one side of the park, edging the River Dore (fishing available), follows the line of the old Golden Valley railway.

Facilities

One central sanitary block with a smaller, refurbished block near the holiday home area which includes private cubicles. Both are fully equipped and include units for disabled guests and families. Laundry rooms. Motorcaravan service point. Play area. Pitch and putt. Tennis, pétanque and croquet. Games room. Winter caravan storage. WiFi (charged). Off site: Riding 3 miles.

Open: All year.

Directions

Park is 1 mile south of Peterchurch on the B4348 road. GPS: 52.02832, -2.9388

Charges guide

Per unit incl. 2 persons and electricity	£ 20.00 - £ 27.00
extra person	£ 4.00
child (5-12 yrs)	£ 2.00

Retford

Trentfield Farm Camping & Caravanning

Church Laneham, Retford DN22 0NJ (Nottinghamshire) T: 01777 228651. E: post@trentfield.co.uk
alanrogers.com/UK3955

A small, friendly, professionally run park. The owners of Trentfield Farm work on the policy of old-fashioned camping and caravanning with all the new amenities and mod-cons! Located in north Nottinghamshire, Trentfield Farm is set between historic Lincoln, Newark, Worksop and Gainsborough, immediately on the banks of the River Trent. It is just within the idyllic hamlet of Church Laneham, an old estate village of the Bishop of York, which is steeped in history. The campsite is level and free draining with 70 grass pitches,16A electricity hook-ups and nearby taps. There is private river frontage with free coarse fishing. Three excellent golf courses are also only a short drive away.

Facilities

The heated toilet block has push-button showers and open style washbasins. Family shower room. No facilities for disabled visitors. Laundry with washing machines, dryer and free spin dryer, iron and freezer for ice-packs. Small 24-hour vending machine with basics. No play area. Free WiFi over much of site. Off site: Sundown Adventureland, Lincoln City and Cathedral, Sherwood Forest and Clumber park, Pureland Japanese Garden. Tennis 1 mile. Riding 1 mile.

Open: Easter - 31 October.

Directions

From A1/A57 roundabout at Markham Moor follow A57 towards Lincoln for 6 miles. Follow Sundown Adventure signs. Take second turning into Laneham and go 1.5 miles through village towards river and ferry. Continue through Church Laneham, past river on right. Go past Manor House Residential Park, up small rise to park. GPS: 53.287685, -0.777497

Charges guide

Per unit incl. 2 persons and electricity	£ 18.50
extra person	£ 4.00

For latest campsite news visit
alanrogers.com

Ripley
Golden Valley Caravan & Camping Park

Coach Road, Golden Valley, Ripley DE55 4ES (Derbyshire) T: 01773 513881.
E: enquiries@goldenvalleycaravanpark.co.uk **alanrogers.com/UK3865**

Golden Valley Caravan & Camping Park is located in the beautiful hamlet of Golden Valley, alongside the Cromford Canal in the Amber Valley area of the Peak District. The site is situated within 26 acres of historic woodland, once a thriving industrial centre for coal, iron foundries and canal workers on the adjacent canal. This secluded woodland site has just 40 pitches on grass or hardstanding for caravans and motorcaravans. There are 24 with independent water supply, electrical connection and mains drainage. There are also two wooded areas for tents and a communal barbecue area. A small fishing pond is available containing carp and it is visited by kingfishers, dragonflies and ducks. The pond is securely fenced to avoid access by young children. There is a great deal of interest in the area including the Midland Railway centre (reduced fares for campers) and many footpaths and cycle ways, including the Cromford canal towpath, and of course throughout the magnificent Peak District National Park.

Facilities

A centrally positioned, heated utility block provides free showers and toilets, facilities for disabled visitors, a laundry room, heated jacuzzi, an indoor playroom and a gym. Bar and café (July/Aug and weekends). Fishing pond. Woodland walks. Play area. Tourist information. Off site: Midland Railway Centre. Denby Pottery. Golf 1 mile. Riding 2 miles. Derby 7 miles. Nottingham 15 miles. Walking and cycling in the Peak District National Park.

Open: All year.

Directions

Leave M1 at exit 26 and follow signs for Matlock and Ripley (A610). At Codnor, turn right at traffic lights, then first right onto Alfreton Road. After a further 2 miles turn left before passing the Newlands Inn to join Coach Road. Site entrance is on left. GPS: 53.05669, -1.37267

Charges guide

Per unit incl. 2 persons and electricity	£ 15.00 - £ 30.00
extra person	£ 5.00 - £ 10.00
child (18 m-16 yrs)	£ 3.00
dog	£ 2.00

Ross-on-Wye
Broadmeadow Caravan & Camping Park

Broadmeadows, Ross-on-Wye HR9 7BW (Herefordshire) T: 01989 768076. E: broadm4811@aol.com
alanrogers.com/UK4320

Ross-on-Wye town centre is within easy walking distance of this modern, spacious park, complete with open views and its own fishing lake. The approach to the site is very unusual, passing through an industrial estate, but eventually you will arrive at a well laid out and pleasant site with facilities of the highest quality. There are 150 large pitches on a mixture of hardstanding and level, open grass; the site is especially good for tents. Each set of four pitches has a service post with water, drain, 16A electricity points and lighting. There may be some traffic noise from the A40 relief road. Seasonal pitches are now available. The market town of Ross-on-Wye is centrally placed for touring Herefordshire, the Wye Valley and the Forest of Dean. The town itself has many facilities such as an indoor swimming pool, putting greens and tennis courts, and lots of good places to eat and drink. Shopping is excellent with a general market held on Thursdays and Saturdays with a farmers' market on the first Friday of each month.

Facilities

Two fully equipped, modern sanitary blocks with baby rooms, family bathrooms each with WC, basin and bath, and a comprehensive unit for disabled visitors. Laundry at each block. Basic motorcaravan service point. Entrance barrier and keypad exit system. Small part-fenced playground. Fenced fishing lake (coarse fishing £8.50 per rod per day – fishing licence not available at reception). Off site: Supermarket 200 yds. Bicycle hire in town. Golf 3 miles. Riding 8 miles.

Open: Easter/1 April - 30 September.

Directions

From A40 relief road turn into Ross at roundabout, take first right into industrial estate, then right in 0.5 miles before supermarket, where site is signed. GPS: 51.91657, -2.57489

Charges guide

Per unit incl. 2 persons and electricity	£ 23.75 - £ 26.50
extra person	£ 5.50
child (2-9 yrs)	£ 3.50
dog	£ 1.75

FREE Alan Rogers Travel Card
Extra benefits and savings - see page 10

Ross-on-Wye
Doward Park Camp Site
Great Doward, Symonds Yat West, Ross-on-Wye HR9 6BP (Herefordshire) T: 01600 890438.
E: enquiries@dowardpark.co.uk **alanrogers.com/UK4360**

This site, which was created around 1997 in a disused quarry, has matured into a very pleasant, peaceful little site, partially terraced, and in a sheltered location. The access roads and the physical proportions of the site make it suitable only for tents, trailer tents and campervans. This site is popular with couples, nature lovers, walkers and young families, but has nothing to offer teenagers. There is a children's play area in Bluebell Wood (unsupervised) at the top of the site with a rope swing and a 'Timber Trak'. Of the 25 pitches for touring (11 with 16A electricity), three are hardstanding for motorcaravans up to 23 feet in length, the remainder are on grass. Five hardstandings are used for seasonal units.

Facilities

A neat central building provides the usual facilities including refurbished hot showers. No designated area for disabled visitors, but toilet facilities have wide access. Freezer for ice packs. Small shop selling basic supplies. Service washing and drying facilities available. Torches are advisable. Bicycle hire. Off site: Variety of inns at both Symonds Yat West and East all offering meals. Fishing 1 mile. Shops and services in Monmouth 4 miles.

Open: 15 March - 31 October.

Directions

From A40 between Ross-on-Wye and Monmouth, turn for Symonds Yat West, and follow signs for Doward Park and Biblins. Turn into narrow lane for 1 mile and site is on right, on sharp left hand bend. GPS: 51.838517, -2.657

Charges guide

Per unit incl. 2 persons
and electricity £ 16.00 - £ 20.00
extra person £ 3.00

Royal Leamington Spa
Harbury Fields Farm Touring Caravan Park
Middle Road, Harbury CV33 9JN (Warwickshire) T: 01926 612457. E: rdavis@harburyfields.co.uk
alanrogers.com/UK4065

This is a delightful, family-run caravan park surrounded by a 222-acre working sheep farm. Peaceful and quiet, it is set in the unspoilt 'Shakespeare countryside'. Located well away from main roads, it is just a mile from the lively village of Harbury, an ancient, prehistoric settlement on a hill near the Fosse Way Roman Road in Warwickshire. There are only 34 spacious pitches (31 on hardstanding, three on grass), all with 16A electricity and eight with full services. Tents are not accepted. The area has a large number of old quarries used historically to extract lyas, a form of limestone used in the manufacture of cement.

Facilities

Two heated toilet blocks have walk-in shower cubicles with washbasin. Separate cubicles with WCs for men and similar for women. Toilet facilities for families and disabled visitors. Washing machine and dryer. Motorcaravan service point. No shop. Off site: Village with pubs, shops, post office and small supermarket. Bus service at end of drive. Fishing and golf 4 miles. Leamington Spa 4 miles.

Open: 2 January - 21 December.

Directions

From the south on the M40, take exit 12 and turn left. After 0.5 miles turn right, then in 3 miles at second roundabout take 4th exit onto B4455 Fosse Way (Harbury). After 2 miles turn right (Harbury) and site is 420 yds. GPS: 52.23985, -1.48689

Charges guide

Per unit incl. 2 persons
and electricity £ 16.40 - £ 23.00

Shrewsbury
Beaconsfield Farm Caravan Park
Battlefield, Shrewsbury SY4 4AA (Shropshire) T: 01939 210370. E: mail@beaconsfield-farm.co.uk
alanrogers.com/UK4410

Just north of the historic market town, a drive of half a mile through open fields lead to this purpose-designed park for adults only (21 years). It is neatly laid out in a rural situation, with a well stocked trout fishing lake and a small coarse pool forming the main feature. The ground has been levelled and grassed to provide 80 well spaced pitches, all have 10A electricity connections, of which 50 are super hardstanding pitches. Two further areas accommodate 49 caravan holiday homes. The park is well lit with a circular tarmac access road, beyond a security barrier.

Facilities

Heated toilet facilities (£2.50 key deposit) are of excellent quality, with roomy, preset showers and hairdryers. Excellent unit for disabled visitors. Laundry facilities. Motorcaravan services. Indoor heated swimming pool with daily open sessions (£3 per person, incl. steam room). Small library. Security barrier and CCTV. WiFi. Only two dogs per unit are accepted. Dog exercise area off site. An adult only park. Car hire available. Accommodation for hire. Off site: Bicycle hire 2 miles.

Open: All year.

Directions

Site is north of Shrewsbury off the A49 Whitchurch road. In the village of Hadnall, turn right opposite the New Inn at camping sign towards Astley and park entrance is 400 yds. on right. Continue down 800 yds. narrow access road with passing places. GPS: 52.770917, -2.704817

Charges guide

Per unit incl. 2 persons
and electricity £ 20.00 - £ 26.00

For latest campsite news visit
alanrogers.com

Shrewsbury

Oxon Hall Touring Park

Welshpool Road, Shrewsbury SY3 5FB (Shropshire) T: 01743 340868. E: oxon@morris-leisure.co.uk

alanrogers.com/UK4430

Oxon Hall is a purpose-built park, well situated for visiting Shrewsbury. Under the same ownership as Stanmore Hall (no. 4400) the site has been developed to a very high standard with mature trees and shrubs providing some shade and shelter. Of the 120 pitches only 105 are in use for touring units, all of which have 16A electric hook-ups, 65 are full service pitches (fresh and waste water facilities, TV hook-up), the others being either grass or with hardstanding. An area is set aside as an adults only section. Some pitches for RV-style units have 32A electric hook-ups. A member of the Best of British group.

Facilities

Toilet facilities here are first rate with washbasins in cubicles, ample showers, baby room, facilities for disabled visitors (all refurbished in 2011), dishwashing room and laundry, all by the entrance in a centrally heated building, also housing reception and the shop. Motorcaravan service point. Up to two dogs per pitch – dog walk on site. Deposit for toilet block key £5. Off site: Supermarket and pub within walking distance. Golf and fishing nearby.

Open: All year.

Directions

From junction of A5 and A458, west of Shrewsbury, follow signs for Oxon park and ride. Park is signed 0.5 miles from junction. GPS: 52.71540, -2.804917

Charges guide

Per person	£ 6.30 - £ 6.70
child (5-15 yrs)	£ 2.20
standard grass pitch	£ 9.00 - £ 10.90
dog (max. 2)	£ 1.00

Skegness

Skegness Sands Touring Site

Winthorpe Avenue, Skegness PE25 1QZ (Lincolnshire) T: 01754 761484. E: info@skegness-sands.com

alanrogers.com/UK3730

This very well organised touring site is part of a much larger caravan holiday home park, but has its own entrance. It is a modern, well appointed site adjacent to the promenade and beach. There are 82 pitches, all level and with 16A electricity; 45 are grass and 37 on gravel hardstandings, four of which are fully serviced. Site lighting is good throughout and there are regular security patrols. The gate to the promenade is kept locked at all times, campers getting a key. The site is a Caravan Club Affiliated Site; members and non-members are all made welcome.

Facilities

The good quality, heated toilet block includes washbasins in curtained cubicles plus three family shower rooms with WC and washbasin and well equipped room for disabled campers. Laundry room. Gas supplies. Hairdressing salon. Indoor heated swimming pool (Spr. B.H-30 Sept; charged). Small modern playground. Off site: Beach 50 yds. Well stocked shop/post office 500 yds. Pubs, fast food outlets and a supermarket are all within easy walking distance. Bus service to Skegness 500 yds.

Open: All year.

Directions

Site is off A52 Boston-Skegness-Mablethorpe road, 1.75 miles north of Skegness town centre. Turn east opposite Garden City pub into Winthorpe Ave. Site entrance is on left at far end of road. Arrivals after 17.00 should contact site. GPS: 53.1668, 0.3495

Charges guide

Per unit incl. 2 persons and electricity	£ 16.60 - £ 24.50
extra person	£ 5.55 - £ 7.60

Sleaford

Low Farm Touring & Camping Park

Spring Lane, Folkingham, Sleaford NG34 0SJ (Lincolnshire) T: 01529 497322. E: lowfarmpark@sky.com

alanrogers.com/UK3770

This quiet, secluded park is a lovely spot to relax or to use as a base for touring Lincolnshire. Jane and Nigel Stevens work hard to make this site a pleasant place to stay and have a well laid out park offering good quality facilities which are kept clean and tidy. The site offers 36 pitches (some occupied by seasonal vans) with 10A electric hook-ups and a field for tents and small rallies. Some hardstandings are available. The site is on the edge of the village of Folkingham with a pub (serving food) and a couple of small shops. For a day at the seaside, Skegness is within easy reach.

Facilities

Central, well maintained toilet block with controllable free showers and open style washbasins. Washing machine. Reception is at the owners' house and a tourist information room with toilets is adjacent. Large field where children can play (also sometimes used by tent campers). Off site: Fishing 5 miles. Golf and riding 10 miles. Shops and supermarkets in Bourne (9 miles) and Sleaford (10 miles).

Open: Easter - mid October.

Directions

Folkingham is 26 miles south of Lincoln on the A15 to Peterborough, 2 miles south of the roundabout junction with the A52 (Nottingham/Grantham/Boston). Park is on southern edge of village; at foot of hill at campsite sign, turn west and site is at end of lane. GPS: 52.88685, -0.411167

Charges guide

Per unit incl. 2 persons and electricity	£ 12.50 - £ 17.50
No credit cards.	

FREE Alan Rogers Travel Card

Extra benefits and savings - see page 10

Slimbridge

Tudor Caravan & Camping Park

Shepherds Patch, Slimbridge GL2 7BP (Gloucestershire) T: 01453 890483. E: info@tudorcaravanpark.co.uk

alanrogers.com/UK4170

This attractive, peaceful campsite is adjacent to the Gloucester-Sharpness Canal. Located behind the Tudor Arms public house, a gate clearly identifies the entrance and the brand new reception is just inside on the right. There are many trees and hedges, particularly surrounding the site, so the canal is not visible. Attractively laid out on two separate fields, there are 75 pitches, all with 16A electricity, and 50 with hardstanding. The old orchard is for long stay or adults only units, with gravel hardstandings, and the more open grassy meadow for family touring units. There is also a rally field beyond the meadow. The adjacent pub has a restaurant and bar (CAMRA award winner every year since 2009) and just across the road, beside the canal, is a café and shop where boats and bicycles can be hired. This is a delightful, peaceful park with plenty to offer: walking, fishing and boating, not to mention ornithology as the Wildfowl and Wetlands Centre founded by Sir Peter Scott at Slimbridge is only 800 yards away.

Facilities

A high quality shower block with underfloor heating provides large shower cubicles, private washing cubicles, baby changing room and facilities for disabled visitors. The other toilet building (can be heated in winter) is located to one side of the orchard and provides all the usual facilities including pushbutton hot showers. Laundry. Gas available. Some site lighting but a torch would be useful. Gate locked 22.30-07.00. WiFi (charged). No charcoal barbecues. Off site: Meals at the Tudor Arms pub. Shop and café in boatyard opposite the site (Easter-Sept), also serves breakfasts. Fishing adjacent. Towpath walks. Berkeley Castle, Frampton and Stroud.

Open: All year.

Directions

From A38 by the junction with A4135 (Dursley), turn west, signed WWT Wetlands Centre Slimbridge. Continue for 1.5 miles turning left into car park of the Tudor Arms. Site entrance is at rear of car park. GPS: 51.735533, -2.395817

Charges guide

Per unit incl. 2 persons and electricity	£ 15.00 - £ 20.50
extra person	£ 3.00
child (under 12 yrs)	£ 1.50
dog	£ 1.00

No credit cards.

Shepherds Patch, Slimbridge, Gloucestershire, GL2 7BP

Welcome to TUDOR CARAVAN PARK

Cotswolds Tourism: Caravan & Camping Site of the Year 2012 (Silver)

- Open All Year
- Caravans, Motorhomes, RVs, Tents
- Separate Adults Only Area
- Beside Gloucester-Sharpness Canal
- Award-winning Pub & Restaurant adjacent
- 800 yards from world-famous Slimbridge WWT

Tel: (01453) 890483   Email: info@tudorcaravanpark.co.uk   Web: www.tudorcaravanpark.com

Spalding

Foreman's Bridge Caravan Park

Sutton Saint James, Spalding PE12 0HU (Lincolnshire) T: 01945 440346. E: foremansbridge@btconnect.com

alanrogers.com/UK3750

Foreman's Bridge is a compact park occupying a large, level and grassy meadow surrounded by trees and high hedges which give it a very secluded feel. The park has 42 level pitches, of which 24 are now occupied by caravan holiday homes (seven for rent). The remainder are touring pitches, all with 16A electricity and gravel hardstanding. Up to half of these are occupied on a seasonal basis. The park could be a useful base from which to explore the Fens and to visit Spalding, famous for its annual flower festival held at the beginning of May. At times there can be noise from military aircraft. Just a 20 minute drive from the site, on the outskirts of Spalding, the Springfields shopping village has some good places to eat, numerous retail outlets and the Festival Garden Centre. From here, there is a new taxi into Spalding town centre. Baytree Garden Centre, close to the village of Moulton, has an owl centre and a large play barn for children. The Butterfly and Wildlife Park in Long Sutton is also worth a visit.

Facilities

The modern, brick-built toilet unit is spacious and kept clean, providing really large individual shower rooms with seats and washbasins (showers on payment). Laundry room. Gas. Fishing possible in the river running past the entrance. Bicycle hire. Two cottages to rent. Winter caravan storage. Off site: Small shop in village 1 mile. Golf 3 miles. Riding 8 miles. Coast 12 miles (The Wash); nearest beach 32 miles.

Open: 1 March - 15 January.

Directions

Sutton St James is 26 miles northeast of Peterborough and 17 miles west of Kings Lynn. From A17 Spalding-Kings Lynn road turn south on B1390 at Long Sutton towards Sutton Saint James for 2 miles. Site entrance is on left immediately after bridge. GPS: 52.75785, 0.088

Charges guide

Per unit incl. 2 persons and electricity	£ 14.00
extra person	£ 3.00
child	£ 2.00

No credit cards.

For latest campsite news visit

alanrogers.com

Stamford
Tallington Lakes Camping & Caravanning
Barholm Road, Tallington, Stamford PE9 4RJ (Lincolnshire) T: 01778 347000. E: info@tallington.com
alanrogers.com/UK3760

This well maintained and attractive 160-acre site surrounds over 200 acres of clean, spring fed water that provides many watersports activities including water-skiing, jet-skiing, sailing, windsurfing, canoeing, pedaloes and angling, along with a pro shop for watersports. In addition there is a 120 m. high, floodlit dry ski slope and a 15 m. tower for climbing and abseiling. Of the 338 pitches, 88 are in a separate area for touring and 46 have 10A electricity. They are level, in groups, separated by some hedging and are either on grass or hardstanding. Some mature trees give a little shade.

Facilities	Directions
The heated sanitary unit has facilities for babies, small children and campers with disabilities. Additional WCs and showers (also used by the water skiers). Laundry facilities. Motorcaravan service point. Bar and restaurant. Swimming and paddling pools (charged). Climbing wall. Go-karting. Watersports. Fishing. Dry-ski slope, snowboard centre and tennis. Small, well fenced, adventure style playground. Off site: Bus stop 1 mile.	From A16, midway between Stamford and Market Deeping, just east of the railway crossing at Tallington, turn north into Barholm Road. Site entrance is on the right in 0.3 miles (site is signed). GPS: 52.67007, -0.37940

Charges guide

Per unit incl. 2 persons and electricity	£ 20.00 - £ 30.00
extra person	£ 5.00

Open: All year.

Stourport-on-Severn
Lickhill Manor Caravan Park
Lower Lickhill Road, Stourport-on-Severn DY13 8RL (Worcestershire) T: 01299 871041.
E: excellent@lickhillmanor.co.uk **alanrogers.com/UK4210**

Lickhill Manor is a well managed touring and holiday site within easy walking distance of the town centre, which is accessed by a footpath along the River Severn. Opportunities exist for fishing and boating. The site is open all year for touring units and there are 120 pitches all with 10A electricity, 57 with hardstanding and some with water and waste water. A large 14-acre rally field with 68 hook-ups is also available for touring units. It is an attractive site with 124 holiday homes, which are well screened from the touring areas, so they are not visually intrusive. There are two excellent play areas for children and a dog exercise field within the park.

Facilities	Directions
An additional sanitary building serves the touring pitches and complements the older unit at the far end of the park. This heated building provides good, modern facilities including a well equipped suite for disabled guests which doubles as a family washroom with facilities for baby changing. Drive-over motorcaravan service point. Gas supplies. Fishing permits are available from site shop. Off site: Stourport shops and pub 10 minutes walk.	From the A451 in Stourport take B4195 northwest towards Bewdley. After 1 mile turn left at crossroads (traffic lights), into Lickhill Road North where site is signed. GPS: 52.343404, -2.299088

Charges guide

Per unit incl. 4 persons and electricity	£ 18.50 - £ 25.00
2 person tent	£ 13.50

Open: All year.

Stratford-upon-Avon
Riverside Park
Tiddington Road, Tiddington, Stratford-upon-Avon CV37 7AB (Warwickshire) T: 01789 292312.
E: riverside@stratfordcaravans.co.uk **alanrogers.com/UK4080**

On the bank of the River Avon, this spacious site has about 225 pitches in total, and about 100 privately owned mobile homes. The 100 touring pitches (no tents) are on level grass, all with 10A electricity hook-ups. There is a small shop and café on site, which serves breakfasts and takeaways in addition to stocking a good selection of basic supplies. A clubhouse that incorporates a bar, playground, games room and TV room is on the adjacent Rayford Park which is under the same management. There is a possible flood risk during periods of inclement weather. A river taxi runs to Stratford from the site.

Facilities	Directions
The main toilet unit has been re-fitted to modern standards and has central heating, spacious preset showers, some washbasins in cubicles, and a child size toilet and shower in the ladies. Wet room style facilities for disabled visitors. Laundry facilities. Slipway and fishing on-site. River launch to Stratford. Gas supplies. No commercial vehicles are accepted. Off site: Buses to Coventry, Warwick and Stratford 5 minutes walk.	From Stratford take B4086 towards Wellesbourne. Site entrance is on left, after one mile, just before Tiddington village (ignore entrance to Rayford Park C.P.). GPS: 52.20023, -1.68213

Charges guide

Per unit incl. 2 persons and electricity	£ 18.00 - £ 25.00
extra person	£ 3.00

Open: 1 April - 31 October.

FREE Alan Rogers Travel Card
Extra benefits and savings - see page 10

Sutton-on-Sea

Cherry Tree Site

Huttoft Road, Sutton-on-Sea LN12 2RU (Lincolnshire) T: 01507 441626. E: info@cherrytreesite.co.uk

alanrogers.com/UK3650

This is a delightful, tranquil, adult only site and is a fine example of a small, good value touring park. It is a 15 minute walk from a Blue Flag beach and a short drive from some of the attractive villages of the Lincolnshire Wolds. A warm welcome awaits from Geoff and Margaret Murray whose attention to detail is evident everywhere. The site is level, the grass is neatly trimmed and well drained, and screening is provided by lines of evergreen hedging. There are 40 good sized pitches, all with10A electricity and hardstanding (no tents) and ten with water and drainage. A member of the Best of British group.

Facilities

The brick-built toilet block, recently extended and refurbished to a high standard, can be heated and is immaculately kept. Controllable hot showers, hairdryers. En-suite unit for disabled visitors (Radar key). Laundry room with washing machine, spin dryer and tumble dryer. Neat reception and separate tourist information cabin. Gas. WiFi over site (charged). Off site: Riding adjacent. Shop and pub 0.6 miles. Beach and fishing 1.5 miles.

Open: 9 March - 4 November.

Directions

Sutton-on-Sea is 15 miles north of Skegness and 40 miles east of Lincoln. The site is 1.5 miles south of the town on A52 coast road, with the entrance leading off a lay-by on the east. GPS: 53.29292, 0.28439

Charges guide

Per unit incl. 2 persons and electricity	£ 17.50 - £ 22.00
extra person	£ 3.50

Tattershall

Tattershall Lakes Country Park

57 Sleaford Road, Tattershall LN4 4LR (Lincolnshire) T: 01526 348800. E: tattershall.holidays@away-resorts.com **alanrogers.com/UK3685**

This extensive park with seven lakes of varying sizes is well kept, offers great opportunities for enthusiasts of watersports and fishing and is only a few hundred yards from the pleasant village of Tattershall. The touring fields are flat and rather featureless but with views across the main lake. There are 269 pitches, numbered but with no hedges or markings to separate them; 180 have 16A electrical connections and 50 also have an individual tap and drainage, plus hardstanding. Fifty lodges and static caravans of varying styles are available for rent and a further 300 are privately owned. The lakeside clubhouse includes a coffee shop serving a variety of meals and snacks, a comfortable bar downstairs where the evening discos and other entertainment take place and, upstairs, another bar overlooking the lake. This houses electronic games, darts and TV, together with a spacious and comfortable lounge.

Facilities

Toilet block with preset showers and open-style washbasins will be under considerable pressure at busy times. En-suite unit for disabled visitors. Washing machines and dryers. A Portacabin provides eight very basic en-suite units (shower, toilet, washbasin), though access is not easy. Small, well stocked shop. Coffee shop serving meals, snacks and takeaways. Two bars. TV and games rooms. Water-skiing and jet ski lakes. Four fishing lakes. Golf course. Archery. Cycle and pedalo hire. Activities and entertainment. Brand new indoor swimming pool and spa complex, complete with lake view hot tubs. WiFi (free). Off site: Tattershall Castle 800 yds. Shops 1 mile.

Open: 1 April - 31 October.

Directions

Tattershall is 22 miles southeast of Lincoln on A153 Sleaford/Horncastle road, 14 miles northeast of Sleaford. Park is on the western edge of the village between the River Witham and Tattershall Castle. GPS: 53.095794, -0.196799

Charges guide

Per unit incl. 6 persons and electricity	£ 4.00 - £ 42.00
dog	£ 1.00

Tewkesbury

Croft Farm Water & Leisure Park

Bredon's Hardwick, Tewkesbury GL20 7EE (Gloucestershire) T: 01684 772321.
E: enquiries@croftfarmleisure.co.uk **alanrogers.com/UK4150**

Croft Farm is an AALA licensed Watersports Centre with Royal Yachting Association approved tuition available for windsurfing, sailing, kayaking and canoeing. The lakeside campsite has 140 level pitches, of which 80 are for touring units with 10A electricity hook-ups. There are 36 gravel hardstandings with very little shade or shelter. An upgrade is planned for the fully equipped gymnasium with qualified instructors, sun bed and sauna. Sports massage, aromatherapy and beauty treatments are available by appointment. The clubhouse has an attractive lakeside terrace and there is a new slipway into the River Avon. Activity holidays for families and groups are organised. Campers can use their own non-powered boats on the lake with reduced launching fees, and there is river fishing. There are plans to include a launch ramp onto the river. Climb Bredon Hill (2 miles) for a panoramic view of the Severn and Avon Valleys. Places of interest include Bredon Barn, pottery and church, and the historic town of Tewkesbury with its abbey, theatre and indoor swimming pool.

Facilities

A recently modernised building has excellent facilities with spacious hot showers. A heated unit in the main building is always open and best for cooler months; this provides further WCs, washbasins and showers, laundry and facilities for disabled visitors. Gas. Watersports centre has shop and conference room. Café/bar (Fri-Sun low season, daily at other times). Takeaway. Gym. Playground. River fishing. Barrier and toilet block key (£5 deposit). Fenced dog exercise area. WiFi in the clubhouse (free to visitors spending £5 or over). Pods and teepees are available to hire. Off site: Pub opposite. Tewkesbury 1.5 miles. Golf 3 miles. Riding 8 miles.

Open: 1 March - 14 November.

Directions

Bredon's Hardwick is midway between Tewkesbury and Bredon on B4080. From M5 exit 9 take A438 (Tewkesbury), at first lights turn right into Shannon Way. Turn right at next lights, into Northway Lane, cross motorway bridge. Turn left into housing estate and cross second bridge. At T-junction turn right on B4080, site is on left opposite Cross Keys Inn. GPS: 52.015967, -2.130267

Charges guide

Per unit incl. 2 persons, electricity and awning	£ 17.00

Discount 10% for 8 nights or more (excl. July, August and B.Hs). Weekends min. 2 nights stay. B.Hs min. 3 nights.

CROFT FARM WATER PARK
BREDONS HARDWICK, TEWKESBURY, GLOS.GL20 7EE
TEL 01684 772 321 - **www.croftfarmleisure.co.uk**

Lakeside Caravan & Camping Park - Water Sports Centre
Log Cabin Clubhouse - Modern Facilities - Camping Pods
Health & Fitness Centre

Woodhall Spa

Bainland Country Park

Horncastle Road, Woodhall Spa LN10 6UX (Lincolnshire) T: 01526 352903. E: bookings@bainland.co.uk
alanrogers.com/UK3690

A family park with many amenities, Bainland has 170 spacious, level pitches in hedged bays (120 touring pitches) grouped in circles and islands and linked by curving roads. There are 51 fully serviced pitches with hardstanding, honeycombed for awning, individual water, drainage and chemical disposal, 16A electricity and TV aerial hook-ups. The remainder of the pitches are either on gravel hardstanding or level grass, all with 10A electricity. The friendly reception is housed in a pleasant Swiss-style building together with the heated indoor pool and jacuzzi, a bistro and spacious bar area. These overlook the 9-hole, par 3 golf course and outdoor bowls area.

Facilities

Three modern, well equipped, heated toilet blocks including a baby room, unisex en-suite shower rooms, family bathroom, fully equipped unit for disabled visitors. Laundry room. Motorcaravan service points. Licensed shop (Feb-Dec). Bistro and bar. Indoor pool (under 16s must be accompanied by an adult). Adventure playground. Trampolines. Crazy golf. Croquet. Games room. Floodlit tennis dome with 3-4 courts including badminton. Par 3, 9-hole golf. Bowls. Leisure activities, including the pool, are individually booked and paid for at reception. Some entertainment in high season. Free WiFi.

Open: All year (in winter, super pitches only).

Directions

Woodhall Spa is 18 miles southeast of Lincoln. Entrance to park is off B1191 Horncastle road 1.5 miles northeast of the village centre and is clearly signed. GPS: 53.158617, -0.183517

Charges guide

Per unit incl. 2 persons and electricity	£ 18.00 - £ 38.00
serviced pitch	£ 20.00 - £ 45.00
extra person	£ 4.00
child (5-12 yrs)	£ 4.00

Special rate for firework display (min. 2 nights, 4/5 Nov). Discounts for senior citizens.

FREE Alan Rogers Travel Card
Extra benefits and savings - see page 10

Woodhall Spa

Glen Lodge Touring Park

Glen Lodge, Edlington Moor, Woodhall Spa LN10 6UL (Lincolnshire) T: 01526 353523

alanrogers.com/UK3692

This quiet, attractive and spacious site is ideal for couples and families who enjoy the rural lifestyle, yet it is only just over a mile from the thriving village of Woodhall Spa which retains much of its old-fashioned charm. All 35 pitches have hardstanding and 10A electricity hook-ups (one or two appeared to need long leads) and are served by shingle roads with some street lighting. The grass and flowerbeds are obviously tended by someone who enjoys gardening. In fact, the whole park has a much-loved feel. Behind the pitches, on one side of the park, is an attractive lawned area with trees and shrubs, whilst on the other side is a field where ball games are permitted. Woodhall Spa has two modern supermarkets and a good range of traditional shops, as well as tearooms, restaurants and pubs. There is also a delightful, old-style cinema called the Kinema in the Woods. Places to visit in the area include the Battle of Britain Memorial Flight, Tattershall Castle, Horncastle with its antiques centre and the city of Lincoln. Skegness is only 26 miles away.

Facilities

The modern heated toilet block (key-pad access) is kept spotlessly clean with controllable showers, vanity style washbasins and piped music. En-suite facilities for disabled visitors. Washing machine and dryer. Off site: Pub serving good food 0.5 miles. Open-air pool, tennis and bowls 1 mile. Shops in village 1.5 miles. Golf and fishing 2 miles. Tattershall Castle 5 miles. Riding and Horncastle 6 miles.

Open: 1 March - 30 November.

Directions

Woodhall Spa is 18 miles southeast of Lincoln. From mini-roundabout in village turn northeast towards Bardney on B1190 (Stixwould Road) past Petwood Hotel. In just over 1 mile at sharp left bend, turn right. Site is 300 yds. on left. GPS: 53.166233, -0.22

Charges guide

Per unit incl. 2 persons and electricity	£ 16.00
extra person (over 4 yrs)	£ 3.00
dog	free

No credit cards.
Discount for over 65s Mon-Thurs.

GLEN LODGE TOURING PARK

Small family run park within a mile of Woodhall Spa, set in beautiful woodland surroundings. Heated toilet/shower block and utility room with washer, dryer and phone. A great combination of peace and tranquillity and yet within easy reach of the seaside town of Skegness. Discounts available Monday to Thursday for senior citizens.

Edlington Moor, Woodhall Spa, Lincolnshire LN10 6UL ▪ Tel/Fax No. 01526 353523

Worksop

Riverside Caravan Park

Central Avenue, Worksop S80 1ER (Nottinghamshire) T: 01909 474118

alanrogers.com/UK3920

A town centre touring park, adjacent to the Worksop cricket ground, this excellent site is attractive and surprisingly peaceful. Riverside is within easy walking distance of the town centre shopping precinct, and the Chesterfield Canal runs close to its northern side offering delightful towpath walks and fishing (children would need to be watched). For those who cannot resist the thwack of leather on willow, this site is ideal. Of the 60 marked level pitches, ten are seasonal and 43 are for touring, mainly on gravel hardstanding, seven are on grass and some are separated by trees and low rails, and all have 10A electric hook-ups.

Facilities

The single sanitary unit near reception can be heated and has all the usual facilities, although showers are on payment (£1 coin). No laundry. Motorcaravan service point. Off site: Fishing 0.5 miles. Several golf courses 1 mile. Bicycle hire 4 miles. Squash and flat or crown green bowling nearby. Campers are made very welcome at the cricket ground clubhouse. One of Worksop's most interesting buildings, the medieval Priory Gatehouse, is open free of charge. Market days are Wed, Fri and Sat.

Open: All year.

Directions

Worksop is 7 miles west of M1 at exit 30 and 4 miles east of A1. Easiest approach is from A57/A60 roundabout west of town – third roundabout from A1. Turn east (at Little Chef) on B6024 towards town centre. Site is well signed. GPS: 53.30600, -1.12867

Charges guide

Per unit incl. 2 persons, awning and electricity	£ 16.00 - £ 18.00

For latest campsite news visit
alanrogers.com

Insurance Service

High quality, low cost insurance you can trust

Motorhome insurance
From only £174

Caravan Insurance **SAVE** UP TO 60%

We've been entrusted with readers' campsite-based holidays since 1968, and they have asked us for good value, good quality insurance.

We have teamed up with Shield Total Insurance – one of the leading names in outdoor leisure insurances – to bring you peace of mind and huge savings. Call or visit our website for a no obligation quote – there's no reason not to – and trust us to cover your valued possessions for you.

Static Caravans - Price Beater GUARANTEE
We guarantee to beat any genuine 'like for like' insurance renewal quote by at least £25. Subject to terms & conditions.

- Caravans - **Discounts up to 60%**
- Motorhomes - **Prices from only £174**
- Park Homes - **Fantastic low rates**
- Tents - **Prices from only £30**

Instant quote

Call **0844 824 6314**

alanrogers.com/insurance

A beautiful and varied region of rolling hills and undulating moors, Yorkshire has a historic past with a wealth of new attractions. Its landscape has inspired famous authors and been the setting for some of Britain's best-loved television programmes.

THE REGION IS DIVIDED INTO NORTH, SOUTH, EAST AND WEST YORKSHIRE

The major attractions of this region are the parks: the Yorkshire Dales National Park comprises 680 square miles of unspoilt countryside with high fells, winding rivers, ancient castles and outstanding views of the surrounding landscapes; the Peak District is noted for its rocky peaks and limestone plateaux; while the North York Moors National Park has miles of open, heather-covered moorland and pretty villages in its valleys. These areas are ideal places for walking, cycling, horse riding and climbing. Or if you prefer to relax and take in the scenery, the North Yorkshire Moors Railway, starting at Pickering, is one of the many steam railways in the region. On the coast, traditional family resorts like Scarborough, Bridlington and Cleethorpes offer the holidaymaker a wide range of activities. Also by the sea is Kingston-upon-Hull, a maritime city with powerful links to Britain's proud seafaring tradition, and the picturesque fishing port of Whitby, once home to Captain James Cook. Elsewhere in the region are the vibrant cities of York, with its wealth of ancient sites including the Minster, Leeds and Sheffield, plus the busy market town of Doncaster.

Places of interest

North: Harrogate; Wensleydale Creamery in Hawes; Jorvik Viking Centre in York; Lightwater Valley Theme Park, near Ripon; Castle Howard near York; Mother Shipton's Cave, Knaresborough; Skipton Castle;

South: Hatfield Waterpark near Doncaster; Tropical Butterfly House and Wildlife Centre in Anston; Sheffield Ski Village, Europe's biggest artificial ski resort; Magna science adventure centre in Rotherham.

East: Bempton Cliffs RSPB Nature Reserve near Bridlington, England's largest seabird colony; market town of Beverley; Captain Cook Museum and abbey in Whitby; Scarborough castle and sea life centre.

West: National Media Museum, Bradford; Royal Armouries Museum, Leeds; Saltaire Victorian village; Brontë Museum, Haworth.

Did you know?

The comedy series, Last of the Summer Wine, was filmed in the Pennine town of Holmfirth and its surrounding countryside.

York is the oldest city in Yorkshire, founded in AD71. The Minster is the largest Gothic cathedral in Northern Europe.

Saltaire was built as a model village during the industrial revolution by Sir Titus Salt.

Bradford was once known as the wool capital of the world. In 1841 there were 38 mills in the town.

Under the pseudonym Ellis Bell, Emily Brontë wrote Wuthering Heights in 1847 at Haworth Parsonage.

Rudston is said to be the oldest inhabited village in England, named after the Rood Stone, a mysterious 4,000-year-old monolith.

Whitby was the inspiration for the Gothic horror novel, Dracula, by Bram Stoker and now holds bi-annual Gothic weekends.

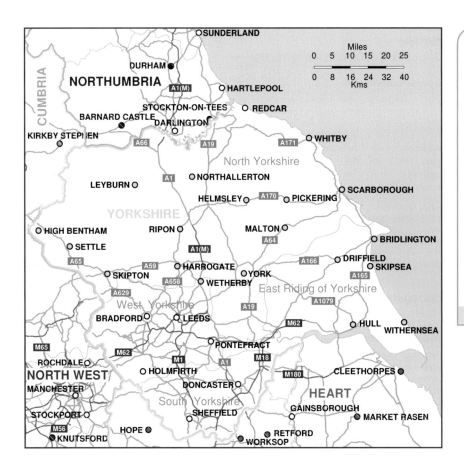

Bridlington
South Cliff Caravan Park

Wilsthorpe, Bridlington YO15 3QN (East Yorkshire) T: 01262 671051. E: southcliff@eastriding.gov.uk

alanrogers.com/UK4498

This traditional style caravan park is part of a large complex owned and operated by the East Riding of Yorkshire Council. There are 193 touring pitches, each with a 16A electricity post; 20 are for tents, the remainder have hardstanding surrounded by grass or, in a few cases, extended to the road. They are in rows across the field, so access for larger units can be tricky when the site is full. Direct access to the seafront is through the vast caravan holiday home park and from there a land train runs a mile along the shore to Bridlington. Here you can visit the historic old town, the harbour with its heritage museum, the Spa Theatre and Ballroom, Sewerby Hall and Gardens and Leisure World. Nearby are Flamborough Head with its lighthouse, and Bempton Cliffs (RSPB).

Facilities

Two toilet blocks (one traditional, one new) provide pushbutton showers, open washbasins (a few in cubicles for ladies). Excellent en-suite units for disabled visitors. Three bathrooms with washbasins and baby changing facilities. No motorcaravan service point. Franchised facilities include a launderette, a well stocked shop (1/3-8/10), a fish and chip shop, and a leisure complex (bar, restaurant, clubroom, games room) offering entertainment evenings in high season and monthly themed weekends (outside August). Ten mobile homes for rent. Dogs are not accepted (except assistance dogs). No large motorhomes. Off site: Golf 0.5 miles. Beach (by car) 1 mile. Shops, pubs and restaurants within 2 miles.

Open: 1 March - 30 November.

Directions

Bridlington is 40 miles east of York via A166/A614. From M62 exit 37, take A614 to Bridlington and turn south on re-routed A165 towards Hull. At roundabout south of town, turn north on newly renumbered A1038; site is signed to right at next roundabout. GPS: 54.0641, -0.2132

Charges guide

Per unit incl. up to 5 persons £ 20.00 - £ 30.00
Discounts in low season and mid seasons.

FREE Alan Rogers Travel Card
Extra benefits and savings - see page 10

Driffield
Thorpe Hall Caravan & Camping Site
Rudston, Driffield YO25 4JE (East Yorkshire) T: 01262 420393. E: caravansite@thorpehall.co.uk
alanrogers.com/UK4510

Just outside the village of Rudston, in the grounds of Thorpe Hall, this pleasant small touring park is six miles from the sea at Bridlington. Enthusiastically managed by Jayne Chatterton, it is set on flat grass, largely enclosed by the old kitchen garden wall. The 78 large pitches have 16A electrical hook-ups and TV connections. A separate field accommodates 14 tents. There are no caravan holiday homes or seasonal pitches. Tourist information leaflets on a range of local walks are provided and Sir Ian MacDonald takes visitors on walks around the estate.

Facilities

The solid, central toilet block was completely refurbished in 2011 and can be heated. Some washbasins are in cabins. Bathroom for disabled visitors and families with young children. Laundry room. Large recycling area. Small shop with gas, essentials and local produce. Games room with pool table and table football. TV room. Large games field. Coarse fishing lake (charged). WiFi (charged).

Open: 1 March - 31 October.

Directions

Site is by the B1253 road, 4.5 miles from Bridlington, on east side of Rudston. GPS: 54.093817, -0.3125

Charges guide

Per unit incl. 2 adults,	
3 children and electricity	£ 16.00 - £ 32.50
tent pitch incl. 2 persons	£ 11.50 - £ 28.50
extra person	£ 3.00

Harrogate
Ripley Caravan Park
Ripley, Harrogate HG3 3AU (North Yorkshire) T: 01423 770050. E: ripleycaravanpark@talk21.com
alanrogers.com/UK4630

Peter and Valerie House are the friendly, resident owners of Ripley Park, a 25-acre grassed caravan park with an indoor heated pool. It accommodates 100 touring units, all with access to electricity, on fairly level grass which undulates in parts. Connected by a circular gravel road, the pitches are marked or spaced (allowing the grass to recover). There are 20 hardstandings. The owners have planted 2,000 trees and these are developing well to provide individual areas and shelter. A pond with ducks provides an attractive feature. In addition, 100 caravan holiday homes occupy a separate area. The park is situated at the gateway to the Yorkshire Dales National Park.

Facilities

At the edge of the touring area, the toilet block can be heated and includes some washbasins in curtained cubicles, 4 individual washing facilities, a baby bath and a separate unit with a shower for disabled visitors. Small laundry. Motorcaravan service point. Shop with gas (limited hours in low seasons). Games room with TV. Nursery playroom. Adventure play equipment and football area. Heated indoor pool (£1 per person) and sauna.

Open: Easter - 31 October.

Directions

About 4 miles north of Harrogate, park access is 150 yds. down the B6165 Knaresborough road from its roundabout junction with the A61. GPS: 54.0369, -1.558833

Charges guide

Per unit incl. 2 persons	
and electricity	£ 16.50 - £ 19.50
extra person	£ 4.00 - £ 5.00

Harrogate
Rudding Holiday Park
Follifoot, Harrogate HG3 1JH (North Yorkshire) T: 01423 870439. E: holiday-park@ruddingpark.com
alanrogers.com/UK4710

The extensive part wooded, part open grounds of Rudding Park are very attractive, peaceful and well laid out. One touring area is sloping but terraces provide level pitches. All 95 touring pitches have 10/16A electricity, 15 have hardstandings with water and a drain and a small number of super pitches are available for touring units. Further pitches are let on a seasonal basis and caravan holiday homes and chalets are in separate areas. On the outer edge of the park is The Deer House, a family pub serving bar meals, with limited opening outside the high season weeks.

Facilities

Two toilet blocks (heated when necessary and may be under pressure at peak times), some washbasins in private cubicles, baby room and bathroom. Laundry rooms. Facilities for disabled visitors. Motorcaravan service point. Shop (6/3-7/11; limited hours). Gas. Restaurant and bar (limited hours outside high season). Heated outdoor swimming and paddling pools (25/5-30/8), supervised (extra charge). Adventure playground. Games room. Golf. WiFi over site (charged).

Open: 4 March - 30 January.

Directions

From junction of A658 and A661 (roundabout), 3 miles southeast of Harrogate take A658 (Leeds). After 0.5 miles turn sharp right onto a road that passes the golf course, holiday park and hotel. All have separate entrances. GPS: 53.97307, -1.49720

Charges guide

Per unit incl. 4 persons	
and electricity	£ 19.00 - £ 37.00
extra person	£ 5.50 - £ 10.50

For latest campsite news visit
alanrogers.com

Helmsley
Foxholme Touring Caravan & Camping Park
Harome, Helmsley YO62 5JG (North Yorkshire) T: 01439 771904. E: reservations@riccalvalecottages.co.uk
alanrogers.com/UK4580

Foxholme is an adults only park suiting those who want a quiet holiday disturbed only by birdsong and passing deer. There are 30 touring pitches set either in an open, slightly sloping field, or between trees on grass. Both areas are attractive and well tended. A further 30 seasonal pitches are arranged amongst the trees. All the pitches have 6A electricity (a few need long leads) and six have hardstanding. Some picnic tables are provided. The site is managed by an on-site warden, with limited reception opening times. Very basic provisions are kept. Wildlife abounds and poppies and other wild flowers enhance this tranquil site. The park is set in quiet countryside and would be a good base for touring, being within striking distance of the moors, the coast and York. There are no on-site activities. There is lighting, but a torch would be useful.

Facilities

The toilet block is an older style building and is clean but basic and showing signs of its age. Some private cubicles. Laundry facilities. Two further small blocks provide WCs only in other parts of the park. Basic motorcaravan service point. Caravan storage. Off site: Riding and golf 3.5 miles. Shops and bicycle hire at Helmsley and Kirkbymoorside, both about 4 miles.

Open: 1 March - 31 October.

Directions

Turn south off A170 between Beadlam (to west) and Nawton (to east) at sign to Ryedale School, then 1 mile to park on left (passing another park on right). From west turn right 400 yds. east of Helmsley, signed Harome, turn left at church, go through village and follow camping signs. Sat nav postcode: YO62 7SD. GPS: 54.23745, -0.990333

Charges guide

Per unit incl. 2 persons and electricity	£ 20.00

No credit cards.

FOXHOLME TOURING CARAVAN PARK
HAROME, HELMSLEY, NORTH YORKSHIRE YO62 5JG
Telephone: (01439) 771 904, or (01439) 771 696
AA 3 PENNANT - CARAVAN CLUB APPROVED - CAMPING CLUB APPROVED

A quiet, rural site for touring vans, motor caravans and some tents. All pitches in well sheltered clearings in the 6 acres of 40 year old woodland. All weather roads, some hardstandings, luxury toilet block graded excellent by the AA, washbasins in cubicles, H&C showers, laundry room, small shop, gas exchange and mains electric hook-ups available.

ADULTS ONLY   BEAUTIFUL COUNTRYSIDE
CLOSE TO THE NORTH YORK MOORS NATIONAL PARK
Please send stamp for brochure to G.C. Binks

Helmsley
Golden Square Caravan & Camping Park
Oswaldkirk, Helmsley, York YO62 5YQ (North Yorkshire) T: 01439 788269.
E: reception@goldensquarecaravanpark.com **alanrogers.com/UK4560**

Golden Square is a popular, high quality, family-owned touring park. Mr. and Mrs. Armstrong are local farmers who have worked hard to turn an old quarry into an exceptionally attractive caravan park with a number of separate, level bays that have superb views over the North York Moors. The 90 touring pitches are not individually separated but they do have markers set into the ground and mainly back on to grass banks. In very dry weather the ground can be hard so steel pegs would be needed (even in wet weather the park is well drained). All pitches have 10A electricity, 24 have drainage and six are deluxe pitches (with waste water, sewerage, electricity, water and TV aerial connections).

Facilities

Two heated toilet blocks have been refurbished and are first rate, one with underfloor heating, with some washbasins in private cubicles. Bathroom (£1) also houses baby facilities. Facilities for disabled visitors. Laundry. Motorcaravan service point. Tourist information room also houses a microwave and an extra iron and board. Shop. Two excellent play areas. Games field and barn with games. Bicycle hire. All year caravan storage. CCTV. Off site: Golf 3 miles. Fishing and riding 5 miles.

Open: 1 March - 31 October.

Directions

From York take B1363 to Helmsley. At Oswaldkirk Bank Top turn left on B1257 to Helmsley. Once on B1257 take second left signed Ampleforth and caravan route to site. Note: caravans are prohibited on Sutton Bank (6 miles west of site). GPS: 54.209333, -1.073783

Charges guide

Per unit incl. 2 persons and electricity	£ 16.00 - £ 24.00

No credit cards.

FREE Alan Rogers Travel Card
Extra benefits and savings - see page 10

High Bentham
Riverside Caravan Park
High Bentham, Lancaster LA2 7FJ (North Yorkshire) T: 01524 261272. E: info@riversidecaravanpark.co.uk
alanrogers.com/UK4715

The pretty, tree-lined approach to Riverside leads into an attractive park, owned by the Marshall family for over 40 years. Nestling in beautiful countryside, alongside the River Wenning, the park has easy access to the Yorkshire Dales and the Lake District. There are 49 marked, level, grassy touring pitches with 16A electricity and TV hook-ups. In addition, there are 12 super pitches on tarmac. An area has been developed for 50 seasonal pitches on gravel. Located away from the touring area are 206 privately owned holiday homes. Tents are not accepted. The smart reception building includes a small shop selling caravan accessories. A member of the Best of British group.

Facilities
The modern toilet block with underfloor heating is centrally situated. Washbasins in cubicles. Unisex showers in a separate area. Toilet and shower room for disabled visitors (Radar key). A new family shower/bathroom (charged). Motorcaravan services. Caravan storage. Outdoor play area for younger children. Large field for ball games. Family games room. The river can be used for fishing (permit from reception) swimming, and small boats. WiFi (charged). Off site: Golf and riding nearby.

Open: All year excl. 15-28 December.

Directions
Leave M6 at exit 34, and take A683 towards Kirkby Lonsdale. After 5 miles take B6480 signed to High Bentham. From the east, take A65 after Settle, the site is signed at B6480, turn left. At Black Bull Hotel follow caravan signs. The park entrance is on right after crossing river bridge. GPS: 54.11311, -2.51066

Charges guide
Per unit incl. 2 persons and electricity	£ 19.25 - £ 25.00
extra person	£ 4.50
child (2-15 yrs)	£ 2.50
dog	£ 1.50

Min. charge per night £ 15.90.
Less 10% for bookings over 7 nights.

Leyburn
Constable Burton Hall Caravan Park
Constable Burton Hall, Leyburn DL8 5LJ (North Yorkshire) T: 01677 450428.
E: caravanpark@constableburton.com alanrogers.com/UK4690

This tranquil park is in beautiful Wensleydale and the emphasis is on peace and quiet, the wardens working to provide a relaxing environment. Being in the grounds of the Hall, it has a spacious, park-like feel to it. On part level, and some a little uneven, well maintained grass, the 120 pitches (40 for touring units) are of a good size and all have 10A electrical connections. There are no pitches for tents. There is no shop on site but milk and newspapers are available to order, and there are shops in nearby Leyburn. Opposite the park entrance is the Wyvill Arms for bar meals. Ball games are not permitted and there is no play area. The gardens of the Hall are open to the public, with a collection of maples and terraced gardens developed by Mrs Vida Burton. The park is ideally placed for visiting the Northern Dales.

Facilities
Two toilet blocks built of local stone and blending in with the local surroundings, have been refurbished recently, are well tiled, kept immaculately clean, and can be heated. Facilities for disabled visitors. Baby room. The former deer barn has been adapted for use as a laundry room and extra washrooms with basins for both men and women. Information leaflets and a few books for visitors can also be found here. Gas supplies. Gates closed 22.00-08.00. WiFi planned for the new season. Off site: Irregular bus service from site gate. Fishing and golf within 5 miles.

Open: Early March - 31 October.

Directions
Park is by the A684 between Bedale and Leyburn, 0.5 miles from the village of Constable Burton on the Leyburn side. GPS: 54.3125, -1.754167

Charges guide
Per unit incl. 2 persons and electricity	£ 18.00 - £ 23.00
extra person	£ 5.00
child (5-16 yrs)	£ 3.00
dog	free

No commercial vehicles.

Constable Burton Hall Caravan Park
01677 450428
caravanpark@constableburton.com

This tranquil park is set in the beautiful grounds of the historic Constable Burton Hall, Wensleydale off the A684

Constable Burton Hall Caravan Park, Leyburn, North Yorkshire, DL8 5LJ

Hull
Burton Constable Holiday Park & Arboretum
The Old Lodges, Sproatley, Hull HU11 4LJ (East Yorkshire) T: 01964 562508. E: info@burtonconstable.co.uk
alanrogers.com/UK4500

The approach to this Holiday Park is set in the grounds of the stately home of Burton Constable, and is most impressive – one of the gatehouses acts as reception and tourist information room. The original 300-acre park, which was landscaped by Capability Brown in the 18th century, and the 90-acre holiday complex, with its well trimmed grass and hedges, has a spacious feel. Much of the park is devoted to holiday homes, but there is a separate touring area on grass, overlooking two sizeable lakes. There are 140 touring pitches, almost all with 10A electricity; there is a separate field for tents and a large hardstanding area for 23 motorcaravans. The coast is only seven miles away.

Facilities

Two heated toilet blocks – one older and small with unisex showers, the newer central block including a laundry room with baby changing. Well equipped room for disabled visitors (Radar key). Shop in the mobile home area. Bar with family room and tables outside overlooking the lakes. Good adventure play area. Fishing. Sailing. Arboretum. Off site: Sproatley with pubs, a shop and the occasional bus 1 mile. Riding 3 miles. Golf 5 miles. Hull 7 miles. Beach 8 miles. Beverley 15 miles. Bridlington 25 miles. York 50 miles.

Open: 1 March - 31 October.

Directions

From the south via M62 or Humber Bridge, take A63 into Hull, then follow signs to A165 Bridlington. On outskirts of Hull turn east on B1238 (Aldborough). At Sproatley, site is signed to left. GPS: 53.80265, -0.199

Charges guide

Per unit incl. 2 persons	
and electricity	£ 16.50 - £ 29.00
extra person	£ 2.00

Malton
Wolds Way Caravan Park
West Farm, West Knapton, Malton YO17 8JE (North Yorkshire) T: 01944 728463. E: info@ryedalesbest.co.uk
alanrogers.com/UK4545

Opened in 2004, this park is located along the top of the Yorkshire Wolds with super panoramic views across the Vale of Pickering to the North Yorks Moors. The one and a half mile tarmac and gravel track from the road to the park is well worth while to reach this peaceful location set amongst glorious countryside. There are 80 level pitches (just 25 for touring units), most with 16A electricity and some with water points. Seating areas, picnic benches and barbecues are provided on the park. There are many footpaths and cycle ways in the area. As well as the obvious attractions of walking the Wolds Way National Trail, the park is well placed for visiting all the local attractions which include Scarborough, Bridlington, Sledmere House and Scampston Hall.

Facilities

A new toilet block is very well appointed and heated. Family bathrooms. Laundry facilities. Very large heated room with sinks, microwave, fridge/freezers, hot drinks machine, TV and tourist information. Room for disabled visitors. Reception also provides a small shop selling basic supplies. Play area. Areas to walk dogs. Caravan storage. A well equipped Finnish style chalet for up to five people is available to rent. Off site: Bus stop 1 mile. Fishing 3 miles. Golf and riding 5 miles. Beach 15 miles.

Open: 1 March - 31 October.

Directions

Park entrance is on the south side of the A64 York-Scarborough road, just past the B1258 turn off and it is signed (may be hidden by foliage). GPS: 54.16633, -0.65425

Charges guide

Per unit incl. 2 persons	
and electricity	£ 14.50 - £ 21.00
extra person (over 15 yrs)	£ 4.00
child (8-14 yrs)	£ 1.50
dog (max. 2)	free

Midweek reductions available.

FREE Alan Rogers Travel Card
Extra benefits and savings - see page 10

Northallerton
Cote Ghyll Caravan & Camping Park

Osmotherley, Northallerton DL6 3AH (North Yorkshire) T: 01609 883425. E: hills@coteghyll.com
alanrogers.com/UK4775

This attractive, family run park is set in a secluded valley, with the higher pitches terraced and the lower ones on a level grassy area either side of the small Cod Beck stream. Of the 80 pitches, 50 are for touring units, all with 10A electricity hook-ups, 12 with full services and hardstanding, plus three larger super pitches. A further 18 pitches are used for caravan holiday homes and 30 are reserved for seasonal units. A simple site with a tranquil setting, Cote Ghyll is highly suited for lovers of peace and quiet, for birdwatching or for more energetic hobbies such as cycling and walking.

Facilities	Directions
Two well-equipped, heated toilet blocks, one new, provide free power showers, vanity style washbasins and hairdryers. Bathroom and facilities for babies and disabled visitors. Laundry room with washing machine, dryer, iron and board. Drying room. Reception provides a small shop for essentials. Gas supplies. Two play areas. WiFi over site (charged). Caravan storage. Off site: Shop and pubs 10 minutes walk. Fishing 1 mile. Beach 18 miles.	Osmotherley is east of the A19. Leave the A19 at A684 exit signed Northallerton and Osmotherley. Go to Osmotherley and site is at the northern end of the village, well signed. GPS: 54.37643, -1.29166

Charges guide

Per unit incl. 2 persons and electricity	£ 19.50 - £ 24.50
extra person	£ 3.00

Open: 1 March - 31 October.

Northallerton
Otterington Park

Station Farm, South Otterington, Northallerton DL7 9JB (North Yorkshire) T: 01609 780656.
E: info@otteringtonpark.com **alanrogers.com/UK4765**

This family-owned, five-acre park is located on a former farm between Thirsk and Northallerton, in the Vale of York. It is ideally placed for visiting the Yorkshire moors and dales, along with local market towns, theme parks and stately homes. Predominantly, it is a flat grass site with gravel hardstandings for 30 touring pitches, with a separate paddock for a further 28 pitches, all with 16A electricity. Privately-owned lodges and static caravans are located in an adjoining park, separated from the touring units by an old, well established, tall hedge. Some minor train noise may be experienced.

Facilities	Directions
One purpose built, clean block in a heated building. Unisex en-suite style shower rooms. Facilities for disabled visitors. Family bathroom with a baby area. Laundry. Drinks/snacks vending machines in reception. Play area. WiFi over site (charged). Off site: Fishing 250 yds. Golf 3 miles. Riding 5 miles. Local bus service to Thirsk and Northallerton run every 2 hours from entrance (not Sun). Several country pubs serving meals within 1 mile.	From A1M join A684 for Leeming Bar and Morton-on-Swale. At roundabout bear right on A167 signed South Otterington and Topcliffe. At South Otterington crossroads (pub) turn left signed Thornton-le-Moor to park in 500 yds. GPS: 54.28771, -1.42046

Charges guide

Per unit incl. 4 persons and electricity	£ 19.00 - £ 23.00
extra person	£ 3.00

Open: 1 March - 31 October.

Pickering
Forest Holidays Spiers House

Cropton Forest, Cropton, Pickering YO18 8ES (North Yorkshire) T: 01751 417591.
E: info@forestholidays.co.uk **alanrogers.com/UK4570**

Forest Holidays is a partnership between the Forestry Commission and The Camping and Caravanning Club. The Spiers House site is set in a wide, natural looking clearing in the middle of Cropton Forest. It is an ideal location for a cycling or walking holiday without having to move your car. The site buildings, built in local stone, are set around a central courtyard with a pedestrian archway leading to the pitches. Sloping fields provide 150 pitches, which include 74 with 10A electricity and 55 with hardstanding. The welcoming reception also incorporates a well stocked shop. Reception provides leaflets for way-marked walks in the forest and orienteering.

Facilities	Directions
The recently refurbished tiled toilet block is spacious and well equipped, and includes private cubicles. Unit for disabled campers. Laundry room with washing machine, dryer and sinks (hot water charged). Well stocked shop. Fish and chip van calls Monday and Friday. Bar with local beer and lager, cider and wine. Bicycle hire. Raised barbecues are permitted. Off site: Pub with home-brewed beer 1 mile. Riding 5 miles. Fishing 7 miles. Golf 12 miles.	From A170 Pickering head westwards towards Helmsley. Turn right signed Cropton and Rosedale (avoiding Cropton village). Forest and park signed after 4 miles. Entrance is via a 500 yd. single track with passing places. GPS: 54.30765, -0.846267

Charges guide

Per unit incl. 2 persons	£ 14.70 - £ 24.40
incl. electricity	£ 19.50 - £ 40.00
extra person	£ 5.10 - £ 6.80

Open: All year.

For latest campsite news visit
alanrogers.com

Pickering
Rosedale Caravan & Camping Park

Rosedale Abbey, Pickering YO18 8SA (North Yorkshire) T: 01751 417272. E: info@flowerofmay.com

alanrogers.com/UK4770

In a beautiful location below Rosedale Moor and on the edge of a popular village, this is a campsite that is highly suitable for walkers. The site itself has a wide entrance on the edge of the village and, as it is within the National Park, the buildings are in the local stone and in keeping with the area. The site gently rises alongside the river, nestling within the valley. There are 120 touring pitches, a few with hardstanding and 72 with 10A electricity connections. There are some caravan holiday homes (private) and seasonal touring pitches in their own areas. The majority have superb views of the surrounding hills. One field is set aside for tents only and many are sited near the river which runs along the edge of the park. The surrounding hillsides are a maze of public footpaths and these and nearby Cropton Forest can all be reached without using your car. In summer, the Dales Bus runs through the village, connecting several of the popular villages. The 13-mile Rosedale circuit follows the route of the old iron ore railway.

Facilities

Sanitary facilities with underfloor heating include free showers and hairdressing units. They may be under a little pressure when the site is very full and are at a distance from some pitches. Facilities for disabled visitors and baby changing. Laundry facilities. Reception provides some basic provisions, sweets, maps and a small selection of camping accessories. Gas supplies. Games room with pool and video games. Large play area with space for ball games. Entrance barrier controlled by card (£10 deposit). Off site: Village with shop, post office, bakery and pubs.

Open: Easter - 3 November.

Directions

Rosedale is signed from A170, 2 miles west of Pickering. Site is in village of Rosedale Abbey, 8 miles north of the A170, adjacent to a Club site with a similar name. GPS: 54.35366, -0.88795

Charges guide

Per unit incl. up to 4 persons (electricity metered)	£ 15.00 - £ 21.00
extra person	£ 3.00
dog	£ 1.00

10% discount on pitch fee for weekly bookings.

Pickering
Overbrook Caravan Park

Maltongate, Thornton-le-Dale, Pickering YO18 7SE (North Yorkshire) T: 01751 474417.
E: enquiry@overbrookcaravanpark.co.uk **alanrogers.com/UK4534**

Situated on the edge of the very pretty village of Thornton-le-Dale, this most attractive, well cared for, adults only site has been developed on a disused railway station. The station building now provides holiday cottages and the caravan park toilet facilities. The site is level with 50 pitches (20 for touring units, the remainder used for seasonal units) arranged either side of a tarmac access road and backed by trees. All are on hardstanding and all have 16A electricity connections. Some pitches are quite small. Neither children nor tents are accepted at this adults only park.

Facilities

The toilet and shower facilities are situated in the old station house. Laundry facilities. Gas supplies. No tents accepted. Only adults are accepted. Off site: Village with bus stop, shops, pubs, fish and chips 800 yds. Bicycle hire 800 yds. Fishing 3 miles. Golf and riding 5 miles. Beach 25 miles.

Open: 1 March - 10 January.

Directions

Thornton-le-Dale is on the A170 Pickering-Scarborough road. In the village follow sign for Malton and park is 800 yds. on the left (follow the stream on the left). GPS: 54.228533, -0.7229

Charges guide

Per unit incl. 2 persons and electricity	£ 18.50 - £ 26.00

No credit cards.

Pickering
Upper Carr Caravan Park

Upper Carr Lane, Malton Road, Pickering YO18 7JP (North Yorkshire) T: 01751 473115.
E: info@uppercarrcaravanpark.co.uk **alanrogers.com/UK4620**

With a central location in the Vale of Pickering, Upper Carr is well placed for the many attractions the area has to offer. The enthusiastic manager is keen to develop it into a family-friendly park, introducing themed weekends and nature trails, and recently a new, reasonably priced restaurant. The park is surrounded by a high, well trimmed hedge which protects it from the wind and deadens the road noise. Upper Carr's six acres provide 80 level pitches, 75 with 10A electricity and some with hardstanding.

Facilities

Recently refurbished, heated toilet blocks have showers (20p) and baby changing facilities. Separate room with WC and washbasin for disabled visitors. Laundry room. Motorcaravan service point. Shop in reception. Restaurant. Play area. Games room. Bicycle hire. Nature trail.

Open: 1 March - 31 October.

Directions

On A169 Pickering-Malton, park is on left 1.5 miles south of Pickering. GPS: 54.222967, -0.769

Charges guide

Per unit incl. 2 adults, 2 children and electricity	£ 12.00 - £ 28.00

FREE Alan Rogers Travel Card
Extra benefits and savings - see page 10

Ripon
Riverside Meadows Country Caravan Park

Ure Bank Top, Ripon HG4 1JD (North Yorkshire) T: 01765 602964. E: info@flowerofmay.com
alanrogers.com/UK4760

Riverside Meadows is a rural park, although the approach to it belies that fact. The short approach from the main road passes a row of houses and a factory, but once they are passed, the park opens up before you and you are once again back in the countryside. There are plenty of caravan holiday homes here but they are, on the whole, quite separate from the 20-25 touring pitches which are mixed amongst a number of seasonal pitches. These pitches, practically all with electrical hook-ups, are mainly on gently sloping grass with 10 hardstandings. A meadow separates the park from the River Ure, a favourite place for strolling and fishing (licences available). Close to Ripon is the Lightwater Valley theme park, and a little further are Fountains Abbey, Harrogate, Knaresborough, the Yorkshire Dales and Thirsk with its market and James Herriot centre. There is lots to do on and off the park for families and couples.

Facilities

The tiled toilet block is quite new and includes a baby room, and a fully fitted shower room for disabled visitors. Laundry facilities. Shop. Bar with snacks. Games room. Well equipped play area. Fishing. WiFi over site (charged). Max. 2 dogs per pitch, contact park first. Off site: Fishing, bicycle hire and riding 800 yds. Golf 1.25 miles. The delightful market town (city) of Ripon with its ancient cathedral is only 20 minutes walk.

Open: Easter/1 April - 31 October.

Directions

At the most northern roundabout on the Ripon bypass (A61), turn onto the A6108 signed Ripon, Masham and Leyburn. Go straight on at mini-roundabout and park is signed on right. GPS: 54.15045, -1.515

Charges guide

Per unit/tent incl. up to	
4 persons (electricity metered)	£ 15.00 - £ 21.00
extra person	£ 3.00

10% discount on pitch fee for weekly bookings.

Ripon
Sleningford Watermill Caravan & Camping Park

North Stainley, Ripon HG4 3HQ (North Yorkshire) T: 01765 635201.
alanrogers.com/UK4588

The watermill buildings are a focal point for this park and house the welcoming reception and some of the facilities. Well spaced touring pitches for tents, caravans, and motorcaravans are set in 14 acres of mature riverside meadow in three distinct areas. Management of the natural habitat of the park is carried out with conservation in mind at all times. The beautiful riverside provides a beach and access for swimming, canoeing and a nature trail. River fishing is possible (fly only). The Ripon Rowel walk passes through the park. Reservation is essential and one night stays are not accepted.

Facilities

Two toilet blocks, one with facilities for disabled visitors (doubles as a family room). Laundry room with local information and brochures. Ice pack freezing service. Shop (essentials and children's fishing nets). Independent canoe hire, trips and courses. Fishing (fly). Max. 2 dogs per pitch. Off site: Pub and restaurant nearby (within safe walking distance). Lightwater Valley theme park 2 miles.

Open: 1 April - 31 October.

Directions

The park is on the A6108 5 miles north of Ripon between the villages of North Stainley and West Tanfield and is clearly signed (brown tourist signs). GPS: 54.199925, -1.571883

Charges guide

Per unit incl. 2 persons	
and electricity	£ 22.00 - £ 27.00

Ripon
Woodhouse Farm Caravan & Camping Park

Winksley, Ripon HG4 3PG (North Yorkshire) T: 01765 658309. E: info@woodhousewinksley.com
alanrogers.com/UK4660

This secluded family park on a former working farm, is only six miles from Ripon and about four from the World Heritage site of Fountains Abbey. It is a very rural park with a spacious feel and various pitching areas are tucked away in woodland areas or around the edges of hedged fields with the centre left clear for children. There are hard roads and most of the 160 pitches have 16A electricity. There are 56 acres in total, 17.5 devoted to the site and 20 acres of woodland for walking.

Facilities

The clean toilet block near the touring pitches includes heating, roomy showers and some washbasins in cabins. Two bathrooms. Facilities for disabled visitors. Farm buildings have a well equipped laundry, reception and shop. Motorcaravan services. Bar (daily) and restaurant (weekends). Takeaway on request. Games room with TV. Play equipment. Fishing. Mountain bike hire. Free WiFi.

Open: Mid March - 31 October.

Directions

From Ripon take Fountains Abbey-Pateley Bridge road (B6265). After 3.5 miles turn right to Grantley and then follow campsite signs for further 1-2 miles. GPS: 54.137417, -1.634667

Charges guide

Per unit incl. 2 persons	
and electricity	£ 19.00 - £ 26.00

For latest campsite news visit
alanrogers.com

Scarborough
Cayton Village Caravan Park

Mill Lane, Cayton Bay, Scarborough YO11 3NN (North Yorkshire) T: 01723 583171.

E: info@caytontouring.co.uk **alanrogers.com/UK4550**

Cayton Village Caravan Park can only be described as a gem. Just three miles from the hustle and bustle of Scarborough, it is a peaceful, attractive haven. Originally just a flat field with caravans around the perimeter, years of hard work have produced a park which is well designed and very pleasing to the eye with quality facilities. The 310 pitches, all with electricity (199 fully serviced) are numbered and everyone is taken to their pitch. A new development, The Laurels, provides 110 hardstanding pitches with 16A electricity, water, waste water, TV connection, and WiFi. The late arrivals area has electrical hook-ups.

Facilities

Four toilet blocks (key code locks) can be heated and have high quality fixtures and fittings. Some showers are preset, others are controllable. Two family shower rooms, family bathroom and baby facilities. Large room for disabled visitors. Two laundry rooms. Reception and shop. Adventure playground. Nature trail and dog walking area. Caravan storage. WiFi at The Laurels. Off site: Fishing 0.5 miles. Bicycle hire 3 miles. Regular bus service from park entrance to Scarborough, Filey and Bridlington.

Open: 1 March - 31 October.

Directions

From A64 Malton-Scarborough road turn right at roundabout (McDonald's) signed B1261 Filey. In Cayton village take second left after Blacksmith's Arms down Mill Lane (at brown tourism sign) and park is 200 yds. on left. From roundabout to park is 2.25 miles. GPS: 54.235733, -0.376117

Charges guide

Per unit incl. 2 persons and electricity	£ 15.00 - £ 30.00
incl. services and hardstanding	£ 19.00 - £ 35.00

Scarborough
Jasmine Park

Cross Lane, Snainton, Scarborough YO13 9BE (North Yorkshire) T: 01723 859240.

E: enquiries@jasminepark.co.uk **alanrogers.com/UK4740**

Jasmine is a very attractive, quiet and well manicured park with owners who go to much trouble to produce many plants to decorate a very colourful entrance. Set in the Vale of Pickering, the park is level, well drained and protected by a coniferous hedge. Of the 126 pitches 71 are for touring units, with 10/16A electricity connections. Fifty-one are super pitches and there are 70 separate pitches for tents. A field is provided for games. Tourist information is provided in a log cabin and the owners are only too happy to advise. This is an excellent, peaceful park for a restful holiday.

Facilities

The heated toilet block is of a high standard and is kept very clean. It includes a room for families and disabled visitors. Laundry room with dishwashing sinks. Motorcaravan service point. Licensed shop selling gas. New play area. Dogs are welcome but there is no dog walk. Caravan storage. WiFi (charged). Off site: Bus service in village 0.5 miles. Riding, golf driving range and 9-hole course 2 miles. Fishing and bicycle hire 5 miles.

Open: 1 March - 31 October.

Directions

Snainton is on the A170 Pickering-Scarborough road and park is signed at eastern end of the village. Turn down Barker's Lane and at the small crossroads turn left and the park is 230 yds. on the left. GPS: 54.218583, -0.575567

Charges guide

Per unit incl. 4 persons, electricity	£ 20.00 - £ 35.00
extra person	£ 2.00
child (under 18 yrs)	£ 1.00

Scarborough
Lebberston Touring Park

Filey Road, Lebberston, Scarborough YO11 3PE (North Yorkshire) T: 01723 585723.

E: info@lebberstontouring.co.uk **alanrogers.com/UK4780**

Lebberston Touring Park is a quiet, spacious touring site and is highly suitable for anyone seeking a quiet relaxing break, such as mature couples or young families (although tents are not accepted). There is no play area or games room, the only concession to children being a large central area with goal posts, so teenagers may get bored. The park itself has a very spacious feel – it is gently sloping and south facing and the views are superb. Of the 125 numbered pitches, 75 are for touring units. All have 10A (some 16A) electricity and 25 are on hardstanding. The circular access road is tarmac.

Facilities

The toilet blocks are of high quality and kept very clean. Large shower cubicles and washbasins in cubicles with curtains. Family bathroom (20p) in one block. Good room for disabled visitors (Radar key). Laundry facilities. Reception sells a few supplies, plus papers, ice cream and gas. Breathable groundsheets only. WiFi over site (charged). Max. 2 dogs. Off site: Golf 600 yds. Beach and fishing 2 miles. Riding 3 miles. Local pub 5 minutes walk.

Open: 1 March - 31 October.

Directions

From A64 Malton-Scarborough road turn right at roundabout (McDonald's, pub and superstore) signed B1261 Filey. Go through Cayton, Killerby and in 4.5 miles site is signed on the left (not easy to see). If you miss the turning, continue to roundabout and turn around. GPS: 54.22502, -0.34343

Charges guide

Per unit incl. 2 persons and electricity	£ 15.50 - £ 27.00

FREE Alan Rogers Travel Card

Extra benefits and savings - see page 10

Scarborough
Flower of May Holiday Park

Lebberston Cliff, Scarborough YO11 3NU (North Yorkshire) T: 01723 584311. E: info@flowerofmay.com
alanrogers.com/UK4520

Situated on the cliff tops, 4.5 miles from Scarborough and 2.5 miles from Filey, Flower of May is a large, family owned park for both touring caravans and caravan holiday homes. The entrance to the park is very colourful and the reception office is light and airy. The park is licensed for 300 touring units of which 200 are fully serviced. The touring pitches are pretty level, arranged in wide avenues, mainly on grass and divided by shrubs. The range of leisure facilities grouped around reception includes an indoor pool with areas for both adults and children, a water flume and a jacuzzi. The main building has two squash courts, ten-pin bowling, table tennis and amusement machines. The leisure centre is also open to the public (concessionary rates for campers) but during high season is only available to local regulars and the caravanners and campers on the park. There are cliff walks down to the beach, but there is an easier walk down from a car park a mile away. Riverside Meadows at Ripon and Rosedale Country Caravan Park near Pickering and Goosewood near York are under the same ownership.

Facilities

Three toilet blocks, all refurbished, provide showers and washbasins in both cabins and vanity style. Baby rooms. Facilities for disabled visitors. Laundry room. Well stocked and licensed shop. Two modern bar lounges, one for families and one for adults only, with discos in season. Café and takeaway fish and chips. Games room with TV. Large adventure playground. Pay and play golf course (£10 a round). Indoor swimming pool. Skateboard ramps. Basketball. Dog exercise area, but numbers and breeds are limited (one per pitch). WiFi throughout the park (charged). Off site: The Plough Inn near the park entrance offers good bar meals. Fishing, boat slipway and riding 2 miles. Bicycle hire 4 miles.

Open: Easter - end October.

Directions

Park is signed from roundabout at junction of A165 and B1261 from where it is 600 yds. GPS: 54.2292, -0.3425

Charges guide

Per unit incl. up to 4 persons (electricity metered)	£ 15.00 - £ 21.00
tent (no electricity)	£ 15.00 - £ 21.00
child (under 3 yrs)	free

10% discount on pitch fee for weekly advance bookings.

Settle
Knight Stainforth Hall Caravan & Camping Park

Little Stainforth, Settle BD24 0DP (North Yorkshire) T: 01729 822200. E: info@knightstainforth.co.uk
alanrogers.com/UK4720

In a very attractive setting, this park is located in the heart of the Yorkshire Dales, the whole area a paradise for hill-walking, fishing and pot-holing and has outstanding scenery. The camping area is on slightly sloping grass, sheltered by mature woodland. There are 100 touring pitches (20 are seasonal), 60 with 16A electricity and water and 25 with hardstanding. A separate area contains 66 privately owned caravan holiday homes. A gate leads from the bottom of the camping field giving access to the river bank where the Ribble bubbles over small waterfalls and rocks and whirls around deep pools. This area is not fenced and children should be supervised, although it is a super location for a family picnic.

Facilities

A modern, heated amenity block provides toilets and showers and includes some washbasins in cubicles. Facilities for disabled visitors and baby changing. Laundry facilities. Motorcaravan service point. Small shop. Games/TV room. Play area with safety base. Fishing (permit from reception). Security barrier. Deposit for key to toilet block and barrier £10. WiFi throughout (charged). Off site: Bicycle hire and golf 3 miles. Riding 6 miles. The Dales Falconry and Conservation Centre, near Settle.

Open: 1 March - 31 October.

Directions

Drive to Settle from A65, through town then west towards Giggleswick. Ignore turning for Stainforth and Horton, and after 200 yds. turn sharp right into Stackhouse Lane (Knight Stainforth). After 2 miles turn right at crossroads. GPS: 54.10025, -2.284833

Charges guide

Per unit incl. 2 persons and electricity	£ 15.00 - £ 18.00
extra person	£ 4.00
child (5-16 yrs)	£ 2.00

For latest campsite news visit
alanrogers.com

Scarborough

Saint Helens in the Park

Wykeham, Scarborough YO13 9QD (North Yorkshire) T: 01723 862771. E: caravans@wykeham.co.uk

alanrogers.com/UK4540

Saint Helens is a high quality touring park with pleasant views, set within 30 acres of parkland. The site is divided into terraces with trees screening each area (one of which is set aside for adults only) and the 130 mainly level, touring pitches have a spacious feel. Electrical hook-ups (16A) are available to most pitches, also in the late arrivals area. A further 170 pitches are occupied seasonal units. Set on a hillside, the park's buildings are built in local stone and all is maintained to a high standard. The Downe Arms, a short stroll away, is known for its good food and family-friendly atmosphere. Some road noise can be expected. Scarborough is only five miles away with its beaches and summer shows, and buses pass the site gates.

Facilities	Directions
Four heated toilet blocks are well equipped and maintained to a high standard. Some washbasins in cabins, free showers and baby baths. Unit for disabled visitors. Good central laundry room. Well stocked shop. Café and takeaway. Small games room. Large dog walking area. Tourist information cabin. Bicycle hire. Caravan storage. Internet café. WiFi thoughout. Off site: Nearby Wykeham Lakes offer fishing (trout and coarse), scuba diving, windsurfing and sailing (in your own boat), 1 mile. Golf and riding 2 miles.	Park access road leads off the A170 (Pickering-Scarborough) road in Wykeham village 2 miles west of junction with B1262. GPS: 54.23795, -0.517044

Charges guide

Per unit incl. 2 persons and electricity	£ 15.90 - £ 26.00
extra person (over 3 yrs)	£ 2.00
dog	£ 1.70

Open: All year excl. 15 January - 13 February.

Sͭ Helens in the Park

250 pitches set in 30 acres of parkland

Adventure playground, excellent shop, games room & amusements. Nearby there is excellent fishing, diving, windsurfing & sailing.

St Helens in the Park - Tel. 01723 862771 - www.sthelenscaravanpark.co.uk

Skipsea

Skipsea Sands Holiday Park

Mill Lane, Skipsea YO25 8TZ (East Yorkshire) T: 0871 664 9812. E: skipsea.sands@park-resorts.com

alanrogers.com/UK4496

This well established holiday park is now owned by Park Resorts and is primarily dedicated to caravan holiday homes, of which there are 625 privately owned and 70 to rent. There is however a pleasantly laid out touring park occupying its own corner of the site and bordered by an attractive duck pond and a large playing area (both well fenced). The 91 marked, level pitches (some occupied by seasonal caravans) are separated by hedges and all have 16A electricity; some also have water, drainage and sewerage connections. The leisure facilities are outstanding and a full daily programme of activities and entertainment is offered for children and adults. Situated on the cliffs on the Yorkshire coast, south of Bridlington, beaches are either a good walk or a short drive away. There is a wide choice of possible days out: Beverley or York, each with its Minster and its horse racing; Spurn Point or Bempton Cliffs.

Facilities	Directions
Two heated toilet blocks have been refurbished, with pushbutton showers, open washbasins and en-suite facilities for disabled visitors. Basic chemical disposal and motorcaravan service point. Washing machines and dryers. Well stocked shop. Bar, coffee shop and restaurant with takeaway. Leisure centre with sports hall, 10-pin bowling, heated indoor swimming pool, jacuzzi, sauna and steam room. Fitness centre with gym and sunbed. Games Kingdom with electronic games and Kids' Zone. Fishing in duck pond (charged). WiFi (charged). Off site: Buses from park gates. Village with shops, pub, restaurant 1 mile. Beach 0.25 mile (on foot) or 4 miles (by car). Golf 3 miles. Boat launching 6 miles. Riding and sailing 9 miles.	Skipsea is 20 miles northeast of Hull and 10 miles south of Bridlington. From Humber Bridge or from M62, take A63 to Hull, east of city follow signs to join A165 towards Bridlington. After 18 miles, turn east on B1249 to Skipsea. In village, turn right then left to site (signed). GPS: 53.98957, -0.20716

Charges guide

Per unit incl. all services	£ 6.00 - £ 30.00
tent pitch	£ 5.00 - £ 25.00
dog	£ 1.00 - £ 3.00

Open: 1 March - 31 October.

For latest campsite news visit

alanrogers.com

Skipton
Howgill Lodge Caravan & Camping Park
Barden, Skipton BD23 6DJ (North Yorkshire) T: 01756 720655. E: info@howgill-lodge.co.uk
alanrogers.com/UK4750

Howgill Lodge is a traditional family park set in the heart of the Yorkshire Dales. Arranged on a sloping hillside, the terraced pitches have fantastic views. It is a small park catering for the needs of walkers, tourers and people who like to just relax. The whole area is a haven for both experienced walkers or the casual rambler, without having to move your car. The 20 touring pitches at the upper part of the park are on hardstanding and have 10A electricity connections. A further 30 pitches on the lower part are mainly grass and for tents. Picnic tables and chairs are provided. There are three mobile homes available to rent. Reception also houses a small shop which sells most of the basics including fresh foods.

Facilities

Heated toilet facilities are at the entrance, near reception. Showers are large and adjustable. Fully equipped laundry room with four additional unisex showers. Outdoor washing lines are provided. Two small blocks housing WCs are lower down the site for the convenience of tent campers. Shop. No play area. Fishing licences are available from reception. Off site: Bus service within walking distance (3 per day). Fishing 1 mile. Bolton Abbey with its beautiful riverside walks 3 miles. Golf, riding and bicycle hire 7 miles. Skipton 8 miles.

Open: 1 April (or Easter) - 31 October.

Directions

Turn off A59 Skipton-Harrogate road at roundabout onto B6160 Bolton Abbey, Burnsall road, through a low (10 ft. 4 in) archway. Three miles past Bolton Abbey at Barden Towers, bear right (Appletreewick and Pateley Bridge). This road is fairly narrow for 1.25 miles (with passing places). Park is signed on right at phone box. GPS: 54.025767, -1.909833

Charges guide

Per unit incl. 2 persons and electricity	£ 18.00 - £ 22.00
family unit incl. electricity	£ 24.00 - £ 28.00

Skipton
Wood Nook Caravan Park
Skirethorns, Threshfield, Skipton BD23 5NU (North Yorkshire) T: 01756 752412. E: enquiries@woodnook.net
alanrogers.com/UK4670

Wood Nook is a family run park in the heart of Wharfedale, part of the Yorkshire Dales National Park. The site includes six acres of woodland with quite rare flora and fauna. Reception is in the farmhouse, as is the small shop. The gently sloping fields have gravel roads and provide 39 touring pitches (30 with gravel hardstanding). All have 10A electricity and nearby water and chemical disposal points. There is also room for 31 tents and there are some caravan holiday homes to let.

Facilities

Converted farm buildings provide dated but clean sanitary facilities which can be heated. Washbasins in cubicles for ladies. Roomy showers (in another building – coin operated). Laundry facilities. Motorcaravan service points. Licensed shop for basics and gifts (from Easter). Gas. Small play area. American motorhomes are taken by prior arrangement. Internet access in reception. WiFi throughout (free). Off site: Fishing and bicycle hire 2 miles. Riding 3 miles. Golf 9 miles. Leisure centre.

Open: 1 March - mid January (dependent on weather).

Directions

Threshfield is 9 miles north of Skipton on the B6265. Continue through village onto B6160 and after garage turn left into Skirethorns Lane. Follow signs for 600 yds, keeping left up narrow lane, then turn right up track for 300 yds. The last 900 yds. is single track – phone ahead to check it is clear. GPS: 54.07267, -2.04199

Charges guide

Per unit incl. 2 persons and electricity	£ 19.00
extra person	£ 3.00

Wetherby
Maustin Caravan Park
Kearby with Netherby, Wetherby LS22 4BZ (North Yorkshire) T: 0113 28 86 23 4. E: judith@maustin.co.uk
alanrogers.com/UK4755

A tranquil site for couples only, this manicured park is set within the North Yorkshire National Park. It offers 25 well spaced pitches sited on grass, all with peaceful, scenic views of the surrounding area. Caravan holiday homes are in a separate area. A bowling club on the site offers membership to all visitors and competitions are held throughout the season. Relax in the comfortable lounge or in the tasteful bar and restaurant area. A covered terrace overlooks the bowling green.

Facilities

One heated, well equipped toilet block has good showers, free hairdryers and roomy toilet and washing cubicles. Good facility for disabled visitors. Laundry room. Kitchen area with freezer. Milk, newspapers, etc. to order at weekends. Bowling club with lounge, bar, restaurant and takeaway (weekends from March). Internet facilities. WiFi over site (charged). Off site: Fishing 2 miles. Riding 3 miles.

Open: All year excl. February.

Directions

From A1 south follow Harewood House signs through Collingham to join A61 (Harrogate). At lights turn right over River Wharfe, right for Kirkby Overblow, then as above. GPS: 53.917464, -1.497488

Charges guide

Per unit incl. 2 persons	£ 18.50
incl. services	£ 21.00

FREE Alan Rogers Travel Card
Extra benefits and savings - see page 10

Whitby
Middlewood Farm Holiday Park

Middlewood Lane, Fylingthorpe, Robin Hood's Bay YO22 4UF (North Yorkshire) T: 01947 880414.
E: info@middlewoodfarm.com **alanrogers.com/UK4532**

Middlewood Farm is a level park, surrounded by hills and with views of the sea from some of the pitches. A short walk through the farm fields and wild flower conservation areas leads to the picturesque old fishing village of Robin Hood's Bay and the sea. The park has 30 touring pitches for caravans and motorcaravans with 10A electricity, 18 with hardstanding and the remainder on grass. There is space for around 130 tents in two areas with 41 electricity connections available and 30 caravan holiday homes to rent. A good beach is only ten minutes walk through the fields.

Facilities

Two splendid toilet blocks have clean facilities and are modern, heated and tiled with free showers and private cabins. Fully equipped laundry room including iron and board. Facilities for babies and disabled visitors. Play area with bark base amongst the tents. WiFi on part of site (charged). Off site: Sandy beach with fishing 0.5 miles (10 mins. walk). Boat launching 2 miles. Golf 7 miles. Shop and public transport in village 5 mins. walk.

Open: 1 March - 31 October.

Directions

From A171 Scarborough-Whitby road turn right (Robin Hood's Bay and Fylingthorpe). Just past 30 mph sign bear right and after 100 yds. turn right into Middlewood Lane. GPS: 54.43012, -0.54670

Charges guide

Per unit incl. 2 persons and electricity	£ 15.00 - £ 25.00
extra person	£ 3.00

No credit cards.

Whitby
Sandfield House Farm Caravan Park

Sandsend Road, Whitby YO21 3SR (North Yorkshire) T: 01947 602660. E: info@sandfieldhousefarm.co.uk
alanrogers.com/UK4528

Although it is set on a hill in undulating countryside on the low cliffs near Whitby, this park provides 200 level pitches, all with electricity. There are 60 pitches for touring caravans, all on hardstanding, and these are mainly set to the front of the park giving wonderful views over the golf course and the sea. Three fully serviced pitches are available. Tents are not accepted here. Whitby is only a mile away and a quarter of a mile walk down a gently sloping track from the park brings you to a two mile long sandy beach. From here it is a gentle stroll along the new promenade to Whitby harbour.

Facilities

Two toilet blocks (one older, one new and very good) have free hot showers. A new block for the 2013 season should be available with the inclusion of facilities for disabled visitors. Laundry room with washing machines, dryers and iron. Off site: Half-hourly bus service to town centre. Golf 200 yds. Fishing 400 yds. Shops and boat launching 800 yds. Railway station 1 mile.

Open: 1 March - 7 November.

Directions

From Whitby follow signs for Sandsend on the A174. The park is on the landward side of the road, opposite the golf course and well signed. GPS: 54.491717, -0.642767

Charges guide

Per unit incl. up to 4 persons and electricity	£ 19.00 - £ 22.00
extra person	£ 2.00

No credit or debit cards.

York
Alders Caravan Park

Home Farm, Alne, York YO61 1RY (North Yorkshire) T: 01347 838722. E: enquiries@homefarmalne.co.uk
alanrogers.com/UK4638

The Alders is located in the village of Alne, nine miles from the centre of York, and has been carefully developed and managed on a working farm in historic parkland. The extra large pitches are arranged in small bays designed to give privacy, and separate the 28 touring pitches from the seasonal units, storage and the camping pods. Service tracks throughout allow site maintenance without compromising privacy. Woodland walks and a water meadow with wild flowers enhance the wonderful peace and tranquillity marred only by the occasional light aircraft.

Facilities

The first rate toilet blocks are heated with family sized shower rooms, one also has a bath (£1 for baths). The newer block includes en-suite bathrooms with bath or shower. Laundry facilities. Provision for disabled visitors. Shop (all season). Gas is sold at reception. Only 2 dogs accepted per pitch. Off site: Floodlit tennis courts in the village. Fishing 2 miles. Golf 3 miles. Riding and bicycle hire 4 miles.

Open: 1 March - 31 October.

Directions

From north on A19: after leaving Easingwold bypass take next right turn (Alne). From south (A19), 5 miles north of Shipton turn left at sign for Alne. In 1.5 miles at T-junction turn left and in 0.5 miles site is signed in the centre of the village. GPS: 54.08185, -1.24105

Charges guide

Per unit incl. 2 persons, 2 children and electricity	£ 17.00
extra person	£ 5.00

For latest campsite news visit
alanrogers.com

Withernsea
Sand le Mere Holiday Village

Southfield Lane, Tunstall HU12 0JF (East Yorkshire) T: 01964 670403. E: info@sand-le-mere.co.uk

alanrogers.com/UK4480

Sand le Mere is an independently run holiday village ideally situated on the east coast of Yorkshire, nestling between beautiful countryside and sandy beaches. The park offers a wide range of facilities and activities to keep the whole family entertained, including a show lounge and an outdoor leisure area. The site is likely to prove popular with fishermen as both fresh water and sea fishing options are available. There are 60 new hardstanding pitches for tourers (all with 16A electricity), 18 of which are fully serviced. A new camping area has electricity hook-ups and new toilet and shower facilities. Just along the coast are the resorts of Hornsea, Bridlington and Scarborough; inland are York and Beverley with their beautiful churches.

Facilities	Directions
One new heated toilet block has excellent showers and WCs. A more dated one awaiting refurbishment is clean and well equipped. Facilities for disabled visitors. Launderette. New (2012) complex with well stocked shop, bar, restaurant and takeaway. Indoor swimming pool (Mar-Nov) with play areas, sauna and steam room. Indoor soft play area. Adventure playgrounds. Gym (charged). Children's club in high season (5-12 yrs). Sea fishing and freshwater fishing (charged). Max. 2 dogs per pitch. WiFi over site (charged). Off site: Golf and riding 6 km.	From Hull take B1242 between Hornsea and Withensea. At Roos, take the turn for Tunstall, where the site is signed. GPS: 53.761592, -0.011233

Charges guide

Per unit incl. 4 persons and electricity	£ 17.00 - £ 24.00
extra person	£ 1.00
dog	free

Open: 1 February - 31 December.

Fabulous Holidays on the Beautiful East Yorkshire Coast

Sand le Mere
HOLIDAY VILLAGE
EAST YORKSHIRE COAST

Sand le Mere is an independently run Holiday Village nestled on the East Coast of Yorkshire and surrounded by stunning countryside, natural parkland & sandy beaches.

We invested over £4m in 2012 in our stunning new facilities including:
• Indoor swimming pool with splash zone & wet play areas.
• Brand new entertainment complex with loads to do and lots of places to eat!

Plus
• Caravan & Luxury Lodge holidays available and a fantastic new touring field.

*Terms and conditions apply. Offer is subject to availability and applies to new bookings only. Check our website or call for more information.

Follow us on Facebook & Twitter

Call us on 01964 670 403 (ALAN ROGERS GUIDE)
Book online www.sand-le-mere.co.uk

Amazing Holidays...
Caravan breaks available from only £85*

Fantastic
£4m
Facilities
Opened 2012

York
Goose Wood Caravan Park

329

Carr Lane, Sutton-on-the-Forest, York YO61 1ET (North Yorkshire) T: 01347 810829.

E: enquiries@goosewood.co.uk **alanrogers.com/UK4640**

Now part of the Flower of May group, Goose Wood has a natural woodland setting. It provides a quiet, relaxed atmosphere from which to explore York itself or the surrounding Yorkshire Dales, Wolds and Moors. The park has a well kept air and a rural atmosphere, with 100 well spaced and marked pitches, all with metered 10A electricity on hardstanding (five also have water and drainage). For children, there is a first rate adventure playground in the trees at one side of the park and for adults, a small coarse fishing lake and attractive, natural woodland for walking. The park is popular with families in high season when it can be busy at weekends.

Facilities	Directions
Tiled and heated, the modern toilet block is spacious and well maintained. An additional unit provides shower rooms, WC and washbasins in cubicles and extra dishwashing sinks. Full facilities for disabled visitors. Laundry room. Motorcaravan service point. Well stocked shop (with gas). Fishing lake. Large adventure playground. Games room. Outdoor table tennis. Dogs (max. two per pitch), to be exercised in nearby woodland. WiFi throughout (charged). Off site: Riding and golf 3 miles. Bicycle hire 6 miles. York 6 miles.	Park is 6 miles north of York; from the A1237 York outer ring-road take the B1363 for Sutton-on-the-Forest and Stillington, taking the first right after the Haxby and Wigginton junction and follow park signs. N.B. Do not use postcode for sat navs; use lat/long or Carr Lane. GPS: 54.0591, -1.0861

Charges guide

Per unit incl. 4 persons (electricity metered)	£ 15.00 - £ 21.00
extra person	£ 3.00

Open: March - 2 January.

York

Moorside Caravan Park

Lords Moor Lane, Strensall, York YO32 5XJ (North Yorkshire) T: 01904 491208

alanrogers.com/UK4610

Strensall is only a few miles from York, one of England's most attractive cities and Moorside Caravan Park will provide a peaceful haven after a day's sightseeing. Children (under 16) are not accepted at this park. It will impress you with its pretty fishing lake, many flowers and the tranquillity (except for the odd passing daytime train). There are 53 marked touring pitches on neat well trimmed grass, most with 6/10A electricity and 22 with hardstanding. The park is very well maintained with a pleasant environment. The small lake is well stocked for coarse fishing and the pitches bordering the lake are the most popular.

Facilities

The purpose built toilet block can be heated and houses immaculately kept facilities with washbasins in cubicles for ladies. Separate, recently constructed facility for disabled visitors. Fully equipped laundry room. Tourist information and books to borrow. Coarse fishing (£3 per day). Caravan storage. Off site: Strensall village with shops and places to eat within a mile. Golf 0.5 miles. Riding 3 miles.

Open: March - end October.

Directions

From the A1237 York outer ring road, take the Strensall turn and head towards Flaxton, past York Golf Club for about half a mile and Park is on left just before a cattle grid. GPS: 54.042733, -1.011683

Charges guide

Per unit incl. 2 persons and electricity	£ 14.00 - £ 17.50

No credit cards.

York

South Lea Caravan Park

The Balk, Pocklington, York YO42 2NX (North Yorkshire) T: 01759 303467. E: info@south-lea.co.uk

alanrogers.com/UK4655

South Lea is situated just off the A1079 road near the delightful market town of Pocklington, about 12 miles from York. A well presented open park with 72 pitches set in 15 acres of flat grassland. Some are hardstanding and all have 16A electricity. The park is divided in to areas by shrubs and hedges, each named after a type of tree. Some areas are in the early stages of planting. The site is ideally positioned for touring the many places of interest in the surrounding area and is within reach of the coast.

Facilities

One toilet block (can be heated) with free showers and hairdryers. There are no facilities for campers with disabilities at present, but these are being planned. Dog showers. Calor Gas supplies. Off site: Pocklington nearby with shops and restaurants, a comprehensive leisure centre and pool. Local airfield for gliders, lessons and pleasure flight. Bus stop at site entrance.

Open: 1 March - 31 October.

Directions

Travelling from the west on the A1079 ignore the first turn off to Pocklington. Stay on the A1079 until you see the signs for the campsite. The turning will be on the left and the site is a short distance down this road on the left. GPS: 53.914298, -0.773592

Charges guide

Per unit incl. 2 persons and electricity	£ 16.00 - £ 20.00

No credit cards.

York

York Meadows Caravan Park

Sheriff Hutton, York YO60 6QP (North Yorkshire) T: 01347 878508.
E: reception@yorkmeadowscaravanpark.com **alanrogers.com/UK4605**

Set in a grassy meadow, this newly created park is surrounded by farmland, half a mile from Sherriff Hutton with its two pubs and village shops. A total of 45 pitches are available, 35 of which are for touring, 30 with hardstanding and electricity (16A) and five super pitches with hardstanding and all services. A further area has room for 38 tents, some with electricity. These are separated from the touring section by trees and a children's play area. The park is a haven for wildlife with trees and meadows all around.

Facilities

The heated toilet facilities are in a single block along with reception and provide a mix of washbasins in cubicles and open vanity units. Separate shower room for disabled visitors. Laundry facilities. Small shop in reception selling essentials. Slides, swings and a zip wire frame (safety surface). WiFi (free but limited reception). Max. 2 dogs. Off site: Fishing 3 miles. Golf 4 miles. City of York 8 miles. Rievaulx Abbey, Castle Howard and Eden Camp within 10 miles. Over 500 square miles of the North York Moors National Park. Yorkshire coast one hour's drive. North York Moors Steam Railway at Pickering.

Open: 1 March - 31 October.

Directions

Join A64 between York and Scarborough. Approximately 8 miles beyond York, heading for Malton, turn left, signposted Flaxton and Sheriff Hutton. At West Lilling turn left for Strensall. Site entrance immediately opposite junction. GPS: 54.0797, -1.0166

Charges guide

Per unit incl. 2 persons and electricity	£ 16.00 - £ 24.00
extra person	£ 3.50
child (5-15 yrs)	£ 1.50

For latest campsite news visit

alanrogers.com

The North West region boasts a wealth of industrial heritage with undiscovered countryside, the vibrant cities of Manchester and Liverpool, the seaside resorts of Blackpool and Morecambe, plus miles of glorious coastline, home to a wide variety of bird species.

THIS REGION INCLUDES: CHESHIRE, LANCASHIRE, MERSEYSIDE, GREATER MANCHESTER AND THE HIGH PEAKS OF DERBYSHIRE

The miles of beautiful, North West countryside offers endless opportunities for recreation. For the more active, the peaceful plains of Cheshire are a walkers' haven with endless trails to choose from. Lancashire is also good walking country, with way-marked paths passing through the outstanding Forest of Bowland, which affords marvellous views over the Lake District in Cumbria and the Yorkshire Dales. Birdwatchers are catered for too, with the coast offering some of the best birdspotting activity in the country, most notably along the Sefton coast and around the Wirral Peninsula. The region's cities have their own charm. Manchester, with its fabulous shopping centres and vibrant nightlife, boasts a rich Victorian heritage; the maritime city of Liverpool has more museums and galleries than any other UK city outside London; Lancaster features fine Georgian buildings and an imposing Norman castle; while Chester is renowned for its medieval architecture and shopping galleries. And offering good, old-fashioned seaside fun is Blackpool. England's most popular seaside resort is packed full of lively entertainment and attractions, such as the white knuckle rides at the pleasure beach, amusement games on the pier and the observation decks in the famous Tower.

Places of interest

Cheshire: Tatton Park in Knutsford; Chester Cathedral and Zoo; Cheshire Military Museum; Lyme Park stately home in Macclesfield; Beeston Castle; Blue Planet Aquarium at Ellesmere Port.

Lancashire: Williamson Park, castle and leisure park in Lancaster; Camelot Theme Park; Blackpool tower and illuminations; Morecambe Bay; Hoghton Tower and National Museum of Football in Preston.

Merseyside: Liverpool Football Club Museum and Tour Centre; The Beatles Story Museum; Speke Hall garden and estate; The Wirral Country Park; Williamson Tunnels Heritage Centre.

Greater Manchester: Imperial War Museum North; Manchester United Football Club Museum; The Lowry; Corgi Heritage Centre in Rochdale; The Trafford Centre.

Did you know?

The first public gallery to open in England was in Liverpool in 1877.

Lancaster Castle is infamous as host to the Pendle witch trials of 1612.

The first passenger railway station was built in Manchester.

Carnforth station was the location for David Lean's 1945 film Brief Encounter.

Ramsbottom holds an annual, two-day chocolate festival in spring.

Morecambe Bay is notorious for its shifting sands and treacherous currents, but can be crossed on foot with a guide.

Opened in 1894, the Blackpool Tower was copied from the Eiffel Tower; the height to the top of the flagpole is 518 feet 9 inches.

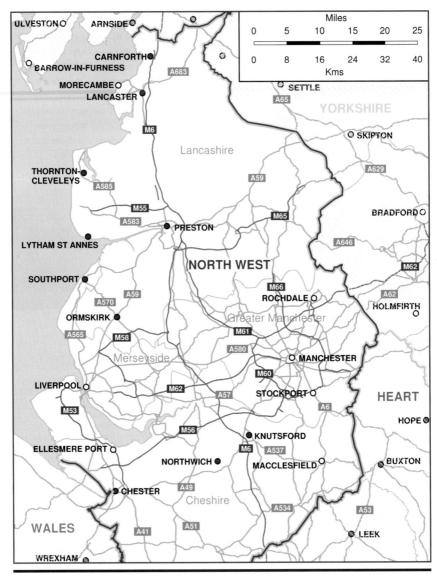

Carnforth

Old Hall Caravan Park

Capernwray, Carnforth LA6 1AD (Lancashire) T: 01524 733276. E: info@oldhallcaravanpark.co.uk

alanrogers.com/UK5271

In a woodland clearing, just five minutes drive from junction 35 of the M6, Old Hall Caravan Park is a gem. Approached along a tree-lined road, this secluded park offers peace and tranquillity. There are 38 touring pitches which are accessed from a circular roadway, all on marked and level hardstandings and with 16A electricity, water and drainage (shared between two pitches). TV hook-ups are available (free). Tents are not accepted. There are 245 privately owned holiday homes which are quite separate from the touring pitches.

Facilities

The central sanitary block is very clean and is heated during cooler months. Vanity style washbasins and large controllable showers. Separate unit for disabled visitors doubles as a family room. Laundry facilities. Gas supplies. Free WiFi over part of site. Off site: Canal fishing 300 yds. Over Kellet 2 miles. Carnforth 3 miles. Historic Lancaster.

Open: 1 March - 10 January.

Directions

From M6 exit 35 take link road signed Over Kellet. Turn left on B6254. At Over Kellet village green turn left signed Capernwray and follow for 1.5 miles. Park is on the right at the end of a 0.5 mile drive. GPS: 54.13958, -2.71357

Charges guide

Per unit incl. electricity	£ 20.00

Carnforth
Silverdale Caravan Park

Middlebarrow Plain, Cove Road, Silverdale LA5 0SH (Lancashire) T: 01524 701508.
E: info@holgates.co.uk **alanrogers.com/UK5350**

This attractive, very high quality park is in an outstanding craggy, part-wooded, hillside location with fine views over Morecambe Bay. It takes 80 touring units, with 339 privately owned caravan holiday homes and 14 to rent, located in woodland away from the touring pitches. With just five grassy pitches for tents (steel pegs required), the remaining large touring pitches are on gravel hardstandings, all with 16A electricity, free TV connection, individual drainage and water points. The main complex with reception and the entrance barrier, provides a well stocked supermarket, lounge bar, restaurant with good value meals and a terrace with views over the bay. There is also an indoor leisure centre. Children have a choice of two adventure playgrounds and plenty of space for ball games. Also on site is a small but challenging pitch and putt course. Everything is completed to the highest standards.

Facilities

Two modern, heated toilet buildings are fully equipped with top quality fittings and include some private cubicles with WC and washbasin. Excellent provision for disabled visitors with a reserved pitch and parking bay adjacent. Launderette. Shop. Gas supplies. Bar and restaurant. Indoor pool (17x17 m, with lifeguard) with spa pool, steam room and sauna. Well equipped gym (charged). Playgrounds. Games room. Pitch and putt course (£2 per person). Facilities are limited mid week in January and early February. Off site: Riding, cycling, golf and fishing all within 4 miles. Morecambe and Lancaster 12 miles.

Open: All year excl. 6 November - 21 December.

Directions

From traffic lights in centre of Carnforth take road to Silverdale under low bridge. After 1 mile turn left signed Silverdale and after 2.5 miles over level crossing, carry on and turn right at T-junction. Follow Holgates sign from here watching for left then right forks (narrow roads). GPS: 54.176603, -2.836034

Charges guide

Per unit incl. 2 adults and all services	£ 31.00
extra person	£ 8.00
extra child (2-17 yrs)	£ 3.00

Minimum stays apply for all B.H. weekends.

AA Campsite of the Year 2011
Winner for England & Overall

Discover an ever-changing landscape

Discover the very best of British holidays in one of our award winning holiday parks and cottages. Situated in the unspoilt Cumbria Lancashire borders, nestled between the Coast and Lake District Mountains.

Holgates
Make the discovery

For all enquiries contact Holgates Caravan Parks
Tel: 01524 701508 or Email: info@holgates.co.uk
Website: www.holgates.co.uk

Carnforth
Bay View Holiday Park

A6 Main Road, Bolton Le Sands, Carnforth LA5 8ES (Lancashire) T: 01524 732854.
E: info@holgatesleisureparks.co.uk **alanrogers.com/UK5270**

Bay View has been developed by the Holgate family into an excellent addition to their group. Situated on the north Lancashire coast, the park is an ideal base for exploring the Lake District, North Yorkshire and the Forest of Bowland. The park is divided into several grassy fields and many of the pitches have stunning views over Morecambe Bay, while others look towards the Lakeland Fells. It is a very open park with little shade. Of the 72 touring pitches, all have 6-15A electricity and are fully serviced. There are also 110 pitches for caravan holiday homes.

Facilities

Three toilet blocks with facilities for disabled visitors. Good laundry. Motorcaravan service point. Shop. An excellent new bar/restaurant with a pool room and children's games room. Playground for young children. Field for ball games. Farm park (animals can be viewed). WiFi (charged). Off site: Fishing 200 yds. Golf and riding 3 miles. Cruises on Lancaster Canal. Leighton Moss RSPB nature reserve. Shopping in nearby Lancaster and Kendal 15 miles.

Open: 1 March - 31 October.

Directions

From M6 exit 35 take the A601M to roundabout and follow signs to Morecambe. Continue through Carnforth and after mini-roundabout look for site sign (at main entrance) in 500 yds. on the right. GPS will take you to rear entrance, which is less accessible. GPS: 54.11602, -2.78791

Charges guide

Per unit with 2 persons, car and electricity	£ 20.00 - £ 25.00
extra person	£ 8.00

FREE Alan Rogers Travel Card
Extra benefits and savings - see page 10

Chester
Manor Wood Country Caravan Park
Coddington, Chester CH3 9EN (Cheshire) T: 01829 782990. E: info@manorwoodcaravans.co.uk
alanrogers.com/UK5220

Arranged on well maintained grass, on farmland with views towards the Welsh hills, this family owned and orientated site has a small swimming pool for use in the summer months. There are 50 level touring pitches with 16A electricity, accessed via tarmac roads. Thirty-nine have hardstandings, 30 have water and drainage. The footpaths and bridle paths from the park will appeal to those with an interest in nature, walking and cycling. Pools on the site allow a range of activities from serious fishing to pond dipping.

Facilities

Heated sanitary unit with showers and washbasins in cubicles. Disabled/family room. Laundry. Covered dishwashing sinks. Basics can be purchased. Small swimming pool (heated May-Sept), adventure play area (6-14 yrs). Games room with pool and table tennis. Tennis court. Security barrier with unrestricted card access. WiFi. Dog walk (2 dogs per pitch) and wellie washing. Gas available. Fishing £5 per rod. Separate, central car parking for a number of pitches. Off site: Restaurant within 1 mile. Golf courses 1.5 and 2 miles. Riding 8 miles. Bicycle hire, Chester and zoo 10 miles.

Open: All year.

Directions

From A41 Whitchurch to Chester Road, take the A534 towards Wrexham, pass Carden Park Hotel and turn opposite Cock o'Barton. After a short distance through Barton the road narrows, bear left and continue for 500 yds. to find the site on the left. Do not rely on sat nav. GPS: 53.087471, -2.829731

Charges guide

Per unit incl. 2 persons and electricity	£ 13.50 - £ 24.00
extra person	£ 3.00
child	£ 3.00

Knutsford
Royal Vale Caravan Park
London Road, Allostock, Knutsford WA16 9JD (Cheshire) T: 01565 722355. E: canistay@royalvale.co.uk
alanrogers.com/UK5245

This brand new, family run site for adults only is located in countryside close to Knutsford, with Tatton Park and other attractions nearby. Expect a relaxed stay on 52 all-weather pitches, each with water, electricity and drainage, attractively arranged around a fully appointed, heated, modern central sanitary unit. There are a further ten grass pitches for tents. Access to the level, gravel and solid hardstandings is via compacted gravel roadways, landscaped on grass with mature and developing hedges and trees.

Facilities

The modern sanitary units include automatic lighting and the eco theme sees low level site lighting and reed beds servicing waste water. Facilities for disabled visitors include separate wet room and a toilet in each of the sanitary units. Laundry. WiFi (charged). Gas available. Off site: Golf 3 miles. Knutsford 3 miles. Tatton Park 6 miles. Jodrell Bank Observatory 6 miles.

Open: All year excl. 8 January - 6 February.

Directions

From south on M6 take exit 18 and follow A50 north towards Holmes Chapel for 4 miles. At Allostock continue 1.2 miles, passing an Alfa Romeo garage on the right and turning left into the park at the old Drover's Arms Pub. GPS: 53.25170, -2.36984

Charges guide

Per unit incl. 2 persons and electricity	£ 24.00

Lancaster
Moss Wood Caravan Park
Crimbles Lane, Cockerham, Lancaster LA2 0ES (Lancashire) T: 01524 791041. E: info@mosswood.co.uk
alanrogers.com/UK5272

Moss Wood is a well established park set in a secluded rural location near the village of Cockerham. You can be sure of a friendly welcome from the park wardens Ian and Sandra when you arrive. A sheltered field has 25 touring pitches on level hardstandings (steel pegs required) with 16A electricity. Most also have water and drainage. Screened from the touring area by a high fence so not visually intrusive are 175 privately owned holiday homes. A purpose-built log cabin houses reception and a shop which sells basic supplies. The approach road to the park is narrow (with passing places) so care should be taken.

Facilities

New centrally located sanitary block (key entry) is kept spotlessly clean and provides vanity style washbasins and roomy, preset showers. Fully equipped facilities for disabled visitors. Covered food preparation area, laundry and dishwashing facilities. Adventure playground. Large field for ball games. Fishing lake (fenced). Woodland dog walking. Off site: Pubs at Cockerham 1 mile. Riding 3 miles. Beach 5 miles. Golf 6 miles. Garstang, historic Lancaster, seaside town of Morecambe and the Lune Valley within easy reach. Local buses stop at end of lane.

Open: 1 March - 31 October.

Directions

Park is 1 mile west of Cockerham on the A588. Leave M6 at exit 33 joining the A6 southbound and follow signs for Cockerham. A588 is 4 miles. Site is signed on the left. GPS: 53.93788, -2.82087

Charges guide

Per unit incl. 2 adults, 2 children and electricity	£ 20.50 - £ 5.50
extra person	£ 3.00
awning	£ 3.00

For latest campsite news visit
alanrogers.com

Lytham Saint Annes

Eastham Hall Caravan Park

Saltcotes Road, Lytham-Saint Annes FY8 4LS (Lancashire) T: 01253 737907. E: info@easthamhall.co.uk

alanrogers.com/UK5295

Eastham Hall is a well established, family run park set in rural Lancashire between the Victorian town of Lytham and the pretty village of Wrea Green. Entering by an electronic barrier system, one sees an area of 150 caravan holiday homes. Quite separate are around 173 pitches for touring units and seasonal rental on open plan, mostly level grass, with 10A electricity. Of these, there are 49 super pitches on hardstanding and grass with full services including 16A electricity. Tents are not accepted. A further five extra large pitches are on grass (units up to 28 feet can be taken). Mature trees border the park and shrubs and bushes separate the various areas. The reception is spacious with lots of tourist information, and at one end there is a large, well stocked shop. The park has no bar or clubhouse, but Lytham is just five minutes by car or a pleasant twenty minute walk. The flat terrain is also ideal for cycling.

Facilities

Three toilet blocks are kept clean and are being updated to include solar panels for heating and private cubicles. Laundry. Excellent facilities for disabled visitors. Gas supplies. Well stocked shop. Adventure play area and large sports field. Barrier (£10 deposit). WiFi throughout park. Off site: Local bus stops at entrance to park. Excellent pub in Wrea Green. Golf and riding 1 mile. Boat launching 2 miles. Shops and restaurants in Lytham, fishing 2.5 miles. Blackpool 6 miles.

Open: 1 March - 31 October.

Directions

From M55 take exit 3 and turn left for Kirkham. At roundabouts follow signs for Wrea Green and Lytham. Continue on B5259 passing Grapes pub and village green. After 1.5 miles cross level crossing (Moss Side) and park is 1 mile on left. GPS: 53.75375, -2.94225

Charges guide

Per unit incl. 1-4 persons	
and electricity	£ 15.00 - £ 28.00
serviced pitch	£ 19.00 - £ 32.00
extra person	£ 2.50
child (5-11 yrs)	£ 1.00
dog	£ 2.00

Eastham Hall Caravan Park - a secluded tranquil Holiday Park

This family run park is a lovely oasis of calm in beautiful rural surroundings. Only 1½ miles from the stylish Victorian town of Lytham, 2 miles from the pretty village of Wrea Green and 6 miles from Blackpool.

01253 737907 • info@easthamhall.co.uk • www.easthamhall.co.uk

Eastham Hall Caravan Park, Saltcotes Road, Lytham St Annes, Lancashire, FY8 4LS

Eastham Hall

Northwich

Lamb Cottage Caravan Park

Dalefords Lane, Whitegate, Northwich CW8 2BN (Cheshire) T: 01606 882302. E: info@lambcottage.co.uk

alanrogers.com/UK5240

At this peaceful, family run, adults only park set in the midst of the lovely Vale Royal area of Cheshire, emphasis is placed on attention to detail. Seasonal and touring caravan pitches are arranged separately on 41 large, landscaped pitches, all with 16A electricity, gravel hardstandings, water and drainage. There are an additional four motorcaravan pitches with hardstandings and electricity. Only breathable ground-sheets are permitted and tents are not accepted. Nearby are Delamere Forest with walking and mountain biking trails, Whitegate Way walking trail, Oulton Park Motor Racing Circuit, castles at Peckforton and Beeston and, within 12 miles, the city of Chester.

Facilities

En-suite toilets, showers and washbasins are housed in a custom built unit, which has extra toilets and washbasins and additional room for disabled guests. Laundry room. All maintained to the highest standards. Recycling of glass and paper. Calor Gas stocked. Fenced dog walk (max. 2 dogs per unit permitted). Pleasant finishing touches include notelets in the payphone booth and a chalet with books, magazines and DVDs to loan and tourist information to take away. WiFi (charged). Off site: Pub serving food within 1 mile. Riding 1.5 miles. Golf 2 miles. Supermarket 3 miles. Fishing 3 miles. Bicycle hire 4 miles.

Open: 1 March - 31 October.

Directions

From M6 exit 19 take A556 towards Chester. After 12 miles turn left at traffic lights (signed Winsford and Whitegate) into Dalefords Lane. Continue for 1 mile and site entrance is on right between a white house and a bungalow. GPS: 53.218244, -2.578655

Charges guide

Per unit incl. 2 persons	
and electricity	£ 20.00 - £ 26.00
extra person	£ 5.00
dog	£ 1.00

FREE Alan Rogers Travel Card
Extra benefits and savings - see page 10

Ormskirk

Abbey Farm Caravan Park

Dark Lane, Ormskirk L40 5TX (Lancashire) T: 01695 572686. E: abbeyfarm@yahoo.com
alanrogers.com/UK5280

This quiet, well equipped, family park beside the Abbey ruins has views over open farmland. It is an ideal base for a longer stay with plenty of interest in the local area, including Ormskirk parish church, unusual for having both a tower and a spire. The park is divided into small paddocks, one of which is for privately owned seasonal units, one for tents, the others for touring units, plus a rally field for special events. The 60 touring pitches, all with 16A electricity, and 12 of which have water and waste water, are on neatly mown level grass, separated by shrubs and colourful flower borders. Mature trees provide some shade.

Facilities

The main toilet block is modern, heated and spotless, providing controllable hot showers. Dual purpose family bathroom with facilities for disabled visitors. A smaller unit has individual shower/WC/washbasin cubicles. Laundry room. Small well stocked shop at reception. Butcher calls twice weekly. Indoor games room. Small adventure playground and large field for ball games. Fishing lake (£2 per rod, per day). WiFi over site (charged). Off site: Local market Thurs. and Sat. Southport 10 miles.

Open: All year.

Directions

From M6 exit 27 take A5209 (Parbold) road. After 5 miles turn left (just before garage) onto B5240, and then first right into Hob Cross Lane, following signs to site. GPS: 53.5698, -2.85665

Charges guide

Per unit incl. 2 persons and electricity	£ 18.20 - £ 19.70
extra person	£ 3.50
child (5-15 yrs)	£ 2.00

Preston

Royal Umpire Caravan Park

Southport Road, Croston, Preston PR26 9JB (Lancashire) T: 01772 600257. E: reception@royalumpire.co.uk
alanrogers.com/UK5290

Royal Umpire is a spacious park near the coast and the M6 for overnight or longer stays. The entrance to the park is past a large, grass area leading to the security barrier with reception immediately to the left; slightly ahead is an unusual sunken garden area that is a pleasing feature. Comprising 60 acres, the park has 189 pitches, almost all with 10A electricity, but a few with 16A. About 75 per cent of the pitches now have gravel hardstanding, some have TV and water connections. Tarmac and gravel roads connect the various pitch areas. There is a shop within 100 yards and a good choice of pubs serving food.

Facilities

Two modern, heated, toilet blocks, one beside reception, the other centrally situated. Fully equipped laundry. Very good facilities for disabled visitors are shared with baby facilities (key access, £20 deposit). Bar (B.Hs only). Takeaway food (weekend, May-Sept). Adventure playground. Children's entertainment (Sat. May-Aug). Field area for ball games. Rally field. Dog exercise area. Free WiFi over part of site. No Charcoal barbecues. Off site: A short walk takes you to the village of Croston.

Open: All year.

Directions

From south use M6 exit 27 onto the A5209 but immediately right on B5250 and follow towards Eccleston, joining A581 at Newtown (5 miles). Site is clearly signed with wide entrance east of Croston. GPS: 53.66669, -2.74827

Charges guide

Per unit incl. 2 adults, 2 children and electricity	£ 16.00 - £ 30.00
extra person	£ 2.50

Southport

Riverside Holiday Park

Southport New Road, Banks, Southport PR9 8DF (Lancashire) T: 01704 228 886.
E: reception@harrisonleisureuk.com **alanrogers.com/UK5285**

Situated by a busy road on the outskirts of the Lancashire coastal town of Southport, Riverside Holiday Park covers 80 acres and has a total of 620 pitches. Of these, 200 are for touring units and tents, 70 with 10A electricity, some with hardstanding. The park is level and open with little shade. A narrow unfenced river runs through the park where fishing in season is possible (licence required). Apart from an outdoor play area for younger children, most of the activities on the park centre around the indoor games room, with live entertainment, a pool room, and a large amusement arcade.

Facilities

Three heated toilet blocks (key entry) only one of which has showers. At busy times these could be stretched and cleaning is variable. Facilities for disabled visitors and babies. Laundry. Well stocked shop. Large bar with TV. Café. Games room. Pool room. Large amusement arcade. Play area. River fishing (with licence). Family club in high season with games, fancy dress, discos etc. Dog walking area. Bus route. WiFi in café. Off site: Beach 5 miles.

Open: All year excl. 1-13 February.

Directions

From the south, M6 exit 26 take M58 to the end, take A59 north towards Preston. From the north, M6 exit 31 take A59 south towards Liverpool/Southport. Both directions, just south of Tarleton, turn west on A565 towards Southport. Park on left in 3 miles. GPS: 53.666955, -2.901056

Charges guide

Per unit incl. electricity	£ 17.00 - £ 25.00

For latest campsite news visit
alanrogers.com

Southport

Willowbank Holiday Home & Touring Park

Coastal Road, Ainsdale, Southport PR8 3ST (Mersey) T: 01704 571566. E: info@willowbankcp.co.uk
alanrogers.com/UK5360

Willowbank Park is well situated for the Sefton coast and Southport, set on the edge of sand dunes amongst mature, wind swept trees. Entrance to the park is controlled by a barrier, with a pass-key issued at the excellent reception building which doubles as a sales office for the substantial, high quality caravan holiday home development. There are 87 touring pitches, 30 on gravel hardstandings, 24 on grass and a further 33 pitches, all with 16A electricity; these are on grass hardstanding using an environmentally friendly reinforcement system. Large units are accepted by prior arrangement. The owners are very well supported by the reception team which has considerable experience in managing the touring park. There could be some noise from the nearby main road. This is a good area for cycling and walking with the Trans Pennine Way being adjacent. The attractions of Southport with its parks, gardens, funfair and shopping are four miles away. Latest arrival time is 21.00.

Facilities	Directions
The purpose built, heated toilet block (refurbished in 2010) is of a high standard including an excellent bathroom for disabled visitors, although the showers are rather compact. Baby room. Laundry. Motorcaravan service point. Play area. Field for ball games. Beauty treatments. WiFi throughout (charged). Off site: Golf and riding 0.5 miles. Beach 1.5 miles. Fishing 4 miles. Bicycle hire 4.5 miles. Martin Mere nature reserve nearby.	Park is 4 miles south of Southport. From Ainsdale on A565 head south for 1.5 miles to second traffic lights (Woodvale) and turn right into Coastal Road to site on left in 150 yds. GPS: 53.5888, -3.044

Open: All year excl. February.

Charges guide

Per unit incl. 2 persons and electricity	£ 14.50 - £ 17.70
hardstanding	£ 1.70
extra person	£ 3.50

Willowbank Holiday Home & Touring Park

* 87 pitches available * Gravel Hardstanding * Grass
* Grass Hardstanding * All with electricity hook up
* Level park throughout * Luxury heated shower and toilet facilities * Laundry Dish washing room * Separate shower and toilet room with wheelchair access * Childrens' play area * Dog exercise area * Strictly no vans or commercial vehicles admitted to the park

Early booking is essential for busy periods and special events such as the Flower Show and Air Show

Willowbank, Coastal Road, Ainsdale, Southport PR8 3ST
Tel: 01704 571566   Fax: 01704 571576   www.willowbankcp.co.uk

---

Thornton-Cleveleys

Kneps Farm Holiday Park

River Road, Stanah, Thornton-Cleveleys FY5 5LR (Lancashire) T: 01253 823632.
E: enquiries@knepsfarm.co.uk **alanrogers.com/UK5300**

A well established park with top class, modern facilities, Kneps Farm is still operated by the family who opened it in 1967. Next to Wyre Country Park, it makes an excellent base from which to explore the area. A VNPR-operated barrier system flanks the reception building which also houses a well stocked shop. The 60 marked and numbered touring pitches are generally on hardstandings, 48 with 16A electricity, and all are accessed from tarmac roads. There are also some grassy pitches and a separate area with 50 caravan holiday homes (most privately owned).

Facilities	Directions
The large, centrally heated sanitary building is warm and inviting with ten individual family bathrooms, each providing a WC, basin and bath/shower. Separate toilet facilities with electric handwash units for men and women. Well equipped room for disabled visitors. Combined baby care/first aid room. Laundry room. Small, well stocked shop. Small, fenced playground. Up to two dogs are accepted per unit. WiFi in reception area. Off site: Sailing 300 yds. Beach and golf 2.5 miles. Fishing 4 miles.	From M55 exit 3, take A585 towards Fleetwood. Turn left at lights, then right at lights by Shell station (for Thornton-Cleveleys), straight across next lights, then right at the next roundabout by River Wyre Hotel. After one mile (past school) turn right at mini-roundabout into Stanah Road, continue across second mini-roundabout and eventually into River Road. Do not use sat nav. GPS: 53.87903, -2.98506

Open: 1 March - 15 November.

Charges guide

Per unit incl. 2 adults, 2 children and electricity	£ 24.50 - £ 30.00

FREE Alan Rogers Travel Card
Extra benefits and savings - see page 10

Want independent campsite reviews at your fingertips?

With spectacular lakes, undulating fells, impressive mountains and lush green valleys, Cumbria is ideal for those who wish to get away from it all and unwind in peaceful, natural surroundings, or for the more active who want to participate in a range of outdoor pursuits.

Cumbria is best known for the beautiful Lake District National Park, with the picturesque valleys and lakes of Windermere, Ullswater and Derwentwater, each with its own distinctive character. Windermere offers no shortage of watersports, whereas Ullswater mainly attracts peaceful sailing boats. While the Lake District is well known, there are also many quiet, undiscovered areas in the region including the wild, rugged moors of the north Pennines and the beautiful Eden Valley, an ideal place for a casual stroll along the riverside footpaths. The western lakes and fells offer more tranquillity. Here the fells drop down to a long and spectacular coastline, with many undiscovered corners from Ennerdale and Eskdale to the sandstone cliffs of St. Bees Head, now part of a designated Heritage Coast. The Lake District peninsulas along the southern coast of Cumbria also display beautiful scenery and are home to a cluster of ancient ruins such as Furness Abbey and the medieval castle built by monks on Piel Island. Rich in heritage, the historic city of Carlisle, which was sited on the Roman-built Hadrian's wall, boasts an impressive castle, Cumbria's only cathedral, a superb Victorian covered market and an array of speciality shops.

Places of interest

Barrow-in-Furness: South Lakes Wild Animal Park; Dalton Castle; Furness Abbey; Piel Island; indoor market.

Carlisle: Citadel and old courts; Tullie House museum and art gallery; cathedral.

Ravenglass: Muncaster Castle with gardens and owl centre; Ravenglass and Eskdale Railway;

Ulverston: the world's only Laurel and Hardy museum.

Kendal: historic riverside town famous for its mint cake and castle ruins; Abbot Hall Art Gallery; Sizergh Castle.

Ambleside: Beatrix Pottery museum; 17th-century Bridge House built over the river.

Windermere: Blackwell Arts & Crafts House; World of Beatrix Potter; Grizedale Forest.

Grasmere: Dove Cottage and Wordsworth Museum; Helm Crag; Gingerbread shop.

Did you know?

Cumbria has the steepest road in England, called the Hardknott Pass.

The Lake District was the inspiration for many poets, writers and artists, including William Wordsworth, Beatrix Potter and John Ruskin.

Windermere is Britain's largest natural lake at 10.5 miles long.

Bassenthwaite is the only real lake in the Lake District! All the others are either meres, (Windermere) or waters (Derwentwater, Coniston Water and Ullswater).

Stretching 73 miles, Hadrian's Wall was built by Romans in the second century.

Kendal's famous mint cake is popular with walkers and was taken on the Transarctic Expedition of 1914-1917.

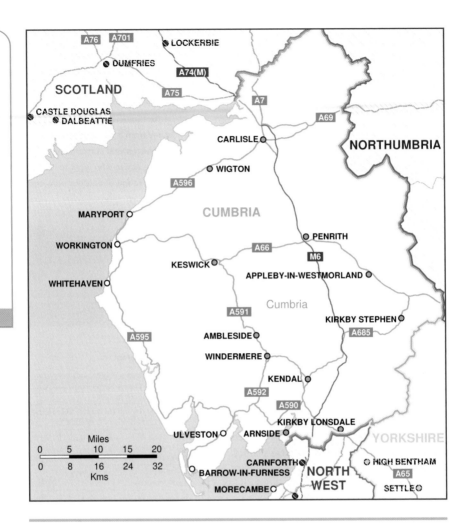

Ambleside

Skelwith Fold Caravan Park

Ambleside LA22 0HX (Cumbria) T: 01539 432277. E: info@skelwith.com

alanrogers.com/UK5520

Skelwith Fold has been developed in the extensive grounds of a country estate taking advantage of the wealth of mature trees and shrubs. The 300 privately owned caravan holiday homes and 150 touring pitches are absorbed into this unspoilt natural environment, sharing it with red squirrels and other wildlife in several discrete areas branching off the central, mile long main driveway. Touring pitches (no tents) are on gravel hardstanding and metal pegs will be necessary for awnings. Electricity hook-ups (10-16A) and basic amenities are available in all areas. Youngsters, and indeed their parents, will find endless pleasure exploring over 90 acres of wild woodland and, if early risers, it is possible to see deer, foxes, etc. at the almost hidden tarn deep in the woods.

Facilities

Three toilet blocks, well situated to serve all areas, have the usual facilities including laundry, drying and ironing rooms. Facilities for disabled visitors. Motorcaravan service point. Well stocked, licensed shop. Battery charging, gas and caravan spares and accessories. Adventure play area. Family recreation area with picnic tables and goal posts in the Lower Glade. Off site: Pubs within walking distance. Fishing 200 m. Ambleside village 2.5 miles. Riding and sailing 3 miles.

Open: 1 March - 15 November.

Directions

From Ambleside take A593 towards Coniston. Pass through Clappergate and on far outskirts watch for B5286 to Hawkshead on left. Park is clearly signed 1 mile down this road on the right. Do not use sat nav to find this park – this will bring you to a locked gate! GPS: 54.41715, -2.995283

Charges guide

Per pitch	£ 20.50 - £ 26.50
incl. electricity	£ 23.50 - £ 29.50
awning	£ 3.00

Discounts for weekly or monthly stays.

Appleby-in-Westmorland

Wild Rose Park

Ormside, Appleby-in-Westmorland CA16 6EJ (Cumbria) T: 01768 351077. E: reception@wildrose.co.uk

alanrogers.com/UK5570

Set in the Eden Valley within easy reach of the Lake District and the Yorkshire Dales, Wild Rose is a well known park. The entrance is inviting with its well mown grass, trim borders and colourful flower displays. It is immediately apparent that this is a much loved park, and this is reflected throughout the site in the care and attention to detail. There are 226 touring pitches all with electricity, however 105 also provide water and waste water, plus the site boasts on-site wardens to ensure that everything is always neat and tidy. Wild Rose deserves its excellent reputation, which the owners strive to maintain and improve. There are five distinct areas on the park providing a variety of pitches and services. Hazel Heights and Egglestone Tiers provide fully serviced super pitches with hardstanding, Braithwaite Fold and the Chesters have pitches with electricity and shared water points. The grass area of Donkey's Nest provides pitches with shared electricity and water. There are five wooden teepees and ten Holiday Home units to rent providing all year round luxurious camping. A member of the Best of British group.

Facilities

Three toilet blocks (two heated) of excellent quality and kept spotlessly clean. Most washbasins are in cubicles. Facilities for babies and disabled visitors. Fully equipped laundry. Motorcaravan service point. Exceptionally well stocked shop incl. gas (1/4-1/11). Licensed restaurant with takeaway and conservatory/coffee lounge (weekends only in low season). Outdoor pool (late May-Sept and open 10.00-18.00). Indoor playroom for under fives. Games room. TV room. Cinema room. Tennis. Bicycle hire. Off site: Fishing 2 miles. Golf and riding 3 miles.

Open: All year.

Directions

Park is signed south off B6260 road 1.5 miles southwest of Appleby. Follow signs to park, towards Ormside. GPS: 54.54893, -2.46422

Charges guide

Per unit incl. 2 persons and electricity	£ 17.00 - £ 27.50
extra person (over 4 yrs)	£ 2.50
'super pitch' incl. mains services and awning	£ 19.00 - £ 29.50

Less 10% for 7 nights or more and for over 60s.

Arnside

Hollins Farm Caravan & Camp Site

Far Arnside, Arnside LA5 0SL (Cumbria) T: 01524 701508. E: Info@hollinsfarm.co.uk

alanrogers.com/UK5595

Improvements continue at Hollins Farm since it was taken over by the Holgate family. In a superb location overlooking Morecambe Bay, it lies between two of North Lancashire's most picturesque coastal villages, Silverdale and Arnside. The park comprises several fields divided by trees. Of the 100 pitches, there are 40 for touring all with 16A electricity, water and TV connections, although large units may have some difficulty negotiating the narrow country lanes. The site's new facilities block is built in local stone and provides visitors with high quality facilities, plus a games room and TV lounge.

Facilities

New facilities block with underfloor heating. Facilities for disabled visitors. Launderette. Games room. TV lounge. Shop (1/3-31/10). Fridge hire. Play area. Caravan storage. Amenities at Silverdale Park (five minutes walk away): bar, restaurant, indoor pool, gym and other leisure facilities (some charges). Off site: Leighton Moss RSPB Nature reserve. Cross Bay walks. Golf 2 miles. Fishing 9 miles.

Open: 14 March - 31 October.

Directions

From M6 exit 35 take the A601(M) and at first roundabout take second exit A6 North. In 2.5 miles take the left turn signed Yealand Redmayne, then follow site signs for Holgates Caravan Park through Silverdale. Hollins Farm is 0.5 miles beyond Holgates. GPS: 54.18077, -2.84352

Charges guide

Per unit incl. 2 persons	£ 26.00 - £ 2~

(219)

Carlisle

Green Acres Caravan Park

High Knells, Houghton, Carlisle CA6 4JW (Cumbria) T: 01228 675418. E: info@caravanpark-cumbria.com

alanrogers.com/UK5640

Green Acres is a small, family run, adults only park. Situated in beautiful, rural surroundings, yet only two miles from junction 44 of the M6, it is perfect for an overnight stop or a longer stay to enjoy Cumbria, Hadrian's Wall and the delights of Carlisle city (four miles away). The Browns have developed Green Acres into an attractive, well maintained and level touring park. There are 30 numbered pitches, all on large hardstandings, arranged in a semicircle, with 10A electricity connections and four serviced pitches (16A). A large camping field includes 12 new hardstanding super pitches on one side for seasonal letting.

Facilities

New toilet block has showers and two additional wetrooms with shower, washbasin and WC. (suitable for disabled visitors). Laundry room with washing machine and tumble dryer. Car/caravan wash area. Caravan storage. Off site: Shop. Golf 3 miles. Fishing 8 miles. Riding and bicycle hire 10 miles.

Open: 1 April - end October.

Directions

Leave M6 at junction 44 and take A689E signed Brampton for 1 mile. Turn left signed Scaleby and site is 1 mile on left. GPS: 54.94505, -2.90728

Charges guide

Per unit incl. 2 persons and electricity	£ 15.00 - £ 19.00
extra person	£ 3.00

Kendal

Waters Edge Caravan Park

Crooklands, Kendal LA7 7NN (Cumbria) T: 015395 67708. E: info@watersedgecaravanpark.co.uk

alanrogers.com/UK5645

Close to the M6 motorway, Waters Edge makes an ideal stopover. However, it is also well worth a longer stay, being centrally situated for visiting the Lake District and the Yorkshire Dales. Surrounded by farmland, the park is long and narrow with one road running down the centre and the pitches on either side. There are 26 level touring pitches, all with hardstanding. These are open and a little on the small side. At each end of the park there are six privately-owned caravan holiday homes. There is a play area for children, but parents of young children would need to be vigilant here as there are well signed but unfenced fast flowing streams at both sides of the park.

Facilities

Centrally located heated toilet block, although a little dated, is spotlessly clean with showers and washbasins in cubicles. Facilities for disabled visitors. Laundry. No motorcaravan service point. Shop for basics. Bar with TV. Off site: Restaurant 300 yds. Riding 3 km. Golf 8 km. Canal and boat trips. Kendal 15 mins. drive.

Open: March - November.

Directions

From M6 exit 36 take A65 (east) (Kirkby Lonsdale) for 300 yds. At next roundabout take 1st exit (Crooklands and Endmoor). Park entrance is 1 mile on the right at Crooklands Motor Co. GPS: 54.24697, -2.7162

Charges guide

Per unit incl. electricity	£ 16.50 - £ 23.80
awning	£ 1.25

Kendal

Ashes Exclusively Adult Caravan Park

New Hutton, Kendal LA8 0AS (Cumbria) T: 01539 731833. E: info@ashescaravanpark.co.uk

alanrogers.com/UK5650

The Ashes is a small, friendly, adult only park in an extremely peaceful setting in the rolling Cumbrian countryside, yet less than three miles from the M6, and only slightly further from Kendal. Thus it is not only a convenient night stop, but also a useful base from which to explore the Lake District and the Yorkshire Dales. A very tidy park, the central grass area is attractively planted with shrubs and bushes and there is an open vista (with little shade). There are 25 hardstanding gravel pitches, all with 10A electrical connections. These are neatly placed around the perimeter with an oval access road. The whole area slopes gently down from the entrance, with some pitches fairly level and others with a little more slope (levelling system for caravans on all pitches). No tents are accepted other than trailer tents.

Facilities

A small, purpose built stone building with a slate roof houses two unisex shower rooms (underfloor heating) and the washing and toilet facilities. New facilities for disabled visitors. Laundry room. No shop. New electronic barrier. TV signal booster. WiFi (charged). Off site: Mr and Mrs Mason have prepared a full information sheet with details of shopping, eating and many other local venues. Supermarket 2 miles. Fishing 2 miles. Golf and riding 3 miles. Bicycle hire and Kendal 4 miles.

Open: 1 March - 4 November.

Directions

From M6 exit 37 follow the A684 towards Kendal for 2 miles. Just past a white cottage turn sharp left at crossroads signed New Hutton. Site is on right in 0.75 miles at a left bend. Only approach and depart using this road. GPS: 54.313133, -2.675

Charges guide

Per unit incl. 2 persons and electricity	£ 19.00 - £ 22.20
extra person (over 18s only)	£ 5.50
extra car/trailer	£ 2.00

Keswick
Castlerigg Hall Caravan & Camping Park

Castlerigg Hall, Keswick CA12 4TE (Cumbria) T: 01768 774499. E: info@castlerigg.co.uk

alanrogers.com/UK5660

This well laid out park was started in the late 1950s by the Jackson family, who over the years have developed and improved the site whilst maintaining its character. Good use has been made of the traditional stone buildings to house the reception and shop, whilst another building houses a modern amenity block along with a really excellent campers' kitchen. Tarmac roads wend their way around the site to the separate tent area of 110 pitches. Gently sloping with some shelter, these pitches have fine views across Keswick, Derwentwater and the western Fells. The 45 caravan pitches tend to be on terraces, again overlooking the lake. Each terrace has a maximum of eight pitches, all on hardstanding and with 10A electricity and nearly all with a water tap and grey water drain. Places to visit include Keswick (about 20 minutes walk), Derwentwater, Ullswater, Penrith, Carlisle and Hadrian's Wall.

Facilities

The main toilet block is beautifully fitted out, fully tiled and heated, with showers, vanity style washbasins (two in cabins) and hair care areas. Unit for disabled visitors (key). Baby area. Fully equipped laundry and dishwashing area. Games room and campers' kitchen complete with microwave, toasters, kettle and hot plates. Two other toilet blocks are older in style but newly decorated and clean. Reception houses tourist information and a well stocked shop (with gas). WiFi over part of site. Off site: Hotel/pub for meals adjacent to site. Fishing, golf, riding, bicycle hire and boat launching, all 2 km.

Open: 11 March - 7 November.

Directions

From Penrith take A66 towards Keswick and Cockermouth. Leave at first sign for Keswick (A591) and follow to junction (A5271). Turn left on A591 (Windermere) and after 1 mile, take small road on right signed Castlerigg and Rakefoot. Park entrance is on right after 400 yds. GPS: 54.5931, -3.112583

Charges guide

Per unit incl. 2 persons and electricity	£ 19.50 - £ 29.00
extra person (over 4 yrs)	£ 3.50 - £ 5.00
tent per adult	£ 6.95 - £ 8.90
dog	£ 1.60 - £ 2.40

Castlerigg Hall
Caravan and Camping Park
the Park with the View. . .
in the heart of the Lakes
Keswick, Cumbria CA12 4TE - English Lake District
Tel: +44 (0)17687 74499   www.castlerigg.co.uk   E-mail: info@castlerigg.co.uk

Kirkby Lonsdale
Woodclose Caravan Park

Kirkby Lonsdale LA6 2SE (Cumbria) T: 01524 271597. E: info@woodclosepark.com

alanrogers.com/UK5605

Woodclose is an established, nine-acre park situated in the Lune Valley, just one mile from the market town of Kirkby Lonsdale. It offers a peaceful and secluded setting catering for walkers, tourers and people who just want to relax. The whole park has a very well cared for appearance with well mown grass, flowering tubs and neat hedges. Screened by a hedge and placed around the perimeter are several seasonal pitches with touring units being placed in the centre. These pitches are numbered and mostly level, some on hardstanding, some on grass, with 16A electricity and digital TV hook-ups.

Facilities

Two toilet blocks are unisex in large, heated, individual rooms with toilets, washbasin and toilet, or washbasin and shower, all well equipped and very clean. Laundry. The second block is in the lower part, again all unisex in cubicles. Facilities for disabled visitors. Shop. Small adventure play area. Bicycle hire. WiFi over site (charged). American motorhomes accepted (limited space). Gates locked 24.00-07.30. Off site: Golf 1 mile. Fishing 7 miles.

Open: 1 March - 1 November.

Directions

From M6 exit 36 take A65 to Kirkby Lonsdale. Site is off the A65 in 6 miles from the motorway. GPS: 54.19835, -2.585017

Charges guide

Per unit incl. 2 persons and electricity	£ 12.50 - £ 23.00
extra person	£ 4.00

FREE Alan Rogers Travel Card
Extra benefits and savings - see page 10

Kirkby Stephen

Pennine View Caravan & Camping Park

Station Road, Kirkby Stephen CA17 4SZ (Cumbria) T: 01768 371717

alanrogers.com/UK5600

Suitable for night halts or longer breaks to visit the Lake District or the Yorkshire Dales, Pennine View is a super small park, well managed and well maintained. With a very attractive rockery at the entrance, the whole site is very neat and tidy. Level, numbered pitches with gravel hardstanding are arranged around the perimeter with grass pitches in the centre. The pitches are of a good size (some being very large) and all are supplied with 16A electricity hook-ups. Pennine View was opened in 1990 and is built on reclaimed land from a former railway goods yard. One end of the park adjoins the River Eden.

Facilities

Built of local stone, the modern toilet block is accessed by a digital keypad and includes individual wash cubicles and deep sink for a baby bath. Both ladies and men have large en-suite units for disabled visitors. Well equipped laundry room. Gas available. Play area. Off site: Nearby hotel offers bar meals. Bicycle hire 300 m. Kirkby Stephen 1 mile (on the Settle-Carlisle railway line). Golf 4 miles.

Open: 1 March - 31 October.

Directions

Park is on the A685 on the southerly outskirts of Kirkby Stephen (just under 1 mile from the town centre). Turn left at small site sign opposite the Croglin Castle hotel. Site is 50 yds. on right. GPS: 54.461667, -2.353367

Charges guide

Per person	£ 6.50 - £ 6.90
pitch	£ 7.00 - £ 8.00

Penrith

Sykeside Camping Park

Brotherswater, Patterdale, Penrith CA11 0NZ (Cumbria) T: 01768 482239. E: info@sykeside.co.uk

alanrogers.com/UK5560

This small touring park is located in a really beautiful, quiet spot in the northern Lakes area (it is just 400 yards from Brotherswater). With views up the Dovedale valley, the park has 100 pitches in the valley floor, mainly for tents. There are 24 for motorcaravans on hardstanding, all with 10A electricity. Pitches are not marked and campers arrange themselves to best enjoy the superb views. The stone-built building, an original barn, near the entrance houses all the facilities. These include the recently extended and refurbished Barn End bar where meals are served.

Facilities

The toilet block includes hot showers and has been refurbished, with a chemical disposal point added. Small launderette and dishwashing room. Self-service shop with camping equipment, gas and an ice-pack service, doubles as reception. Cosy, licensed bar and restaurant (daily in summer, weekends only in winter). Bunkhouse accommodation for 30 persons in various groupings. Fishing nearby. Free WiFi in bar area. Off site: Bicycle hire 3 miles. Good sailing on Ullswater 4 miles. Riding 8 miles. Golf 10 miles. The Brotherswater Inn is adjacent.

Open: All year.

Directions

From M6 exit 40 take A66 towards Keswick. At first roundabout take A592 and follow signs for Ullswater and Glenridding, continue to Brotherswater and Sykeside is on the right of the A592. The entrance is behind Brotherswater Inn. GPS: 54.4985, -2.9255

Charges guide

Per tent incl. 2 persons and car	£ 13.50 - £ 23.50
motorcaravan incl.	
2 persons and electricity	£ 17.50 - £ 25.00
child (5-15 yrs)	£ 2.00 - £ 2.50

Penrith

Westmorland Caravan Park

Tebay, Orton, Penrith CA10 3SB (Cumbria) T: 01539 711322. E: caravans@westmorland.com

alanrogers.com/UK5590

For caravans, motorcaravans and trailer tents only, this is the ideal stopover for anyone heading either north or south, near the M6 motorway, but far enough away for the traffic noise not to be too disturbing. There are 80 level pitches on gravel, divided into bays of about six or seven units (25 are for touring units). All touring pitches have 16A electricity. The bays are backed by grassy banks alive with rabbits and birds – a long list in the office describes the large variety of birds to be seen on the site. There is good site lighting and a late arrivals area.

Facilities

The heated toilet block is basic but kept very clean and includes washbasins and showers. Bathroom for disabled visitors with ramped access. Family room. Laundry. Reception sells gas. Dog walk. Off site: Shops and restaurants five minutes walk away at the motorway service area. Fishing 2 miles. Golf 17 miles. Within 30 minutes drive are the market towns of Appleby, Penrith and Kendal. Boat rides on Ullswater.

Open: 9 March - 4 November.

Directions

From the M6, exit for Tebay services (site signed) just north of exit 38. Site is accessible from the services travelling north or south. GPS: 54.4477, -2.606467

Charges guide

Per unit incl. 4 persons	
and electricity	£ 18.50 - £ 22.00
child	free
awning	£ 2.50

For latest campsite news visit

alanrogers.com

Penrith
Cove Camping Park

Ullswater, Watermillock, Penrith CA11 0LS (Cumbria) T: 01768 486549. E: info@cove-park.co.uk

alanrogers.com/UK5620

Cove Camping is a delightful, small site, some of the 50 pitches having great views over Lake Ullswater. The grass is well trimmed, there are ramps to keep speeds down to 5 mph. and the site is well lit. There are 21 touring pitches with 10A electricity hook-ups, and 29 tent pitches, seven of which have electricity. The rest of the park is quite sloping and some terracing has been carried out to give pitches with a lake view. Refuse and recycling bins are hidden behind wooden fencing. The park is well situated for walking, boating, fishing and pony trekking. The road up from the A592 is narrow, but a self imposed, one-way system is generally adhered to and the warden will advise on a different way to leave the site.

Facilities

The recently refurbished toilet block is immaculate and heated in cooler months, providing adjustable showers, some washbasins in cabins and, for ladies, a hairdressing area with stool and a baby changing unit. Foyer containing a freezer (free), and tourist information. Laundry with washing machine, dryer and an iron. Gas supplies. Small, grass based play area. Off site: Shop nearby. Fishing 1.5 miles. Riding 3 miles. Golf 6 mile. Bicycle hire 3 miles (will deliver).

Open: March - 31 October.

Directions

We advise using the following directions rather than GPS. From A66 Penrith-Keswick road, take A592 south (Ullswater). Turn right at Brackenrigg Inn and follow road uphill for 1.5 miles to park on left. This road is narrow, large unit should telephone park for an alternative route. GPS: 54.604283, -2.881883

Charges guide

Per unit incl. 2 persons and electricity	£ 20.00 - £ 28.00
tent incl. 2 persons	£ 14.00 - £ 22.00
child (5-17 yrs)	£ 2.00
dog (max. 2)	free

Penrith
Waterfoot Caravan Park

Pooley Bridge, Penrith CA11 0JF (Cumbria) T: 01768 486302. E: enquiries@waterfootpark.co.uk

alanrogers.com/UK5610

Waterfoot is a quiet family park for caravans and motorcaravans only. It is set in 22 acres of partially wooded land, developed in the fifties from a private estate. The 146 private caravan holiday homes are quite separate from the 34 touring pitches. Lake Ullswater is only about 400 yards away and a half mile stroll through bluebell woods brings you to the village of Pooley Bridge. Waterfoot's touring pitches are arranged very informally in a large clearing. Most are level, there are some hardstandings and all have 10A electricity. The park no longer accepts American RVs. There is a bar in a large, imposing mansion, in the past a family home then a golf hotel. Public footpaths lead straight from the park.

Facilities

The heated toilet block includes washbasins and preset showers in cubicles. New facilities for disabled visitors. Large, light and airy dishwashing room and fully equipped laundry. Small shop selling basics, gas and newspapers. Bar with strictly enforced, separate family room open weekend evenings in low season and every evening in high season. Large fenced field with play equipment to suit all ages and goal posts for football and a new play park. Off site: Fishing 0.5 miles. Riding 1.5 miles. Golf 5 miles. Pooley Bridge has a post office/general store, hotels and restaurants.

Open: 1 March - 14 November.

Directions

Do not use GPS. Please use the following directions. From M6 exit 40, take A66 signed Keswick. After 0.5 miles at roundabout take A592 signed Ullswater and site is on right after 4 miles. GPS: 54.614017, -2.83115

Charges guide

Per unit incl. all persons and electricity	£ 19.00 - £ 30.50

 FREE Alan Rogers Travel Card
Extra benefits and savings - see page 10

Penrith
Lowther Holiday Park

Eamont Bridge, Penrith CA10 2JB (Cumbria) T: 01768 863631. E: alan@lowther-holidaypark.co.uk

alanrogers.com/UK5625

Sitting on the banks of the River Lowther this holiday park occupies 50 acres of rural, wooded parkland, home to the rare red squirrel. There are 400 caravan holiday homes and lodges around the park, together with 70 touring pitches. A proportion of these are taken by seasonal lets. Marked and numbered, on mostly level ground between mature trees, all have 10A electricity and hardstanding. A separate elevated grass area is available for tents. There is a small touring office with 24 hour security next to the holiday home sales office, where a well stocked shop also sells some caravan accessories.

Facilities

Two central toilet blocks provide large, preset showers. Fully equipped bathroom with baby changing. Drive through motorcaravan service. Laundry. Full facilities for disabled visitors (Radar key). Licensed shop. Squirrel Inn with restaurant and games room. Play areas. Fly fishing (permit from office). Activity weekends. Live entertainment and children's parties. Max. two dogs per unit.

Open: 7 March - 13 November.

Directions

From M6 exit 40 take A66 towards Scotch Corner for 1 mile. At roundabout take A6 south for 1 mile towards Shap. Lowther is on the right as you pass through Eamont Bridge. GPS: 54.647667, -2.737017

Charges guide

Per unit incl. 6 persons
and electricity £ 23.00 - £ 30.00

Penrith
The Quiet Site Caravan & Camping Park

Watermillock, Penrith CA11 0LS (Cumbria) T: 07768 727016. E: info@thequietsite.co.uk

alanrogers.com/UK5630

The Quiet Site is a secluded, family run park operating as a carbon neutral company. It is situated on a hillside in the Lake District National Park with views over the fells and just 1.5 miles from Lake Ullswater. There are 100 unmarked touring pitches, most with hardstanding and 60 with electricity. All have been terraced to provide level surfaces. The camping area is undulating. In a separate part of the park screened by mature trees, there are 23 privately-owned caravan holiday homes. There are two cottages to rent and recent additions are timber camping pods, an alternative to bringing your own tent.

Facilities

The toilet block provides preset showers and open style washbasins, three bathrooms and two private shower rooms. Bathroom with facilities for disabled visitors. Baby area. Laundry. Motorcaravan services. Well stocked shop at reception. Gas supplies. Bar (weekends only in low season). TV and games room. Excellent adventure play area. Caravan storage. WiFi. American motorhomes would find access very difficult.

Open: All year.

Directions

From M6, exit 40, take A66 (Keswick) for 1 mile, then A592 (Ullswater) for 4 miles. Turn right at Lake junction, still on A592 (Windermere). After 1 mile turn right (at Brackenrigg Inn) and follow for 1.5 miles to site on right (large units phone for alternative route). GPS: 54.604683, -2.882783

Charges guide

Per unit incl. 2 persons,
awning and electricity £ 16.00 - £ 30.00
Camping Cheques accepted.

Penrith
Ullswater Caravan, Camping & Marine Park

Watermillock, Penrith CA11 0LR (Cumbria) T: 017684 86666. E: info@uccmp.co.uk

alanrogers.com/UK5635

Located within the Lake District National Park, Ullswater Caravan Park is centrally situated for touring the many attractions of this glorious area. It has 220 pitches, 58 for touring units, the remainder used for holiday homes. All have 10A electricity, 50 also have water and drainage. Some are situated very close to the bar and are also overlooked by mobile homes with little privacy. At the far end of the park, other pitches are in a more wooded area. In between is a large grassy space for tents. There are occasional glimpses of the lake through the trees. Attractive, self-catering holiday cottages are available for rent.

Facilities

Two toilet blocks, both recently refurbished, have facilities for babies and disabled visitors. Laundry. Recently refurbished reception and shop with off-licence. Bar and games room open to 20.00 at busy times. Well equipped playground for younger children. WiFi. Off site: Walks in the hills above the park. Steamer rides on the lake from Pooley Bridge 2 miles.

Open: 1 March - 14 November.

Directions

From M6 exit 40 take A66 west (Keswick). At first roundabout (Rheged) take second exit (Ullswater) on A592. At T-junction turn right, still on A592, and after Brackenrigg Inn continue downhill to telephone box on right, and sign for church. Turn right here and up to entrance on right. GPS: 54.5978, -2.87482

Charges guide

Per unit incl. 2 persons
and electricity £ 17.00 - £ 26.00
extra person £ 3.50 - £ 5.00

For latest campsite news visit
alanrogers.com

Penrith
Flusco Wood Touring Caravan Park

Flusco, Penrith CA11 0JB (Cumbria) T: 01768 480020. E: info@fluscowoodtouringpark.co.uk
alanrogers.com/UK5670

Flusco Wood Caravan Park is still being developed but everything is to a very high standard. Set amongst woodland with the 22 touring pitches in bays, this park will meet the needs of those requiring a quiet holiday (with plenty of walks from the site) and also those travelling up or down the M6 looking for a quiet night's rest. All pitches have electricity and water and are on hardstanding, with an area near reception with hardstandings for motorcaravans. Recent additions here include new log cabins (privately owned), with more planned. A member of the Countryside Discovery group.

Facilities

A log cabin style building houses very clean, heated facilities including preset showers and vanity style washbasins (1 cubicle). Large en-suite shower rooms for families and disabled visitors. Dishwashing sinks under cover. Laundry, drying room and boot washing sink. Second log cabin serves as reception/shop with basic supplies, gas and daily newspapers. Play equipment on bark. Grass area for ball games. Off site: Pub and P.O. store 2 miles. Fishing, bicycle hire and golf 4 miles.

Open: 22 March - 31 October.

Directions

From M6 junction 40 take A66 west towards Keswick. Go straight on at first roundabout, after 2.5 miles take right turn at top of hill (Flusco, Recycling Centre). After 0.5 miles road turns right up hill (narrow), site is on left at the top. GPS: 54.655408, -2.841346

Charges guide

Per unit incl. 2 persons and electricity	£ 18.50 - £ 21.50

Wigton
Stanwix Park Holiday Centre

Greenrow, Silloth CA7 4HH (Cumbria) T: 01697 332666. E: enquiries@stanwix.com
alanrogers.com/UK5505

Stanwix Park is a family run holiday park with absolutely everything anyone could want for a memorable holiday all year round. The park has 111 caravan holiday homes and chalets for rent, together with 212 which are privately owned. These are mostly located around the central complex. In addition at either end of the park, there are 121 fully serviced (10A electricity) pitches for touring units and tents, some on grass, some with hardstanding. A warm welcome awaits in the main reception, with lots of local and tourist information. Motorcaravans over eight metres only accepted by prior arrangement.

Facilities

The two heated and spotlessly clean sanitary blocks. Large en-suite bathrooms, showers, vanity style washbasins and a unit in each for disabled visitors. Campers' kitchen. Laundry. Gas sales. Well stocked shop (6/3-15/11). Bars with evening entertainment (6/3-15/11). Restaurant with takeaway (all year). TV and snooker room. Indoor leisure centre. Outdoor swimming pool (31/5-1/9). 10-pin bowling centre. Amusement arcade. Soft play area. Minigolf. Tennis. Bicycle hire. Free WiFi over part of site. Dogs max. 2. Off site: Beach 1 mile. Bus service 1 mile in Silloth.

Open: All year.

Directions

From south, take exit 41 from the M6 and follow B5305 to Silloth. From north on A74/M6 take exit 44 and A595 and A596 to Wigton. On entering Silloth, turn left following signs for park. Entrance is on the right. GPS: 54.8614, -3.388333

Charges guide

Per person	£ 4.20 - £ 5.00
child (under 5 yrs)	£ 2.70 - £ 3.30
pitch	£ 12.90 - £ 16.20

Wigton
Hylton Caravan Park

Silloth, Wigton CA7 4AY (Cumbria) T: 01697 332666. E: ericstanwix@stanwix.com
alanrogers.com/UK5506

Hylton Caravan Park is owned and managed by the Stanwix family and although it is only a short walk away from the livelier Stanwix Park, it is a peaceful haven for people who prefer the 'quiet life'. The only activity is an adventure park for children which is not visible from the touring area. Divided by a circular road, the 170 privately owned caravan holiday homes are visible but not intrusive. There are 90 open plan, mostly level touring and tent pitches, all fully serviced and with 10A electricity.

Facilities

A high quality toilet block is superbly fitted out and includes toilets, showers, vanity style washbasins, extra large bathrooms and a separate cubicle for disabled visitors. Dishwashing under cover. Fully equipped laundry. Gas sales. Max. 2 dogs per pitch. Off site: Shops within walking distance. Entertainment and amenities at Stanwix Park. Silloth golf course. Bowling. Fishing 1 mile.

Open: 1 March - 15 November.

Directions

On entering Silloth, turn left following signs to Hylton Caravan Park. GPS: 54.868333, -3.39835

Charges guide

Per person	£ 4.20 - £ 5.00
child (under 5 yrs)	£ 2.70 - £ 3.30
pitch	£ 10.40 - £ 13.00

FREE Alan Rogers Travel Card
Extra benefits and savings - see page 10

Wigton

The Larches Caravan Park

Mealsgate, Wigton CA7 1LQ (Cumbria) T: 01697 371379. E: thelarches@hotmail.co.uk

alanrogers.com/UK5510

Mealsgate and The Larches lie on the Carlisle-Cockermouth road, a little removed from the hectic centre of the Lake District, yet with easy access to it (and good views towards it) and to other attractions nearby. This quiet, family run, adults only park takes 45 touring units of any type, 42 of which have 10A electricity, water and drainage. These pitches are in grassy areas with tall, mature trees, shrubs and accompanying wildlife. Some are sloping and irregular, others on marked hardstandings. There are currently a few privately owned holiday homes and there are plans to extend this area of the park. On arrival visitors are loaned very comprehensive tourist information brochures. There are bus routes to Carlisle and Keswick, walks from the park and good restaurants nearby. This is an ideal haven for couples – only adult visitors are accepted.

Facilities

Recently refurbished toilet facilities provide en-suite facilities for both sexes. Separate unit for disabled visitors can be heated. Campers' kitchen with microwave (free). Laundry room. Small shop selling mainly camping accessories, gas and off-licence. Small indoor heated pool (June-Aug). Wildlife pond. Caravan storage. Off site: Riding 1.5 miles. Golf 3.5 miles. Bicycle hire 7 miles. Fishing 8 miles.

Open: 1 March - 31 October.

Directions

Park entrance is south off the A595 (Carlisle-Cockermouth road) just southwest of Mealsgate. GPS: 54.763267, -3.2358

Charges guide

Per unit incl. 2 persons	
and electricity	£ 19.00 - £ 22.00
extra person	£ 4.00 - £ 5.00
awning or extra car	£ 2.50 - £ 3.50
backpacker	£ 8.50 - £ 9.50

Discounts for senior citizens and bookings over 7 nights. No credit cards.

Advantage all the way

alan rogers

Travel Card

Got yours yet?

Extra benefits and savings - see page 10

For latest campsite news visit

alanrogers.com

Windermere
Hill of Oaks Caravan Park

Tower Wood, Windermere LA12 8NR (Cumbria) T: 01539 531578. E: enquiries@hillofoaks.co.uk

alanrogers.com/UK5615

This park on the banks of Lake Windermere lives up to its name, Hill of Oaks. Set on a hillside in mature woodland, the park offers families a safe natural environment with nature walks through the managed ancient woodlands, as well as six jetties for boat launching and access to watersports activities (jet skis are not allowed). The road into the park passing the farmhouse is long, winding and narrow, so long outfits should ring ahead for a different access, reception being about half a mile from the entrance. Although the park is situated on Lake Windermere the touring pitches nestle within the trees, not actually by the lake. All 43 have 16A electricity, digital TV hook-up and hardstanding. Most are large enough to take a car and boat and three large super pitches also have water and a drain. Tents are not accepted at Hill of Oaks. The entrance barrier is open from 08.00 till dusk with a security code being provided for exit. There is a new reception and shop selling basics, with a tourist information room adjacent. These are on the lakeside in wooden chalet-type buildings with an abundance of hanging baskets and flowers.

Facilities

The central tiled toilet block, recently refurbished, is very clean and heated. Vanity style washbasins, controllable showers and free hairdryers. Baby changing. Laundry. Unit for disabled visitors. Motorcaravan service point. Shop for basics. Two fenced play areas, one for toddlers and adventure style for over 5s. Picnic areas. Fishing (licence required). WiFi (charged). Off site: Fell Foot Park and Gardens 1 mile. Golf 4 miles. Riding hire 6 miles.

Open: 1 March - 14 November.

Directions

From M6 exit 36 head west on A590 (Barrow and Newby Bridge). Follow A590 to roundabout signed Bowness and turn right on A592 for 3 miles. Site is signed on left. GPS: 54.30755, -2.9454

Charges guide

Per pitch	£ 17.50 - £ 37.50
awning	£ 4.00
boat	£ 3.95 - £ 10.50

Lake District Estates present...

Woodclose Park — Situated in Kirkby Lonsdale, between the Yorkshire Dales and the Lake District National Park. woodclosepark.com

Waterfoot Park — Nestling in the grounds of a Georgian mansion, overlooking Ullswater, in the Lake District National Park. waterfootpark.co.uk

Hill of Oaks — Exclusive lake frontage on Windermere, with boat launching and access to watersport activities. hillofoaks.co.uk

Windermere
Park Cliffe Camping & Caravan Estate

Birks Road, Windermere LA23 3PG (Cumbria) T: 01539 531344. E: info@parkcliffe.co.uk

alanrogers.com/UK5545

This beautiful park is situated in the heart of the Lake District National Park and is well managed and maintained by the welcoming staff. The 70 touring pitches are open, unshaded, on gravel hardstanding with 10A electricity, water and drainage. There are some seasonal units and three mobile homes for hire. Five pods have been sited. Tucked away in a valley are privately owned mobile homes. Two areas have been set aside for 100 tent pitches, 25 of which have 6A electric hook-ups (steel pegs required).

Facilities

Two blocks of toilets and showers are heated and very clean. Full facilities for disabled visitors. Baby room. Four private bathrooms for hire (min. 3 days), and one by the hour. Laundry. Motorcaravan service point. Bar, restaurant and takeaway. Shop. Games room. Outdoor adventure play area (recently refurbished) is set secluded to one side of tourers, a public footpath runs through to Moor How. Off site: Fellfoot Country Park with (sail) boat launching, walking, climbing, cycling and many other activities.

Open: 1 March - 11 November.

Directions

From M6 exit 36 take A590 to Newby Bridge. Turn right on A592 for 3.6 miles then right again. Site is signed shortly on the right. Caravans and trailers must approach Park Cliffe from Newby Bridge direction on A592 - extremely tight turn from north. GPS: 54.312517, -2.9375

Charges guide

Per unit incl. 2 persons and electricity	£ 25.00 - £ 30.00
extra person	£ 5.00

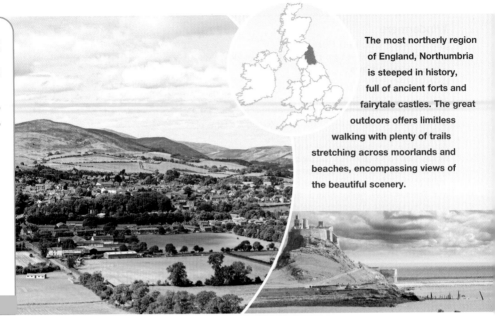

The most northerly region of England, Northumbria is steeped in history, full of ancient forts and fairytale castles. The great outdoors offers limitless walking with plenty of trails stretching across moorlands and beaches, encompassing views of the beautiful scenery.

THE REGION COMPRISES: NORTHUMBERLAND, DURHAM, TYNE AND WEAR, AND TEESIDE

The 400 square mile Northumberland National Park is one of the most peaceful and remote places in England. With endless walks across moorlands and hills, it stretches south from the Cheviot Hills, through the Simonside Hills, to the crags of Whin Sill, where it engulfs a section of the historic Hadrian's Wall, built by the Romans to mark the northern limit of their empire. The Pennine Way was the country's first official long-distance path and is still the longest. At 268 miles, it stretches from the Peak National Park to the border. The coastline is not to be forgotten, with mile upon mile of deserted, sandy beaches, with resorts that still have an old fashioned feel to them, such as Whitley Bay, South Shields and Seaton Carew. The majestic castles of Bamburgh, and Dunstanburgh can be seen for miles along the Northumberland coast. Surrounded on three sides by the river Wear, the small, historic city of Durham is dominated by England's greatest Norman cathedral. With cobbled medieval streets and restricted car access, it is a popular place with visitors. Further north is the bustling city of Newcastle. Home to an array of cosmopolitan restaurants and bars, music venues, and fabulous architecture, it also boasts a lively nightlife.

Places of interest

Northumberland: Bamburgh Castle; Alnwick Castle and gardens; Berwick-upon-Tweed; Lindisfarne Priory on Holy Island; Newbiggin Maritime Centre; Dunstanburgh Castle; Corbridge Roman sites at Hadrian's Wall.

Durham: Durham Castle and Cathedral; Barnard Castle; Beamish Museum; Diggerland at Langley Park; Harperley POW Camp; Crook Hall and Gardens.

Tyne and Wear: New Metroland indoor theme park and shopping complex; 700-year-old Holy Jesus Hospital, Newcastle. with Life Science Centre, Discovery Museum and Castle Keep; Gibside forest garden.

Teeside: Kirkleatham Owl Centre; Darlington Railway Centre and Museum; Guisborough Hall; Saltburn Smugglers Heritage Centre; Captain Cook Birthplace Museum, Marton.

Did you know?

Alnwick Castle was used as the setting for Hogwarts in the Harry Potter films.

Stretching from Wallsend to Bowness-on-Solway, Hadrian's Wall is 81 miles long.

Middlesbrough Teesside Transporter Bridge was built in 1911 and is the only one of its kind in England, with a gondola capable of carrying nine cars and 200 passengers.

In the past 300 years Berwick has changed hands between the Scottish and the English no less than 13 times.

Anthony Gormley's Angel of The North has a wingspan of 54 metres and is visited by 150,000 people every year.

Sir Malcolm Campbell's first speed record of 138 mph was set on Saltburn sands on 17 June 1922.

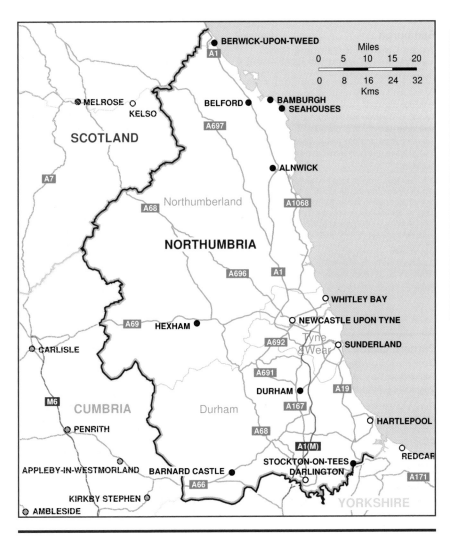

Alnwick

Dunstan Hill Camping & Caravanning Club Site

Dunstan Hill, Dunstan, Alnwick NE66 3TQ (Northumberland) T: 01665 576310

alanrogers.com/UK5770

Off a quiet lane between Embleton and Craster this is a rural site with a tree belt to shelter it from the north wind and has access to the beach via a level footpath through the fields, across the golf course and past the ruins of Dunstanburgh Castle. This is just over a mile by car. With gravel access roads, the peaceful site has 150 level, well spaced pitches, 80 with 16A electricity. Reception is manned by very helpful managers and there is an area for outside parking and late arrivals at the entrance. This is a wonderful area to visit, with its unspoilt beaches and the whole area is steeped in history.

Facilities

Two very clean and well maintained toilet blocks have some washbasins in cubicles, hairdryers (20p) and a washroom for children with deep sinks. Fully equipped facility for disabled visitors in one block, a laundry in the other. Small shop for gas and basics. Bread and milk to order and a mobile shop and the paper man visit. Fish and chip van (Fri). Well stocked tourist information room. Small play area. Torches are useful. WiFi (charged). Off site: Good eating places nearby including Craster (world famous fish restaurant). Beach, fishing and golf 1.5 miles. Riding 8 miles. Bicycle hire 10 miles.

Open: 29 March - 5 November.

Directions

From A1 just north of Alnwick take the B1340 or B6347 (further north) for Embleton. Site is signed in Embleton village. Avoid signs to Dunstanburgh Castle and follow those for Craster. Site is (south) on the left after 0.5 miles. GPS: 55.4855, -1.6291

Charges guide

Per person	£ 7.75 - £ 9.45
child (6-18 yrs)	£ 2.70 - £ 2.95
non-member pitch fee	£ 7.10

FREE Alan Rogers Travel Card
Extra benefits and savings - see page 10

Bamburgh

Waren Caravan & Camping Park

Waren Mill, Bamburgh NE70 7EE (Northumberland) T: 01668 214366. E: waren@meadowhead.co.uk

alanrogers.com/UK5750

Developed from 100 acres of privately-owned, undulating heath and woodland, Waren Park is a large, spacious family site with marvellous views over Northumberland's golden beaches and the sea. A large section of caravan holiday homes is separate from a self-contained, four-acre touring area. Enclosed by sheltering banks, this provides 150 reasonably level pitches, 100 with 16A electrical connections. Wooden wigwams are also available for rent. As well as the spacious grounds to wander in, there is much to see nearby: historic castles, the Farne Islands, the Cheviot Hills and miles of sandy beaches.

Facilities

The older toilet facilities have been refurbished and include four family en-suite shower rooms, a family bathroom and facilities for disabled visitors. A newer block situated in a separate static holiday home section also provides good facilities. Laundry room. Motorcaravan service point. Licensed shop. Bar with terrace serving bar meals (all season). Gaming machine room with pool table. Patio area. Children's play park and playing fields. Splash pool (June-Sept). WiFi. Off site: Beach 500 yds. excellent for birdwatching, unsuitable for bathing. Safe bathing 4 miles.

Open: 14 March - 31 October.

Directions

Follow B1342 from the A1 to Waren Mill towards Bamburgh. After Budle Bay turn right and follow signs. GPS: 55.60045, -1.75487

Charges guide

Per unit incl. 2 persons and electricity	£ 17.50 - £ 22.50
extra person (over 5 yrs)	£ 5.00
1-man tent (no car)	£ 9.75 - £ 12.50
dog	£ 3.00

Less 10% for bookings of 7 days or over.

Barnard Castle

Doe Park Touring Caravan Park

Cotherstone, Barnard Castle DL12 9UQ (Co. Durham) T: 01833 650302. E: info@doepark.co.uk

alanrogers.com/UK5710

The Lamb family will make you very welcome and personally take you to your pitch at Doe Park. The camping fields have a lovely open aspect with wonderful views and the 70 pitches are spacious with well mown grass, all with 10A electricity, 60 with hardstanding. This is Hannah Hauxwell country and the Dales, less frequented than other upland areas, provide wonderful walking country; indeed part of the Pennine Way runs near this peaceful site. The park's reception is a new wooden cabin at the entrance to the pitch area and is well stocked with tourist information guides.

Facilities

With toilet facilities at the farmhouse, two well kept blocks are closer to the pitches. Built in local stone, these are fully tiled with the newest one heated. Washbasins in cabins and adjustable showers. Well appointed unisex unit for disabled visitors. Small laundry. Eggs and milk are available from the farmhouse. Gas and battery charging. River fishing on site. Dogs by arrangement only.

Open: 1 March - 31 October.

Directions

Follow B6277 from Barnard Castle in direction of Middleton in Teesdale. The farm is signed on left just after Cotherstone village. GPS: 54.578217, -1.99235

Charges guide

Per unit incl. 2 persons and electricity	£ 15.50 - £ 20.00
extra person (over 6 yrs)	£ 1.50 - £ 2.00

No credit cards.

For latest campsite news visit
alanrogers.com

Belford
South Meadows Caravan Park
South Meadows, Belford NE70 7DP (Northumberland) T: 01668 213326. E: g.mcl@btinternet.com
alanrogers.com/UK5755

South Meadows is set in the north Northumberland countryside, within walking distance of the village of Belford with its market cross and old coaching inn. Covering six acres of level grass, there are 150 hardstanding pitches, most with 13A electricity, water and TV aerial point. At present 60 pitches are available for touring units. A further area can accommodate 50 tents. The manager is environmentally aware and encourages recycling. Determined that visitors have a relaxing holiday, he will site your caravan using his own towing equipment. There is an area especially for disabled visitors with wider paths and safety features including a 24 hour telephone directly to the manager's home on site.

Facilities

The fully tiled toilet block is excellent, heated in cool weather, with washbasins in cabins and roomy showers (free). Three family shower rooms. An additional Portacabin style toilet block is open in one area for the summer months. Hairdryers. Full facilities for disabled visitors. Laundry with washing machines, dryers and iron plus a baby unit. Food preparation and cooking area. Coffee shop (weekends, incl. Sun. roast) and takeaway (daily until 16.00). Play area. Caravan storage and servicing. Off site: Village with pub and shops, golf 0.5 miles. Riding and beach 3 miles. Alnwick Castle.

Open: All year.

Directions

Turn off A1, 15 miles from Alnwick to Belford village and park is signed at the southern end. GPS: 55.590967, -1.822583

Charges guide

Per unit incl. 2 persons	
and electricity	£ 19.00 - £ 24.00
tent per adult	£ 5.00 - £ 10.00
extra person	£ 6.00 - £ 10.00
child (2-16 yrs)	£ 3.50 - £ 4.50

No credit cards.

Berwick-upon-Tweed
Chainbridge Touring Caravan Site
Bankhead Villa, Horncliffe, Berwick-upon-Tweed TD15 2XT (Northumberland) T: 07554 953697.
E: stay@chainbridgecaravansite.co.uk **alanrogers.com/UK5785**

This beautifully laid out L-shaped park is for adults only and quietly situated down a non-classified road which leads to a chain bridge over the River Tweed, linking Scotland and England. The owners are very welcoming and many visitors return time and time again. The park offers 16 hardstanding touring pitches off a gravel driveway. All have electricity (16A) and fresh water. With very little noise from all but the birds this is a very tranquil site. Berwick-upon-Tweed is on the doorstep, just four miles away, and just inland you'll find Northumberland's fine sandy beaches.

Facilities

Three unisex toilets provide washbasins and showers with underfloor heating. No dedicated facilities for disabled visitors. Coin operated washing machine and dryers. Kitchen with sink, freezer and microwave. Motorcaravan service point. TV room and lounge. Trout fishing. Riverside walks. Cycle paths. WiFi (limited area). Off site: Beach, bicycle hire and golf all within 4 km. Riding 5 km. Berwick-upon-Tweed 4 miles. Holy Island, Alnwick Castle and Gardens, Hadrian's Wall and the Scottish Borders. Edinburgh by car or train from Berwick.

Open: 1 March - 30 November.

Directions

From the A1 turn off onto A698, after approximately 2 miles turn right and follow brown tourist signs for Honey Farm. From the west turn off the A698 towards Horncliffe and follow signs for Honey Farm. Site is down a narrow road before road weight and width limits apply. GPS: 55.7474, -2.10489

Charges guide

Per unit incl. 2 persons	
and electricity	£ 17.00 - £ 22.00

No credit cards.

Been to any good campsites lately?
We have

alan rogers

The UK's market leading independent guides to the best campsites
Also available on iPad **alanrogers.com/digital**

FREE Alan Rogers Travel Card
Extra benefits and savings - see page 10

Berwick-upon-Tweed

Ord House Country Park

East Ord, Berwick-upon-Tweed TD15 2NS (Northumberland) T: 01289 305288. E: enquiries@ordhouse.co.uk

alanrogers.com/UK5800

Ord House is a 40-acre park for 260 privately-owned holiday homes and 74 touring caravan and tent pitches. The park has a very well cared for appearance throughout, with well mown grass and colourful arrays of flowering bushes. Ord House itself, an 18th-century mansion, has been tastefully converted to provide a bar, lounge bar and family room. The touring pitches, 67 with 16A electricity, are in small sections, from the secluded, walled orchard to the more open areas nearer the toilet blocks. There are 39 hardstanding pitches, each with electricity, water and drainage, with 12 in the walled garden.

Facilities

The main, modern toilet building is of excellent quality and cleanliness, very well maintained and can be heated. Two good large family bathrooms (with two showers, a bath, WC and washbasin). Two rooms for disabled visitors. Large well equipped laundry. Motorcaravan service point. Gas supplies. Bar, bar food and family room. Crazy golf. Draughts. Play area. Commercial vehicles are not accepted. Dogs accepted by prior arrangement. Free WiFi.

Open: All year.

Directions

From A1 Berwick bypass take East Ord exit and follow signs. GPS: 55.75416, -2.03348

Charges guide

Per unit incl. up to 4 persons and electricity	£ 17.00 - £ 28.00
extra person (over 5 yrs)	£ 2.50
tent pitch	£ 12.50 - £ 23.00
dog	free - £ 1.50

Durham

Finchale Abbey Touring Park

Finchale Abbey Farm, Brasside, Durham DH1 5SH (Co. Durham) T: 01913 865528.
E: Godricawatson@hotmail.com **alanrogers.com/UK5715**

At the end of a very narrow no-through road is the Finchale Abbey (English Heritage). This adults only park is situated alongside it with the ruins forming a scenic backdrop. It offers 43 pitches, 34 of which are hardstanding, all with 10A electricity. There are also three large, fully serviced super pitches. Privately owned mobile homes are positioned on the upper level above the touring pitches. A tarmac road within the park allows for easy access to the pitches which are off to both sides. The River Wear runs along one side of the park.

Facilities

The single, heated toilet block includes facilities for disabled visitors. All facilities are modern and very clean. Motorcaravan service point. Small shop for essentials. Small café with takeaway food. River fishing (permits from shop). Swimming and canoeing in the river (guests to bring own equipment). Walks in the woods and along the river bank. WiFi in reception area. Off site: Golf 800 m. Arnison Centre (1.5 miles) with full shopping facilities. Cocken Lodge driving range (10 mins. walk).

Open: All year.

Directions

From the A1 junction 63, turn onto the A167 for approximately 4 miles, turn left at the roundabout, direction Arnison Centre. Follow signs for Finchale Abbey from there. Please note some signs say Finchale Abbey and some say Finchale Priory (both are same). GPS: 54.818101, -1.5423

Charges guide

Per unit incl. 2 persons and electricity	£ 20.00 - £ 25.00
extra person	£ 3.00

Durham

Durham Grange Caravan Club Site

Meadow Lane, Durham DH1 1TL (Co. Durham) T: 01913 844778

alanrogers.com/UK5705

Fully refurbished and landscaped, this park offers 76 flat spacious pitches, 59 are hardstanding and eight fully serviced. Easy access to the A1M and the A690 make it an ideal stopover for those travelling north or south or for visiting the historic cathedral city of Durham, the Beamish museum or Gateshead Metro centre. A coppice of mature trees and newly planted shrubs mask road noise and make an attractive dog walking area. The park has been redesigned with attention to detail in all areas offering pockets of privacy and a central area with picnic tables and benches.

Facilities

The single toilet block is a heated building with free showers, hairdryers, and private cubicles. Laundry and food preparation area. Separate baby area and facilities for disabled visitors are via a key entry system. Shop in reception with limited supplies; bread, milk and papers to order. Gas. Secure caravan storage. WiFi (charged). Off site: Large supermarket 2 miles. Park and ride (07.00-19.00) into Durham city centre 800 yds.

Open: All year.

Directions

From A1M exit 62 turn left for Durham city (A690). After 20 yds. turn right (across dual carriageway A690), and continue along A690 to next exit 2 miles and return on A690 left hand turn (signed just before A1M). GPS: 54.79545, -1.53065

Charges guide

Per person	£ 5.10 - £ 6.90
pitch incl. electricity (non-member)	£ 13.10 - £ 14.90

Durham
Strawberry Hill Caravan Park

Running Waters, Old Cassop, Durham DH6 4QA (Co. Durham) T: 01913 723457. E: info@strawberryhf.co.uk

alanrogers.com/UK5700

This park is owned and managed by Howard and Elizabeth who are experienced caravanners. They have terraced their site to offer panoramic views over the fields and woodland from all the pitches. The park is licensed to accommodate more units but the owners prefer to offer space to visitors by providing generous pitches on either grass or hardstanding. There are 50 touring pitches (with 16A electric hook-ups), including ten on hardstanding, plus a separate terrace for tents. At present the new landscaping on the park offers limited shade.

Facilities

The single toilet block can be heated and is kept very clean. Free showers. Laundry. Facilities for disabled visitors incorporating a baby care area. Small but well stocked shop in reception. Gas. Off site: Buses (Durham-Hartlepool) from entrance. Country pub with meals 1 mile. Large hypermarket 3 miles. Riding 5 miles. Park and ride (07.00-19.00) into Durham city centre operates nearby.

Open: 1 March - 30 December.

Directions

From A1M exit 61 follow signs for Peterlee. At next roundabout take first left (A688). Straight on at next roundabout then right at the next (A181). Park is 2 miles on the left as you go up a hill on a dual carriageway. GPS: 54.75326, -1.47809

Charges guide

Per unit incl. 2 persons and electricity (meter)	£ 16.00 - £ 18.00
extra person	£ 4.00

Hexham
Causey Hill Caravan Park

Causey Hill, Hexham NE46 2JN (Northumberland) T: 01434 602834. E: causeyhill@dalyparks.co.uk

alanrogers.com/UK5805

Causey Hill Caravan Park is situated at the top of a steep hill overlooking Hexham. It is mainly occupied by mobile homes, in excess of 100, but also offers a small touring area which is well separated above them. There are 20 hardstanding pitches for touring, all with 16A electricity and water. Plenty of grassy areas surround the pitches and trees have been recently planted. Barbecue and picnic areas are provided and walks amongst wildflowers and wildlife are possible in the woodland.

Facilities

The heated toilet block is near reception and quite a walk from the touring area. Facilities for disabled visitors (key access). Laundry room. Small play area. Woodland walks. WiFi throughout (charged). Off site: Bicycle hire, fishing and golf all within 1 mile. Restaurants, supermarkets, swimming pool and theatre in Hexham just over 1 mile. Hexham Racecourse 800 m. Hadrian's Wall 5 miles. Newcastle and The Metro Centre 20 miles.

Open: March - October.

Directions

From Hexham town centre, follow the B6306 Blanchland Road to Hexham Racecourse, turn right at the sign. GPS: 54.957128, -2.118709

Charges guide

Per unit incl. 2 persons and electricity	£ 20.00
child	free
No credit cards.	

Hexham
Fallowfield Dene Caravan & Camping Park

Acomb, Hexham NE46 4RP (Northumberland) T: 01434 603553. E: info@fallowfielddene.co.uk

alanrogers.com/UK5810

Although only 2.5 miles from Hexham, Fallowfield Dene Caravan Park is very secluded, situated in mature woodland at the end of a no-through road. Set in woodland glades (formerly a Victorian lead mine), each with a Roman name (Hadrian's Wall is close), are 118 seasonal pitches and 32 touring pitches, all with 16A electricity. A further ten tent pitches have been added, suitable for smaller tents, and a barbecue area with views of woodland and fields. The park entrance, with a new reception and shop, is neat, tidy and very colourful. There is no play area or games field, but the surrounding woods are a paradise for children.

Facilities

Brick built toilet blocks (one for each sex) are central and heated in cool weather. Well tiled and kept very clean, there are washbasins in cabins and free hairdryers. Fully equipped room for disabled visitors. Laundry room with dishwashing sinks. Baby bath. Motorcaravan service point. Small shop for essentials, including gas. Barrier card £5 deposit. WiFi. Off site: Good restaurant five minutes walk. Supermarkets and other shops at Hexham and Corbridge. Fishing and riding 3 miles. Golf 5 miles.

Open: 14 March - 1 November.

Directions

From A69 Newcastle-Carlisle road, take A6079 north signed Bellingham and Rothbury. At village of Acomb, site is signed to right. Follow site signs for 1.5 miles. Then turn left down a single track road with passing places. GPS: 55.00166, -2.09470

Charges guide

Per unit incl. 2 persons and electricity	£ 20.00 - £ 21.00
extra person	£ 3.50

Seahouses

Seafield Caravan Park

Seahouses NE68 7SP (Northumberland) T: 01665 720628. E: info@seafieldpark.co.uk

alanrogers.com/UK5745

The park is situated just across the road from the sea and rock pools. The site has caravans to rent and pitches for 18 touring units (no tents). All the pitches have concrete bases, water, waste, sewerage and 20A electricity, but none has a sea view. A number of small gates give immediate access to Seahouses with its excellent range of shops and eating places. The large site is attractive with landscaped gardens, pools and a stream among the caravans. The private mobile homes are set apart from those available to rent. Its location in Seahouses makes it an ideal base for visiting the Farne Islands and many other interesting and historical places such as Alnwick Castle and gardens, Craster (kippers), Bamburgh and Lindisfarne on Holy Island. The fee includes free access to the Ocean Club facilities – 20 m. swimming pool, children's pool, spa, steam room, sauna and fitness suite. There is a licensed coffee shop, a children's nature trail and outdoor play area.

Facilities

The single toilet block is housed in an old building but is of the highest standard inside with a family bathroom, controllable showers with door and ample changing space. The block has heating, hairdryers (charged) and the latest in hand dryers. There is a well equipped baby room. Laundry and dishwashing. Snack bar/takeaway. Swimming pool, children's pool, spa, steam room, sauna, fitness suite and coffee shop in Ocean Club. Play area. Bicycle hire. WiFi over site. Off site: Immediate access to Seahouses with all amenities.

Open: All year (excl. 10/1-8/2).

Directions

On entering Seahouses from the south take road to Bamburgh and site is on left just past road down to harbour. GPS: 55.583162, -1.657171

Charges guide

Per unit incl. 2 persons and electricity	£ 25.00 - £ 48.00
extra person	£ 8.00
child (2-15 yrs)	£ 5.00

Stockton-on-Tees

White Water Caravan Club Park

Tees Barrage, Stockton-on-Tees TS18 2QW (Teeside) T: 01642 634880

alanrogers.com/UK5740

Being part of the multi-million pound development at the Tees Barrage, this pleasantly landscaped club site caters for all tastes, especially watersports enthusiasts. The Tees Barrage has transformed 11 miles of the Tees, providing clean, non-tidal water for many activities. The site itself provides 115 pitches, hedged with bushes, all with 16A electricity connections, and includes 21 fully serviced pitches set within bays and hedges (fresh water and waste disposal). The adjoining White Water Course (Britain's largest purpose-built canoe course) provides facilities for both advanced and beginner canoeists.

Facilities

The central, heated toilet block of high quality includes washbasins in cubicles, baby changing facilities and a good unit for disabled visitors. Laundry room. Motorcaravan service point. Play area on fine gravel. Family room with TV and pool table. Off site: Supermarket 6 minutes. Hotel near the entrance. Retail and leisure park, just across Barrage bridge, with 14-screen cinema, 10-pin bowling, shops and fast food outlets.

Open: All year.

Directions

From A1(M1) take A66 for Darlington and follow until you pick up signs for Teeside Retail Park and the Tees Barrage. Cross railway bridge and the Barrage bridge, then first right to site on left in 400 yds. GPS: 54.567869, -1.286039

Charges guide

Per person	£ 3.90 - £ 5.85
child (5-16 yrs)	£ 1.30 - £ 2.05
pitch incl. electricity (non member)	£ 12.70 - £ 15.00

Use Camping Cheques on 16 top quality UK parks
all at £13.95 per night

£**13.95** /night
single tariff
2 people

Cambridgeshire	Parklands
Cornwall	Wooda Farm Park
	Carlyon Bay
Cumbria	The Quiet Site
Devon	Cofton Country Holidays
	River Dart Country Park
	Riverside Caravan Park
	Whitehill Country Park
Dorset	Newlands
Hampshire	Shamba
Ireland	Adare Caravan & Camping Park
	Cong Caravan & Camping Park
Isle of Wight	The Orchards
Norfolk	Waverney
Suffolk	Westwood Caravan Park
Peak District	Rivendale

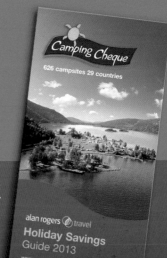

www.campingcheque.co.uk
FREE Holiday Savings Guide
01580 214002

Land of ancient myths and Celtic legends, Wales is a small and compact country boasting a diverse landscape, from lakes and mountains, rivers and valleys to beautiful coastlines and rolling wooded countryside. It offers superb opportunities for an active holiday.

Wales' biggest asset is undoubtedly its countryside, home to three National Parks that make up almost a quarter of the country's total area. Snowdonia National Park in the north combines dramatic mountain scenery with glacial valleys, lakes and streams, while in the south the Brecon Beacons boast mountains, moorlands, forests and wooded gorges with deep caves. The surrounding area of the Wye Valley on the borders with England is a designated Area of Outstanding Natural Beauty; as are the Gower Peninsula, the Lleyn Peninsula, the Anglesey Coast and the Clwydian Range. The endless miles of largely unspoilt and beautiful Pembrokeshire coastline in the west have some of the finest long beaches in Europe, with pretty little bays plus the lively traditional seaside resorts of Tenby and Whitesand. Further inland is the secluded and pretty Gwaun Valley. The capital of Wales, Cardiff, has many attractions, including its newly developed waterfront, the Millennium Stadium. Castles can be seen all over Wales, ranging from tiny stone keeps to huge medieval fortresses; some of the best preserved are Caernarfon, Conwy and Harlech, all built by Edward I.

Places of interest

North: Isle of Anglesey; Portmeirion Italianate village; Llandudno; Colwyn Bay; Caernarfon, Conwy and Harlech castles; Ffestiniog and Welsh Highland railways.

West: Oakwood Park, Wales' only theme park; the National Botanic Gardens at Aberglasney; Dolaucothi Goldmines; historic, stone-walled Aberaeron.

Mid: Brecon Beacons National Park; the lakes of the Elan Valley; picturesque seaside town of Barmouth; Machynlleth, 'ancient capital of Wales' and the nearby Centre for Alternative Technology.

South: Caerphilly's enormous medieval castle; Cardiff, capital of Wales; seaside resorts of Tenby and Saundersfoot; National Botanic Garden of Wales, Llanarthne.

Did you know?

The origins of the Red Dragon flag may date back to the Roman period, when the dragon was used by military cohorts.

St. David's in Pembrokeshire is Britain's smallest city by virtue of its cathedral to the patron saint of Wales.

There are many sites in Wales linked to the legend of King Arthur: Castell Dinas Brân, near Llangollen, is reputed to be the resting place of the Holy Grail.

The Welsh name for Snowdon, Yr Wyddfa, means burial place.

The Welsh ruler Owen Glendower was the last native Welshman to be given the title Prince of Wales in 1400.

The Welsh language is one of Europe's oldest languages and shares its roots with Breton, Gaelic and Cornish.

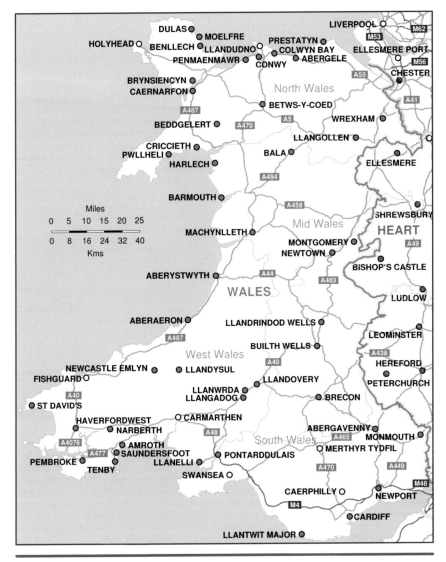

North Wales

Mid Wales

WALES

HEART

West Wales

South Wales

Aberaeron

Aeron Coast Caravan Park

North Road, Aberaeron SA46 0JF (Ceredigion) T: 01545 570349. E: enquiries@aeroncoast.co.uk

alanrogers.com/UK6280

Aeron Coast is a family holiday park with a wide range of recreational facilities, on the west coast of Wales. Although it has a high proportion of caravan holiday homes (200 privately owned), touring units of all types are provided for in two fields separated from the beach and sea by a high bank (although the best beach is on the south side of this traditional fishing village). Pitches are on level grass with all units regularly and well spaced in lines in traditional style. The main attraction of the park is its excellent provision for families, both in and out of doors.

Facilities	Directions
Two modern toilet blocks offer excellent facilities including large family showers. Facilities for disabled visitors and babies (in one block). Basic motorcaravan service point. Heated swimming pools (1/6-15/9). Club house (from Easter, 12.00-14.00 and from 19.00) serving bar meals and takeaway in school holiday periods. Entertainments room. Shop at the petrol station at the entrance. Only one dog per unit. Off site: Beach and fishing 1 mile.	Park is on northern outskirts of Aberaeron village with entrance on the right beside a petrol station. Brown signpost. GPS: 52.2445, -4.254917

Open: 1 March - 31 October.

Charges guide

Per unit incl. 4 persons	
and electricity	£ 16.00 - £ 26.00
extra person (over 2 yrs)	£ 4.00
dog	£ 1.00

FREE Alan Rogers Travel Card
Extra benefits and savings - see page 10

Abergavenny
Pont Kemys Caravan & Camping Park

Chainbridge, Abergavenny NP7 9DS (Monmouthshire) T: 01873 880688. E: info@pontkemys.com

alanrogers.com/UK5914

Pont Kemys is an attractive, peaceful touring park neatly arranged on the banks of the River Usk, only four miles from the town of the same name. There are 65 touring pitches, both on grass and with hardstanding, arranged around the perimeter of the park and within the central area. All have 16A electric hook-ups. An adult only area provides 21 fully serviced pitches. This is a quiet site with few amenities. Reception contains a small shop selling basic provisions, plus gas and camping supplies. Free WiFi is planned. The Chainbridge pub and a bar/restaurant at the local golf club are within walking distance. Entrance to the site is limited to units of less than 35 ft. due to access. Plenty of activities are possible in the local area, including fishing, pony trekking, canoeing and rock climbing.

Facilities

The modern sanitary block is neat and clean. Baby room. Toilet/shower for disabled visitors. Laundry room. Kitchen area with microwave. Basic provisions and camping items from reception. Gas. TV lounge. Simple play area. Max. 2 dogs per pitch. Separate dog walking area. Off site: Pub and golf club bar/restaurant within walking distance. Golf 400 m. Fishing 4 miles. Usk 4 miles. Many of South Wales' attractions such as the Millennium Stadium, Cardiff, the Big Pit Museum and the many castles are accessible by car.

Open: March - October.

Directions

From M4 exit 24 travel north on A449 and turn off into Usk. Take B4598 (Abergavenny) for 4 miles, cross Chainbridge and park is 300 yds. on right. From Abergavenny follow one-way system (Monmouth), turn left on B4598 (do not join the A40 dual carriageway). After 4 miles turn right for Usk at Charthouse pub, then 2.5 miles to park. GPS: 51.746567, -2.946556

Charges guide

Per unit incl. 2 persons and electricity	£ 17.00 - £ 19.00
extra person	£ 3.00
child (5-12 yrs)	£ 2.00
dog (max. 2)	£ 1.00

Abergele
Hunters Hamlet Caravan Park

Sirior Goch Farm, Betws-yn-Rhos, Abergele LL22 8PL (Conwy) T: 01745 832237. E: huntershamlet@aol.com

alanrogers.com/UK6650

This small, family owned park is licensed for all units except tents (trailer tents are allowed). On a gently sloping hillside providing beautiful panoramic views, one area provides 15 well spaced pitches with hardstanding and 10A electricity, with access from a circular, hardcore road. A more recent area has been developed next to this of a similar design but with eight fully serviced super pitches (water, waste water, sewage, TV and 16A electricity). Shrubs and bushes at various stages of growth enhance both areas. A natural play area incorporating rustic adventure equipment set amongst mature beech trees with a small bubbling stream is a children's paradise. The site operates a no football policy. Milk and papers can be ordered and the Hunters will do their best to meet your needs. The park is well situated to tour Snowdonia and Anglesey and is within easy reach of Llandudno and Rhyl.

Facilities

The heated toilet block has fully tiled facilities including showers en-suite with toilets for both sexes. A sunroom to the rear houses laundry and dishwashing (hot and cold), washing machine and dryer, iron and board, freezer and fridge. Family bathroom (metered) and basic toilet and shower facilities for disabled visitors. Play area. WiFi over site (free). All year caravan storage. Max. 2 dogs per pitch. Off site: Fishing and golf 2 miles. Beach 3.5 miles. Sailing and boat launching 7 miles. Riding 10 miles.

Open: 1 March - 31 October.

Directions

From Abergele take A548 south for almost 3 miles; turn onto B5381 in direction of Betws-yn-Rhos and park is on left after 0.5 miles. GPS: 53.248833, -3.6068

Charges guide

Per unit incl. 2 persons and electricity	£ 18.00 - £ 21.00
super pitch	£ 23.00 - £ 26.00
extra person	£ 4.00
child (at school)	£ 2.00
Less £5 on weekly bookings.	

For latest campsite news visit
alanrogers.com

Abergele
Plas Farm Caravan Park

Plas-yn-Betws, Betws-yn-Rhos, Abergele LL22 8AU (Conwy) T: 01492 680254.
E: info@plasfarmcaravanpark.co.uk **alanrogers.com/UK6685**

An attractive and welcoming site has been created as a series of terraces behind a working farm. Situated on the edge of the Snowdonia National Park, Plas Farm perfectly blends the campsite into the surrounding countryside. Sian and John Jones will give you a warm welcome and you get an immediate feel for the beautiful surroundings. The view is different from each of the terraces, and from the bottom terrace a woodland walk circles the site and is used as a dog walk. The 50 pitches all have 10/16A electric hook-ups and 46 are fully serviced. On a separate field there is provision for 30 tents, some with electricity. Access could be difficult for large outfits, so telephoning in advance is recommended. The Conwy Valley is an ideal location for adults and children alike, offering hill walking, golfing, rambling, tennis, sailing and watersports. You can visit the Welsh Mountain Zoo and narrow-gauge railways. Regular sea angling trips operate from the Conwy Quay and the Conwy River hosts an abundance of trout and salmon.

Facilities

Two new toilet blocks (2011) have a mixture of cubicles and open washbasins, showers and toilets for both sexes. For disabled visitors there is a shower, toilet and washbasin. Family room with further facilities and baby changing. Laundry with washing machine, tumble dryer and ironing. Play area with low-level climbing frame. WiFi over site (charged). An area has been created above the site with benches to sit and admire the views. Off site: Pub within one mile of the site. Fishing and golf 2 miles. Riding 10 miles.

Open: 1 March - 31 October.

Directions

Heading towards North Wales, leave the A55 at exit 24 on thr A547 through Abergele town centre. Continue straight over mini-roundabout at Tesco and next mini-roundabout. After 0.5 miles, turn left (Rhyd-y-Foel/Dolwen). After 3 miles at crossroads, turn left on B5381 for 0.5 miles and turn left signed Abergele and site which is 200 yds. on the left. GPS: 53.252515, -3.651064

Charges guide

Per unit incl. 2 persons and electricity	£ 13.00 - £ 19.50
extra person	£ 5.00 - £ 6.00
child (3-16 yrs)	£ 2.00 - £ 3.00
dog	£ 1.00

Plas-yn-Betws • Betws-yn-Rhos
Abergele • Conwy LL22 8AU
Tel. 01492 680 254
info@plasfarmcaravanpark.co.uk
www.plasfarmcaravanpark.co.uk

A quiet touring caravan and camping site set in the picturesque, tranquil surroundings of Betws-yn-Rhos, surrounded by history, natural beauty and coastline.

Abergele
Ty Mawr Holiday Park

Towyn Road, Towyn, Abergele LL22 9HG (Conwy) T: 01745 832079.
E: holidaysales.tymawr@park-resorts.com **alanrogers.com/UK6655**

Ty Mawr Holiday Park is located close to the many attractions of the North Wales Coast and the Snowdonia National Park. The touring area has a refurbished toilet block. The pool complex has also been completely renovated during 2011 to provide an excellent indoor pool and flume. There is some traffic noise from the road adjacent to the meadow. Large outfits can be accommodated, but if they exceed 6 m. they are required to pay for two pitches. There is a large proportion of privately-owned and rental caravan holiday homes which are neatly sited on well manicured grass pitches.

Facilities

Two well maintained, functional blocks which can be heated serve the main touring area with Portacabin style units on the open meadows. They are regularly cleaned. Washbasins are open style, preset showers have curtains and hooks, but no seats. Baby rooms. Facilities for disabled visitors (key). Launderette. Ice pack service. Shop. Bar with meals, cafeteria and takeaway. Indoor pool. Multisport courts. Excellent play areas and children's clubs. Evening family entertainment. WiFi (charged). Off site: Beach 0.25 miles. Bicycle hire 0.5 miles. Golf, riding and boat launching 3 miles. Fishing 6 miles. The island of Anglesey and the historic towns of Conwy and Caernarfon are within easy reach.

Open: Mid March - end October.

Directions

Take the A55 in a westerly direction into North Wales and take exit for Abergele. Follow signs for A548 Rhyl towards Towyn. Shortly after Towyn turn right into site. GPS: 53.29867, -3.55442

Charges guide

Per pitch	£ 5.00 - £ 33.00
incl. electricity	£ 8.00 - £ 36.00
dog	£ 1.00 - £ 3.00

Units over 6 metres in length are charged for 2 pitches.

 FREE Alan Rogers Travel Card
Extra benefits and savings - see page 10

Aberystwyth

Glan-y-Mor Leisure Park

Clarach Bay, Aberystwyth SY23 3DT (Ceredigion) T: 01970 828900. E: glanymor@sunbourne.co.uk

alanrogers.com/UK6290

Follow the road to Clarach Bay and on the seafront is Glan-y-Mor, a busy, holiday style park with an enviable situation. On a wet day you may not wish to go far with the comprehensive leisure centre on site – it is open eight months of the year with reduced entry fee for campers. Although the balance of pitches is very much in favour of caravan holiday homes (3:1) which dominate the open park and bay, there are 50 touring pitches, 45 with 10A electricity and four new super pitches. They are rather small and are pressed together in two small sections on the lower part of the park.

Facilities

The heated toilet block is on the lower touring area with a laundry room, plus a toilet for disabled guests. A Portacabin type block (high season only) is on the ridge ground. A suite including shower for disabled visitors is in a block in the upper static site, with further facilities at the leisure centre (Radar key). Motorcaravan service point. Gas supplies. Supermarket. Play area. Large sports field. Swimming pool. Licensed restaurant and takeaway (from Easter). WiFi (charged). Off site: Golf (reduced rates).

Open: 1 March - 31 October.

Directions

Clarach is signed west from the A487 (Aberystwyth-Machynlleth) in village of Bow Street (narrow bridge). Follow signs over crossroads to beach and park. Access for caravans from Aberystwyth on B4572 is difficult. GPS: 52.43625, -4.08025

Charges guide

Per unit incl. up to 6 persons and electricity	£ 15.00 - £ 26.50

Top camping area max. charge £10 plus £2 electricity.

Amroth

Pantglas Farm Caravan Park

Tavernspite, Pembrokeshire, Amroth SA34 0NS (Pembrokeshire) T: 01834 831618. E: pantglasfarm@btinternet.com **alanrogers.com/UK5974**

A secluded, rural, family run park with a nice atmosphere, Pantglas Farm is four miles from the coast with extensive views over rolling countryside and down to the sea. Set in three gently sloping paddocks spread over 14 acres, there are 83 generously sized, fairly level pitches with 10A electricity on gravel hardstanding. This is a popular and attractive site close to the main resorts but enjoying a more tranquil atmosphere. An on-site clubhouse also has a lounge with TV and a games room, with some simple entertainment activities arranged at Bank Holidays, some weekends and in high season.

Facilities

Two toilet blocks (one can be heated) are of a good standard including large controllable showers and some washbasins in cubicles. Facilities for disabled visitors include a wet room. Laundry facilities. Gas supplies. Licensed clubhouse (opening times vary). Play area. Games field. Games room. TV lounge. WiFi over site (charged). Off site: Fishing 1 mile. Supermarket, golf and riding 3 miles. Beaches at Amroth and Pendine 3 miles.

Open: 23 March - 19 October.

Directions

From A477 Tenby-Pembroke road turn right at Red Roses crossroads to Tavernspite for 1.25 miles. At village pump take middle road. Site is 0.5 miles on left. GPS: 51.778317, -4.645417

Charges guide

Per unit incl. 2 persons and electricity	£ 19.00 - £ 21.00
extra person	£ 3.00

Credit cards accepted with surcharge.

Bala

Glanllyn Lakeside Caravan & Camping Park

Llanuwchllyn, Bala LL23 7ST (Gwynedd) T: 01678 540227. E: info@glanllyn.com

alanrogers.com/UK6345

This 16-acre site lying alongside the southern end of Bala lake has 204 pitches. With around 40 seasonal units, this leaves 164 tourist pitches, 94 of which have electric hook-ups. In this location, virtually all the pitches have wonderful views of the lake or the surrounding mountain sides. The terrain is grassy, fairly open and level, but with natural terraces. There are around 19 individual hardstandings and a further hardstanding area by the beach is a favourite with motorcaravanners. The site is served by main tarmac access roads with speed bumps.

Facilities

Complex of three modern sanitary buildings (one can be heated and is used in low season) with preset showers. Facilities for babies and suite for disabled campers (key code access). Laundry room. Motorcaravan service point. Shop at reception (Easter-Oct). Gas supplies. Adventure style playground. Only 2 dogs per unit permitted. Breathable groundsheets only and only for min. 3-day stay. Off site: Bicycle hire, pool and golf in Bala 3 miles.

Open: Easter - mid October.

Directions

From Bala take A494 southwest towards Dolgellau for 3 miles, entrance is on left, on a right hand bend. GPS: 52.877667, -3.64665

Charges guide

Per unit incl. 2 persons and electricity	£ 21.00 - £ 29.00
tent pitch incl. 2 persons	£ 15.00 - £ 19.00
extra person	£ 6.00

For latest campsite news visit

alanrogers.com

Bala
Pen-y-Bont Touring & Camping Park
Llangynog Road, Bala LL23 7PH (Gwynedd) T: 01678 520549. E: penybont-bala@btconnect.co.uk
alanrogers.com/UK6340

This is a pretty little park with 59 touring pitches, 47 of which have hardstanding. Connected by circular gravel roads, they are intermingled with trees and tall trees edge the site. Electricity connections (16A) are available, including 11 for tents, and there are 28 serviced pitches with hardstanding, electricity, water and drainage. There are also pitches for 25 seasonal units. The park entrance, the building that houses reception and the shop provide quite a smart image. With views of the Berwyn mountains, Pen-y-bont has a peaceful, attractive and useful location being the closest park to Bala town.

Facilities	Directions
The toilet block includes washbasins in cubicles and spacious hot showers. Two new cubicles with washbasin and WC. Separate laundry room and an en-suite unit for disabled visitors, that doubles as a baby room, operated by key (£5 deposit). Outside covered area with fencing and concrete floor for dishwashing sinks and bins. Motorcaravan service point. Shop. Bicycle hire. Caravan storage. WiFi (charged). Off site: Fishing 200 yds. Boat launching, golf and riding 2 miles. Mon. market in Bala.	Park is 0.5 miles southeast of Bala village on the B4391. Bala is between Dolgellau and Corwen on the A494. GPS: 52.901717, -3.590117

Open: 15 March - 27 October.

Charges guide

Per unit incl. 2 persons and electricity	£ 19.00 - £ 23.00
tent pitch incl. 2 persons	£ 15.50 - £ 20.50
extra person	£ 7.50
child (4-16 yrs)	£ 4.00

Barmouth
Hendre Mynach Touring Caravan & Camping Park
Llanaber, Barmouth LL42 1YR (Gwynedd) T: 01341 280262. E: mynach@lineone.net
alanrogers.com/UK6370

A neat and tidy family park, colourful flowers and top rate facilities make an instant impression on arrival down the steep entrance to this park (help is available to get out if you are worried). Of the 240 pitches, 60 are for touring guests and are allocated in various areas, with substantial tenting areas identified. All 60 touring pitches are fully serviced with electricity, water taps and waste water. The beach is only 100 yards away but is separated from the park by a railway line. It can be crossed by pedestrian operated gates, which could be a worry for those with young children.

Facilities	Directions
Two toilet blocks, one modern and one traditional, both offer excellent facilities including spacious showers (free) and washbasins in cubicles. An extension to the traditional block provides facilities for disabled visitors. Motorcaravan service point. Well stocked shop incorporating a snack bar and takeaway (Easter-1/11). WiFi. Off site: Beach 100 m. Fishing, boat launching and bicycle hire within 0.5 miles. Riding 5 miles. Golf 9 miles.	Park is off the A496 road north of Barmouth in village of Llanaber with entrance down a steep drive. GPS: 52.73300, -4.06618

Open: All year excl. 10 January - 28 February.

Charges guide

Per unit incl. 2 persons and electricity	£ 15.00 - £ 30.00
extra person	£ 4.00

Plus £2 per night for certain weekends.

Barmouth
Islawrffordd Caravan Park
Talybont, Barmouth LL43 2AQ (Gwynedd) T: 01341 247269. E: info@islawrffordd.co.uk
alanrogers.com/UK6385

If you like to park up and have all amenities within easy access, then this site is ideal. Family owned and run since being established in 1957, Islawrffordd Caravan Park offers the very best in quality, which is evident as you enter the park. There are 75 fully serviced touring pitches (some seasonal) and 30 tent pitches. The fully serviced pitches all have courtesy light, electricity, fresh and waste water points and chemical disposal. Facilities include a well stocked minimarket, a bar/restaurant, takeaway and indoor swimming pool with sauna, jacuzzi and tanning suite. The site has private access to a sandy beach.

Facilities	Directions
The immaculate, modern toilet facilities have underfloor heating and climate control, a toilet for disabled visitors (Radar key) and baby changing room. Launderette. The toilet block and the entrance and exit of the park are activated by a key fob (deposit required). WiFi throughout (charged). Off site: Sea fishing trips from Barmouth. Golf at Royal St Davids Golf Club is 15 minutes away in Harlech. Pony trekking is about 30 minutes drive away.	Approximately four miles north of Barmouth, turn off the main A496 on to Fford Glan Mor Road, over a narrow railway bridge, past the Talybont Railway Halt and neighbouring campsites. The park is almost at the end and is signed to the left. GPS: 52.772491, -4.100299

Open: All year.

Charges guide

Per serviced pitch incl. 5 persons	£ 32.50
tent pitch incl. up to 5 persons	£ 28.50

FREE Alan Rogers Travel Card
Extra benefits and savings - see page 10

Barmouth
Trawsdir Touring Caravans & Camping Park
Llanaber, Barmouth LL42 1RR (Gwynedd) T: 01341 280999. E: enquiries@trawsdir.co.uk

alanrogers.com/UK6380

With sea views from almost every pitch and with a backdrop of hills, this campsite has something for everyone, young and old alike. Entrance and exit via the site barrier, and access to the facilities are by a key fob. A well equipped children's play area with safety surface is close to reception. Of the 142 touring pitches, 70 are for tents (48 with electricity) while the remaining 72 are fully serviced and can take RVs. The campsite has a large dog walking field and from the corner of the site is a lit walk to the Wayside Inn, avoiding the main road. A member of the Best of British group.

Facilities

Two toilet blocks are furnished to a very high standard, however one is kept in reserve for when cleaning is being done except for the busiest times. Facilities for disabled visitors with good access (Radar key). Baby changing facilities in both male and female toilets. Laundry. Shop. WiFi (charged). Off site: Sea fishing trips from Barmouth. Golf 20 minutes away in Harlech. A private beach is available at sister site across the road.

Open: 1 March - 6 January.

Directions

From Barmouth follow signs for Harlech (do not take beach road), pass through the town. After town, pass church, up the hill and leave the 40 mph speed limit. Pass Caerddaniel Holiday Park and Wayside Inn. Trawsdir entrance is just beyond on right hand side. GPS: 52.749871, -4.080361

Charges guide

| Per unit incl. 4 persons and electricity | £ 17.00 - £ 32.00 |

Beddgelert
Forest Holidays Beddgelert
Caernarfon Road, Beddgelert LL55 4UU (Gwynedd) T: 01766 890288. E: info@forestholidays.co.uk

alanrogers.com/UK6590

Forest Holidays is a partnership between the Forestry Commission and The Camping and Caravanning Club. This well equipped site is in the heart of Snowdonia, set in a marvellous, natural, wooded environment on the slopes of Snowdon. Well equipped and well managed, the site provides 204 pitches – tents in a semi-wooded field area and caravans amongst the trees with numbered hardstandings, and 105 places with 10/16A electricity. Tents may pitch where they like in their areas leaving six metres between units or there are six new grass pitches with electrical hook-ups for tents. Metal tent pegs may be best (available from the shop). Free maps of the forest walks are provided in reception.

Facilities

Two fully equipped and modern sanitary toilet blocks provide large, free hot showers. Laundry equipment is in one block. Toilet and washbasin for disabled visitors. Excellent drive-through motorcaravan service point. Shop (Easter-end Sept). Adventure playground. Common room. Off site: Pub within walking distance (under 1 mile) and other eating places nearby. Bicycle hire 1 mile.

Open: All year.

Directions

Site is clearly signed to the left 1 mile north of Beddgelert on the A4085 Caernarfon road. GPS: 53.02075, -4.119767

Charges guide

Per unit incl. 2 persons	£ 12.30 - £ 26.60
incl. electricity	£ 17.00 - £ 37.00
extra person	£ 4.50 - £ 6.80

Benllech
Plas Uchaf Caravan & Camping Park
Benllech Bay, Benllech LL74 8NU (Isle of Anglesey) T: 01407 763012

alanrogers.com/UK6636

This spacious, family run, campsite is set in 16 acres of flat, well mown grass with 12 hardstandings. A separate area for 60 tents is provided. Within the park there are woodland walks and a play route for children, an attractive play area with robust play equipment and a dog walk. All in an open, rural setting this park offers a safe haven for young families to enjoy. The pitches are set around the perimeter of six individual areas, each with picnic tables for communal use and all 110 touring pitches offer electricity (10/16A) and a water supply. Motorcaravans over 26 ft. are not accepted. Large outfits are advised to phone in advance. A new reception/games room and walkers' accommodation are planned.

Facilities

Three clean, traditional style sanitary blocks have separate facilities for men and women, with hot showers (charge), open style washbasins, hairdryers and small baths. Baby areas. Facilities for disabled visitors are planned for the new building. Limited laundry. Large playing field, play equipment and dog walk. Freezer facilities. Off site: Shops, bars, restaurants, fishing, golf, sandy beach, riding and sailing all within 1 mile.

Open: 14 March - 14 October.

Directions

From the Britannia Bridge take the A5025. In Benllech turn left onto the B5108. After the fire station on left, turn first right and the park is signed. GPS: 53.32676, -4.23956

Charges guide

| Per unit incl. 2 persons and electricity | £ 16.00 - £ 20.00 |

No credit cards.

For latest campsite news visit
alanrogers.com

Betws-y-Coed
Riverside Touring Park

Old Church Road, Betws-y-Coed LL24 0AL (Gwynedd) T: 01690 710310. E: riverside@morris-leisure.co.uk

alanrogers.com/UK6615

This is a delightful, peaceful, eight-acre caravan park owned and operated by the Morris Leisure Group. It is set just a five minute walk away from the village of Betws-y-Coed, a perfect location to visit the stunning Snowdonia National Park. Betws-y-Coed is widely acclaimed as one of the most attractive villages in Great Britain. There are a total of 120 spacious pitches, 61 for mobile homes and 59 for tourers (all hardstanding; 20 are super pitches and there are a few grass tent pitches). All have 16A electricity and TV. A member of the Caravan Club affiliated scheme (non-members very welcome).

Facilities

The heated toilet block (key access) has walk-in style shower cubicles. Separate cubicles with WCs. Facilities for children and disabled visitors. Laundry facilities. Motorcaravan service point. A digital TV booster system is available. Security barrier is closed 22.00-07.00. Dog walk (max. 2 per unit). No arrivals before 13.00. No gazebos. Off site: Village with supermarket. Fishing 1 mile. Golf 4 miles. Boat launching 5 miles. Ffestiniog railway.

Open: 18 February - 3 January.

Directions

From southeast turn right off A5 (Llangollen-Betws-y-Coed) in Betws village and follow signs Riverside, Railway Museum and Golf Club. Site entrance on left just after railway station. GPS: 53.093264, -3.799234

Charges guide

Per unit incl. 2 persons	
and electricity	£ 22.60 - £ 25.30
extra person	£ 6.60 - £ 7.00

Brecon
Pencelli Castle Caravan & Camping Park

Pencelli, Brecon LD3 7LX (Powys) T: 01874 665451. E: pencelli@tiscali.co.uk

alanrogers.com/UK6040

This high quality park is on the edge of Pencelli village. Set in the grounds of an old castle amidst the Brecon scenery, the park has both atmosphere and character. It offers excellent facilities in peaceful, rural tranquillity. The owners, Liz and Gerwyn Rees, have retained the country charm but have added an all embracing range of spacious, heated, luxury facilities, attractively enhanced by potted plants, etc. There are three touring fields. The Orchard has some fully serviced pitches with hardstanding, amongst shrubs, fruit trees and a stone cider mill. The Oaks taking a mix of motorcaravans, caravans and tents and the Meadow for tents only (with boot and bike wash) are bordered by majestic trees and the Monmouthshire and Brecon Canal. All the fields are level with neatly mown grass and tarmac access roads. The historic manor house, that dates back to 1583, is adjacent to arched barns that house an increasing collection of vintage farm machinery including carts and rare tractors. A path leaves the village to reach the top of the Brecon Beacons or there is an easy towpath ramble to Tal-y-Bont.

Facilities

The toilet block is very well designed and includes some private cubicles, two large fully equipped rooms for families and disabled visitors incorporating double showers, baby changing and bath facilities. Laundry. Drying room with lockers. Information and planning room. Motorcaravan service point. Small shop. Playground and nature trail for children. Bicycle hire. WiFi throughout (free). Only assistance dogs accepted. Off site: The Royal Oak Inn 100 yds. Riding 2 miles. Golf and bicycle hire 5 miles.

Open: 16 February - 27 November.

Directions

From the A40 south after Brecon bypass take the B4558 at signs for Llanfrynach and later Pencelli (narrow bridge). If travelling north on A40, approach via Tal-y-Bont. Site is at south end of Pencelli. GPS: 51.914783, -3.317867

Charges guide

Per unit incl. 2 persons	
and electricity	£ 16.80 - £ 27.60
extra person	£ 6.50 - £ 8.00
child (5-15 yrs)	£ 4.75 - £ 6.50

FREE Alan Rogers Travel Card
Extra benefits and savings - see page 10

Brynsiencyn
Fron Caravan & Camping Park
Brynsiencyn, Anglesey LL61 6TX (Isle of Anglesey) T: 01248 430310. E: mail@froncaravanpark.co.uk
alanrogers.com/UK6635

A traditional, all touring campsite in a peaceful rural location, Fron has panoramic views over the surrounding countryside. From the entrance gate a tarmac drive passes through a two-acre, level, grassy paddock, which is reserved for 35 large sized tent and trailer tent pitches. The drive leads up to the old farmhouse which houses reception and a well stocked shop. Behind the farmhouse is another two-acre, sloping paddock with 40 caravan and motorcaravan pitches, five with hardstandings, and 57 electricity hook-ups (10A). A heated swimming pool is well controlled by the owners.

Facilities

Toilet facilities are in three units of varying ages and designs. These include a unit for ladies with some basins in cubicles, good hot showers with dividers (20p), a baby area and a suite for disabled campers. Laundry facilities. Motorcaravan service point. Heated swimming pool (30x14 ft; May-Sept). Gas stocked. Max. 2 dogs per pitch. Torches useful. Off site: Brynsiencyn Village (0.5 miles) has a hotel and Spar shop with ATM. Fishing 1.5 miles. Riding 3 miles. Golf 4 miles.

Open: Easter/1 April (whichever is earlier) - end September.

Directions

Cross Britannia Bridge and take first slip road (Llanfairpwll A4080), then next left (Newborough and Brynsiencyn). Continue on A4080 for 5 miles, turning right in village at Groeslon Hotel. Continue through Brynsiencyn for 1 mile to site at western end of village. The entrance requires a wide sweep for a car and caravan. GPS: 53.176217, -4.28785

Charges guide

Per unit incl. 2 persons and 2 children	£ 22.00
extra person	£ 6.00

No credit cards.

Builth Wells
Fforest Fields Caravan & Camping Park
Hundred House, Builth Wells LD1 5RT (Powys) T: 01982 570406. E: office@fforestfields.co.uk
alanrogers.com/UK6320

This secluded park is set on a family hill farm within seven acres in the heart of Radnorshire. This is simple country camping and caravanning at its best, with no clubhouse, swimming pool or games room. The facilities include 80 large pitches on level grass on a spacious and peaceful, carefully landscaped field by a stream. Electrical connections (mostly 16A) are available and there are 17 hardstanding pitches, also with electricity. Several additional areas without electricity are provided for tents. There are two new lakes, one for boating and fly fishing, the other for coarse fishing.

Facilities

The toilet facilities are acceptable with baby bath, dishwashing and laundry facilities including washing machines and a dryer. Milk, eggs, orange juice and gas are sold in reception, otherwise there are few other on-site facilities. Fishing. Torches are useful. WiFi throughout. Off site: Pub at Hundred House village 1 mile. Bicycle hire and golf 5 miles. Riding 10 miles.

Open: Easter - October.

Directions

Park is 4 miles east of Builth Wells near the village of Hundred House on A481. Follow brown signs. Do not use postcode on sat nav. GPS: 52.17121, -3.31621

Charges guide

Per unit incl. 2 persons and electricity	£ 18.00
extra person	£ 3.00

No credit cards.

Caernarfon
Plas Gwyn Caravan & Camping Park
Llanrug, Caernarfon LL55 2AQ (Gwynedd) T: 01286 672619. E: info@plasgwyn.co.uk
alanrogers.com/UK6620

In a beautiful location, this traditional, family run touring site is within the grounds of a house that was built in 1785 in the Georgian style with a colonial style veranda. The 30 touring caravan pitches are set around the perimeter of a slightly sloping grass field, and there are 8 hardstandings for motorcaravans. There are 36 pitches with 16A electricity hook-ups, of which 17 also provide water and waste water. A separate tent field has 10 pitches. Two 'timber tents' offer a touch of luxury camping. A separate field houses five caravan holiday homes for rent. A member of the Countryside Discovery group.

Facilities

An older style building houses the toilet facilities (fittings are modern) which are kept neat and tidy. Controllable hot showers. Laundry room. No dedicated facilities for babies and disabled visitors. Drive-over motorcaravan service point. Gas stocked. Reception stocks basic food items, etc. Breakfast 'butties' made to order and delivered. WiFi. Minimal site lighting so torches useful. Off site: Golf 1 mile. Riding 2.5 miles. Bicycle hire 3 miles. Fishing 4 miles.

Open: 1 March - 31 October.

Directions

Site is on A4086, 3 miles from Caernarfon, and 2.5 miles from Llanberis, well signed with easy access. GPS: 53.146733, -4.212233

Charges guide

Per unit incl. 2 persons and electricity	£ 17.50 - £ 21.00
tent pitch	£ 13.00 - £ 28.50
extra person	£ 3.00

For latest campsite news visit
alanrogers.com

Caernarfon
Bryn Gloch Caravan & Camping Park

Betws Garmon, Caernarfon LL54 7YY (Gwynedd) T: 01286 650216. E: eurig@bryngloch.co.uk

alanrogers.com/UK6600

Bryn Gloch is a well kept, family owned touring park in the impressive Snowdonia area – an unusual feature is the mountain railway which passes through the park. Neat and quiet, it takes some 160 units on five flat, wide meadows with some breathtaking views. With tarmac access roads and free areas allowed in the centre for play, of the 152 touring pitches, 80 have hardstanding, 10A electricity, water and drainage. In addition, there are 15 caravan holiday homes. Fishing is possible on the river bordering the park with a barbecue and picnic area, adventure play area and field for ball games. Tourist information is provided in the complex by the reception/shop and the park is very popular with walkers and cyclists. Caernarfon with its famous castle is five miles.

Facilities	Directions
The two very clean and modern main toilet blocks include washbasins in cabins, large showers, a family bathroom (hot water £1), baby room and complete facilities for visitors with disabilities (coded access). The far field has a Portacabin style unit containing all facilities, for use in peak season. Well equipped laundry and separate drying room. Motorcaravan service point and car wash. Shop (1/3-31/10). TV and games rooms with computer, pool tables and amusement machines. Minigolf. Entrance barrier with coded access. WiFi. Off site: Pub 1 mile. Riding 2.5 miles. ATM at garage in Ceathro 3 miles. Bicycle hire and golf 5 miles.	From Caernarfon take A4085 signed Beddgelert. Park is just beyond Waunfawr, 5.6 miles southeast of Caernarfon. After crossing river bridge, the entrance is immediately on the right, opposite St Garmon church. GPS: 53.095183, -4.1884

Charges guide

Per unit incl. 2 persons	
and electricity	£ 18.00 - £ 28.00
extra person	£ 4.00
child (3-16 yrs)	£ 2.00
dog (max. 2)	£ 1.00

Open: All year, limited facilities 1 November - 28 February.

AWARD WINNING SITE within Snowdonia National Park
TOURING, TENT & MOTORHOME PITCHES - STATIC CARAVANS FOR HIRE - SEASONAL PITCHES

Nestled in a picturesque valley on the banks of the river Gwyrfai and overlooked by Snowdonia mountain ranges. Facilities; Elec Hook-ups, luxury toilet/shower block, disabled fac. shop/off licence Close by local pub/restaurant, Water sports, Climbing, Walking, Horse Riding. **BrynGloch** **01286 650216** camping & caravanning park **www.campwales.co.uk**

Caernarfon
Tafarn Snowdonia Parc Brewpub & Campsite

Waunfawr, Caernarfon LL55 4AQ (Gwynedd) T: 01286 650409. E: info@snowdonia-park.co.uk

alanrogers.com/UK6605

Set on the banks of the River Gwyrfai and amongst spectacular scenery, this no frills campsite is adjacent to the station for the Welsh Highland Railway. There are 32 grass pitches, (20 with 16A electricity) of variable size. They are set in an open field and serviced by two clean shower and toilet blocks (refurbished in 2010). Enjoy riverside walks and free fishing (licence required) before calling in at the adjoining pub with its own microbrewery (listed in the CAMRA Good Beer guide) and home cooked food. Children are well catered for with a family room in the pub, two gardens (one safe for toddlers) and a playground. The campsite is located four miles from the foot of Snowdon.

Facilities	Directions
One small toilet block in main camping field. A second block with separate showers and toilets for men and ladies, together with laundry facilities, is reached via a footbridge over the railway track. Both have been upgraded, but may become stretched when site is full. Full bar, restaurant and takeaway facilities. TV. Games room. Playground. Free fishing (licence required). Off site: Riding 800 yds. Golf 3 miles. Beach and sailing 5 miles.	From Caernarfon take the A4085 for 4 miles and campsite is on the left. The entrance is at the far end of pub/railway station car park. GPS: 53.10611, -4.20176

Charges guide

Per unit incl. 2 persons and electricity	£ 22.00
children and dogs	free

Open: All year.

FREE Alan Rogers Travel Card
Extra benefits and savings - see page 10

Cardiff

Cardiff Caravan Park

Pontcanna Fields, via Sophia Close, Cardiff CF11 9XR (Cardiff) T: 02920 398362.
E: cardiffcaravanpark@cardiff.gov.uk **alanrogers.com/UK5925**

Run by the city council, this popular site is set within acres of parkland, one mile from the city centre, ideal for visiting the many attractions of the city of Cardiff. The campsite has 61 touring pitches which are on a fairly open area, with 43 on a grasscrete surface with 16A electric hook-ups, the remainder are on grass. There is a public right of way through the site. Security is good with an on-site warden 24 hours a day, and security cameras (infrared) constantly scanning the whole area. Large units should phone ahead to arrange for access.

Facilities	Directions
Two heated buildings each with key code entry systems, the one by reception has a laundry and facilities for disabled campers. Both have controllable hot showers. Baby facilities. Bicycle hire (the site specialises in cycles adapted for disabled visitors). Riding can be arranged. Off site: The Millennium Stadium, Glamorgan County Cricket Ground, Cardiff Bay. Shops and services within easy walking distance. Fishing 0.25 mile. Golf 4 miles. Open: All year.	From the A48 turn south on A4119 (Cardiff Road). Pass church on left following signs for SWALEC Stadium. At next traffic lights turn into Sophia Close and Gardens. Turn left at Institute of Sport and pass County Cricket Ground on right. Continue along avenue to site on left. GPS: 51.49155, -3.20313

Charges guide

Per unit incl. electricity	£ 22.00 - £ 25.00
tent	£ 9.00 - £ 25.00

Colwyn Bay

Bron-Y-Wendon Touring Caravan Park

Wern Road, Llanddulas, Colwyn Bay LL22 8HG (Conwy) T: 01492 512903.
E: stay@northwales-holidays.co.uk **alanrogers.com/UK6690**

Bron-Y-Wendon is right by the sea between Abergele and Colwyn Bay on the beautiful North Wales coast. This is a quiet park which, by its own admission, is not really geared up for the family unit – there is no playground here. The park is manicured to the highest standards and caters for a large number of seasonal caravans on pitches with gravel bases which are kept very tidy. There are a further 65 grass based, and 85 hardstanding touring pitches, all with 16A electricity and tarmac access roads, 25 also with water and waste water. All pitches have coastal views and the sea and beach are just a short walk away. Trailer tents are accepted, but not other tents.

Facilities	Directions
Two toilet blocks, both with heating, provide excellent facilities including men's and women's shower rooms separate from the toilets and washbasins. Good facilities for disabled visitors. Laundry with washing machines and dryers. Mobile shop visits daily. Gas supplies. WiFi (charged). Off site: Llanddulas village with shops and pubs. Fishing 1 mile. Golf 4 miles. Riding 6 miles. Open: All year.	From A55 Chester-Conwy road turn at Llanddulas interchange (A547), junction 23. Turn right opposite Shell garage and park is 400 yds, signed on coast side of the road. GPS: 53.29185, -3.6445

Charges guide

Per unit incl. 2 persons and electricity	£ 20.00 - £ 24.00
extra person	£ 2.00 - £ 3.00

Conwy

Bron Derw Touring Park

Llanrwst, Conwy LL26 0YT (Conwy) T: 01492 640494. E: info@bronderw-wales.co.uk
alanrogers.com/UK6644

Nestling between the mountains and the edge of the small village of Llanrwst, Bron Derw has two camping areas, one for adults only and one for families. The 43 pitches (all with 16A electric supply) are well spaced out on hardstandings around the edge of the site, giving a feeling of spaciousness which matches the surrounding countryside. It is a family run site and this shows in the level of service and welcome which is received. Larger outfits can be accommodated, but it is advisable to phone ahead to make sure an adequate pitch is available.

Facilities	Directions
Two very modern and well apportioned blocks, one in each area. The adults only block was opened in 2011. Both have facilities for disabled visitors, and laundry facilities at the rear. Motorcaravan service point. Utility room. Off site: Within the Snowdonia National Park and only 20 minutes drive to the coastal resorts of North Wales. Fishing within 1 mile. Marin Trail mountain biking route 2 miles. Tree Top Adventure within 4 miles. Golf and bicycle hire 4 miles. Betws-y-Coed 5 miles. Open: 1 March - 31 October.	From the coast follow the A55 on to A470 for Betws-y-Coed and Llanrwst. In Llanrwst turn left into Parry Road then turn left again at T-junction. Take first farm entrance on the right signed Bron Derw and continue up the drive to the campsite. GPS: 53.143639, -3.797126

Charges guide

Per unit incl. 2 persons and electricity	£ 17.00 - £ 19.00
extra person	£ 4.00

For latest campsite news visit
alanrogers.com

Criccieth
Llanystumdwy Camping & Caravanning Club Site
Tyddyn Sianel, Llanystumdwy, Criccieth LL52 0LS (Gwynedd) T: 01766 522855

alanrogers.com/UK6580

Overlooking mountains and sea, Llanystumdwy is one of the earliest Camping & Caravanning Club sites. It is an attractive, sloping site with well manicured grass areas surrounded by trees and with good facilities. The wardens are very helpful and know their site and can advise on the most suitable pitch. There are 70 pitches in total (20 ft. spacing), 45 with 10A electricity connections, spaced over two fields with mainly caravans in the top field with four hardstandings for motorcaravans, tents are sited lower down. Some road noise may be experienced by those in tents on the lower field.

Facilities

A purpose-built toilet block to one side includes excellent, full facilities for disabled visitors, one washbasin each in a cubicle for male and female and extra large sinks. Facilities for babies. Laundry (taps with fitting for disabled campers). Gas supplies. WiFi over site (charged). Off site: Riding and fishing 0.5 miles. Beach 3 miles.

Open: March - October.

Directions

Follow A497 from Criccieth west and take second right to Llanystumdwy. Site is on the right. GPS: 52.920867, -4.27885

Charges guide

Per person	£ 5.53 - £ 8.17
non-member pitch fee	£ 7.10

Dulas
Tyddyn Isaf Caravan & Camping Park
Lligwy Bay, Dulas LL70 9PQ (Isle of Anglesey) T: 01248 410203

alanrogers.com/UK6637

This warm, welcoming family site cascades down the hillside from the bar/restaurant at the top of the site to the beach. The site has had the same owners for over 30 years. Lligwy Bay, with its sandy beach and sheltered waters, is ideal for children to play on and is accessible from the site. There are 80 touring pitches (of which 40 are seasonal) all with 16A electricity. The tent pitches (some with 10A electricity) are on separate fields. The site has been influenced by the clientele who have visited over the years. The owners insist that all visitors are escorted to their pitch and, if required, helped with siting.

Facilities

Two toilet blocks with free electric showers (timed; activated by a key-fob). Laundry facilities. The upper toilet block can be overstretched in peak times. A third toilet block is next to the bar. Shop selling basics. Bar serving snacks and main meals, takeaway food (mid May-mid Sept). Wi-Fi. Off site: Golf is a short drive away. Sea- and freshwater fishing. Numerous cycle paths and walks including the coastal walk to Moelfre. Anglesey has its own vineyard producing some excellent wines.

Open: Easter - 20 October.

Directions

From A55 Drive over Britannia bridge onto Anglesey. Look for turning (Benllech and Amlwch). Drive to roundabout and follow A5025 through Pentraeth and then Benllech, at second roundabout turn left and on to Brynrefail, turn right opposite gift shop. Follow signs for Tyddyn Isaf, half a mile down the lane. GPS: 53.3625, -4.27545

Charges guide

Per unit incl. 2 adults, 2 children and electricity	£ 22.00 - £ 29.00

No credit cards.

Harlech
Barcdy Caravan & Camping Park
Talsarnau, Harlech LL47 6YG (Gwynedd) T: 01766 770736. E: anwen@barcdy.co.uk

alanrogers.com/UK6350

Barcdy is partly in a sheltered vale, partly on a plateau top and partly in open fields edged by woods. There are fells to the rear and marvellous views across the Lleyn peninsula in one direction and towards the Snowdon range in another. The Roberts family opened to their first visitors over 60 years ago, and still welcome them today. The park provides for all tastes with level or sloping grass pitches, either secluded in the valley or enjoying the view from the plateau or the lower field. There are 92 pitches, including 20 that are fully serviced for touring caravans with electricity (16A) and 40 for tents, 10 with 10A electricity, plus 30 caravan holiday homes. A member of the Countryside Discovery group.

Facilities

Two toilet blocks, the one at the top of the valley opened in high season only, include large, comfortable showers, that open direct to the outside. Two family shower rooms at each block, one for each sex. Hot water is free to the washbasins, dishwashing sinks and showers. WiFi over site (charged). Dogs are not accepted. Off site: Fishing 0.5 miles. Riding 4 miles. Golf 4 and 6 miles.

Open: 1 April - 31 October.

Directions

Park is just off the A496 between villages of Llandecwyn and Talsarnau, 4 miles north of Harlech. If approaching from Porthmadog do not attempt to use toll road if towing or over 2 tons. GPS: 52.912983, -4.0524

Charges guide

Per unit incl. 2 persons and electricity	£ 16.00 - £ 22.00

 FREE Alan Rogers Travel Card
Extra benefits and savings - see page 10

Harlech
Min-y-Don Holiday Home & Touring Park

Beach Road, Harlech LL46 2UG (Gwynedd) T: 01766 780286. E: manager@minydonholidayhomepark.co.uk

alanrogers.com/UK6365

Set within the Snowdonia National Park, this super park was totally rebuilt for the 2009 season to a standard that others will strive to achieve. It is a level site with first class facilities and providing 82 well drained grass touring pitches, all with full services, including waste water and sewerage connections (seven with hardstanding for large motorcaravans). Tents are not accepted. In a separate area there are 112 caravan holiday homes. With three miles of golden sand beaches and the Snowdon mountain range as a backdrop, Min-y-Don overlooks the famous Royal St David's Golf Course.

Facilities

New toilet facilities are excellent with private cabins and underfloor heating. Large separate unit for disabled visitors. Two private bathrooms for rent. Motorcaravan services. Laundry facilities. Play area. Football pitch. Bike track. Putting green. WiFi (free). Off site: Supermarket and leisure centre 800 yds. Harlech with shops, pubs and restaurants within walking distance. Beach nearby. Coastal train. Bus service. Portmeirion. Snowdon.

Open: 1 March - 31 October.

Directions

From Barmouth go north on the A496 to Harlech. Go over level crossing and turn left into Beach Road. From the north on the A496 in Harlech, right into Beach Road before level crossing. Park is on the right in 400 yds. GPS: 52.862366, -4.11526

Charges guide

Per person	£ 5.50 - £ 7.00
child (5-15 yrs)	£ 2.00 - £ 3.50
pitch	£ 6.50 - £ 13.00

Harlech
Woodlands Caravan Park

Harlech LL46 2UE (Gwynedd) T: 01766 780419. E: info@woodlandsparkharlech.com

alanrogers.com/UK6355

This delightful little site is lovingly tended by its owners and has just 18 pitches for tourists, all with gravel hardstanding and 10A electric hook-ups, for caravans and motorcaravans only. Tents are not accepted. There are also 22 privately owned holiday homes, and three holiday cottages. However, the location of this site certainly makes up for its diminutive size, nestling under the massive rock topped by Harlech Castle, now a designated World Heritage Site. The narrow lane running alongside the site up to the old town above, is the steepest hill in Britain. The Blue Flag beach is only 500 yards away.

Facilities

The modern stone built toilet facilities are heated, clean and tidy with controllable showers (50p), vanity style washbasins, a small laundry with a baby changing area, but with no dedicated facilities for disabled visitors. Chemical disposal point but no motorcaravan service point. WiFi. Off site: Golf 0.25 miles. Steam train pleasure trips (July/Aug). Harlech Castle. The town also has a theatre and cinema. Fishing and riding 3 miles. Portmeirion, location of the cult TV series, The Prisoner, 8 miles. Barmouth (market Thu. and Sun) 10 miles.

Open: 1 March - 31 October.

Directions

From Barmouth take A496 to Harlech and continue downhill past Royal St David's Golf Course. Fork right immediately before railway crossing, and site is 200 yds. on right. DO NOT turn towards town centre which is on B4573, it is very narrow and congested. GPS: 52.86155, -4.107633

Charges guide

Per unit incl. 2 persons and electricity	£ 17.00 - £ 23.00

No credit or debit cards.

Haverfordwest
Creampots Touring Caravan & Camping Park

Broadway, Broad Haven, Haverfordwest SA62 3TU (Pembrokeshire) T: 01437 781776. E: creampots@btconnect.com **alanrogers.com/UK5992**

This peacefully located and beautifully manicured, garden-like park is ideal for couples and families, and is a convenient base within easy reach of beaches or for touring the local area. Creampots has 72 spacious, level pitches all with 10A electric hook-ups, including 21 with gravel hardstanding, and pitches for tents. There is a separate field and an overflow area taking 30 tents for the August peak holiday time. This is an ideal location for the local attractions.

Facilities

The single small white-washed sanitary unit is a modern building which can be heated. Two free hot showers per sex, open style washbasins. Washbasin and WC for disabled campers. These facilities were clean and tidy but may come under pressure at peak times. Tiny laundry room. Gas supplies. Off site: Shop, post office, pub with hot food in Broad Haven 1 mile. Fishing and boat launching 1 mile. Beach 1.5 miles. Riding 4 miles.

Open: March - October.

Directions

The site is 5 miles west of Haverfordwest. From Haverfordwest take B4341 to Broad Haven, at Broadway follow brown tourist sign on left. GPS: 51.777333, -5.072283

Charges guide

Per unit incl. 2 persons and electricity	£ 19.45 - £ 24.15
dog	free

For latest campsite news visit
alanrogers.com

Haverfordwest
Redlands Touring Caravan & Camping Park

Hasguard Cross, Little Haven, Haverfordwest SA62 3SJ (Pembrokeshire) T: 01437 781300.
E: info@redlandscamping.co.uk **alanrogers.com/UK5994**

This peaceful, family run site is located in the heart of the Pembrokeshire countryside, close to many lovely sandy beaches. Redlands takes around 80 touring units in three areas divided by banks topped with pine trees, 32 hardstandings and 69 with 10A electricity. The first two areas take 60 caravans or motorcaravans and include 32 hardstandings, the third takes 19 tents on a level grassy meadow. There are fine views across rolling countryside to St Brides Bay. Reception has a small shop which is open only in peak periods. Breathable groundsheets must be used. American RVs – advance booking only. A sandy beach and the Pembrokeshire Coastal Path are 1.5 miles away.

Facilities

The traditional style toilet block is well kept and heated early and late season. It has all the usual requirements including two extra shower, basin and WC suites. Large utility room with washing machine, dryer and spin dryer. Ironing is free, and there are sinks for laundry and dishes. Shop. Freezers. Wet suit washing area. Dogs are welcome (max. 2 high season) but must be kept on lead. Off site: Summer bus service. Fishing and boat launching 1.5 miles. Shops and ATM in Broadhaven 2 miles. Riding and sailing 5 miles. Golf 6 miles. Coastal bus service.

Open: 1 March - mid December.

Directions

Site 6.5 miles southwest of Haverfordwest. From Haverfordwest take the B4327 road towards Dale and site is on the right at Hasguard Cross. N.B. Do not approach via Broad Haven. GPS: 51.755567, -5.112383

Charges guide

Per unit incl. 2 persons and electricity	£ 17.70 - £ 22.95
extra person	£ 4.50
dog (max. 2, 1st free)	free - £ 1.00

No credit cards.

Llandovery
Erwlon Caravan & Camping Park

Brecon Road, Llandovery SA20 0RD (Carmarthenshire) T: 01550 721021. E: peter@erwlon.co.uk
alanrogers.com/UK5955

Just outside Llandovery and on the edge of the Brecon Beacons National Park, Erwlon is an attractive and welcoming campsite. Of the 110 pitches, seven are used for privately owned caravan holiday homes, 33 have seasonal caravans and 70 are for touring units. Most are on hardstanding with electricity connections and 12 have water and a drain as well. There is a flat field for tents at the bottom of the park with some electrical outlets, an open-sided, covered area for eating, food preparation and bicycle storage. The site has a relaxed atmosphere where consideration for others minimises the need for formal rules. It is ideal for young families, walkers, cyclists and fishermen. Gold mines and the National Showcaves Centre for Wales (including dinosaur park) are within an easy drive. A member of the Best of British group.

Facilities

New heated toilet block with washbasins in cabins, 4 family rooms (basin, shower, toilet) and a room for families and disabled visitors which includes a baby unit. Combined, well equipped laundry and dishwashing room. Motorcaravan service point. Fridge freezer. Fishing. Bicycle hire. WiFi (charge). Off site: Supermarket 500 yds. Town amenities (shops, pubs, restaurants and indoor pool) within 1 mile. Golf 1 mile. Riding 8 miles. Beaches about 25 miles.

Open: All year.

Directions

Park is half a mile outside the town boundary of Llandovery on the A40 to Brecon. GPS: 51.99491, -3.78076

Charges guide

Per unit incl. 2 persons	£ 13.00 - £ 16.00
incl. services	£ 16.00 - £ 19.00
extra person	£ 1.50 - £ 2.00
dog	free

No credit cards.

FREE Alan Rogers Travel Card
Extra benefits and savings - see page 10

Llandrindod Wells

Dolswydd Caravan Park

Dolswydd, Pen-y-Bont, Llandrindod Wells LD1 5UB (Powys) T: 01597 851267.
E: Hughes@dolswydd.freeserve.co.uk **alanrogers.com/UK6250**

Dolswydd is on the edge of a pretty, traditional working farm. A tranquil site with excellent views of the Welsh hills and surrounding area, it has modern facilities and 25 good spacious pitches mainly on hardstandings, all with 16A electrical connections. The Hughes family extends a warm and friendly welcome to their little park, surrounded by hills and wandering sheep, which is ideal as a touring base or for a one night stop, but booking is recommended, especially at peak times, Bank Holidays and during the Victorian Festival (last week in August). A footpath leads from the back of the site to the rear of the local pub which offers good, home cooked food.

Facilities

Modern facilities include lots of hot water, dishwashing, laundry, and a WC/washroom for disabled campers. Fishing in the river alongside the site (free, but licence required). Off site: Within walking distance are the local pub and garage. Riding 1 mile. Golf and bicycle hire 5 miles.

Open: Easter - end October.

Directions

Pen-y-Bont is 2 miles east of the junction of the A44 and A483 roads at Crossgates. Take A44 (Kington). Go through Pen-y-Bont and immediately after crossing cattle grid, site is on right. On arrival drive across farm cattle grid and reception is at second farmhouse. GPS: 52.15857, -3.18773

Charges guide

Per unit incl. 2 persons and electricity	£ 12.00
dog	free

Llandysul

Brynawelon Touring & Camping Park

Sarnau, Llandysul SA44 6RE (Ceredigion) T: 01239 654584. E: info@brynaweloncp.co.uk
alanrogers.com/UK6005

Paul and Liz Cowton have turned Brynawelon into a friendly, attractive and well appointed campsite. It is in a stunning rural location within two miles of the Ceredigion coast with its beaches, and close to the River Teifi with plenty of water based activities. All the 40 pitches have electricity hook-ups and of these, 25 are serviced hardstanding pitches (electricity, water and waste). A number of all-weather pitches for tents have been added recently. The remainder are on level grass. The park has ample room for children to play, an enclosed play area, an indoor games room with TV, and a sauna next to reception.

Facilities

Modern toilet block with toilets, showers, washbasins in cabins, two full suites in each side and a separate room for families and disabled visitors. Laundry/kitchen. Enclosed play area. Games room with table football, electronic games, TV and library. Sauna (charged). Dog walking area. WiFi (charged). Off site: Shops and pub 1 mile. Links with local farm shop (pre-order delivery, voucher scheme). Beach 1 mile. Fishing 2 miles. Golf and riding 3 miles. Dolphin trips at New Quay 10 miles.

Open: March - 31 October.

Directions

Travelling north on the A487 from Cardigan turn right (southeast) at the crossroads in Sarnau village, signed Rhydlewis. Site is on the left after 650 yds. Note: the cross-country approach is not advised. GPS: 52.13001, -4.45401

Charges guide

Per unit incl. 2 persons and electricity	£ 15.00
incl. 4 persons, hardstanding and services	£ 25.00

No credit cards.

Llanelli
Pembrey Country Park Caravan Club Site
Pembrey, Llanelli SA16 0EJ (Carmarthenshire) T: 01554 834369
alanrogers.com/UK5940

Set on the edge of a 520-acre country park, this popular Caravan Club site enjoys a wonderful location with a vast range of outdoor activities, including the use of a seven-mile stretch of safe, sandy beach a mile away. Well sheltered, the site is set in 12-acre grounds and provides 130 touring pitches, of which 68 are on hardstanding for caravans and motorcaravans. All are equipped with 16A electricity. Thoughtful landscaping has included the planting of many species of trees and a circular, one-way tarmac road provides easy access. RAF jets do practise in this area (although becoming less frequent and generally not flying at the weekend).

Facilities

The toilet block is of an excellent standard including washbasins in cubicles, facilities for disabled visitors and a baby room. Fully equipped laundry room. Dishwashing room and further sinks under cover. Motorcaravan service point. Gas available. Local tradesmen visit each morning selling milk, bread and newspapers. New play area. Late arrivals area (with electricity). Off site: Amenities of the country park. Shops 1 and 2.5 miles. Beach 1 mile (dogs are restricted on the beach May-Sept).

Open: 23 March - 7 January.

Directions

Leave M4 at exit 48 onto A4138 (Llanelli). After 4 miles turn right onto A484 at roundabout (Carmarthen). Continue for 7 miles to Pembrey. Follow brown country park signs in preference to sat nav. The country park is signed off the A484 in Pembrey village; site entrance is on right 100 yds. before park gates. GPS: 51.681817, -4.297417

Charges guide

Per person	£ 5.40 - £ 7.60
pitch incl. electricity (non-member)	£ 13.20 - £ 17.50

Llangadog
Abermarlais Caravan Park
Llangadog SA19 9NG (Carmarthenshire) T: 01550 777868. E: aberma@tiscali.co.uk
alanrogers.com/UK5960

Apart from the attractions of south or mid Wales for a stay, this sheltered, family run park could also double as a useful transit stop close to the main holiday route for those travelling to Pembrokeshire. In a natural setting, up to 88 touring units are accommodated in one fairly flat, tapering, five-acre grass field edged by mature trees and a stream. Pitches are numbered and generously spaced around the perimeter and on either side of a central, hedged spine at the wider end, with 48 electrical hook-ups (10A) and some hardstanding. Backpackers have a small, separate area. A torch would be useful.

Facilities

The one small toilet block is older in style, but is clean, bright, cheerful and adequate with controllable showers. Dishwashing sinks but no laundry facilities (nearest about 5 miles). Motorcaravan service point. Shop doubles as reception. Gas supplies. Play area with tennis and volleyball nets and play equipment. Off site: Restaurants nearby. Pubs, shops, etc. at Llangadog. Fishing 2 miles.

Open: 14 March - 14 November.

Directions

Park is on the A40, between the junctions with the A4069 and A482, between Llandovery and Llandeilo. GPS: 51.951583, -3.9003

Charges guide

Per person	£ 2.00
child (5-16 yrs)	£ 1.25
pitch incl. electricity and awning	£ 10.00

Llangollen
Ty-Ucha Farm Caravan Park
Maesmawr Road, Llangollen LL20 7PP (Denbighshire) T: 01978 860677
alanrogers.com/UK6700

Only a mile from Llangollen, Ty Ucha has a rather dramatic setting, nestling under its own mountain and with views across the valley to craggy Dinas Bran castle. It is a neat, ordered park, carefully managed by the owner and providing 40 pitches (30 with 10A electrical hook-up) for caravans and motorcaravans only (tents are not accepted). They are well spaced around a large, grassy field with an open centre for play. One side slopes gently and is bounded by a stream and wood in which a nature trail has been made. Because of overhead cables, kite flying is forbidden; no bike riding either.

Facilities

The single toilet block, although of Portacabin style, is clean and well maintained and can be heated. It includes two metered showers for each sex (a little cramped). Dishwashing sink with cold water outside. No laundry facilities but there is a launderette in Llangollen. Games room. Late arrivals area. Note: tents are not accepted. Off site: Golf and hotel with reasonably priced meals 0.5 mile. Fishing 1 mile.

Open: Easter - October.

Directions

Park is signed off A5 road, 1 mile east of Llangollen (250 yds). Do not approach from Birch Hill using sat nav but proceed to Maesmawr Road. GPS: 52.96546, -3.14569

Charges guide

Per unit incl. 2 persons and electricity	£ 15.00
extra person	£ 2.00

No credit cards.

FREE Alan Rogers Travel Card
Extra benefits and savings - see page 10

Llantwit Major

Acorn Camping & Caravanning

Ham Lane South, Llantwit Major CF61 1RP (Vale of Glamorgan) T: 01446 794024.
E: info@acorncamping.co.uk **alanrogers.com/UK5927**

A peaceful, family owned, rural site, Acorn is situated on the Heritage Coast, one mile from the beach and the historic town of Llantwit Major. The 105 pitches are mostly on grass, with a few private and rental mobile homes at the far end, leaving around 90 pitches for touring units, including eight gravel hardstandings and 71 electric hook-ups (10A). There is a separate area for tents. Reception houses a very well stocked shop which includes groceries and essentials, souvenirs, children's toys, camping gear, a delicatessen and takeaway meals cooked to order. There is occasional aircraft noise. Site lighting is kept to a minimum to allow guests to enjoy the night sky – a torch might be useful.

Facilities

A warm, modern building houses spacious shower cubicles with washbasins, ample WCs, a family/baby room, and a suite for disabled campers. Laundry facilities. Drinks machine. Shop. Gas. Snooker room. Games room (charged). Play area with free trampoline. WiFi (free). Off site: Glamorgan Heritage Coastal Footpath. Llanerch Vineyard. Cosmeston Lakes Country Park at Penarth. Beach and sea fishing 1 mile. Riding 2 miles. Lake 4 miles. Golf and boat launching 9 miles.

Open: 5 February - 4 December.

Directions

From east on M4 exit 33 follow signs to Cardiff airport, take B4265 for Llantwit Major. Turn left at lights, through Broverton and left into Ham Lane East, finally left into Ham Manor Park and signs to site. From west: M4 exit 35, turn south on A473 for 3 miles, then left on A48. Turn right at Pentre Meyrick (Llantwit Major) on B4268/70. Left at roundabout on B4265, over mini-roundabout, right at lights into Llanmaes Road, left at mini-roundabout, continue around back of the town, left at mini-roundabout, and right into Ham Lane East then South. Follow site signs. GPS: 51.40409, -3.48181

Charges guide

Per unit incl. 2 persons and electricity	£ 16.00 - £ 17.00
extra person	£ 4.75

Machynlleth

Morben Isaf Touring & Holiday Home Park

Derwenlas, Machynlleth SY20 8SR (Powys) T: 01654 781473. E: manager@morbenisaf.co.uk
alanrogers.com/UK6245

Morben Isaf provides 13 touring pitches with multi-services, all with 16A electricity, water tap, waste water drain and a satellite TV hook-up. There is further grassy space below the touring pitches, beyond the fishing lake, which is normally used as a playing field and football pitch but can accommodate around 10 tents which do not need any services. On a lower level, behind the site manager's bungalow, and barely visible from the touring site, are 87 privately owned caravan holiday homes. There is a new play area suitable for children up to 10 years old. Also on the site is an unfenced coarse fishing lake which campers are free to use. Machynlleth is a market town, home of Owain Glyndwr's fifteenth century Welsh Parliament building and the Celtica Centre, and is also close to the Tal-y-Llyn Steam Railway, the Centre for Alternative Technology, Corris Craft Centre and King Arthur's Labyrinth. Adjacent to the site is the Dyfi Osprey Project visitor centre – for the first time in 2007, a nest platform was erected and was occupied by a pair of ospreys. This park is in a convenient location for an overnight halt, or a short stay whilst visiting all these attractions.

Facilities

Small but well equipped, heated modern toilet block includes spacious controllable showers, baby changing and child seats in both ladies' and men's. Facilities for disabled campers. Well equipped laundry. Internet access (free). Off site: Pub serving hot food 1.5 miles. Leisure Centre, shops and services in Machynlleth 3 miles (market on Wed). Dyfi Osprey Project visitor centre adjacent. Centre for Alternative Technology 6 miles.

Open: Mid March - 31 October.

Directions

Site is 3 miles southwest of Machynlleth beside A487. GPS: 52.570067, -3.91145

Charges guide

Per unit incl. 2 persons and electricity	£ 19.00
tent (2 persons)	£ 12.50

For latest campsite news visit
alanrogers.com

Llanwrda
Springwater Lakes

Harford, Llanwrda SA19 8DT (Carmarthenshire) T: 01558 650788. E: bookings@springwaterlakes.com
alanrogers.com/UK5880

Set in 20 acres of Welsh countryside, Springwater offers a selection of fishing lakes to keep even the keenest of anglers occupied. However, it is not just anglers who will enjoy this site – it is a lovely base to enjoy the peace and tranquillity of this part of Wales. Springwater offers 40 spacious, flat pitches either on grass or 30 gravel hardstanding, all with 16A electricity and ten fully serviced pitches, plus ten tent pitches. Malcolm and Shirley Bexon are very proud of their site and welcome all visitors with a smile. This is not a site for children unless they enjoy fishing (no play areas). If you want to learn about fishing Malcolm or Mark will be happy to help.

Facilities

The modern, heated, toilet block is very clean and includes facilities for disabled visitors (there is also wheelchair access to the lakes for fishing). Fishing. Tackle/bait shop. Off site: Spar shop and garage 500 yds. (other shops 5 miles). Riding 2 miles. Golf 4 miles.

Open: 1 March - 31 October.

Directions

From A40 at Llanwrda take A482 to Lampeter. After 6 miles go through village of Pumsaint and site is 2 miles further on the left, just before garage shop. GPS: 52.067417, -3.98225

Charges guide

Per unit incl. 2 persons and electricity	£ 16.00 - £ 22.50
extra person (over 3 yrs)	£ 6.00
dog	free - £ 2.00

No credit cards.

Moelfre
Home Farm Caravan Park

Marianglas, Anglesey LL73 8PH (Isle of Anglesey) T: 01248 410614. E: enq@homefarm-anglesey.co.uk
alanrogers.com/UK6640

A tarmac drive through open fields and a barrier/intercom system leads to this neatly laid out, quality park, with caravan holiday homes to one side. Nestling below what was once a Celtic hill fort, later decimated as a quarry, the park is edged with mature trees and farmland. A circular, tarmac access road leads to the 102 well spaced and numbered touring pitches. With five types available, there are pitches for everyone; ranging from grass with no electricity, to oversized, deluxe hardstandings with electricity, water tanks/taps, waste water drain and TV hook-ups. All electricity is 16A and there are separate well maintained grass fields/areas for tents. Some areas are slightly sloping. The 'pièce de résistance' must be the children's indoor play area, large super adventure play equipment, complete with tunnels and bridges on safe rubber matting, not to mention an outside fenced play area and fields available for sports and walking. Various beaches, sandy and rocky, are within a mile. A member of the Best of British group.

Facilities

Two purpose built toilet blocks, one part of the reception building, are of similar design, can be heated and are maintained to a high standard. En-suite provision for visitors with disabilities (with key). Excellent small bathroom for children with baby bath and curtain for privacy. Family room (with key). Laundry room. Motorcaravan service point. Ice pack service. A new reception building with shop provides basic essentials, gas and some caravan accessories. Indoor and outdoor play areas. TV and pool table. Small library. Hard tennis (extra charge) with racquet hire. WiFi (charged). Off site: Beach 1 mile. Restaurants, shops and ATM at Benllech 2 miles. Fishing and golf 2 miles. Riding 8 miles.

Open: April - October.

Directions

From the Britannia Bridge take second exit left signed Benllech and Amlwch on the A5025. Two miles after Benllech keep left at roundabout and park entrance is 300 yds. on the left beyond the church. GPS: 53.34055, -4.256367

Charges guide

Per unit incl. 2 persons and electricity	£ 19.50 - £ 33.50
extra person	£ 4.00 - £ 6.50
child (3-15 yrs)	£ 2.25 - £ 4.25
dog (max. 2)	£ 1.00 - £ 2.00

FREE Alan Rogers Travel Card
Extra benefits and savings - see page 10

Monmouth
Glen Trothy Caravan & Camping Park
Mitchel Troy, Monmouth NP25 4BD (Monmouthshire) T: 01600 712295. E: enquiries@glentrothy.co.uk
alanrogers.com/UK5890

Glen Trothy is a pretty park on the banks of the River Trothy and visitors are greeted by an array of colourful flowerbeds and tubs around the entrance and reception area. Three fields provide level touring and tent pitches. The first and largest field has a circular gravel road with seasonal pitches arranged on the outer side and touring pitches on the inner side. These have slabs for vehicle wheels and electricity hook-ups. The second field, just past the toilet block, has pitches for trailer tents and tents only (16 with electricity), whilst the camping field is for tents only (no cars are allowed on this area).

Facilities

Some improvements have been made to the sanitary block (possibly stretched at peak times). Facilities for disabled visitors. Laundry facilities. Tourist information in hut opposite reception. Small play area. Free fishing (from the camping field only). Dogs are not accepted. Off site: Golf, canoeing, shopping and supermarkets at the historic town of Monmouth 1.5 miles. The Wye Valley and the Forest of Dean are nearby for outings.

Open: 1 March - 31 October.

Directions

At Monmouth, take A40 east to Abergavenny. Exit at first junction and at T-junction, where site is signed, turn left onto B4284. Follow signs for Mitchel Troy. Site is on right just past village sign. GPS: 51.790967, -2.7341

Charges guide

Per unit incl. 2 persons and electricity	£ 12.00 - £ 18.00
extra person	£ 3.00

Montgomery
Daisy Bank Touring Caravan Park
Snead, Montgomery SY15 6EB (Powys) T: 01588 620471. E: enquiries@daisy-bank.co.uk
alanrogers.com/UK6330

For adults only, this pretty, tranquil park in the Camlad Valley has panoramic views, and is an ideal base for walkers. Attractively landscaped with traditional English flower beds and many different trees and shrubs, this small park has been carefully developed. The Welsh hills to the north and the Shropshire hills to the south overlook the three fields which provide a total of 83 pitches. The field nearer to the road (perhaps a little noisy) is slightly sloping but there are hardstandings for motorcaravans, while the second field is more level. All pitches have 16A electricity, water and waste water drainage and TV hook-up. Two camping pods were added in 2011 with plans to add some more.

Facilities

The well equipped, heated toilet block now incorporates modern, en-suite units and facilities for disabled visitors. A second block was added in 2010 incorporating four en-suite units and two WCs. Laundry facilities. Shop in reception. Gas supplies. Brick barbecues. Small putting green (free loan of clubs and balls). Bicycle hire. Small library. WiFi. Off site: Supermarket 2 miles. Many eating places nearby. Fishing 3 miles. Golf and riding 10 miles.

Open: All year.

Directions

Site is by the A489 road 2 miles east of Churchstoke towards Craven Arms. GPS: 52.529917, -3.0297

Charges guide

Per unit incl. 2 persons and all services	£ 18.00 - £ 27.00
extra person	£ 5.00
tent (per person)	£ 9.00 - £ 11.00
dog	£ 1.00

Montgomery
Smithy Park
Abermule, Montgomery SY15 6ND (Powys) T: 01584 711280. E: info@smithypark.co.uk
alanrogers.com/UK6305

Smithy Park is set in four acres of landscaped grounds bordered by the River Severn and the Shropshire Union Canal, in the tranquil rolling countryside of central Wales. It does have 60 privately owned caravan holiday homes, but beyond these is a separate touring area which has the benefit of being closest to the river with the best views and a small picnic and seating area on the bank. This area has 26 fully serviced hardstanding pitches (16A electricity, water, waste water and satellite TV hook-ups). A timber chalet provides all the sanitary facilities, and is located in one corner of the touring area.

Facilities

The timber clad chalet building provides two good sized showers per sex, washbasins in cubicles, a family room suitable for the less able (there is a step up to the building). Additional toilet and washbasin in a new building by reception. Utility room with laundry facilities. Fishing in the river Severn. Gas stocked. Fenced playground. WiFi (charged). Off site: Supermarkets and all other services in Newtown 3 miles. Golf 3 miles. Riding 5 miles.

Open: 1 March - 31 October.

Directions

Site is 3 miles north of Newtown in the village of Abermule. Turn off the A483 into village, and turn down the lane beside the Waterloo Arms, opposite the village shop and Post Office. Site is at end of lane. GPS: 52.544217, -3.238717

Charges guide

Per unit incl. 2 persons and electricity	£ 20.00 - £ 27.00
extra person	£ 4.00

For latest campsite news visit
alanrogers.com

Narberth
Little Kings Park

Amroth Road, Ludchurch, Narberth SA67 8PG (Pembrokeshire) T: 01834 831330.
E: littlekingspark@btconnect.com **alanrogers.com/UK5975**

This superb family run park has a number of attributes to make your stay both comfortable and memorable. There are stunning views over Carmarthen Bay to the Gower and beyond to the coast of Somerset and North Devon. At night no fewer than seven lighthouses can be seen blinking out their warnings. A touring field provides 56 well spaced, large touring pitches all with 10A electricity, 21 with gravel hardstanding and fully serviced. A further seven pitches are in a different area. There are 60 pitches for tents in an adjoining paddock with 31 electricity hook-ups.

Facilities

Two modern toilet blocks include controllable hot showers (20p for 6 minutes 30p for 9), open style washbasins, a family shower room and a full suite for disabled visitors. Laundry rooms. Shop with bakery. Takeaway, bar and restaurant with conservatory (evenings only; low season at B.Hs and weekends only). Covered, heated swimming pool. Games rooms. Playground. Ball games area. Gas supplies. WiFi (charged). Off site: Supermarket at Kilgetty 2.5 miles. Fishing 1.5 miles. Riding 4 miles. Golf 8 miles.

Open: 1 March - 31 October.

Directions

Site is 5 miles southeast of Narberth. From the A477 Carmarthen to Pembroke road, 2 miles after Llanteg at petrol station, turn left towards Amroth, Wiseman's Bridge, Ludchurch. After 1 mile, at crossroads, turn right (signed Ludchurch, Narberth) and park is 800 yds. GPS: 51.751517, -4.6879

Charges guide

Per unit incl. 2 persons and electricity	£ 15.00 - £ 26.00
extra person (over 3 yrs)	£ 2.20

Newcastle Emlyn
Cenarth Falls Holiday Park

Cenarth, Newcastle Emlyn SA38 9JS (Ceredigion) T: 01239 710345. E: enquiries@cenarth-holipark.co.uk
alanrogers.com/UK6010

The Davies family has developed an attractively landscaped, part wooded holiday home park with 89 units (one for rent). A neat well cared for, sheltered area at the top of the park provides 30 touring pitches, accessed via a tarmac road. All are on shingle hardstanding with 16A electricity (so unsuitable for tents). A sunken, kidney shaped outdoor pool with landscaped surrounds and sunbeds is a focal point. The Coracles Health and Country Club provides an indoor pool, spa, sauna and steam rooms and fitness suite. It also provides a bar with evening meals. A member of the Best of British group.

Facilities

The excellent sanitary block is accessed by key and uses a 'P.I.R.' system that controls heating, lighting, water and air freshener on entry. Provision for disabled visitors (doubling as a family room). Laundry facilities. Gas supplies. Outdoor pool (late May-late Sept). Coracles Health and Country Club (see above). Play area. Games room with pool table and electronic games. WiFi over site (charged). Off site: Fishing and shop within 0.5 miles. Riding 7 miles. Bicycle hire 8 miles. Golf 10 miles.

Open: 1 March - mid November.

Directions

Follow A484 Cardigan-Newcastle Emlyn road and park is signed before Cenarth village. GPS: 52.0499, -4.531717

Charges guide

Per unit incl. up to 4 people and electricity	£ 17.00 - £ 27.00
extra person	£ 2.00

Newport
Cwmcarn Forest Drive Campsite

Cwmcarn, Crosskeys, Newport NP11 7FA (Newport) T: 01495 272001. E: cwmcarn-vc@caerphilly.gov.uk
alanrogers.com/UK5930

This forest site, run by Caerphilly Council, is set in a narrow, sheltered valley with magnificent wooded slopes. The park is not only central for the many attractions of this part of Wales, but there is also much of the natural environment to enjoy including a small fishing lake and the seven mile forest drive. The site has a slightly wild feel, but is well located and has 27 well spaced, flat pitches, most with 15A electricity (three with concrete hardstanding), spread over three small fields between the new Visitor Centre and the small lake. Three timber camping pods have been added with another three planned.

Facilities

The single, heated toilet block includes toilet facilities for disabled visitors, laundry facilities, small cooker and fridge. The Visitors' Centre has a coffee shop. Guided walks and the popular Twrch (9 miles) mountain bike trail. Timber camping pods. WiFi. Dogs accepted by prior arrangement. Large units (over 24 ft) not accepted due to access. Off site: Shops within 1 mile. Riding 2 miles.

Open: All year excl. 23 December - 2 January.

Directions

Cwmcarn Forest Drive is well signed from exit 28 on the M4. From the Midlands and the 'Heads of the Valleys' road (A465), take A467 south to Cwmcarn. GPS: 51.63771, -3.11877

Charges guide

Per unit incl. 2 persons and electricity	£ 14.00 - £ 18.00
extra person	£ 4.00 - £ 6.00

FREE Alan Rogers Travel Card
Extra benefits and savings - see page 10

Newport
Tredegar House Country Park Caravan Club Site
Coedkernen, Newport NP10 8TW (Newport) T: 01633 815600

alanrogers.com/UK6060

This immaculate Caravan Club site is ideally situated for breaking a journey or for longer stays. It can accommodate 79 units, all with 16A electricity hook-up and 68 with gravel hardstanding, four fully serviced. A further grass area is allocated for tents, with its use limited to families and couples – no single sex groups are accepted. The site itself is set within the gardens and park of Tredegar House, a 17th-century house and country park which is open to the public. The entrance gates are locked at dusk so contact the site reception for details of latest arrival times. Some road noise may be expected at times.

Facilities

The sanitary block is of an excellent standard and includes washbasins in cubicles. Facilities for disabled visitors, babies and toddlers. Laundry. Motorcaravan service point. Calor gas available. Tredegar House visitors' centre with tea rooms, gift shop and craft workshops (open Easter-Sept). Adventure play area in the park. WiFi (charged). Off site: Supermarket 0.5 miles. Newport 3 miles.

Open: All year.

Directions

From M4 take exit 28 or from A48 junction with the M4 follow brown signs for Tredegar House. The caravan park is indicated to the left at the house entrance. GPS: 51.56148, -3.03341

Charges guide

Per person	£ 4.30 - £ 6.20
pitch incl. electricity (non-member)	£ 12.90 - £ 16.00

Newtown
Cringoed Caravan Park
Cringoed, Llanbrynmair, Newtown SY19 7DR (Powys) T: 01650 521237. E: enquiries@cringoed.co.uk

alanrogers.com/UK6240

Cringoed is a pleasant, peaceful, small park with a river to one side, hills on the other and trees at either end. There are 30 spacious pitches available for touring and these are in a level open field, each with hardstanding and 16A electricity. About 36 caravan holiday homes are placed at either end of the site, some amongst trees and some in a newer, more open area. There are also ten tent pitches, some with electricity. This site is within easy reach of some of mid-Wales' best scenery and not far from the coast. Paul and Sue Mathers continue landscaping the site and will make you very welcome.

Facilities

The single toilet block is neat, modern and quite adequate. Laundry and dishwashing. Adventure play area. Small tourist information room. WiFi (free). Off site: Shops 1 mile (ATM at Spar in Carno 6 miles). Bicycle hire 1 mile. Fishing 5 miles. Golf 8 miles. Riding 12 miles.

Open: 7 March - 30 November.

Directions

From the A470 between Newton and Machynlleth in the village of Llanbrynmair take the B4518 signed Staylittle (caravan signs). After 1 mile just before bridge turn right, go over site bridge and turn right into site. GPS: 52.598333, -3.644383

Charges guide

Per unit incl. 2 persons and electricity	£ 14.00 - £ 17.00
No credit cards.	

Pembroke
Freshwater East Caravan Club Site
Trewent Hill, Freshwater East, Pembroke SA71 5LJ (Pembrokeshire) T: 01646 672341

alanrogers.com/UK5990

Located within the Pembrokeshire Coast National Park, this Caravan Club site is open to non-members (for all units). The park is flanked by trees on one side with a mix of grass and hardstanding tiered pitch areas to choose from. There are a total of 130 pitches, 65 hardstanding, all with 16A electrical hook-ups. There are a few pitches for tents. The beach and the Pembroke Coastal Path are just a few minutes walk. This is an excellent area for walking with magnificent cliff views. Note: TV aerial connections are available, but you will need your own extension cable.

Facilities

The two heated toilet blocks are modern and clean with washbasins in cubicles, and free hairdryers or sockets for your own. Facilities for disabled visitors. Fully equipped laundry rooms. Waste point for motorcaravans. Gas supplies. Reception keeps basic food items. Information kiosk. Small play area. WiFi. Off site: Beach 400 yds. Shop 0.5 miles. Public transport 1 mile. Fishing 5 miles.

Open: 30 March - 8 October.

Directions

From east on A477, fork left 1.25 miles past Milton onto A4075 Pembroke road. In Pembroke immediately (after railway bridge) turn sharp left at roundabout on A4139 Tenby road. In Lamphey turn right onto B4584 (Freshwater East). In 1.75 miles turn right (Stackpole, Trewent) and after 400 yds. right into lane at Club sign. Do not tow to the beach area. GPS: 51.645262, -4.872512

Charges guide

Per person	£ 4.60 - £ 6.20
pitch incl. electricity (non-member)	£ 13.50 - £ 16.00

For latest campsite news visit
alanrogers.com

Penmaenmawr
Tyddyn Du Touring Park

Conwy Old Road, Penmaenmawr LL34 6RE (Conwy) T: 01492 622300. E: stay@tyddyndutouringpark.co.uk

alanrogers.com/UK6695

This attractively landscaped, adults only, five-hectare campsite is conveniently situated close to the A55 and positioned on a hillside with panoramic views across Conwy Bay to The Great Orme at Llandudno and Puffin Island. Offering peace and quiet in a superb location between mountains and the sea and being within easy reach of Conwy, Snowdonia National Park and many historic regions of north Wales, this is an ideal base for exploring the area. Tarmac roads connect the three levels which are tiered to maximise the views for everyone. There are 92 touring pitches on grass or hardstanding and all have 16A electricity. No arrivals before 14.00 please and visitors under the age of 18 are not allowed on site.

Facilities

Two well maintained sanitary blocks provide showers, open style washbasins and hairdryers. En-suite facilities for disabled visitors (Radar key). Motorcaravan service point (care needed to access). Well equipped laundry room. Small library. £5 (cash only) refundable deposit for entry card. WiFi (charged). Off site: Golf 0.5 mile. Pub at entrance to park. Shops and restaurants within 1 mile. Sandy beach 10-15 minutes walk. Fishing and sailing 1 mile. Conwy 4 miles. Llandudno 9 miles.

Open: 22 March - 31 October.

Directions

From the A55 take exit 16 and at roundabout signed Penmaenmawr turn immediately sharp left into Ysguborwen Road. Entrance to park is 300 yds. on the right. GPS: 53.27425, -3.90632

Charges guide

Per unit incl. 2 adults and electricity	£ 22.00 - £ 25.00
extra person (over 18 yrs)	£ 2.00
awning	free

Pontarddulais
River View Touring Park

The Dingle, Llanedi, Pontarddulais SA4 0FH (Carmarthenshire) T: 01269 844876.
E: info@riverviewtouringpark.com **alanrogers.com/UK5945**

Nestling in the valley of the River Gwili, River View is an attractive, quiet and friendly park made up of three fields: one by the river which is kept mainly for adults and two on a plateau up a steep slope on the opposite side of the lane. Particular care has been taken to protect the natural environment. There are 65 level, generously sized pitches of which 49 are touring pitches, the remainder seasonal. All have 16A electricity, 44 have hardstanding and 6 are fully serviced. This is a popular rural retreat for young families and older couples. The park is close to the end of the M4. This allows easy access and there is plenty to do or see in the near vicinity, including castles, gardens, beaches, wildfowl reserves and a water park. A Site of Special Scientific Interest is located immediately at the back of the park. The bird life visible from the site is varied and includes buzzards and red kites, and dippers on the river. The toilet block, including an en-suite family room with baby changing facilities and one for disabled visitors, is modern and equipped to a very high standard, including underfloor heating and automatic lighting.

Facilities

The modern, heated, toilet block is spotless with spacious showers, family room and suite for disabled visitors. Laundry with sinks, washing machine, tumble dryer, iron and ironing board. Small shop for basics and local fresh produce. Large grassy recreation area on main field. Fishing. Off site: Golf, shop, bar and restaurant 1 mile. Bicycle hire 5 miles. Beach 12 miles.

Open: 4 March - 20 November.

Directions

From M4 exit 49 take A483 signed Llandeilo. Take the first turn left (after layby) and park is on left after 300 yds. GPS: 51.75817, -4.06288

Charges guide

Per unit incl. 2 persons and electricity	£ 15.00 - £ 19.00
incl. services	£ 18.00 - £ 22.00
extra person	£ 3.50 - £ 4.50
child (under 4 yrs)	£ 1.00 - £ 2.00
dog	£ 1.50 - £ 2.00
No credit cards.	

FREE Alan Rogers Travel Card
Extra benefits and savings - see page 10

Prestatyn

Nant Mill Family Touring Caravan & Tenting Park

Gronant Road, Prestatyn LL19 9LY (Denbighshire) T: 01745 852360. E: nantmilltouring@aol.com

alanrogers.com/UK6660

This traditional style, family owned and run park of around seven acres, takes some 150 units arranged over four fields. There are some distant sea views to be had from many pitches. These are carefully allocated to ensure that the largest, central, sloping field is reserved for families. A smaller more intimate field for tents only is to one side of this and two small paddocks on the other side are for couples who might prefer a quieter, more level location. There are 96 electrical connections (10A) but tents are not permitted on pitches with hook-ups. The pitches nearer the road may experience some noise.

Facilities

The main toilet block is older in style but very well kept, with showers, open style washbasins and baby changing facilities. Extra showers in a small Portacabin style unit. Showers are free, with a £1 deposit for the cubicle key (return after each shower). Facilities for disabled visitors. Laundry facilities. Playground and play field. WiFi. No touring vehicles over 26 ft. Off site: Beach, sea fishing, golf, shops all 0.5 miles.

Open: End March - mid October.

Directions

Site entrance is 0.5 mile east of Prestatyn on A548 coast road. GPS: 53.33765, -3.3932

Charges guide

Per unit incl. 2 persons and electricity	£ 18.25 - £ 21.25
extra person (over 3 yrs)	£ 2.00
dog (max. 1)	free

No credit/debit cards.

Pwllheli

Bolmynydd Camping Park

Llanbedrog, Pwllheli LL53 7UP (Gwynedd) T: 07882 850 820. E: info@bolmynydd.co.uk

alanrogers.com/UK6585

The drive to Bolmynydd is not for the faint hearted. The roads are extremely narrow with plenty of bends, and are accessible only by cars and small VW-style camper vans; the site is not licensed for touring caravans or motorcaravans. However, the campsite is ideal for tents and offers spectacular views . With 16 seasonal caravan pitches and 40 tent pitches, the owners request that you telephone ahead to discuss access and availability.

Facilities

One clean sanitary block, maintained to a high standard (may be under pressure in peak season). Separate modern showers, toilets and open style washbasins. Baby bath in well equipped laundry room. No motorcaravan service point. WiFi over site. Off site: Ten minutes walk to small supermarket and pub. Riding, beach and sailing 400 yds. Fishing 1 mile. Golf 3 miles.

Open: Easter/1 April (whichever is earliest) - 31 October.

Directions

From Pwllheli take the A499 toward Abersoch. After 4 miles pass through Llanbedrog and at the campsite sign turn sharp left. Continue for half a mile, site is on the left. Do not follow sat nav into the village of Llanbedrog, instead proceed past and turn at the brown sign. GPS: 52.85231, -4.48844

Charges guide

Per unit incl. 2 persons	£ 20.00 - £ 22.00
electricity	£ 5.00

No credit cards.

Pwllheli

Hafan y Môr Holiday Park

Pwllheli LL53 6HJ (Gwynedd) T: 07949 642 534

alanrogers.com/UK6575

One of Haven's flagship parks, Hafan y Môr has a substantially redeveloped leisure and activity area. The park is set on the coast with direct access to the beach. A full range of clubs is provided for toddlers to teens and there is a popular splash zone and adventure playground. This is a large park with 700 caravan holiday homes, either for rent or privately owned. The site has been well designed with hedges, trees, planting, green spaces and lakes. The 74 touring pitches are in a separate area and all have 16A electricity, with a choice of hardstanding or grass. Tents are not accepted on this site.

Facilities

Sanitary facilities are in new Portacabin style units. Two children's units, two family shower units, three baby changing units. Facilities for disabled visitors. Laundry facilities. Two supermarkets. Gift shop. Sweet shop. Hire shop. Bars. Starbucks coffee bar. Restaurant. Lakeside Inn. Fish and chips, Burger King. Fast food takeaway. Indoor pool with flumes and slides. Sporting facilities and coaching. Entertainment and activities including clubs for children. WiFi (charge). Off site: Llyn peninsula beaches.

Open: March - 2 November.

Directions

From the Midlands and the south M54 to Telford. A5 past Oswestry and Llangollen. Take A494 to Bala. In Bala turn right for Porthmadog. Turn left at roundabout in Porthmadog, signed Criccieth and Pwllheli. Park is on the left, 3 miles out of Criccieth. GPS: 52.906137, -4.334579

Charges guide

Contact site.

For latest campsite news visit

alanrogers.com

Saint Davids
Caerfai Bay Caravan & Tent Park
Caerfai Road, Saint Davids SA62 6QT (Pembrokeshire) T: 01437 720274. E: info@caerfaibay.co.uk

alanrogers.com/UK5995

About as far west as one can get in Wales, St Davids is Britain's smallest city, noted for its cathedral and Bishop's Palace. This cliff-top park in west Wales has direct access to the Pembrokeshire Coastal Path and a magnificent sandy beach is just a few minutes away, down the path from the car park by the site entrance. Altogether there are 105 touring pitches (incl. 78 for tents) and 45 electric hook-ups (10A), with 16 hardstandings. Main access roads are tarmac. The camping area is spread over three open and sloping fields (chocks are often necessary). All have magnificent views over St Brides Bay. The caravan field also has a small number of holiday homes and is closest to reception. The second and third fields are for tents and motorcaravans, almost all on grass with a few hardstandings available. Caerfai farm shop is across the lane (opens end of May), and other shops and services are just a mile away. Site lighting is deliberately minimal, so a torch would be useful.

Facilities
Three main heated buildings house the sanitary facilities, one by reception contains facilities for disabled visitors and families, dish washing facilities, laundry, cooking facilities (hot plate, microwave and fridge). Adjacent a small new block offers 3 unisex cubicles (WC and basin). The third, in the tent field, includes 4 family rooms, dish washing, microwave, fridge, toaster, wet suit washing and drying area. Motorcaravan services. Bicycle storage. Gas. Barbecue stands for hire. Dog walking area. WiFi (charged). Off site: Walk the Pembrokeshire coastal path, visit Ramsey Island Bird and Grey Seal Reserve. St Davids Cathedral and Oriel Y Parc Visitor Centre/Gallery. Sea fishing 400 yds. Boat launching 1.5 and 3 miles. Golf 2 miles. Riding 10 miles.

Open: 1 March - 14 November.

Directions
From Haverfordwest take the A487 to St Davids. On passing the city boundary, turn left into lane immediately before the Oriel Y Parc Visitor Centre/Gallery (site signed), and continue on for 0.75 miles to site entrance on right. GPS: 51.872983, -5.2569

Charges guide
Per unit incl. 2 persons and electricity	£ 16.00 - £ 22.50
extra person	£ 4.50
child (3-12 yrs)	£ 3.00
dog	£ 1.00

Discounts for early payment, and for senior citizens in low season.

Saundersfoot
Moreton Farm Leisure Park
Moreton, Saundersfoot SA69 9EA (Pembrokeshire) T: 01834 812016. E: moretonfarm@btconnect.com

alanrogers.com/UK5980

Moreton Farm has been developed in a secluded valley, a 10-20 minute walk from Saundersfoot and four miles from Tenby. It provides 30 caravan (all with 16A electricity, and including 17 with hardstanding) and 30 tent pitches on two sloping, neatly cut grass fields, with 12 pine holiday lodges and four cottages for letting occupying another field. The site is approached under a railway bridge (height 10 ft. 9 ins, width across the top 6 ft. 6 ins, but with alternative access over the railway line for slightly larger vehicles just possible). There are a few trains during the day, none at night. This is a quiet family site. Pembroke and Carew castles and a variety of visitor attractions are close.

Facilities
The toilet blocks (which can be heated) are light and airy, providing preset hot showers (on payment). Unit for disabled visitors with ramp (shower, toilet and washbasin). Baby bath. Laundry facilities. Fenced, outside clothes drying area. Small shop for basics and gas. Playground. Bicycle hire can be arranged. No dogs or other pets are accepted. Off site: Fishing and riding 1 mile. Golf 4 miles.

Open: 1 March - 31 October.

Directions
From A477 Carmarthen-Pembroke road take A478 for Tenby at Kilgetly. Park is signed on left after 1.5 miles. Watch carefully for sign and park is 0.5 miles up poorly made-up road and under bridge. GPS: 51.711983, -4.727683

Charges guide
Per unit incl. 2 persons and electricity	£ 16.00 - £ 21.00
extra person	£ 2.00

Tenby

Manorbier Country Park

Station Road, Manorbier, Tenby SA70 7SN (Pembrokeshire) T: 01834 871952.
E: enquiries@countrypark.co.uk **alanrogers.com/UK5985**

With sandy beaches, castles and the Pembrokeshire Coastal Path nearby, Manorbier is well located for a holiday in southwest Wales. There are 50 generously sized touring pitches, all with electric hook-up and hardstanding, including four fully serviced super pitches. The park also accommodates about 100 caravan holiday homes, of which 36 are for rent. Leisure amenities are very good with a wellness centre that incorporates an indoor pool, health suite, a gym and tennis facilities. Family entertainment is organised in the bar complex which also houses a restaurant and takeaway. Children will enjoy the adventure play park and toddler play area, and will enjoy meeting 'JC and Gerry the Bear'. Larger units should book in advance and motorcaravans over 25 ft. are not accepted.

Facilities

A single building at one end of the car parking area provides all toilet facilities. It can be heated and has hot showers (on payment), a multi-purpose room suitable for families, babies and disabled campers. Laundry facilities. Shop. Bar, restaurant and takeaway. Wellness centre with indoor heated swimming and paddling pools, jacuzzi, sauna and steam room, vertical solarium, gym and tennis (all charged). Adventure play park and toddler play area. WiFi (free). Dogs are not accepted. Larger units should book in advance and motorcaravans over 25 ft. are not accepted. Off site: Adjacent garden centre restaurant. Fish and chip bar opposite. Bicycle hire, boat launching, sailing and beach 1.5 miles. Golf and riding 3 miles.

Open: 1 March - 30 November.

Directions

From Tenby take A4139 towards Pembroke, passing through Penally and Lydstep. At crossroads (Manorbier signed to left) continue straight on following signs to the station. Turn right by Baptist Chapel into Station Road, and continue to site entrance (do not go into Manorbier village). GPS: 51.657917, -4.794283

Charges guide

Per unit incl. up to 4 persons	
and electricity	£ 14.00 - £ 36.00
full service pitch	£ 17.00 - £ 39.00
extra person	£ 2.00

Tenby

Trefalun Park

Devonshire Drive, Saint Florence, Tenby SA70 8RD (Pembrokeshire) T: 01646 651514. E: trefalun@aol.com
alanrogers.com/UK5982

Only four miles from Tenby and the beaches of Carmarthen Bay, Trefalun Park is an open, well laid out campsite with a friendly atmosphere engendered by the owners. There are 90 touring pitches here which are mainly level, although the park has gentle slopes. The pitches are generously sized with 10/16A electricity available. Hardstandings have been created for 64 pitches, some with full services. Three caravan holiday homes are available also for rent. This park will suit those, particularly families, looking for a quiet holiday and also the more active who favour walking, cycling or watersports.

Facilities

Modern heated toilet block, with some washbasins in cabins. Water to showers and laundry is metered (20p). Separate, fully equipped suite for disabled visitors and families. Separate baby room. Laundry. Motorcaravan services planned. Play area. Gas. Off site: Fishing, riding and wildlife park 600 yds. Shop, pub (with food) and outdoor pool 1.5 miles. Golf 3 miles. Tenby with all town facilities, beach, boat launching and sailing 4 miles.

Open: 2 April - 28 October.

Directions

From the A477 at Sageston (4 miles east of Pembroke) turn southeast just to the east of the village on B4318 signed for the Wildlife Park. Trefalun Park is signed to the left after 2.5 miles, opposite the entrance to the Wildlife Park. GPS: 51.69326, -4.75340

Charges guide

Per unit incl. 2 persons	
and electricity	£ 14.50 - £ 22.00
with services	£ 16.50 - £ 25.00
extra person	£ 2.50

For latest campsite news visit
alanrogers.com

Wrexham
James' Caravan Park

Ruabon, Wrexham LL14 6DW (Wrexham) T: 01978 820148. E: ray@carastay.demon.co.uk

alanrogers.com/UK6680

Open all year, this park has attractive, park-like surroundings with mature trees and neat, short grass. However, edged by two main roads it is subject to some road noise. The park has over 40 pitches, some level and some on a slope, with informal siting giving either a view or shade. Electricity (6/10A) is available all over, although a long lead may be useful. Being so conveniently positioned, this is an ideal stopover site. Tourist information and a free freezer for ice packs are in the foyer of the toilet block. This is a useful park with easy access from the A483 Wrexham-Oswestry road.

Facilities

The heated toilet block offers roomy showers but would benefit from updating. Cleaning variable. En-suite facilities for visitors with disabilities complete with special 'clos-o-mat' toilet! Motorcaravan service point. Gas available. Off site: The village is a 10 minute walk with a Spar shop, fish and chips, a restaurant, launderette and four pubs. Golf 3 miles.

Open: All year.

Directions

Park is at junction of A483/A539 Llangollen road and is accessible from the west-bound A539. GPS: 52.98286, -3.04093

Charges guide

Per unit incl. 2 persons and electricity	£ 15.00
extra person	£ 2.00
awning	£ 2.00
gazebo	£ 5.00
dog	£ 1.00

No credit cards.

James Caravan Park

Idyllic Park with mature trees, well cared for grass, renovated buildings and all modern facilities

ray@carastay.demon.co.uk • Tel: 01978 820148 • Ruabon, LL14 6DW

Wrexham
Plassey Leisure Park

Eyton, Wrexham LL13 0SP (Wrexham) T: 01978 780277. E: enquiries@plassey.com

alanrogers.com/UK6670

Plassey Leisure Park has been carefully developed over the past 50 years. Improvements include landscaping, car parking and low level lighting installed around the park. A new area for 15 privately owned holiday homes has been recently created. Originally a dairy farm, the park is set in 247 acres of the Dee Valley and offers an extensive range of activities. It has been divided into discreet areas with 120 pitches around the edges. There are 90 touring pitches with 16A electrical connections, 30 pitches are fully serviced and 50 have hardstanding. Five further areas accommodate 120 seasonal caravans. There is much to do and to look at in the rural setting at Plassey. A member of the Best of British group.

Facilities

Some refurbished toilet facilities are supplemented by a new heated block with individual washbasin cubicles, a room for disabled visitors and families. Laundry. Motorcaravan services. Shop (with gas). Club room with games room for children. Heated indoor pool with sun bed, sauna and new viewing area (charged). Adventure play area. Nine hole golf course. Fishing lakes. Wildlife meadow and countryside footpaths. Bicycle hire. No skateboards or footballs permitted. Winter caravan storage. Luxury holiday home for hire. WiFi throughout (charged). Off site: Riding 2 miles.

Open: February - November.

Directions

Follow brown and cream signs for The Plassey from the A483 Chester-Oswestry bypass onto the B5426 and park is 2.5 miles. Also signed from the A528 Marchwiel-Overton road. GPS: 52.997883, -2.966317

Charges guide

Per unit incl. 2 persons	
and electricity	£ 16.50 - £ 26.50
incl. services	£ 19.50 - £ 33.50
extra person (over 5 yrs)	£ 4.50
dog	£ 2.00

Includes club membership, coarse fishing, badminton and table tennis (own racquets and bats required).

Been to any good campsites lately?
We have

You'll find them here...

The UK's market leading independent
guides to the best campsites

Also available on iPad **alanrogers.com/digital**

From gentle rolling hills and rugged coastlines, to dramatic peaks, punctuated with beautiful lochs, Scotland is a land steeped in history that provides superb opportunities to enjoy wild, untamed and spectacular scenery.

Probably the most striking thing about Scotland is the vast areas of uninhabited landscape. Southern Scotland boasts beautiful fertile plains, woodlands and wild sea coasts. It also has a rich heritage with ancient castles, abbeys and grand houses. Further north are the Trossachs with their heather-clad hills, home of Rob Roy, the folk hero. The Highlands and Islands, including Skye, Mull and Islay, have some of the most dramatic landscapes in Europe, dominated by breathtaking mountain ranges, such as Ben Nevis and the Grampians, plus deep glistening lochs, the largest being Loch Ness, where the monster reputedly lives. And lying at the very edge of Europe, the islands of the Inner and Outer Hebrides share a rugged, natural beauty with unspoilt beaches and an abundance of wildlife. The two largest cities, Edinburgh and Glasgow, have their own unique attractions. The capital, Edinburgh, with magnificent architecture, comprises the Medieval Old Town and the Georgian New Town, with the ancient castle standing proudly in the middle. A short distance to the west, Glasgow has more parks and over 20 museums and galleries, with works by Charles Rennie Mackintosh scattered around the city.

Places of interest

Lowlands: National Gallery of Scotland and Edinburgh Castle; Glasgow Science Centre; Stirling Castle; New Lanark World Heritage Site; Kelso Abbey.

Heart of Scotland: fishing town of Oban; Stirling Castle and Wallace Monument; Loch Lomond; Pitlochry; university town of St Andrews; Aberdeen; Dunfermline Abbey; fishing villages of Crail and Anstruther; Famous Grouse Experience in Crieff.

Highlands and Islands: Fort William; 600 ft. Eas a Chual Aluinn waterfall near Kylesku; the Cairngorms; Highland Wildlife Part at Kingussie; Inverness; Aviemore; Lochalsh Woodland Gardens; Malt Whisky Trail, Moray; Dunvegan Castle on the Isle of Skye.

Did you know?

Dunfermline Abbey is the final resting place of 22 kings, queens, princes and princesses of Scotland, including Robert the Bruce.

Whales can be seen off the west coast of the Highlands, and the Moray Firth is home to bottle-nosed dolphins.

Many famous ships were built at Clydebank, including the Cutty Sark and the Lusitania.

Since 1861, every day (except on Sundays), the one o'clock gun has boomed out from Edinburgh castle.

Charles Rennie Mackintosh, famous architect and designer, was born in Glasgow in 1868.

The first organised fire brigade was established in Edinburgh in 1824.

The Forth Railway Bridge is 8,296 ft. long.

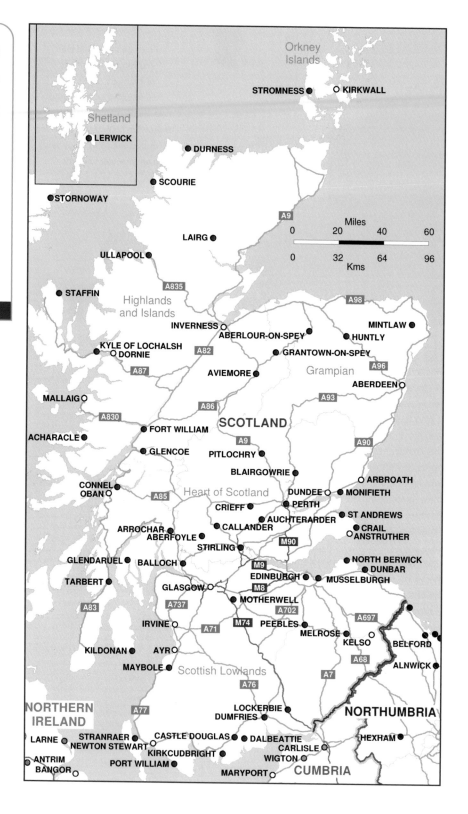

For latest campsite news visit
alanrogers.com

Aberfoyle
Trossachs Holiday Park
Aberfoyle FK8 3SA (Stirling) T: 0800 1971192. E: info@trossachsholidays.co.uk

alanrogers.com/UK7230

Nestling on the side of a hill, three miles south of Aberfoyle, this is an excellent base for touring this famously beautiful area. Lochs Lomond, Ard, Venachar and others are within easy reach, as are the Queen Elizabeth Forest Park and, of course, the Trossachs. Very neat and tidy, there are 45 well laid out and marked pitches arranged on terraces with hardstanding. All have electricity and most also have water, drainage and TV connections. There is also a large area for tents. There are trees between the terraces and lovely views across the valley. The adjoining oak and bluebell woods are a haven for wildlife, with wonderful walks. You will receive a warm welcome from the friendly staff at this well run, family park.

Facilities

A timber building houses sanitary facilities providing a satisfactory supply of toilets, showers and washbasins, the ladies' area being rather larger, with two private cabins. Laundry room. Well stocked shop (all season). Games room with TV. Play equipment (on gravel). Off site: Golf, boat launching and fishing 3 miles. Sailing 6 miles. Discount scheme arranged with a local leisure centre provides facilities for swimming, sauna, solarium, badminton, tennis, windsurfing, etc.

Open: 1 March - 31 October.

Directions

Park is 3 miles south of Aberfoyle on the A81 road, well signed. GPS: 56.140133, -4.3555

Charges guide

Per unit incl. 2 persons and electricity	£ 15.00 - £ 19.00
incl. all services	£ 17.00 - £ 21.00
tent pitch incl. 2 persons	£ 14.50 - £ 18.50
extra person	£ 4.00

Aberlour-on-Spey
Aberlour Gardens Caravan & Camping Park
Aberlour-on-Spey AB38 9LD (Moray) T: 01340 871586. E: info@aberlourgardens.co.uk

alanrogers.com/UK7540

This pleasant park is within the large walled garden of the Aberlour Estate on Speyside. The owners have made many improvements to the sheltered, five-acre, family run park which provides a very natural setting amidst spruce and Scots pine. Of the 73 level pitches, 35 are for touring leaving the remainder for holiday homes and seasonal units. All pitches have 10A electrical connections and 16 are all-weather pitches. This is an ideal area for walking, birdwatching, salmon fishing and pony trekking, or for following the only Malt Whisky Trail in the world, while Aberlour has a fascinating old village shop – a time capsule. A member of the Best of British group.

Facilities

The toilet facilities are now a little dated (there are plans for refurbishment). Facilities for visitors with disabilities can also be used as family or baby changing room. Laundry facilities. Motorcaravan service point. Small licensed shop stocking basics and with an information area. Play area. WiFi throughout (charged). Off site: Swimming and bicycle hire 1 mile. Fishing 1 and 5 miles. Golf 4 miles.

Open: 1 March - 28 December.

Directions

Turn off A95 midway between Aberlour and Craigellachie onto unclassified road. Site signed in 500 yds. Vehicles over 10'6" high should use the A941 Dufftown road (site signed). GPS: 57.47485, -3.1986

Charges guide

Per unit incl. 2 persons and electricity	£ 18.75 - £ 23.40
extra person (over 5 yrs)	£ 2.50
backpacker and tent (per person)	£ 8.40 - £ 9.90
dog	free

FREE Alan Rogers Travel Card
Extra benefits and savings - see page 10

Acharacle
Resipole Farm Holiday Park
Loch Sunart, Acharacle PH36 4HX (Highland) T: 01967 431235. E: info@resipole.co.uk
alanrogers.com/UK7800

This quiet, open five-hectare park is marvellously set on the shores of Loch Sunart, eight miles from Strontian, on the Ardnamurchan peninsula. It is a must for anyone seeking peace and tranquillity and really worth the journey. With wonderful views across the water and regularly visited by wild deer, Resipole Farm offers a good base for exploring the whole of this scenic area or, more locally, for fishing, boating (launching from the site's own slipway) and walking in the unspoilt countryside. There are 48 level and well drained touring pitches here, 40 with 10/16A electricity. Tents are sited by the hedges.

Facilities

The central, modern sanitary block can be heated and is kept very clean. Excellent provision for disabled visitors. Laundry facilities. Motorcaravan service point. Caravan storage. Art gallery and studios. Fishing. WiFi in some areas (free).

Open: Easter/1 April - 31 October.

Directions

From A82 Fort William road, take Corran ferry located 5 miles north of Ballachulish and 8 miles south of Fort William. Leaving ferry, turn south along the A861. Park is on the north shore of Loch Sunart, 8 miles west of Strontian. Single track road for 8 miles approaching Resipole. GPS: 56.710933, -5.720217

Charges guide

Per unit incl. 2 persons and electricity	£ 19.00
extra person	£ 3.00

Arrochar
Forest Holidays Ardgartan
Ardgartan, Arrochar G83 7AR (Dunbartonshire) T: 01301 702293. E: fe.holidays@forestry.gsi.gov.uk
alanrogers.com/UK7260

Forest Holidays is a partnership between the Forestry Commission and The Camping and Caravanning Club. Ardgartan is a rugged site in the Argyll Forest Park. Splendidly situated with mountains all around and lovely views of Loch Long, there are lots of sightseeing and activity opportunities. The 175 pitches are in sections which are well divided by grass giving an uncrowded air. Most with hardstanding and marked by numbered posts, they are accessed from hard surfaced roads and 54 have electrical hook-ups. There are additional grass areas for tents. Midges can be a problem in this area of Scotland.

Facilities

The main toilet block is opposite the reception and shop. It includes facilities for disabled visitors and babies. Launderette. Play equipment (bark surfaces). Raised barbecues are allowed. Bicycle hire. Fishing. Boat launching. Off site: Arrochar village with fuel, general stores and a restaurant 2 miles.

Open: All year.

Directions

From A82 Glasgow-Crianlarich road take A83 at Tarbet signed Arrochar and Cambletown. Site is 2 miles past Arrochar, the entrance on a bend. GPS: 56.188783, -4.781667

Charges guide

Per unit incl. 2 persons	£ 15.00 - £ 29.00
incl. electricity	£ 20.00 - £ 35.00
extra person	£ 4.00 - £ 6.00
child (5-16 yrs)	£ 2.00 - £ 3.50

Auchterarder
Grand Eagles Caravan Park
Nether Coul, Auchterarder PH3 1ET (Perth and Kinross) T: 01764 663119. E: info@grandeagles.co.uk
alanrogers.com/UK7270

This is a charming small park, purpose designed and landscaped. In a sheltered position, it is conveniently situated for exploring central Scotland and the Highlands with many leisure activities close at hand (particularly golf) and within walking distance of the village (1 mile). The 21 original pitches, all with 6A electricity and hardstanding, 12 fully serviced, are well spaced around the edge of the elongated, level grass park. Marked pitches with grass frontage back on to raised banks which are planted with trees. Further pitches have been developed to one side of the site.

Facilities

Toilet facilities (with key system) include controllable, well equipped hot showers. A toilet for disabled visitors is provided in both the male and female units. Laundry room with sink and washing machine; an iron can be provided. Fishing. Caravan storage. Off site: Village and golf 1 mile. Bicycle hire and riding 4 miles. The historic cities of Perth and Stirling are less than half an hour's drive away.

Open: All year.

Directions

Park is between the A9 and A824 roads east of Auchterarder village, only 2 miles from the main road. It is reached by turning on to the B8062 (Dunning) road from the A824. GPS: 56.304333, -3.676167

Charges guide

Per unit incl. up to 4 persons and electricity	£ 19.50
extra person (over 5 yrs)	£ 2.00

No credit cards.

For latest campsite news visit
alanrogers.com

Aviemore

Forest Holidays Glenmore

Aviemore PH22 1QU (Highland) T: 01479 861271. E: info@forestholidays.co.uk

alanrogers.com/UK7680

Forest Holidays is a partnership between the Forestry Commission and The Camping and Caravanning Club. This site is attractively laid out in a fairly informal style in several adjoining areas connected by narrow, part gravel, part tarmac roads, with access to the lochside. One of these areas, the Pinewood Area, is very popular and has 32 hardstandings (some distance from the toilet block). Of the 220 marked pitches on fairly level, firm grass, 122 have 16A electricity. This site, with something for everyone, would be great for family holidays. The Glenmore Forest Park lies close to the sandy shore of Loch Morlich.

Facilities

New toilet and shower blocks. Next to the site is a range of amenities including a well stocked shop (open all year), a café serving a variety of meals and snacks, and a Forestry Commission visitor centre and souvenir shop. Barbecues are not permitted in dry weather. Bicycle hire. Fishing. Sandy beach (Blue Flag). Off site: The Aviemore centre with a wide range of indoor and outdoor recreation activities including skiing 7 miles. Golf within 15 miles.

Open: All year.

Directions

Immediately south of Aviemore on B9152 (not the A9 bypass) take B970 then follow sign for Cairngorm and Loch Morlich. Site entrance is on right past the loch. If travelling in winter, prepare for snow. GPS: 57.167033, -3.694717

Charges guide

Per unit incl. 2 persons	£ 14.50 - £ 30.00
incl. electricity	£ 19.50 - £ 35.00
extra person	£ 2.75 - £ 4.50

Balloch

Lomond Woods Holiday Park

Tullichewan, Old Luss Road, Balloch G83 8QP (West Dunbartonshire) T: 01389 755000.
E: lomondwoods@holiday-parks.co.uk **alanrogers.com/UK7240**

A series of improvements over the last few years has made this one of the top parks in Scotland. Almost, but not quite, on the banks of Loch Lomond, this landscaped, well planned park is suitable for both transit or longer stays. There are 110 touring units on well spaced, numbered pitches on flat or gently sloping grass. All have hardstanding and 10A electrical connections and 27 have water and waste water too. Watersports activities and boat trips are possible on Loch Lomond.

Facilities

The single large, heated, well kept toilet block includes some showers with WCs, baths for ladies, a shower room for disabled visitors and two baby baths. Covered dishwashing sinks. Launderette. Motorcaravan service points. Games room with TV, table tennis and pool table. Playground. American motorhomes accepted with prior notice. WiFi over site (charged). Off site: Fishing and boat launching 400 yds. Riding 4 miles. Golf 5 miles. Restaurants, bar meals and buses in Balloch (5 minutes).

Open: All year.

Directions

Turn off A82 road 17 miles northwest of Glasgow on A811 Stirling road. Site is in Balloch at southern end of Loch Lomond and is well signed. GPS: 56.00155, -4.592233

Charges guide

Per unit incl. up to 2 persons and electricity	£ 20.00 - £ 24.00
incl. mains services and awning	£ 22.00 - £ 26.00
extra person	£ 3.00

Blairgowrie

Nethercraig Caravan Park

By Alyth, Blairgowrie PH11 8HN (Perth and Kinross) T: 01575 560204.
E: nethercraigholidaypark@btconnect.com **alanrogers.com/UK7280**

Nethercraig is a family run touring park, attractively designed and beautifully landscaped, with views across the Strathmore valley to the long range of the Sidlaw hills. The 40 large touring pitches are accessed from a circular, gravel road, all with 10A electrical connections and all but one with hardstanding (for awnings too). In addition, there are five large pitches for tents on flat grass. There is a personal welcome for all visitors at the attractive modern reception building and shop which provides the necessary essentials, gas and tourist information.

Facilities

The central, purpose built toilet block is well equipped and maintained, and can be heated. Unit for disabled visitors (entry by key). Separate sinks for dishwashing and clothes in the laundry room (metered hot water), plus a washing machine, dryer and iron, and clothes line. Shop. Play area. Small football field. Fishing. Caravan storage. Off site: Fishing 2 miles. Golf within 4 miles. Riding 4 miles. Boat launching 6 miles.

Open: 15 February - 13 January.

Directions

From A926 Blairgowrie-Kirriemuir road, at roundabout south of Alyth join B954 (Glenisla). Follow caravan signs for 4 miles and turn right onto unclassified road (Nether Craig). Park is on left after 0.5 miles. GPS: 56.6614, -3.1998

Charges guide

Per unit incl. 2 persons and electricity	£ 15.00 - £ 18.00
extra person	£ 1.00

FREE Alan Rogers Travel Card
Extra benefits and savings - see page 10

Callander

The Gart Caravan Park

Stirling Road, Callander FK17 8LE (Perth and Kinross) T: 01877 330002. E: enquiries@theholidaypark.co.uk
alanrogers.com/UK7220

Gart Caravan Park is situated within the Loch Lomond and Trossachs National Park, just a mile from the centre of Callander. Surrounded by mature trees, this attractive, family run park is peaceful and spacious. All is kept in a pristine condition and a very warm welcome awaits on arrival with a superb information pack given to all. The 128 all grass touring pitches are reasonably level, open plan and marked, with 16A electricity, water and drain. Tents and pup tents are not accepted, groundsheets are not permitted. Privately owned caravan holiday homes are located away from the touring section near the river which runs for 200 yards along the park boundary.

Facilities

Modern heated central facilities are immaculate, kept spotlessly clean with toilets and showers, plus extra areas with showers, baby changing and hair washing basins. Separate facilities for disabled visitors. Fully equipped laundry. Drive-over motorcaravan service point. Gas sales. No shop on site but a breakfast car arrives at 09.00 with papers and basic provisions. Large adventure play area, part undercover. Separate field for ball games. Free fishing (not Sundays). Max. two dogs permitted. Off site: Supermarket 200 yds. Golf, bus service and bicycle hire 1 mile. Riding 6 miles.

Open: 1 April - 15 October.

Directions

From the south take M9. Near Stirling, leave at exit 10 and follow A84 through Doune. Park is on the left, 1 mile before Callander town centre. GPS: 56.2365, -4.1891

Charges guide

Per unit incl. services	£ 23.00
awning	£ 2.00
Reduced rates for the over 50s.	
Loyalty card.	

Castle Douglas

Barlochan Caravan Park

Palnackie, Castle Douglas DG7 1PF (Dumfries and Galloway) T: 01557 870267.
E: info@gillespie-leisure.co.uk alanrogers.com/UK6945

Barlochan Caravan Park is situated on a hillside overlooking the Urr Estuary on the Solway Coast close to Dalbeattie and Castle Douglas, with the small village of Palnackie being a short walk away. Set on terraces, level, marked and numbered, most of the touring and tent pitches are on grass with a limited number of hardstandings available. There are 21 with 16A electrical connections. In addition, 55 holiday homes (five for hire) are positioned on terraces high above the touring areas and screened by mature shrubs and trees. Just to the left of the entrance there is a minigolf course and an adventure play area screened from the park with mature trees. The sheltered outdoor swimming pool is popular. Through the village, under a mile from the park, there is a coarse fishing lake which is free for visitors to the park. Dalbeattie Forest nearby provides miles of walking and mountain bike trails. Castle Douglas is just 9 miles away and gardeners will enjoy an afternoon at the well known Threave Gardens.

Facilities

The refurbished sanitary facilities are kept spotlessly clean. Shower cubicles have recently been made larger, suitable for wheelchair entry, but if required there is also a separate unit with WC and basin. Fully equipped laundry with outside drying area. Reception and well stocked shop. Heated outdoor swimming pool and terrace. Large games room and TV room. Minigolf. Off site: Fishing 300 yds. Bicycle hire 3 miles. Golf 7 miles. Riding and beach 10 miles. Village pub nearby. Dalbeattie Forest for cycling and walking.

Open: Easter/1 April - 31 October.

Directions

From Dumfries take A711 west to Dalbeattie. Continue through Dalbeattie for 0.5 miles and bear left at T-junction signed Auchencairn. Site is 2 miles on the right. GPS: 54.895023, -3.842564

Charges guide

Per unit incl. 2 persons and electricity	£ 17.00 - £ 22.50
extra person	£ 2.50
child (4-15 yrs)	£ 1.50
dog	£ 2.00

For latest campsite news visit
alanrogers.com

Castle Douglas
Loch Ken Holiday Park

Parton, Castle Douglas DG7 3NE (Dumfries and Galloway) T: 01644 470282.
E: office@lochkenholidaypark.co.uk **alanrogers.com/UK6940**

Loch Ken Holiday Park sits right on the shore of the loch, adjacent to the RSPB bird reserve and the Galloway Forest Park – it is a peaceful haven in an Area of Outstanding Natural Beauty. This is a family owned park with 40 touring pitches and 33 caravan holiday homes, ten of which are for rent. The touring pitches, all with 10A electricity, are quite separate and are arranged in a mostly open plan way on a large, neatly mown grass area beside the water. Some of this area is gently undulating. Mature trees border the park and provide an area for walking dogs.

Facilities

The toilet block has been completely refurbished to modern standards and was exceptionally clean when we visited. Separate facilities in a modern Portacabin unit are provided in the tent area. Facilities for disabled visitors. Gas supplies. Well stocked shop. Good play area. Bicycles, canoes and dinghies for hire. Boat launching (permit from reception). Fishing (permit). Off site: Buses stop at the entrance, but are limited. Skiing 0.5 miles. Golf and riding 7 miles. Bars and restaurants in Castle Douglas 9 miles. Kirkcudbright 15 miles.

Open: 1 March - 31 October.

Directions

From Castle Douglas take the A713 north for 7 miles. Site entrance is on left in Parton. GPS: 55.0104, -4.05568

Charges guide

Per unit incl. 2 persons, 2 children under 10 yrs and electricity	£ 17.00 - £ 22.00
tent, no electricity	£ 12.00 - £ 17.00
extra person	£ 2.00
dog	£ 2.00

Castle Douglas
Mossyard Caravan Park

Gatehouse of Fleet, Castle Douglas DG7 2ET (Dumfries and Galloway) T: 01557 840226.
E: enquiry@mossyard.co.uk **alanrogers.com/UK6890**

Mossyard is a family run park set within a working farm right beside the sea in a sheltered bay. The park and farmhouse appear together suddenly over the horizon as you approach, with some breathtaking views across the Solway where the Galloway Hills and the waters of Fleet Bay meet. There are 37 grass touring pitches, 12 for caravans and motorcaravans on an elevated area that slopes in parts. The remaining 25 pitches for any unit are on a level field which adjoins the beach but is a little way from the sanitary facilities. Electrical connections (16A) are available to all.

Facilities

Some of the farm buildings around the main farmhouse have been utilised for the toilet facilities, which are of traditional design. Showers are coin-operated (20p). Roomy facilities for disabled visitors can also be used as a family bathroom. Purpose built building with laundry, dishwashing area and information room with freezer and fridge for visitors' use. No shop. Off site: Gatehouse of Fleet with shops, pubs and restaurants 4 miles. Riding 1 mile. Bicycle hire and golf 5 miles.

Open: 30 March - 3 November.

Directions

Take A75 road from Dumfries towards Stranraer and park is signed to the left, 4 miles west of Gatehouse of Fleet, 1 mile down a single track farm road. GPS: 54.840183, -4.26015

Charges guide

Per unit incl. 2 persons and electricity	£ 16.50 - £ 18.50

Connel
Oban Camping & Caravanning Club Site

Barcaldine, By Connel PA37 1SG (Argyll and Bute) T: 01631 720348
alanrogers.com/UK7810

Owned by the Camping and Caravanning Club, this site at Barcaldine, 12 miles north of Oban, is a small, intimate site taking 75 units. Arranged within the old walled garden of Barcaldine House, the walls give it some protection from the wind and make it quite a sun trap. There are 23 level, fairly small pitches with hardstanding and 52 electrical hook-ups (16A). (It can be wet underfoot in bad weather). Being a small site, it has a very cosy feel to it, due no doubt to the friendly welcome given to new arrivals.

Facilities

The central toilet block can be heated and is kept very clean with free hot showers, hairdryers and plenty of washbasins and WCs. Excellent unit for disabled visitors. Laundry. Motorcaravan service point. Small shop open a few hours each day for basic provisions and gas. Small play area. WiFi throughout (charged). Off site: Sea Life Centre 2 miles. Bus every hour outside gate.

Open: 29 March - 5 November.

Directions

Entrance is off the A828 road on south side of Loch Creran, 6 miles north of Connel Bridge. From the south, go past Barcaldine House and site is 300 yds. on right. GPS: 56.5265, -5.309933

Charges guide

Per person	£ 5.95 - £ 9.35
child (6-18 yrs)	£ 2.70 - £ 2.95
non-member pitch fee	£ 7.10

FREE Alan Rogers Travel Card
Extra benefits and savings - see page 10

Crail

Sauchope Links Park

Crail KY10 3XJ (Fife) T: 01333 450460. E: info@sauchope.co.uk

alanrogers.com/UK7285

Sauchope Links Park is a member of the Largo Leisure Parks group with a good range of facilities on offer, notably a heated swimming pool, an indoor recreation room and a play area for children. The site's location is very attractive with miles of rocky shore to be explored. Pitches here are grassy and of a good size. A number of fully serviced pitches are available and also hardstandings. Alternatively, a number of mobile homes and micro lodges (small wooden chalets) are available for rent.

Facilities

Small shop. Games room. Play areas. Tourist information. Mobile homes and other accommodation for rent. Off site: Top class golf at Crail golf club, the seventh oldest in the world and the Royal and Ancient club at St Andrews needs little introduction. Walking and cycle tracks. Fishing. Riding. Scone Palace. Craigtoun Country Park.

Open: 21 March - 31 October.

Directions

Approaching from St Andrews on the A918, on entering Crail at a sharp right hand corner, turn left down an unclassified road. Site is signed 400 yds. on right. Follow signs to the site, which is down by the sea. GPS: 56.261606, -2.612724

Charges guide

Per unit incl. 2 persons and electricity	£ 16.00 - £ 22.00
extra person	£ 5.00

Crieff

Braidhaugh Holiday Park

South Bridgend, Crieff PH7 4DH (Perth and Kinross) T: 01764 652951. E: info@braidhaugh.co.uk

alanrogers.com/UK7275

Braidhaugh is a member of the Largo Leisure Parks group and is situated on the banks of the River Earn among the scenic surroundings of Perthshire. There are 39 touring pitches, all with electricity, water and drainage. The site is well located for exploring Central Scotland, as well as being within walking distance of shops, restaurants, places of interest and many sporting facilities. The Earn is renowned for its salmon and trout fishing and permits can be purchased from the reception. The small shop stocks the essentials and a larger supermarket is close at hand. The beautiful countryside surrounding the park offers many country walks in all directions and this is also excellent mountain biking terrain.

Facilities

Small shop. Games room. Play areas. Fishing. WiFi (charged). Tourist information. Mobile homes and other accommodation for rent. Off site: Top class golf (courses at Muthill, Crieff and Comrie). Walking and cycle tracks. Fishing. Riding. Leisure centre.

Open: All year.

Directions

Approaching from Perth, drive through Crieff and turn left onto the A822 (Stirling). At the bottom of the hill cross a bridge over the River Earn. Turn right immediately after the bridge and take the first right to enter park. GPS: 56.366771, -3.853455

Charges guide

Per unit incl. 2 persons and electricity	£ 20.00 - £ 23.00

Dalbeattie

Glenearly Caravan Park

Dalbeattie DG5 4NE (Dumfries and Galloway) T: 01556 611393. E: enquiries@glenearlycaravanpark.co.uk

alanrogers.com/UK6870

Glenearly is owned and managed by Mr and Mrs Jardine. Rurally located, it has been tastefully developed from farmland into a touring and mobile home, all year park. There are 39 marked, open pitches, all with 16A electrical connections and TV, most on hardstandings. Seasonal units use some pitches. Walls and shrubs divide the touring section from the caravan holiday homes (two for rent), with mature trees around the perimeter. There are attractive views over the hills and forest of Barhill and buzzards, yellow wagtails, woodpeckers and goldfinch are some of the birds that can be seen, along with the park's own donkeys and ponies. This is a very well kept, well designed park.

Facilities

Situated in the centre of the touring area, the toilets and showers are fitted out to a high standard. Unit for disabled visitors and families. Laundry room with washing machines and dryer and an outside drying area. Large games room. Play area. Max. 2 dogs accepted. Off site: Shops, pubs, restaurants, etc. at Dalbeattie. Golf 1 mile. Fishing and riding 5 miles. Beach 5 miles. Bicycle hire 10 miles.

Open: All year.

Directions

From Dumfries take A711 towards Dalbeattie. 6 miles beyond Beeswing, after passing sign for Edingham Farm, park is signed with entrance on right (beside a bungalow). GPS: 54.944867, -3.822283

Charges guide

Per unit incl. 2 persons and electricity	£ 16.50 - £ 18.50
extra person (over 5 yrs)	£ 2.00

For latest campsite news visit
alanrogers.com

Dalbeattie
Sandyhills Bay Leisure Park

Sandyhills, Dalbeattie DG5 4NY (Dumfries and Galloway) T: 01387 780257. E: info@gillespie-leisure.co.uk
alanrogers.com/UK6880

Sandyhills Bay is a small, quiet park beside a sheltered, sandy beach. Reception is on the left through a car park used by visitors either walking the hills or enjoying the beach. Beyond is a large flat camping area, above which, divided by a tree lined hedge, are 60 pitches, 36 taken by holiday homes situated around the perimeter. The 24 touring pitches, most with 16A electricity connections are in the centre of the flat grass area. Wooden wigwams with a terrace and picnic bench are available to rent. This is an excellent family park, with the beach and a children's play area on the park. Within walking distance, at Barend, is an approved riding centre suitable for all the family. There is a well stocked licensed shop and a takeaway with table and chairs outside from where you can enjoy the well kept garden and splendid views across the Solway.

Facilities	Directions
The sanitary facilities are of traditional design, situated in one central block to the side of the touring area. Laundry room (tokens from reception). Shop. Adventure play area by the beach. Visitors can also use the facilities at Brighouse Bay, the largest park in the Gillespie Group. Barrier at entrance and beach car park (returnable deposit). Off site: Golf and riding 500 yds. Bicycle hire 2 miles. Fishing 10 miles.	From Dumfries take A710 Solway coast road (about 16 miles). Site is on left just after signs for Sandyhills. GPS: 54.879017, -3.731033

Open: Easter/1 April - 31 October.

Charges guide

Per unit incl. 2 persons	
and electricity	£ 17.00 - £ 22.50
extra person	£ 3.00
child (4-15 yrs)	£ 1.75
dog	£ 2.00

Dumfries
Southerness Holiday Village

Southerness, Dumfries DG2 8AZ (Dumfries and Galloway) T: 01387 880256.
E: enquiries@parkdeanholidays.co.uk **alanrogers.com/UK6875**

Set beside a two mile stretch of sandy beach, at the foot of the beautiful Galloway Hills, is Southerness Holiday Village. Part of the Parkdean Group, it is a large park with the main emphasis on caravan holiday homes. However, there are also 100 open plan pitches for caravans, motorcaravans and tents. Set away from the static units, these are divided into two areas, some on level hardstanding with water connection, others on grass and all with 16A electrical connections. The light and airy reception office displays local information including a weekly 'What's On' programme as the main leisure complex is located a short walk from the touring area.

Facilities	Directions
A modern toilet block provides en-suite facilities throughout (key entry). Well maintained, it is kept very clean by on-site wardens. Excellent unit for disabled visitors. Well equipped laundry. Shop. Bar with large TV. Bistro, takeaway and coffee shop. Indoor swimming pool. Indoor soft play area. Amusement arcade. Comprehensive evening entertainment programme. Outdoor adventure play area. Nature trails. Beach. Off site: Golf course adjacent. Fishing 2.5 miles. Bicycle hire 3 miles. Riding 9 miles. Coastal drive to Rockcliffe and Kippford.	From Dumfries take A710 Solway Coast road for 10 miles. Sign for Holiday Village is on the left. GPS: 54.87613, -3.60037

Open: Before Easter - 31 October.

Charges guide

Per unit incl. 4 persons	£ 14.00 - £ 31.50
incl. services	£ 16.00 - £ 35.50
extra person	£ 2.50 - £ 3.50
dog	£ 2.00 - £ 3.00

FREE Alan Rogers Travel Card
Extra benefits and savings - see page 10

Dunbar
Belhaven Bay Caravan & Camping Park

Belhaven Bay, West Barns, Dunbar EH42 1TU (East Lothian) T: 01368 865956.
E: belhaven@meadowhead.co.uk **alanrogers.com/UK7065**

Located in the John Muir Country Park, Belhaven Bay Caravan Park is just one mile from the historic town of Dunbar, where the ancient castle ruin stands guard over the town's twin harbours. This is an excellent family park with easy access to the beach and to the clifftop trail which has spectacular views capturing the beauty of the countryside and seascapes. The park's 66 caravan holiday homes (five for rent) are located quite separately from the touring and tent areas. These are surrounded by mature trees and are arranged in large open bays. There is a new tent and touring area with electricity points, so now there are 60 reasonably level, mostly grass touring pitches, 48 with 10A electricity available.

Facilities

Facilities are central and include a unit for disabled visitors. Laundry room. Motorcaravan service point. Reception also has a small shop and tourist information. Cyber Café and WiFi. Play area and ball game area. Off site: Bus stop at entrance. Golf 1 mile. Riding and boat launching 2 miles.

Open: 13 March - 31 October.

Directions

From the A1 (north or south) exit at the Thistley Cross roundabout west of Dunbar. Park is 1 mile down the A1087 towards Dunbar.
GPS: 55.996767, -2.545117

Charges guide

Per unit incl. 2 persons and electricity	£ 17.50 - £ 26.50
extra person (over 5 yrs)	£ 5.00

Dunbar
Thurston Manor Leisure Park

Innerwick, Dunbar EH42 1SA (East Lothian) T: 01368 840643. E: info@thurstonmanor.co.uk
alanrogers.com/UK7075

In a rural setting and nestling at the foot of the Lammermuir hills, this holiday park offers either a restful or a lively stay. It is close to historic Dunbar with its beaches, harbour and ruined castle. The 129 touring pitches are set away from the 510 holiday homes. All have 10A electricity connections. Thirty of these are super pitches with electricity, water and drainage. The indoor heated swimming pool and leisure complex offer space to relax and work out. There are woodland walks, safe play areas for children and fishing in a well stocked pond.

Facilities

The clean, well equipped and fully heated sanitary block provides constant hot water for showering, dishwashing and family bathing. Mini market. Restaurant and sports bar. Leisure centre with heated swimming pool (10x6 m), sauna, steam room, fitness room and solarium. Children's play areas. Live family entertainment. WiFi. Off site: Riding and beach 2 miles. Bicycle hire 4 miles. Golf 5 miles.

Open: 1 March - 7 January.

Directions

From north or south on the A1 take the Innerwick turnoff (near Dunbar). Follow the road for half a mile. Thurston Leisure Park is on the right hand side.
GPS: 55.959847, -2.46221

Charges guide

Per unit incl. 2 persons and electricity	£ 19.00 - £ 29.75
extra person	£ 2.00

Durness
Sango Sands Oasis Caravan & Camping Site

Durness via Lairg IV27 4PZ (Highland) T: 01971 511726. E: keith.durness@btinternet.com
alanrogers.com/UK7735

Sango Sands Oasis is a quiet, ten-acre site overlooking the beautiful Sango Bay, a Blue Flag beach. The site was established by the family in 1978 and they have worked hard improving the facilities over the years. There are 82 pitches for tents and touring caravans, 48 with 16A electricity hook-ups. The land is well drained and fairly level. It is possible to see whales, porpoise, dolphins and seals from the site plus a variety of sea birds which nest nearby. An ideal area for walkers, including the less adventurous, there are numerous marked paths and there is an excellent variety of angling, from rivers to the sea.

Facilities

Traditional toilet and shower blocks are lit at night but a torch may be useful. Free showers with curtains. Showers and toilets are separate. With the beach so close don't be surprised to find sand in the showers. En-suite facilities for disabled visitors. Laundry. Campers' kitchen with cooking rings. Café, bar and licensed restaurant. TV. Games room with pool and darts. Off site: Grocery stores, post office, ATM, fuel and gas supplies in the village. Visitors' Centre. Golf 1.5 miles. Boat launching 2 miles.

Open: All year.

Directions

From Thurso take the North Coast road (A836 to Tongue, becoming A838 to Durness). Site is on right as you go through village. From Ullapool follow A835 north to Ledmore Junction and turn left on A837. After 8 miles turn right (A894 to Laxford Bridge). Turn left on A838. Durness is 19 miles further. Site on left going through the village. GPS: 58.56449, -4.74221

Charges guide

Per person	£ 6.50
electricity	£ 3.70

For latest campsite news visit
alanrogers.com

Edinburgh
Linwater Caravan Park

West Clifton, East Calder, Edinburgh EH53 0HT (Edinburgh) T: 01313 333326. E: linwater@supanet.com

alanrogers.com/UK7045

This delightful, small, family run park is set in the countryside but is still close to the city of Edinburgh. The park is level and the 60 large touring pitches are a mixture of grass and hardstanding; 49 have 16A electricity connections. Parts of the park are screened off by trees and fences. Two sides are sheltered by trees and shrubs and one side is open with views over fields. With just the occasional sound of aircraft from the airport, it is difficult to believe that you are so close to a major city. Linwater is a useful park for visiting Edinburgh and areas outside the city. The reception area has a wealth of information on places to visit. Just four miles down the road is a park and ride scheme and the purchase of a Day Saver ticket is a cheap way to get into Edinburgh and to explore the area. The Falkirk Wheel, houses, castles and gardens are all within easy reach.

Facilities	Directions
The modern and well maintained heated sanitary block has private cabins. Facilities for disabled visitors. Laundry. Gas supplies. Milk, bread and newspapers to order (by 21.00 for the next morning). Home produced free range eggs and bacon from reception. Sand pit. Four timber tents for hire. Free WiFi in reception area. Off site: Fishing 1 mile.	From the A720 Edinburgh bypass, leave at sign for Wilkieston on the A71. In Wilkieston turn right at traffic lights (park signed). Continue to next sign indicating left and site 1 mile further on the right. GPS: 55.91104, -3.43588

Open: Mid March - early November.

Charges guide

Per unit incl. 2 persons and electricity	£ 16.00 - £ 21.00
tent incl. 2 persons	£ 14.00 - £ 18.00

A family-run touring park just west of Edinburgh with easy access to Edinburgh, Royal Highland Showground and Falkirk Wheel. Excellent amenities and lovely walks to Canal and Country Park. Call in on your way north or south, or stay awhile, you will be most welcome.

Linwater Caravan Park, West Clifton, East Calder, West Lothian, EH53 0HT
Tel: 0131 333 3326
queries@linwater.co.uk
www.linwater.co.uk

Edinburgh
Edinburgh Caravan Club Site

35-37 Marine Drive, Edinburgh EH4 5EN (Edinburgh) T: 01313 126874

alanrogers.com/UK7050

Situated as it is on the northern outskirts and within easy reach of the city of Edinburgh, this large, busy Caravan Club site (open to non members) provides an ideal base for touring. Enter the site through rather grand gates to find the visitors' car park and reception to the left. There are 146 large, flat pitches (142 hardstandings, 12 with water tap and waste water disposal) with 16A electricity hook-ups and TV aerial, and provision for 50 tents in a separate field (hook-ups available) with a covered cooking shelter and bicycle stands close by. As the bushes planted around the site mature, there will be shade. The nearest hotel/restaurant is under a mile away, and the Firth of Forth bridge about two miles. The Royal Yacht Britannia and many other attractions can be found in the city.

Facilities	Directions
Two well kept, heated toilet blocks provide washbasins in cubicles, hairdryers and hand dryers, an en-suite room for disabled campers, plus a baby and toddler room with child size facilities. Each block houses a dishwashing and vegetable preparation area, and a laundry. Drying room. No shop, but milk, bread, and newspapers can be ordered, with ice creams and gas from reception. Fenced play area. Boules. Dog walk in the only natural wood in Edinburgh (part of the site). WiFi. Off site: Bicycle hire nearby. Health club (with Internet access) 400 yds. – ask at site for introduction card.	Turn right off A720 at Gogar roundabout at end of bypass (City Centre, A8). Turn left onto A902 (Forth Road Bridge), then right onto A90. At Blackhall junction lights fork left into Telford Road (A902). At Crewe Toll roundabout turn left (B9085) and at T-junction (after bridge) turn right at lights towards Leith (A901). Turn left at lights (Silverknowes, Davidson's Mains). In half a mile at roundabout turn right into Marine Drive. Site is half a mile on the left. GPS: 55.97755, -3.2645

Open: All year.

Charges guide

Per person	£ 5.10 - £ 6.90
child (5-16 yrs)	£ 1.55 - £ 2.55
pitch incl. electricity (non member)	£ 13.10 - £ 16.60

FREE Alan Rogers Travel Card
Extra benefits and savings - see page 10

Edinburgh

Mortonhall Caravan & Camping Park

38 Mortonhall Gate, Frogston Road East, Edinburgh EH16 6TJ (Edinburgh) T: 01316 641533.
E: mortonhall@meadowhead.co.uk **alanrogers.com/UK6990**

Mortonhall Park makes a good base to see the historic city of Edinburgh and buses to the city leave from the park entrance every ten minutes (parking in Edinburgh is not easy). Although only four miles from the city centre, Mortonhall is in quiet mature parkland, in the grounds of the Mortonhall estate, and easy to find with access off the bypass. There is room for 250 units, mostly on numbered pitches on a slight slope with nothing to separate them, but marked by jockey wheel points. Over 180 places have 10/16A electricity, several with hardstanding, water and drainage as well, and there are many places for tents.

Facilities

Two modern toilet blocks, but the only cabins are in the third excellent facility at the top of the park, which has eight unisex units incorporating shower, washbasin and WC. Further basic facilities are added for the high season. Facilities for disabled visitors. Motorcaravan services. Laundry room. Bar/restaurant. Shop. Games and TV rooms. Play area. Late arrivals area. Torches useful. Internet access. WiFi (charged). Off site: Riding, golf courses and driving range 2 miles. Bicycle hire 4 miles.

Open: 20 March - 4 January.

Directions

Park is well signed south of the city, 5 minutes from A720 city bypass. Take the Mortonhall exit from the Straiton junction and follow camping signs. Entrance road is alongside the Klondyke Garden Centre. GPS: 55.902889, -3.181705

Charges guide

Per unit incl. 2 persons and electricity	£ 16.50 - £ 29.00
tent pitch (4 persons)	£ 13.50 - £ 24.75
extra person (5 yrs and over)	£ 5.00

Fort William

Glen Nevis Caravan & Camping Park

Glen Nevis, Fort William PH33 6SX (Highland) T: 01397 702191. E: camping@glen-nevis.co.uk
alanrogers.com/UK7830

Just outside Fort William, in a most attractive and quiet situation with views of Ben Nevis, this spacious park is used by those on active pursuits as well as sightseeing tourists. It comprises eight quite spacious fields, divided between caravans, motorcaravans and tents (steel pegs required). It is licensed for 250 touring caravans but with no specific tent limits. The large touring pitches, many with hardstanding, are marked with wooden fence dividers, 174 with 13A electricity and 100 also have water and drainage. The park becomes full in the peak months but there are vacancies each day. If reception is closed (possible in low season) you site yourself. There are regular security patrols at night in busy periods. The park's own modern restaurant and bar with good value bar meals is a short stroll from the park, open to all. A well managed park with bustling, but pleasing ambiance, watched over by Ben Nevis. Around 1,000 acres of the Glen Nevis estate are open to campers to see the wildlife and explore this lovely area.

Facilities

The four modern toilet blocks with showers (extra showers in two blocks); and units for disabled visitors. An excellent block in Nevis Park (one of the eight camping fields) has some washbasins in cubicles, showers, further facilities for disabled visitors and a second large laundry room. Motorcaravan service point. Shop (Easter-mid Oct), barbecue area and snack bar (May-mid Sept). Play area. Off site: Pony trekking, golf and fishing nearby.

Open: 15 March - 31 October.

Directions

Turn off A82 to east at roundabout just north of Fort William following camp sign. GPS: 56.804517, -5.073917

Charges guide

Per unit incl. 2 persons and electricity	£ 15.20 - £ 22.30
extra person	£ 1.80 - £ 3.20
child (5-15 yrs)	£ 1.00 - £ 1.60
dog	free

Glen Nevis Caravan and Camping Park

AA Campsite of the Year for Scotland 2006

Glen Nevis, Fort William, PH33 6SX - 01397 702 191 - glen-nevis.co.uk

For latest campsite news visit
alanrogers.com

Fort William
Linnhe Lochside Holidays

Corpach, Fort William PH33 7NL (Highland) T: 01397 772376. E: relax@linnhe-lochside-holidays.co.uk

alanrogers.com/UK7850

This quiet well run park has a very peaceful situation overlooking Loch Eil, and it is beautifully landscaped with wonderful views. There are individual pitches with hardstanding for 65 touring units (12 seasonal) on terraces leading down to the water's edge. They include 32 with 16A electricity connection, water and drainage, plus 30 with 10A electricity only. A separate area on the lochside takes 15 small tents (no reservation). There are also 60 caravan holiday homes and 14 centrally heated pine chalets for hire. Fishing is free on Loch Eil and you are welcome to fish from the park's private beach or bring your own boat and use the slipway and dinghy park. About five miles from Fort William on 'The Road to the Isles', the park is conveniently placed for touring the Western Highlands. Easily accessible are Ben Nevis and the Nevis range (cable car to 2,000 ft), geological, Jacobite and Commando museums, distillery visits, seal island trips, the Mallaig steam railway and the Caledonian Canal.

Facilities

Toilet facilities are excellent, heated in the cooler months and include baths (£1). Dishwashing room. First class laundry and separate outdoor drying room (charged per night). Self-service, licensed shop (end May-end Sept). Gas supplies. Barbecue area. Toddlers' play room and two well equipped play areas on safe standing. Large motorcaravans are accepted but it is best to book first. Caravan storage. Max. 2 dogs per pitch. Off site: Bicycle hire 2.5 miles. Riding, golf and skiing 5 miles.

Open: 15 December - 31 October.

Directions

Park entrance is off A830 Fort William-Mallaig road, 1 mile west of Corpach. GPS: 56.847817, -5.16025

Charges guide

Per unit incl. 2 persons and electricity	£ 17.75 - £ 21.00
extra person	£ 3.25
child (3-15 yrs)	£ 2.00
dog	£ 1.25

Seasonal rates available.

Corpach, Fort William Scotland PH33 7NL

Touring, camping, chalets and caravans. Fantastic views. Wildlife and free fishing. Friendly 4 star park.

Tel. 01397772376 ● www.linnhe-lochside-holidays.co.uk

Glendaruel
Glendaruel Caravan Park

Glendaruel PA22 3AB (Argyll and Bute) T: 01369 820267. E: mail@glendaruelcaravanpark.co.uk

alanrogers.com/UK7860

Glendaruel is in South Argyll, in the area of Scotland bounded by the Kyles of Bute and Loch Fyne, yet is less than two hours by road from Glasgow and serviced by ferries from Gourock and the Isle of Bute. There is also a service between Tarbert and Portavadie. Set in the peaceful wooded gardens of the former Glendaruel House, in a secluded glen surrounded by the Cowal hills, it makes an ideal base for touring this beautiful area. The park takes 35 units on numbered hardstandings with 10A electricity connections, plus 15 tents, on flat oval meadows bordered by mature trees.

Facilities

The toilet block is ageing but kept very neat and tidy and can be heated. Washing machine and dryer. A covered area has dishwashing sinks and picnic tables for use in bad weather. Shop (limited hours in low season). Gas available. Games room with pool table, table tennis and video games. Behind the laundry is a children's play centre for under 12s and additional play field. Fishing. Torches advised. Off site: Sea fishing and boat slipway 5 miles, adventure centre (assault courses, abseiling and rafting) and sailing school close by. Golf 12 miles.

Open: 28 March - 26 October.

Directions

Entrance is off A886 road 13 miles south of Strachur. Alternatively by Gourock to Dunoon ferry, then on B836 which joins the A886 4 miles south of the park (not recommended for touring caravans). Ignore sat nav which takes you down narrow back roads. Note: contact park for discount arrangements with Western Ferries (allow 7 days for postage of tickets). GPS: 56.033967, -5.212833

Charges guide

Per unit incl. 2 persons and electricity	£ 19.00

Glencoe

Invercoe Caravan & Camping Park

Invercoe, Glencoe PH49 4HP (Argyll and Bute) T: 01855 811210. E: holidays@invercoe.co.uk

alanrogers.com/UK7790

On the edge of Loch Leven, surrounded by mountains and forest, Iain and Lynn Brown are continually developing this attractively located park in its magnificent historical setting. It provides 63 pitches for caravans, motorcaravans and tents on level grass (can be a bit wet in bad weather) with gravel access roads (some hardstandings). You choose your own numbered pitch, those at the loch side being very popular. The only rules imposed are necessary for safety because the owners prefer their guests to feel free and enjoy themselves. This is a park you will want to return to again and again. There is much to do for the active visitor with hill walking, climbing, boating, pony riding and sea loch or fresh water fishing in this Area of Outstanding Natural Beauty.

Facilities

The well refurbished toilet block can be heated. Dishwashing under cover, excellent laundry facilities with a drying room. New large under cover eating area. Motorcaravan service point comprising multi-drainage point, fresh water, dustbins, and chemical disposal point. Shop (Easter-end Oct). Play area with swings. Fishing. New fore-shore hardstanding with slipway. WiFi. Off site: The village with pub and restaurant is within walking distance. Visitors' Centre at Glencoe 2 miles. Bicycle hire 2 miles. Golf 3 miles.

Open: All year.

Directions

Follow A82 Crianlarich-Fort William road to Glencoe village and turn onto the B863; park is 0.5 miles along, well signed. GPS: 56.686567, -5.105983

Charges guide

Per unit incl. 2 persons and electricity	£ 19.00 - £ 23.00
extra person	£ 4.00
child (3-15 yrs)	£ 2.00

Senior citizens less £1 per person outside July/Aug.

Grantown-on-Spey

Grantown-on-Spey Caravan Park

Seafield Avenue, Grantown-on-Spey PH26 3JQ (Highland) T: 01479 872474.
E: warden@caravanscotland.com alanrogers.com/UK7670

This excellent park is peacefully situated on the outskirts of the town, with views of the mountains in the distance. There are 125 well tended gravel and grass pitches for caravans and motorcaravans, all with 10/16A electricity and 69 offer fresh and waste water facilities. In addition to this, a number of super pitches also offer 16A electricity, WiFi and individual Sky TV box. A further 12 pitches are used for seasonal occupation and there is space for 50 or more tents. The park is affiliated to the Caravan Club. Trees and flowers are a feature of this attractive, landscaped location. The wardens escort visitors to their pitch and will help to site caravans if necessary. Caravan holiday homes are located in a separate area of the park.

Facilities

The modern toilet and shower block is complete with laundry and drying room. A further block provides good, clean toilet facilities, with new washing cabins for ladies. Facilities for disabled visitors. Laundry room. Motorcaravan service point. Gas, ice creams, cold drinks and camping accessories available at reception. Games room with table tennis and pool table. WiFi over site (charged). Caravan and motorcaravan secure storage. Off site: Fishing, golf and mountain bike hire within 1 mile. Riding 3 miles.

Open: All year incl. Christmas and New Year.

Directions

Go into the town. Turn north at Bank of Scotland. Park straight ahead half a mile. GPS: 57.3348, -3.618617

Charges guide

Per unit incl. 2 persons and 10A electricity	£ 18.30 - £ 28.00
small 2-man tent	£ 10.00 - £ 15.00
extra person	£ 1.00 - £ 3.00

For latest campsite news visit
alanrogers.com

Huntly
Huntly Castle Caravan Park
The Meadow, Huntly AB54 4UJ (Aberdeenshire) T: 01466 794999. E: enquiries@huntlycastle.co.uk
alanrogers.com/UK7550

Huntly Caravan Park was opened in '95 and its hardworking owners, the Ballantynes, are justly proud of their neat, well landscaped 15 acre site that is affiliated to the Caravan Club (non members welcome). The 10 level grass and 50 hardstanding touring pitches are separated and numbered, with everyone shown to their pitch. Arranged in three bays with banks of heathers and flowering shrubs separating them, most pitches have 16A electrical hook-ups and 15 are fully serviced with water and waste water. Two bays have central play areas and all three have easy access to a toilet block, as has the camping area. The park also has 40 privately owned caravan holiday homes (three to hire).

Facilities

The three heated toilet blocks are well designed and maintained, with washbasins (in cubicles for ladies) and large showers. Each block also has a family shower room, dishwashing sinks and a room for disabled visitors. Laundry room. Milk and papers may be ordered at reception. Activity centre (charged and facilities are also open to the public; open weekends and all local school holidays). WiFi (charged). Off site: Huntly is 10 minutes walk. Fishing, golf and bicycle hire within 1 mile. Riding 5 miles.

Open: 26 March - 28 October.

Directions

Site is well signed from A96 Keith-Aberdeen road. GPS: 57.45205, -2.7916

Charges guide

Per unit incl. 2 persons and electricity	£ 17.80 - £ 23.45
extra person	£ 5.40 - £ 7.10
child (5-16 yrs)	£ 1.65 - £ 2.75

Kildonan
Seal Shore Camping & Touring Site
Kildonan, Isle of Arran KA27 8SE (North Ayrshire) T: 01770 820320. E: enquiries@campingarran.com
alanrogers.com/UK7025

A warm welcome awaits here on the island of Arran from the resident owner, Maurice Deighton and his daughter. Located on the southernmost point of the island, this is a quiet and peaceful park situated along its own private beach with wonderful sea views. The open, grassy area, sloping in parts, takes caravans, motorcaravans and tents with ten electricity connections (16A). The reception doubles as a shop selling basics with a TV room adjacent. There are communal picnic and barbecue areas. The Kildonan Hotel is next door serving restaurant and bar meals. Permits are available for loch fishing and charters available from the owner, a registered fisherman. Golfers can choose from seven courses.

Facilities

The good toilet block is clean and tidy and includes full facilities for disabled visitors that double as a baby room. Laundry room with washing machine, dryers and iron. Indoor dishwashing with fridge and freezer for campers' use. Shop. Camping gas. Beach. Fishing. Sailing. Covered barbecue area. Off site: Nearest golf course at Whiting 6 miles. Heritage Museum in Brodick and to the North of the island, Lochranza castle and distillery.

Open: March - October.

Directions

From Brodick take A841 south for 12 miles to sign for Kildonan. Site is downhill, on the seashore, next to the Kildonan Hotel. GPS: 55.44100, -5.11397

Charges guide

Per unit incl. 2 persons and electricity	£ 19.00 - £ 34.00
extra person	£ 6.00
child (5-15 yrs)	£ 3.00
tent pitch	£ 1.00 - £ 4.00

Got yours yet?
Extra benefits and savings - see page 10

Kirkcudbright
Brighouse Bay Holiday Park

Brighouse Bay, Borgue, Kirkcudbright DG6 4TS (Dumfries and Galloway) T: 01557 870267.
E: info@gillespie-leisure.co.uk **alanrogers.com/UK6950**

Hidden away within 1,200 exclusive acres, on a quiet, unspoilt peninsula, this spacious family park is only some 200 yards through bluebell woods from an open, sandy bay. Over 90 per cent of the 210 touring caravan pitches have 10/16A electricity, some with hardstanding and some with water, drainage and TV aerial. The three tent areas are on fairly flat, undulating ground and some pitches have electricity. There are 120 self-contained holiday caravans and lodges of which about 30 are let, the rest privately owned. On-site leisure facilities include a golf and leisure club with 16.5 m. pool, water features, jacuzzi, steam room, fitness room, games room, golf driving range, bowling and clubhouse bar and bistro. The 18-hole golf course extends onto the headland with superb views. The TRSS Approved Pony Trekking Centre, offers treks for beginners, hacks for the more experienced and riding lessons. This is a well run park of high standards and a member of the Best of British group.

Facilities

The large, well maintained main toilet block includes 10 unisex cabins with shower, basin and WC, and 12 with washbasin and WC. A second, excellent block has en-suite shower rooms (one for disabled visitors). Baby room. Laundry facilities. Motorcaravan service point. Gas. Licensed shop. Bar, restaurant and takeaway. Golf and Leisure Club. Play area. Pony trekking. Quad bikes, boating pond, 10-pin bowling, putting. Nature trails. Fishing. Caravan storage. Leisure facility bookings.

Open: All year.

Directions

In Kirkcudbright turn onto A755 and cross river bridge. In 400 yds. turn left onto B727 at international camping sign. GPS: 54.7875, -4.1291

Charges guide

Per unit incl. 2 persons and electricity	£ 19.50 - £ 26.00
extra person	£ 3.00

Four individual holiday parks with excellent family facilities on the Galloway Coast of SW Scotland

Brighouse Bay
9 and 18 hole golf courses. Driving range. Indoor and toddlers pools. Games, steam, jacuzzi and fitness rooms. Quad bikes. Sea and coarse fishing. Pony trekking. All-weather bowling green.

Seaward   **Barlochan**   **Sandyhills**
Each Park offers its own unique blend of character and style to help you to relax in the way that suits you best. Excellent accommodation and unique on-park facilities, offering a destination suited to you - whatever your wishes - in one of Scotland's most beautiful holiday destinations.
• Tourers, motorhomes and tents all catered for.   • Holiday homes and lodges for sale or hire.

To find out more call **01557 870 267** or visit
www.gillespie-leisure.co.uk

Kirkcudbright
Seaward Caravan Park

Dhoon Bay, Kirkcudbright DG6 4TJ (Dumfries and Galloway) T: 01557 870267. E: info@gillespie-leisure.co.uk
alanrogers.com/UK6900

Seaward Caravan Park is little sister to the much larger Brighouse Bay Holiday Park, 3.5 miles away. Set in an idyllic location overlooking the bay, this park is suitable for all units. The terrain is slightly undulating, but most of the numbered pitches are flat and of a good size. There are 35 pitches (21 hardstandings) designated for caravans and motorcaravans, a further 14 for tents, plus 43 caravan holiday homes (six for hire). All of the pitches for touring units have electricity connections and 12 are also serviced with water and drainage. This is a quiet park with excellent views over the sea, ideally suited for that relaxing holiday or for touring the region.

Facilities

The principal toilet block is to the rear of the touring area. Four rooms with en-suite facilities are also suitable for disabled visitors. Baby room. Laundry facilities. No motorcaravan services (but waste water tank emptying available). The reception/shop stocks basics. Unsupervised heated outdoor swimming pool (1/5-30/9). Central play area with picnic tables. Games room. Pitch and putt (charged). Off site: Beach and fishing adjacent.

Open: 1 March - 31 October.

Directions

In Kirkcudbright turn onto A755 signed Borgue. Go over river bridge and after 400 yds. turn left onto B727 at international camping sign. Proceed with caution when turning right into site entrance as the turn is tight. GPS: 54.819767, -4.082117

Charges guide

Per unit incl. 2 persons and electricity	£ 17.50 - £ 23.00
extra person	£ 2.50

For latest campsite news visit
alanrogers.com

Kyle of Lochalsh

Reraig Caravan Site

Balmacara, Kyle of Lochalsh IV40 8DH (Highland) T: 01599 566215. E: warden@reraig.com

alanrogers.com/UK7760

This is a small, level park close to Loch Alsh with a wooded hillside behind (criss-crossed with woodland walks). Set mainly on well cut grass, it is sheltered from the prevailing winds by the hill and provides just 45 numbered pitches. There are 10A electrical connections and 35 hardstandings (two without electricity). Tents you can stand in are not accepted. Small tents are permitted at the discretion of the owner, so it would be advisable to telephone first if this affects you. Reservations are not taken so it may be best to arrive before late afternoon in July and August.

Facilities

The single sanitary block is kept immaculately clean. Children have their own low basins. Controllable hot showers are on payment (10p for 2 minutes). Sinks for laundry and dishwashing. A slope replaces the small step into the ladies and sink rooms. Motorcaravan drainage point. WiFi throughout (charged). Off site: Adjacent to the park is the Balmacara Hotel (with bar), shop (selling gas), sub-post office and off-licence.

Open: 1 May - 30 September.

Directions

On A87, park is 2 miles west of the junction with the A890, beside the Balmacara hotel.
GPS: 57.283133, -5.626517

Charges guide

Per unit incl. 2 persons and electricity	£ 15.40
extra person (13 yrs or over)	£ 3.00
awning (May, June, Sept only)	£ 3.00

Lairg

Woodend Camping & Caravan Park

Achnairn, Lairg IV27 4DN (Highland) T: 01549 402248

alanrogers.com/UK7720

Woodend is a delightful, small park overlooking Loch Shin and perfect for hill walkers and backpackers. Peaceful and simple, it is owned and run single-handedly by Mrs Cathie Ross, who provides a warm Scottish welcome to visitors. On a hill with open, panoramic views across the Loch to the hills beyond and all around, the large camping field is undulating and gently sloping with some reasonably flat areas. The park is licensed to take 55 units and most of the 30 electrical hook-ups (16A) are in a line near the top of the field, close to the fenced play area which has several items of equipment on grass.

Facilities

The sanitary facilities are of old design but kept very clean and are quite satisfactory. Laundry with two machines and a dryer. Kitchen with dishwashing sinks and eating room for tent campers. Reception is at the house, Sunday papers, daily milk and bread may be ordered. Fishing licences for the Loch (your catch will be frozen for you). Off site: Mountain bikes can be hired in Lairg 5 miles. Several scenic golf courses within 20-30 miles.

Open: 1 April - 30 September.

Directions

Achnairn is near the southern end of Loch Shin. Turn off the A838 single track road at signs for Woodend. From the A9 coming north take the A836 at Bonar Bridge, 11 miles northwest of Tain.
GPS: 58.080267, -4.44705

Charges guide

Per unit incl. electricity	£ 10.00 - £ 12.00
tent	£ 8.00 - £ 10.00

No credit cards.

Lerwick

Clickimin Caravan & Camp Site

Clickimin Leisure Complex, Lochside, Lerwick ZE1 0PJ (Shetlands) T: 01595 741000.
E: clickimin.centre@srt.org.uk **alanrogers.com/UK7980**

The caravan and camping site is in the grounds of the Clickimin leisure complex, but it is not dominated by the building with its swimming pool and restaurant, etc. The site is arranged in two tiers which are well laid out with a tarmac road in the centre of each tier. The lower grass tier is separated into areas by shrubs and provides a camping area for 30 tents. The upper tier has 50 touring pitches, each with a large gravel area and divided from its neighbour by a wide, impressed concrete section for sitting out. A small lamp post with electricity, water and waste disposal points is provided at each pitch.

Facilities

The modern toilet block is clean and includes a toilet and shower cubicle for disabled visitors. Large, warm and well equipped laundry and drying room with an area for food preparation. Bar (evenings). Café and takeaway. Heated indoor and outdoor swimming pools. Off site: Shop and bicycle hire within 1 mile. Golf 3 miles. Riding 12 miles.

Open: May - September.

Directions

Site is on the west side of Lerwick and is signed as you start to leave Lerwick. Take the A969 north or south. Just before leaving the town is the road North Lochside (turn south) or South Lochside (turn north). Clickimin Leisure Centre is on this road.
GPS: 60.15348, -1.15934

Charges guide

Per unit incl. electricity	£ 11.10
tent	£ 5.30 - £ 9.90

FREE Alan Rogers Travel Card
Extra benefits and savings - see page 10

Lockerbie
Hoddom Castle Caravan Park

Hoddom, Lockerbie DG11 1AS (Dumfries and Galloway) T: 01576 300251. E: hoddomcastle@aol.com

alanrogers.com/UK6910

The park around Hoddom Castle is landscaped, spacious and well laid out on mainly sloping ground with many mature and beautiful trees, originally part of an arboretum. The drive to the site is just under a mile long with a one way system. Many of the 120 numbered pitches have good views of the castle and have gravel hardstanding with grass for awnings. Most have 16A electrical connections. In front of the castle are flat fields used for tents and caravans with a limited number of electricity hook-ups. The oldest part of Hoddom Castle itself is a 16th-century Borders Pele Tower, or fortified Keep. This was extended to form a residence for a Lancashire cotton magnate, became a youth hostel and was then taken over by the army during WW2. Since then parts have been demolished but the original Border Keep still survives, unfortunately in a semi-derelict state. The site's bar and restaurant have been developed in the courtyard area from the coach houses, and the main ladies' toilet block used to be the stables. Amenities include a comfortable bar lounge with a TV. The park's nine-hole golf course is in an attractive setting alongside the Annan river, where fishing is possible for salmon and trout (tickets available). Coarse fishing is also possible elsewhere on the estate. This is a peaceful base from which to explore historic southwest Scotland.

Facilities

The main toilet block can be heated and is very well appointed. Washbasins in cubicles, 3 en-suite cubicles with WC and basin (one with baby facilities) and an en-suite shower unit for disabled visitors. Two further tiled blocks, kept very clean, provide washbasins and WCs only. Well equipped laundry room at the castle. Motorcaravan service point. Licensed shop at reception (gas available). Bar, restaurant and takeaway (restricted opening outside high season). Games room. Large, grass play area. Crazy golf. Mountain bike trail. Fishing. Golf. Guided walks (high season). Caravan storage. Off site: Tennis nearby.

Open: 1 April - 30 October.

Directions

Leave A74M at exit 19 (Ecclefechan) and follow signs to park. Leave A75 at Annan junction (west end of Annan bypass) and follow signs. GPS: 55.041367, -3.311

Charges guide

Per unit incl. 2 persons	£ 11.50 - £ 18.50
incl. electricity	£ 14.50 - £ 21.50
extra person	£ 3.00
child (7-16 yrs)	£ 1.50

• Fishing
• Walking
• Golf
• Cycle Hire

ENQUIRIES: The Warden, Hoddom Castle, Hoddom, Lockerbie DG11 1AS
Tel: 01576 300251 • www.hoddomcastle.co.uk • Email: hoddomcastle@aol.com

For latest campsite news visit
alanrogers.com

Maybole

The Ranch Holiday Park

Culzean Road, Maybole KA19 8DU (South Ayrshire) T: 01655 882446

alanrogers.com/UK7015

This holiday park is situated in the Ayrshire countryside, a mile from the small town of Maybole. The Ranch, a Caravan Club affiliated site, is managed by the McAuley family. The park is beautifully set out with 65 spacious touring pitches, all with 16A electricity connections and on level hardstanding. There are also 100 caravan holiday homes with one for rent. The superb facilities include a private leisure centre with an indoor heated pool, sauna, solarium and well equipped gym. Adjacent is a small, fenced play park for toddlers and to the rear is an enclosed play area for older children.

Facilities

Modern sanitary facilities, recently rebuilt, are well located. Kept spotlessly clean, there are washbasins in cubicles and large showers. Facilities for disabled visitors. Well equipped laundry (includes exchange library for books and magazines). Small shop in reception with information area. Indoor heated pool, sauna, solarium and gym. WiFi throughout (charged). Off site: Golf courses at Turnberry. Fishing at Mochram Loch 1.5 miles. Beach 2 miles.

Open: All year.

Directions

From Maybole turn onto B7023 (signed Culzean Maidens) for 1 mile and site is signed on left. GPS: 55.3559, -4.7061

Charges guide

Per unit incl. 2 persons and electricity	£ 12.60 - £ 21.40
extra person	£ 4.10 - £ 6.20
child	£ 1.30 - £ 2.20

Melrose

Melrose Gibson Park Caravan Club Site

High Street, Melrose TD6 9RY (Borders) T: 01896 822969

alanrogers.com/UK7030

This is an ideal transit park, being so close to the A68, but is also a perfect base for exploring this southern area of Scotland. Edinburgh is only 35 miles away by car or on one of the regular buses which run from the park entrance, so an ideal day trip. This small, three-acre park has only 60 touring pitches plus, unusually, an extra 12 tent pitches (summer only) next to the adjacent rugby pitch. All touring pitches have 16A electricity and TV connections (otherwise it is a bad signal here), 57 have hardstanding and ten are serviced with water and drainage. A one-way system on the tarmac roads is in operation.

Facilities

First rate, heated toilet facilities are in a new building with spacious showers and washbasins in cabins, and have a very pleasing finish. Laundry facilities. Separate room with shower and WC for disabled visitors. Motorcaravan service point. Gas is available. WiFi. Security barrier (operated by card). Off site: Shops, pubs, restaurants and historic buildings in Melrose, a five minute walk away.

Open: All year.

Directions

Turn left off A68 Jedburgh-Lauder road at roundabout 2.5 miles past Newton St Boswell onto A6091 Galashiels road. In 3.25 miles at roundabout turn right onto B6374 to Melrose (not at first turning into town). Site is on right at filling station opposite Melrose Rugby Club. GPS: 55.598017, -2.72413

Charges guide

Per person	£ 4.60 - £ 6.20
pitch incl. electricity (non-members)	£ 13.15 - £ 16.00

Mintlaw

Aden Country Park Caravan Park

Station Road, Mintlaw AB42 5FQ (Aberdeenshire) T: 01771 623460

alanrogers.com/UK7530

Aden Country Park is owned by the Aberdeenshire local authority and is open to the public. The caravan and camping site is on one side of the park. Beautifully landscaped and well laid out with trees, bushes and hedges, it is kept very neat and tidy. It provides 48 numbered pitches for touring units, with varying degrees of slope (some level) and all with 16A electrical hook-ups, plus an area for tents. There are also 12 caravan holiday homes. The council plan to lease the campsite to private owners from 2012. The park is in a most attractive area and one could spend plenty of time enjoying all it has to offer.

Facilities

The modern toilet block is clean, with good facilities for disabled visitors. It can be heated and provides free, preset hot showers, hairdryer for ladies, and a baby bath, but no private cabins. Laundry facilities (metered). Motorcaravan service point. Gas supplies. Small shop in reception area. Restaurant in the Heritage Centre. Games areas. Play equipment. Dog exercise area. Off site: Shops in Mintlaw 0.5 miles. Fishing 1 mile. Riding 2 miles.

Open: Easter - 25 October.

Directions

Approaching Mintlaw from west on A950 road, park is shortly after sign for Mintlaw station. From east, go to the western outskirts of village and entrance is on left – Aden Country Park and Farm Heritage Centre. GPS: 57.52475, -2.026117

Charges guide

Per unit incl. electricity	£ 17.50 - £ 20.00
tent (2 persons)	£ 9.00 - £ 9.50

FREE Alan Rogers Travel Card
Extra benefits and savings - see page 10

Monifieth

Riverview Holiday Park

Marine Drive, Monifieth DD5 4NN (Angus) T: 01382 535471. E: info@riverview.co.uk

alanrogers.com/UK7410

A quiet, family park, Riverview overlooks a long sandy beach and has magnificent views over the River Tay towards the Kingdom of Fife and yet is within walking distance of Monifieth town. The park is neatly set out with flowering shrubs and bushes dividing 40 numbered touring pitches. Some enjoying river views, they are grassy and level, each with 16A electricity and two also with water and drainage. Bordering the park are 46 privately owned caravan holiday homes and four to rent. At the entrance to the park is a small reception office and separate tourist information room and a leisure suite with sauna, steam baths and gym (charged). A member of the Best of British group.

Facilities	Directions
The spotlessly clean amenity block (key entry) has open washbasins, one in a cabin with WC, and preset showers. Baby bath. Full facility for disabled visitors. Laundry. Leisure suite. Games room and play area. Adventure play area. Off site: Picnic areas and small boat slipway adjacent. Opposite the Riverview recreation park offers football pitches, putting, crazy golf, tennis, bowling as well as a well equipped adventure play park. Golf 800 yds. Fishing 2 miles. Riding 3 miles. Dundee city 5 miles.	From Dundee follow signs for Monifieth on the A930, after passing Tesco. Turn right at sign for golf course and right again under railway bridge. Park is signed on the left. GPS: 56.47995, -2.811533

Open: 1 April - 31 October.

Charges guide

Per unit incl. 2 adults and 2 children	£ 20.00 - £ 23.00
extra person	£ 2.00
awning	£ 3.00

Motherwell

Strathclyde Country Park Caravan Club Site

Strathclyde Country Park, 366 Hamilton Road, Motherwell ML1 3ED (North Lanarkshire) T: 01698 402060. E: strathclydepark@northlan.gov.uk **alanrogers.com/UK7000**

The 1,200-acre Country Park is a large green area less than 15 miles from the centre of Glasgow. This Caravan Club site has been entirely rebuilt and features 107 all-weather hardstanding pitches. There are 12 serviced pitches and additional space for 50 tents. The warden's accommodation and toilet blocks are clad in wood to blend in with their surroundings. This site is suitable as a stopover or for longer stays (max. 14 days) and is ideal as a base for visiting Glasgow. The city will be hosting the 2014 Commonwealth Games. The site is close to the motorway, so some traffic noise should be expected.

Facilities	Directions
Two brand new toilet blocks with all facilities. Enclosed sinks for dishwashing and food preparation. Provision for babies and disabled visitors. Laundry facilities. Motorcaravan services. Shop in reception sells basic provisions. Play area for young children. Woodland walk. WiFi. Off site: Bar and restaurant facilities 100 yds. Fishing 400 yds. Bus 1 mile.	Take exit 5 from the M74 and follow sign for A275 Strathclyde Country Park. Turn first left for site. GPS: 55.803917, -4.046733

Open: March - January.

Charges guide

Per caravan pitch incl. 2 persons and electricity	£ 14.75

No credit cards.

Musselburgh

Drum Mohr Caravan Park

Levenhall, Musselburgh EH21 8JS (East Lothian) T: 01316 656867. E: bookings@drummohr.org

alanrogers.com/UK6980

This family owned, attractively laid out touring park is on the east side of Edinburgh. It is a secluded, well kept modern park, conveniently situated for visits to Edinburgh, the Lothian and Borders regions. It has been carefully landscaped and there are many attractive plants, flowers and hedging. There are 120 individual pitches, 40 with hardstanding, for touring units of any type, well spaced out on gently sloping grass in groups of 12 or more, marked with white posts. All have electric hook-ups and 13 are fully serviced with water and waste water connections. Free space is left for play and recreation.

Facilities	Directions
The two toilet blocks are clean, attractive, of ample size and can be heated. Free hot water to washbasins (one cabin for men, two for ladies in each block) and to showers and laundry sinks. Baby changing. Laundry facilities in each block. Motorcaravan service point. Shop (bread and papers to order). Playground. Dog walk. Security barrier with code access. WiFi (on payment). Bothy for hire. Off site: Golf adjacent. Beach 6 miles.	From Edinburgh follow A1 signs for Berwick-on-Tweed for 6-7 miles. Turn off for Wallyford and follow camp and Mining Museum signs. From south follow A1 taking junction after Tranent village (A199 Musselburgh). Follow signs. GPS: 55.950033, -3.011667

Open: All year.

Charges guide

Per unit incl. 2 persons and electricity	£ 18.00 - £ 25.00

For latest campsite news visit

alanrogers.com

North Berwick
Tantallon Caravan & Camping Park

Tantallon Road, North Berwick EH39 5NJ (East Lothian) T: 01620 893348. E: tantallon@meadowhead.co.uk

alanrogers.com/UK7060

Tantallon is a large park with views over the Firth of Forth and the Bass Rock. The park has 147 quite large, grass touring pitches in two lower, more sheltered areas (Law Park), with the rest having good views at the top (Bass Park). Many have some degree of slope. There are 75 electrical connections (10A) and ten pitches also with water and waste water. Each area has its own sanitary facilities, the top block a little way from the end pitches. About 55 caravan holiday homes for sale or hire are in their own areas. Wooden wigwams are also available. This is a mature, well managed park with good facilities.

Facilities

Bass Park has 8 unisex units with shower, washbasin and toilet. The other areas have open washbasins. Two heated units for disabled visitors. Good launderette. Motorcaravan service point. Reception sells newspapers at weekends. Games room with TV. Internet access in reception and WiFi. Playground. Putting green. Dogs are only accepted by prior arrangement. Off site: Supermarket, beaches and fishing within walking distance. Golf next door.

Open: 13 March - 31 October.

Directions

Park is beside the A198 just to the east of North Berwick, which is between Edinburgh and Dunbar. It is easily accessible from the A1.
GPS: 56.05575, -2.690833

Charges guide

Per unit incl. 2 persons and electricity	£ 17.75 - £ 28.75
extra person (over 5 yrs)	£ 5.00

Peebles
Crossburn Caravan Park

Edinburgh Road, Peebles EH45 8ED (Borders) T: 01721 720501. E: enquiries@crossburncaravans.co.uk

alanrogers.com/UK6960

A peaceful, friendly small park, suitable as a night stop, Crossburn is on the south side of the A703 road, half a mile north of the town centre. The entrance has a fairly steep slope down to reception and the shop which also sells a very large selection of caravan and camping accessories. Passing the caravans for sale and the holiday homes you might think that this is not the site for you, but persevere as the touring area is very pleasant, with attractive trees and bushes. Of the 40 pitches, all have 16A electricity, 20 have hardstanding and eight are fully serviced. There is also a sheltered area for tents.

Facilities

One toilet block, with washbasins in cubicles and spacious, controllable free showers. Campers' kitchen (key at reception). Shop. Adjacent is a large games room with snooker table and games machines. Good play area. Riverside dog walk. Card operated barrier (£10 deposit). Off site: Buses from site gate or in Peebles (a short walk).

Open: Easter/1 April - October.

Directions

Park is by the A703 road, 0.5 miles north of Peebles.
GPS: 55.662167, -3.193333

Charges guide

Per pitch	£ 22.00 - £ 24.00
hiker or cyclist plus tent	£ 9.00

Perth
Noah's Ark Caravan Park

Newhouse Farm, Perth PH1 1QF (Perth and Kinross) T: 01738 580661. E: info@perthcaravanpark.co.uk

alanrogers.com/UK7265

Noah's Ark Caravan Park is situated on the outskirts of Perth and enjoys panoramic views over the surrounding Grampian mountains. This is a good base for a golfing break, with no less than five excellent courses within a short distance, including St Andrews and Gleneagles. There are 46 touring pitches here. These are grassy and of a good size. All have electrical connections. A further eight tent pitches are available (some with electricity). The site also has a number of Microlodge Hobbit Houses. These are unique wooden chalets, fully equipped to a high standard (even with a TV). On-site amenities include a Play Barn for children, which also houses a restaurant, karting, bowling and a golf driving range.

Facilities

Two sanitary blocks are adjacent in one corner of the park, one of wood construction, the other Portacabin style. Family shower and bathrooms. Facilities for disabled visitors. Motorcaravan service point. Gas. Noah's Galley café. Children's Play Barn. Karting. Golf driving range. Bowling. Minigolf. Local takeaway meals are delivered. WiFi throughout (free). Microlodges for rent. Off site: Golf (five courses including Gleneagles and St Andrews). Perth (bus service). Fishing. Walking and mountain biking.

Open: 1 March - 31 October.

Directions

The site is on the outskirts of Perth. Approaching from Inverness on A9, turn right at Inveralmond roundabout and then, having passed St Johnstone football club, follow signs for Noah's Ark.
N.B. Do not use postcode for sat nav.
GPS: 56.397285, -3.49119

Charges guide

Per unit incl. 2 persons and electricity	£ 20.00 - £ 22.00
extra person	£ 2.00

FREE Alan Rogers Travel Card
Extra benefits and savings - see page 10

Scotland

Pitlochry
Blair Castle Caravan Park

Blair Atholl, Pitlochry PH18 5SR (Perth and Kinross) T: 01796 481263. E: mail@blaircastlecaravanpark.co.uk
alanrogers.com/UK7300

This attractive, well kept park is set in the grounds of Blair Castle, the traditional home of the Dukes of Atholl. It has a wonderful feeling of spaciousness with a large central area left free for children's play or for general use. There is space for 250 touring units, all with 10/16A electricity connections, 63 with hardstanding and 44 fully serviced pitches with water and waste water facilities. Caravan holiday homes, 85 privately owned and 25 for hire, are in separate areas. A quality park, quiet at night and well managed. The castle is open to the public and the beautiful grounds and gardens are free to those staying on site.

Facilities

The five toilet blocks can be heated and are of excellent quality and very clean. Large hot showers, some incorporating WC and washbasin, and further cubicles with WC and washbasin. Facilities for disabled visitors. Baby changing mats. Laundry. Motorcaravan service point. Shop. Games room. WiFi in some areas (charged). Gas supplies. Large motorhomes accepted (max. 30 ft. or 5 tons). Off site: Riding, golf and fishing all 0.5 miles.

Open: 27 February - 26 November.

Directions

From A9 just north of Pitlochry take B8079 into Blair Atholl. Park is in grounds of Blair Castle, well signed. GPS: 56.767039, -3.845791

Charges guide

Per unit incl. 2 persons	
and electricity	£ 20.00 - £ 23.00
extra person	£ 2.00
child (5-14 yrs)	£ 1.50

Pitlochry
The River Tilt Park

Golf Course Road, Blair Atholl, Pitlochry PH18 5TB (Perth and Kinross) T: 01796 481467.
E: stuart@rivertilt.co.uk **alanrogers.com/UK7295**

This good quality, family owned park is set on the banks of the River Tilt, a short walk from the village of Blair Atholl, where the 16th-century Blair Castle stands proud. There are 54 privately owned caravan holiday homes. Two central areas have been set aside for touring caravans, motorcaravans and tents, with 31 pitches mostly with hardstanding. Divided by mature shrubs and hedges, all have 10A electricity connections, 18 have water and a drain. One of the areas is reserved for those with dogs. The Steadings Spa provides an indoor pool, solarium, steam room, spa pool and multigym, plus Waves hair salon.

Facilities

The toilet block is centrally situated (with key entry) and provides en-suite toilet and washbasin cabins and individual large preset showers, one suitable for disabled visitors. Baby facilities. Laundry. Motorcaravan service point. Bar and restaurant. Leisure spa complex with indoor pool, etc. Hair salon. Tennis. WiFi throughout (free). Max. 2 dogs per pitch. Off site: Private fishing and golf adjacent. Bicycle hire 0.5 miles. Riding 1.5 miles.

Open: Two weeks after Easter - 10 November.

Directions

From the A9 just north of Pitlochry, take B8079 into Blair Atholl and follow signs for River Tilt. GPS: 56.76538, -3.83962

Charges guide

Per unit incl. 2 persons	
and electricity	£ 16.00 - £ 20.00
extra person	£ 1.50
child	£ 1.00

Pitlochry
Tummel Valley Holiday Park

Tummel Bridge, Pitlochry PH16 5SA (Perth and Kinross) T: 01882 634221.
E: enquiries@parkdeanholidays.co.uk **alanrogers.com/UK7305**

Set in the Tay Forest Park on the banks of the River Tummel, this large family holiday park is part of the Parkdean Group. Divided into two areas by the roadway, the main emphasis is on chalets to let on the side that overlooks the river. Privately owned caravan holiday homes and touring pitches are on the other, quieter side. The 26 touring pitches, open plan with hardstanding, electricity hook-up and a shared water point, overlook a small fishing lake, which is an added attraction for all the family. On arrival, you should turn right and park, then cross back to book in.

Facilities

The very clean toilet block (recently refurbished) has vanity style washbasins, preset showers and a bathroom in each section. Good facilities for disabled visitors. Laundry. No motorcaravan service point. Shop. Entertainment complex with bar and terrace, restaurant and takeaway. Indoor heated pool and toddlers' splash pool. Solarium and sauna. Amusements. All weather sports court. Adventure play area. Crazy golf. Nature trails. Bicycle hire. Fishing. Max. 2 dogs per unit. Off site: Golf and riding 10 miles.

Open: Late March/Easter - 31 October.

Directions

Travel through Pitlochry. After 2 miles turn left on B8019 to Tummel Bridge (10 miles). Park is on both the left and right. Touring units should turn right and park, then return to reception on the left. GPS: 56.70742, -4.02002

Charges guide

Per unit incl. 4 persons	
and electricity	£ 13.00 - £ 32.00
dog	£ 2.00 - £ 3.00

Port William
Kings Green Caravan Park

South Street, Port William DG8 9SG (Dumfries and Galloway) T: 01988 700489. E: kingsgreencp@gmail.com
alanrogers.com/UK6885

Kings Green Caravan Park is now owned and run by the Port William Community Association. Kept very natural and situated beside the sea overlooking Luce Bay and the Mull of Galloway, it is within walking distance of Port William, well known for its harbour and fishing community. The all grass, open site provides 30 marked and numbered pitches for caravans, motorcaravans and tents (21 with 10A electricity). On arrival visitors are given a welcome pack. If reception is not open, you are invited to park and details of reserved pitches are placed on the notice board.

Facilities

The small toilet block (key entry) is kept very clean and has vanity style washbasins, free electric showers and hair dryers. Facilities for disabled visitors include WC and washbasin (Radar key). New Laundry. Large play and ball game area adjacent. Off site: Shops, restaurants and bars in Port William. Walks and cycle routes. Fishing 50 yds. Sailing 600 yds. Golf 2 miles. Riding 3 miles.

Open: 30 March - 31 October.

Directions

From Dumfries, take A75 to Newton Stewart. Follow A714 to Wigtown, then B7085 to Port William. GPS: 54.755967, -4.581533

Charges guide

Per unit incl. 2 persons and electricity	£ 12.00 - £ 13.00

Saint Andrews
Craigtoun Meadows Holiday Park

Mount Melville, Saint Andrews KY16 8PQ (Fife) T: 01334 475959. E: craigtoun@aol.com
alanrogers.com/UK7290

This attractively laid out, quality park has individual pitches and good facilities and although outnumbered by caravan holiday homes, the touring section is an important subsidiary. Its facilities are both well designed and comprehensive. With 56 units taken on gently sloping land, caravans go on individual hardstandings with grass alongside for awnings on most pitches. All caravan pitches are large (130 sq.m) and are equipped with 16A electricity, water and drainage. There are 15 larger patio pitches with summer house, barbecue patio, picnic table and chairs, partially screened. Tents are taken on a grassy meadow at one end, also with electricity available.

Facilities

An excellent, centrally heated, luxury sanitary building serves the touring area. All washbasins are in cabins and each toilet has its own basin. Showers are unisex, as are two bathrooms, with hand and hair dryers. Facilities for disabled visitors and babies. Launderette. Licensed restaurant (restricted hours in low season). Games room. Playground, play field and woodland. Information room. Dogs and other pets are not accepted. Off site: Golf and bicycle hire 1.5 miles. Fishing 5 miles. Riding 6 miles.

Open: 15 March - 31 October.

Directions

From M90 exit 8 take A91 to St Andrews. Just after sign for Guardbridge (to left, A919), turn right at site sign and sign for Strathkinness. Go through village, over crossroads at end of village, left at next crossroads, then 0.75 miles to park. GPS: 56.324617, -2.83745

Charges guide

Per unit incl. 2 persons and electricity	£ 20.00 - £ 25.50
tent	£ 17.00 - £ 20.00

Scourie
Scourie Caravan & Camping Park

Harbour Road, Scourie IV27 4TG (Highland) T: 01971 502060
alanrogers.com/UK7730

Mr Mackenzie has carefully nurtured this park over many years, developing a number of firm terraces with 60 pitches which gives it an attractive layout – there is nothing regimented here. Perched on the edge of the bay in an elevated position, practically everyone has a view of the sea and a short walk along the shore footpath leads to a small sandy beach. The park has tarmac and gravel access roads, with well drained grass and hardstanding pitches, some with 10A electric hook-ups. A few are on an area which is unfenced from the rocks (young children would need to be supervised here).

Facilities

The toilet facilities can be heated. Showers have no divider or seat. Laundry. Motorcaravan service point. The Anchorage restaurant at the entrance to the park (used as reception at quiet times) serves meals cooked to order. Boat launching. Fishing permits can be arranged. Off site: Village with shop and post office, gas is available from the petrol station and mobile banks visit regularly.

Open: Easter/1 April - 30 September, but phone first to check.

Directions

Park is by Scourie village on A894 road in northwest Sutherland. GPS: 58.351417, -5.156767

Charges guide

Per unit incl. 2 persons	£ 12.00 - £ 16.00
electricity	£ 2.00
extra person	£ 2.50
child (3-16 yrs)	£ 1.50
No credit cards.	

FREE Alan Rogers Travel Card
Extra benefits and savings - see page 10

Staffin

Staffin Caravan & Camping Site

Staffin IV51 9JX (Isle of Skye) T: 01470 562213. E: staffincampsite@btinternet.com

alanrogers.com/UK7750

This small camping site is just outside Staffin, where the broad sweep of the bay is dotted with working crofts running down to the sea. With 50 pitches, 26 with 16A electricity, some slope but many are reasonably level, with improved hardstanding for caravans and motorcaravans. The entrance to the site from the main road is by a single track road. A marked walk from the site leads to the seashore and slipway (good for walking dogs). Skye has many activities to offer and for the truly dedicated walker the Cuillins are the big attraction and the hills above Staffin are demanding in places!

Facilities

The modern sanitary block includes large, controllable showers. There are some hot water dishwashing sinks and a laundry. Large hardstanding area has a motorcaravan service point. Gas available. Bicycle hire. Off site: Staffin village with a large shop (open six days a week) and a restaurant 400 yds. The Columbia centre in the village provides Internet access. Fishing and boat launching 1 mile. Riding 9 miles.

Open: 1 April - 30 September.

Directions

Site is 15 miles north of Portree on A855 (2 miles of single track at the start), just before 40 mph. signs on the right. GPS: 57.622017, -6.196

Charges guide

Per unit incl. 2 persons and electricity	£ 11.50 - £ 13.50
extra person	£ 1.50

No credit cards.

Stirling

Witches Craig Caravan Park

Blairlogie, Stirling FK9 5PX (Stirling) T: 01786 474947. E: info@witchescraig.co.uk

alanrogers.com/UK7320

Witches Craig is a neat and tidy park, nestling under the Ochil Hills. All 60 pitches have 10A electricity and hardstanding, seven of these being large (taking American-style motorhomes easily). Reasonably level, the park covers five well maintained acres with the grass beautifully manicured. Being by the A91, there is some daytime road noise. Trees have been planted to try to minimise this but the further back onto the park you go, the less the traffic is heard. The area has a wealth of historic attractions, starting with the Wallace Monument which practically overlooks the park. Stirling is known as the 'Gateway to the Highlands' and its magnificent castle is world renowned.

Facilities

The modern, heated toilet block is well maintained, and includes one cubicle with washbasin and WC each for ladies and men. Free controllable showers. Baby bath and mat. Good unit for disabled visitors. Motorcaravan service point. Laundry facilities. Bread, milk, drinks and papers are available daily (supermarket 2.5 miles). Play area. Field for team games. Free WiFi. Off site: Golf 1 mile. Riding and bicycle hire 2 miles, Fishing 3 miles. Castles, museums, cathedrals and parks within 10 miles.

Open: 1 April - 31 October.

Directions

Park is on the A91, 3 miles northeast of Stirling. GPS: 56.148033, -3.898667

Charges guide

Per unit incl. 2 persons and electricity	£ 19.50 - £ 22.50
extra person	£ 2.00
child (2-13 yrs)	£ 1.00
awning (no groundsheet)	£ 2.00

Stornoway

Laxdale Holiday Park

6 Laxdale Lane, Stornoway HS2 0DR (Isle of Lewis) T: 01851 706966. E: info@laxdaleholidaypark.com

alanrogers.com/UK7920

Whilst not in the most scenic of locations, this good park is well placed for touring. Surrounded by trees, it is on the edge of Stornaway (ferry port) and is well laid out with a tarmac road running through the centre. A level hardstanding area for touring caravans has 14 electricity hook-ups plus two for tents and a grassy area for tents gently slopes away to the trees and boundary. There are five holiday caravans and a self-catering holiday bungalow available for rent on the site, plus a bunkhouse. The site is centrally situated in an ideal spot for touring the Isle of Lewis with easy access to all parts of the island.

Facilities

The well maintained and modern toilet block is heated and raised above the hardstanding area. Access is via steps or a gravel path to the ramp. Good (but narrow) showers (50p). Laundry. WiFi in reception (charged). Off site: Bus stop 200 yds. The fishing port of Stornoway has a range of shops and restaurants. New sports centre with swimming pool. Library with free Internet access.

Open: 1 April - 31 October.

Directions

From Stornoway take the A857 for 1 mile then take the second turning on the left past the hospital. GPS: 58.22738, -6.39254

Charges guide

Per unit incl. 2 persons and electricity	£ 15.00 - £ 20.00

Credit cards accepted (over £50).

For latest campsite news visit
alanrogers.com

Stranraer
Aird Donald Caravan Park

London Road, Stranraer DG9 8RN (Dumfries and Galloway) T: 01776 702025. E: enquiries@aird-donald.co.uk
alanrogers.com/UK7020

Aird Donald is a good stopping off point when travelling to and from the Irish ferries, but it is also useful for seeing the sights around Stranraer. This tidy park comprises 12 acres surrounded by conifers, flowering trees and shrubs, and the 300 yard drive is lit and lined with well trimmed conifers. There are grass areas for caravans and tents, and hardstandings with electricity hook-up (these are very handy for hardy winter touring units). A small play area caters for young children, but the local leisure centre is only a walk away and provides swimming, table tennis, gym and a theatre.

Facilities

Two toilet blocks, the new block is modern and heated. Kept very clean, this one is kept locked with a key deposit of £5. There are two types of shower, an electric one which is metered (50p) and two others which are free. Washbasins are in vanity units, ladies having one in a cubicle. Unit for disabled visitors has a washbasin and WC. The original block has been renovated but is more basic with free showers and open all the time. Small laundry. Motorcaravan services. Play area.

Open: All year.

Directions

Enter Stranraer on A75 road. Watch for narrow site entrance on left entering town, opposite school. GPS: 54.90185, -5.006217

Charges guide

Per unit incl. 2 persons and electricity	£ 18.00
extra person	£ 1.00

No credit cards.

Stromness
Point of Ness Caravan & Camping Site

Well Park, Ness Road, Stromness KW16 3DN (Orkney) T: 01856 873535. E: recreation@orkney.gov.uk
alanrogers.com/UK7950

This quiet site is in an idyllic position bounded by the sea on one side (an entrance to the harbour). It is sheltered by the land from the open sea and has views to the mountains and the island of Hoy. There is a rocky beach close by and walks from the site. It is a level, firm grassy site, protected from the small drop to the sea by a low fence. Access to the steps to the sea is gained by a gate in the fence. Whilst being located at one end of Orkney, it is still easy to visit the Churchill Barriers and the Italian Chapel as well as the closer Maes Howe and Skara Brae sites. Regular ferries come into Stromness from Thurso.

Facilities

The well maintained traditional style toilet block has good sized showers (20p) with curtains separating the changing area. Well equipped laundry. Telephone and tourist information. Lounge for campers is at one end of the block. Off site: Fishing, golf and bicycle hire all nearby.

Open: 28 April - 30 September.

Directions

Site is just west of Stromness and is signed from the town. Campers can walk along the high street to the site on the edge of the town. Caravans and motorcaravans are advised to take the road at the back of the town. GPS: 58.95443, -3.30041

Charges guide

Per pitch	£ 8.30
tent	£ 4.40 - £ 7.95

No credit cards.

Tarbert
Muasdale Holiday Park

Muasdale, Tarbert PA29 6XD (Argyll and Bute) T: 01583 421207. E: enquiries@muasdaleholidays.com
alanrogers.com/UK7250

Muasdale Touring Park has a beachside location with fine views of the sea and islands, between Campbeltown and Tarbert on Kintyre's west coast. This is a small, friendly site of just 16 pitches with ten for touring units, five for tents and one used for a caravan holiday home to rent. The pitches are situated on a level, grass field, all with unobstructed sea views. All have electrical connections. You are advised to anchor tents and awnings securely as the winds are sometimes strong and gusty. The beach is a magnificent expanse of white sand with rock pools and an abundance of wildlife.

Facilities

The single Portacabin style toilet block is clean, heated and adequate. No specific facilities for disabled visitors or babies. Laundry facilities. Games room. Direct beach access. Sea swimming and fishing. Canoeing. WiFi (in the games room; charged). Accommodation to rent. Off site: Well stocked village shop 100 yds. Kintyre Way walking trail. Whisky distilleries. Golf.

Open: April - mid October.

Directions

Approaching from Glasgow (Erskine Bridge), take the A82 (Crianlarich), past Loch Lomond. At Tarbet take A83 (Campbeltown), through Inveraray, Lochgilphead and Tarbert (Loch Fyne) and on to Muasdale Village. Site signed. GPS: 55.597307, -5.686058

Charges guide

Per unit incl. 2 persons and electricity	£ 16.00 - £ 18.00

FREE Alan Rogers Travel Card
Extra benefits and savings - see page 10

Ullapool

Ardmair Point Caravan Park

Ardmair Point, Ullapool IV26 2TN (Highland) T: 01854 612054. E: sales@ardmair.com

alanrogers.com/UK7710

This spectacularly situated park, overlooking the little Loch Kanaird, just round the corner from Loch Broom, has splendid views all round. The 68 touring pitches are arranged mainly on grass around the edge of the bay, in front of the shingle beach. Electrical hook-ups (10A) are available and some gravel hardstandings are on the other side of the access road, just past the second toilet block. Tent pitches, together with cheaper pitches for some touring units are in a large field behind the other sanitary facilities. Scuba diving is popular at Loch Kanaird because the water is so clear. Seals and otters are regularly seen in the bay and the whole area is full of interest, including visits to Inverewe Gardens and the Isle Martin bird and seal colonies.

Facilities

Two toilet blocks, both with good facilities. One block has wonderful views from the large windows in the launderette and dishwashing rooms. Large en-suite rooms for disabled visitors. Motorcaravan service point. Shop. Play area. Fishing. Sailing and boating (with your own boat). Off site: Ullapool for shopping 3 miles. Golf and bicycle hire 3 miles.

Open: 1 April - late September, depending on the weather.

Directions

Park is off the A835 road, 3 miles north of Ullapool. GPS: 57.933967, -5.197017

Charges guide

Per unit incl. 2 persons
and electricity   £ 15.00 - £ 20.00

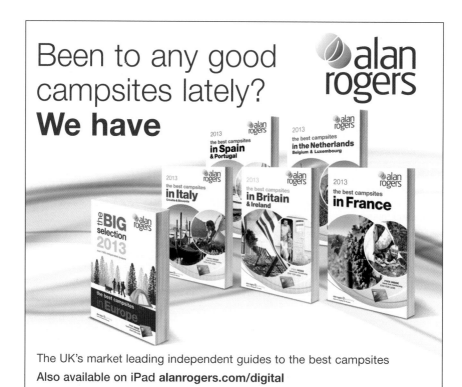

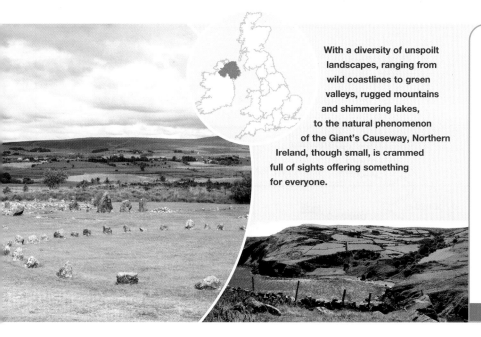

With a diversity of unspoilt landscapes, ranging from wild coastlines to green valleys, rugged mountains and shimmering lakes, to the natural phenomenon of the Giant's Causeway, Northern Ireland, though small, is crammed full of sights offering something for everyone.

NORTHERN IRELAND COMPRISES THE FOLLOWING COUNTIES: ANTRIM, ARMAGH, DOWN, FERMANAGH, LONDONDERRY AND TYRONE

The rugged coastline of the Causeway Coast and the nine Glens of Antrim in the north, is an Area of Outstanding Natural Beauty, with white sandy shores and little bays, tranquil forests and romantic ruins and castles, full of tales of the ancient Irish Giants and other myths and legends. At over 60 million years old, with a mass of 4,000 tightly-packed basalt columns, each a polygon shape, the Giant's Causeway is a popular attraction. One of the most beautiful regions is in the west around Londonderry, a delightful walled city set on a hill on the banks of the Foyle estuary. Further south is the beautiful region of Fermanagh, with glistening lakes and little islands all surrounded by lush green fields, hillsides and forests. The large lake of Lough Erne is to be found here: made up of two channels, the lower and upper Loughs, the meeting point of these channels is Enniskillen, a town steeped in history, boasting numerous preserved buildings including a castle. Across to the eastern shores lies the ancient Kingdom of Down, with its endless miles of spectacular coastline, little fishing villages, country parks and the Mountains of Mourne. And, ringed by hills, sea lough and river valley is Belfast, a bustling city full of theatres, concert halls, art galleries and restaurants.

Places of interest

Antrim: Antrim Lough Shore Park; Rathlin Island; Giant's Causeway; Dunluce Castle near Portrush; Carrick-a-Rede Rope Bridge.

Belfast & environs: Belfast zoo and castle; Irish Linen Centre in Lisburn; Carrickfergus Castle; Crown Liquor Saloon.

Armagh: Gosford Forest Park near Markethill; Lough Neagh Discovery Centre on Oxford Island; Ardress House.

Down: County Museum and Downpatrick Cathedral; Mourne Mountains; Tollymore and Castlewellan forest parks; Ballycopeland Windmill near Millisle.

Fermanagh: Enniskillen Castle and Castle Coole; village of Belleek; Marble Arch Caves, near Lough Macnean; Devenish Island on Lough Erne.

Londonderry: St Columb's Cathedral; Tower Museum; Mural Tours; Foyle Valley Railway Centre in Derry.

Tyrone: Omagh; Beaghmore stone circles near Cookstown; Dungannon; Sperrin Mountains.

Did you know?

Northern Ireland measures 85 miles from north to south and is about 110 miles wide.

The world's most famous ship, the Titanic, was built in Belfast.

Legend has it that the rugged Giant's Causeway was built by Finn McCool, the legendary Irish Giant, when he travelled to Scotland to bring back his sweetheart.

At 2,240 yards, an Irish mile is 480 yards longer than a standard English mile.

Mountsandel near Coleraine is where Ireland's first known house was built 9,000 years ago.

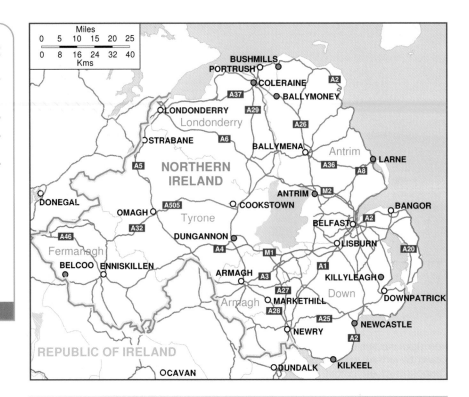

Ballymoney
Drumaheglis Caravan Park

36 Glenstall Road, Ballymoney BT53 7QN (Co. Antrim) T: 028 2766 0280. E: drumaheglis@ballymoney.gov.uk

alanrogers.com/UK8340

A caravan park which continually maintains high standards, Drumaheglis is popular throughout the season. Situated on the bank of the lower River Bann, approximately four miles from the town of Ballymoney, it appeals to watersports enthusiasts and makes a very good base for exploring this scenic corner of Northern Ireland. This attractive site is well laid out with trees, shrubs, flower beds and tarmac roads. There are 35 serviced pitches for touring units with hardstanding, 5/16A electricity, water points and drainage. The marina offers facilities for boat launching, water skiing, cruising, canoeing and fishing. Getting out and about can take you to the Giant's Causeway, seaside resorts such as Portrush or Portstewart, the sands of Whitepark Bay, the Glens of Antrim and the picturesque villages of the Antrim coast road. Ballymoney is a popular shopping town and the Joey Dunlop Leisure Centre has a high-tech fitness studio, sports hall, etc. There is much to see and do within this borough and of interest is the Ballymoney Museum in Townhead Street.

Facilities

Modern toilet blocks are very clean and well maintained. Facilities for disabled visitors. Baby changing facilities and four en-suite shower rooms. Washing machine and dryer. Basic shop. Play area. Barbecue and picnic areas. Barrier with key system. Fishing. Boat launching. Off site: Marina. Bus service from park entrance. Bicycle hire and golf 4 miles. Riding 6 miles. Beach 10 miles.

Open: 17 March - end October.

Directions

From A26/B62 Portrush-Ballymoney roundabout continue for 2 miles on the A26 towards Coleraine. Site is clearly signed; follow international camping signs. GPS: 55.07212, -6.59082

Charges guide

Per unit incl. electricity	£ 24.00
tent pitch	£ 16.00

Antrim
Six Mile Water Caravan & Camping Park

Lough Road, Antrim BT41 4DG (Co. Antrim) T: 028 9446 4963. E: sixmilewater@antrim.gov.uk
alanrogers.com/UK8330

Six Mile Water is located at the Lough Shore Park and is adjacent to the Antrim Forum leisure complex, a major amenity area that includes swimming pools, a bowling green, an adventure playground for children, fitness and health gyms and sports fields. Managed by Antrim Borough Council, the park is easily accessible when travelling to and from the ports of Belfast and Larne, making it perfect for stopovers. There are 37 pitches with 13A electricity, arranged in a herringbone layout of hardstandings with grass for awnings, a grass area for eight tents to one side, plus picnic and barbecue areas. Advance booking is advisable. Six Mile Water is central for sightseeing in the area including the Antrim Castle Gardens and Clotworthy Arts Centre, and for shopping in Antrim town. The Lough Shore Park offers visitors boating and water activities and boat launching on the beautiful Lough Neagh, as well as walking and cycling the Lough Shore Trail which takes in 25 places of interest along its 128 mile cycle route. The nearby golf club also offers a 20 bay driving range.

Facilities

The small, modern toilet block provides toilets, washbasins and showers and facilities for disabled campers. Baby changing unit. Laundry room. TV lounge and games room. Fishing and boat launching. Off site: The facilities of Lough Shore Park, including a café, open all year round. Antrim Forum leisure centre. Bus service 1 mile. Shops, pubs and restaurants within 1.5 miles. Golf 1.5 miles. Riding 6 miles.

Open: March - October and weekends in Feb. and Nov.

Directions

Site is 1 mile south of the city centre. Follow signs for Antrim Forum and Lough Shore Park. On the Dublin road, turn off into Lough Road. Pass Antrim Forum and park is at the end of the road (with speed bumps). GPS: 54.71533, -6.23375

Charges guide

Per unit incl. electricity	£ 21.00 - £ 23.00
tent	£ 15.00 - £ 22.00

Six Mile Water Caravan and Camping Park
Lough Road, Antrim, Northern Ireland, BT41 4DG

Situated on the shores of Lough Neagh, an ideal base for Northern Ireland.
On-site facilites include: TV lounge, games room, modern toilet and shower block, WiFi internet access, fully equipped laundry room, electric hook-up for 37 pitches and 8 camping sites. Maximum stay 14 nights. Open March - October and weekends only during February and November.

Tel: 028 9446 4963   Email: sixmilewater@antrim.gov.uk
www.antrim.gov.uk/caravanpark

Belcoo
Rushin House Caravan Park

Holywell, Belcoo, Enniskillen BT93 5DU (Co. Fermanagh) T: 028 6638 6519.
E: enquiries@rushinhousecaravanpark.com **alanrogers.com/UK8515**

Although situated in Northern Ireland, this park, opened in 2007, is almost on the border with the Republic of Ireland. It has been carefully landscaped from farmland that sloped down to the tranquil Lough MacNean. There are 24 fully serviced pitches on hardstanding which form a friendly circle surrounding a fairy thorn tree. There is also a small camping area. The toilet block, boat jetty, picnic tables and play areas are only a short walk away from the pitches. The helpful owners live on site and are on call most of the time. This park provides a peaceful haven to relax after returning from days out in lovely Fermanagh. At the farm entrance are the stark ruins of Templerushin Church and nearby is Saint Patrick's Holy Well.

Facilities

Heated toilet block, beautifully appointed, with laundry and adjoining kitchen area. Separate facilities for disabled campers. Payphone. Boat jetty. Play area. All-weather sports facility. Picnic area. Tourist information. Off site: Golf course nearby. Charming twin border towns of Belcoo and Blacklion with shops and restaurants. Within 25 miles are historic Enniskillen, Marble Arch caves, Belleek Pottery, two National Trust properties, and the dramatic countryside of Fermanagh, Donegal and Sligo.

Open: 11 March - 31 October.

Directions

From Enniskillen follow the A4 for 13 miles to Belcoo. Turn right on to the B52 towards Garrison and in 1 mile you will see the signs for Rushin House. GPS: 54.306584, -7.89505

Charges guide

Per unit incl. services	£ 24.00
extra person	£ 3.00

FREE Alan Rogers Travel Card
Extra benefits and savings - see page 10

Bushmills
Ballyness Caravan Park
40 Castlecatt Road, Bushmills BT57 8TN (Co. Antrim) T: 028 2073 2393. E: info@ballynesscaravanpark.com
alanrogers.com/UK8360

Ballyness is immaculately cared for and is designed with conservation in mind. In keeping with the surrounding countryside, it is extensively planted with native trees and shrubs. A pathway encircles several ponds which attract local wildlife and birds. The overall appearance of this eight hectare park, with its white stone pillared entrance gate and broad tarmac drive is attractive. There are 48 pitches, all on hardstanding with electricity, water and drainage. Privately-owned caravan holiday homes are placed away from the touring pitches.

Facilities

One spotlessly clean and well decorated, cottage style heated sanitary block (key coded). Facilities for disabled visitors (toilet and shower). Shop for basic food supplies, gas and campers' essentials. Family room with bath. Laundry room. Play area and play park. WiFi. Games/TV room. Off site: Bus service 0.5 miles. Bicycle hire, beach and fishing 1 mile. Boat launching and championship golf courses 1.5 miles. Riding 5 miles.

Open: 16 March - 31 October.

Directions

From M2 follow A26. At Ballymoney turn right on B66 towards Dervock and turn left. Stay on B66 and site is 5.5 miles on right. GPS: 55.20121, -6.52096

Charges guide

Per unit incl. 2 persons, electricity, water and drainage	£ 22.00
extra person (over 6 yrs)	£ 1.00
awning or pup tent	£ 2.00

Bushmills
Bush Caravan Park
97 Priestland Road, Bushmills BT57 8UJ (Co. Antrim) T: 028 2073 1678. E: bushcaravanpark@tiscali.co.uk
alanrogers.com/UK8350

A good base for touring the North Antrim Coast, this family run park is only minutes away from two renowned attractions, the Giant's Causeway and the Old Bushmills Distillery. Located just off the main Ballymoney-Portrush Road (B62), it is approached by a short drive. The park is partly surrounded by mature trees and hedging, but views across the countryside can still be appreciated. Tarmac roads lead to 47 well laid out and spacious pitches with hardstanding and 16A electricity, or to a grass area for pup tents. Unique features on site are murals depicting the famed scenery, sights and legends of the Causeway Coast. Occasional barbecues, tours to the distillery and coastal trips are organised.

Facilities

The toilet block (opened by key pad) is modern, clean and equipped to a high standard. Facilities include controllable showers with excellent provision for visitors with disabilities (can also be used by families). Washing machine and dryer. Central play area. Recreation room for all ages. Off site: Riding 2 miles. Golf, beach and fishing 3 miles. Bicycle hire and boat launching 4 miles.

Open: Easter - 31 October.

Directions

From the A26 turn onto the B62 for 7 miles. Turn onto the B17 Priestlands Road and site is immediately on the left. GPS: 55.17103, -6.57114

Charges guide

Per unit incl. 2 persons and electricity	£ 20.00
awning	£ 2.00

Coleraine
Tullans Farm Holiday Park
46 Newmills Road, Coleraine BT52 2JB (Co. Londonderry) T: 028 7034 2309. E: tullansfarm@hotmail.com
alanrogers.com/UK8590

A well run family park convenient for the Causeway coast, Tullans Farm has a quiet, heart of the country feel, yet the university town of Coleraine is within a mile, the seaside resorts of Portrush and Portstewart five miles and a shopping centre a five minute drive. The toilet block is clean and attractive flower displays add to the park's well cared for appearance. Around the park roads are gravel and the 36 pitches are on hardstanding; all with 10A electricity, water and drainage. In season the owners organise barbecues, barn dances and line dancing. A central building houses the reception, toilet block and TV room. Plans have been passed to provide caravan holiday home accommodation.

Facilities

The toilet and shower rooms, including a family shower unit, are spacious, modern and include facilities for visitors with disabilities. Laundry and washing up room with sinks, washing machine, dryers and fridge. Play areas. TV lounge. Games room. Barn used for indoor recreation. Snooker room for adults. Caravan storage. Off site: Public transport in Coleraine 1 mile. Fishing and riding 1.5 miles. Golf, beach and bicycle hire 5 miles.

Open: March - 30 September.

Directions

From the Lodge Road roundabout (south end of Coleraine) turn east onto A29 Portrush ring road and proceed for 0.5 miles. Turn right at sign for park and Windy Hall. GPS: 55.12557, -6.63923

Charges guide

Per unit incl. all persons, electricity and awning	£ 20.00
tent	£ 10.00 - £ 18.00

For latest campsite news visit
alanrogers.com

Dungannon
Dungannon Park

Moy Road, Dungannon BT71 6DY (Co. Tyrone) T: 028 8772 8690. E: dpreception@dungannon.gov.uk
alanrogers.com/UK8550

This small touring park nestles in the midst of a 70-acre park with a multitude of tree varieties, brightly coloured flower beds and a charming 12-acre fishing lake. The 12 touring pitches, some with lake views, are on hardstanding each with dedicated water, waste and 16A electricity connections. Hedging provides some separation. There is an unmarked grass area for tents. Run by Dungannon Council the park, which has tennis courts, football and cricket pitches, lies about a mile south of Dungannon town.

Facilities

Sanitary facilities are to the rear of the Amenity Centre and include showers (by token), washbasins, baby changing mat and spacious unit for disabled visitors. Laundry room with washing machine and dryer, dishwashing area and chemical disposal unit. Excellent play area. TV lounge. Tennis. Fishing. Walking. Orienteering. Off site: Bus stop and shop at main entrance to park. Restaurants, shops, leisure facilities in Dungannon. Interesting walking and cycling in Clogher Valley. Local markets.

Open: 1 March - 31 October.

Directions

From M1 exit 15 join A29 towards Dungannon. Turn left at second traffic lights signed Dungannon Park. GPS: 54.390217, -6.757967

Charges guide

Per unit incl. services	£ 15.00

Kilkeel
Chestnutt HolidayPark

3 Grange Road, Kilkeel, Newry BT34 4LW (Co. Down) T: 028 4176 2653. E: info@chestnuttholidayparks.com
alanrogers.com/UK8410

Chestnutt Caravan Park is one of the best in the southernmost corner of Northern Ireland. There are two areas designated for touring units, one on each side of the entrance road and all pitches have electricity, light, water and waste. The park is surrounded by dramatic scenery and unspoilt countryside and is an attractive choice for a beach based holiday. The adjacent beach, with lifeguard, tennis court, small football pitch and play park will keep youngsters happy all day. The backdrop of the Mourne Mountains to the north gives the area shelter.

Facilities

Each touring section has its own toilet block with token operated showers. The large well equipped laundry (also token operated), toilets and full facilities for disabled campers have been completely refurbished. Shop, restaurant and takeaway (all open Easter weekend, Jul/Aug). Tennis court. Small football pitch. Play area. WiFi over site (small charge). Off site: Mountain and coastal walks and country parks. Sea canoeing and other watersports, sea fishing and golf are all available nearby.

Open: 17 March - 31 October.

Directions

From the north follow the A2 from Newcastle and at Kilkeel follow signs for Cranfield West and then Chestnutt Holiday Park. From Newry, pass through Rostrevor and 6 miles further you will see signs for Cranfield West. GPS: 54.030864, -6.068868

Charges guide

Per unit incl. awning and electricity	£ 20.00

Kilkeel
Cranfield Caravan Park

123 Cranfield Road, Cranfield West, Kilkeel BT34 4LJ (Co. Down) T: 028 4176 2572.
E: jimchestnut@btconnect.com **alanrogers.com/UK8405**

On the shores of Carlingford Lough, with direct access to a Blue Flag beach, this friendly, family-run park immediately impresses with its well cared for flower beds, neat hedging, cordyline palms and the elegant building which incorporates the family home and reception. Despite the many privately owned caravan holiday homes on site, touring pitches are kept separate and are situated towards the park entrance. Most pitches have a sea view, hardstanding and all have tower units providing 10A electricity hook-ups, water, waste water point and TV outlet. Tents are not accepted.

Facilities

A modern, heated toilet block (entrance by key) is well maintained with tiled walls/floors, preset showers (token) and open style washbasins. Excellent suite for disabled visitors doubles as a family room, also a night WC (by key). Dishwashing sinks and well equipped laundry in a separate building. Play area (outside park). Sea fishing, boat launching and beach (with lifeguard). WiFi (charged).

Open: 17 March - 30 September.

Directions

Travelling southeast on A2 Newry-Kilkeel Road turn right 5.5 miles after passing through Rostrevor onto local road, signed Cranfield/Greencastle. If approaching from Kilkeel follow signs for Cranfield West. GPS: 54.029933, -6.0683

Charges guideguide

Per unit incl. all persons and electricity	£ 22.00
awning	£ 2.00

FREE Alan Rogers Travel Card
Extra benefits and savings - see page 10

Kilkeel

Sandilands Caravan Park

30 Cranfield Road, Cranfield East, Kilkeel BT34 4LJ (Co. Down) T: 028 4176 3634.
E: info@chestnuttholidayparks.com **alanrogers.com/UK8407**

In the very popular area of Cranfield, Sandilands is set slightly apart from its neighbours, looking south east over the Irish Sea rather than Carlingford Lough. The park largely comprises privately owned caravan holiday homes, but has an attractive and enclosed area for 30 touring units. It makes the most of its coastal plain situation to the immediate south of the Mourne Mountains. Kilkeel and the mountain foothills can be reached in a few minutes by car.

Facilities

Laundry and toilet block (entrance to all facilities by key) is well maintained. It has preset showers (token) and open style washbasins and a night WC. There are no dedicated facilities for disabled visitors. Play area and small football pitch. Off site: Sea fishing and boat launching nearby. Pretty village of Rostrevor, well known for its ceilidhs and Irish music 7 miles. Kilkeel and Annalong are interesting fishing towns.

Open: 17 March - 31 October.

Directions

From the north leave the A2 in the middle of Kilkeel and follow signs for Cranfield East until the sign for Sandilands appears on the left. From Newry pass through Rostrevor and after 6 miles look for signs to Cranfield East. GPS: 54.029932, -6.058391

Charges guide

Per unit incl. services	£ 19.00
awning	£ 1.00

Killyleagh

Delamont Country Park Camping & Caravanning Club Site

Delamont Country Park, Downpatrick Road, Killyleagh BT30 9TZ (Co. Down) T: 028 4482 1833.
E: delamont.site@thefriendlyclub.co.uk **alanrogers.com/UK8460**

This is Northern Ireland's first Camping and Caravanning Club site and is now one of the country's more popular sites. Facilities on the campsite itself are excellent and it has an orderly, neat and tidy appearance. Reception stands beside the entrance to the site and the sanitary block towards the rear. The 65 all weather pitches on level terrain all have electricity, plus water and waste hook-ups. The site is surrounded by trees and the rich vegetation of the country park, and the young shrubs and trees around the pitches are slowly maturing.

Facilities

The single modern toilet block, with heating, has wash cubicles and a baby bath. En-suite facilities for disabled visitors. Laundry sinks, washing machine and dryer; dishwashing inside. Small shop area selling basics. Adventure playground and miniature railway in country park. Free admittance to country park for campers. WiFi (charged). Off site: Fishing and riding 1 mile. Golf 4 miles. Tyrella beach 7 miles.

Open: 15 March - 12 November.

Directions

From Belfast follow the A22 southeast to village of Killyleagh. Pass through village and site entrance is on left after 1 mile. GPS: 54.38656, -5.67657

Charges guide

Per unit incl. 2 persons and electricity	£ 15.50 - £ 22.45
non member pitch fee	£ 7.10

Larne

Carnfunnock Country Park Caravan Park & Campsite

Coast Road, Ballygally, Larne BT40 2QG (Co. Antrim) T: 028 2827 0541. E: carnfunnock@larne.gov.uk
alanrogers.com/UK8310

In a magnificent parkland setting overlooking the Irish Sea and Scotland, what makes this touring site popular are its scenic surroundings and convenient location. It is 3.5 miles north of the market town of Larne on the famed Antrim Coast Road and offers 31 level super pitches, including three extra long pitches, all with hardstanding, water, 16A electricity, drainage, individual pitch lighting and ample space for an awning. The site has a neat appearance with a tarmac road following through to the rear where a number of pitches are placed in a circular position with allocated space for tents.

Facilities

A small building beside the entrance gates houses the toilet facilities (entry by key) which have had a major refurbishment and are kept very clean. There are shower units, a family bathroom and facilities for disabled visitors. Baby changing room. Off site: Facilities of the adjacent Country Park include: gift shop, restaurant and coffee shop, adventure playground, maze, putting green, 9-hole golf course, forest walks and much more. Fishing and boat launching 400 yds. Riding 7 miles.

Open: 16 March - 4 November.

Directions

From ferry terminal in Larne, follow signs for Coast Road and Carnfunnock Country Park; well signed on A2 coast road. GPS: 54.888193, -5.845231

Charges guide

Per caravan or motorcaravan incl. electricity and awning	£ 19.00 - £ 22.00
tent incl. 2 persons	£ 11.50 - £ 12.50
tent (per extra person)	£ 2.00

For latest campsite news visit
alanrogers.com

Larne
Curran Caravan Park

131 Curran Road, Larne BT40 1DD (Co. Antrim) T: 028 2827 3797. E: robinsonsservicestation@hotmail.co.uk

alanrogers.com/UK8320

Attractive garden areas add to the charm of this small, neat park which has recently been purchased by the owner of the garage/shop opposite. It is very conveniently situated for the ferry terminal and only a few minutes walk from the sea. The new owner has been making some upgrades and now provides four hardstanding pitches for motorcaravans. The 34 pitches, all with 14A electricity connections, give reasonable space off the tarmac road and there is a separate tent area of 1.5 acres. Larne market is on Wednesdays. You may consider using this site as a short term base for discovering the area as well as an ideal overnight stop, especially for early or late ferry crossings. The warden can usually find room for tourists so reservations are not normally necessary.

Facilities

The toilet block is clean and adequate without being luxurious but there are no facilities for disabled visitors. Laundry room with dishwashing facilities. Bowls and putting adjacent and also play areas with good equipment and safety surfaces. Late arrivals can call at the garage if open. Off site: Train station and bus stop within a few minutes walk. Many other amenities are very close including a shop (100 yds), restaurants, tennis and a leisure centre with swimming pool (300 yds). Boat launching 500 yds. Bicycle hire 0.5 miles. Golf 2 miles.

Open: Easter - 31 October.

Directions

Immediately after leaving the ferry terminal, turn right and follow camp signs. Site is 400 yds. on the left. GPS: 54.84995, -5.80818

Charges guide

Per caravan, motorcaravan or large tent incl. electricity and awning	£ 15.00
tent	£ 10.00

Newcastle
Tollymore Forest Caravan Park

178 Tullybrannigan Road, Newcastle BT33 OPW (Co. Down) T: 028 4372 2428

alanrogers.com/UK8420

This popular park, for touring units only, is located within the parkland of Tollymore Forest which is noted for its scenic surroundings. The forest park is approached by a majestic avenue of Himalayan cedars and covers an area of almost 500 hectares. Situated two miles from the beaches and resort of Newcastle, it is backed impressively by the Mourne mountains. The open grassy site is attractively laid out with hardstanding pitches, 72 of which have 6A electricity. The Forestry Service Rangers are very helpful and ensure that the caravan site is efficiently run and quiet, even when full. Exploring the park is part of the pleasure of staying here and the stone bridges and entrance gates are of particular interest. The picturesque Shimna and Spinkwee rivers rise in the Mournes and flow through the park. Tree lovers appreciate the arboretum with its many rare species.

Facilities

The timbered toilet blocks have wash cubicles, showers, dishwashing and laundry area. Fishing (permit required). Off site: Confectionery shop and tea room nearby in high season. Small grocery shop a few yards from the exit gate of the park with gas available.

Open: All year.

Directions

Approach Newcastle on the A24. Before entering the town, at roundabout, turn right on to A50 signed Castlewellan and follow signs for Tollymore Forest Park. GPS: 54.22630, -5.93449

Charges guide

Per unit incl. car and persons	£ 10.50 - £ 15.50
electricity	£ 1.50

FREE Alan Rogers Travel Card
Extra benefits and savings - see page 10

Famed for its folklore, traditional music, and friendly, hospitable people, the Republic of Ireland offers spectacular scenery contained within a relatively compact area. With plenty of beautiful areas to discover, and a decidedly relaxed pace of life, it is an ideal place to unwind.

IRELAND IS MADE UP OF FOUR PROVINCES: CONNAUGHT, LEINSTER, MUNSTER AND ULSTER, COMPRISING 32 COUNTIES, 26 OF WHICH FALL IN THE REPUBLIC OF IRELAND

Ireland is the perfect place to indulge in a variety of outdoor pursuits while taking in the glorious scenery. There are plenty of way-marked footpaths, which lead through woodlands, across cliffs, past historical monuments and over rolling hills. The dramatic coastline, with its headlands, secluded coves and sandy beaches, is fantastic for watersports: from sailing to windsurfing, scuba diving and swimming; or for just simply relaxing and watching the variety of seabirds that nest on the shores. The Cliffs of Moher, in particular, is a prime location for birdwatching and Goat Island, just offshore, is where puffins make their nesting burrows. Fishing is another popular activity; the country is full of pretty streams, rivers, hidden lakes and canals, which can all be explored by hiring a boat. In the south, the beautiful Ring of Kerry is one of the most visited regions. This 110-mile route encircles the Inveragh Peninsula, and is surrounded by mountains and lakes. Other sights include the Aran Islands, home to some of the most ancient Christian and pre-Christian remains in Ireland, and the Rock of Cashel, with its spectacular group of medieval buildings; not to mention the bustling cities of Dublin, Galway and Cork.

Places of interest

Connaught: Boyle Abbey; Connemara National Park; Céide Fields at Ballycastle; Kylemore Abbey; Aran Islands; Galway city; Westport; Sligo Abbey; megalithic tombs of Carrowmore.

Leinster: Wicklow Mountains National Park; Rock of Cashel; Killkenny Castle; Guinness brewery, Trinity College and National Museum in Dublin; Dunmore Cave at Ballyfoyle; Wexford Wildfowl Reserve.

Munster: harbour towns of Kinsale and Clonakilty; Blarney Castle in Cork; historical city of Limerick with 13th-century castle fortress and old town; Ring of Kerry; Bunratty Castle; Cliffs of Moher; Killarney National Park.

Ulster: Glenveagh National Park; Slieve League, the highest sea cliffs in Europe; Donegal Castle; Newmills Corn and Flax Mills in Letterkenny.

Did you know?

The official currency of the Republic of Ireland is the Euro.

The international dialling code for the Republic of Ireland is 00 353 (then drop the first '0' of the number).

The Blarney Stone, reputedly cast with a spell by a witch to reward a king who saved her from drowning, is said to bestow the gift of eloquence on all those who kiss it.

The harp is a symbol of the Irish people's love of music: since Medieval times it has been the official emblem for Ireland.

Hurling is the oldest native sport.

On display in Trinity College, the Book of Kells is one of the oldest books in the world, written around the year 800 AD.

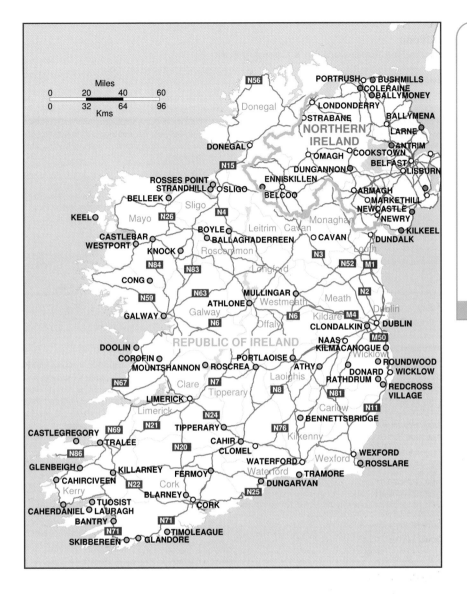

Digital iPad editions

alan rogers

Available on the App Store

FREE Alan Rogers bookstore app - digital editions of all 2013 guides
alanrogers.com/digital

Athlone

Lough Ree (East) Caravan & Camping Park

Ballykeeran, Athlone (Co. Westmeath) T: 090 647 8561. E: athlonecamping@eircom.net

alanrogers.com/IR8960

This touring park is alongside the Breensford river, screened by trees but reaching the water's edge. The park is discreetly located behind Ballykeeran's main street. The top half of the site is in woodland and after the reception and sanitary block, Lough Ree comes into view and the remaining pitches run down to the shoreline. There are 60 pitches, most on hardstanding and all with 6A electricity. With fishing right on the doorstep there are boats for hire locally and the site has its own private mooring buoys, plus a dinghy slip and harbour. A restaurant and 'singing' pub are close.

Facilities

The toilet block is clean and the recently refurbished ladies' toilets, unisex showers (€ 1) and facilities for disabled visitors are all excellent. Dishwashing sinks outside. Laundry room (wash and dry € 8). A wooden chalet houses a pool room with open fire and campers' kitchen (no cooking facilities). Off site: Riding 4 km. Bicycle hire 5 km. Golf 8 km.

Open: 1 April - 30 September.

Directions

From Athlone take N55 towards Longford for 4.8 km. Park is in Ballykeeran. Prepare to take a left turn on a sharp, right-hand curve, the park is then clearly signed. GPS: 53.44815, -7.88992

Charges guide

Per unit incl. 2 persons and electricity	€ 21.00 - € 23.00
extra person	€ 4.00

No credit cards.

Athy

Forest Farm Caravan & Camping Park

Dublin Road, Athy (Co. Kildare) T: 059 863 1231. E: forestfarm@eircom.net

alanrogers.com/IR9080

This site makes an excellent stopover if travelling from Dublin to the southeast counties. It is also ideally placed to visit local places of interest including the Shackleton exhibition, the Japanese Gardens and the Irish National Stud. Part of a working farm, the campsite spreads to the right of the modern farmhouse, which also provides B&B and holiday apartments. The owners have cleverly utilised their land to create a site which offers 64 unmarked touring pitches on level ground. Of these, 32 are for caravans, all with electricity and ten with hardstanding, and 32 places are available for tents.

Facilities

The centrally located, red brick toilet block is heated and double glazed. Spacious shower unit for disabled visitors. Family room with shower and WC. Laundry room. Campers' kitchen with fridge/freezer, cooker, table and chairs. Comfortable, large lounge/games room (a TV can be provided). Sand pit and picnic tables. Off site: Shop, bar and restaurant 3 km. Golf courses nearby. Coarse and game fishing 4 km.

Open: All year.

Directions

From exit 3 of M9 head west towards Athy on the N78. Pass Athy and turn left at roundabout onto R418 signed Kilcullen. The site is signed on right after 3 km. and approached along a 500 m. avenue of tall pines. GPS: 53.0139, -6.9256

Charges guide

Per unit incl. 2 persons	€ 18.00 - € 20.00
extra person	€ 4.00
hiker, cyclist or motorcyclist incl. tent	€ 6.00

Ballaghaderreen

Willowbrook Camping & Caravan Park

Kiltybranks, Ballaghaderreen (Co. Roscommon) T: 094 986 1307. E: info@willowbrookpark.com

alanrogers.com/IR8815

This is a campsite with a difference. Willowbrook is a small family run caravan and camping park, which offers a unique holiday in an unspoiled part of Ireland. It has eight hardstanding pitches with electricity and a central level grass area without power, all with ample water points. An additional tenting area is available in the adjoining field. The main difference is that meditation, Tai Chi and other relaxation techniques, all adding to the tranquillity of the setting, are organised by Dave and Lin Whitefield whose aim is to ensure their guests relax and unwind in this idyllic hideaway.

Facilities

The toilet block is immaculate and lit at night, with separate shower cubicles. Shower and toilet facilities for disabled campers at reception (some distance from pitches). Laundry room. Campers' kitchen with microwave, kettle and toaster. Library and reading room with TV. Archery. Martial arts room. Fishing. Torches useful. Off site: Local sporting activities available include tennis, golf and fishing.

Open: All year.

Directions

Take R293 from Ballaghaderreen towards Castlerea and Ballyhaunis, then R325 over the bridge. Bear left, still towards Castlerea and Ballyhaunis for 1.5 km. Turn right at sign to site in 500 m. GPS: 53.86672, -8.60214

Charges guide

Per unit incl. 2 persons and electricity	€ 23.50
family tent incl. 2 adults and 2 children	€ 23.00

No credit cards.

For latest campsite news visit

alanrogers.com

Bantry
Eagle Point Caravan & Camping Park
Ballylickey, Bantry (Co. Cork) T: 027 506 30. E: eaglepointcamping@eircom.net
alanrogers.com/IR9510

Midway between the towns of Bantry and Glengarriff, the spectacular peninsula of Eagle Point juts into Bantry Bay. The first impression is of a spacious country park rather than a campsite. As far as the eye can see this 20-acre, landscaped, part-terraced park, with its vast manicured grass areas separated by mature trees, shrubs and hedges, runs parallel with the shoreline providing lovely views. Suitable for all ages, this is a well run park mainly for touring units, with campers pitched mostly towards the shore. It provides 125 pitches with 6A electricity, although many are seasonally occupied.

Facilities

Three well maintained, well designed toilet blocks are of a high standard. Laundry. Motorcaravan services. Play area. Tennis. Football field, well away from the pitches. Fishing. Boat launching. Supermarket at park entrance. Dogs are not accepted. WiFi. Off site: Golf 2 km. Bicycle hire 6 km. Riding 10 km.

Open: 20 April - 24 September.

Directions

Take N71 to Bandon, then R586 Bandon to Bantry. From Bantry take N71 to Glengarriff. 6.4 km. further; or N22 Cork to Macroom, R584 to Ballylickey Bridge, N71 to Glengarriff. Entrance opposite Cronins petrol station. GPS: 51.718333, -9.455278

Charges guide

Per unit incl. 2 persons and electricity	€ 29.00 - € 32.00
extra person	€ 10.00

Belleek
Belleek Park Caravan & Camping
Belleek, Ballina (Co. Mayo) T: 096 715 33. E: lenahan@belleekpark.com
alanrogers.com/IR8750

Belleek has a quiet woodland setting, only minutes from Ballina, a famed salmon fishing centre. With excellent pitches and toilet block, the family owners are committed to ensuring that it is immaculate at all times. From the entrance gate, the park is approached by a drive that passes reception and leads to 80 well spaced pitches. With a very neat overall appearance, 50 pitches have hardstanding and electricity hook-ups, and you may choose your pitch. Sports facilities within a short distance of the park include a swimming pool, tennis and bicycle hire. There is a Blue Flag beach at Ross.

Facilities

Spotlessly clean, tastefully decorated toilet block providing showers (€ 1 token). Baby bath. Facilities for disabled campers. Laundry facilities. Reception includes a shop and a tea room also serving breakfast. Campers' kitchen and emergency accommodation with beds provided. TV room. Games room. Play area. Ball game area. Tennis. Barbecue area. Free WiFi over site. Off site: Fishing 1 km. Bicycle hire 2 km. Golf 3.5 km. Beach 10 km.

Open: 1 March - 1 November, by arrangement all year.

Directions

Take R314 Ballina-Killala road. Park is signed on right after 3 km. GPS: 54.1345, -9.1585

Charges guide

Per unit incl. 2 persons and electricity	€ 23.00
extra person	€ 5.00
child	€ 2.50
hiker/cyclist and tent	€ 9.00

Bennettsbridge
Nore Valley Park
Annamult, Bennettsbridge (Co. Kilkenny) T: 056 772 7229. E: norevalleypark@eircom.net
alanrogers.com/IR9230

This lovely site is set on a grassy hill overlooking the valley of the River Nore, with a woodland setting behind. Situated on a working farm, it offers 70 touring pitches, 50 of which have 6A electricity. There is an additional area for tents and four mobile homes for rent. The owners, Samuel and Isobel, are proud of their park and her baking and jams must be sampled. An attractive courtyard houses several unusual facilities including a sand pit and a straw loft play area for wet weather. Animal park, outdoor chess, tractor rides and go-karts in the fields. There is easy access to Waterford city, famous for its crystal.

Facilities

The modern toilet block is kept clean and can be heated. Two units suitable for disabled visitors. Laundry room with washing machine and dryer. Motorcaravan services. The original block in the courtyard is used mainly in the low season. Shop (basic items such as milk, bread and camping gaz) and café (June-Aug). Comfortable lounge. Games room. Play area. Minigolf. Off site: Bennettsbridge 3 km. Outdoor pursuits nearby. Riding 6 km. Golf 10 km.

Open: 1 March - 31 October.

Directions

From Kilkenny take R700 to Bennettsbridge. Just before the bridge turn right at sign for Stoneyford and after 3 km. site is signed Nore Valley Park. GPS: 52.56307, -7.19506

Charges guide

Per unit incl. 2 persons and electricity	€ 22.00 - € 24.00
extra person	€ 4.00

FREE Alan Rogers Travel Card
Extra benefits and savings - see page 10

Blarney

Blarney Caravan & Camping Park

Stone View, Blarney (Co. Cork) T: 021 451 6519. E: con.quill@camping-ireland.ie

alanrogers.com/IR9480

There is a heart of the country feel about this 'on the farm' site, yet the city of Cork is only an 8 km. drive. What makes this friendly, family run park so appealing is its secluded location and neatly laid out, open appearance. The terrain on the three acre park is elevated and gently sloping, commanding views towards Blarney Castle and the surrounding mountainous countryside. The 80 pitches, 39 of which have hardstanding and 10A electrical connections, are with caravans near the entrance with tents pitched slightly further away. There are gravel roads, well tended young shrubs and a screen of mature trees.

Facilities

Excellent toilet facilities are housed in converted farm buildings. Reception and small shop are now at entrance. Good facilities for disabled visitors. Laundry room. Campers' kitchen. Motorcaravan service point. Shop (1/6-31/8). TV lounge. Internet and WiFi throughout (free). Delightful 18-hole golf and pitch and putt course. Off site: Bar 100 m. Within easy reach of the ports of Cork and Rosslare.

Open: 25 March - 28 October.

Directions

Site is 8 km. northwest of Cork, just off the N20. Take N20 from Cork for 6 km. and then left on R617 to Blarney. Site clearly signed at Top Filling station in village, in 2 km. GPS: 51.94787, -8.54622

Charges guide

Per unit incl. 2 persons	
and electricity	€ 25.00 - € 27.00
extra person	€ 6.50
child (under 14 yrs)	€ 3.00 - € 3.50

Boyle

Lough Key Caravan & Camping Park

Lough Key Forest Park, Boyle (Co. Roscommon) T: 071 966 2212. E: info@loughkey.ie

alanrogers.com/IR8825

This caravan and camping park is set deep in the 320 hectares of the Lough Key Forest Park. Comprising mixed woodland including giant red cedar, beech, ash and oak trees, the forest is bounded by Lough Key and incorporates several of its islands. The rustic design of the main building on the park (which houses reception, a campers' kitchen, a lounge, and the sanitary and laundry facilities) blends well with the wooded environment. The well landscaped, five-hectare site provides space for 52 touring units with electricity connections and ample water points, and many of the pitches are within woodland.

Facilities

The main toilet block includes metered hot showers (€ 2). Facilities for disabled campers (key required). Campers' kitchen and sheltered eating area. Laundry. Play area in the centre of the park with adventure type play equipment in a hedged area, plus seating for parents. Forest walks and trails. Boat tours and boat hire. Security barrier closed at night. Site security patrol. Off site: Local shop will deliver to site. Restaurant at Rockingham harbour. Nearby town of Boyle for bars and restaurants 3 km.

Open: 1 April - mid September.

Directions

Park is 4 km. east of Boyle on the N4 Dublin-Sligo Road. Note: there is a height restriction (3 m) on the signed exit from the park towards Boyle, but there is an alternative route to the N4. GPS: 53.98125, -8.235167

Charges guide

Per unit incl. 2 persons and electricity	€ 25.00

No credit cards.

Caherdaniel

Wave Crest Caravan & Camping Park

Caherdaniel (Co. Kerry) T: 066 947 5188. E: wavecrest@eircom.net

alanrogers.com/IR9560

It would be difficult to imagine a more dramatic location than Wave Crest's on the Ring of Kerry coast. Huge boulders and rocky outcrops tumble from the park entrance on the N70 down to the seashore which forms the most southern promontory on the Ring of Kerry. There are spectacular southward views from the park across Kenmare Bay to the Beara peninsula. Sheltering on grass patches in small coves that nestle between the rocks and shrubbery, are 65 hardstanding pitches and 20 on grass offering seclusion. Electricity connections are available (13A). This park would suit older people looking for a quiet, relaxed atmosphere.

Facilities

Two blocks house the sanitary and laundry facilities and include hot showers on payment (€ 1). Small shop and takeaway service (June-Sept). Small play area. Fishing and boat launching. Off site: Riding 1 km. Bicycle hire and golf 10 km. Small beach near and Derrynane Hotel with bar and restaurant.

Open: All year.

Directions

On the N70 (Ring of Kerry), 1.5 km. east of Caherdaniel. GPS: 51.75881, -10.09112

Charges guide

Per unit incl. 2 persons and electricity	€ 27.00
extra person	€ 6.00
child	€ 2.00

Cahir
The Apple Camping & Caravan Park
Moorstown, Cahir (Co. Tipperary) T: 052 744 1459. E: con@theapplefarm.com
alanrogers.com/IR9410

This fruit farm and campsite combination offers an idyllic country holiday venue in one of the most delightful situations imaginable. For touring units only, it is located off the N24, midway between Clonmel and Cahir. The park has 32 pitches in a secluded situation behind the barns; they are mostly grass with 14 hardstandings and 25 electricity connections (13A, Europlug). Entrance is via a 300 m. drive flanked by the orchard fields and various non-fruit tree species, which are named and of interest to guests who are free to spend time walking the paths around the farm.

Facilities

Toilet facilities, kept very clean, quite modern in design and with heating, comprise showers, washbasins with mirrors, electric points, etc. in functional units occupying two corners of the large floor space. Facilities for disabled visitors. Also in the barn are dishwashing sinks, washing machine and a fridge/freezer for campers to use. Good drive-on motorcaravan service point. Good tennis court (free). Play area. Dogs are not accepted. WiFi (free). Off site: Fishing, golf, and riding 6 km. Bicycle hire 9 km.

Open: 1 May - 30 September.

Directions

Park is 300 m. off main N24, 9.6 km. west of Clonmel, 6.4 km. east of Cahir.
GPS: 52.37663, -7.84262

Charges guide

Per unit incl. 2 persons and electricity	€ 15.50
extra person	€ 6.50
child	€ 4.50

No charge per unit. Less 20% for groups of 4 or more.

Cahirciveen
Mannix Point Camping & Caravan Park
Cahirciveen (Co. Kerry) T: 066 947 2806. E: mortimer@campinginkerry.com
alanrogers.com/IR9610

A tranquil, beautifully located seashore park, it is no exaggeration to describe Mannix Point as a nature lovers' paradise. Situated in one of the most spectacular parts of the Ring of Kerry, overlooking the bay and Valentia Island, the rustic seven-acre park commands splendid views in all directions. The park road meanders through the level site and offers 42 pitches of various sizes and shapes, many with shelter and seclusion. There are 42 electrical connections (10A) available. A charming, old flower bedecked fisherman's cottage has been converted to provide facilities including reception, excellent campers' kitchen and a cosy sitting room with turf fire.

Facilities

Toilet and shower facilities were clean when we visited. Modern and well equipped campers' kitchen and dining area. Comfortable campers' sitting room. Laundry facilities with washing machines and dryer. Motorcaravan service point. Picnic and barbecue facilities. Fishing and boat launching from site. Off site: Bicycle hire 800 m. Riding 3 km. Pubs, restaurants and shops 15 mins. on foot.

Open: 15 March - 15 October.

Directions

Park is 300 m. off the N70 Ring of Kerry road, 800 m. southwest of Cahirciveen (or Cahersiveen) on the road towards Waterville.
GPS: 51.941517, -10.24465

Charges guide

Per unit incl. 2 persons and electricity	€ 27.00
extra person	€ 6.00

No credit cards.

Castlebar
Carra Caravan & Camping Park
Belcarra, Castlebar (Co. Mayo) T: 094 903 2054. E: post@mayoholidays.com
alanrogers.com/IR8790

This is an ideal location for those seeking a real Irish village experience in a 'value for money' park. Small, unpretentious and family run, it is located in Belcarra, a regular winner of the Tidiest Mayo Village award. Nestling at the foot of a wooded drumlin, it is surrounded by rolling hills and quiet roads which offer an away from it all feeling, yet Castlebar the county's largest town is only an 8 km. drive. On the pleasant 1.5-acre park, the 20 unmarked touring pitches, 15 with electric hook-up (13A Europlug), are on flat ground enclosed by ranch fencing and shaded in parts by trees.

Facilities

The new toilet block has well equipped showers (€ 1). En-suite facility for disabled visitors. Combined kitchen with fridge/freezer, sink, table, chairs, washing machine and dryer. Comfortable lounge with TV. Horse-drawn caravans for hire. Off site: Village shops, a post office and cosy bar with Irish music most Friday nights. Leisure centre and tennis court. Free fishing area. Golf 8 km.

Open: 31 March - 10 November.

Directions

From Castlebar follow the N84 towards Ballinrobe. On the outskirts of Castlebar, 100 m. after the railway bridge turn left for Belcarra (Ballycarra) 8 km. Site is at south end of village by a garage and a plumber's merchant. GPS: 53.79950, -9.21699

Charges guide

Per unit incl. all persons and electricity	€ 16.00

No credit cards.

FREE Alan Rogers Travel Card
Extra benefits and savings - see page 10

Castlebar

Lough Lannagh Caravan Park

Old Westport Road, Castlebar (Co. Mayo) T: 094 902 7111. E: info@loughlannagh.ie

alanrogers.com/IR8810

Lough Lannagh is an attractive holiday village on the lake shore, which offers quality accommodation, self-catering cottages and a caravan park. A new lakeside path takes you into Castlebar (15 minute stroll) with its many restaurants, pubs, theatres and shops. County Mayo's main attractions are also within a short drive. The caravan park has 20 touring pitches, well laid out in a separate dedicated corner of the village, all on hardstanding with electric connections. There is a separate grass area for tents. One reception area serves all and is situated to the right of the security barrier; check in prior to 18:00.

Facilities	Directions
One modern heated sanitary block provides washbasins and well equipped, preset showers. En-suite unit for disabled visitors. Laundry room with sink, washing machines and dryers near reception. Café (serving breakfast). Fitness suite (free entry; over 18s only admitted). Boules. Badminton. Tennis. Lakeside circular walk.	To get to Castlebar take the N5, N60 or N84. At Castlebar ring road follow directions for Westport. Site is signed on all approach roads to the Westport roundabout. GPS: 53.8491, -9.3119

Charges guide

Per unit incl. 2 persons, electricity and hardstanding	€ 21.00 - € 24.00
extra person	€ 3.00

Open: April - September.

Castlegregory

Anchor Caravan Park

Castlegregory (Co. Kerry) T: 066 713 9157. E: anchorcaravanpark@eircom.net

alanrogers.com/IR9550

Of County Kerry's three long, finger like peninsulas which jut into the sea, Dingle is the most northerly. Anchor Caravan Park is 20 km. west of Tralee, the main town, and under 4 km. south of Castlegregory on Tralee Bay. Its situation, just 150 m. from a fine sandy beach, provides ideal opportunities for safe bathing, boating and shore fishing. A secluded and mature, five acre park, it is enclosed by shrubs and trees that give excellent shelter. There are 30 pitches, all with electric hook-ups and some also with drainage and water points. Although there are holiday homes for hire, these are well apart from the touring pitches. The approach roads to the park are narrow and may be difficult for larger units.

Facilities	Directions
Toilet facilities (entry by key) are kept very clean and provide showers on payment (€ 0,50), two private cabins, some low level basins and a toilet with handrail. No facilities for disabled campers. Laundry facilities (incl. drying room, clothes lines and ironing). Campers' kitchen with fridges, freezers and seating. Motorcaravan services. Two play areas. Games and TV rooms. Off site: Beautiful sandy beach 2 minutes. Fishing 2 km. Riding 3 km.	From Tralee follow N86 Dingle coast road for 19 km. At Camp take R560 towards Castlegregory. Park is signed from Camp. GPS: 52.24393, -9.98579

Charges guide

Per unit incl. 2 persons and electricity	€ 20.00 - € 22.00
extra person	€ 5.00
No credit cards.	

Open: Easter - 30 September.

Clondalkin

Camac Valley Tourist Caravan & Camping Park

Green Isle Road, Clondalkin Dublin 22 (Co. Dublin) T: 014 640 644. E: reservations@camacvalley.com

alanrogers.com/IR9100

Opened in 1996, this campsite is not only well placed for Dublin, but also offers a welcome stopover if travelling to the more southern counties from the north of the country, or vice versa. Despite its close proximity to the city, and the distant noise from the dual carriageway, being located in the 300-acre Corkagh Park gives it a 'heart of the country' atmosphere. There are 163 pitches on hardstandings for caravans laid out in bays and avenues, all with electrical connections, drainage and water points. Maturing trees and shrubs separate pitches and roads are of tarmac. Beyond the entrance gate and forecourt stands an attractive, timber-fronted building housing the site amenities.

Facilities	Directions
Heated sanitary facilities include good sized showers (token). Facilities for disabled visitors. Baby room. Laundry. Shop and coffee bar. Playground with wooden play frames and safety base. Fishing. Electronic gate controlled from reception and 24-hour security. Off site: Bicycle hire 1.5 km. Golf 6 km. Riding 9 km.	Site is in Corkah Park, 4 km. west of M50 exit 9, just off N7 Nass Road on the north side. It is clearly signed from both directions at the new R136 turnoff. GPS: 53.30445, -6.41533

Charges guide

Per unit incl. 2 persons and electricity	€ 25.00 - € 27.00
extra person	€ 5.00

Open: All year.

For latest campsite news visit

alanrogers.com

Cong

Cong Caravan & Camping Park

Lisloughrey, Quay Road, Cong (Co. Mayo) T: 094 954 6089. E: info@quietman-cong.com

alanrogers.com/IR8740

It would be difficult to find a more idyllic and famous spot for a caravan park than Cong. Situated close to the shores of Lough Corrib, Cong's scenic beauty was immortalised in the film, The Quiet Man. This well kept park is 1.6 km. from the village of Cong, near the grounds of the magnificent and renowned Ashford Castle. Reception, shop and the hostel, stand to the fore of the site. Toilet facilities and the holiday hostel accommodation are entered from the courtyard area. The 40 grass pitches, 36 with electricity, are placed at a higher level to the rear, with the sheltered tent areas below and to the side. The park can be crowded and busy in high season.

Facilities

Toilet facilities are kept clean and are heated when necessary. Hot showers with curtains (€ 1 charge). Good facilities for disabled visitors. Campers' kitchen. Launderette service. Shop. Catering is a feature – full Irish and continental breakfast, dinner and packed lunch may be ordered, and home baked bread and scones for sale in the shop. Barbecue, games room and extensive play area. TV lounge. WiFi planned for 2013. Off site: Riding, golf and bicycle hire within 2 km. Fishing, sailing and boat slipway 500 m.

Open: All year.

Directions

Leave N84 road at Ballinrobe to join R334/345 signed Cong. Turn left at end of the R345 (opposite entrance to Ashford Castle), slow down take next road on right (about 300 m) and the park is on right (200 m). GPS: 53.53945, -9.27263

Charges guide

Per unit incl. 2 persons
and electricity   € 20.00 - € 25.00

Camping Cheques accepted.

Corofin

Corofin Village Camping & Caravan Park

Main Street, Corofin (Co. Clare) T: 065 683 7683. E: info@corofin.camping.com

alanrogers.com/IR9460

This compact green oasis in the centre of the village of Corofin occupies one acre and adjoins the family's hostel. The owners, Jude and Marie Neylon, live on the site and have a policy of always having a family member on hand at all times. They are very environmentally aware and have excellent recycling facilities. The 16 touring pitches all have electricity and there are ample water points. The site now includes a small separate tent area which is quite private and well sheltered. A campers' kitchen, laundry room and the TV and games room are separate to the hostel facilities. This little site is neat and well maintained and makes an ideal base for sightseeing throughout Clare. It is a peaceful location, yet central for the restaurants, takeaway, shops and pubs in the village.

Facilities

The sanitary block is bright and clean with free hot showers. Separate facilities for disabled campers. Laundry room with washing machine and dryer. Campers' kitchen. TV and games room. CCTV security. Free WiFi. Torches useful. Site is not suitable for large units. Off site: Fishing and boat launching 2 km. Riding 8 km. Bicycle hire 10 km. Golf 20 km. Beach 20 km.

Open: 1 April - 30 September.

Directions

Corofin village is 12 km. from Ennis, from where you take the N85 towards Ennistymon and after 2 km. (well signed) turn right onto R476. Site is in the centre of the village. GPS: 52.9407, -9.058933

Charges guide

Per unit incl. 2 persons and electricity	€ 25.00
extra person	€ 5.00
child	€ 3.00

No credit cards.

FREE Alan Rogers Travel Card
Extra benefits and savings - see page 10

Donard

Moat Farm Caravan & Camping Park

Donard (Co. Wicklow) T: 045 404 727. E: moatfarm@ireland.com

alanrogers.com/IR9160

Providing a true feel of the countryside, this park is part of a working sheep farm. It offers incredible vistas across a scenic landscape, yet is within driving distance of Dublin and Rosslare. Driving into the village of Donard you little suspect that alongside the main street lies a pleasant, well cared for and tranquil five acre campsite. The entrance is approached by way of a short road where the ruins of a medieval church sit high overlooking the forecourt and reception. There are 40 pitches for caravans and tents. Spacious pitches with hardstanding line both sides of a broad avenue, incorporating ample space for awnings and all with electricity and drainage. A large field takes tents and further caravans. Those with larger units are advised to contact the site to check accessibility.

Facilities

The toilet block is kept very clean and includes spacious showers. Facilities for visitors with disabilities. Well equipped laundry room. Good quality campers' kitchen. Large recreation/entertainment room with open fire. Three large barbecues and patio area. Caravan storage. Off site: Mountain climbing and sites of archaeological interest nearby. Fishing 3 km. Golf and riding 13 km. Bicycle hire 15 km.

Open: 17 March - 14 September.

Directions

Park is 16.5 km. south of Blessington. Leave the M50 Dublin ring motorway at exit 10 to join N81 southwest for 19 km. to Blessington. Continue on N81 for a further 16.5 km. and turn left at Old Toll House pub onto local road and follow signs to park in Donard village (3.5 km). GPS: 53.0212, -6.61562

Charges 2013

Per unit incl. 2 persons and electricity	€ 23.00
extra person	€ 5.00
child	€ 3.00
motorcyclist, cyclist or hiker incl. tent	€ 10.00

No credit cards.

Doolin

Nagle's Doolin Camping & Caravan Park

Doolin (Co. Clare) T: 065 707 4458. E: ken@doolincamping.com

alanrogers.com/IR9465

This neat and tidy seaside site is located just one kilometre from the cliffs of Moher, and a short ferry ride from the sparsely populated Aran Islands. The nearby village of Doolin, famed for its traditional music, has a good range of shops, restaurants and pubs. The four-hectare site, which has spectacular views over the bay to Conemara, has 99 pitches, including 76 level hardstandings (with 10A electricity, water and drainage) and grass pitches for tents. They are not separated by hedges, but the site is divided into bays by limestone walls. There is excellent WiFi coverage over the whole site. Walkers and nature lovers will be in their element among the rare species of flowers and insects found in this limestone region known as the Burren. Doolin itself is home to a number of traditional pubs with lively, impromptu music sessions featuring musicians from Ireland and overseas. A complete contrast is offered by the many signposted coastal walks along the eight-kilometre headland, with its panoramic views towards the Aran Islands, just 20 minutes away by high speed ferry.

Facilities

One modern, well equipped toilet block is unheated but has good facilities including en-suite unit for disabled visitors. Laundry with 3 washers and 3 dryers (charged). Kitchen with cooking rings (charged), fridge/freezer and sinks with hot water. Shop (June-Aug). Motorcaravan service point. Gas. WiFi throughout. Off site: Pitch and putt, boat launching and ferry to Aran Islands all 300 m. Fishing, riding, bicycle hire, shops, hot food and bars within 1-2 km. Golf 10 km.

Open: Open from St Patrick's weekend to mid/end October (check with site).

Directions

From Limerick take N85 round Ennis to Ennistymon, then N67 towards Lisdoonvarna. After 11 km. turn left for Doolin and then Doolin Pier. Site signed. From Galway take N18 and then in 20 km. N67 to Lisdoonvarna and follow signs as above. GPS: 53.01677, -9.402

Charges guide

Per unit incl. 2 persons and electricity	€ 21.00 - € 23.00
extra person	€ 7.00
child	€ 3.00

DOOLIN CAMPING
NAGLE'S CAMPING & CARAVAN PARK
Situated on the verge of the Atlantic between the Cliffs of Moher and the Burren.
The site is only 100m from Doolin Pier, ferry port to the Aran Islands
Tel. +353 (0)65 707 4458 | www.doolincamping.com | ken@doolincamping.com

Dungarvan
Casey's Caravan & Camping Park
Clonea, Dungarvan (Co. Waterford) T: 058 419 19

alanrogers.com/IR9330

This is a very large park by Irish standards. Set on 20 acres of flat grass, edged by mature trees, this family run park is well managed and offers 284 pitches which include 110 touring pitches all with electrical hook-ups and 60 with hardstanding. There is even a large, open and flat field without services for high season overspill arrivals. The remainder are occupied by caravan holiday homes. There is direct access from the park to a sandy, Blue Flag beach with a resident lifeguard during July and August. A highly recommended leisure centre is adjacent should the weather be inclement. The park is 5.5 km. from Dungarvan, a popular town for deep sea angling, from where charter boats can be hired and three, 18-hole golf courses are within easy driving distance. Suggested drives include the scenic Vee, the Comeragh Mountain Drive and the coast road to Tramore – the last having a series of magical coves and the remains of old copper mines. The pretty 'English' village of Lismore and the picturesque and historic town of Youghal, once home to Sir Walter Raleigh, are each about 30 km. drive away.

Facilities

The central toilet block (key system), has good facilities kept spotlessly clean. Showers on payment (€ 1). Small laundry with washing machine and dryer. A further modern block provides an excellent campers' kitchen, laundry room and toilet for disabled visitors. Large adventure play area. Large, well equipped games room. TV lounge. Minigolf. Gas supplies. Full time security staff in high season. Tiny tots play area for those under 4 yrs. WiFi throughout (free). Off site: Two village stores near the beach. Hotel for food and drink. Golf 5 km. Fishing 4 km.

Open: 5 April - 9 September.

Directions

From Dungarvan centre follow R675 east for 3.5 km. Look for signs on the right to Clonea Bay and site. Site is 1.5 km. GPS: 52.094767, -7.546167

Charges guide

Per unit incl. 2 persons and electricity	€ 29.00 - € 33.00
extra person	€ 7.00 - € 8.00
child	€ 3.00
hiker, biker, cyclist	€ 10.00 - € 10.50

No credit cards.

Fermoy
Blackwater Valley Caravan & Camping Park
Mallow-Killarney Road, Fermoy (Co. Cork) T: 025 321 47. E: blackwatervalleycaravanpark@gmail.com

alanrogers.com/IR9470

The location of this park provides the best of both worlds, as it backs onto green fields adjacent to the Blackwater river, yet is within 200 metres of Fermoy town. Pat and Nora Ryan live overlooking the park which ensures supervision and prompt attention. Well situated for touring, there are 25 pitches, all with hardstanding and 13A electricity connections. Water taps are convenient to all pitches. Considerable additional space for tents is available towards the rear of the park. There are five caravan holiday homes to rent. Fermoy provides local amenities, such as a cinema, restaurants and pubs, many hosting traditional music. The town park has a leisure centre with pool, and a play area is 100 metres on foot.

Facilities

Modern, tiled toilet block provides the usual facilities including an en-suite shower room for disabled visitors. Laundry room. Campers' kitchen with cooking facilities and dining area. TV and games room. Motorcaravan service point. Off site: Fishing adjacent. Internet access 100 m. Bicycle hire 1 km. Golf 3.5 km. Beach 35 km.

Open: 15 March - 31 October.

Directions

In Fermoy town take N72 for Mallow. Park is 200 m. from the junction. GPS: 52.141498, -8.281873

Charges guide

Per unit incl. 2 persons and electricity	€ 24.00
extra person	€ 6.00
child	€ 3.00

No credit cards.

Galway

Salthill Caravan Park

Knocknacarra, Salthill, Galway (Co. Galway) T: 091 523 972. E: info@salthillcaravanpark.com

alanrogers.com/IR8870

Salthill Caravan Park was first opened in 1960, and has been run by the O'Malley family ever since. The park comprises five acres of mobile homes and a three-acre campsite, near to the water's edge. The park has superb views over Galway Bay, and has access to a shingle beach, just 100 m. distant. The 49 touring pitches are grassy and open, all with 10A electrical connections and 35 hardstanding. Adjacent to the site, there is a pleasant coastal pathway which leads to Galway City and sandy beaches (800 m). Off site, there is a friendly pub (200 m) and a well stocked, large supermarket (600 m). Salthill beach is actually several sandy Blue Flag beaches separated by rocky outcrops. Windsurfing, kayaking and paddle boarding are all popular, and courses are available nearby. The Galway Atlantiquaria is Ireland's premier aquarium, and boasts more than 170 species of fresh water and marine life. Galway City is renowned for its important Arts festival in July, when the city welcomes over 100,000 visitors for a varied programme of visual art, music, theatre and dance.

Facilities

One (unheated) toilet block in the middle of the touring pitches also contains a washing machine and dryer (5 euros each), sinks (hot water charged). Showers by reception (on payment). No facilities for disabled visitors. Limited grocery items in reception. New children's playground. Games room. Dogs are not accepted.
Off site: Watersports. Pub 200 m. Fishing, beach and golf 500 m. Supermarket 600 m. Bicycle hire 3 km. Riding 4 km.

Open: 1 April - 29 September.

Directions

The site is 1 mile west of Salthill. From the N6 (bypassing Galway City) follow signs to Clifden, R338 to its junction with R337 at traffic lights. Turn right and follow R337 (large supermarket on right) to its junction with R336, turn left (south) and site is 200 m. on left. GPS: 53.256798, -9.104914

Charges guide

Per unit incl. 2 persons and electricity	€ 25.00 - € 30.00
extra person	€ 5.00
child	free - € 3.00
dog	free

Glandore

The Meadow Camping Park

Glandore (Co. Cork) T: 028 332 80. E: meadowcamping@eircom.net

alanrogers.com/IR9500

The stretch of coast from Cork to Skibbereen reminds British visitors of Devon before the era of mass tourism. This is rich dairy country, the green of the meadows matching the emerald colours of the travel posters. Thanks to the warm and wet Gulf Stream climate, it is also a county of gardens and keen gardeners. The Meadow is best described not as a site but as a one-acre garden surrounded, appropriately, by lush meadows. The owners, who live on the park, have cleverly arranged room for 19 pitches, 14 with 6A electric hook-ups (12 Europlug), among the flower beds and shrubberies of their garden. There are 12 hardstandings. Among the homely features are a campers' kitchen and dining area.

Facilities

Facilities are limited but well designed and maintained with brand new solar panels. Showers on payment. Washing machine and dryer. Larger units may be accepted depending on length and available space; contact park before arrival. Football and cycling are not permitted on the park. WiFi (charged). Off site: Fishing, swimming, boat launching and sailing at Glandore 2 km. Riding 5 km. Bicycle hire 10 km. Golf 19 km.

Open: Easter - 15 September.

Directions

Park is 1.5 km. east of Glandore, off N71 road, on R597 midway between Leap and Rosscarbery (coast road). Approach roads are very narrow. GPS: 51.56693, -9.09702

Charges guide

Per unit incl. 2 persons and electricity	€ 23.00
extra person	€ 6.00
child (under 16 yrs)	€ 3.00
No credit cards.	

Glenbeigh
Glenross Caravan & Camping Park
Ring of Kerry, Glenbeigh (Co. Kerry) T: 087 137 6865. E: glenross@eircom.net
alanrogers.com/IR9600

Its situation on the spectacular Ring of Kerry and the Kerry Way footpath gives Glenross an immediate advantage, and scenic grandeur around every bend of the road is guaranteed as Glenbeigh is approached. Quietly located before entering the village, the park commands stunning views of Rossbeigh Strand, (within walking distance) and the Dingle Peninsula. On arrival, a good impression is created with the park being well screened from the road, with a new stone entrance and gates. With 30 touring pitches, 27 with hardstanding and all with 10A electricity (Europlug), and six caravan holiday homes, the park is attractively laid out. Dedicated small tent area.

Facilities	Directions
Well maintained modern toilet block includes facilities for laundry. Motorcaravan service point. Shelter for campers and new dining area. Bar, restaurant and takeaway (all season). Games room. Bicycle hire. Free WiFi over site. Off site: Playground at Blue Flag Rossbeigh beach (5 minutes). Watersports and tennis nearby. Riding and fishing 200 m.	Park is on the N70 Killorglin-Glenbeigh road, on the right just before entering the village. GPS: 52.05887, -9.93198

Open: 6 April - 24 September.

Charges guide

Per unit incl. 2 persons and electricity	€ 29.00 - € 30.00
extra person	€ 8.00

No credit cards.

Keel
Keel Sandybanks Caravan & Camping Park
Keel, Achill Island (Co. Mayo) T: 098 432 11. E: info@achillcamping.com
alanrogers.com/IR8730

This is a park offering a taste of island life and the opportunity to relax in dramatic, scenic surroundings. Achill, Ireland's largest island, is 24 km. long and 19 km. wide and is connected to the mainland by a bridge. The wide open site is situated beside the Blue Flag beach near Keel village. Although there are static holiday mobile homes on this site, the 84 touring pitches are kept separate. There are 50 pitches with hardstanding and some are located at the perimeter fence overlooking the beach. Although sand based, the ground is firm and level. There is direct access to the beach which is supervised by lifeguards.

Facilities	Directions
Two modern, heated toilet blocks, one at the entrance gate beside reception and the other in a central position. Facilities include WCs, washbasins and hot showers (on payment). Hairdryers. Laundry. En-suite facilities for disabled visitors at reception block. Play area. TV/games room. Watersports on Keel Strand and Lough. Fishing trips. WiFi over site (charged). Off site: Village with a food shop, takeaway, restaurants and music in the pubs.	From Achill Sound follow the R319 for 13 km. Site is on the left before Keel village. GPS: 53.97535, -10.0779

Open: Easter - mid September.

Charges guide

Per unit incl. 2 persons and electricity	€ 18.00 - € 21.00
child	€ 2.00
extra person	€ 3.00

Killarney
Donoghues White Villa Farm Caravan & Camping Park
Lissivigeen, Killarney-Cork Road N22, Killarney (Co. Kerry) T: 064 662 0671. E: killarneycamping@eircom.net
alanrogers.com/IR9630

This is a very pleasing, small touring park, surrounded by green fields, yet only five minutes away from Killarney town. There are many trees and shrubs around the park, but dominant is a magnificent view of the MacGillicuddy's Reeks. There are 30 pitches for caravans and tents, 20 with hardstanding and a grass area for awnings, electricity (10A Europlug), water points and night lighting. One pitch is designated for disabled campers with a specially adapted en-suite facility. Unusually, old school desks are placed in pairs around the site as picnic tables, plus an antique green telephone box.

Facilities	Directions
The sandstone coloured toilet block is kept spotlessly clean and houses showers (€ 1), a good toilet/shower room for disabled visitors (key access). Laundry room. Motorcaravan service area. Campers' kitchen with TV. Play area. Max. 2 dogs (not certain breeds). Daily coach tours from park. WiFi over site (free). Off site: Pub with restaurant 1 km. Bicycle hire 3 km. Riding and golf 4 km. Killarney town 5 mins. away, and National Park 10 mins.	From Killarney take N22 Cork road, through Park Road roundabout, pass Supervalu and downhill. Continue on N22 up hill to N22/N72 roundabout. Park is 200 m. further. GPS: 52.04724, -9.45358

Open: 6 May - 30 September.

Charges guide

Per unit incl. 2 persons and electricity	€ 22.00 - € 23.00
extra person	€ 6.00

No credit cards.

FREE Alan Rogers Travel Card
Extra benefits and savings - see page 10

Killarney

Fleming's White Bridge

Ballycasheen Road, Killarney (Co. Kerry) T: 064 663 1590. E: info@killarneycamping.com

alanrogers.com/IR9620

The main road from Cork to Killarney (N22) runs through the gentle valley of the River Flesk. Between the two sits Fleming's White Bridge camping park. Its ten-hectare site is within comfortable walking distance of Killarney centre. Surrounded by mature, broad-leafed trees, the park is flat, landscaped and generously adorned with flowers and shrubs. It comprises 92 pitches, the majority for touring caravans, on well kept grass pitches with electricity hook-ups, although some have concrete hardstanding and some pitches are reserved for tents.

Facilities

Three toilet blocks are of a high standard. Motorcaravan service point. Campers' drying room and two laundries. Small shop (1/6-1/9). Two TV rooms and a games room. Fishing (advice and permits provided). Canoeing (own canoes). Bicycle hire. Woodland walks. Off site: Swimming pool and Leisure Centre 0.5 km. Kayaking 1.5 km. Golf 2 km. Riding and Killarney National Park 3 km.

Open: 15 March - 29 October.

Directions

From Cork and Mallow: at N72/N22 junction continue towards Killarney and take first turn left (Ballycasheen Road). Proceed for 300 m. to archway entrance on left. GPS: 52.05595, -9.47458

Charges guide

Per unit incl. 2 persons and electricity	€ 30.00
extra person	€ 8.00
child	€ 3.00
No credit cards.	

Killarney

Fossa Caravan & Camping Park

Fossa, Killarney (Co. Kerry) T: 064 663 1497. E: fossaholidays@eircom.net

alanrogers.com/IR9590

This park is in the village of Fossa, ten minutes by car or bus (six per day) from Killarney town centre. Fossa Caravan Park has a distinctive reception building and hostel accommodation, a stimulating play area and shop. The park is divided in two – the touring caravan area lies to the right, tucked behind the main building and to the left is an open grass area mainly for campers. Touring pitches, with 10/15A electricity and drainage, have hardstanding and are angled between shrubs and trees in a garden setting. To the rear at a higher level and discreetly placed are 30 caravan holiday homes, sheltered by the thick foliage of the wooded slopes which climb high behind the park.

Facilities

Modern toilet facilities include showers on payment. En-suite unit for campers with disabilities. Laundry room. Campers' kitchen. Shop. Takeaway (8/7-25/8). TV lounge. Tennis. Play area. Picnic area. Games room. Security patrol. Off site: Fishing and golf 3 km. Bicycle hire 5 km. Woodland walk into Killarney. A visit to Killarney National Park is highly recommended.

Open: 1 April - 30 September.

Directions

Approaching Killarney from all directions, follow signs for N72 Ring of Kerry/Killorglin. At last roundabout join R562/N72. Continue for 5.5 km. and Fossa is second park to right. GPS: 52.07071, -9.58573

Charges guide

Per unit incl. 2 persons and electricity	€ 22.00 - € 26.00
extra person	€ 6.00
hiker/cyclist incl. tent	€ 8.00 - € 9.00

Killarney

Killarney Flesk Caravan & Camping Park

Muckross Road, Killarney (Co. Kerry) T: 064 663 1704. E: killarneylakes@eircom.net

alanrogers.com/IR9640

At the gateway to the National Park and Lakes, near Killarney town, this family run, seven-acre park has undergone extensive development and offers high quality standards. Pitches vary in size and spacing and have 10A electricity. Many pitches have a good grass area for awnings, and 11 also have dedicated electricity, water and drainage. The grounds are neat and tidy with a feeling of space. The toilet block is central to most pitches and camp security appears to be tight. This site would appeal to young people wanting to be close to the action in Killarney.

Facilities

Modern, clean toilet blocks are well equipped. Baby room. En-suite facility for disabled campers (key operated). Laundry room. Campers' kitchen. Games room. Night time security checks. Winter caravan storage. Off site: Adjacent hotel (same ownership) with bar and restaurant. Fishing 300 m. Boat launching 2 km.

Open: 17 April - 30 September.

Directions

From Killarney follow the N71 and signs for Killarney National Park. Site is 1.5 km. on the left beside the Victoria House Hotel. GPS: 52.04304, -9.49954

Charges guide

Per unit incl. 2 persons and electricity	€ 29.00 - € 30.00
extra person	€ 8.50
child (under 14 yrs)	€ 3.00

Kilmacanogue
Valley Stopover & Caravan Park
Killough, Kilmacanogue (Co. Wicklow) T: 012 829 565. E: rowanbb@eircom.net
alanrogers.com/IR9140

In a quiet, idyllic setting in the picturesque Rocky Valley, this small, neat, family run park is convenient for the Dublin ferries. Situated in the grounds of the family home, covering under an acre, it can be used either as a transit site or for a longer stay. It will appeal to those who prefer the small, certificated type of site. There are grassy pitches, eight hardstandings and a total of ten electric hook-ups, a separate area for three tents, two water points, night lighting and a security gate. Staying here, you are only minutes from Enniskerry which lies in the glen of the Glencullen river. You can enjoy a delight of forest walks, or visit Powerscourt, one of the loveliest gardens in Ireland, as well as the nearby Powerscourt waterfall. To reach the sea, travel 6 km. to Bray, one of the oldest seaside resorts in the country.

Facilities

Sanitary facilities, clean when we visited, are housed in one very small unit and consist of two WCs with washbasins, mirrors, etc. and a shower (free). Laundry sink, spin dryer. Campers' kitchen. Full cooked Irish breakfast in the family house. Off site: Riding 3 km. Golf 7 km. Fishing 16 km.

Open: Easter - 31 October.

Directions

Turn off N11 Dublin-Wexford road at Kilmacanogue, following signs for Glendalough. Continue for 1.6 km. and take right fork signed Waterfall. Park is second opening on the left in 200 m. Narrow entrance off road requires care. GPS: 53.1671, -6.1634

Charges guide

Per unit incl. 2 persons and electricity	€ 20.00
extra person	€ 1.25

Knock
Knock Caravan & Camping Park
Main Street, Knock (Co. Mayo) T: 094 9388100. E: caravanpark@knock-shrine.ie
alanrogers.com/IR8780

This park is in a sheltered, landscaped area immediately south of the world famous Shrine that receives many visitors. Comfortable and clean, the park has neatly trimmed lawns with tarmac roads and surrounded by clipped trees. The 70 touring pitches are of average size on hardstanding and 52 have 15A electrical connections. There is also an overflow field. Because of the religious connections of the area, the site is very busy in August and there are unlikely to be any vacancies at all for 14-16 August. Besides visiting the Shrine and Knock Museum, it is also a good centre for exploring County Mayo.

Facilities

Two heated toilet blocks have good facilities for disabled visitors and a nice sized rest room attached, hot showers and adequate washing and toilet facilities. Laundry room. Gas supplies. TV rooms. Playground. Free WiFi over site. Off site: Adjacent Shrine and Basilica with a restaurant in the grounds. Fishing 5 km. Golf and riding 11 km.

Open: 1 March - 31 October.

Directions

Exit from the N17 at the Knock bypass and from the roundabout follow signs to the site which is just south of the village. GPS: 53.79391, -8.91387

Charges guide

Per unit incl. 2 persons and electricity	€ 23.00 - € 25.00
extra person	€ 2.00 - € 2.50
child	€ 1.00

No credit cards.

FREE Alan Rogers Travel Card
Extra benefits and savings - see page 10

Lauragh
Creveen Lodge Caravan & Camping Park
Healy Pass, Lauragh (Co. Kerry) T: 064 668 3131. E: info@creveenlodge.com
alanrogers.com/IR9570

The Healy Pass is the well known scenic summit of the R574 road that crosses the Beara Peninsula, shortening the original journey from Kenmare Bay in the north to Bantry Bay in the south by nearly 70 km. As this narrow coast road starts to climb steeply, on the mountain foothills you will arrive at Creveen Lodge, a working hill farm with a quiet, homely atmosphere. The park provides 20 attractive pitches, 16 with 10A electricity and an area of hardstanding for motorcaravans. To allow easy access, the steep farm track is divided into a simple one-way system. Creveen Lodge, commanding views across Kenmare Bay, is divided among three gently sloping fields separated by trees. The park is carefully tended with neat rubbish bins and rustic picnic tables informally placed. Although not so famed as the Iveragh Peninsula, around which runs the Ring of Kerry, the northern Beara is a scenically striking area of County Kerry. This is walking and climbing countryside and nearby is Derreen Gardens.

Facilities

Well appointed and maintained, the small toilet block provides token operated showers (€ 1). Communal room with cooking facilities, a fridge, freezer, TV, ironing board, fireplace, tables and chairs. Reception is in the farmhouse. Play area. Off site: Water sports, riding, 'Seafare' cruises, shops and a restaurant nearby. Fishing 2 km. Bicycle hire and boat launching 9 km.

Open: Easter - 31 October.

Directions

Park is on the Healy Pass road (R574) 1.5 km. southeast of Lauragh. GPS: 51.75562, -9.76193

Charges guide

Per unit incl. 2 persons and electricity	€ 22.00
extra person	€ 3.00
child	€ 1.00

No credit cards.

Mountshannon
Lakeside Holiday Park
R352, Mountshannon (Co. Clare) T: 061 927225. E: lakesidecamping@gmail.com
alanrogers.com/IR9464

This woodland park is set by the shore of beautiful Lough Derg and is a twenty minute stroll from the village of Mountshannon. This is a site for those who like to camp close in a natural setting. The 45 touring pitches, all with 8A electricity, are set by the water's edge and also in a separate area in the woods, close to the facilities buildings and reception. Caravan holiday homes and timber camping lodges and huts are mostly tucked away in the woodland. Although the pitches are small and close together, the site has large, open spaces for games and sports. It has two little harbours and kayaks, rowing boats and motorboats may be rented on an hourly or daily basis at one of these. Wildlife and birds are everywhere and you may get a glimpse of a sea eagle or of Rusty, one of the resident red squirrels.

Facilities

Spacious preset showers (€ 1) are in one of a cluster of small, unheated facility buildings, which also include the toilets, laundry and dishwashing; these are clean but basic. Disabled visitors' toilet (key at reception). Campers' kitchen and TV/lounge area. Large games field. Tennis court. Boat hire. Fishing. Birdwatching. Dogs are not accepted in July/August. Some site lighting but torch advised. Reservations essential and photo ID required. Off site: The village of Mountshannon (within 2 km) has a newsagent, grocery and deli, a café/restaurant and pubs with live music on some evenings.

Open: 1 May - 1 October.

Directions

Site signed off R352 Scarriff-Portumna road just northeast of Mountshannon village. Note: this road is very narrow with only a few passing places. GPS: 52.92775, -8.42061

Charges guide

Per unit incl. 2 persons and electricity		€ 20.00 - € 23.00
extra person		€ 5.00
child		€ 3.00
dog (not July/Aug)		free

For latest campsite news visit
alanrogers.com

Mullingar
Lough Ennell Camping & Caravan Park
Tudenham Shore, Mullingar (Co. Westmeath) T: 044 934 8101. E: eamon@caravanparksireland.com
alanrogers.com/IR8965

Natural, rustic charm is the visitor's first impression on arrival at Lough Ennell Caravan Park. Set in 18 acres of mature woodland beside a Blue Flag lake, Eamon and Geraldine O'Malley run this sheltered and tranquil park with their family, who live on the site. They receive a blend of visitors – seasonal residents in camping holiday homes (private and to rent), caravanners and motorcaravanners and there are ample areas for tents. Pitches are varied, sheltered with trees and natural shrubbery, and with gravel or gravel and grass combinations. There are 44 touring pitches with electricity (7A Europlug) available on 25 hardstanding and grass pitches, with water points on or nearby all pitches; there are also 80 tent pitches. The site is a paradise for fishermen, with brown trout, rainbow trout, pike, tench, roach, perch, rudd and bream available. There is also one lake stocked with carp. Just an hour from Dublin, it provides a good holiday base or a useful stopover en-route to the West of Ireland. The watersports permitted on the lake include canoeing, sailing, windsurfing, boating, water skiing, fishing and safe swimming. The woodlands offer ample opportunities for walking and cycling. The site has several other lakes within a 10 to 15 minute drive. Some are coarse fishing only, while others are stocked lakes with multiple varieties of fish. Other activities might include tennis, riding, golf, dog racing and, of course, forest walks. Belvedere House and Tullynally Castle are nearby and the large town of Mullingar, known as the capital of the lake lands, is just 6 km.

Facilities

The toilet block provides toilets, washbasins and hot showers (€1 coin). Additional dishwashing areas are around the park. Laundry. Small shop (all season). Café and coffee shop with takeaway. TV and games room. Play areas and area for ball games. Small lakeside beach. Fishing. Late arrivals area outside. Security including CCTV. Some breeds of dog are not accepted. Off site: Golf 1.5 km. Riding 4 km. Bicycle hire 6 km. Bus service 8 km. Boat hire on Lough Ennell and other lakes.

Open: Easter/1 April - 30 September.

Directions

From N4 take the N52. Follow signs for Belvedere House and take turn 300 m. south of Belvedere House (signed for site). Continue to the shores of Lough Ennell and turn left. If in difficulty, telephone the site. GPS: 53.466111, -7.375278

Charges guide

Per unit incl. 2 persons and electricity	€ 23.00 - € 25.00
extra person	€ 5.00
child	€ 3.00
No credit cards.	

Portlaoise
Laois Caravan and Camping
Clondouglas, Mountrath Road, Portlaoise (Co. Laois) T: 086 339 0867. E: ti.brenn1@gmail.com
alanrogers.com/IR9040

Opened in 2011 and set on a family run farm, this small site is conveniently situated for the Dublin to Limerick M7 motorway. It is less than 15 km. from the Slieve Bloom mountains, a Mecca for walkers, and 6 km. from the centre of Portlaoise. There are seven touring pitches with hardstanding, 16A electricity and water set to one edge of a camping field. Children can enjoy farm animals such as sheep, goats, chickens and pigs, and perhaps help feed lambs, and find eggs (even chocolate ones at Easter). There is some distant noise from the motorway, and mainline trains pass behind the farm. It would make a good stopover between Dublin and Cork or Limerick.

Facilities

A new timber-clad toilet block is tiled and heated, and has three family rooms with WC and shower. One also has a bath and is equipped for disabled visitors. Laundry room. Kitchen/lounge with cooking and dishwashing facilities, satellite TV, extensive library, comfortable seating and table tennis. Motorcaravan service point. Off site: Karting and angling 14 km. Horse-drawn caravans, guided walking tours 25 km.

Open: March - September.

Directions

From motorway M7 take exit 18 head southwest on R445 (signed Castletown-Mountrath). Site is on left in 1.5 km. GPS: 53.0082, -7.372083

Charges guide

Per unit incl. 2 persons and electricity	€ 24.00
extra person	€ 10.00
child (3rd free)	€ 3.00

FREE Alan Rogers Travel Card
Extra benefits and savings - see page 10

Rathdrum

Hidden Valley Caravan & Camping Park

Rathdrum (Co. Wicklow) T: 086 727 2872. E: info@irelandholidaypark.com

alanrogers.com/IR9155

This pleasant, level park occupies over seven hectares on both banks of the pretty Avonmore River near the small town of Rathdrum. It has 100 pitches arranged around a boating pond. The pitches are mostly concrete hardstandings with a few on grass. All have safe 16A electricity hook-ups and close access to a water tap and waste drainage. Across a fine footbridge is a large, flat area for tents – most of them used by families at holiday time. Spring 2010 saw major landscaping work on what must now be regarded as one of the best camping park play areas in Ireland.

Facilities

Well equipped, very modern toilet block finished in local slate. Facilities for visitors with disabilities. Motorcaravan service point. Laundry. Hobs for cooking. Small shop. Takeaway. Fishing in the river may be arranged. Play park. Canoes and boats for hire on lake. Bicycle hire. Log cabins for rent. Dogs must be kept on a lead. WiFi. Off site: Golf and riding within 5 miles. Beach within 15 miles. The pretty town of Avoca (TV's Ballykissangel) and Powerscourt House and Waterfall within easy reach.

Open: 1 April - 30 September.

Directions

Leave M11 at exit signed Rathnew. From this village follow signs for Rathdrum (c.15 mins). Over bridge approaching Rathdrum turn right immediately at large new apartment building. Park gate is on right. GPS: 52.938693, -6.22898

Charges guide

Per unit incl. 2 persons and electricity	€ 26.00 - € 28.00
extra person	€ 6.00

Redcross Village

River Valley Caravan & Camping Park

Redcross Village (Co. Wicklow) T: 040 441 647. E: info@rivervalleypark.ie

alanrogers.com/IR9150

In the small country village of Redcross, in the heart of County Wicklow, you will find this first rate, family run park. Based here you are within easy reach of beauty spots such as the Vale of Avoca (Ballykissangel), Glendalough and Powerscourt, plus the safe beach of Brittas Bay. The 160 touring pitches are divided into separate, well landscaped areas with an adults only section. All have 6/10A electricity connections and offer a choice of hardstanding or grass – you select your pitch. A late arrivals area has electricity hook-ups, water and night lighting.

Facilities

All sanitary blocks are of the highest quality, modern and well designed. Excellent facilities for disabled visitors. Showers are on payment (€ 1 token). Laundry area. Campers' kitchen. Motorcaravan service points. Gas supplies. Inn and restaurant. TV and games room. Tennis courts. Par 3 golf course. Beer garden with entertainment for children (July/Aug). Sports complex. Playgrounds. WiFi (free). New archery range and mini wildlife walk for 2013.

Open: Mid March - end October.

Directions

From Dublin follow N11 Wexford road south, bypassing Ashford and Rathnew. After The Beehive pub look out for Doyle's pub on right. Turn right at pub and continue for 5 km. to park at top of Redcross village. GPS: 52.8884, -6.14528

Charges guide

Per unit incl. 2 persons and electricity	€ 25.00 - € 27.00
extra person	€ 6.00

Roscrea

Streamstown Caravan & Camping Park

Streamstown, Roscrea (Co. Tipperary) T: 050 521 519. E: streamstowncaravanpark@eircom.net

alanrogers.com/IR9420

This family run site, set on a dairy farm in the centre of Ireland, has been open for over 40 years. It is conveniently situated off the M7 Dublin-Limerick road and makes a good overnight halt or for a longer stay if you are seeking a quiet, restful location with little to disturb the peace. There are 27 touring pitches, ten with hardstanding and separated by low hedges. The remainder are on grass and more suitable for units with awnings. This is a working farm and the owners, who are friendly and welcoming, have made some attractive improvements. Roscrea town provides all services.

Facilities

The sanitary facilities, very clean when we visited, are housed in a modern block. Showers (free), toilets and washbasins (two washbasins are in cubicles). Facilities for disabled visitors in family shower room. Good laundry room. Good campers' kitchen with fridge/freezer, electric cooker and TV. Small play area. TV, pool table and games room. Caravan storage. Accommodation to rent. A torch would be useful. Off site: Fishing 1.5 km. Golf 5 km.

Open: Easter - 1 October, (other times by arrangement).

Directions

Leave M7 at Roscrea exit. From Roscrea follow signs for R491 Shinrone. Continue towards Shinrone following site signs for 2.5 km. and site entrance is on left. GPS: 52.95720, -7.83937

Charges guide

Per unit incl. 2 persons and electricity	€ 24.00
extra person	€ 4.50

For latest campsite news visit
alanrogers.com

Rosses Point

Greenlands Caravan & Camping Park

Rosses Point (Co. Sligo) T: 071 917 7113. E: noelineha@eircom.net

alanrogers.com/IR8690

Just off the N15 road and 8 km. west of Sligo town, this is a well run park at Rosses Point, in the sand hills adjoining a championship golf course. The 120 pitches (100 for touring units, all with 10A electricity) are thoughtfully laid out with small tents placed to the front of reception and the hardstanding touring pitches separated from the trailer tent pitches which occupy the rear. The ground is undulating and adds interest to the overall appearance. Your view depends on where you are pitched – look towards Coney Island and the Blackrock lighthouse which guards the bay, take in the sight of Benbulben Mountain or appreciate the seascape and the water lapping the resort's two bathing beaches.

Facilities	Directions
Modern toilet facilities are kept exceptionally clean, with hot showers (€ 1 token). Washing machine, dryer and iron. Motorcaravan service point. Campers' kitchen. Information point and TV room by reception. Play area and sand pit for children. Outdoor chess and draughts. Internet in reception. Night security. Off site: Golf 50 m. Shop, restaurant and evening entertainment in village.	From Sligo city travel 800 m. north on N15 road, turn left onto R291 signed Rosses Point. Continue for 6.5 km. and park is on right after village. GPS: 54.30628, -8.56889

Open: Easter - 14 September.

Charges guide

Per unit incl. 2 persons and electricity	€ 24.00 - € 26.00
extra person	€ 5.00

Rosslare

Saint Margaret's Beach Caravan & Camping Park

Lady's Island, Rosslare Harbour (Co. Wexford) T: 053 913 1169. E: info@campingstmargarets.ie

alanrogers.com/IR9170

'This park is loved', was how a Swedish visitor described this family-run, environmentally-friendly caravan and camping park, the first the visitor meets near the Rosslare ferry port. Landscaping with flowering containers and maze-like sheltered camping areas and a pretty sanitary block all demonstrate the Traynor family's attention to detail. The 27 touring pitches all have 6/10A electricity, are sheltered from the fresh sea breeze and ferries can be seen crossing the Irish sea. Just metres away, the safe, sandy beach (part of the Wexford coastal path) curves around in a horseshoe shape ending in a small pier and slipway. Tourist information on the area is provided in the well stocked shop.

Facilities	Directions
The toilet block is spotless. Laundry room. Campers' kitchen including toaster, microwave and TV. Shop (June-Aug). Fresh milk and bread daily. Mobile homes for rent. Sun/TV room. Free WiFi over site. Courtesy bicycles. Off site: Walking, beach and fishing. Boat slipway 2.5 km. Pitch and putt 2 km. Riding 6 km. Pubs and restaurants. The JFK Arboretum, Johnstown Castle and Gardens, the Irish National Heritage Park, Kilmore Quay and Marina.	From the N25 south of Wexford town, outside village of Tagoat, follow signs for Lady's Island and Carne. After 3 km. pass Butler's Bar and take next left and continue for 2.5 km. Site is well signed. GPS: 52.206433, -6.356417

Open: Mid March - 31 October.

Charges guide

Per unit incl. 2 persons and electricity	€ 20.00 - € 24.00
extra person	€ 2.50

Roundwood

Roundwood Caravan & Camping Park

Roundwood (Co. Wicklow) T: 012 818 163. E: info@dublinwicklowcamping.com

alanrogers.com/IR9130

In the heart of the Wicklow mountains, the hospitable owner of this park maintains high standards. It is neatly laid out with rows of trees dividing the different areas and giving an attractive appearance. There are 44 hardstanding pitches for caravans and motorcaravans, some sloping, all with 6A electricity, plus 33 pitches for tents, arranged off tarmac access roads. There are excellent walks around the Varty Lakes and a bus service to Dublin city. Nearby are the Wicklow Mountains and the Sally Gap, Glendalough, Powerscourt Gardens and many other places of natural beauty. This site is well placed for the ferry ports.

Facilities	Directions
The sanitary block is kept clean, with adequate washing and toilet facilities, plus spacious showers (€ 1). Good laundry facilities, but machines are not self-service. Motorcaravan service point. Campers' kitchen and dining room. TV room. Adventure playground. WiFi (charged). Bicycle hire. Off site: Village has shops, pubs, restaurants, takeaway food, and a Sunday market. Fishing within 1 km.	Turn off N11 Dublin-Wexford road at Kilmacanogue towards Glendalough, then 15 km. to Roundwood. Park is north side of village. GPS: 53.06924, -6.22269

Open: End of April - 31 August.

Charges guide

Per unit incl. 2 persons and electricity	€ 28.00 - € 30.00
extra person	€ 8.00 - € 9.00

No credit cards.

FREE Alan Rogers Travel Card
Extra benefits and savings - see page 10

Skibbereen
The Hideaway Camping & Caravan Park
Skibbereen (Co. Cork) T: 028 222 54. E: skibbereencamping@eircom.net
alanrogers.com/IR9505

A sister park to The Meadow at Glandore, the Hideaway is ideally situated as a touring base for the West Cork region. It is a well run site under the constant supervision of the owners and although it enjoys tranquil surroundings, including preserved marshland, it is only ten minutes walk from the busy market town of Skibbereen. The Hideaway is a two-hectare, touring only park with 60 pitches, including 50 with hardstanding and 6A electric hook-up. The remainder are for tents. Shrubs and low hedges divide the park giving an open feel overall and commanding views across the fields and hills. One long building houses reception, the toilet facilities and a games room.

Facilities

The modern toilet block has non-slip floors, well equipped showers (on payment). Baby room with bath. En-suite unit for disabled visitors. Laundry. Campers' dining room. Motorcaravan service point. Adventure play area. WiFi (charged). Football and cycling not permitted on the park. WiFi (charged). Off site: Bicycle hire 1 km. Fishing 1.6 km. Golf 2 km. Riding 4 km.

Open: Easter - 15 September.

Directions

From Skibbereen town centre take R596 (signed Casteltownsend). Site is on the left after 1 km. GPS: 51.54167, -9.26008

Charges guide

Per unit incl. 2 persons and electricity	€ 23.00
extra person	€ 6.00
child (under 16 yrs)	€ 3.00

No credit cards.

Strandhill
Strandhill Caravan & Camping Park
Strandhill (Co. Sligo) T: 071 916 8111. E: strandhillcvp@eircom.net
alanrogers.com/IR8695

This seaside park is located on 20 acres of undulating grass on a sandy base, with natural protection from the onshore breezes of the famous Strandhill beach. There are 55 hardstanding pitches for caravans and motorcaravans, with electricity and ample water points, and two camping areas for tents, one with views of the sea and the second more sheltered. Throughout the site many hollows provide ideal pitches for tents. Strandhill, world recognised as a surfing Mecca, also provides activities for all the family. There are miles of sandy beach and dunes, and the Knocknarea Mountain is popular for walking.

Facilities

The toilet block is clean and fresh with hot showers (token €1.50), hand dryers and hairdryer. New reception building includes TV room, games room, campers' kitchen, laundry and a well equipped facility for disabled visitors. WiFi over part of site (charged). Automatic gate and door control. Off site: Children's playground adjacent. Public transport from village. Shops, restaurants, takeaway, pubs and ATM just beyond the park's boundary in the village. Strandhill golf course 500 m. Bicycle hire within 1 km. Riding 2 km.

Open: Easter - 30 September.

Directions

Strandhill is 8 km. west of Sligo city on the R292. Site is on the airport road. GPS: 54.27242, -8.60448

Charges guide

Per unit incl. 2 persons	€ 20.00
plus 2 children	€ 22.00
electricity (10A)	€ 4.00
extra person	€ 3.00 - € 5.00

Timoleague
Sextons Caravan and Camping Park
R600 Timoleague/Clonakility Road, Bandon (Co. Cork) T: 023 884 6347. E: info.sextons@gmail.com
alanrogers.com/IR9490

Sexton's is an unpretentious site that has been in existence for over 40 years. At the time of writing, the owners were proud of their recently completed reception, allowing the old shop area to be converted into a comfortable lounge area for campers. They are also very confident that their plans to convert a part of the laundry into an en-suite facility for use by campers with disabilities will enhance their status. The 2.5-hectare park contains 50 pitches for touring vans and tents, 30 of these on gravel hardstanding and the remainder on well kept lawn grass.

Facilities

Two small toilet blocks with free showers are in old farm buildings. Small shop (1/5-30/9). Gas. Small but comfortable campers' kitchen with local TV. Sitting room for campers. Laundry. Internet and WiFi (charged). Small playground, football field and games room. Bicycle hire can be arranged. Off site: Beaches, riding, boat launching, fishing and golf, all within 6 km.

Open: 15 March - 30 September.

Directions

Take the N71 into Clonakilty, then follow the R600 towards Timoleague for 5 km. The site is on the right. Look for John Wayne statue guarding the entrance. GPS: 51.635006, -8.800821

Charges guide

Per unit incl. 2 persons and electricity	€ 23.00
extra person	€ 5.00

No credit cards.

For latest campsite news visit
alanrogers.com

Tipperary
Ballinacourty House Caravan & Camping Park

Glen of Aherlow, Tipperary (Co. Tipperary) T: 062 565 59. E: info@camping.ie

alanrogers.com/IR9370

Ballinacourty House and its cobble-stoned courtyard form the centrepiece of this south facing park with views of the Galtee Mountains. Accessed by a tree-lined lane, the reception area is in part of the renovated 18th-century building, as is the adjoining restaurant. The park is level with 26 touring pitches with 6A electricity and 19 grassy pitches for tents. Some areas are shaded and there are open spaces to accommodate rallies and larger groups. Self-catering cottages and B&B are also available. This tranquil site is very appealing to families with young children. It is an excellent base from which to tour the Rock of Cashel, the Mitchelstown Caves, Swiss Cottage and the towns of Tipperary, Cahir and Cashel. The management has recently begun to keep farm animals in an enclosed part of the park and intends to enhance the estate's entire old walled garden.

Facilities

Sanitary facilities provide free hot water and showers. Baby room. Laundry with ironing facilities. Campers' kitchen. Ice pack freezing. Licensed restaurant (early booking advised). Motorcaravan services. Gas supplies. Frisbee golf. TV and games rooms. Picnic benches. Tennis. Play area. Off site: Riding, fishing and golf.

Open: Easter - last Sunday in September.

Directions

Follow the N24 from Tipperary or Cahir to Bansha. Turn on to R663 for 11 km, passing Glen Hotel after 10 km. Follow signs for Ballinacourty House. GPS: 52.41614, -8.21047

Charges guide

Per unit incl. 2 persons	
and electricity	€ 24.00 - € 27.00
extra person	€ 5.00
child	€ 4.00

Tipperary
The Glen of Aherlow Caravan & Camping Park

Newtown, Glen of Aherlow (Co. Tipperary) T: 062 565 55. E: rdrew@eircom.net

alanrogers.com/IR9400

The owners of one of Ireland's newest parks, George and Rosaline Drew, are campers themselves and have set about creating an idyllic park in an idyllic location. This three-hectare park is set in one of Ireland's most picturesque valleys and is open all year. There are beautiful views of the wooded and hilly areas of Slievenamuck and the Galtee Mountains. There are 42 large and level touring pitches, with both hardstanding and grass places, each pair sharing a double hook-up 10A post and water point. The Drew family is happy to welcome large groups and rallies, and large units can be accommodated. The new stone-built reception, shop and coffee bar beside the gate should now be complete. The excellent facilities are located in a purpose-built toilet block.

Facilities

The modern toilet block includes free showers and facilities for disabled visitors. Motorcaravan service point. Laundry room with ironing. Campers' kitchen. Recreation and TV rooms. Shop, bicycle hire and Internet café planned. Off site: Holiday homes to rent 300 m. Restaurant nearby. Outdoor activities. Fishing in Aherlow River. Golf and riding 7 km.

Open: All year.

Directions

From Tipperary town take N24 to Bansha, then R663 to Newtown. Continue through village and pass Coach Road Inn to park in 300 m. GPS: 52.4161, -8.2105

Charges guide

Per unit incl. 2 persons and electricity	€ 28.00
extra person	€ 6.00
child (2-18 yrs)	€ 2.00

FREE Alan Rogers Travel Card
Extra benefits and savings - see page 10

Insurance Service

High quality, low cost insurance you can trust

Motorhome insurance
From only £174

Caravan Insurance
SAVE
UP TO 60%

We've been entrusted with readers' campsite-based holidays since 1968, and they have asked us for good value, good quality insurance.

We have teamed up with Shield Total Insurance – one of the leading names in outdoor leisure insurances – to bring you peace of mind and huge savings. Call or visit our website for a no obligation quote – there's no reason not to – and trust us to cover your valued possessions for you.

Static Caravans - Price Beater **GUARANTEE**

We guarantee to beat any genuine 'like for like' insurance renewal quote by at least £25. Subject to terms & conditions.

- Caravans - **Discounts up to 60%**
- Motorhomes - **Prices from only £174**
- Park Homes - **Fantastic low rates**
- Tents - **Prices from only £30**

Instant quote

Call **0844 824 6314**

alanrogers.com/insurance

Alan Rogers Insurance Services is a trading name of Alan Rogers Travel Limited which is an Appointed Representative of ITC Compliance Ltd and is authorised and regulated by the Financial Services Authority. Insurance products featured in this advertisement are provided by Shield Total Insurance which is a trading name of Vantage Insurance Services Limited (VISL). VISL is a subsidiary of Vantage Holdings Ltd and is authorised and regulated by the Financial Services Authority. VISL is registered in England No. 3441136. Registered Office: 41 Eastcheap, London EC3M 1DT.

Tralee
Woodlands Park Touring Caravan & Camping Park

Dan Spring Road, Tralee, Co. Kerry (Co. Kerry) T: 066 712 1235. E: woodlandstralee@gmail.com

alanrogers.com/IR9650

This family run park is located in the heart of Kerry, on the gateway to the Dingle peninsula and just north of the Ring of Kerry and Killarney. Woodlands is an ideal base, only ten minutes walk from Tralee town centre via the town park and famous rose garden. Located on a 16-acre elevated site approached by a short road and a bridge that straddles the River Lee; once on site the town seems far removed with a countryside environment taking over. Hedging, trees, grazing fields and the distant Slieve Mish Mountain create the setting. There are 135 pitches including 85 super pitches with hardstanding, electricity (10A), water and drainage and a grass area. The park has a landscaped entrance and tropical shrubs, cordyline palms and flower beds have been planted around the park. The owners of Woodlands have designed and equipped their park to a high standard including a clubhouse. The town park is home to the Kerry County Museum and Siamsa Tire, the National Folk Theatre of Ireland, with nightly performances. In addition to the river, there is a canal bank walk to Blennerville village and its windmill.

Facilities

Excellent, heated sanitary facilities include sizeable showers (€ 1 token) and provision for disabled guests. Campers' kitchen. Laundry room with washing machines and dryer. Gas for sale. Motorcaravan service point. Club house with café/snack bar. Shop. Games room. TV and adult only room. Free WiFi over part of site. Fenced adventure play area. Public telephone on site. Off site: Aqua Dome nearby (discounted family pass for campers). Golf 6 km. Riding 2 km. Blue Flag beaches on the Dingle Peninsula. Sailing 10 km.

Open: All year.

Directions

Site is 1 km. southwest of Tralee town centre. From N21/N69/N86 junction south of Tralee follow site signs for 2.4 km. to park, 200 m. off the N86 Tralee-Dingle road. Site is 300 m. east of the Aqua Dome GPS: 52.26157, -9.70338

Charges guide

Per unit incl. 2 persons	
and electricity	€ 23.00 - € 25.00
extra person	€ 6.00
child (under 16 yrs)	€ 3.00

Award Winning Touring Park perfect for family holiday's and an ideal base to explore beautiful Co. Kerry. Enjoy the quiet Woodland Setting just a few minutes stroll to Tralee town centre. **Alan Rogers Welcome Award runners up 2011**

www.kingdomcamping.com

Tramore
Newtown Cove Camping & Caravan Park

Newtown Road, Tramore (Co. Waterford) T: 051 381 979. E: info@newtowncove.com

alanrogers.com/IR9340

Well run and friendly, this very attractive small park is only five minutes walk from the beautiful Newton Cove. It offers views of the famous and historic Metal Man and is 2.5 km. from Tramore beach and 11 km. from Waterford. Neatly set out on gently sloping grass are 40 pitches, with the abundance of shrubs and bushes reflecting the efforts of the owners. All pitches have 10A electrical connections, some with hardstanding also, and access is by well lit, tarmac roads. There are around 50 privately owned caravan holiday homes. A modern building at the entrance houses reception, the amenities and additional sanitary facilities. The busy holiday resort of Tramore, with a wide range of shops and eating houses, is close and there is a choice of many delightful cliff walks in the immediate vicinity.

Facilities

The main sanitary block at the bottom end of the site provides good, clean facilities including a bathroom. Showers on payment (token from reception). Excellent motorcaravan services. Campers' kitchen with cooking facilities, sheltered eating area, lounge and small laundry. Small shop (1/7-30/8). TV room. Games room. Small play area. Off site: Beach 400 m. Fishing 400 m. Golf 800 m.

Open: Easter - 25 September.

Directions

From Tramore on R675 coast road to Dungarvan. Turn left 2 km. from town centre, following signs. GPS: 52.14763, -7.17274

Charges guide

Per unit incl. 2 persons	
and electricity	€ 24.00 - € 29.00
extra person	€ 6.00
hiker, cyclist or motorcyclist	€ 8.00 - € 11.00

FREE Alan Rogers Travel Card
Extra benefits and savings - see page 10

Tuosist

Beara Camping The Peacock

Coornagillagh, Tuosist (Co. Kerry) T: 064 668 4287. E: bearacamping@eircom.net

alanrogers.com/IR9580

Five minutes from Kenmare Bay, The Peacock is a unique location for campers who appreciate the natural world, where disturbance to nature is kept to a minimum. This five-acre site offers simple, clean and imaginative camping facilities. Located on the Ring of Beara, bordering the counties of Cork and Kerry, visitors will be treated with hospitality by a Dutch couple, Bert and Klaske van Bavel, almost more Irish than the Irish, who have made Ireland their home and run the site with their family. The variety of accommodation at Beara Camping includes a hostel, caravan holiday homes, secluded hardstanding pitches with electricity and level grass areas for tenting. In addition, there are cabins sleeping two or four people and hiker huts sleeping two, ideal to avoid a damp night or to dry out.

Facilities

Three small blocks, plus facilities at the restaurant provide toilets, washbasins and free hot showers. Laundry service for a small fee. Campers' kitchens and sheltered eating area. Restaurant and takeaway (May-Oct). No pets in rental accommodation or tents. Off site: Public transport from the gate during the summer months. Pub and shop 900 m. Riding 6 km. Golf 12 km. Boating, fishing and sea angling 200 m. Beach (pebble) 500 m.

Open: 1 April - 31 December.

Directions

From the N22, 17 km. east of Killarney, take the R569 south to Kenmare. In Kenmare take R571, Castletownbere road and site is 12 km. GPS: 51.8279, -9.7356

Charges guide

Per unit incl. 2 persons and electricity	€ 22.50
extra person	€ 3.50
child (0-10 yrs)	€ 2.00

Westport

Westport House Caravan & Camping Park

Westport House Country Park, Westport (Co. Mayo) T: 098 277 66. E: camping@westporthouse.ie

alanrogers.com/IR8770

Located in the grounds of an elegant country estate, this is a popular park. In an attractive, sheltered area of the parkland, set in the trees, are 95 pitches, 70 with hardstanding and 10/12A electricity. Outside the peak season, the site may not be fully open, and some facilities such as the bar and café may not be available. Westport House and an adventure park are nearby on the estate and campsite visitors get a 20 per cent discount on all tickets. There are also special family rates for three days camping, along with an annual pass to the adventure park. Free activities available on site include a recreation room, tennis, table tennis, pitch and putt, fishing, Pirates Den (soft play area), playground, sand pit, movie nights and teen disco at weekends. Additionally, there is Westport House, an 18th-century historic home with original architecture, antiques and art as well as tours and tea rooms.

Facilities

Toilet facilities are provided at various points on the site, plus a 'super-loo' located in the farmyard buildings. Facilities for disabled visitors. Laundry facilities. Café and bar with food and musical entertainment at weekends. Fishing. Tennis. Westport House and Country Park. Dog owners should contact site. Free WiFi over site. Off site: Within 5 km. of the estate are an 18-hole golf course and deep sea angling on Clew Bay.

Open: April - September, but contact site first.

Directions

Take R335 Westport-Louisburgh road, then follow signs for Westport Quay, turn in sharp right through gates of Westport House and continue through estate following signs for camping. GPS: 53.8053, -9.5395

Charges guide

Per unit incl. 2 persons and electricity	€ 24.00 - € 26.00
extra person	€ 4.00
hiker or cyclist	€ 9.50
Family weekend rates in June.	

For latest campsite news visit
alanrogers.com

A visit to the Channel Islands offers a holiday in part of the British Isles, yet in an area which has a definite continental flavour. All the islands have beautiful beaches and coves, pretty scenery and fascinating histories.

THE CHANNEL ISLANDS ARE MADE UP OF THE ISLANDS OF: JERSEY, GUERNSEY, SARK, HERM AND ALDERNEY

The largest of the Channel Islands is Jersey, which is also the most commercial with more entertainment on offer. It has long stretches of safe beaches for swimming and water-based activities such as windsurfing and banana rides. Caravans and motorcaravans are allowed on Jersey, but with a number of limitations (for example, length of stay, the width and length of the unit). A permit is required, which is obtained as part of the booking procedure with the campsite of your choice. You must book in advance but the campsite owner will advise you on all aspects of your visit.

Guernsey will suit those who prefer a quieter, more peaceful holiday. Caravans and motorcaravans are not allowed here. Guernsey too has wide, sandy beaches plus sheltered coves. The historic, harbour town of St Peter Port has steep and winding cobbled streets, with plenty of shops, cafés and restaurants.

For those who want total relaxation, one of the smaller islands – Sark or Herm, would be ideal. No cars are permitted on either of these islands. Explore on foot, by bicycle or horse-drawn carriage.

Shopping on all the islands has the advantage of no VAT – particularly useful when buying cameras, watches or alcohol.

Places of interest

Jersey: St Helier; Jersey Zoo; Jersey war tunnels; Elizabeth Castle; German Underground Hospital in St Lawrence; Samarès Manor in St Clement; Shell Garden at St Aubin; Battle of Flowers Museum in St Ouen.

Guernsey: Castle Cornet at St Peter Port Harbour; Victor Hugo's House; Guernsey Folk Museum; German Occupation Museum; Fort Grey Shipwreck Museum; Saumarez Park.

Sark: La Coupée; La Seigneurie, with old dovecote and gardens; Gouliet and Boutique Caves; Le Pot on Little Sark; Venus Pool; Little Sark Village.

Herm: This tiny island has beautiful, quiet, golden beaches and a little harbour village and hotel. Arrive by ferry from Guernsey for a wonderful day out.

Did you know?

Jersey has been associated with knitting for nearly 400 years.

The Channel Islands were the only part of the British Isles to be occupied by the Germans during the Second World War.

Herm island is just one and a half miles long and only half a mile wide.

Le Jerriais is the native language of Jersey, a blend of Norse and Norman French.

Note: The reciprocal health services agreement between the British Government and the Channel Islands ended in April 2009. The EHIC card does not cover emergency health care as the Channel Islands are not part of the EU. Travel insurance is now essential.

Castel

Fauxquets Valley Campsite

Candie Road, Castel, Guernsey GY5 7QL (Guernsey) T: 01481 255460. E: info@fauxquets.co.uk

alanrogers.com/UK9780

Situated in the rural centre of the island, Fauxquets is in a pretty sheltered valley, hidden down narrow lanes away from busy roads and run by the Guille family. It was once a dairy farm, but the valley side has now been developed into an attractive campsite, with the old farm buildings as its centre. Plenty of trees, bushes and flowers have been planted to separate pitches and to provide shelter around the various fields which are well terraced. The 86 touring pitches are of a good size, most marked, numbered and with electricity, and there is lots of open space. There are also 15 smaller places for backpackers. The site has 23 fully equipped tents for hire, but there are no tour operators. The Haybarn licensed restaurant and bar provides breakfast, morning coffee and cake and evening meals. There is plenty of room to sit around the heated swimming pool, including a large grassy terrace with sun beds provided.

Facilities

Good toilet facilities have controllable showers, some washbasins in private cabins with a shower, baby bath and changing unit. Dishwashing facilities under cover and a tap for free hot water. Laundry room with free irons, boards and hairdryers. Heated swimming pool (20x45 ft) with paddling pool. Restaurant and bar (25/6-7/9). Small shop with ice-pack hire and gas. TV room. Table football and table tennis. Small play area and play field. Bicycle hire. Torches useful. Off site: Riding and golf 2 miles. Fishing, sailing and boat launching 3 miles.

Open: April - 15 September.

Directions

From harbour take second exit from roundabout. At top of hill, turn left at 'filter in turn' into Queens Road, then right at next filter. Follow straight through lights, down hill past hospital, through pedestrian lights and straight on at next lights at top of hill. Continue for 0.75 miles, then turn right opposite sign for German Hospital. Fourth left is pedestrian entrance, cars carry on for 400 yds. to gravel entrance on left. GPS: 49.46812, -2.58843

Charges guide

Per person	£ 8.50 - £ 10.50
child (4-14 yrs)	£ 6.00 - £ 7.50
electricity (6A)	£ 3.50

Herm Island

Seagull Campsite

The Administration Office, Herm Island GY1 3HR (Herm) T: 01481 750000. E: reservations@herm.com

alanrogers.com/UK9830

This tiny site, and indeed the island of Herm, will appeal to those who are looking for complete tranquillity and calm. Reached by boat (20 minutes and about £11 return fare for adults, £5.50 for children) from Guernsey, the 300-acre island allows no cars, only tractors, on its narrow roads and paths (no bicycles either). The campsite is a twenty minute uphill walk from the harbour, but your luggage will be transported for you by tractor. It consists of several terraced areas offering a total of 90 pitches, and 26 fully equipped tents for hire on flat grass areas. There are no electricity hook-ups. Bring your own tent and equipment or hire both (but not bedding, crockery and lighting) from the site. One is free to stroll around the many paths, through farmland, heath and around the coast, with its beautiful beaches.

Facilities

Small, modern, but open, toilet block. Hot showers (£1 payment – there is a shortage of water on Herm). Laundry facility and small kitchen. Freezer for ice-packs. No dogs or pets are allowed. Torches useful. Off site: The harbour village is about ten minutes walk for small shop, gas, a post office, pub, restaurants and café. Fishing on the island.

Open: May - first w/end in September.

Directions

Reached by boat from St Peter Port – report to Administration Office on arrival. Do not take your car as it is unlikely you will be able to park long term in St Peter Port. GPS: 49.46997, -2.445745

Charges guide

Per person	£ 7.00
child (under 14 yrs)	£ 3.50
transportation of luggage	£ 7.50

Equipped tents for hire. Groups of single people not accepted.

For latest campsite news visit
alanrogers.com

Saint Martin
Beuvelande Camp Site
Beuvelande, Saint Martin, Jersey JE3 6EZ (Jersey) T: 01534 853575. E: info@campingjersey.com
alanrogers.com/UK9720

What a pleasant surprise we had when we called here – the outstanding sanitary building gives campers facilities often associated with top class hotels. A licensed restaurant with a covered terrace area is also situated in this building, open morning and evening all season, but perhaps a few less hours at quiet times. There are 150 pitches, 60 with fully equipped tents for hire, but with plenty of space for those with their own. Cars may be parked next to your tent. One hundred pitches have electric hook ups (5/10A). Torches would be useful. Car and bicycle hire can be arranged. This family run park prides itself on quality, cleanliness and hospitality.

Facilities

The toilet block is fully tiled and spotlessly clean, with controllable showers, two fully equipped bathrooms for disabled visitors, and a baby room. Plenty of dishwashing facilities and a laundry. Well stocked shop (08.00-19.00 at peak times; stocks gas). Licensed restaurant. Outdoor heated swimming pool (41x17 ft) with a sun terrace and small waterslide. Play area and large playing field. Games room with arcade games and pool. TV room. Evening entertainment. Ice pack and battery charging services (small charge). Off site: Beach and sailing 1.5 miles. Fishing, golf and riding within 2 miles.

Open: 1 April - 30 September.

Directions

On leaving the harbour by Route du Port Elizabeth, take A1 east through tunnel and A17. At fourth set of traffic lights turn left on A6. Continue to Five Oaks and on to St Martin's RC church, then right into La Longue Rue, right again Rue de L'Orme then left to site. GPS: 49.21294, -2.05615

Charges guide

Per person	£ 10.00
child (2-14 yrs)	£ 7.00

Single sex groups not accepted.

Saint Martin
Rozel Camping Park
Rozel, Saint Martin, Jersey JE3 6AX (Jersey) T: 01534 855200. E: rozelcampingpark@jerseymail.co.uk
alanrogers.com/UK9710

This family owned park is within walking distance of the famous Jersey Zoo and the pretty harbour and fishing village of Rozel, where the north coast cliff path commences. There are two main camping areas providing 130 pitches, of which 120 have 10/16A electricity and 16 are used for fully equipped tents to hire. Some pitches, mainly for smaller tents are arranged on terraced areas. The remainder are on a higher, flat field where pitches are arranged in bays with hedges growing to separate them into groups. The site has provided easy access for caravans and motorcaravans, plus chemical and grey waste disposal facilities. In addition to package deals for tent hire and travel, the site offers a good range of camping equipment for hire on a daily basis. Boats are accepted by prior arrangement.

Facilities

Two first rate, heated sanitary buildings include a bathroom for disabled visitors with a shower, toilet and washbasin. Family shower room with small heater for cooler weather. Fully equipped laundry. Shop. Takeaway (peak season). Swimming pool (June-Sept) with children's pool and sunbathing areas. Play area. Crazy golf. Games room, reading and TV room. Torches useful. Bicycles for hire can be delivered to the site. Off site: Fishing 1 mile. Beach 2 miles. Riding 3 miles. Golf 4 miles.

Open: 21 May - 9 September.

Directions

Leave harbour by Route du Port Elizabeth, take A1 east through tunnel and A17. At fourth set of lights turn left on A6. Keep in middle lane. Continue to Five Oaks and on to St Martin's church. Turn right, then immediately left at The Royal pub on B38 to Rozel, continue to end of road, turn right and park is on right. GPS: 49.23841, -2.05058

Charges guide

Per person	£ 8.80 - £ 9.20
child (4-11 yrs)	£ 5.00
electricity	£ 2.00

Tent hire and travel packages.

FREE Alan Rogers Travel Card
Extra benefits and savings - see page 10

Saint Sampson's
Vaugrat Camping

Route de Vaugrat, Saint Sampson's, Guernsey GY2 4TA (Guernsey) T: 01481 257468.
E: enquiries@vaugratcampsite.com **alanrogers.com/UK9770**

Vaugrat Camping is a neat, well tended site, close to the beach in the northwest of the island. Owned and well run by the Laine family, it is centred around attractive and interesting old granite farm buildings dating back to the 15th century, with a gravel courtyard and pretty flower beds. It provides 150 pitches (six with electricity) on flat, grassy meadows that are mostly surrounded by trees, banks and hedges to provide shelter. Tents are arranged around the edges of the fields, giving open space in the centre, and while pitches are not marked, there is sufficient room and cars may be parked next to tents. Only couples and families are accepted. It also offers 30 fully equipped tents for hire. Housed in the old farmhouse, now a listed building, are the reception area and shop, where fresh croissants are baked every morning. There are plans to include caravans and motorcaravans subject to permission.

Facilities

Well kept sanitary facilities are in two buildings. The first block is in the courtyard, with hot showers on payment. Unit for disabled visitors with shower, basin and toilet (six inch step into building). Laundry facilities. Second block near the camping fields provides toilets, washbasins and dishwashing facilities. Shop with ice pack hire and gas (open at certain times by arrangement). Café serving breakfast only. Dogs are not accepted. Torches may be useful. Off site: Bus service within easy reach. Car or bicycle hire can be arranged. Fishing, riding and golf within 1.5 miles. Hotel and bar nearby.

Open: May - September.

Directions

On leaving St Peter Port, turn right onto coast road for 1.5 miles. At filter turn left into Vale Road. Straight over at two sets of lights then first left by church. Follow to crossroads (garage opposite) turn right. Carry on past Peninsula Hotel, then second left, signed for site. Site on left after high stone wall with concealed entrance. GPS: 49.49584, -2.55433

Charges guide

Per person	£ 10.50
child (3-13 yrs)	£ 7.70
electricity	£ 6.00

Families and couples only. Fully equipped tents to hire (details from site).

Sark
Pomme de Chien Campsite

Sark GY9 0SB (Sark) T: 01481 832316. E: rangjill@hotmail.com
alanrogers.com/UK9870

'The island where time stands still' is an apt description of Sark, one of the smallest inhabited Channel Islands, some 45 minutes from Guernsey by boat. Situated five minutes from the shops and ten from the beach, the Pomme de Chien campsite is small with only 50 pitches, of which eight are occupied by fully equipped tents for rent. The remainder are for campers with their own tents (no caravans, motorcaravans or trailer tents of course). The pitches are large, on fairly level ground, but none have electricity hook-ups. There is a warm welcome from the owners Chris and Jill Rang with the famous charm of Sark. Although you cannot take your car to the island, the Condor service via Guernsey means you can get there in a little over three hours, either with your own small tent or you could hire one of the site's own (equipment includes everything you are likely to need except bedding and a torch).

Facilities

Modern sanitary block with free hot showers (large, with bench and hook), toilets and washbasins. Dishwashing sinks are outside. Outside washing line. Dogs are not accepted. Torches are necessary. Baggage can be transferred from the harbour to the site by tractor trailer, at a cost of £1 per item. Off site: Bicycle hire 5 minutes. Beach and fishing a 10 minute walk.

Open: All year.

Directions

Take the tractor-drawn 'train' up Harbour Hill (90p; you can walk but it is a ten minute hike). Once at the top take road leading off left, then second right, and follow the lane to the site entrance. Reception is at house with white gates. GPS: 49.43665, -2.36331

Charges guide

Per person	£ 7.50
child	£ 5.00

No credit cards.

For latest campsite news visit
alanrogers.com

Want independent campsite reviews at your fingertips?

Holiday Caravans and Chalets

Over recent years many of the campsites featured in this guide have added large numbers of high quality caravan holiday homes, chalets and lodges. Many park owners believe that some former caravanners and motorcaravanners have been enticed by the extra comfort this type of accommodation can now provide, and that maybe this is the ideal solution to combine the freedom of camping with all the comforts of home.

Quality is consistently high and, although the exact size and inventory will vary from park to park, if you choose any of the parks detailed here, you can be sure that you're staying in some of the best quality and best value caravan holiday homes or chalets available.

Home comforts are provided and typically these include a fridge with freezer compartment, gas hob, proper shower – often a microwave and CD player too, but do check for details. All caravan holiday homes and chalets come fully equipped with a good range of kitchen utensils, pots and pans, crockery, cutlery and outdoor furniture. Many even have an attractive wooden sundeck or paved terrace – a perfect spot for outdoors eating or relaxing with a book and watching the world go by. An efficient heating system is invariably included and some models may also incorporate air conditioning.

Regardless of model, colourful soft furnishings are the norm and a generally breezy décor helps to provide a real holiday feel.

Although some parks may have a large number of different accommodation types, we have restricted our choice to one or two of the most popular accommodation units (either caravan holiday homes or chalets) for each of the parks listed.

The caravan holiday homes here will be of modern design, and recent innovations such as pitched roofs undeniably improve their appearance.

Design will invariably include clever use of space and fittings/furniture to provide for comfortable holidays – usually light and airy, with big windows and patio-style doors, fully equipped kitchen areas, a shower room with shower, washbasin and WC, cleverly designed bedrooms and a comfortable lounge/dining area (often incorporating a sofa bed).

In general, modern campsite chalets incorporate all the best features of caravan holiday homes in a more traditional, wood-clad structure, sometimes with the advantage of an upper mezzanine floor for an additional bedroom.

Our selected parks offer a massive range of different types of caravan holiday home and chalet, and it would be impractical to inspect every single accommodation unit. Our selection criteria, therefore, primarily takes account of the quality standards of the campsite itself.

However, there are a couple of important ground rules:

- Featured caravan holiday homes must be no more than 5 years old.
- Chalets no more than 10 years old.
- All listed accommodation must, of course, fully conform with all applicable local, national and European safety legislation.

For each park we have given details of the type, or types, of accommodation available to rent, but these details are necessarily quite brief. Sometimes internal layouts can differ quite substantially, particularly with regard to sleeping arrangements, where these include the flexible provision for 'extra persons' on sofa beds located in the living area.

These arrangements may vary from accommodation to accommodation, and if you're planning a holiday which includes more people than are catered for by the main bedrooms you should check exactly how the extra sleeping arrangements are to be provided!

Charges

An indication of the tariff for each type of accommodation featured is also included, indicating the variance between the low and high season tariffs. However, given that many parks have a large and often complex range of pricing options, incorporating special deals and various discounts, the charges we mention should be taken to be just an indication. We strongly recommend therefore that you confirm the actual cost when making a booking.

We also strongly recommend that you check with the park, when booking, what (if anything) will be provided by way of bed linen, blankets, pillows etc. Again, in our experience, this can vary widely from park to park.

On every park a fully refundable deposit (usually between £100 and £250) is payable on arrival. There may also be an optional cleaning service for which a further charge is made. Other options may include sheet hire (typically £20 per unit) or baby pack hire (cot and high chair).

UK0380 Wooda Farm Holiday Park

⊙ see report page 19

Poughill, Bude EX23 9HJ

AR1 – HOLLY – Mobile Home

Sleeping: 2 bedrooms, sleeps 5: 1 double, 2 singles, sofa bed, pillows and blankets provided

Living: living/kitchen area, heating, TV, shower, WC

Eating: fitted kitchen with hobs, oven, microwave, grill, fridge, freezer

Outside: table & chairs

Pets: not accepted

AR2 – BRAMBLES – Bungalow

Sleeping: 4 bedrooms, sleeps 7: 2 doubles, 3 singles, pillows and blankets provided

Living: living/kitchen area, heating, TV, shower, separate WC

Eating: fitted kitchen with hobs, oven, microwave, grill, dishwasher, fridge, freezer

Outside: table & chairs

Pets: not accepted

Other (AR1 and AR2): cot, highchair to hire

Open: 23 March - 3 November

Weekly Charge	AR1	AR2
Low Season *(from)*	£ 336	£ 575
High Season *(from)*	£ 854	£ 1295

UK0970 Cofton Country Holidays

⊙ see report page 59

Starcross, Dawlish EX6 8RP

AR1 – ASHBURN – Mobile Home

Sleeping: 3 bedrooms, sleeps 6: 1 double, 4 singles, pillows and blankets provided

Living: living/kitchen area, heating, TV, shower, separate WC

Eating: fitted kitchen with hobs, oven, microwave, grill, fridge, freezer

Outside: table & chairs

Pets: not accepted

AR2 – THE COACHING HOUSE – Cottage

Sleeping: 3 bedrooms, sleeps 6: 2 doubles, 2 singles, pillows and blankets provided

Living: living/kitchen area, heating, TV, shower, separate WC

Eating: fitted kitchen with hobs, oven, microwave, grill, dishwasher, fridge, freezer

Outside: table & chairs

Pets: not accepted

Other (AR1 and AR2): bed linen, cot, highchair to hire

Open: All year

Weekly Charge	AR1	AR2
Low Season *(from)*	£ 325	£ 375
High Season *(from)*	£ 865	£ 930

UK1780 Freshwater Beach Holiday Park

▶ see report page 85

Burton Bradstock, Bridport DT6 4PT

AR1 – BUDGET – Mobile Home	**AR2 – SUPER DELUXE – Mobile Home**
Sleeping: 3 bedrooms, sleeps 6: 1 double, 4 singles, pillows and blankets provided	Sleeping: 3 bedrooms, sleeps 6: 1 double, 4 singles, pillows and blankets provided
Living: living/kitchen area, heating, TV, shower, WC	Living: living/kitchen area, heating, TV, shower, WC
Eating: fitted kitchen with hobs, oven, grill, fridge, freezer	Eating: fitted kitchen with hobs, oven, microwave, grill, fridge, freezer
Outside: table & chairs	Outside: table & chairs
Pets: not accepted	Pets: not accepted

Open: 15 March - 9 November

Weekly Charge	AR1	AR2
Low Season *(from)*	£ 210	£ 350
High Season *(from)*	£ 690	£ 980

UK2920 Bay View Park

▶ see report page 134

Old Martello Road, Pevensey Bay BN24 6DX

AR1 – FESTIVAL SUPER – Mobile Home	**AR2 – RICHMOND DELUXE – Mobile Home**
Sleeping: 2 bedrooms, sleeps 6: 1 double, 2 singles, sofa bed, pillows and blankets provided	Sleeping: 2 bedrooms, sleeps 6: 1 double, 2 singles, sofa bed, pillows and blankets provided
Living: living/kitchen area, heating, TV, shower, separate WC	Living: living/kitchen area, heating, TV, shower, WC
Eating: fitted kitchen with grill, fridge	Eating: fitted kitchen with grill, fridge
Outside: table & chairs	Outside: table & chairs
Pets: not accepted	Pets: not accepted

Other (AR1 and AR2): bed linen, cot, highchair to hire

Open: 1 March - 31 October

Weekly Charge	AR1	AR2
Low Season *(from)*	£ 265	£ 299
High Season *(from)*	£ 573	£ 635

UK3435 Woodlands Caravan Park

Holt Road, Upper Sheringham NR26 8TU

▶ see report page 161

AR1 – THE HAY SHED – Bungalow

Sleeping: 3 bedrooms, sleeps 10: 2 doubles, 2 singles, sofa bed, pillows and blankets provided

Living: living/kitchen area, heating, TV, shower, separate WC

Outside: 4 sun loungers

Pets: not accepted

AR2 – THE MALTING HOUSE – Bungalow

Sleeping: 3 bedrooms, sleeps 8: 2 doubles, 2 singles, sofa bed, pillows and blankets provided

Living: living/kitchen area, heating, TV, shower, WC, separate WC

Outside: 4 sun loungers

Pets: not accepted

Open: All year

Weekly Charge	AR1	AR2
Low Season (from)	£ 500	£ 500
High Season (from)	£ 1200	£ 1200

UK3850 Rivendale Caravan & Leisure Park

Buxton Road, Alsop-en-le-Dale, Ashbourne DE6 1QU

▶ see report page 168

AR1 – LODGE

Sleeping: 2 bedrooms, sleeps 6: 1 double, 2 singles, sofa bed, pillows and blankets provided

Living: living/kitchen area, heating, TV, shower, WC, separate WC

Eating: fitted kitchen with hobs, oven, microwave, grill, fridge, freezer

Outside: table & chairs, barbecue

Pets: accepted (with supplement)

AR2 – FAMILY POD

Sleeping: 1 bedroom, sleeps 4

Living: heating

Pets: accepted (with supplement)

Other (AR1 and AR2): bed linen, cot, highchair to hire

Open: 1 February - 5 January

Weekly Charge	AR1	AR2
Low Season (from)	£ 350	£ 350
High Season (from)	£ 560	£ 350

UK4520 Flower of May Holiday Park
Lebberston Cliff, Scarborough YO11 3NU

▶ see report page 202

AR1 – 4 BERTH GOLD – Mobile Home

Sleeping: 2 bedrooms, sleeps 4: 1 double, 2 singles, pillows and blankets provided

Living: living/kitchen area, heating, TV, shower, WC

Eating: fitted kitchen with hobs, oven, microwave, grill, fridge, freezer

Pets: not accepted

AR2 – 6 BERTH GOLD – Mobile Home

Sleeping: 3 bedrooms, sleeps 6: 1 double, 4 singles, pillows and blankets provided

Living: living/kitchen area, heating, TV, shower, WC

Eating: fitted kitchen with hobs, oven, microwave, grill, fridge, freezer

Pets: not accepted

Other (AR1 and AR2): bed linen to hire

Open: 28 March - 3 November

Weekly Charge	AR1	AR2
Low Season (from)	£ 360	£ 415
High Season (from)	£ 610	£ 660

UK4640 Goose Wood Caravan Park
Carr Lane, Sutton-on-the-Forest, York YO61 1ET

▶ see report page 207

AR1 – ELM – Mobile Home

Sleeping: 2 bedrooms, sleeps 4: 1 double, 2 singles, pillows and blankets provided

Living: living/kitchen area, heating, TV, shower, WC

Eating: fitted kitchen with hobs, oven, microwave, grill, dishwasher, fridge, freezer

Outside: table & chairs

Pets: accepted (with supplement)

AR2 – LAUREL/BIRCH – Mobile Home

Sleeping: 3 bedrooms, sleeps 6: 1 double, 4 singles, pillows and blankets provided

Living: living/kitchen area, heating, TV, shower, WC

Eating: fitted kitchen with hobs, oven, microwave, grill, dishwasher, fridge, freezer

Outside: table & chairs

Pets: accepted (with supplement)

Other (AR1 and AR2): bed linen to hire

Open: 1 March - 2 January

Weekly Charge	AR1	AR2
Low Season (from)	£ 290	£ 312
High Season (from)	£ 450	£ 480

Low Cost Flights

An Inexpensive Way To Arrive At Your Campsite

Many campsites are conveniently served by a wide choice of low cost airlines. Cheap flights can be very easy to find and travellers increasingly find the regional airports often used to be smaller, quieter and generally a calmer, more pleasurable experience.

Low cost flights can make campsites in more distant regions a much more attractive option: quicker to reach, inexpensive flights, and simply more convenient.

Campsites are seeing increased numbers of visitors using the low cost flights and are adapting their services to suit this clientele. An airport shuttle service is not uncommon, meaning you can take advantage of that cheap flight knowing you will be met at the other end and whisked to your campsite. No taxi queues or multiple drop-offs.

Obviously, these low cost flights are impractical when taking all your own camping gear but they do make a holiday in campsite owned accommodation much more straightforward. The low cost airline option makes caravan holiday home holidays especially attractive: pack a suitcase and use bed linen and towels provided (which you will generally need to pre-book).

Open All Year

The following parks are understood to accept caravanners and campers all year round. It is always wise to phone the park to check as the facilities available, for example, may be reduced.

England

South West England
Cornwall

Bodmin	UK0270	Mena
Bodmin	UK0306	Ruthern Valley
Looe	UK0006	Tencreek H.P.
Newquay	UK0165	Monkey Tree
Newquay	UK0540	Carvynick
Padstow	UK0430	Padstow
Redruth	UK0114	Globe Vale
Saint Ives	UK0030	Ayr
Saint Martins-Looe	UK0320	Polborder House
Saltash	UK0440	Dolbeare
Truro	UK0012	Killiwerris
Truro	UK0180	Carnon Downs
Truro	UK0185	Cosawes

South West England
Devon

Braunton	UK0710	Hidden Valley
Dawlish	UK0970	Cofton
Dawlish	UK1010	Lady's Mile
Drewsteignton	UK1250	Woodland Springs
Ilfracombe	UK0690	Stowford Farm
Modbury	UK0820	Moor View
Newton Abbot	UK0980	Lemonford
Paignton	UK0870	Beverley
Plymouth	UK0810	Riverside *(Plymouth)*
South Molton	UK0745	Riverside *(S Molton)*
Tavistock	UK0790	Harford Bridge
Tavistock	UK0795	The Old Rectory

South West England
Somerset, Wiltshire, West Dorset

Bath	UK1460	Newton Mill
Bishop Sutton	UK1510	Chew Valley
Bridgwater	UK1306	Mill Farm
Bristol	UK1440	Baltic Wharf
Martock	UK1420	Southfork
Minehead	UK1301	Westermill Farm
Salisbury	UK1640	Greenhill Farm
Salisbury	UK1650	Coombe
Salisbury	UK1655	Church Farm
Sparkford	UK1500	Long Hazel
Taunton	UK1340	Cornish Farm
Taunton	UK1350	Quantock Orchard
Taunton	UK1520	Waterrow
Westbury	UK1630	Brokerswood
Weymouth	UK1820	Bagwell Farm

Southern England

Banbury	UK2600	Barnstones
Bere Regis	UK2050	Rowlands Wait
Bletchingdon	UK2590	Greenhill Farm
Cowes	UK2530	Waverley
Fordingbridge	UK2290	Sandy Balls
Oxford	UK2595	Diamond Farm
Wareham	UK2030	Wareham Forest

South East England

Ashford	UK3040	Broadhembury
Bexhill-on-Sea	UK2955	Kloofs
Brighton	UK2930	Brighton Caravan Club Site
Canterbury	UK3070	Canterbury
Chertsey	UK2810	Chertsey
Folkestone	UK3090	Black Horse
Horsham	UK2940	Honeybridge
Hurstpierpoint	UK2942	Apollo Sun Club
Marden	UK3030	Tanner Farm
Redhill	UK2800	Alderstead Heath
Washington	UK2950	Washington

London

Abbey Wood	UK3260	Abbey Wood
Crystal Palace	UK3270	Crystal Palace

East of England

Beccles	UK3380	Waveney River
Bury-Saint Edmunds	UK3345	The Dell
Great Yarmouth	UK3382	Rose Farm
Great Yarmouth	UK3485	Clippesby
Hunstanton	UK3520	Searles
Ipswich	UK3310	Low House
Norwich	UK3455	Deer's Glade
Peterborough	UK3580	Ferry Meadows
Pidley	UK3575	Stroud Hill
Swaffham	UK3470	Breckland
Woodbridge	UK3322	Run Cottage

Heart of England

Ashbourne	UK3854	Peak Gateway
Bridgnorth	UK4400	Stanmore Hall
Buxton	UK3845	Clover Fields
Coleford	UK4160	Christchurch
Coventry	UK4075	Hollyfast
Grantham	UK3765	Woodland Waters
Grantham	UK3775	Wagtail C.P.
Ludlow	UK4395	Ludlow Touring Park

Open All Year continued

Lutterworth	UK3890	Stanford Hall
Matlock	UK3815	Lickpenny
Melton Mowbray	UK3895	Eye Kettleby
Meriden	UK4070	Somers Wood
Moreton-in-Marsh	UK4130	Moreton-in-Marsh
Newark	UK3940	Smeaton's Lakes
Newark	UK3945	Milestone
Nottingham	UK3935	Thornton's Holt
Oakham	UK3903	Rutland
Peterchurch	UK4300	Poston Mill
Ripley	UK3865	Golden Valley
Shrewsbury	UK4410	Beaconsfield
Shrewsbury	UK4430	Oxon Hall
Skegness	UK3730	Skegness Sands
Slimbridge	UK4170	Tudor
Stamford	UK3760	Tallington Lakes
Stourport-on-Severn	UK4210	Lickhill Manor
Woodhall Spa	UK3690	Bainland
Worksop	UK3920	Riverside *(Worksop)*

Yorkshire

Ormskirk	UK5280	Abbey Farm

North West England

Preston	UK5290	Royal Umpire

Cumbria

Appleby-in-Westmorland	UK5570	Wild Rose
Penrith	UK5560	Sykeside
Penrith	UK5630	The Quiet Site
Wigton	UK5505	Stanwix Park

Northumbria

Belford	UK5755	South Meadows
Berwick-upon-Tweed	UK5800	Ord House
Durham	UK5705	Durham Grange
Durham	UK5715	Finchale Abbey
Stockton-on-Tees	UK5740	White Water

Wales

Barmouth	UK6385	Islawrffordd
Beddgelert	UK6590	Beddgelert
Caernarfon	UK6600	Bryn Gloch

Caernarfon	UK6605	Tafarn Snowdonia
Cardiff	UK5925	Cardiff
Colwyn Bay	UK6690	Bron-Y-Wendon
Llandovery	UK5955	Erwlon
Montgomery	UK6330	Daisy Bank
Newport	UK6060	Tredegar House
Wrexham	UK6680	James'

Scotland

Arrochar	UK7260	Ardgartan
Auchterarder	UK7270	Grand Eagles
Aviemore	UK7680	Glenmore
Balloch	UK7240	Lomond Woods
Crieff	UK7275	Braidhaugh
Dalbeattie	UK6870	Glenearly
Durness	UK7735	Sango Sands
Edinburgh	UK7050	Edinburgh
Glencoe	UK7790	Invercoe
Grantown-on-Spey	UK7670	Grantown
Kirkcudbright	UK6950	Brighouse Bay
Melrose	UK7030	Melrose Gibson Park
Musselburgh	UK6980	Drum Mohr
Stranraer	UK7020	Aird Donald

Northern Ireland

Newcastle	UK8420	Tollymore

Republic of Ireland

Athy	IR9080	Forest Farm
Ballaghaderreen	IR8815	Willowbrook
Caherdaniel	IR9560	Wave Crest
Clondalkin	IR9100	Camac Valley
Cong	IR8740	Cong
Tipperary	IR9400	Glen of Aherlow
Tralee	IR9650	Woodlands

Channel Islands

Sark	UK9870	Pomme de Chien

Dogs

For the benefit of those who want to take their dogs with them or for people who do not like dogs at the parks they visit, we list here the parks that have indicated to us that they do not accept dogs. If you are planning to take your dog we do advise you to phone the park first to check – there may be limits on numbers, breeds, etc. or times of the year when they are excluded.

Never – these parks do not accept dogs at any time:

UK0065	Wayfarers	35	UK3120	Gate House Wood	140
UK0115	Tehidy	37	UK4100	Hoburne Cotswold	171
UK0250	Pentewan Sands	35	UK4498	South Cliff	193
UK0302	South Penquite	19	UK5890	Glen Trothy	254
UK0306	Ruthern Valley	17	UK5980	Moreton Farm	259
UK0785	South Breazle	69	UK5985	Manorbier	260
UK0870	Beverley	70	UK6040	Pencelli Castle	243
UK0940	Holmans Wood	54	UK6350	Barcdy	247
UK1075	Golden Coast	77	UK7290	Craigtoun Meadows	285
UK1150	Ruda	55	UK9770	Vaugrat	322
UK1490	Greenacres	97	UK9830	Seagull	320
UK2130	Grove Farm	109	UK9870	Pomme de Chien	322
UK2300	Ashurst	105	IR8870	Salthill	306
UK2590	Greenhill Farm	108	IR9410	The Apple	301
UK3060	Yew Tree	131	IR9510	Eagle Point	299

Sometimes – these parks do not accept dogs at certain times of the year or have other restrictions, contact park:

UK0010	Chacewater	43	UK3110	Quex	130
UK0030	Ayr	40	UK3485	Clippesby	153
UK0215	Sun Haven Valley	31	UK4496	Skipsea Sands	204
UK0280	Eden Valley	18	UK4520	Flower of May	202
UK0710	Hidden Valley	52	UK4770	Rosedale	199
UK0735	Woolacombe Sands	80	UK5350	Silverdale	211
UK0850	Galmpton	54	UK5710	Doe Park	230
UK0860	Whitehill	69	UK5750	Waren	230
UK1540	Batcombe Vale	97	UK5930	Cwmcarn Forest	255
UK2270	Oakdene Forest	118	UK5995	Caerfai Bay	259
UK2500	Heathfield Farm	111	UK6280	Aeron Coast	237
UK2510	Whitecliff Bay	106	UK6290	Glan-y-Mor	240
UK2572	Swiss Farm	113	UK6660	Nant Mill	258
UK2590	Greenhill Farm	108	UK9710	Rozel	321
UK3095	Little Satmar	136	IR8770	Westport House	318

Fishing

We are pleased to include details of parks which provide facilities for fishing on site. Many other parks, particularly in Scotland and Ireland, are in popular fishing areas and have facilities within easy reach. Where we have been given details, we have included this information in the reports. It is always best to contact parks to check that they provide for your individual requirements.

England

UK5280	Abbey Farm	214
UK3680	Ashby Park	175
UK1540	Batcombe Vale	97
UK2180	Beacon Hill	116
UK4410	Beaconsfield	184
UK2610	Bo Peep	105
UK2965	Brakes Coppice	129
UK4320	Broadmeadow	183
UK1630	Brokerswood	101
UK4500	Burton Constable	197
UK1665	Burton Hill	94
UK3855	Callow Top	167
UK5785	Chainbridge	231
UK1545	Cheddar Bridge	91
UK2810	Chertsey	132
UK2875	Chichester Lakeside	132
UK3845	Clover Fields	170
UK0970	Cofton	59
UK1125	Crealy Meadows	61
UK4150	Croft Farm	189
UK3455	Deer's Glade	159
UK5710	Doe Park	230
UK1590	Exe Valley	93
UK3895	Eye Kettleby	179
UK2915	Fairfields Farm	135
UK4380	Fernwood	172
UK5715	Finchale Abbey	232
UK2221	Fishery Creek	112
UK3750	Foreman's Bridge	186
UK1780	Freshwater Beach	85
UK3970	Glencote	176
UK1740	Golden Cap	86
UK1075	Golden Coast	77
UK3865	Golden Valley	183
UK4640	Goose Wood	207
UK2590	Greenhill Farm	108
UK1640	Greenhill Farm	97
UK2130	Grove Farm	109
UK0790	Harford Bridge	75
UK2360	Hill Cottage	110
UK5615	Hill of Oaks	227
UK4100	Hoburne Cotswold	171
UK1480	Home Farm	87
UK3300	Homestead Lake	150
UK3055	Hop Farm	139
UK2900	Horam Manor	137
UK2820	Horsley	134
UK2700	Hurley	113
UK4090	Island Meadow	174
UK3430	Kelling Heath	162
UK4190	Kingsgreen	177
UK4720	Knight Stainforth	202
UK4210	Lickhill Manor	187
UK3480	Little Lakeland	154
UK5625	Lowther	224
UK4310	Luck's All	175
UK5220	Manor Wood	212
UK0415	Meadow Lakes	40
UK0270	Mena	18
UK3945	Milestone	180
UK0750	Minnows	76
UK0165	Monkey Tree	31
UK4610	Moorside	208
UK5272	Moss Wood	212
UK0425	Mother Ivey's Bay	34
UK0685	Newberry Valley	54
UK2465	Ninham	121
UK1570	Northam Farm	83
UK3400	Old Brick Kilns	152
UK1390	Old Oaks	92
UK5600	Pennine View	222
UK0250	Pentewan Sands	35
UK1090	Peppermint Park	58
UK0235	Porth Beach	30
UK4300	Poston Mill	182
UK3850	Rivendale	168
UK0950	River Dart	49
UK4715	Riverside (Lancaster)	196
UK0745	Riverside (South Molton)	73
UK5285	Riverside (Southport)	214
UK4080	Riverside (Stratford)	187
UK1150	Ruda	55
UK4480	Sand le Mere	207
UK0695	Sandaway	62
UK2290	Sandy Balls	110
UK3410	Sandy Gulls	158
UK3520	Searles	154
UK1330	Secret Valley	84
UK4588	Sleningford Watermill	200
UK3940	Smeaton's Lakes	181
UK0302	South Penquite	19
UK3575	Stroud Hill	160
UK2572	Swiss Farm	113
UK3760	Tallington Lakes	187
UK3030	Tanner Farm	138
UK3685	Tattershall Lakes	188
UK4510	Thorpe Hall	194
UK3655	Thorpe Park	171
UK4345	Townsend	176
UK0530	Trethiggey	30
UK0170	Trevella	26
UK0220	Trevornick	32

Bicycle Hire

We understand that the following parks have bicycles to hire on site or can arrange for bicycles to be delivered. However, we would recommend that you contact the park to check as the situation can change.

England

UK1415	Alpine Grove	87
UK3855	Callow Top	167
UK3485	Clippesby	153
UK3455	Deer's Glade	159
UK4360	Doward Park	184
UK3390	Dower House	151
UK1590	Exe Valley	93
UK3895	Eye Kettleby	179
UK3750	Foreman's Bridge	186
UK4560	Golden Square	195
UK1490	Greenacres	97
UK3904	Greendale Farm	181
UK1640	Greenhill Farm	97
UK1725	Hawkchurch	51
UK0210	Hendra	27
UK3430	Kelling Heath	162
UK0802	Langstone Manor	74
UK0475	Lower Polladras	24
UK0750	Minnows	76
UK3330	Moat Barn	164
UK2465	Ninham	121
UK2270	Oakdene Forest	118
UK1390	Old Oaks	92
UK1350	Quantock Orchard	99
UK0950	River Dart	49
UK2315	Riverside *(Hamble)*	112
UK0025	Roselands	42
UK2050	Rowlands Wait	107
UK0306	Ruthern Valley	17
UK4540	Saint Helens	204
UK0695	Sandaway	62
UK2290	Sandy Balls	110
UK5745	Seafield	234
UK3520	Searles	154
UK2120	South Lytchett Manor	117
UK4570	Spiers House	198
UK5505	Stanwix Park	225
UK3685	Tattershall Lakes	188
UK3655	Thorpe Park	171
UK1575	Unity	88
UK4620	Upper Carr	199
UK1580	Warren Farm	83
UK3380	Waveney River	148
UK2510	Whitecliff Bay	106
UK5570	Wild Rose	219
UK5605	Woodclose	221
UK3500	Woodhill	151
UK0805	Woodovis	74

Wales

UK5925	Cardiff	246
UK6330	Daisy Bank	254
UK6345	Glanlynn	240
UK6040	Pencelli Castle	243
UK6340	Pen-y-Bont	241
UK6685	Plas Farm	239
UK6670	The Plassey	261

Scotland

UK7260	Ardgartan	266
UK6950	Brighouse Bay	278
UK7680	Glenmore	267
UK6940	Loch Ken	269
UK7000	Strathclyde	282
UK7230	Trossachs	265

Republic of Ireland

IR9620	Flemings	308
IR9400	Glen of Aherlow	316
IR9600	Glenross	307
IR9155	Hidden Valley	312
IR9640	Killarney Flesk	308
IR8965	Lough Ennell	311
IR9130	Roundwood	313
IR9490	Sextons	314

Channel Islands

UK9780	Fauxquets	320

Golf

We understand that the following parks have facilities for playing golf on site. Where facilities are within easy reach and we have been given details, we have included this information in the individual reports. However, we recommend that you contact the park to check that they meet your requirements.

England

UK3690	Bainland	189
UK2920	Bay View	134
UK0540	Carvynick	32
UK0720	Easewell Farm	78
UK4520	Flower of May	202
UK1750	Highlands End	86
UK3230	Lee Valley	145
UK3320	Moon & Sixpence	164
UK1020	Oakdown	72
UK4300	Poston Mill	182
UK4710	Rudding	194
UK3520	Searles	154
UK4070	Somers Wood	179
UK0690	Stowford Farm	63
UK3685	Tattershall Lakes	188
UK3655	Thorpe Park	171
UK0220	Trevornick	32
UK1575	Unity	88
UK0380	Wooda Farm	19

Wales

UK6385	Islawrffordd	241
UK6670	The Plassey	261

Scotland

UK6950	Brighouse Bay	278
UK6910	Hoddom Castle	280
UK7265	Noah's Ark	283

Northern Ireland

UK8310	Carnfunnock	294

Republic of Ireland

IR9150	River Valley	312

Horse Riding

We understand that the following parks have horse riding stables on site. Where facilities are within easy reach and we have been given details, we have included this information in the individual reports. However, we recommend that you contact the park to check that they meet your requirements.

England

UK1370	Burrowhayes	95
UK2900	Horam Manor	137
UK0360	Lakefield	21
UK1306	Mill Farm	84
UK2290	Sandy Balls	110
UK0690	Stowford Farm	63
UK1575	Unity	88
UK0735	Woolacombe Sands	80
UK1060	Yeatheridge	55

Scotland

UK6950	Brighouse Bay	278

Boat Launching

We understand that the following parks have boat slipways on site. Where facilities are within easy reach and we have been given details, we have included this information in the individual reports. However, we recommend that you contact the park to check that they meet your requirements.

England

UK4500	Burton Constable	197
UK2810	Chertsey	132
UK4150	Croft Farm	189
UK3290	Fen Farm	150
UK2221	Fishery Creek	112
UK5615	Hill of Oaks	227
UK3055	Hop Farm	139
UK2700	Hurley	113
UK4210	Lickhill Manor	187
UK4310	Luck's All	175
UK0750	Minnows	76
UK0250	Pentewan Sands	35
UK4080	Riverside (Stratford)	187
UK3760	Tallington Lakes	187
UK3685	Tattershall Lakes	188
UK2520	Thorness Bay	109
UK3380	Waveney River	148
UK2510	Whitecliff Bay	106

Wales

UK6345	Glanlynn	240
UK6385	Islawrffordd	241

Scotland

UK7260	Ardgartan	266
UK7710	Ardmair Point	288
UK6950	Brighouse Bay	278
UK7850	Linnhe Lochside	275
UK6940	Loch Ken	269
UK6890	Mossyard	269
UK7250	Muasdale	287
UK7800	Resipole	266
UK7410	Riverview	282
UK7025	Seal Shore	277

Northern Ireland

UK8405	Cranfield	293
UK8340	Drumaheglis	290
UK8515	Rushin House	291
UK8407	Sandilands	294
UK8330	Six Mile Water	291

Republic of Ireland

IR9510	Eagle Point	299
IR9464	Lakeside (Mountshannon)	301
IR8965	Lough Ennell	311
IR8960	Lough Ree	298
IR9610	Mannix Point	301
IR9560	Wave Crest	300

Adults Only

We list here the parks that have indicated to us that they do not accept children at any time during the year, at certain times, or in certain areas of their park.

England

UK4410	Beaconsfield	184
UK1770	Bingham Grange	87
UK3470	Breckland	162
UK3040	Broadhembury	128
UK0010	Chacewater	43
UK5785	Chainbridge	231
UK1545	Cheddar Bridge	91
UK3650	Cherry Tree	188
UK1510	Chew Valley	82
UK3845	Clover Fields	170
UK1590	Exe Valley	93
UK3895	Eye Kettleby	179
UK5715	Finchale Abbey	232
UK4580	Foxholme	195
UK5640	Green Acres	220
UK3904	Greendale Farm	181
UK0012	Killiwerris	44
UK5240	Lamb Cottage	213
UK3450	Little Haven	159
UK3695	Long Acres	169
UK1500	Long Hazel	98
UK1355	Lowtrow Cross	98
UK3330	Moat Barn	164
UK0820	Moor View	66
UK1390	Old Oaks	92
UK4534	Overbrook	199
UK1680	Plough Lane	92
UK5245	Royal Vale	212
UK3410	Sandy Gulls	158
UK4070	Somers Wood	179
UK3575	Stroud Hill	160
UK5650	The Ashes	220
UK5510	The Larches	226
UK3420	Two Mills	158
UK1520	Waterrow	100
UK0065	Wayfarers	35
UK0900	Widdicombe Farm	70
UK1250	Woodland Springs	60
UK0915	Woodville	68
UK2620	Wysdom	108
UK3555	Wyton Lakes	155

Wales

UK6330	Daisy Bank	254
UK6695	Tyddyn Du	257

Been to any good campsites lately?
We have

You'll find them here...

The UK's market leading independent
guides to the best campsites

Also available on iPad alanrogers.com/digital

... also here...

101 great campsites, ideal for your specific
hobby, pastime or passion

Also available on iPad **alanrogers.com/digital**

Want independent campsite reviews at your fingertips?

You'll find them here...

Over 3,000 in-depth campsite reviews at
www.alanrogers.com

...and even here...

FREE

The Alan Rogers
Travel Card

Across the Alan Rogers guides you'll find a network of thousands of quality inspected and selected campsites. We also work with numerous organisations, including ferry operators and tourist attractions, all of whom can bring you benefits and save you money.

Our brand **NEW** Travel Card binds all this together, along with exclusive extra content in our cardholders' area at **alanrogers.com/travelcard**

Advantage all the way

Carry the Alan Rogers Travel Card on your travels and save money all the way.
Enjoy exclusive offers on many partner sites - as well as hotels, apartments and campsite accommodation. We've even teamed up with Camping Cheque, the low season discount scheme, so you can load your card with Cheques before you travel. So register today - hundreds of campsites already have special offers just for you.

Holiday **discounts**, **free** kids' meals, **free** cycle hire, **discounted** meals, **free** sports activities, **free** gifts on arrival, **free** wine with meals, **free** wifi, **free** tennis, **free** spa day, **free** access to local attractions.

Check out all the offers at **alanrogers.com/travelcard**
and present your card on arrival.

Benefits that add up

- Offers and benefits on many Alan Rogers campsites across Europe

- Save up to 60% in low season on over 600 campsites

- Savings on rented accommodation and hotels at over 400 locations

- Free cardholders' magazine

- Exclusive cardholders' area on our website – exchange opinions with other members

- Discounted ferries

- Savings on Alan Rogers guides

- Travel insurance deals

Register today - and start saving

Step 1
Register at www.**alanrogers.com/travelcard**
(you can now access exclusive content on the website).

Step 2
You'll receive your activated card, along with a Welcome email containing useful links and information.

Step 3
Start using your card to save money or to redeem benefits during your holiday.

Register now at
alanrogers.com/travelcard

Want independent campsite reviews at your fingertips?

Insurance Service

High quality, low cost insurance you can trust

Motorhome insurance
From only £174

Caravan Insurance
SAVE UP TO 60%

We've been entrusted with readers' campsite-based holidays since 1968, and they have asked us for good value, good quality insurance.

We have teamed up with Shield Total Insurance – one of the leading names in outdoor leisure insurances – to bring you peace of mind and huge savings. Call or visit our website for a no obligation quote – there's no reason not to – and trust us to cover your valued possessions for you.

Static Caravans - Price Beater GUARANTEE
We guarantee to beat any genuine 'like for like' insurance renewal quote by at least £25. Subject to terms & conditions.

- Caravans - **Discounts up to 60%**
- Motorhomes - **Prices from only £174**
- Park Homes - **Fantastic low rates**
- Tents - **Prices from only £30**

Instant quote
Call **0844 824 6314**

alanrogers.com/insurance

Alan Rogers Insurance Services is a trading name of Alan Rogers Travel Limited which is an Appointed Representative of ITC Compliance Ltd and is authorised and regulated by the Financial Services Authority. Insurance products featured in this advertisement are provided by Shield Total Insurance which is a trading name of Vantage Insurance Services Limited (VISL). VISL is a subsidiary of Vantage Holdings Ltd and is authorised and regulated by the Financial Services Authority. VISL is registered in England No. 3441136. Registered Office: 41 Eastcheap, London EC3M 1DT.

Getting the most from off peak touring

£**13.95**/night
single tariff
2 people

There are many reasons to avoid high season, if you can. Queues are shorter, there's less traffic, a calmer atmosphere and prices are cheaper. And it's usually still nice and sunny!

And when you use Camping Cheques you'll find great quality facilities that are actually open and a welcoming conviviality.

Did you know?

Camping Cheques can be used right into mid-July and from late August on many sites. Over 90 campsites in France alone accept Camping Cheques from 20th August.

Save up to 60% with Camping Cheques

Camping Cheque is a fixed price scheme allowing you to go as you please, staying on over 600 campsites across Europe, always paying the same rate and saving you up to 60% on regular pitch fees. One Cheque gives you one night for 2 people + unit on a standard pitch, with electricity. It's as simple as that.

Special offers mean you can stay extra nights free (eg 7 nights for 6 Cheques) or even a month free for a month paid! Especially popular in Spain during the winter, these longer-term offers can effectively halve the nightly rate. See Site Directory for details.

Check out our amazing Ferry Deals!

Why should I use Camping Cheques?

- It's a proven system, recognised by all 600+ participating campsites
  - so no nasty surprises.

- It's flexible, allowing you to travel between campsites, and also countries, on
  a whim - so no need to pre-book. (It's low season, so campsites are rarely full,
  though advance bookings can be made).

- Stay as long as you like, where you like - so you travel in complete freedom.

- Camping Cheques are valid 2 years - so no pressure to use them up.
  (If you have a couple left over after your trip, simply keep them for the following
  year, or use them up in the UK).

Tell me more... (but keep it brief!)

Camping Cheques was started in 1999 and has since grown in popularity each
year (nearly 2 million were used last year). That should speak for itself. There
are 'copycat' schemes, but none has the same range of quality campsites that
save you up to 60%.

Ask for your **FREE** continental road map,
which explains how Camping Cheque works

01580 214002

FREE

downloadable Site Directory
alanrogers.com/directory

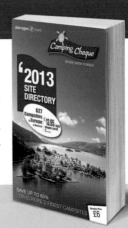

campingcheque.co.uk

Start 2013
in real style...

The **ONLY SHOW** in the spring where the leading caravan and motorhome manufacturers will be displaying their **NEW 2013 SEASON MODELS.**

The Spring
CARAVAN &
CAMPING SHOW
19-24 FEB 2013 · NEC BIRMINGHAM

SUPPORTERS:

WWW.SPRINGCARAVANANDCAMPINGSHOW.CO.UK

The **NATIONAL SHOW** at the NEC where you'll see the **NEW 2014 SEASON** caravan and motorhome models from all the leading manufacturers.

...and end it
truly inspired.

The
MOTORHOME &
CARAVAN SHOW
15-20 OCT 2013 · NEC BIRMINGHAM

SUPPORTERS:

WWW.MOTORHOMEANDCARAVANSHOW.CO.UK

ORGANISED BY: NCC events

Regions of Britain & Ireland

Scotland
page 263

Northern
Ireland
page 289

Northumbria
page 228

Cumbria
page 217

North West
England
page 209

Yorkshire
page 192

Republic of Ireland
page 296

Heart of England
page 165

Wales
page 236

East of England
page 146

Southern
England
page 103

South West England
page 16

South East
England
page 127

London
page 142

Channel Islands
page 319

351

Town & Village Index

Index by Campsite Number

England

Index by Campsite Number continued

Index by Campsite Number continued

359

Index by Campsite Number continued

Channel Islands

Index by Campsite Region, County & Name

England

South West England

Cornwall

Devon